Frommer's®
Maui

My Maui

By Jeanette Foster

OVER THE PAST FEW DECADES, THE TRAVEL WORLD HAS "DISCOVERED" MAUI.
But my love affair with the Valley Isle—a terrible nickname that doesn't do this sensuous place justice—goes back to the time when Waikiki was "the" Hawaii destination, when Maui was unknown to anyone outside of the state.

It's hard to overstate Maui's opulent beauty, which glossy travel magazines have well documented. Seeing the first rays of the sun appear over the horizon atop the 10,000-foot Haleakala volcano can be a religious experience. But Maui snares unsuspecting visitors through their other senses as well. Through the intoxicating aroma of just-bloomed ginger after a rain squall. The song of a gentle breeze through a row of swaying palm trees. The luscious first bite of a ripe mango, sticky juice streaming down your chin. The way the luxurious, warm waters of the Pacific feel as your body floats effortlessly over a rainbow of tropical fish.

Legends tell us that gods and goddesses once walked the island, and that Maui gets its name from a demigod who snared the sun and made it promise to slow down its daily journey across the sky. The sumptuousness of this small island can only be experienced by walking the aina (land), just as the gods once did. I've walked this land, and Maui is as close to heaven as I'm going to get.

HANA HIGHWAY (left) Maui's most famous road, the Hana Highway, is a destination in itself, not just the route to one. Hugging the windy, rocky coastline, this 50-mile road traverses awe-inspiring seascapes, tumbling waterfalls, and lush rainforests.

Thousands of cars take this wiggle of a road every day. Too many of them rush to "get there," not realizing there is no "there"—the road is the "there." Take your time, stop to smell the ginger, jump in a freshwater pool, and watch the clouds float by.

MOLOKINI (above) Like a crescent moon fallen from the sky, the remains of the crater of Molokini, about halfway between Maui and the uninhabited island of Kahoolawe, is a dream destination for snorkel and dive enthusiasts. Tilted so that only the thin rim of its southern side shows above water in a perfect semicircle, Molokini stands like a scoop against the tide, and serves, on its concave side, as a natural sanctuary for tropical fish.

SILVERSWORD (left) The silversword, a rare plant, grows high on the slopes of 10,000ft. Haleakala and blooms only once a year (between July and September). A relative of the sunflower family, the silversword looks like a pine cone with a fountain of red-petaled, daisy-like flowers that turn silver soon after blooming.

PROTEA (below) Originally from South Africa, and looking more like something from outer space, proteas come in more than 40 different varieties, ranging from pincushions (pictured) to something resembling a bouquet of feathers. Grown on the slopes of Haleakala, proteas are a long-lasting cut flower, and will last up to a year if dried.

KAHAKULOA (above) Nestled in a crevice between two steep hills, along the very narrow Kahekili Highway, is the picturesque village of Kahakuloa, composed of a few weather-worn houses, a church with a red-tile roof, and vivid green taro patches. The village gets its name from the 636ft. high "Kahakuloa" (or tall lord) Head rising at the edge of the bay.

LEIS (right) Nothing says Hawaii like a lei. The tropical beauty of the delicate garland, the delicious sweet fragrance of the blossoms, the sensual way the flowers curl softly around your neck—getting lei'd in Hawaii is a sensuous experience.

WINDSURFING AT HOOKIPA (left) With constant wind and endless waves, Hookipa Beach Park, on Maui's windward side, attracts top windsurfers from around the globe. The best place to watch these athletes leap over the waves is on the grassy cliffs above the beach. They take to the water after noon (board surfers claim the waves in the morning).

IAO NEEDLE (below) Jetting up at an impressive 2,250ft., the Iao Needle is actually the eroded remnant of a basaltic core that sits in the volcanic caldera of the West Maui Mountains. Before Westerners came to Maui, the Needle was a sacred place where Hawaiians came to honor their gods. They named the valley where the Needle stands Iao, or "supreme light."

HUMPBACK WHALE (above) Visitors to Maui come in all sizes. Maui's largest visitors—the humpback whales—are also its most faithful, arriving every year around December and staying until April. Humpbacks migrate from Alaska to the Hawaiian Islands to mate and calve. As big as a city bus and weighing several tons each, these frolicking leviathans are easy to spot from shore, off the coasts of Maui, Molokai and Lanai.

SURFING PEAHI (right) The massive waves at Peahi, which the local residents call Jaws (because the waves can eat you up), have always been there—but for years, they were too far off shore, too big, coming in too fast for surfers to catch and ride them. About a decade ago, surfers like Laird Hamilton started experimenting, using jet boats to tow a surfer far offshore and bring him up to speed, before whipping him into the path of these giants (some waves as high as 60ft.). Jaws has been conquered.

ONELOA BEACH (left) The Hawaiians called this white-sand beach "Oneloa," which means long sand. The local residents know it as "Big Beach," and at 3,300ft. long and 100ft. wide it is one of Maui's most popular. When the water is calm, this picture-perfect beach is great for swimming, fishing, and surfing. Snorkeling is great at the north end, around Puu Olai, a 360ft. cinder cone. But when a storm rolls in, the waves can lash the shore with a strong rip current around the steep drop-off, making it dangerous for inexperienced open-ocean swimmers.

HALEAKALA (above) Driving, hiking, or biking through the otherworldly landscape of Haleakala (House of the Sun) National Park is an experience not to be missed. Here you can hike above the clouds and peer down into Haleakala crater, which, at 7.5 miles long by 2.5 miles wide by 3,000ft. deep, is big enough to swallow Manhattan. To the Hawaiians, 10,000ft. Haleakala, a dormant volcano, was a spiritual place where kahuna (priests) performed rituals. Today it's home to two of Hawaii's most endangered species: nene (Hawaiian geese) and silversword plants.

Maui History & Legends

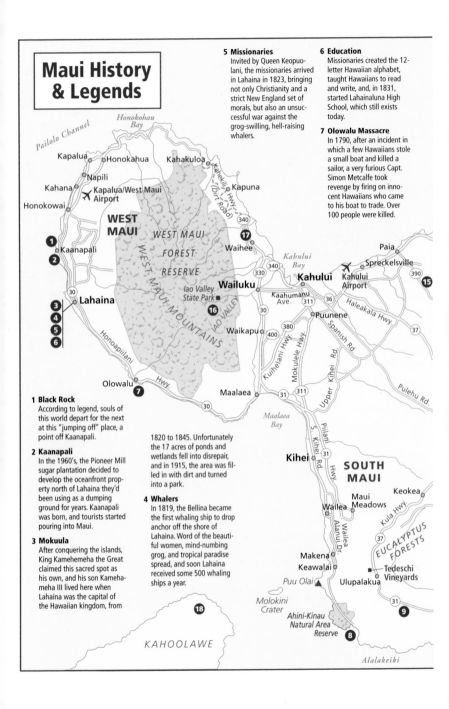

5 Missionaries
Invited by Queen Keopuo-lani, the missionaries arrived in Lahaina in 1823, bringing not only Christianity and a strict New England set of morals, but also an unsuccessful war against the grog-swilling, hell-raising whalers.

6 Education
Missionaries created the 12-letter Hawaiian alphabet, taught Hawaiians to read and write, and, in 1831, started Lahainaluna High School, which still exists today.

7 Olowalu Massacre
In 1790, after an incident in which a few Hawaiians stole a small boat and killed a sailor, a very furious Capt. Simon Metcalfe took revenge by firing on innocent Hawaiians who came to his boat to trade. Over 100 people were killed.

1 Black Rock
According to legend, souls of this world depart for the next at this "jumping off" place, a point off Kaanapali.

2 Kaanapali
In the 1960's, the Pioneer Mill sugar plantation decided to develop the oceanfront property north of Lahaina they'd been using as a dumping ground for years. Kaanapali was born, and tourists started pouring into Maui.

3 Mokuula
After conquering the islands, King Kamehameha the Great claimed this sacred spot as his own, and his son Kamehameha III lived here when Lahaina was the capital of the Hawaiian kingdom, from 1820 to 1845. Unfortunately the 17 acres of ponds and wetlands fell into disrepair, and in 1915, the area was filled with dirt and turned into a park.

4 Whalers
In 1819, the Bellina became the first whaling ship to drop anchor off the shore of Lahaina. Word of the beautiful women, mind-numbing grog, and tropical paradise spread, and soon Lahaina received some 500 whaling ships a year.

8 La Perouse
The first European explorer to set foot on Maui was Admiral Comte de la Perouse, in 1786. He didn't like the "burning climate" of Kihei and sailed off.

9 Cape Kinau
Overlooking La Perouse Bay is the site of the last lava flow on Maui, estimated to have occurred in the 1790's.

10 Haleakala
Maui, the demi-god whom the island is named after, is said to have stood atop Haleakala and lassoed the sun to slow down its daily path across the sky.

11 Sugar
The first successful sugar plantation, once the largest industry on Maui, was started by George Wilfong in 1849, along the Hana coast.

12 Kuiki Hill
Kaahumanu, born in a cave in this prominent point on Hana Bay in 1768, had a huge impact on Hawaiian culture despite such humble beginnings. After the death of her husband Kamehameha in 1820, she helped end Hawaii's *kapu* (taboo) system by sitting down and eating with men—a major *kapu* at the time.

13 Piilanihale Heiau
This *heiau* (temple), the largest in the state was named for one of Maui's greatest chiefs, Piilani, who united the island of Maui in the 15th century.

14 1946 Tsunami
In 1946, an earthquake in the Aleutian Islands caused a tsunami that slammed into the Hana coastline, devastating the village of Hamoa and sweeping clean most of the buildings on the Keanae Peninsula.

15 Haiku Ditch
Claus Spreckels changed the face of Maui when he built the 30-mile Haiku Ditch in 1878. The ditch brought 50 million gallons of water a day from rain-rich Haiku to arid, dry Puunene to irrigate his sugar fields.

16 Kepaniwai
In 1790, in his effort to gain control of all the Hawaiian islands, Kamehameha and his men fought and won a bloody battle in Iao Valley that left the Iao Stream blocked with fallen bodies, giving the area the name Kepaniwai, or "damming of the waters."

17 Halekii-Pihana Heiau
These two *heiau*, built in 1240, sit on a hill with a commanding view of central Maui and Haleakala. Kahekili, the last chief of Maui, lived here.

18 Kahoolawe
The U.S. military took over this island, a sacred site to Hawaiians, during World War II and used it as a bombing target until 1993, when it was returned to the state.

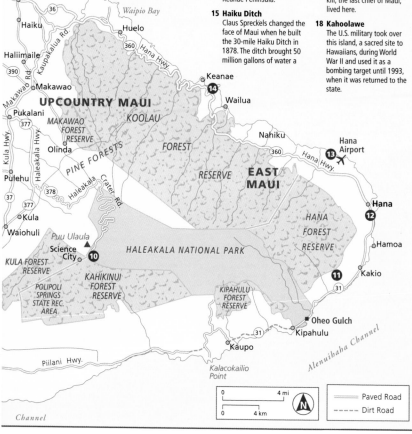

The Road to Hana

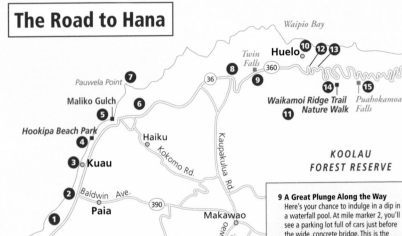

Waipio Bay

Huelo ⑩ ⑫ ⑬

Twin Falls 360 ⑧ ⑨

Pauwela Point ⑦ 36 ⑭ ⑮

Maliko Gulch ⑥ *Waikamoi Ridge Trail* *Puahokamoa Nature Walk* *Falls*

⑤ ⑪

Hookipa Beach Park ④

Haiku *Kokomo Rd.*

③ **Kuau** *Kaupakulua Rd.* **KOOLAU FOREST RESERVE**

② Baldwin Ave. 390

Paia **Makawao**

①

Makawao Ave.

36 *Halaeakala Hwy.*

Airport To Kahului 37

1 Before You Start
Fill up your gas tank before you get to Paia. Gas in Paia is very expensive, and it's the last place for gas until you get to Hana.

2 Paia
The former plantation village of Paia was once a thriving sugar-mill town. Today, chic eateries and trendy shops stand next door to mom-and-pop establishments.

3 Kuau
After you leave Paia you'll pass the Kuau Mart on your left. The road then bends into an S-turn; in the middle of the S is the entrance to Mama's Fish House and an adjacent small sandy cove. Ocean access is treacherous, but the beach is a great place to sit and soak up some sun.

4 Hookipa Beach Park
A mile from Mama's, just before mile marker 9, is a place known around the world as one of the greatest windsurfing spots on the planet: Hookipa Beach Park.

5 Maliko Gulch
At mile marker 10, look for the road on your right, which goes under the bridge and past a rodeo arena, and on to the rocky beach at Maliko Bay. The 1946 tidal wave wiped out the once-thriving community at the mouth of the bay. If the surf is up, it's a great place to watch the waves.

6 Haiku
Around mile marker 11, you'll pass through the rural area of Haiku, with banana patches, cane grass blowing in the wind, and forests of guava trees, avocados, and kukui trees. This was once a thriving pineapple area, but lately million-dollar homes have become the new crop.

7 Jaws
If it's winter and the waves are up, stop here to watch expert surfers battle the mammoth waves off Pauwela Point at an area known as Jaws (as in, the waves can chew you up). To get there, turn left off the Hana Highway at Hahana Road, between mile markers 13 and 14. Park where the paved road ends, and hike about a mile and a half along the private dirt road (Maui Land and Pine property) to the ocean. Practice aloha-don't park in the pineapple fields, and hands off the pineapples.

8 Change in Miles
At mile marker 16, the curves begin, one right after another. Slow down and enjoy the view of bucolic rolling hills, mango trees, and vibrant ferns. After mile marker 16, the road is still called the Hana Highway, but the number changes from Highway 36 to Highway 360, and the mile markers go back to 0.

9 A Great Plunge Along the Way
Here's your chance to indulge in a dip in a waterfall pool. At mile marker 2, you'll see a parking lot full of cars just before the wide, concrete bridge. This is the entrance to Twin Falls; pull over on the mountain side and park. Be aware that this is private property and trespassing is illegal in Hawaii. If you decide that you want to "risk it," from the gate here you have a 3 to 5 minute walk to the first waterfall and pool, then you can continue on another 10 to 15 minutes to the second, larger waterfall and pool (don't go in if it has been raining).

10 Hidden Huelo
Just before mile marker 4 on a blind curve, look for a double row of mailboxes on the left-hand side by the pay phone. Down the road lies a hidden Hawaii, where ocean waves pummel soaring lava cliffs and serenity prevails. Only a few hundred people live among the scattered homes on this windswept land. The lone tourist attraction in Huelo is the historic 1853 Kaulanapueo Church.

11 Koolau Forest Reserve
After Huelo, you'll reach the edge of the lush Koolau Forest Reserve. The coastline here gets about 60 to 80 inches of rain a year, and farther up the mountain, the rainfall is 200 to 300 inches a year. Here you will see 20- to 30-foot-tall guava trees, mangos, java plums, and avocados the size of softballs.

12 Dangerous Curves
About a half mile after mile marker 6, there's a sharp U-curve in the road, going uphill. The road is practically one lane here, so sound your horn at the start of the U-curve to let approaching cars know you are coming. Take this curve, as well as those coming up in the next several miles, very slowly.

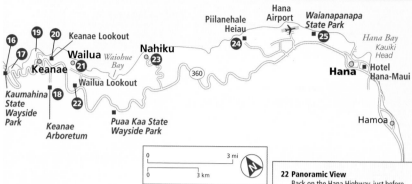

Hana
Airport

Piilanehale
Heiau

Waianapanapa
State Park

Keanae Lookout

16
19
20

17

Wailua *Waiohue
Bay*

Nahiku

24

Hana Bay
Kauiki
Head

25

Keanae

21

23

360

Hana

Hotel
Hana-Maui

Wailua Lookout

Kaumahina
State
Wayside
Park

18

22

Puaa Kaa State
Wayside Park

Keanae
Arboretum

Hamoa

0   3 mi
0   3 km

13 Kaaiea Bridge
Just before mile marker 7 is a forest of
waving bamboo. For the best view, pull
over at the Kaaiea Bridge, just after mile
marker 7, and look back.

14 Family Hike
At mile marker 9, there's a small state
wayside area with restrooms, a pavilion,
picnic tables, and a barbecue area. The
well-marked Waikamoi Ridge Trail is an
easy three-quarter-mile loop that meanders through eucalyptus, ferns, and hala
trees.

15 Warning-Use Caution
As you approach the 11 mile marker, the
highway becomes a congested one-lane
road due to all the cars parked along it
(they're stopping for Puohokomoa Falls,
which I no longer recommend because
it's overrun with tourists), so drive
slowly and safely through this area.

16 Photo Op
Just past mile marker 12 is the Kaumahina (Moonrise) State Wayside Park. Not
only is this a good pit stop (restrooms
are available here) and a wonderful
place for a picnic (with tables and barbecue area), but the view of the rugged
coastline makes an excellent photo-you
can see all the way down to the jutting
Keanae Peninsula.

17 Honomanu Bay Beach Park
Turn left just after mile marker 14; the
rutted dirt-and-cinder road takes you
down to the rocky black-sand beach of
Honomanu. There are no facilities here,
but it's a popular site among surfers and
net fishermen. There are strong rip currents offshore, so swimming is best in
the stream inland from the ocean. Stand
on the beach and turn to look back on
the steep cliffs covered with vegetation.

18 Keanae Arboretum
Between mile markers 16 and 17
you'll see a cluster of bunkhouses
belonging to the YMCA Camp Keanae.
A quarter-mile down is the Keanae
Arboretum. You can visit the arboretum, swim in the pools of Piinaau
Stream, or press on along a mile-long
trail into Keanae Valley and a lovely
tropical rainforest.

19 Keanae Peninsula
The old Hawaiian village of Keanae
stands out against the Pacific like a
place time forgot. The native Hawaiians who live here still grow taro and
pound it into poi, pluck opihi (limpet)
from tide pools along the jagged
coast, and cast throw-nets at schools
of fish.

20 Yet Another Photo Op
Just past mile marker 17 is a wide
spot on the ocean side of the road
where you can see the entire Keanae
Peninsula's checkerboard pattern of
green taro fields and its ocean boundary etched in black lava.

21 Wailua
After the Keanae School, around mile
marker 18, look for the Wailua Road
on the left. This will take you through
the hamlet of homes and churches of
Wailua, including the blue and white
Coral Miracle Church, home of the
Our Lady of Fatima Shrine. According
to legend, in 1860, the men of this village were building a church by diving
for coral to make the stone; an arduous project. A freak storm hit the area
and deposited the coral from the deep
on a nearby beach. If you look back at
Haleakala from here, on your left you
can see the spectacular Waikani Falls.

22 Panoramic View
Back on the Hana Highway, just before
mile marker 19, is the Wailua Valley
State Wayside Park, on the right side of
the road. Climb up the stairs for a view
of the Keanae Valley, waterfalls, and Wailua Peninsula. For a better view of the
Wailua Peninsula, continue down the
road about a quarter-mile, to the pull-off
area on the ocean side.

23 Nakihu
Just after mile marker 25 is a narrow 3-
mile road leading to the remains of the
old Hawaiian community of Nahiku. This
once was a thriving village of thousands; today, the beautiful, remote area
is home to fewer than a hundred-mostly
wealthy mainland residents visiting their
luxurious vacation homes. At the turn of
the 20th century, this site saw brief commercial activity as home of the Nahiku
Rubber Co.

24 Piilanihale Heiau
Turn toward the ocean on Ulaino Road,
by mile marker 31. Drive down the
paved road (which turns into a dirt road)
to the first stream (about 1[bf]1/2 miles).
If the stream is flooded, go back. If you
can forge the stream, cross it and park
on the right side of the road by the huge
breadfruit trees. The Piilanihale Heiau,
believed to be the largest in the state,
measures 340 feet by 415 feet, and it
was built in a unique terrace design. Historians believe that Piilani's two sons
and his grandson built the mammoth
temple sometime in the 1500s.

25 Waianapanapa State Park
At mile marker 32, just on the outskirts
of Hana, shiny black-sand Waianapanapa Beach appears like a vivid dream,
with bright-green jungle foliage on three
sides and cobalt-blue water lapping at
its feet. The 120-acre park includes sea
cliffs, lava tubes, arches, camping, picnic
pavilions, restrooms, showers, drinking
water, and hiking trails.

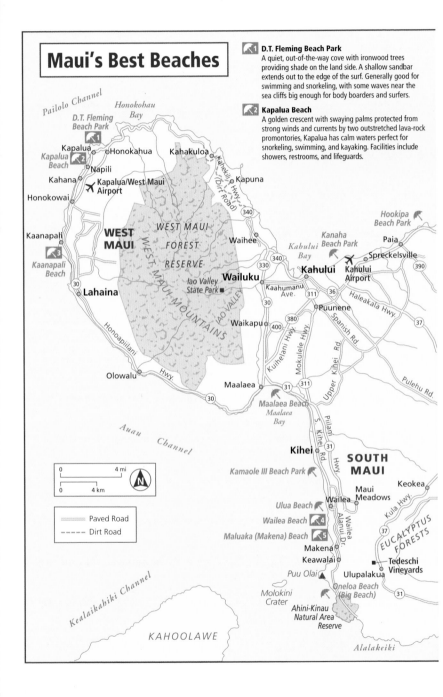

Maui's Best Beaches

1 D.T. Fleming Beach Park
A quiet, out-of-the-way cove with ironwood trees providing shade on the land side. A shallow sandbar extends out to the edge of the surf. Generally good for swimming and snorkeling, with some waves near the sea cliffs big enough for body boarders and surfers.

2 Kapalua Beach
A golden crescent with swaying palms protected from strong winds and currents by two outstretched lava-rock promontories, Kapalua has calm waters perfect for snorkeling, swimming, and kayaking. Facilities include showers, restrooms, and lifeguards.

Pailolo Channel

Honokohau Bay

D.T. Fleming Beach Park 1

Kapalua
Kapalua Beach 2
Napili
Kahana
Honokowai

Honokahua
Honokahua

Kahakuloa

Kapuna

Kaanapali
Kaanapali Beach 3

Kapalua/West Maui Airport

WEST MAUI

WEST MAUI FOREST RESERVE

Kahekili Hwy. (Dirt Road)

340

330   340

Waihee

Hookipa Beach Park

Kanaha Beach Park
Kahului Bay

Paia
Spreckelsville

390

Kahului

Kahului Airport

Lahaina

30

WEST MAUI MOUNTAINS

Iao Valley State Park

IAO VALLEY

Wailuku

Kaahumanu Ave.

30

311   36

Puunene

Haleakala Hwy.

37

Honoapiilani Hwy.

Waikapu

380   400

Olowalu

Maalaea

31   311

Maalaea Beach
Maalaea Bay

Kuihelani Hwy.

Mokulele Hwy.

Upper Kihei Rd.

Spanish Rd.

Pulehu Rd.

30

Auau Channel

Kihei

SOUTH MAUI

Kamaole III Beach Park

Maui Meadows

Keokea

0   4 mi
0   4 km

N

Paved Road
Dirt Road

Ulua Beach
Wailea Beach 4
Maluaka (Makena) Beach 5

Wailea

S Kihei Rd.

Piilani Hwy.

Wailea Alanui Dr.

Kula Hwy.

37

EUCALYPTUS FORESTS

Makena

Keawalai

Tedeschi Vineyards

Puu Olai

Ulupalakua

Molokini Crater

Oneloa Beach (Big Beach)

31

Kealaikahiki Channel

Ahini-Kinau Natural Area Reserve

KAHOOLAWE

Alalakeiki

3 Kaanapali Beach

Four-mile-long Kaanapali boasts grainy gold sand as far as the eye can see. A paved beach walk links hotels and condos, open-air restaurants, and the Whalers Village shopping center. Summertime swimming is excellent, and snorkeling is great around Black Rock, in front of the Sheraton.

4 Wailea Beach

This gold-sand, crescent-shaped beach is big, wide, and protected on both sides by black-lava points. From the beach, the view out to sea is magnificent, framed by neighboring Kahoolawe and Lanai and the tiny crescent of Molokini; you can often spot whales from shore here in season (Dec–Apr), and catch unreal sunsets nightly. The clear waters tumble to shore in waves just the right size for gentle riding, with or without a board.

5 Maluaka Beach (Makena Beach)

This wide, palm-fringed crescent of golden sand is set between two black-lava points and bounded by big sand dunes topped by a grassy knoll. Makena offers great swimming when it's flat and placid, excellent bodysurfing when the waves come rolling in, and lovely vistas of Molokini Crater and Kahoolawe off in the distance.

6 Hamoa Beach

This half-moon-shaped, gray-sand beach (a mix of coral and lava) in a truly tropical setting sits below 30-foot black-lava sea cliffs. An unprotected beach open to the ocean, Hamoa is often swept by powerful rip currents. Surf breaks offshore and rolls ashore, making it a popular surfing and bodysurfing area. The calm left side is best for snorkeling in the summer.

7 Waianapanapa State Park

This state park is perhaps best known for its black-sand beach (actually small black pebbles). Swimming is generally unsafe due to strong waves and rip currents, but it's a great spot for picnicking, hiking along the shore, and simply sitting and relaxing.

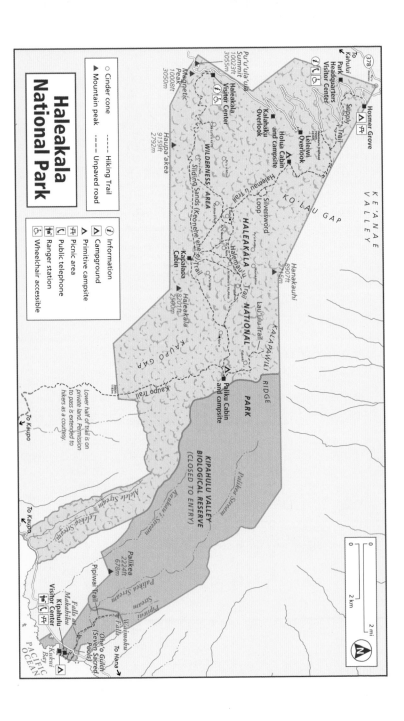

Haleakala National Park

Legend:
- ○ Cinder cone
- ▲ Mountain peak
- ---- Hiking Trail
- --- Unpaved road

- ⓘ Information
- △ Campground
- ▲ Primitive campsite
- ⛏ Picnic area
- ☎ Public telephone
- Ranger station
- ♿ Wheelchair accessible

To Kahului
378
Park Headquarters
Visitor Center
Supply Trail
Hosmer Grove

Pu'u'ula'ula
Summit
10023ft
3055m

Leleiwi
Overlook

Magnetic
Peak
10008ft
3050m

Haleakala
Visitor Center

Kalahaku
Overlook

Holua Cabin
and campsite

Halemau'u Trail

Silversword
Loop

WILDERNESS AREA

Sliding Sands (Keonehe'ehe'e) Trail

Haupa'akea
9159ft
2792m

KO'OLAU GAP

KE'ANAE
VALLEY

Hanakauhi
8907ft
2715m

HALEAKALA

NATIONAL

Kapalaoa
Cabin

Halemau'u Trail

Lau'ulu Trail

KALAPAWILI
RIDGE

Haleakala
8201ft
2590m

KAUPO GAP

Kaupo Trail

Lower half of trail is on
private land. Permission
to pass is extended to
hikers as a courtesy.

To Kaupo

To Kaupo

Paliku Cabin
and campsite

PARK

KIPAHULU VALLEY
BIOLOGICAL RESERVE
(CLOSED TO ENTRY)

Palikea
Stream

Palikea
7224ft
678m

Pipiwai Trail

Kipahulu
Visitor Center

Palikea Stream

Pipiwai Stream

Falls at
Makahiku

Waimoku
Falls

'Ohe'o Gulch
(Seven Sacred
Pools)

To Hana

Kuloa
Bay

PACIFIC
OCEAN

Nu'ele Stream

Lelekea Stream

Kukui Stream

0 ___ 2 mi
0 ___ 2 km

N

Frommer's®

Maui

2009

by Jeanette Foster

Here's what the critics say about Frommer's:

"Amazingly easy to use. Very portable, very complete."

—*Booklist*

"Detailed, accurate, and easy-to-read information for all price ranges."
—*Glamour Magazine*

"Hotel information is close to encyclopedic."

—*Des Moines Sunday Register*

"Frommer's Guides have a way of giving you a real feel for a place."
—*Knight Ridder Newspapers*

WILEY

Wiley Publishing, Inc.

Published by:

Wiley Publishing, Inc.

111 River St.
Hoboken, NJ 07030-5774

ISBN 978-0-470-28560-2
Editor: Leslie Shen, with Christine Ryan
Production Editor: Suzanna R. Thompson
Cartographer: Elizabeth Puhl
Photo Editor: Richard Fox
Production by Wiley Indianapolis Composition Services

For information on our other products and services or to obtain technical support, please contact our Customer Care Department within the U.S. at 800/762-2974, outside the U.S. at 317/572-3993 or fax 317/572-4002.

Wiley also publishes its books in a variety of electronic formats. Some content that appears in print may not be available in electronic formats.

Manufactured in the United States of America

5 4 3 2 1

Contents

4 Suggested Maui Itineraries   87

5 Where to Stay   103

6 Where to Dine   142

7 Fun On & Off the Beach   173

List of Maps

Acknowledgments

Special thanks to Priscilla Life, the best researcher in Hawaii.

An Invitation to the Reader

In researching this book, we discovered many wonderful places—hotels, restaurants, shops, and more. We're sure you'll find others. Please tell us about them, so we can share the information with your fellow travelers in upcoming editions. If you were disappointed with a recommendation, we'd love to know that, too. Please write to:

Frommer's Maui 2009
Wiley Publishing, Inc. • 111 River St. • Hoboken, NJ 07030-5774

An Additional Note

Please be advised that travel information is subject to change at any time—and this is especially true of prices. We therefore suggest that you write or call ahead for confirmation when making your travel plans. The authors, editors, and publisher cannot be held responsible for the experiences of readers while traveling. Your safety is important to us, however, so we encourage you to stay alert and be aware of your surroundings. Keep a close eye on cameras, purses, and wallets, all favorite targets of thieves and pickpockets.

About the Author

A resident of the Big Island, **Jeanette Foster** has skied the slopes of Mauna Kea—during a Fourth of July ski meet, no less—and gone scuba diving with manta rays off the Kona Coast. A prolific writer widely published in travel, sports, and adventure magazines, she's also a contributing editor to *Hawaii* magazine, the editor of *Zagat's Survey to Hawaii's Top Restaurants,* and the Hawaii chapter author of *1,000 Places to See in the USA and Canada Before You Die.* In addition to writing this guide, Jeanette is the author of *Frommer's Maui; Frommer's Kauai; Frommer's Hawaii with Kids; Frommer's Portable Big Island; Frommer's Honolulu, Waikiki & Oahu; Frommer's Maui Day by Day;* and *Frommer's Honolulu & Oahu Day by Day.*

Other Great Guides for Your Trip:

Frommer's Maui Day by Day
Frommer's Portable Maui
Frommer's Kauai
Frommer's Hawaii
Frommer's Hawaii with Kids
Frommer's Honolulu & Oahu Day by Day
Hawaii For Dummies
Maui For Dummies

Frommer's Star Ratings, Icons & Abbreviations

Every hotel, restaurant, and attraction listing in this guide has been ranked for quality, value, service, amenities, and special features using a **star-rating system.** In country, state, and regional guides, we also rate towns and regions to help you narrow down your choices and budget your time accordingly. Hotels and restaurants are rated on a scale of zero (recommended) to three stars (exceptional). Attractions, shopping, nightlife, towns, and regions are rated according to the following scale: zero stars (recommended), one star (highly recommended), two stars (very highly recommended), and three stars (must-see).

In addition to the star-rating system, we also use **seven feature icons** that point you to the great deals, in-the-know advice, and unique experiences that separate travelers from tourists. Throughout the book, look for:

Finds	Special finds—those places only insiders know about
Fun Fact	Fun facts—details that make travelers more informed and their trips more fun
Kids	Best bets for kids and advice for the whole family
Moments	Special moments—those experiences that memories are made of
Overrated	Places or experiences not worth your time or money
Tips	Insider tips—great ways to save time and money
Value	Great values—where to get the best deals

The following **abbreviations** are used for credit cards:

AE	American Express	DISC	Discover	V	Visa
DC	Diners Club	MC	MasterCard		

Frommers.com

Now that you have this guidebook to help you plan a great trip, visit our website at **www.frommers.com** for additional travel information on more than 4,000 destinations. We update features regularly to give you instant access to the most current trip-planning information available. At Frommers.com, you'll find scoops on the best airfares, lodging rates, and car rental bargains. You can even book your travel online through our reliable travel booking partners. Other popular features include:

- Online updates of our most popular guidebooks
- Vacation sweepstakes and contest giveaways
- Newsletters highlighting the hottest travel trends
- Podcasts, interactive maps, and up-to-the-minute events listings
- Opinionated blog entries by Arthur Frommer himself
- Online travel message boards with featured travel discussions

What's New in Maui

Big, big changes are hitting the travel industry, especially on the tropical isle of Maui, as this book goes to press. Airlines are shutting down, charging a premium for window and aisle seats, and imposing fees for a second (and, in some cases, first) checked bag; hotel prices are rising; and the cost of gas (especially in Hawaii) has skyrocketed.

But in my experience, travelers are people who want to experience a new place and culture. They want to live it, breathe it, and incorporate these experiences into their lives to make them richer and fuller. Travelers travel. Period. So despite the woes of the airlines, and regardless of the increase in prices, nothing stops this breed from living life. And generally, such travelers are Frommer's readers. Here's where I come in: This guide lets you in on how to get the most out of your travel dollar, how to make the most out of your limited time, and how to experience the Maui of your dreams.

PLANNING YOUR TRIP TO MAUI In 2008, both **Aloha Airlines** and **ATA Airlines** shut down, taking 16% of the seats from the U.S. mainland to Hawaii out of the market (not to worry, other air carriers are replacing those seats as fast as they can) and leaving nearly 1,000 fewer seats a week in the interisland market.

Just as Aloha Airlines was closing, another mode of transportation was opening. At press time, the **Hawaii Superferry** (© **877/HI-FERRY** [443-3779]; www. hawaiisuperferry.com), after a few stumbling starts, had just begun interisland service between Honolulu and Maui, with plans to add service between Honolulu and Kauai and between Honolulu and the Big Island. Although not as fast as the 30-minute interisland flights (the Superferry takes 3 hr. from Honolulu to Maui), and at slightly higher ticket prices, the Superferry does offer the option of taking a vehicle interisland. However, if you're prone to seasickness, the Superferry may not be for you, especially in the winter months of November through March, when big ocean swells and strong winds move into Hawaii's waters.

VOG As if there weren't already enough changes to digest, Madame Pele, the volcano goddess, has done it again on the Big Island. In addition to the nearly continuous eruption (since Jan 3, 1983) on the side of Mauna Loa from the Kilauea vent, in 2008 she erupted from the main Halemaumau Crater in Hawaii Volcanoes National Park. This was a very different **volcano eruption:** While past eruptions generally consisted of curtains of fire, with lava shooting several hundred feet into the air and then slowly rolling down the side of the volcano into the ocean, the 2008 eruption from Halemaumau made the earth shake, threw rocks (some the size of Volkswagens) into the air, and spit a pink ash into the sky that rained back to earth, covering nearby communities. The recent episode also raised the level of hazardous sulfur dioxide. How does that affect your trip to Maui (or Molokai or Lanai)? Beware that the vog (caused by gases released from the eruption of volcano) can, on occasion, blanket the state, not just the Big Island of Hawaii where the volcano is erupting.

WHERE TO STAY Despite all the hoopla in the press, Maui County has *not* shut down **B&Bs** or **vacation rentals.** However, the Maui County (which consists of Maui, Molokai, and Lanai) Planning Commission is reviewing the requirements for permits for bed-and-breakfasts and vacation rentals. As we went to press, neither the Planning Commission (which is a regulatory body that does not make law, only offers suggestions to the County Council) nor the Maui County Council had passed any firm recommendations or laws on how to regulate these two entities in the future.

All of the B&Bs and vacation rentals recommended in this book have been in operation for years, all are reputable, and all have followed the law in paying state and county taxes. However, because there is no predicting what the government will do, please be sure to contact the B&B or vacation rental you are interested in—ideally, way in advance of your trip—to make sure you will get the accommodations of your choice.

In 2008, the **Ritz-Carlton Kapalua** reopened after an extensive $160-million renovation that transformed the hotel into an even more elegant property, with a focus on a Hawaiian (vs. the former European) theme. All guest rooms now have the latest technology, including flatscreen LCD TVs, DVD players, iPod docking stations, and wireless Internet access (included in the resort fee). The penthouse floor has been converted into Residential Suites (with kitchens, living rooms, and separate bedrooms), available for guests. Other transformations include upgrades to the signature 10,000-square-foot, three-tiered pool; a new children's pool; an Environmental Education Center; and a new 17,500-square-foot

Waihua Spa, with 15 treatment rooms, saunas, whirlpool with lava-stone walls, and fitness center. See p. 120.

WHERE TO DINE If you want a real Maui dining experience, sign up for **Tour da Food** (© 808/242-8383; www.tourdafood.com). Chef Bonnie Friedman takes foodies off the tourist path to discover the culinary treasures (from snack shacks to restaurants to markets and manufacturers) that make up Maui's unique cuisine. Accompanied by Bonnie's wonderful commentary on Maui's multicultural food options and its colorful history, you will eat some of the island's most yummy food (which you never would have discovered on your own). See p. 151.

OUTDOOR ACTIVITIES Although Maui's volcano, **Haleakala,** is *not* erupting, there are changes afoot here. The national park is continuing its evaluation of the impact of commercial downhill bicycle rides inside the park. As we went to press, the five bicycle companies that have downhill tour permits will be allowed to continue their operations inside the park, while the remaining operators must simply start their tours outside the park to prepare to ride down the mountain. Be sure to check with the tour operator when you book—ask whether the downhill tour actually starts inside or outside the park. For more on biking in the park, see p. 200.

MAUI AFTER DARK The Grammy-winning **Masters of Hawaiian Slack Key Guitar Concert Series** (© 888/669-3858; www.slackkey.com) brings the best of Hawaiian music to the Napili Kai Beach Resort every Wednesday night at 7:30pm. Host George Kahumoku, Jr., introduces a new slack-key master every week. Not only are there incredible Hawaiian music and singing, but George and his guest also "talk story" about old Hawaii, music, and Hawaiian culture. Not to be missed. See p. 256.

MOLOKAI After the demise of Aloha Airlines and ATA Airlines, the next giant closure of the year came when **Molokai Ranch,** owner of a third of the island and the largest employer on Molokai, shut down all operations: cattle ranching, the Lodge at Molokai Ranch, the Beach Village at Molokai Ranch, its restaurants, and a few shops in Maunaloa, leaving the planned community looking like a ghost town. However, Molokai Ranch and its operations were just one aspect of the "most Hawaiian" island, which is still as beautiful as ever and still beckons to those looking for a cultural experience, stepping back in time to old Hawaii.

LANAI In addition to the **Four Seasons** taking over the management of the **Lodge at Koele** and the **Manele Bay** resorts, the other big change on Lanai is that renowned Maui chef Bev Gannon (Haliimaile General Store, Joe's) has redesigned the menu at the new **Lanai City Grille,** located in the **Hotel Lanai.** The menu focuses on whatever is in season and fresh that day, with fish, seafood, meats, and rotisserie chicken among the offerings. See p. 303.

1

The Best of Maui

Maui, also called the Valley Isle, is just a small dot in the vast Pacific Ocean, but it has the potential to offer visitors unforgettable experiences: floating weightless through rainbows of tropical fish, standing atop a 10,000-foot volcano watching the sunrise color the sky, and listening to the raindrops in a bamboo forest.

Whether you want to experience the "real" Hawaii, go on a heart-pounding adventure, or simply relax on the beach, this book is designed to help you create the vacation of your dreams.

It can be bewildering to plan your trip with so many options vying for your attention. To make your task easier, this chapter highlights what I consider the very best that Maui has to offer.

1 The Best Beaches

- **D. T. Fleming Beach Park:** This quiet, out-of-the-way beach, located north of the Ritz-Carlton hotel, starts at the 16th hole of the Kapalua golf course (Makaluapuna Point) and rolls around to the sea cliffs on the other side of the cove. Ironwood trees provide shade on the land side. Offshore, a shallow sandbar extends out to the edge of the surf. The waters are generally good for swimming and snorkeling, but sometimes, off near the sea cliffs, the waves are big enough to suit body boarders and surfers. See p. 173.

- **Kapalua Beach:** On an island of many great beaches, this one takes the prize. A golden crescent with swaying palms protected from strong winds and currents by two outstretched lava-rock promontories, Kapalua has calm waters that are perfect for snorkeling, swimming, and kayaking. Even though it borders the Kapalua Resort, the beach is long enough for everyone to enjoy. Facilities include showers, restrooms, and lifeguards. See p. 176.

- **Kaanapali Beach:** Four-mile-long Kaanapali stands out as one of Maui's best beaches, with grainy gold sand as far as the eye can see. Most of the beach parallels the sea channel, and a paved beach walk links hotels and condos, open-air restaurants, and the Whalers Village shopping center. Summertime swimming is excellent. The best snorkeling is around Black Rock, in front of the Sheraton; the water is clear, calm, and populated with brilliant tropical fish. See p. 176.

- **Wailea Beach:** This is the best gold-sand, crescent-shaped beach on Maui's sun-baked southwestern coast. One of five beaches within Wailea Resort, Wailea Beach is big, wide, and protected on both sides by black-lava points. It serves as the front yard for the Four Seasons Resort, Maui's most elegant hotel, and the Grand Wailea Resort, its most outrageous. From the beach, the view out to sea is magnificent, framed by neighboring Kahoolawe and Lanai and the tiny crescent of Molokini. The clear waters tumble to shore in waves just the right size for gentle riding, with or without a board. All the beaches on the west and south coasts are great for spotting whales, but Wailea, with its fairly flat sandy beach that gently slopes down to the ocean, provides exceptionally good whale-watching from shore in season (Dec–Apr). See p. 177.

- **Maluaka Beach (Makena Beach):** On the southern end of Maui's resort coast, development falls off dramatically, leaving a wild, dry countryside punctuated by green kiawe trees. This wide, palm-fringed crescent of golden sand is set between two black-lava points and bounded by big sand dunes topped by a grassy knoll. Makena can be perfect for swimming when it's flat and placid, but it can also offer excellent bodysurfing when the waves come rolling in. Molokini and Kahoolawe can be seen off in the distance. See p. 178.

- **Waianapanapa State Park:** In east Maui, a few miles before Hana, the 120 acres of this state park offer 12 cabins, a caretaker's residence, a picnic area, a shoreline hiking trail, and, best of all, a black-sand beach (it's actually small black pebbles). Swimming is generally unsafe, though, due to strong waves and rip currents. But it's a great spot for picnicking, hiking along the shore, and simply sitting and relaxing. See p. 179.

- **Hamoa Beach:** This half-moon-shaped, gray-sand beach (a mix of coral and lava) in a truly tropical setting is a favorite among sunbathers, snorkelers, and bodysurfers in Hana. The 100-foot-wide beach is about 900 feet long and sits below 30-foot black-lava sea cliffs. An unprotected beach open to the ocean, Hamoa is often swept by powerful rip currents. The surf breaks offshore and rolls in, making this a popular surfing and bodysurfing area. The calm left side is best for snorkeling in the summer. See p. 179.

- **Hulopoe Beach (Lanai):** This golden, palm-fringed beach off the south coast of Lanai gently slopes down to the azure waters of a Marine Life Conservation District, where clouds of tropical fish flourish and spinner dolphins come to play. A tide pool in the lava rocks defines one side of the bay, while the other is lorded over by the Four Seasons Lanai at Manele Bay, which sits prominently on the hill above. Offshore, you'll find good swimming, snorkeling, and diving; on shore, there's a full complement of beach facilities, from restrooms to camping areas. See p. 304.

2 The Best Maui Experiences

- **Taking the Plunge:** Don mask, fins, and snorkel to explore the magical underwater world, where kaleidoscopic clouds of tropical fish flutter by exotic corals; a sea turtle might even come over to check you out. Molokini is everyone's favorite snorkeling destination (see "Snorkel Cruises to Molokini," p. 186), but the shores of Maui are lined with magical spots as well (see "Beaches," p. 173). Can't swim? No problem: Hop on a submarine with **Atlantis Adventures** (© **800/548-6262**; p. 187) for a plunge beneath the waves without getting wet.

- **Hunting for Whales on Land:** No need to shell out megabucks to go out to sea in search of humpback whales—you can watch these majestic mammals breach and spy-hop from shore. I recommend scenic McGregor Point, at mile marker 9 along Honoapiilani Highway, just outside Maalaea in

Maui

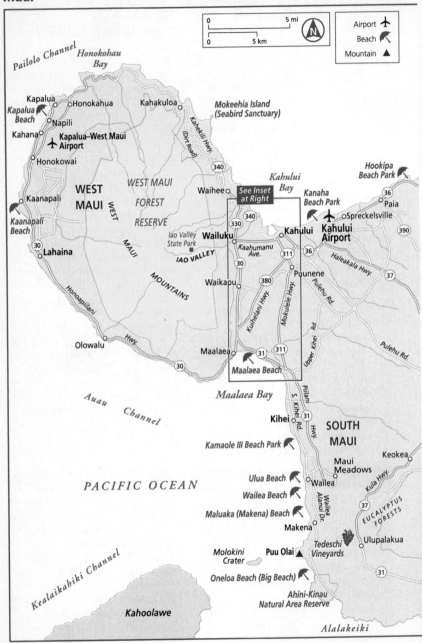

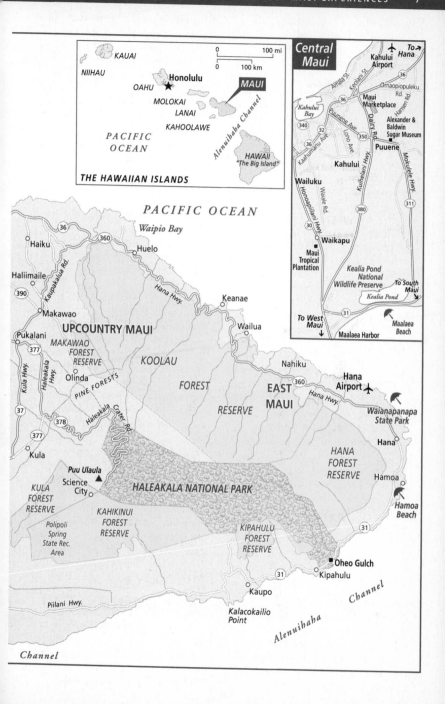

south Maui. The humpbacks arrive as early as November, but the majority travel through Maui's waters from mid-December to mid-April. See "Whale-Watching" (p. 187).

- **Watching the Windsurfers:** World-championship contests are held at Hookipa, on the north shore, one of the greatest windsurfing spots on the planet. Sit on a grassy bluff or stretch out on the sandy beach, and watch the world's top-ranked windsurfers twirling and dancing on the wind and waves like colorful butterflies. See "Windsurfing" (p. 189) and "Driving the Road to Hana" (p. 228).

- **Experiencing Maui's History:** Wander the historic streets of the old whaling town of Lahaina, where the 1800s are alive and well thanks to the efforts of the Lahaina Restoration Society. Drive the scenic Kahekili Highway, where the preserved village of Kahakuloa looks much as it did a century ago. Stand in awe at Piilanihale, Hawaii's largest *heiau* (temple), located just outside Hana. See "Lahaina & West Maui" coverage, beginning on p. 207.

- **Greeting the Rising Sun from Haleakala's Summit:** Bundle up in warm clothing, fill a thermos full of hot java, and drive up to the summit to watch the sky turn from inky black to muted charcoal as a small sliver of orange forms on the horizon. Standing at 10,000 feet, breathing in the rarefied air, and watching the first rays of light streak across the sky is a mystical experience of the first magnitude. See "House of the Sun: Haleakala National Park" (p. 221).

- **Exploring a Different Hawaii— Upcountry Maui:** On the slopes of Haleakala, cowboys, farmers, ranchers, and other country people make their homes in serene, neighborly communities like Makawao, Kula, and Ulupalakua—worlds away from the bustling beach resorts. Acres of onions, lettuce, tomatoes, carrots, cabbage, and flowers cover the hillsides. Maui's only winery is located here, offering the perfect place for a picnic. See "More in Upcountry Maui" (p. 226).

- **Driving Through a Tropical Rainforest:** The Hana Highway is not just a drive but an adventure: Stop along the way to plunge into icy mountain ponds filled by cascading waterfalls; gaze upon vistas of waves pummeling soaring ocean cliffs; inhale the sweet aroma of blooming ginger; and take a walk back in time, catching a glimpse of what Hawaii looked like before concrete condos and fast-food joints washed ashore. See "Driving the Road to Hana" (p. 228).

- **Taking a Day Trip to Lanai:** From Lahaina, join **Trilogy** (© **888/MAUI-800** [6284-800]) for a snorkel cruise to Lanai, or take the **Expeditions Maui–Lanai Passenger Ferry** over and rent a four-wheel-drive jeep on your own. It's a two-for-one island experience: Board in Lahaina Harbor and admire Maui from offshore; then get off at Lanai and go snorkeling in the clear waters, tour the tiny former plantation island, and catch the last ferry home. See "Day Cruises to Lanai" (p. 180) and chapter 12.

3 The Best Adventures

Branch out while you're in Maui. Do something you wouldn't normally do— after all, you're on vacation. Some of the following adventures are a bit pricey, but these splurges are worth every penny.

- **Skimming over the Ocean in a Kayak:** Glide silently over the water, hearing only the sound of your paddle dipping beneath the surface. This is the way the early Hawaiians traveled along the coastline. You'll be eye level and up close and personal with the ocean and the coastline, exploring areas you can't get to any other way. Venture out on your own or go with an experienced guide—either way, you won't be sorry. See "Ocean Kayaking" (p. 181).

- **Scuba Diving:** You're in love with snorkeling and the chance to view the underwater world, but it's just not enough—you want to get closer and see even more. Take an introductory scuba dive: After a brief lesson on how to use the diving equipment, you'll plunge into the deep to swim with the tropical fish and go eyeball to eyeball with other marine critters. See "Scuba Diving" (p. 184).

- **Exploring a Lava Tube:** Most people come to Maui to get outdoors and soak up some Hawaiian sunshine, but don't miss the opportunity to see firsthand how volcanic islands were formed. With **Maui Cave Adventures** (✆ **808/248-7308**), you can hike into the subterranean passages of a huge, extinct lava tube with 40-foot ceilings—an offbeat adventure and a geology lesson you won't soon forget. See "Spelunking" (p. 202).

- **Seeing the Stars from Inside a Volcanic Crater:** Driving up to see the sunrise is a trip you'll never forget, but to *really* experience Haleakala, plan to hike in and spend the night. To get a feel for why the ancient Hawaiians considered this one of the most sacred places on the island, you simply have to wander into the heart of the dormant volcano, where you'll find some 27 miles of hiking trails, two camping sites, and three cabins. See "Hiking & Camping" (p. 189) and "House of the Sun: Haleakala National Park" (p. 221).

- **Hiking to a Waterfall:** There are waterfalls and then there are *waterfalls:* The magnificent 400-foot Waimoku Falls, in Oheo Gulch outside of Hana, are worth the long drive and the uphill hike you have to take to get there. The falls are surrounded by lush green ferns and wild orchids, and you can even stop to take a dip in the pool at the top of Makahiku Falls on the way. See "Hiking & Camping" (p. 189).

- **Flying over the Remote West Maui Mountains:** Your helicopter streaks low over razor-thin cliffs, then flutters past sparkling waterfalls and down into the canyons and valleys of the inaccessible West Maui Mountains. There's so much beauty to absorb that it all goes by in a rush. You'll never want to stop flying over this spectacular, surreal landscape—and it's the only way to see the dazzling beauty of the prehistoric area of Maui. See "By Air, Land & Sea: Guided Island Adventures" (p. 203).

- **Taking a Drive on the Wild Side:** Mother Nature's wild side, that is—on the Kahekili Highway on Maui's northeast coast. This back-to-nature experience will take you past ancient Hawaiian *heiau* (temples); along steep ravines; and by rolling pastures, tumbling waterfalls, exploding blowholes, crashing surf, and jagged lava coastlines. You'll wander through the tiny Hawaiian village of Kahakuloa and around the "head" of Maui to the Marine Life Conservation Area of Honolua-Mokuleia and on to the resort of Kapalua. You'll remember this adventure for years. See "Lahaina & West Maui" in chapter 8.

- **Riding a Mule to Kalaupapa:** Even if you have only 1 day to spend on Molokai, spend it on a mule. The **Molokai Mule Ride** ✰ (✆ **800/567-7550**) trek from "topside" Molokai to the Kalaupapa National Historical Park (Father Damien's world-famous leper colony) is a once-in-a-lifetime adventure. The cliffs are taller than 300-story skyscrapers, and the narrow 3-mile trail includes 26 dizzying switchbacks, but Buzzy Sproat has never lost one of his trustworthy mules (or any riders) on the difficult trail. The mules make the trek daily, rain or shine. See "The Legacy of Father Damien: Kalaupapa National Historical Park" (p. 286).

4 The Best of Underwater Maui

An entirely different Maui greets anyone with a face mask, snorkel, and fins. Under the sea, you'll find schools of brilliant tropical fish, green sea turtles, quick-moving game fish, slack-jawed moray eels, and prehistoric-looking coral. It's a kaleidoscope of color and wonder.

- **Black Rock:** This spot, located on the Kaanapali Beach just off the Sheraton Maui Resort, is excellent for beginning snorkelers during the day and for scuba divers at night. Schools of fish congregate at the base of the rock and are so used to snorkelers that they go about their business as if no one were around. If you take the time to look closely at the crannies of the rock, you'll find lion fish in fairly shallow water. At night (when a few outfitters run night dives here), lobsters, Spanish dancers, and eels come out. See "Kaanapali Beach" (p. 176).

- **Olowalu:** When the wind is blowing and the waves are crashing everywhere else, Olowalu, the small area 5 miles south of Lahaina, can be a scene of total calm—perfect for snorkeling and diving. You'll find a good snorkeling area around mile marker 14. You might have to swim about 50 to 75 feet; when you get to the large field of finger coral in 10 to 15 feet of water, you're there. You'll see a turtle-cleaning station, where turtles line up to have small cleaner wrasses pick off small parasites. This is also a good spot to see crown-of-thorns starfish, puffer fish, and lots of juvenile fish. See "Snorkeling" (p. 185) and "Lahaina & West Maui" (p. 207).

- **Hawaiian Reef:** Scuba divers love this area off the Kihei-Wailea coast because it has a good cross section of topography and marine life typical of Hawaiian waters. Diving to depths of 85 feet, you'll see everything from lava formations and coral reef to sand and rubble, plus a diverse range of both shallow- and deepwater creatures. See "An Expert Shares His Secrets: Maui's Best Dives" (p. 182).

- **Third Tank:** Scuba divers looking for a photo opportunity will find it at this artificial reef, located off Makena Beach at 80 feet. This World War II tank acts like a fish magnet—because it's the only large solid object in the area, any fish or invertebrate looking for a safe home comes here. Surrounding the tank is a cloak of schooling snappers and goatfish just waiting for a photographer with a wide-angle lens. It's small, but Third Tank is loaded with more marine life per square inch than any site off Maui. See "An Expert Shares His Secrets: Maui's Best Dives" (p. 182).

- **Molokini:** Shaped like a crescent moon, this islet's shallow concave side serves as a sheltering backstop against sea currents for tiny tropical fish; on its opposite side is a deepwater cliff inhabited by spiny lobsters, moray eels, and white-tipped sharks. Neophyte snorkelers report to the concave side; experienced scuba divers, the cliff side. Either way, the clear water and abundant marine life make this islet off the Makena coast one of Hawaii's most popular dive spots. See "Watersports" (p. 179).

- **Ahihi-Kinau Natural Preserve:** Fishing is strictly *kapu* (forbidden) in Ahihi Bay (at the end of the road in south Maui), and the fish seem to know it—they're everywhere in this series of rocky coves and black-lava tide pools. The black, barren, lunarlike land stands in stark contrast to the green-blue water, which is home to a sparkling mosaic of tropical fish. Scuba divers might want to check out **La Pérouse Pinnacle** in the middle of La Pérouse Bay; clouds of damselfish and triggerfish will greet you on the surface. See "Snorkeling" (p. 185) and "An Expert Shares His Secrets: Maui's Best Dives" (p. 182).

5 The Best Golf Courses

- **Kaanapali Golf Resort** (© 808/661-3691): All golfers, from high handicappers to near-pros, will love these two challenging courses. The North Course is a true Robert Trent Jones, Sr., design: an abundance of wide bunkers; several long, stretched-out tees; and the largest, most contoured greens on Maui. The South Course is an Arthur Jack Snyder design; although shorter than the North Course, it requires more accuracy on the narrow, hilly fairways. Just like its sibling course, it has a water hazard on its final hole, so don't tally up your score card until you sink your final putt. See p. 198.

- **Kapalua Resort** (© 877/527-2582): Kapalua is probably the best nationally known golf resort in Hawaii, due to the PGA Mercedes-Benz Championship played here each January. The Bay Course and the Village Course are vintage Arnold Palmer designs; the Plantation Course is a strong entry from Ben Crenshaw and Bill Coore. All sit on Maui's wind-swept northwestern shore, at the rolling foothills of Puu Kukui, the summit of the West Maui Mountains. See p. 198.

- **Makena Golf Courses** (© 808/879-3344): Here you'll find 36 holes by "Mr. Hawaii Golf"—Robert Trent Jones, Jr.—at his best. Add to that spectacular views: Molokini islet looms in the background, humpback whales gambol offshore in winter, and the tropical sunsets are spectacular. The South Course has magnificent views (bring your camera) and is kinder to golfers who haven't played for a while. The North Course is more difficult but also more stunning. The 13th hole, located partway up the mountain, has a view that makes most golfers stop and stare. The next hole is even more memorable: a 200-foot drop between tee and green. See p. 199.

- **Wailea Golf Club** (© 888/328-MAUI [6284]): On the sunbaked south shore of Maui stands Wailea Resort, *the* hot spot for golf in the islands. You'll find great golf at these three resort courses: The Blue Course is an Arthur Jack Snyder design, while the Emerald and Gold courses are both by Robert Trent Jones, Jr. All boast outstanding views of the Pacific and the mid–Hawaiian Islands. See p. 199.

- **The Lanai Courses:** For quality and seclusion, nothing in Hawaii can touch Lanai's two golf-resort offerings. The **Experience at Koele** (© 800/321-4666), designed by Ted Robinson and Greg Norman, and the **Challenge at Manele** (© 800/321-4666), a wonderful Jack Nicklaus course with ocean views from every hole, rate among Hawaii's best courses. Both are tremendous fun to play, with the Experience featuring the par-4 8th hole, which drops some 150 yards from tee to fairway, and the Challenge boasting the par-3 12th, which plays from one cliff side to another over a Pacific inlet—one of the most stunning holes in Hawaii. See p. 308.

6 The Best Luxury Hotels & Resorts

- **Hyatt Regency Maui Resort & Spa** (© **800/233-1234** or 808/661-1234; www.maui.hyatt.com): Spa-goers will love Hawaii's first oceanfront spa. The 806 rooms of this fantasy resort, spread out among three towers, have very comfortable separate sitting areas and private lanais with eye-popping views. This huge place covers some 40 acres; even if you don't stay here, you might want to walk through the expansive tree-filled atrium and the parklike grounds. See p. 110.

- **Kaanapali Alii** (© **800/642-6284** or 808/661-3330; www.kaanapali-alii. com): The height of luxury, these oceanfront condominium units (right on Kaanapali Beach) combine all the amenities of a luxury hotel (including a 24-hr. front desk) with the convenience of a condominium. One-bedroom units (1,500 sq. ft.) start at $395 for four people. The beachside recreation area includes a swimming pool, a separate children's pool, a whirlpool, gas barbecue grills and picnic areas, exercise rooms, saunas, and tennis courts. See p. 111.

- **Sheraton Maui Resort** (© **866/716-8109** or 808/661-0031; www.sheraton-maui.com): Offering the best location on Kaanapali Beach, recent renovations, and a great hassle-free experience, the Sheraton is my pick of Kaanapali hotels. This is the place for travelers who just want to arrive, have everything ready for them, and get on with their vacation. (Sheraton has a "no-hassle" check-in: The valet takes you and your luggage straight to your room, which means no time wasted standing in line at registration.) See p. 111.

- **Ritz-Carlton Kapalua** (© **800/262-8440** or 808/669-6200; www.ritzcarlton.com): With its great location, style, and loads of hospitality, this is the best Ritz anywhere. Situated on the coast below the picturesque West Maui Mountains, this grand, breezy hotel overlooks the Pacific Ocean and Molokai across the channel. The natural setting, on an old coastal pineapple plantation, is the picture of tranquillity. The service is legendary, the golf courses are daunting, and the nearby beaches are perfect for snorkeling, diving, and just relaxing. See p. 120.

- **The Fairmont Kea Lani Maui** (© **800/659-4100** or 808/875-4100; www.fairmont.com/kealani): This all-suite luxury hotel in Wailea has 840-square-foot suites featuring kitchenettes with microwaves and coffeemakers, living rooms with high-tech media centers and pullout sofa beds (great if you have the kids in tow), marble wet bars, and spacious bedrooms. The oversize marble bathrooms have separate showers big enough for a party. Large lanais off the bedrooms and living rooms overlook the pools and lawns, with views that sweep right down to the white-sand beach. See p. 129.

- **Four Seasons Resort Maui at Wailea** (© **800/334-MAUI** [6284] or 808/874-8000; www.fourseasons.com/maui): This is the ultimate beach hotel for latter-day royals, offering excellent cuisine, spacious rooms, gracious service, and Wailea Beach—one of Maui's best gold-sand beaches—right outside the front door. Every room has at least a partial ocean view from a private lanai. The luxury suites are as big as some Honolulu condos and full of marble and deluxe appointments. See p. 130.

- **Grand Wailea Resort Hotel & Spa** (© **800/888-6100** or 808/875-1234; www.grandwailea.com): There's nothing subtle or understated about it, but many travelers adore this over-the-top fantasy resort. It has 10,000 tropical plants in the lobby; a fabulous pool with slides, waterfalls, and rapids; Hawaii's largest spa; plush oceanview rooms; and a superb location on a gorgeous stretch of beach. See p. 130.

- **Hotel Hana-Maui** (© **800/321-HANA** [4262] or 808/248-8211; www.hotelhanamaui.com): Picture Shangri-La, Hawaiian style: 66 acres rolling down to the sea in a remote Hawaiian village, with two pools and access to one of the best beaches in Hana. This is the atmosphere, the landscape, and the culture of old Hawaii set in the latest accommodations of the 21st century. A white-sand beach just a 5-minute shuttle ride away, top-notch wellness center, and numerous activities (horseback riding, mountain bicycling, tennis, pitch-and-putt golf) all add up to make this one of the top resorts in the state. See p. 137.

- **Four Seasons Resort Lanai at Manele Bay** (Lanai; © **800/321-4666** or 808/565-2000; www.fourseasons.com/lanai): The high-end resort chain Four Seasons took over management of this 236-unit property after a multimillion-dollar makeover. Facing the deep-blue Pacific, this luxury resort has become even more luxurious. The remodeled rooms (most with an ocean view) now feature 40-inch flatscreen TVs and huge marble bathrooms. The nearly beachfront hotel (a 2-min. stroll puts you on the sands of one of Hawaii's best beaches) also has many pluses for families: child-care programs, a teen center, and an excellent fitness program and pampering spa. Add to that great golf, plenty of tennis, and all the ocean activities you can think of. See p. 299.

- **Four Seasons Resort Lanai, The Lodge at Koele** (Lanai; © **800/321-4666** or 808/565-4000; www.fourseasons.com/lanai): After some $50 million in renovations, the Four Seasons took over management of the former Lodge at Koele. All of the 102 guest rooms were totally renovated, with new carpeting, furniture, and fabrics, plus luxuries such as signature Four Seasons beds, 42-inch flatscreen TVs, and high-speed Internet access. This inn, which resembles a grand English country estate, was built in 1991 and needed the renovation. The new look is spectacular. See p. 300.

7 The Best Moderately Priced Accommodations

- **The Plantation Inn** (© **800/433-6815** or 808/667-9225; www.theplantationinn.com): Attention, romance-seeking couples: You need look no further. This charming Lahaina hotel looks like it's been here 100 years or more, but looks can be deceiving. The Victorian-style inn is actually of 1990s vintage—an artful deception. The rooms are romantic to the max, tastefully done with period furniture, hardwood floors, stained glass, ceiling fans, and four-poster canopy beds. The rooms wrap around the large pool and deck; also on site are a spa and an elegant pavilion lounge, where breakfast is served, all starting at $169 double. See p. 107.

- **Lahaina Inn** (© **800/669-3444** or 808/661-0577; www.lahainainn.com): If the romance of historic Lahaina catches your fancy, a stay here will really complete the experience. Built in 1938 as a general store, it has been restored as a charming, antiques-filled inn right in the heart of town, with room rates as low as $150. Downstairs, you'll find one of Hawaii's most popular storefront bistros, David Paul's Lahaina Grill. See p. 109.

- **Kahana Sunset** (© **800/669-1488** or 808/669-8011; www.kahanasunset. com): This is a great choice for families, featuring a series of wooden condo units stair-stepping down the side of a hill to a postcard-perfect white-sand beach. The units feature full kitchens, washer/dryers, large lanais with terrific views, and sleeper sofas (starting at $165 for up to four people). See p. 116.

- **Punahoa Beach Apartments** (© **800/ 564-4380** or 808/879-2720; www. punahoabeach.com): This small oceanside Kihei condo complex is hidden on a quiet side street; the grassy lawn out front rolls about 50 feet down to the beach. You'll find great snorkeling just offshore and a popular surfing spot next door, with shopping and restaurants all within walking distance. Every well-decorated unit features a lanai with fabulous ocean views, starting at $116 off season. See p. 125.

- **Paniolo Hale** (Molokai; © **800/367- 2984** or 808/553-8334; www.molokai-vacation-rental.com or www.paniolo hale.org): This is far and away Molokai's most charming lodging and probably its best value. The two-story old-Hawaii ranch-house design is airy and homey, with oak floors and walls of folding-glass doors that open to huge screened verandas. The condos start at just $105 for two. See p. 270.

- **Hotel Lanai** (Lanai; © **800/795- 7211** or 808/565-7211; www.hotel lanai.com): This simple, down-home, plantation-era relic has recently been Laura Ashley–ized. The Hotel Lanai is homey, funky, and fun—and, best of all, a real bargain (starting at $139 for two) compared to its ritzy neighbors. See p. 300.

8 The Best Bed & Breakfasts

- **Old Wailuku Inn at Ulupono** (© **800/305-4899** or 808/244-5897; www.mauiinn.com): Located in historic Wailuku, the most charming town in central Maui, this restored 1924 former plantation manager's home is the place to stay if you're looking for a night in the old Hawaii of the 1920s. The guest rooms are spacious, with exotic ohia-wood floors and traditional Hawaiian quilts. The morning meal is a full gourmet breakfast served on the enclosed back lanai or on a tray delivered to your room if you prefer. Rates start at $150. See p. 103.

- **Guest House** (© **800/621-8942** or 808/661-8085; www.mauiguesthouse. com): This is one of the great bed-and-breakfast deals in Lahaina: a charming inn offering more amenities than the expensive Kaanapali hotels just down the road. The spacious home features floor-to-ceiling windows, parquet floors, and a large swimming pool. Guest rooms have quiet lanais and romantic Jacuzzis. Breakfasts are a gourmet affair. All units are $169 double. See p. 108.

- **Nona Lani Cottages** (© **800/ 733-2688** or 808/879-2497; www. nonalanicottages.com): Picture this: a grassy expanse dotted with eight cottages tucked among palm, fruit, and sweet-smelling flower trees, right across the street from a white-sand beach. This is one of the great hidden deals in Kihei. The cottages are tiny but contain everything you'll need. At $105 a night, this is a deal. See p. 127.

- **Pineapple Inn Maui** (© 877/ **212-MAUI** [6284] or 808/298-4403; www.pineappleinnmaui.com): Opened in late 2004, this charming inn (only four rooms, plus a darling two-bedroom cottage) is not only an exquisite find, but also a terrific value (rates start at $119 a night). Located in the residential Maui Meadows area, with panoramic ocean views, the two-story inn features a giant saltwater pool and Jacuzzi overlooking the ocean. Each of the soundproof rooms is expertly decorated with a small kitchenette, comfy bed, free wireless Internet access, TV/VCR, and an incredible view off your own private lanai. See p. 128.

- **Two Mermaids on Maui B&B** (© **800/598-9550** or 808/874-8687; www.twomermaids.com): Two avid scuba divers are the hosts at this very friendly Kihei B&B, professionally decorated in brilliant, tropical colors, complete with hand-painted art of the island (above and below the water) in a quiet neighborhood just a short 10-minute walk from the beach. Comfy rooms start at $115, including breakfast. See p. 128.

- **What a Wonderful World B&B** (© **800/943-5804** or 808/879-9103; www.amauibedandbreakfast.com): Another one of Kihei's best B&Bs offers a great central location in town—just ½ mile to Kamaole II Beach Park, 5 minutes from Wailea golf courses, and convenient to shopping and restaurants. All rooms boast cooking facilities and private

entrances, bathrooms, and phones. A family-style breakfast (eggs Benedict, Alaskan waffles, skillet eggs with mushroom sauce, fruit blintzes) is served on the lanai, which has views of white-sand beaches, the West Maui Mountains, and Haleakala. From $89 double. See p. 128.

- **Ekena** (© **808/248-7047**; www.ekena maui.com): Situated on 8½ acres in the hills above Hana, this Hawaiian-style wooden pole house, with 360-degree views of the coastline, the ocean, and Hana's verdant rainforest, is perfect for those in search of a quiet, peaceful vacation. Inside, the elegantly furnished home features floor-to-ceiling sliding-glass doors and a fully equipped kitchen (starting at $225 for two); outside, hiking trails into the rainforest start right on the property. Beaches, waterfalls, and pools are mere minutes away. See p. 138.

- **Hamoa Bay House & Bungalow** (©**808/248-7884;**www.hamoabay. com): This enchanting retreat sits on 4 verdant acres within walking distance of Hamoa Beach, just outside Hana. The romantic 600-square-foot Balinese-style cottage has a full kitchen and hot tub. This very private place is perfect for honeymooners. The price? Just $225. See p. 139.

- **Heavenly Hana Inn** (© **808/248-8442;** www.heavenlyhanainn.com): Just a stone's throw from the center of Hana is this tiny Japanese-style inn, where no attention to detail has been spared. Flowers are everywhere, ceiling fans keep the rooms cool, and the delicious gourmet breakfast is served in a setting filled with art. The 2 acres of grounds are impeccable, with tiny bridges over a meandering stream and Japanese gardens. Rooms start at $190. See p. 140.

- **Aloha Beach House** (Molokai; © **888/828-1008** or 808/828-1100;

www.molokaivacation.com): Nestled on the lush East End of Molokai is this Hawaiian-style beach house sitting right on the white-sand beach of Waialua. Perfect for families, the impeccably decorated two-bedroom, 1,600-square-foot property has a huge open living/dining/kitchen area that opens onto an old-fashioned porch for meals or just sitting in the comfy chairs and watching the clouds roll by. Just $290 for up to five people. See p. 272.

9 The Best Resort Spas

- **Spa Moana at the Hyatt Regency Maui Resort & Spa** (© 800/233-1234 or 808/661-1234; www.maui.hyatt.com): The island's first oceanfront spa, this 20,000-square-foot facility offers an open-air exercise lanai, wet-treatment rooms, massage rooms, a relaxation lounge, sauna and steam rooms, a Roman pool illuminated by overhead skylights, and a duet treatment suite for couples. See p. 110.

- **Spa at the Ritz-Carlton Kapalua** (© 800/262-8440 or 808/669-6200; www.ritzcarlton.com): Book a massage on the beach. The spa itself is welcoming and wonderful, but there is nothing like smelling the salt in the air and feeling the gentle caress of the wind in your hair while experiencing a true Hawaiian massage. See p. 120.

- **Spa Kea Lani at the Fairmont Kea Lani Maui** (© 800/659-4100 or 808/875-4100; www.fairmont.com/kealani): This intimate, Art Deco boutique spa (just a little over 5,000 sq. ft., with nine treatment rooms), which opened in 1999, is the place for personal and private attention. The fitness center next door is open 24 hours (a rarity in Hawaiian resorts) with a personal trainer on duty some 14 hours a day. See p. 129.

- **Spa at the Four Seasons Resort Maui at Wailea** (© 800/334-MAUI [6284] or 808/874-8000; www.fourseasons.com/maui): Imagine the sound of the waves rolling on Wailea Beach as you are soothingly massaged in the privacy of your cabana, tucked in among the beachside foliage. This is the place to come to be absolutely spoiled. Yes, there's an excellent workout area and tons of great classes, but the specialty here is hedonistic indulgence. See p. 130.

- **Spa Grande at the Grand Wailea Resort Hotel & Spa** (© 800/888-6100 or 808/875-1234; www.grandwailea.com): This is Hawaii's biggest spa, at 50,000 square feet and with 40 treatment rooms. The spa incorporates the best of the Old World (romantic ceiling murals, larger-than-life Roman-style sculptures, mammoth Greek columns, huge European tubs), the finest Eastern traditions (a full Japanese-style traditional bath and various exotic treatments from India), and the lure of the islands (tropical foliage, ancient Hawaiian treatments, and island products). It has everything from a top fitness center to a menu of classes and is constantly on the cutting edge of the latest trends. See p. 130.

- **Spa at the Four Seasons Resort Lanai at Manele Bay** (Lanai; © 800/321-4666 or 808/565-2000; www.fourseasons.com/lanai): The new spa facility here features a variety of massages, facials, wraps, and scrubs (don't miss the signature Ali'i banana-coconut scrub). In addition, the Four Seasons has added a 1,500-square-foot fitness center (with one of the best ocean views in the resort) that features the latest cardiovascular and strength-training equipment, free weights, and a wood-floor studio for classes (spinning, yoga, Pilates, and meditation). See p. 299.

⌒Moments Pampering in Paradise

Hawaii's spas have raised the art of relaxation and healing to a new level. The traditional Greco-Roman-style spas, with lots of marble and big tubs in closed rooms, have evolved into airy, open facilities that embrace the tropics. Spa-goers in Hawaii are looking for a sense of place, steeped in the culture. They want to hear the sound of the ocean, smell the salt air, and feel the caress of the warm breeze. They want to experience Hawaiian products and traditional treatments they can get only in the islands.

The spas of Hawaii, once nearly exclusively patronized by women, are now attracting more male clients. There are also special massages for children and pregnant women, and some spas have created programs to nurture and relax brides on their big day.

Today's spas offer a wide diversity of treatments. Massage options include Hawaiian lomilomi, Swedish, aromatherapy (with sweet-smelling oils), craniosacral (massaging the head), shiatsu (no oil, just deep thumb pressure on acupuncture points), Thai (another oil-less massage involving stretching), and hot stone. There are even side-by-side massages for couples. The truly decadent might try a duo massage—not one, but two massage therapists working on you at once.

Body treatments, for the entire body or just the face, involve a variety of herbal wraps, masks, or scrubs using a range of ingredients from seaweed to salt to mud, with or without accompanying aromatherapy, lights, and music.

After you have been rubbed and scrubbed, most spas offer an array of water treatments—a sort of hydromassage in a tub with jets and an assortment of colored crystals, oils, and scents.

Those are just the traditional treatments. Most spas also offer a range of alternative healthcare like acupuncture and chiropractic, and more exotic treatments like ayurvedic and siddha from India or reiki from Japan. Some offer specialized, cutting-edge treatments, like the Grand Wailea Resort's full-spectrum color-light therapy pod (based on NASA's work with astronauts).

Once your body has been pampered, spas also offer a range of fitness facilities (weights, racquetball, tennis, golf, and so on) and classes (such as yoga, aerobics, spinning, tai chi, and kickboxing). Several offer adventure fitness packages (from bicycling to snorkeling). For the less active, most spas also have salons dedicated to hair and nail care.

If all this sounds a bit overwhelming, not to worry: All the spas in Hawaii have individual consultants who will help you design an appropriate treatment program to fit your individual needs.

Of course, all this pampering doesn't come cheap. Massages are generally $180 to $275 for 50 minutes and $265 to $300 for 80 minutes, body treatments are in the $150-to-$250 range, and alternative healthcare treatments can be as high as $200 to $300. But you may think it's worth the expense to banish your tension and stress.

10 The Best Restaurants

- **Mañana Garage** (℃ 808/873-0220): It's great fun dining here, and the food is fantastic, too. Tuck in to fabulous *arepas* (cornmeal-cheese griddle cakes with smoked salmon), fried green tomatoes, excellent ceviche, and a host of new flavors in a colorful, edgy, industrial atmosphere. You'll dine among vertical garage doors, table bases made from hubcaps, cobalt walls, and chrome accents, with *Buena Vista Social Club* on the sound system and very hip servers who will bring you the best desserts in this neck of the woods—Kahului, of all places! See p. 142.

- **A Saigon Cafe** (℃ 808/243-9560): Jennifer Nguyen's unmarked dining room in an odd corner of Wailuku is always packed, a tribute to her clean, crisp Vietnamese cuisine—and the Maui grapevine. Grab a round of rice paper and wrap your own Vietnamese "burrito" of tofu, noodles, and vegetables. See p. 144.

- **A. K.'s Café** (℃ 808/244-8774; www.akscafe.com): Chef Elaine Rothermel has a winner with this tiny cafe in the industrial district of Wailuku. It may be slightly off the tourist path, and the decor isn't much to look at, but it is well worth the effort to find this delicious eatery, with creative cuisine coming out of the kitchen—most of it healthy. Prices are so eye-poppingly cheap, you might find yourself wandering back here again during your vacation. See p. 145.

- **David Paul's Lahaina Grill** (℃ 808/667-5117): Endlessly popular and universally appreciated for its high quality, David Paul's is still most folks' favorite Maui eatery—even without David Paul. No one seems to tire of the kalua duck he turned into a Maui institution, or the Kona coffee–roasted rack of lamb, or the much-imitated tequila shrimp. The menu changes often, but thank goodness the room doesn't: Its pressed-tin ceilings and 1890s decor continue to intrigue. See p. 146.

- **Gerard's** (℃ 808/661-8939; www.gerardsmaui.com): Proving that French is fabulous, particularly in the land of sushi and sashimi, Gerard Reversade is the Gallic gastronome who delivers ecstasy with every bite. From the rack of lamb to the spinach salad and oyster mushrooms in puff pastry, every meal is memorable. The fairy lights on the veranda in the balmy outdoor Lahaina setting are the icing on the gâteau. See p. 148.

- **Mala Ocean Tavern** (℃ 808/667-9394; www.malaoceantavern.com): Perched right on the ocean, this tiny "tavern" is the brainchild of Mark and Judy Ellman, owners of Maui Tacos and Penne Pasta Café. They use healthy, organically grown food and fresh fish to make intriguing dishes. The atmosphere could not be more enticing, with just a handful of tables out on the oceanfront lanai and several more tables in the warmly decorated interior. The staff is helpful and efficient, and the food is outstanding. See p. 150.

- **Son'z Maui at Swan Court** (℃ 808/667-4506; www.sonzmaui.com): For 30 years, the Swan Court was *the* dining experience at the Hyatt Regency Maui Resort, and under Tri-Star Restaurant Group it's even better. The restaurant already had perhaps the most romantic location in Maui, overlooking a man-made lagoon with white and black swans swimming by and the rolling surf of the Pacific in the distance. The culinary team's creative dishes, coupled with fresh local ingredients, have made it a must for every Maui visitor. See p. 153.

- **Roy's Kahana Bar & Grill** (© 808/669-6999; www.roysrestaurant.com): This restaurant bustles with young, hip servers impeccably trained to deliver blackened ahi or perfectly seared lemon-grass *shutome* (broadbill swordfish) hot to your table, in rooms that sizzle with cross-cultural tastings. See p. 156.

- **Pineapple Grill** (© 808/669-9600): This is the best new restaurant on Maui—if you only had a single night to eat on the island, I'd send you here. In fact, if you eat here at the beginning of your Maui trip, you might end up coming back! Chef Ryan Luckey is a genius at turning fresh local ingredients into culinary masterpieces such as the Maui-style seafood paella with Portuguese sausage and Kula herbs. See p. 158.

- **Plantation House Restaurant** (© 808/669-6299): Plantation House features teak tables, a fireplace, open sides, mountain and ocean views, and chef Alex Stanislaw's love for Mediterranean flavors and preparations. It's a friendly, comfortable restaurant with great food, including sublime eggs Mediterranean at breakfast, and polenta, crab cakes, fish, pork tenderloin, filet mignon, and other delights at dinner. The ambience is superb. See p. 158.

- **Sansei Seafood Restaurant & Sushi Bar** (© 808/669-6286 in Kapalua, 879-0004 in Kihei; www.sansei hawaii.com): Relentlessly popular, Sansei serves sushi and then some: hand rolls warm and cold, udon and ramen, and the signature Asian rock-shrimp cake with the oh-so-complex lime-chile butter and cilantro pesto. This place is flavor central—simplicity is not its strong suit, so be prepared for some busy tasting. See p. 158.

- **Joe's** (© 808/875-7767; www.bev gannonrestaurants.com): The impressive view spans the Wailea golf course, tennis courts, ocean, and Haleakala—a worthy setting for Beverly Gannon's style of American home cooking with a regional twist (also see "Haliimaile General Store," below). The hearty staples include excellent mashed potatoes, lobster, fresh fish, and filet mignon, but the meatloaf (a whole loaf, like Mom used to make) upstages them all. See p. 165.

- **Haliimaile General Store** (© 808/572-2666; www.haliimailegeneral store.com): Bev Gannon, one of the 12 original Hawaii Regional Cuisine chefs, is still going strong at her foodie haven in the pineapple fields. You'll dine at tables set on old wood floors under high ceilings. The food, a blend of eclectic American with ethnic touches, bridges Hawaii with Gannon's Texas roots and puts an innovative spin on Hawaii Regional Cuisine. Examples include sashimi napoleon and the house salad—island greens with mandarin oranges, onions, toasted walnuts, and blue-cheese crumble. See p. 165.

- **Moana Bakery & Cafe** (© 808/579-9999; www.members.aol.com/moanacafe): In the unlikely location of Paia, the Moana gets high marks for its stylish concrete floors, high ceilings, booths and cafe tables, and fabulous food. Don Ritchey, formerly a chef at Haliimaile General Store, has created the perfect Paia eatery, a casual bakery/cafe that highlights his stellar skills. It may not look like much from the outside, but don't be fooled. This innovative eatery serves breakfast, lunch, and dinner and offers live entertainment at night. See p. 169.

- **Colleen's at the Cannery** (© 808/575-9211; www.colleensinhaiku.com):

Way, way, way off the beaten path lies this chic, fabulous find in the rural Haiku Cannery Marketplace. It's worth the drive to enjoy Colleen's fabulous culinary creations, such as wild-mushroom ravioli with sautéed portobello mushrooms, tomatoes, herbs, and a roasted-pepper coulis. See p. 170.

- **Old Lahaina Luau** (© 800/248-5828 or 808/667-1998; www.old lahainaluau.com): It's not exactly a restaurant, but it's certainly an unforgettable dining experience. Maui's best luau serves top-quality food that's as much Pacific Rim as authentically Hawaiian, served from an open-air thatched structure. It's one-third entertainment, one-third good food, and one-third ambience. See p. 260.

- **Ihilani** (Lanai; © 808/565-2296; www.fourseasons.com/manelebay/dining): During their tenures here, a number of top Hawaii chefs (such as Philippe Padovani and Edwin Goto) have added their own style to the menu, which melds Mediterranean with Island cuisine. The result is one of Lanai's top gourmet restaurants. The latest incarnation of this classy restaurant, overlooking the resort and the ocean beyond, is traditional Italian cuisine that is actually reasonably priced. Not to be missed. See p. 301.

- **Lanai City Grille** (Lanai; © 808/565-7211): Celebrated Maui chef Bev Gannon (Haliimaile General Store, Joe's) redesigned the menu in this cute eatery, where the decor consists of pine-paneled walls, chintz curtains, and a fireplace. The menu sticks to whatever is in season and fresh that day, from the fish and seafood to the rotisserie chicken. See p. 303.

- **Pele's Other Garden** (Lanai; © 808/565-9628): You don't have to spend a fortune at the high-priced eateries in the two resorts on Lanai: This charming bistro in the heart of Lanai City has a full-scale New York deli (yummy pizzas), and you can also get box lunches and picnic baskets to go. Dinner is now served on china on cloth-covered tables—a real dining room! See p. 304.

11 The Best Shops & Galleries

- **Summerhouse** (© 808/871-1320): Bright and sassy tropical wear and the jewelry and accessories to go with it are a cut above at Kahului's Summerhouse. T-shirts are tailored and in day-to-evening colors, while dresses are good for either the office or a night out. See p. 243.

- **Bailey House Museum Shop** (© 808/244-3326): You can travel Hawaii and peruse its past with the assemblage of made-in-Hawaii items at this museum gift shop in Wailuku. Tropical preserves, Hawaiian music, pareu, prints by esteemed Hawaiian artists, cookbooks, hatbands, and magnificent wood bowls reflect a discerning standard of selection. Unequaled for Hawaiian treasures on Maui. See p. 244.

- **Brown-Kobayashi** (© 808/242-0804): At this quiet, tasteful, and elegant Asian shop in Wailuku, the selection of antiques and collectibles changes constantly but reflects an unwavering sense of gracious living. There are old and new European and Hawaiian objects, from koa furniture (which disappears fast) to lacquerware, Bakelite jewelry, Peking glass beads, and a few priceless pieces of antique ivory. See p. 244.

- **Village Galleries** (© 808/661-4402 in Lahaina, 808/669-1800 in Kapalua): Maui's oldest galleries have maintained high standards and the respect of a public that is increasingly impatient with clichéd island art. On exhibit are the finest contemporary Maui artists in all media, with a discerning selection of handcrafted jewelry. In Lahaina, the contemporary gallery has a larger selection of jewelry, ceramics, glass, and gift items, as well as paintings and prints. See p. 248 and 250.

- **Hui No'eau Visual Arts Center** (© **808/572-6560**): Half the experience is the center itself, one of Maui's historic treasures: a strikingly designed 1917 *kamaaina* (native-born, or old-timer) estate on 9 acres in Makawao; two of Maui's largest hybrid Cook and Norfolk pines; and an arts center with classes, exhibitions, and demonstrations. The gift shop is as memorable as the rest of it. You'll find one-of-a-kind works by local artists, from prints to jewelry and pottery. See p. 251.

- **Viewpoints Gallery** (© **808/572-5979**): I love this airy, well-designed Makawao gallery and its helpful staff, which complement the fine Maui art: paintings, sculpture, jewelry, prints, woods, and glass. This is Maui's only fine-arts cooperative, showcasing the work of dozens of local artists. See p. 253.

- **Hana Coast Gallery** (© **808/248-8636**): This gallery is a good reason to go to Hana: It's an aesthetic and cultural experience that informs as it enlightens. Tucked away in the posh hideaway Hotel Hana-Maui, the 3,000-square-foot gallery is known for its high level of curatorship and commitment to the cultural art of Hawaii. It's devoted entirely to Hawaiian artists, who display their sculptures, paintings, prints, feather work, stonework, and carvings. See p. 254.

- **Dis 'N Dat** (Lanai; © **866/DIS-N-DAT** [347-6328]): This is my favorite shop on Lanai, where Barry (Dis) and Susie (Dat) have collected the unusual, the bizarre, and the hilariously funny. You'll find everything from finely crafted teak and exotic wood sculptures and carvings to mobiles and wind chimes (the more outrageous, the better), plus an impressive line of handmade jewelry, stained glass, and more. See p. 313.

- **The Local Gentry** (Lanai; © **808/565-9130**): This wonderful Lanai boutique features clothing and accessories that are not the standard resort-shop fare. You'll find fabulous silk aloha shirts by Iolani, Putumayo separates (perfect for Hawaii) in easy-care fabrics, a fabulous line of silk aloha shirts by Tiki, top-quality hemp-linen camp shirts, inexpensive sarongs, fabulous socks, and the Tommy Bahama line for men and women. There are also great T-shirts, swimwear, jewelry, bath products, picture frames, jeans, chic sunglasses, offbeat sandals, and wonderful children's clothes. See p. 314.

2

Maui in Depth

Since the Polynesians ventured across the Pacific to the Hawaiian Islands more than 1,000 years ago, these floating jewels have continued to call visitors from around the globe.

Located in one of the most remote and isolated places on the planet, Maui, as part of the Hawaiian Islands chain, floats in the warm waters of the Pacific, blessed by a tropical sun and cooled by gentle year-round trade winds—creating what might be the most ideal climate imaginable. Centuries of the indigenous Hawaiian culture have given the people of the islands the "spirit of aloha," a warm, welcoming attitude that invites visitors to come and share this exotic paradise. Mother Nature has carved out verdant valleys, hung brilliant rainbows in the sky, and trimmed the islands with sandy beaches in a spectrum of colors, from white to black to even green and red.

Visitors are drawn to Maui not only for its incredible beauty, but also for its opportunities for adventure: bicycling down a 10,000-foot dormant volcano, swimming in a sea of rainbow-colored fish, hiking into a rainforest, or watching whales leap out of the ocean as you tee off on one of the country's top golf courses. Others come to rest and relax in a land where the pace of life moves at a slower rate and the sun's rays soothe and allow both body and mind to regenerate and recharge.

Venturing to Maui is not your run-of-the-mill vacation, but rather an experience in the senses that will remain with you, locked into your memory, way, way, way after your tan fades. Years later, a sweet smell, the warmth of the sun on your body, or the sound of the wind through the trees will take you back to the time you spent in the islands.

Incidentally, Maui is the only island in the Hawaiian chain named after a god—well, actually a demigod (half man, half god). Hawaiian legends are filled with the escapades of Maui, who had a reputation as a trickster. In one story, Maui is credited with causing the birth of the Hawaiian Islands when he threw his "magic" fishhook down to the ocean floor and pulled the islands up from the bottom of the sea. Another legend tells how Maui lassoed the sun to make it travel more slowly across the sky so that his mother could more easily dry her clothes. Maui's status as the only island to carry the name of a deity seems fitting, considering its reputation as the perfect tropical paradise, or as Hawaiians say, *Maui no ka oi* ("Maui is the best").

1 Maui Today

A CULTURAL RENAISSANCE A conch shell sounds, a young man in a bright feather cape chants, torchlight flickers at sunset on the beach, and hula dancers begin telling their graceful centuries-old stories. It's a cultural scene out of the past come to life once again—for Hawaii is enjoying a renaissance of hula, chant, and other aspects of its ancient culture.

The biggest, longest, and most elaborate celebrations of Hawaiian culture are the Aloha Festivals, which encompass more than 500 cultural events from August to October. "Our goal is to teach and share our culture," says Gloriann Akau, a former manager of the Aloha Festivals. "In 1946, after the war, Hawaiians needed an identity. We were lost and needed to regroup. When we started to celebrate our culture, we began to feel proud. We have a wonderful culture that had been buried for a number of years. This brought it out again. Self-esteem is more important than making a lot of money."

In 1985, native Hawaiian educator, author, and *kupuna* (respected elder) George Kanahele started integrating Hawaiian values into hotels like Maui's Kaanapali Beach Hotel. "You have the responsibility to preserve and enhance the Hawaiian culture, not because it's going to make money for you, but because it's the right thing to do," Kanahele told the Hawaii Hotel Association. "Ultimately, the only thing unique about Hawaii is its Hawaiianess. Hawaiianess is our competitive edge."

From general managers to maids, resort employees went through hours of Hawaiian cultural training. They held focus groups to discuss the meaning of aloha—the Hawaiian concept of unconditional love—and applied it to their work and their lives. Now many hotels have joined the movement and instituted Hawaiian programs. No longer content with teaching hula as a joke, resorts now employ a real *kumu hula* (hula teacher) to instruct visitors and have a *kupuna* (elder) take guests on treks to visit *heiau* (temples) and ancient petroglyph sites.

THE QUESTION OF SOVEREIGNTY

The Hawaiian cultural renaissance has also made its way into politics. Many *kanaka maoli* (native people) are demanding restoration of rights taken away more than a century ago when the U.S. overthrew the Hawaiian monarchy. Their demands were not lost on President Bill Clinton, who was picketed at a Democratic political fundraiser at Waikiki Beach in July 1993. Four months later, Clinton signed a document stating that the U.S. Congress "apologizes to Native Hawaiians on behalf of the people of the United States for the overthrow of the Kingdom of Hawaii on January 17, 1893, with the participation of agents and citizens of the United States, and deprivation of the rights of Native Hawaiians to self-determination."

But even neo-nationalists aren't convinced that complete self-determination is possible. Each of the 30 identifiable sovereignty organizations (and more than 100 splinter groups) has a different stated goal, ranging from total independence to nation-within-a-nation status, similar to that of Native Indians. In 1993, the state legislature created a Hawaiian Sovereignty Advisory Commission to "determine the will of the native Hawaiian people." The commission plans to pose the sovereignty question in a referendum open to all over 18 with Hawaiian blood, no matter where they live. The question still remains unanswered.

2 Looking Back at Maui

Paddling outrigger canoes, the first ancestors of today's Hawaiians followed the stars and birds across the sea to Hawaii, which they called "the land of raging fire." Those first settlers were part of the great Polynesian migration that settled the vast triangle of islands stretching between New Zealand, Easter Island, and Hawaii. No one is sure exactly when they came to Hawaii from Tahiti and the Marquesas Islands, some 2,500 miles to the south, but a bone fishhook found at the southernmost tip of the Big Island has been carbon-dated to A.D. 700. Chants claim that the Mookini Heiau, also on the Big Island, was built in A.D. 480. Some recent archaeological digs at Maluuluolele Park in Lahaina even predate that.

All we have today are some archaeological finds, some scientific data, and ancient chants to tell the story of Hawaii's past. The chants, especially the *Kumulipo*, which is the chant of creation and the litany of genealogy of the *alii* (high-ranking chiefs) who ruled the islands, talk about comings and goings between Hawaii and the islands of the south, presumed to be Tahiti. In fact, the channel between Maui, Kahoolawe, and Lanai is called *Kealaikahiki,* or "the pathway to Tahiti."

Around 1300, the transoceanic voyages stopped for some reason, and Hawaii began to develop its own culture in earnest. The settlers built temples, fish ponds, and aqueducts to irrigate taro plantations. Sailors became farmers and fishermen. Each island was a separate kingdom. The *alii* created a caste system and established taboos. Violators were strangled. High priests asked the gods Lono and Ku for divine guidance. Ritual human sacrifices were common.

Maui's history, like that of the rest of Hawaii, was one of wars and conquests, with one king taking over another king's land. The rugged terrain of Maui and the water separating Maui, Molokai, Lanai, and Kahoolawe made for natural boundaries of kingdoms. In the early years, there were three kingdoms on Maui: Hana, Waikulu, and Lahaina. The chants are not just strict listings of family histories. Some describe how a ruler's pride and arrogance can destroy a community. For example, according to the chants, Hana's King Hua killed a priest in the 12th century, and as a result the gods sent a severe drought to Hana as a punishment.

Three centuries later, another ruler came out of Hana who was to change the course of Maui's history: Piilani, the first ruler to unite all of Maui. His rule was a time not only of peace but also of community construction projects. Piilani built fish ponds and irrigation fields and began creating a paved road some 4 to 6 feet wide around the entire island. Piilani's sons and grandson continued these projects and completed the *Alalou,* the royal road that circled the united island. They also completed Hawaii's largest *heiau* (temple) to the god of war, Piilanihale, which still stands today.

Maui was a part of a pivotal change in Hawaii's history: After conquering Maui in 1795, Kamehameha united all of the islands into one kingdom. It started in 1759, when yet another battle over land was going on. This time Kalaniopuu, a chief from the Big Island, had captured Hana from the powerful Maui chief Kahikili. Kahikili was busy overtaking Molokai when the Big Island chief stole Hana from him. The Molokai chief escaped and fled with his wife to Hana, where the Big Island chief welcomed him. A few years later, the Molokai chief and his wife had a baby girl in Hana, named Kaahumanu, who later married Kamehameha.

THE "FATAL CATASTROPHE"   No ancient Hawaiian ever imagined a *haole* (a white person; literally, one with "no breath") would ever appear on one of these "floating islands." But then one day in 1778, just such a person sailed into Waimea Bay on Kauai, where he was welcomed as the god Lono.

The man was 50-year-old Capt. James Cook, already famous in Britain for "discovering" much of the South Pacific. Now on his third great voyage of exploration, Cook had set sail from Tahiti northward across uncharted waters to find the mythical Northwest Passage that was said to link the Pacific and Atlantic oceans. On his way, Cook stumbled upon the Hawaiian Islands quite by chance. He named them the Sandwich Islands, for the Earl of Sandwich, first lord of the admiralty, who had bankrolled the expedition.

Overnight, Stone Age Hawaii entered the age of iron. Nails were traded for fresh water, pigs, and the affections of Hawaiian women. The sailors brought syphilis, measles, and other diseases to which the Hawaiians had no natural immunity, thereby unwittingly wreaking havoc on the native population.

After his unsuccessful attempt to find the Northwest Passage, Cook returned to Kealakekua Bay on the Big Island, where a fight broke out over an alleged theft, and the great navigator was killed by a blow to the head. After this "fatal catastrophe," the British survivors sailed home. But Hawaii was now on the sea charts, and traders on the fur route between Canada and China anchored in Hawaii to get fresh water. More trade—and more disastrous liaisons—ensued.

Two more sea captains left indelible marks on the islands. The first was American John Kendrick, who in 1791 filled his ship with sandalwood and sailed to China. By 1825, Hawaii's sandalwood forests were gone, enabling invasive plants to take charge. The second captain was Englishman George Vancouver, who in 1793 left cows and sheep, which spread out to the high-tide lines. King Kamehameha I sent for cowboys from Mexico and Spain to round up the wild livestock, thus beginning the islands' *paniolo* (cowboy) tradition.

The tightly woven Hawaiian society began to unravel after the death in 1819 of King Kamehameha I, who had used guns seized from a British ship to unite the islands under his rule. One of his successors, Queen Kaahumanu, abolished old taboos, such as that of women eating with men, and opened the door for religion of another form when she converted to Christianity.

STAYING TO DO WELL   In 1819, the first whaling ship dropped anchor in Lahaina. Sailors on the *Bellina* were looking for fresh water and supplies, but they found beautiful women, mind-numbing grog, and a tropical paradise. A few years later, in 1823, the whalers met rivals for this hedonistic playground: the missionaries. The God-fearing missionaries arrived from New England bent on converting the pagans. They chose Lahaina because it was the capital of Hawaii.

Intent on instilling their brand of rock-ribbed Christianity in the islands, the missionaries clothed the natives, banned them from dancing the hula, and nearly dismantled their ancient culture. They tried to keep the whalers and sailors out of the bawdy houses, where a flood of whiskey quenched fleet-size thirsts and where the virtue of native women was never safe.

The missionaries taught reading and writing, created the 12-letter Hawaiian alphabet, started a printing press in Lahaina, and began writing the islands' history, which until then had existed only as an oral account in memorized chants. They also started the first school in Lahaina, which still exists today: the Lahainaluna High School.

Children of the missionaries became the islands' business leaders and politicians. They married Hawaiians and stayed on in the islands, causing one wag to remark that the missionaries "came to do good and stayed to do well."

In Lahaina's heyday, some 500 whaling ships a year dropped anchor in the Lahaina Roadstead. In 1845, King Kamehameha III moved the capital of Hawaii from Lahaina to Honolulu, where more commerce could be accommodated in the natural harbor there. Some whaling ships starting skipping Lahaina for the

Is Everyone Hawaiian in Hawaii?

The plantations brought so many different people to Hawaii that the state is now a rainbow of ethnic groups: Living here are Caucasians, African Americans, American Indians, Eskimos, Japanese, Chinese, Filipinos, Koreans, Tahitians, Vietnamese, Hawaiians, Samoans, Tongans, and other Asian and Pacific Islanders. Add a few Canadians, Dutch, English, French, Germans, Irish, Italians, Portuguese, Scottish, Puerto Ricans, and Spaniards. Everyone's a minority here.

In combination, it's a remarkable potpourri. Many people retain an element of the traditions of their homeland. Some Japanese Americans in Hawaii, generations removed from the homeland, are more traditional than the Japanese of Tokyo. And the same is true of many Chinese, Koreans, Filipinos, and others, making Hawaii a kind of living museum of various Asian and Pacific cultures.

larger port of Honolulu. Fifteen years later, the depletion of whales and the emergence of petroleum as a more suitable oil signaled the beginning of the end of the whaling industry.

KING SUGAR EMERGES When the capital of Hawaii moved to Honolulu, Maui might have taken a back seat in Hawaii's history had it not been for the beginning of a new industry: sugar. In 1849, George Wilfong, a cantankerous sea captain, built a mill in Hana and planted some 60 acres of sugar cane, creating Hawaii's first sugar plantation. At that time the gold rush was on in California, and sugar prices were wildly inflated. Wilfong's harsh personality and the demands he placed on plantation workers did not sit well with the Hawaiians. In 1852, he imported Chinese immigrants to work in his fields. By the end of the 1850s, the gold rush had begun to diminish, and the inflated sugar prices dropped. When Wilfong's mill burned down, he finally called it quits.

Sugar production continued in Hana, however. In 1864, two Danish brothers, August and Oscar Unna, started the Hana Plantation. Four years later they imported Japanese immigrants to work the fields.

Some 40 miles away, in Haiku, two sons of missionaries, Samuel Alexander and Henry Baldwin, planted 12 acres of this new crop. The next year, Alexander and Baldwin added some 5,000 acres in Maui's central plains and started Hawaii's largest sugar company. They quickly discovered that without the copious amounts of rainfall found in Hana, they would need to get water to their crop, or it would fail. In 1876, they constructed an elaborate ditch system that brought water from rainy Haiku some 17 miles away to the dry plains of Wailuku, a move that cemented the future of sugar in Hawaii.

Around the same time, another sugar pioneer, Claus Spreckels, bought up property in the arid desert of Puunene from Hawaiians who sold him the "cursed" lands at a very cheap price. The Hawaiians were sure they had gotten the better part of the deal because they believed that the lands were haunted.

Spreckels was betting that these "cursed" lands could be very productive if he could get water rights up in the rainy hills and bring that water to Puunene, just as Alexander and Baldwin had done. But first he needed that water. Thus began a series of late-night poker games with the then-king Kalakaua. Spreckels's gamble paid off: Not only did he beat the king at poker (some say he cheated), but

Do You Have to Speak Hawaiian in Hawaii?

Almost everyone here speaks English. But many folks in Hawaii now speak Hawaiian as well. All visitors will hear the words *aloha* and *mahalo* (thank you). If you've just arrived, you're a *malihini*. Someone who's been here a long time is a *kamaaina*. When you finish a job or your meal, you are *pau* (finished). On Friday it's *pau hana,* work finished. You eat *pupu* (Hawaii's version of hors d'oeuvres) when you go *pau hana.*

The Hawaiian alphabet, created by the New England missionaries, has only 12 letters: the five regular vowels (*a, e, i, o,* and *u*) and seven consonants (*h, k, l, m, n, p,* and *w*). The vowels are pronounced in the Roman fashion: that is, *ah, ay, ee, oh,* and *oo* (as in "too")—not *ay, ee, eye, oh,* and *you,* as in English. For example, *huhu* is pronounced *who-who.* Most vowels are sounded separately, though some are pronounced together, as in Kalakaua: Kah-lah-*cow*-ah.

Below are some basic Hawaiian words that you'll often hear in Hawaii and see throughout this book. For a more complete list of Hawaiian words, go to www.geocities.com/~olelo/hltableofcontents.html or www.hisurf.com/hawaiian/dictionary.html.

alii Hawaiian royalty
aloha greeting or farewell
halau school
hale house or building
heiau Hawaiian temple or place of worship
kahuna priest or expert
kamaaina old-timer
kapa tapa, bark cloth
kapu taboo, forbidden
keiki child
kupuna respected elder
lanai porch or veranda
lomilomi massage
mahalo thank you
makai a direction, toward the sea
mana spirit power
mauka a direction, toward the mountains
muumuu loose-fitting gown or dress
ono delicious
pali cliff
paniolo Hawaiian cowboy(s)
wiki quick

he also built the elaborate 30-mile Haiku Ditch system, which transported 50 million gallons of water a day from rainy Haiku to dry Puunene.

The big boost to sugar not only on Maui but also across the entire state came in 1876, when King Kalakaua negotiated the Sugar Reciprocity Treaty with the United States, giving the Hawaiian sugar industry a "sweet" deal on prices and tariffs.

In 1891, King Kalakaua visited chilly San Francisco, caught a cold, and died in the royal suite of the Sheraton Palace. His sister, Queen Liliuokalani, assumed the throne.

A SAD FAREWELL   On January 17, 1893, a group of American sugar planters and missionary descendants, with the support of U.S. Marines, imprisoned Queen Liliuokalani in her own palace, where she later penned the sorrowful lyric "Aloha Oe," Hawaii's song of farewell. The monarchy was dead.

A new republic was established, controlled by Sanford Dole, a powerful sugar-cane planter. In 1898, through annexation, Hawaii became an American territory ruled by Dole. His fellow sugarcane planters, known as the Big Five, controlled banking, shipping, hardware, and every other facet of economic life on the islands.

Planters imported more contract laborers from Puerto Rico (in 1900), Korea (in 1903), and the Philippines (1907–31). Most of the new immigrants stayed on to establish families and become a part of the islands. Meanwhile, the native Hawaiians became a landless minority in their homeland.

For nearly a century on Hawaii, sugar was king, generously subsidized by the U.S. federal government. The sugar planters dominated the territory's economy, shaped its social fabric, and kept the islands in a colonial plantation era with bosses and field hands.

WORLD WAR II & ITS AFTERMATH   On December 7, 1941, Japanese Zeros came out of the rising sun to bomb American warships based at Pearl Harbor, on the island of Oahu. This was the "day of infamy" that plunged the United States into World War II.

The attack brought immediate changes to the islands. Martial law was declared, stripping the Big Five cartel of its absolute power in a single day. Japanese Americans and German Americans were interned. Hawaii was "blacked out" at night, Waikiki Beach was strung with barbed wire, and Aloha Tower was painted in camouflage.

During the postwar years, the men of Hawaii returned after seeing another, bigger world outside of plantation life and rebelled. Throwing off the mantle of plantation life, the workers struck for higher wages and improved working conditions. Within a few short years after the war, the white, Republican leaders who had ruled since the overthrow of the monarchy were voted out of office, and labor leaders in the Democratic Party were suddenly in power.

TOURISM & STATEHOOD   In 1959, Hawaii became the last star on the Stars and Stripes, the 50th state of the union. But that year also saw the arrival of the first jet airliners, which brought 250,000 tourists to the fledgling state.

Tourism had already started on Maui shortly after World War II, when Paul I. Fagan, an entrepreneur from San Francisco who had bought the Hana Sugar Co., became the town's angel.

Fagan wanted to retire to Hana, so he focused his business acumen on this tiny town with big problems. Years ahead of his time, he thought tourism might have a future in Hana, so he built a small six-room inn, called Kauiki Inn, which later became the Hotel Hana-Maui. When he opened it in 1946, he said it was for first-class, wealthy travelers (just like his

Pidgin: 'Eh Fo' Real, Brah

If you venture beyond the tourist areas, you might hear another local tongue: pidgin English, a conglomeration of slang and words from the Hawaiian language. "Broke da mouth" (tastes really good) is the favorite pidgin phrase and one you might hear; "'Eh fo' real, brah" means "It's true, brother." You could be invited to hear an elder "talk story" (relating myths and memories). But because pidgin is really the province of the locals, your visit to Hawaii is likely to pass without your hearing much pidgin at all.

friends). Not only did his friends come, but he also pulled off a public-relations coup that is still talked about today. Fagan owned a baseball team, the San Francisco Seals. He figured they needed a spring-training area, so why not use Hana? He brought out the entire team to train in Hana, and, more important, he brought out the sportswriters. The sportswriters penned glowing reports about the town, and one writer gave the town a name that stuck: "Heavenly Hana."

However, it would be another 3 decades before Maui became a popular visitor destination in Hawaii. Waikiki was king in the tourism industry, seeing some 16,000 visitors a year by the end of the 1960s, and some four million a year by the end of the 1970s. In 1960, Amfac, owner of Pioneer Sugar Co., looked at the area outside of Lahaina that was being used to dump sugar-cane refuse and saw another use for the beachfront land. The company decided to build a manicured, planned luxury resort in the Kaanapali area. They built it, and people came.

A decade later, Alexander & Baldwin, now the state's largest sugar company, looked at the arid land they owned south of Kihei and also saw possibilities: The resort destination of Wailea was born.

By the mid-1970s, some one million visitors a year were coming to Maui. Ten years later, the number was up to two million.

At the beginning of the 21st century, the visitor industry replaced agriculture as Maui's number-one industry. Maui is the second-largest visitor destination in Hawaii. For 12 years in a row, the readers of *Condé Nast Traveler* and *Travel + Leisure* magazines have voted Maui the "Best Island in the World."

Hawaii was at record-breaking visitor counts (6.9 million) in 2000. Then September 11, 2001, sent a blow to Hawaii—tourism dropped abruptly, sending Hawaii's economy into a tailspin. But people eventually started traveling again, and in 2003, visitor arrivals were up to 6.3 million. By 2005, Hawaii's economy was recovering, the number of visitors to the state shot up to 6.75 million, business was booming in construction, and real-estate sales were higher than ever.

Just 3 years later, the economic pendulum swung the opposite way. Real estate in Hawaii, as on the mainland, dropped in value and sales plummeted. A record number of visitors, some nine million, had come to Hawaii in 2007, but the economic downturn in 2008 saw the closure of Aloha Airlines (which had served Hawaii for 61 years before closing) and ATA Airlines, as well as the shutting down of all operations (both cattle ranch and visitor accommodations) of Molokai Ranch, that island's largest employer and land owner.

3 The Lay of the Land

The first Hawaiian islands were born of violent volcanic eruptions that took place deep beneath the ocean's surface about 70 million years ago—more than 200 million years after the major continental land-masses had been formed. As soon as the islands emerged, Mother Nature's fury began to carve beauty from barren rock. Untiring volcanoes spewed forth rivers of fire that cooled into stone. Severe tropical storms, some with hurricane-force winds, battered and blasted the cooling lava rock into a series of shapes. Ferocious earthquakes flattened, shattered, and reshaped the islands into precipitous valleys, jagged cliffs, and recumbent flatlands. Monstrous surf and gigantic tidal waves rearranged and polished the lands above and below the reaches of the tide.

It took millions of years for nature to shape the familiar form of Diamond Head on Oahu, Maui's majestic peak of Haleakala, the waterfalls of Molokai's northern side, the reefs of Hulopoe Bay on Lanai, and the lush rainforests of the Big Island. The result is an island chain like no other—a tropical dreamscape of a landscape rich in flora and fauna, surrounded by a vibrant underwater world.

THE FLORA OF THE ISLANDS

Hawaii is filled with sweet-smelling flowers, lush vegetation, and exotic plant life.

AFRICAN TULIP TREES Even from afar, you can see the flaming red flowers on these large trees, which can grow to be more than 50 feet tall. The buds hold water, and Hawaiian children use the flowers as water pistols.

ANGEL'S TRUMPETS These small trees can grow up to 20 feet tall, with an abundance of large (up to 10-in. diameter) pendants—white or pink flowers that resemble, well, trumpets. The Hawaiians call them *nana-honua,* which means "earth gazing." The flowers, which bloom continually from early spring to late fall, have a musky scent. *Warning:* All parts of the plant are poisonous and contain a strong narcotic.

ANTHURIUMS Anthuriums originally came from the tropical Americas and the Caribbean islands. There are more than 550 species, but the most popular are the heart-shaped red, orange, pink, white, and purple flowers with tail-like spathes. Look for the heart-shaped green leaves in shaded areas. These exotic plants have no scent but will last several weeks as cut flowers. Anthuriums are particularly prevalent on the Big Island.

BANYAN TREES Among the world's largest trees, banyans have branches that grow out and away from the trunk, forming descending roots that grow down to the ground to feed and form additional trunks, making the tree very stable during tropical storms. The banyan in the courtyard next to the old courthouse in Lahaina, Maui, is an excellent example of a spreading banyan—it covers ⅔ acre.

BIRDS-OF-PARADISE These natives of Africa have become something of a trademark of Hawaii. They're easily recognizable by the orange and blue flowers nestled in gray-green bracts, looking somewhat like birds in flight.

BOUGAINVILLEA Originally from Brazil, these vines feature colorful, tissue-thin bracts, ranging in color from majestic purple to fiery orange, that hide tiny white flowers.

BREADFRUIT TREES A large tree—more than 60 feet tall—with broad, sculpted, dark-green leaves, the famous breadfruit produces a round, head-size green fruit that's a staple in the diets of all Polynesians. When roasted or baked, the whitish-yellow meat tastes somewhat like a sweet potato.

BROMELIADS   There are more than 1,400 species of bromeliads, of which the pineapple plant is the best known. "Bromes," as they're affectionately called, are generally spiky plants ranging in size from a few inches to several feet in diameter. They're popular not only for their unusual foliage, but also for their strange and wonderful flowers. Used widely in landscaping and interior decoration, especially in resort areas, bromeliads are found on every island.

COFFEE   Hawaii is the only state that produces coffee commercially. Coffee is an evergreen shrub with shiny, waxy, dark-green pointed leaves. The flower is a small, fragrant white blossom that develops into ½-inch berries that turn bright red when ripe. Look for coffee at elevations above 1,500 feet on the Kona side of the Big Island and on large coffee plantations on Kauai, Molokai, Oahu, and Maui.

GINGER   White and yellow ginger flowers are perhaps the most fragrant in Hawaii. Usually found in clumps growing 4 to 7 feet tall in areas blessed by rain, these sweet-smelling, 3-inch-wide flowers are composed of three dainty petal-like stamens and three long, thin petals. Ginger was introduced to Hawaii in the 19th century from the Indonesia-Malaysia area. Look for white and yellow ginger from late spring to fall. If you see ginger on the side of the road, stop and pick a few blossoms—your car will be filled with a divine fragrance the rest of the day.

Other members of the ginger family frequently seen in Hawaii include red, shell, and torch ginger. Red ginger consists of tall green stalks with foot-long red "flower heads." The red "petals" are actually bracts, which protect the 1-inch-long white flowers. Red ginger, which does not share the heavenly smell of white ginger, lasts a week or longer when cut. Look for red ginger from spring through late fall. Shell ginger, which originated in India and Burma, thrives in cool, wet mountain forests. These plants, with their pearly white, clamshell-like blossoms, bloom from spring to fall.

Perhaps the most exotic ginger is the red or pink torch ginger. Cultivated in Malaysia as seasoning, torch ginger rises directly out of the ground. The flower stalks, which are about 5 to 8 inches in length, resemble the fire of a lighted torch. This is one of the few types of ginger that can bloom year-round.

HELICONIA   Some 80 species of the colorful heliconia family came to Hawaii from the Caribbean and Central and South America. The bright yellow, red, green, and orange bracts overlap and appear to unfold like origami birds. The most obvious heliconia to spot is the lobster claw, which resembles a string of boiled crustacean pincers. Another prolific heliconia is the parrot's beak: Growing to about hip height, it's composed of bright-orange flower bracts with black tips. Look for parrot's beaks in spring and summer.

HIBISCUS   The 4- to 6-inch hibiscus flowers bloom year-round and come in a range of colors, from lily white to lipstick red. The flowers resemble crepe paper, with stamens and pistils protruding spire-like from the center. Hibiscus hedges can grow up to 15 feet tall. The yellow hibiscus is Hawaii's official state flower.

JACARANDA   Beginning around March and sometimes lasting until early May, these huge lacy-leaved trees metamorphose into large clusters of spectacular lavender-blue sprays. The bell-shaped flowers drop quickly, leaving a majestic purple carpet beneath the tree.

MACADAMIA   A transplant from Australia, macadamia nuts have become a commercial crop in recent decades in Hawaii, especially on the Big Island and Maui. The large trees—up to 60 feet tall—bear a hard-shelled nut encased in a leathery husk, which splits open and dries when the nut is ripe.

MONKEYPOD TREES   The monkeypod is one of Hawaii's most majestic trees; it grows more than 80 feet tall and 100 feet across. Seen near older homes and in parks, the leaves of the monkeypod drop in February and March. Its wood is a favorite of woodworking artisans.

NIGHT-BLOOMING CEREUS   Look along rock walls for this spectacular night-blooming flower. Originally from Central America, this vinelike member of the cactus family has green scalloped edges and produces foot-long white flowers that open as darkness falls and wither as the sun rises. The plant also bears an edible red fruit.

ORCHIDS   To many minds, nothing says Hawaii more than orchids. The most widely grown variety—and the major source of flowers for leis and garnish for tropical libations—is the vanda orchid. The vandas used in Hawaii's commercial flower industry are generally lavender or white, but they grow in a rainbow of colors, shapes, and sizes. The orchids used for corsages are the large, delicate cattleya; the ones used in floral arrangements—you'll probably see them in your hotel lobby—are usually dendrobiums.

PANDANUS (HALA)   Called *hala* by Hawaiians, pandanus is native to Polynesia. Thanks to its thick trunk, stiltlike supporting roots, and crown of long, swordlike leaves, the hala tree is easy to recognize. In what is quickly becoming a dying art, Hawaiians weave the *lau* (leaves) of the hala into hats, baskets, mats, bags, and the like.

PLUMERIA   Also known as frangipani, this sweet-smelling, five-petal flower, found in clusters on trees, is the most popular choice of lei makers. The Singapore plumeria has five creamy-white petals, with a touch of yellow in the center. Another popular variety, ruba—with

flowers from soft pink to flaming red—is also used in leis. When picking plumeria, be careful of the sap from the flower—it's poisonous and can stain clothes.

PROTEA   Originally from South Africa, this unusual oversize shrub comes in more than 40 different varieties. The flowers of one species resemble pincushions; those of another look like a bouquet of feathers. Once dried, proteas will last for years.

SILVERSWORD   This very uncommon and unusual plant is seen only on the Big Island and in the Haleakala Crater on Maui. The rare relative of the sunflower family blooms between July and September. The silversword in bloom is a fountain of red-petaled, daisylike flowers that turn silver soon after blooming.

TARO   Around pools, near streams, and in neatly planted fields, you'll see these green heart-shaped leaves, whose dense roots are a Polynesian staple. The ancient Hawaiians pounded the roots into poi. Originally from Sri Lanka, taro not only is a food crop, but is also grown for ornamental reasons.

THE FAUNA OF THE ISLANDS

When the first Polynesians arrived in Hawaii between A.D. 500 and 800, scientists say they found some 67 varieties of endemic Hawaiian birds, a third of which are now believed to be extinct. They did not find any reptiles, amphibians, mosquitoes, lice, fleas, or even a cockroach.

There were only two endemic mammals: the hoary bat and the monk seal. The **hoary bat** must have accidentally blown to Hawaii at some point, from either North or South America. It can still be seen during its early evening forays, especially around the Kilauea Crater on the Big Island.

The **Hawaiian monk seal,** a relative of warm-water seals found in the Caribbean and the Mediterranean, was nearly slaughtered into extinction for its skin and oil

Leapin' Lizards!

Geckos are harmless, soft-skinned, insect-eating lizards that come equipped with suction pads on their feet, enabling them to climb walls and windows to reach tasty insects such as mosquitoes and cockroaches. You'll see them on windows outside a lighted room at night or hear their cheerful chirp.

during the 19th century. These seals have recently experienced a minor population explosion; sometimes they even turn up at various beaches throughout the state. They're protected under federal law by the Marine Mammals Protection Act. If you're fortunate enough to see a monk seal, just look; don't disturb one of Hawaii's living treasures.

The first Polynesians brought a few animals from home: dogs, pigs, and chickens (all were for eating), as well as rats (stowaways). All four species are still found in the Hawaiian wild today.

BIRDS

More species of native birds have become extinct in Hawaii in the last 200 years than anywhere else on the planet. Of 67 native species, 23 are extinct and 30 are endangered. Even the Hawaiian crow, the **alala,** is threatened.

The **aeo,** or Hawaiian stilt—a 16-inch-long bird with a black head, black coat, white underside, and long pink legs—can be found in protected wetlands like the Kanaha Wildlife Sanctuary (where it shares its natural habitat with the Hawaiian coot) and Kealia Pond on Maui.

The **nene** is Hawaii's state bird. It's being brought back from the brink of extinction through strenuous protection laws and captive breeding. A relative of the Canada goose, the nene stands about 2 feet high and has a black head and yellow cheeks. The approximately 500 nene in existence can be seen in only three places: on Maui at Haleakala National Park, and on the Big Island at Mauna Kea State Recreation Area bird sanctuary and on the slopes of Mauna Kea.

The Hawaiian short-eared owl, the **pueo,** which grows to between 12 and 17 inches, can be seen at dawn and dusk. According to legend, spotting a pueo is a good omen.

SEA LIFE

Approximately 680 species of fish are known to inhabit the waters around the Hawaiian Islands. Of those, approximately 450 species stay close to the reef and inshore areas.

CORAL   The reefs surrounding Hawaii are made up of various coral and algae. The living coral grows through sunlight that feeds specialized algae, which, in turn, allow the development of the coral's calcareous skeleton. The reef, which takes thousands of years to develop, attracts and supports fish and crustaceans, which use it for food and habitat. Mother Nature can batter the reef with a strong storm, but humans have proven far more destructive.

The corals most frequently seen in Hawaii are hard, rocklike formations named for their familiar shapes: antler, cauliflower, finger, plate, and razor coral. Some coral appears soft, such as tube coral; it can be found in the ceilings of caves. Black coral, which resembles winter-bare trees or shrubs, is found at depths of more than 100 feet.

REEF FISH   Of the approximately 450 types of reef fish here, about 27% are native to Hawaii and are found nowhere else in the world. During the millions of years it took for the islands to sprout up from the sea, ocean currents—mainly from Southeast Asia—carried thousands of marine animals and plants to Hawaii's reef; of those, approximately 100 species adapted and thrived. You're likely to spot one or more of the following fish while underwater.

Angelfish can be distinguished by the spine, located low on the gill plate. These fish are very shy; several species live in colonies close to coral.

Blennies are small, elongated fish, ranging from 2 to 10 inches long, with the majority in the 3- to 4-inch range. Blennies are so small that they can live in tide pools; you might have a hard time spotting one.

Butterflyfish, among the most colorful of the reef fish, are usually seen in pairs (scientists believe they mate for life) and appear to spend most of their day feeding. There are 22 species of butterflyfish, of which three (bluestripe, lemon or milletseed, and multiband or pebbled butterflyfish) are endemic. Most butterflyfish have a dark band through the eye and a spot near the tail resembling an eye, meant to confuse their predators (moray eels love to lunch on them).

Moray and **conger eels** are the most common eels seen in Hawaii. Morays are usually docile except when provoked or when there's food around. Unfortunately, some morays have been fed by divers and now associate divers with food; thus, they can become aggressive. But most morays like to keep to themselves. While morays may look menacing, conger eels look downright happy, with big lips and pectoral fins (situated so that they look like big ears) that give them the appearance of a perpetually smiling face. Conger eels have crushing teeth so they can feed on crustaceans; because they're sloppy eaters, they usually live with shrimp and crabs that feed off the crumbs they leave.

Parrotfish, one of the largest and most colorful of the reef fish, can grow up to 40 inches long. They're easy to spot—their front teeth are fused together, protruding like buck teeth that allow them to feed by scraping algae from rocks and coral. The rocks and coral pass through the parrotfish's system, resulting in fine sand. In fact, most of the white sand found in Hawaii is parrotfish waste; one large parrotfish can produce a ton of sand a year. Native parrotfish species include yellowbar, regal, and spectacled.

Scorpion fish are what scientists call "ambush predators": They hide under camouflaged exteriors and ambush their prey. Several kinds sport a venomous dorsal spine. These fish don't have a gas bladder, so when they stop swimming, they sink—that's why you usually find them "resting" on ledges and on the ocean bottom. They're not aggressive, but be very careful where you put your hands and feet in the water so as to avoid those venomous spines.

Surgeonfish, sometimes called *tang,* get their name from the scalpel-like spines located on each side of the body near the base of the tail. Several surgeonfish, such as the brightly colored yellow tang, are boldly colored; others are adorned in more conservative shades of gray, brown, or black. The only endemic surgeonfish—and the most abundant in Hawaiian waters—is the convict tang, a pale white fish with vertical black stripes (like a convict's uniform).

Wrasses are a very diverse family of fish, ranging in length from 2 to 15 inches. Wrasses can change gender from female to male. Some have brilliant coloration that changes as they age. Several types of wrasse are endemic to Hawaii: Hawaiian cleaner, shortnose, belted, and gray (or old woman).

GAME FISH   Hawaii is known around the globe as *the* place for big-game fish—marlin, swordfish, and tuna. Six kinds of **billfish** are found in the offshore waters around the islands: Pacific blue marlin, black marlin, sailfish, broadbill swordfish, striped marlin, and shortbill spearfish. Hawaii billfish range in size from the 20-pound shortbill spearfish and striped marlin to the 1,805-pound Pacific blue marlin, the largest marlin ever caught with rod and reel in the world.

Tuna ranges in size from small (1 lb. or less) mackerel tuna used as bait (Hawaiians call them *oioi*) to 250-pound yellowfin ahi tuna. Other local species of tuna are big-eye, albacore, kawakawa, and skipjack.

Other types of fish, also excellent for eating, include **mahimahi** (also known as dolphin fish or dorado), in the 20- to 70-pound range; **rainbow runner,** from 15 to 30 pounds; and **wahoo** (ono), from 15 to 80 pounds. Shoreline fishermen are always on the lookout for **trevally** (the state record for a giant trevally is 191 lb.), **bonefish, ladyfish, threadfin, leatherfish,** and **goatfish.** Bottom fishermen pursue a range of **snapper**—red, pink, gray, and others—as well as **sea bass** (the state record is a whopping 563 lb.) and **amberjack** (which weigh up to 100 lb.).

WHALES   Humpback whales are popular visitors who come to Hawaii to mate and calve every year, beginning in November and staying until spring—April or so—when they return to Alaska. On every island, you can take winter whale-watching cruises that will let you observe these magnificent leviathans up close. You can also spot them from shore—humpbacks grow to up to 45 feet long, so when one breaches (jumps out of the water), you can see it for miles.

Humpbacks are among the biggest whales found in Hawaiian waters, but other whales—such as pilot, sperm, false killer, melon-headed, pygmy killer, and beaked—can be seen year-round, especially in the calm waters off the Big Island's Kona Coast.

SHARKS   Yes, there *are* sharks in Hawaii, but you more than likely won't see one unless you're specifically looking. About 40 different species of sharks inhabit the waters surrounding Hawaii, ranging from the totally harmless whale shark (at 60 ft., the world's largest fish), which has no teeth and is so docile that it frequently lets divers ride on its back, to the not-so-docile, extremely uncommon great white shark. The most common sharks seen in Hawaii are white-tip or gray reef sharks (about 5 ft. long) and black-tip reef sharks (about 6 ft. long).

HAWAII'S ECOSYSTEM PROBLEMS

Officials at Hawaii Volcanoes National Park on the Big Island saw a potential problem a few decades ago with people taking a few rocks home with them as "souvenirs." To prevent this problem from escalating, the park rangers created a legend that the fiery volcano goddess, Pele, would punish these souvenir-seekers with bad luck. There used to be a display case in the park's visitor center filled with letters from people who had taken rocks from the volcano, relating stories of all the bad luck that followed. Most begged Pele's forgiveness and instructed the rangers to please return the rock to the exact location that was its original home.

Unfortunately, Hawaii's other ecosystem problems can't be handled as easily.

MARINE LIFE   Hawaii's beautiful and abundant marine life has attracted so many visitors that they threaten to overwhelm it. A great example of this is **Molokini,** a small crater off the coast of Maui. Twenty-five years ago, one or two small six-passenger boats made the trip once a day to Molokini; today it's not uncommon to sight 20 or more boats, each carrying 20 to 49 passengers, moored inside the tiny crater. One tour operator has claimed that, on some days, it's so crowded that you can actually see a slick of suntan oil floating on the surface of the water.

Hawaii's **reefs** have faced increasing impact over the years as well. Runoff of soil and chemicals from construction, agriculture, and erosion can blanket and choke a reef, which needs sunlight to survive. Human contact with the reef can also upset the ecosystem. Coral, the basis of the reef system, is very fragile; snorkelers and divers grabbing onto it can break off pieces that took decades to form. Feeding the fish can also upset the balance of the ecosystem (not to mention upsetting the digestive systems of the fish). In areas where they're fed, the normally shy reef fish become more aggressive, surrounding divers and demanding food.

FLORA The rainforests are among Hawaii's most fragile environments. Any intrusion—from hikers carrying seeds on their shoes to the rooting of wild boars—can upset the delicate balance of these complete ecosystems. In recent years, development has moved closer and closer to the rainforests. On the Big Island, people have protested the invasion of bulldozers and the drilling of geothermal wells in the Wao Kele O Puna rainforest for years.

FAUNA The biggest impact on the fauna in Hawaii is the decimation of native birds by feral animals, which have destroyed the bird's habitats, and by mongooses that have eaten the birds' eggs and young. Government officials are vigilant about snakes because of the potential damage they can do to the remaining bird life.

A recent pest introduced to Hawaii is the coqui frog. That loud noise you hear after dark, especially on the eastern side of the Big Island and various parts of Maui, including the Kapalua Resort area and on the windward side of the island, is the cry of the male coqui frog looking for a mate. A native of Puerto Rico, where the frogs are kept in check by snakes, the coqui frog came to Hawaii in some plant material, found no natural enemies, and has spread across the Big Island and Maui. A chorus of several hundred coqui frogs is deafening (it's been measured at 163 decibels, or the noise level of a jet engine from 100 ft.). In some places, like Akaka Falls, on the Big Island, there are so many frogs that they are now chirping during daylight hours.

4 Maui in Popular Culture: Books, Film & Music

In addition to the books discussed below, you may want to peruse *Frommer's Maui Day by Day.* Those planning an extended trip to Hawaii should check out *Frommer's Honolulu, Waikiki & Oahu; Frommer's Honolulu & Oahu Day by Day; Frommer's Kauai; Frommer's Hawaii;* and *Frommer's Hawaii with Kids* (all published by Wiley Publishing, Inc.).

BOOKS
FICTION

The first book people think about is James A. Michener's *Hawaii* (Fawcett Crest, 1974). This epic novel manages to put the island's history into chronological order, but remember, it is still fiction, and very sanitized fiction, too. For a more contemporary look at life in Hawaii today, one of the best novels is *Shark Dialogues,* by Kiana Davenport (Plume, 1995). The novel tells the story of Pono, the larger-than-life matriarch, and her four daughters of mixed races. Davenport skillfully weaves legends and myths of Hawaii into the "real life" reality that Pono and her family face in the complex Hawaii of today. Lois-Ann Yamanaka uses a very "local" voice and stark depictions of life in the islands in her fabulous novels *Wild Meat and the Bully Burgers* (Farrar, Straus, Giroux, 1996), *Blu's Hanging* (Avon, 1997), and *Heads by Harry* (Avon, 1999).

NONFICTION

Mark Twain's writing on Hawaii in the 1860s offers a wonderful introduction to Hawaii's history. One of his best books is *Mark Twain in Hawaii: Roughing It in the Sandwich Islands* (Mutual Publishing, 1990). A great depiction of the Hawaii of 1889 is *Travels in Hawaii,* by Robert Louis Stevenson (University of Hawaii Press, 1973).

For contemporary voices on Hawaii's unique culture, one of the best books to get is *Voices of Wisdom: Hawaiian Elders Speak,* by M. J. Harden (Aka Press, 1999). Some 24 different *kahuna* (experts) in their fields were interviewed about their talent, skill, or artistic practice. These living treasures talk about how Hawaiians of yesteryear viewed nature, spirituality and healing, preservation and history, dance and music, arts and crafts, canoes, and the next generation.

Native Planters in Old Hawaii: Their Life, Lore, and Environment (Bishop Museum Press, Honolulu, 2004) was originally published in 1972 but is still one of the most important ethnographic works on traditional Hawaiian culture, portraying the lives of the common folk and their relationship with the land before the arrival of Westerners. This revised edition, with a great index that allows you to find anything, is an excellent resource for anyone interested in Hawaii.

The just-released *Honolulu Stories: Two Centuries of Writing,* edited by Gavan Daws and Bennett Hymer (Mutual Publishing, 2008), is a fascinating 1,000-plus-page book filled with the writings of various authors over the past 200 years. More than 350 selections—ranging from short stories, excerpts from novels, and scenes from plays, musicals, and operas to poems, songs, Hawaiian chants, cartoons, slams, and even stand-up comedy routines—are contained in this must-read for anyone interested in Hawaii. The authors range from Hawaiian kings and queens to Hawaiian chefs and commoners, including some well-known writers (translated from seven different languages)—all telling their own stories about Honolulu.

FLORA & FAUNA Because Hawaii is so lush with nature and blessed with plants, animals, and reef fish seen nowhere else on the planet, a few reference books can help you identify what you're looking at and make your trip more interesting. In the botanical world, Angela Kay Kepler's *Hawaiian Heritage Plants* (A Latitude 20 Book, University of Hawaii Press, 1998) is the standard for plant reference. In a series of essays, Kepler weaves culture, history, geography, botany, and even spirituality into her vivid descriptions of plants. You'll never look at plants the same way. There are great color photos and drawings to help you sort through the myriad species. Another great resource is *Tropicals,* by Gordon Courtright (Timber Press, 1988), which is filled with color photos identifying everything from hibiscus and heliconia to trees and palms.

The other necessary reference to have in Hawaii is one that identifies the colorful reef fish you will see snorkeling. The best of the bunch is John E. Randall's *Shore Fishes of Hawaii* (University of Hawaii Press, 1998). Two other books on reef-fish identification, with easy-to-use spiral bindings, are *Hawaiian Reef Fish: The Identification Book,* by Casey Mahaney (Blue Kirio Publishing, 1993), and *Hawaiian Reef Fish,* by Astrid Witte and Casey Mahaney (Island Heritage, 1998).

To learn everything you need to identify Hawaii's unique birds, try H. Douglas Pratt's *A Pocket Guide to Hawaii's Birds* (Mutual Publishing, 1996).

For fans of the Hawaiian lei, *Na Lei Makamae: The Treasured Lei,* by Marie McDonald and Paul Weissich (University of Hawaii Press, 2003), is a comprehensive work on this incredible art form. McDonald is one of Hawaii's top lei makers, and Weissich is the director emeritus of Honolulu Botanical Gardens; together they cover some 88 flowers and plants used for leis.

HISTORY There are many great books on Hawaii's history, but one of the best places to start is with the formation of the Hawaiian Islands, vividly described in David E. Eyre's *By Wind, By Wave: An Introduction to Hawaii's Natural History* (Bess Press, 2000). In addition to chronicling the natural history of Hawaii, Eyre describes the complex interrelationships among the plants, animals, ocean, and people. He points out that Hawaii has become the "extinction capital of the world," but rather than dwelling on that fact, he urges readers to do something about it and carefully spells out how.

For an even more complete tome, get the University of Hawaii Press's *Hawaiian Natural History, Ecology, and Evolution* (2002), by Alan C. Ziegler. Readers can trace the natural history of the Hawaiian archipelago through the book's 28 chapters or focus on specific topics such as island formation by plate tectonics, plant and animal evolution, flightless birds and their fossil sites, Polynesian migrational history and ecology, the effects of humans and exotic animals on the environment, current conservation efforts, and the contributions of the many naturalists who visited the islands over the centuries and the stories behind their discoveries.

For a history of "precontact" Hawaii (before Westerners arrived), David Malo's *Hawaiian Antiquities* (Bishop Museum Press, 1976) is the preeminent source. Malo was born around 1793 and wrote about the Hawaiian lifestyle at that time, as well as the beliefs and religion of his people. It's an excellent reference book, but not a fast read. For more readable books on old Hawaii, try *Stories of Old Hawaii,* by Roy Kakulu Alameida (Bess Press, 1997), on myths and legends; *Hawaiian Folk Tales,* by Thomas G. Thrum (Mutual Publishing, 1998); and *The Legends and Myths of Hawaii,* by His Hawaiian Majesty King David Kalakaua (Charles E. Tuttle Company, 1992).

The best story of the 1893 overthrow of the Hawaiian monarchy is told by Queen Liliuokalani, in her book *Hawaii's Story by Hawaii's Queen, Liliuokalani* (Mutual Publishing, 1990). When it was written, it was an international plea for justice for her people, but it is a poignant read even today. It's also a must-read for people interested in current events and the recent rally for sovereignty in the 50th state. Two contemporary books on the question of Hawaii's sovereignty are Tom Coffman's *Nation Within: The Story of America's Annexation of the Nation of Hawaii* (Epicenter, 1998) and Thurston Twigg-Smith's *Hawaiian Sovereignty: Do the Facts Matter?* (Goodale, 2000), which explores the opposite view. Twigg-Smith, former publisher of the statewide newspaper *The Honolulu Advertiser,* is the grandson of Lorrin A. Thurston, one of the architects of the 1893 overthrow of the monarchy. His so-called "politically incorrect" views present a different look on this hotly debated topic.

For more recent history, Lawrence H. Fuchs's *Hawaii Pono* (Bess Press, 1991) is a carefully researched tome on the contributions of each of Hawaii's main immigrant communities (Chinese, Japanese, and Filipino) between 1893 and 1959.

An insightful look at history and its effect on the Hawaiian culture is *Waikiki, A History of Forgetting & Remembering,* by Andrea Feeser (University of Hawaii Press, 2006). A beautiful art book (designed by Gaye Chan), this is not your typical coffee-table book, but a different look at the cultural and environmental history of Waikiki. Using historical texts, photos, government documents, and interviews, this book lays out the story of how Waikiki went from a self-sufficient agricultural area to a tourism mecca, detailing the price that was paid along the way.

Another great cultural book recently released is Davianna Pomaikai McGregor's *Na Kua'aina: Living Hawaiian Culture* (University of Hawaii Press, 2007). I love this book for so many reasons—first, it focuses not on the Hawaiian royalty, but on the common people of Hawaii and how they lived. McGregor, a professor of ethnic studies at UH, examines how people lived in rural lands and how they kept the Hawaiian traditions alive. She describes the cultural significance of each area (the island of Molokai; Hana, Maui; and Puna, Hawaii), the landscape, the Hawaiian gods who lived there, the chants and myths about the area, and how the westernization of the area has changed the land and the Hawaiian people.

FILM

My favorite films made in Hawaii but about other places are:

- **Bird of Paradise:** Delmer Daves's 1951 remake of the 1932 film stars Debra Paget as an island princess who falls in love with a visiting Frenchman (Louis Jourdan) against the wishes of her people. It was filmed on the island of Kauai with a new technology called Technicolor.
- **The Devil at Four O'Clock:** Mervyn LeRoy directed this 1961 story about faith and redemption (filmed on Maui), which tells the story of an alcoholic priest (Spencer Tracy) who enlists the aid of three condemned convicts (one played by Frank Sinatra) to help in the rescue of native children threatened by an erupting volcano.
- **Donovan's Reef:** John Ford directed this 1963 John Wayne romantic comedy about two ex-Navy men who

remain on a South Seas island (played by Kauai) after World War II. "Guns" Donovan (Wayne) runs the local bar, while Doc Dedham (Jack Warden) has married a local princess. A former shipmate (Lee Marvin) arrives, followed by a high-society Bostonian (Elizabeth Allen).

- **The Enemy Below:** This classic story (released in 1957) of a U.S. destroyer chasing a German submarine during World War II stars Robert Mitchum and Curt Jurgens in the lead roles as the American and German captains. While all of the ocean scenes take place in the North Atlantic, they were actually filmed in Hawaii.
- **Islands in the Stream:** Filmed on Kauai, this 1977 movie tells the story of Ernest Hemingway's last published novel. Set on the island of Bimini in the Caribbean, it is about artist Thomas Hudson's renewed relationship with his three young sons and former wife.
- **Joe Versus the Volcano:** This least well-known of the Tom Hanks/Meg Ryan movies is a romantic comedy filmed in 1990. John Shanley's film tells the tale of a hypochondriac who, when told that he is dying, accepts an offer to throw himself into the volcano of a remote tropical island. En route, however, he learns that there are many reasons to keep on living.
- **Jurassic Park:** Filmed on the islands of Kauai and Oahu, Steven Spielberg's 1993 megahit, which was billed as "an adventure 65 million years in the making," is the story of dinosaurs on the loose at the site of the world's only dinosaur farm and theme park, where creatures from the past are produced using harvested DNA.
- **The Karate Kid, Part II:** In one of those instances where the sequel is actually better than the original, this

1986 movie takes our hero Daniel LaRusso (Ralph Macchio) and his mentor, Mr. Miyagi (Pat Morita), to Miyagi's homeland, Okinawa, to visit his dying father and confront his old rival. An entire Okinawan village was re-created on Oahu's Windward Coast.

- *King Kong:* John Guillermin's 1976 version of the classic story of the great ape and the girl (Jessica Lange) was filmed on parts of Kauai rarely seen by visitors or residents.

- *The Lost World: Jurassic Park:* In Steven Spielberg's 1997 follow-up to *Jurassic Park,* dinosaurs have been bred and then escaped following the abandonment of the project in the first installment. The sequel features much more Hawaiian scenery than the original.

- *Mister Roberts:* John Ford's 1955 comedy-drama, set aboard an insignificant ship stationed in the Pacific during World War II, was nominated for three Academy Awards, including Best Picture. Jack Lemmon won the Oscar for Best Supporting Actor for his role as Ensign Pulver. The film also stars Henry Fonda in the title role and James Cagney as Captain Morton.

- *None But the Brave:* Frank Sinatra directed and starred in this 1965 story of American and Japanese soldiers who, when stranded on a tiny Pacific island during World War II (filmed on Kauai), must make a temporary truce and cooperate to survive. This was the only film directed by Sinatra.

- *Outbreak:* Wolfgang Petersen directed this 1995 tale of a lethal virus that is transported to the United States by an African monkey host. Federal agencies rush to find an antidote before the planet's population is wiped out. The scenes of the African

village were filmed near the Wailua River on Kauai.

- *Planet of the Apes:* Tim Burton's 2001 remake of the 1968 science-fiction classic, which starred Charlton Heston, is more faithful to the original Pierre Boulle novel, but also much more dark and sinister. Exterior battle scenes were filmed on lava fields on the Big Island of Hawaii.

- *Raiders of the Lost Ark:* Filmed on Kauai, Steven Spielberg's 1981 film follows archaeologist Indiana Jones on a search for the Ark of the Covenant, which is also sought by the Nazis under orders from Hitler.

- *Six Days Seven Nights:* Ivan Reitman's 1998 adventure-comedy is about a New York magazine editor and a gruff pilot who are forced to put aside their dislike for each other in order to survive after crash-landing on a deserted South Seas island (filmed on Kauai). It stars Harrison Ford and Anne Heche.

- *South Pacific:* The 1958 motion-picture adaptation of the Rodgers and Hammerstein musical was filmed on Kauai. The film has an all-star cast, with Rossano Brazzi and Mitzi Gaynor in the lead roles. It was nominated for three Academy Awards but won only for Best Sound.

- *Uncommon Valor:* Ted Kotcheff's 1983 story tells of a retired Marine colonel (Gene Hackman) who reunites his son's former unit to organize a secret raid on a Vietnamese prison camp, where he hopes to rescue his son and other American MIAs. The climactic scenes set in Laos were filmed on the island of Kauai.

- *The Wackiest Ship in the Army:* Richard Murphy directed this 1960 comedy set during World War II and filmed on Kauai and Oahu. The crew and captain (played by Jack Lemmon) are sent on a secret mission in waters patrolled by the Japanese. The film was based on the true story of a mission ordered by Army Gen. Douglas MacArthur.

- **Waterworld:** Kevin Costner directed and starred in this 1995 film about a future in which the polar ice caps have melted, leaving most of the world's surface deep beneath the oceans. The survivors live poorly on the water's surface, dreaming of finding "dry land." Some of the water scenes were filmed off Kauai. The final and most beautiful scenes in the movie were filmed in the Waipio Valley on the Big Island.

My favorite films made in Hawaii and about Hawaii are:

- **Blue Hawaii:** Chad Gates (Elvis Presley), upon discharge from the Army, returns to Hawaii to enjoy life with his buddies and girlfriend, against the wishes of his parents, who want him to work for the family business. Presley, Joan Blackman, and Angela Lansbury make this 1961 film a classic, with great music and beautiful Hawaiian scenery from the early 1960s.
- **50 First Dates:** This 2004 romantic comedy stars Drew Barrymore and Adam Sandler in a story about a young woman (Barrymore) who has lost her short-term memory in a car accident and who now relives each day as if it were October 13. She follows the same routine every day, until she meets Henry Roth (Sandler), who falls in love with her and seeks a way to forge a long-term relationship.
- **From Here to Eternity:** Fred Zinnemann's 1953 multiple-Oscar winner, set in pre–World War II Hawaii, tells the story of several Army soldiers stationed on Oahu on the eve of Pearl Harbor. The film won Best Picture,

Best Supporting Actor (Frank Sinatra), Best Supporting Actress (Donna Reed), and five other awards.
- **Hawaii:** George Roy Hill's 1966 adaptation of the James Michener novel features amazing island scenery and stars Julie Andrews, Max von Sydow, and Richard Harris. It is a great introduction to the early history of Hawaii.
- **Honeymoon in Vegas:** Andrew Bergman's 1992 comedy starring James Caan, Nicolas Cage, Sarah Jessica Parker, and Pat Morita is primarily set in Las Vegas, but has a wonderful segment shot on Kauai at the fictional home of millionaire Tommy Korman (Caan).
- **In Harm's Way:** Otto Preminger's 1965 classic drama of the war in the Pacific focuses on several Navy officers (and the women in their lives) who are suddenly catapulted into the war following the Japanese attack on Pearl Harbor. It stars John Wayne, Kirk Douglas, Patricia Neal, Tom Tryon, and Paula Prentiss.
- **Molokai: The Story of Father Damien:** This 1999 film follows the life of Belgian priest Damien de Veuster from 1872, the year before his arrival in Kalaupapa, through his years ministering to the patients with Hansen's disease at Kalaupapa, until his death at the Molokai settlement in 1889.
- **Pearl Harbor:** Michael Bay's 2001 film depicts the time before, during, and after the December 7, 1941, Japanese attack (with the best re-creation of the Pearl Harbor attack ever put on film) and tells the story of two best friends and the woman they both love.
- **Picture Bride:** Japanese director Kayo Hatta presents this 1995 film about a Japanese woman who travels to Hawaii to marry a man that she

has never met, but only seen through photos and letters. She soon discovers that he is twice her age and that much turmoil awaits her in her new home. Beautifully filmed on the North Shore of Oahu and the Hamakua Coast of the Big Island, with a special appearance by Toshiro Mifune.

- **Tora! Tora! Tora!:** This 1970 film tells the story of the Japanese attack on Pearl Harbor as seen from both the American and the Japanese perspectives.

MUSIC

Hawaiian music ranges from traditional ancient chants and hula to slack-key guitar, to contemporary rock and a new genre, Jawaiian, a cross of reggae, Jamaican, and Hawaiian. To listen to Hawaiian music, check out Hawaiian 105 (www.hawaiian105.com). Below are my picks for Hawaiian music.

- **Best of the Gabby Band,** by Gabby Pahinui (traditional Hawaiian)

- **Gently Weeps,** by Jake Shimabukuro (contemporary Hawaiian)
- **Hapa,** by Hapa (contemporary Hawaiian)
- **Hawaiian Blossom,** by Raiatea Helm (traditional Hawaiian)
- **Hawaiian Tradition,** by Amy Hana-iali'i Gilliom (traditional Hawaiian)
- **Honolulu City Lights,** by Keola & Kapono Beamer (contemporary Hawaiian)
- **Legends of Hawaiian Slack Key Guitar,** by various artists (a collection of slack-key guitar music and a 2007 Grammy winner)
- **Masters of Hawaiian Slack Key Guitar, Vol. 1,** by various artists (a collection of slack-key guitar music and a 2006 Grammy winner)
- **Na Leo Hawaii Kaniko,** by the Master Chanters of Hawaii (chanting)
- **Na Pua O Hawaii,** by Makaha Sons (contemporary Hawaiian)
- **Wonderful World,** by Israel Kamaka-wiwo'ole (contemporary Hawaiian)

5 Eating & Drinking on Maui

TRIED & TRUE: HAWAII REGIONAL CUISINE

Peter Merriman, a founding member of Hawaii Regional Cuisine (HRC) and a recipient of the James Beard Award for Best Chef: Northwest/Hawaii (along with George Mavrothalassitis of Chef Mavro Restaurant), describes the current trend in Hawaii as a refinement, a tweaking upward, of everything from fine dining to down-home local cooking. This means sesame- or nori-crusted fresh catch on plate-lunch menus, and *huli-huli* chicken at five-diamond eateries, paired with Beaujolais and leeks and gourmet long rice.

At the same time, says Merriman, HRC, the style of cooking that put Hawaii on the international culinary

map, has become watered down, a buzz-word: "A lot of restaurants are paying lip service."

As it is with things au courant, it is easy to make a claim but another thing to live up to it. As Merriman points out, HRC was never solely about technique; it is equally about ingredients and the chef's creativity and integrity. "We continue to get local inspiration," says Merriman. "We've never restricted ourselves." If there is a fabulous French or Thai dish, chefs like Merriman will prepare it with local ingredients and add a creative edge that makes it distinctively Hawaii Regional.

HRC was established in the mid-1980s in a culinary revolution that catapulted Hawaii into the global epicurean arena. The international training, creative vigor, fresh ingredients, and cross-cultural menus of the 12 original HRC chefs have made the islands a dining destination applauded nationwide. (In a tip of the toque to island tradition, *ahi*—a word ubiquitous in Hawaii—has replaced *tuna* on many chic New York menus.)

Here's a sampling of what you can expect to find on a Hawaii Regional menu: seared Hawaiian fish with *lilikoi* shrimp butter; taro-crab cakes; Pahoa corn cakes; Molokai sweet-potato or breadfruit vichyssoise; Ka'u orange sauce and Kahua Ranch lamb; fern shoots from Waipio Valley; Maui onion soup and Hawaiian bouillabaisse, with fresh snapper, Kona crab, and fresh aquacultured shrimp; blackened ahi summer rolls; herb-crusted onaga; and gourmet Waimanalo greens, picked that day. You may also encounter locally made cheeses, squash and taro risottos, Polynesian *imu*-baked foods, and guava-smoked meats. If there's pasta or risotto or rack of lamb on the menu, it could be nori (red algae) linguine with opihi (limpet) sauce, or risotto with local seafood served in taro cups, or rack of lamb in cabernet and hoisin sauce (fermented soybean, garlic, and spices). Watch for ponzu sauce, too; it's lemony and zesty, much more flavorful than the soy sauce it resembles.

PLATE LUNCHES & MORE: LOCAL FOOD

At the other end of the spectrum is the vast and endearing world of "local food." By that I mean plate lunches and poke, shave ice and saimin, bento lunches and manapua—cultural hybrids all.

Reflecting a polyglot population of many styles and ethnicities, Hawaii's idiosyncratic dining scene is eminently inclusive. Consider surfer chic: Barefoot in the sand, in a swimsuit, you chow down on a **plate lunch** ordered from a lunch wagon, consisting of fried mahimahi, "two scoops rice," macaroni salad, and a few

leaves of green, typically julienned cabbage. (Generally, teriyaki beef and shoyu chicken are options.) Heavy gravy is often the condiment of choice, accompanied by a soft drink in a paper cup or straight out of the can. Like **saimin**—the local version of noodles in broth topped with scrambled eggs, green onions, and sometimes pork—the plate lunch is Hawaii's version of high camp.

But it was only a matter of time before the humble plate lunch became a culinary icon in Hawaii. These days, even the most chichi restaurant has a version of this modest island symbol (not at plate-lunch prices, of course), while vendors selling the real thing—carb-driven meals served from wagons—have queues that never end.

Because this is Hawaii, at least a few licks of poi—cooked, pounded taro (the traditional Hawaiian staple crop)—are a must. Other **native foods** include those from before and after Western contact, such as laulau (pork, chicken, or fish steamed in ti leaves), kalua pork (pork cooked in a Polynesian underground oven known here as an *imu*), lomi salmon (salted salmon with tomatoes and green onions), squid luau (cooked in coconut milk and taro tops), poke (cubed raw fish seasoned with onions and seaweed and the occasional sprinkling of roasted kukui nuts), haupia (creamy coconut pudding), and kulolo (steamed pudding of coconut, brown sugar, and taro).

Bento, another popular quick meal available throughout Hawaii, is a compact, boxed assortment of picnic fare usually consisting of neatly arranged sections of rice, pickled vegetables, and fried chicken, beef, or pork. Increasingly, however, the bento is becoming more health conscious, as in macrobiotic or vegetarian brown-rice bentos. A derivative of the modest lunch box for Japanese immigrants who once labored in the sugar and pineapple fields, bentos are dispensed everywhere, from department stores to corner delis and supermarkets.

Also from the plantations comes **manapua,** a bready, doughy sphere filled with tasty fillings of sweetened pork or sweet beans. In the old days, the Chinese "manapua man" would make his rounds with bamboo containers balanced on a rod over his shoulders. Today you'll find white or whole-wheat manapua containing chicken, vegetables, curry, and other savory fillings.

The daintier Chinese delicacy **dim sum** is made of translucent wrappers filled with fresh seafood, pork hash, and vegetables, served for breakfast and lunch in Chinatown restaurants. The Hong Kong–style dumplings are ordered fresh and hot from bamboo steamers rolled on carts from table to table. Much like hailing a taxi in Manhattan, you have to be quick and loud for dim sum.

For dessert or a snack, particularly on Oahu's North Shore, the prevailing choice is **shave ice,** the Island version of a snow cone. Particularly on hot, humid days, long lines of shave-ice lovers gather for heaps of finely shaved ice topped with sweet tropical syrups. (The sweet-sour *li hing mui* flavor is a current favorite.) The fast-melting mounds, which require prompt, efficient consumption, are quite the local summer ritual for sweet tooths. Aficionados order shave ice with ice cream and sweetened adzuki beans plopped in the middle.

AHI, ONO & OPAKAPAKA: A HAWAIIAN SEAFOOD PRIMER

The seafood in Hawaii has been described as the best in the world. And why not? Without a doubt, the islands' surrounding waters, including the waters of the remote northwestern Hawaiian Islands, and a growing aquaculture industry contribute to the high quality of the seafood here.

The reputable restaurants in Hawaii buy fresh fish daily at predawn auctions or from local fishermen. Some chefs even catch their ingredients themselves. "Still wiggling" and "just off the hook" are the ultimate terms for freshness in Hawaii.

Although some menus include the Western description for the fresh fish used, most often the local nomenclature is listed, turning dinner into a confusing, quasiforeign experience for the uninitiated. To help familiarize you with the menu language of Hawaii, here's a basic glossary of Island fish:

ahi   yellowfin or big-eye tuna, important for its use in sashimi and poke at sushi bars and in Hawaii Regional Cuisine

aku   skipjack tuna, heavily used by local families in home cooking and poke

ehu   red snapper, delicate and sumptuous, yet lesser known than opakapaka

hapuupuu   grouper, a sea bass whose use is expanding

hebi   spearfish, mildly flavored, and frequently featured as the "catch of the day" in upscale restaurants

kajiki   Pacific blue marlin, also called *au,* with a firm flesh and high fat content that make it a plausible substitute for tuna

kumu   goatfish, a luxury item on Chinese and upscale menus, served en papillote or steamed whole, Oriental style, with scallions, ginger, and garlic

mahimahi   dolphin fish (the game fish, not the mammal) or dorado, a classic sweet, white-fleshed fish requiring vigilance among purists because it's often disguised as fresh when it's actually "fresh-frozen"—a big difference

monchong   bigscale or sickle pomfret, an exotic, tasty fish, scarce but gaining a higher profile on Hawaiian Island menus

nairagi   striped marlin, also called *au,* good as sashimi and in poke, and often substituted for ahi in raw-fish products

onaga   ruby snapper, a luxury fish, versatile, moist, and flaky

ono   wahoo, firmer and drier than the snappers, often served grilled and in sandwiches

opah   moonfish, rich and fatty, and versatile—cooked, raw, smoked, and broiled

opakapaka   pink snapper, light, flaky, and luxurious, suited for sashimi, poaching, sautéing, and baking; the best-known upscale fish

papio   jack trevally, light, firm, and flavorful, and favored in Island cookery

shutome   broadbill swordfish, of beef-like texture and rich flavor

tombo   albacore tuna, with a high fat content, suitable for grilling

uhu   parrotfish, most often encountered steamed, Chinese style

uku   gray snapper of clear, pale-pink flesh, delicately flavored and moist

ulua   large jack trevally, firm-fleshed and versatile

3

Planning Your Trip to Maui

Maui has so many places to explore, things to do, and sights to see that it's hard to know where to start—that's where I come in. In the pages that follow, I've compiled everything you need to know to plan your ideal trip to Maui: information on airlines, seasons, a calendar of events, how to make camping reservations, and much more (even how to tie the knot).

For additional help in planning your trip and for more on-the-ground resources in Maui, please turn to the appendix.

1 Visitor Information

For advance information on traveling in Maui, contact the **Maui Visitors Bureau,** 1727 Wili Pa Loop, Wailuku, Maui, HI 96793 (© **800/525-MAUI** [6284] or 808/244-3530; fax 808/244-1337; www. visitmaui.com).

The **Kaanapali Beach Resort Association** is at 2530 Kekaa Dr., Suite 1-B, Lahaina, HI 96761 (© **800/245-9229** or 808/661-3271; fax 808/661-9431; www. kaanapaliresort.com).

The state agency responsible for tourism is the **Hawaii Visitors & Convention Bureau (HVCB),** Waikiki Business Plaza, 2270 Kalakaua Ave., Suite 801, Honolulu, HI 96815 (© **800/GO-HAWAII** [464-2924] or 808/923-1811; www.gohawaii.com).

If you want information about working and living in Maui, contact the **Maui Chamber of Commerce,** 250 Alamaha St., Unit N-16A, Kahului, HI 96732 (© **808/871-7711;** www.mauichamber. com).

INFORMATION ON MAUI'S PARKS
NATIONAL PARKS The islands of Maui and Molokai have one national park each: **Haleakala National Park,**

P.O. Box 369, Makawao, HI 96768 (© **808/572-4400;** www.nps.gov/hale); and **Kalaupapa National Historical Park,** P.O. Box 2222, Kalaupapa, HI 96742 (© **808/567-6802;** www.nps.gov/ kala). For more information, see "Hiking & Camping" in chapters 7 and 11.

STATE PARKS To find out more about state parks on Maui and Molokai, contact the **Hawaii State Department of Land and Natural Resources,** 1151 Punchbowl St., No. 130, Honolulu, HI 96813 (© **808/587-0300;** www.hawaii. gov), which can provide information on hiking and camping. For free topographic trail maps, call the State Department of Forestry at © **808/984-8100.**

COUNTY PARKS For information on Maui County Parks, contact **Maui County Parks and Recreation,** 1580-C Kaahumanu Ave., Wailuku, HI 96793 (© **808/270-7230;** www.co.maui.hi.us/ departments/Parks/Recware).

HAWAII ON THE WEB
Below are some of the best Hawaii-specific websites for planning your trip.

- **Maui Visitors Bureau (www.visit maui.com):** An excellent all-around

Tips   What to Pack

Maui is very informal: You'll get by with shorts, T-shirts, and sneakers at most attractions and restaurants; a casual sundress or a polo shirt and khakis are fine even in the most expensive places. Dinner jackets for men are required only in some of the fine-dining rooms of a very few ultra-exclusive resorts, such as the Lodge at Koele on Lanai—and they'll cordially provide you with a jacket if you don't bring your own. Aloha wear is acceptable everywhere, so you may want to plan on buying an aloha shirt or a muumuu (a Hawaiian-style dress) while you're in Maui.

So bring T-shirts, shorts, long pants, a couple of bathing suits, tennis shoes, and rubber water shoes or flip-flops. Don't forget a long-sleeved cover-up (to throw on at the beach when you've had enough sun for the day). If you plan on hiking, bring hiking boots and several pairs of good socks. You might also want to bring binoculars for whale-watching.

The tropical sun poses the greatest threat to anyone who ventures into the great outdoors, so be sure to pack **sun protection:** a good pair of sunglasses, strong sunscreen, a light hat, and a canteen or water bottle if you'll be hiking—you'll easily dehydrate in the tropical heat, so figure on carrying 2 liters of water per day on any hike. Campers should bring water-purification tablets or devices. Also see "Health" and "Safety," later in this chapter.

Don't bother overstuffing your suitcase with 2 whole weeks' worth of clothes: Maui has **laundry facilities** almost everywhere (except Hana). If your accommodations don't have a washer and dryer or laundry service (most do), there will most likely be a laundry nearby.

One last thing: **It really can get cold on Maui.** If you plan to see the sunrise from the top of Haleakala, bring a warm jacket. Even in summer when it's 80°F (27°C) at the beach, 40°F (4°C) upcountry temperatures are not uncommon. It's always a good idea to bring long pants and a windbreaker, sweater, or light jacket. And be sure to toss some **rain gear** in your suitcase if you'll be in Maui any time between November and March.

guide to travel tips, Hawaiian culture, activities, tours, lodging, family vacations and events, weddings, and honeymoons. Info on Molokai and Lanai is also listed—but keep in mind that only members of the MVB are listed.

- **Planet Hawaii** (**www.planet-hawaii. com**): An island-by-island guide to activities, lodging, shopping, culture, the surf report, weather, and more. Mostly you'll find short listings with links to other websites.
- **Maui Island Currents** (**www.island currents.com**): Specializing in arts

and culture, Island Currents gives the most detailed lowdown on current exhibitions and performance art. Gallery listings are organized by town, while in-depth articles highlight local artists. You can consult restaurant reviews from the *Maui News* "Best of Maui" poll for suggestions and prices.

- **Maui Net** (**www.maui.net**): The clients of this Internet service provider are featured in this extensive directory of links to accommodations, activities, and shopping. The activities section has links to golf, hiking, airborne activities, and ocean adventures, such as scuba and snorkeling. These links lead to outfitters' sites, where you can learn more and set up excursions before you arrive in paradise.

- **Molokai Visitors Association** (**www.molokai-hawaii.com**): This is a very complete site for activities, events, nightlife, accommodations, and family vacations. Enjoy the landscape by viewing a virtual photo tour, get driving times between various points, and learn about local history.

- **Lanai Visitors Bureau** (**www.visit lanai.net**): Find everything you wanted to know about the island of Lanai, from activities and accommodations to maps, a calendar of events, and even romance.

- **Hawaiian Language** (**www.geocities. com/~olelo/hltableofcontents.html**): This fabulous site has not only easy lessons on learning the Hawaiian language, but also a great cultural calendar, links to other Hawaii websites, a section on the hula, and lyrics (and translations) to Hawaiian songs.

2 Entry Requirements

PASSPORTS

New regulations issued by the Department of Homeland Security now require virtually every air traveler entering the U.S. to show a passport. As of January 23, 2007, all persons, including U.S. citizens, traveling by air between the United States and Canada, Mexico, Central and South America, the Caribbean, and Bermuda are required to present a valid passport. As of January 31, 2008, U.S. and Canadian citizens entering the U.S. at land and sea ports of entry from within the Western Hemisphere will need to present government-issued proof of citizenship, such as a birth certificate, along with a government-issued photo ID, such as a driver's license. A passport is not required for U.S. or Canadian citizens entering by land or sea, but it is highly encouraged to carry one.

For information on how to obtain a passport, see the "Passports" section in the appendix.

VISAS

The U.S. State Department has a **Visa Waiver Program (VWP)** allowing citizens of the following countries to enter the United States without a visa for stays of up to 90 days: Andorra, Australia, Austria, Belgium, Brunei, Denmark, Finland, France, Germany, Iceland, Ireland, Italy, Japan, Liechtenstein, Luxembourg, Monaco, the Netherlands, New Zealand, Norway, Portugal, San Marino, Singapore, Slovenia, Spain, Sweden, Switzerland, and the United Kingdom. (*Note:* This list was accurate at press time; for the most up-to-date list of countries in the VWP, consult www.travel.state.gov/visa.) Canadian citizens may enter the United States without visas; they will need to show passports (if traveling by air) and proof of residence, however. *Note:* Any passport issued on or after October 26, 2006, by a VWP country must be an **e-Passport** for VWP travelers to be eligible to enter the U.S. without a visa. Citizens of these nations also need to present a round-trip air or cruise ticket upon arrival. E-Passports contain computer chips capable of storing biometric information, such as the required digital photograph of the holder. (You can identify an e-Passport by the symbol on the bottom center cover of your passport.) If your passport doesn't have this feature, you can still travel without a visa if it is a valid passport issued before October 26, 2005, and includes a machine-readable

Tips Hey, No Smoking in Hawaii

Well, not *totally* no smoking, but Hawaii has one of the toughest laws against smoking in the U.S. It's against the law to smoke in public buildings, including airports, shopping malls, grocery stores, retail shops, buses, movie theaters, banks, convention facilities, and all government buildings and facilities. There is no smoking in restaurants, bars, or nightclubs. Most bed-and-breakfasts prohibit smoking indoors, and more and more hotels and resorts are becoming smoke-free even in public areas. Also, there is no smoking within 20 feet of a doorway, window, or ventilation intake (so no hanging around outside a bar to smoke—you must go 20 ft. away). Even some beaches have no-smoking policies (and at those that do allow smoking, you'd better pick up your butts and not use the sand as your own private ashtray—or else face stiff fines). Breathing fresh, clear air is "in," while smoking in Hawaii is "out."

zone, or between October 26, 2005, and October 25, 2006, and includes a digital photograph. For more information, go to **www.travel.state.gov/visa**.

Citizens of all other countries must have (1) a valid passport that expires at least 6 months later than the scheduled end of their visit to the U.S., and (2) a tourist visa, which may be obtained without charge from any U.S. consulate.

As of January 2004, many international visitors traveling on visas to the United States will be photographed and fingerprinted on arrival at Customs in airports and on cruise ships in a program created by the Department of Homeland Security called **US-VISIT.** Exempt from the extra scrutiny are visitors entering by land or those (mostly in Europe; see above) that don't require a visa for short-term visits. For more information, go to the Homeland Security website at **www.dhs.gov/dhspublic**.

For specifics on how to get a visa, see "Visas" in the appendix (p. 322).

MEDICAL REQUIREMENTS

Unless you're arriving from an area known to be suffering from an epidemic (particularly cholera or yellow fever), inoculations or vaccinations are not required for entry into the United States.

CUSTOMS
WHAT YOU CAN BRING INTO THE U.S.

Every visitor 21 or older may bring in, free of duty, the following: (1) 1 liter of wine or hard liquor; (2) 200 cigarettes, 100 cigars (but not from Cuba), or 3 pounds of smoking tobacco; and (3) $100 worth of gifts. These exemptions are offered to travelers who spend at least 72 hours in the United States and who have not claimed them within the preceding 6 months. It is forbidden to bring into the country almost any meat products (including canned, fresh, and dried meat products such as bouillon, soup mixes, and such). Generally, condiments including vinegars, oils, spices, coffee, tea, and some cheeses and baked goods are permitted. Avoid rice products, as rice can often harbor insects. Bringing fruits and vegetables is not advised, though not prohibited. Customs will allow produce depending on where you got it and where you're going after you arrive in the U.S. Foreign tourists may carry in or out up to $10,000 in U.S. or foreign currency with no formalities; larger sums must be declared to U.S. Customs on entering or leaving, which includes filing form CM 4790. For details regarding U.S. Customs and Border Protection, consult your nearest U.S. embassy or consulate, or **U.S. Customs** (www.customs.ustreas.gov).

WHAT YOU CAN TAKE HOME FROM MAUI

Canadian Citizens: For a clear summary of Canadian rules, write for the booklet *I Declare,* issued by the Canada Border Services Agency (© **800/461-9999** in Canada, or 204/983-3500; www.cbsa-asfc.gc.ca).

U.K. Citizens: For information, contact **HM Revenue & Customs** at © **0845/010-9000** (or 020/8929-0152 from outside the U.K.), or consult the website at www.hmce.gov.uk.

Australian Citizens: A helpful brochure available from Australian consulates and Customs offices is *Know Before You Go.* For more information, call the **Australian Customs Service** at © **1300/363-263,** or log on to www.customs.gov.au.

New Zealand Citizens: Most questions are answered in a free pamphlet available at New Zealand consulates and Customs offices: *New Zealand Customs Guide for Travellers, Notice no. 4.* For more information, contact **New Zealand Customs Service,** The Customhouse, 17–21 Whitmore St., Box 2218, Wellington (© **04/473-6099** or 0800/428-786; www.customs.govt.nz).

3 When to Go

Most visitors don't come to Maui when the weather's best in the islands; rather, they come when it's at its worst everywhere else. Thus, the **high season**—when prices are up and resorts are often booked to capacity—is generally from mid-December through March or mid-April. The last 2 weeks of December, in particular, are the prime time for travel to Maui. If you're planning a holiday trip, make your reservations as early as possible, expect crowds, and prepare to pay top dollar for accommodations, car rentals, and airfare. Whale-watching season begins in January and continues through the rest of winter, sometimes lasting into May.

The **off season,** when the best rates are available and the island is less crowded, is spring (mid-Apr to mid-June) and fall (Sept to mid-Dec)—a paradox, since these are the best seasons to be in Maui, in terms of reliably great weather. If you're looking to save money, or if you just want to avoid the crowds, this is the time to visit. Hotel rates and airfares tend to be significantly lower during the off season, and good packages and special deals are often available.

Note: If you plan to come to Maui between the last week in April and early May, be sure to book your accommodations, interisland air reservations, and car rentals in advance. In Japan, the last week of April is called **Golden Week** because three Japanese holidays take place one after the other. The islands are especially busy with Japanese tourists during this time.

Due to the large number of families traveling in **summer** (June–Aug), you won't get the fantastic bargains of spring and fall. However, you'll still do much better on packages, airfare, and accommodations than you will in the winter months.

CLIMATE

Because Maui lies at the edge of the tropical zone, it technically has only two seasons, both of them warm. There's a dry season that corresponds to **summer** (Apr–Oct) and a rainy season in **winter** (Nov–Mar). It rains every day somewhere in the islands any time of the year, but the rainy season sometimes brings enough gray weather to spoil your tanning opportunities. Fortunately, it seldom rains in one

How's the Weather?

Well, it depends which side of the island you're on: the leeward side or the windward side. The charts below show the average monthly temperatures in Wailea (on the leeward side) and Hana (on the windward side), plus the average number of rainy days in each month.

	Jan	Feb	Mar	Apr	May	June	July	Aug	Sept	Oct	Nov	Dec
Wailea												
Temp. (°F)	73	69	69	71	73	75	77	77	77	75	73	71
Temp. (°C)	23	21	21	22	23	24	25	25	25	24	23	22
Rainy days	3	2	2	1.7	0.6	0.1	0.1	0.3	0.3	0.8	1.7	1.7
Hana												
Temp. (°F)	73	70	70	71	72	74	75	75	76	75	73	71
Temp. (°C)	23	21	21	22	22	23	24	24	24	24	23	22
Rainy days	10.6	13.5	10.1	7.3	7.3	6.7	8.4	9.6	7.3	10.1	9.9	12.1

spot for more than 3 days straight, and rainy days often just consist of a mix of clouds and sun, with very brief showers.

The **year-round temperature** doesn't vary much more than 15°, but it depends on where you are. Maui's **leeward** sides (the west and south) are usually hot and dry, whereas the **windward** sides (east and north) are generally cooler and moist. If you want arid, sunbaked, desertlike weather, go leeward. If you want lush, often wet, junglelike weather, go windward. Your best bets for total year-round sun are the Kihei–Wailea and Lahaina–Kapalua coasts.

Maui is also full of **microclimates,** thanks to its interior valleys, coastal plains, and mountain peaks. If you travel into the mountains, the climate can change from summer to winter in a matter of hours because it's cooler the higher you go. In other words, if the weather doesn't suit you, just go to the other side of the island—or head into the hills.

HOLIDAYS

When Hawaii observes holidays (especially those over a long weekend), travel between the islands increases, interisland airline seats are fully booked, rental cars are at a premium, and hotels and restaurants are busier.

Federal, state, and county government offices are closed on all federal holidays; for a list, see the appendix.

State and county offices are also closed on local holidays, including Prince Kuhio Day (Mar 26), honoring the birthday of Hawaii's first delegate to the U.S. Congress; King Kamehameha Day (June 11), a statewide holiday commemorating Kamehameha the Great, who united the islands and ruled from 1795 to 1819; and Admissions Day (third Fri in Aug), which honors the admittance of Hawaii as the 50th state on August 21, 1959.

Other special days celebrated in Hawaii by many people but which involve no closing of federal, state, or county offices are the Chinese New Year (which generally falls in Jan or Feb; in 2009, it's Jan 26), Girls' Day (Mar 3), Buddha's Birthday (Apr 8), Father Damien's Day (Apr 15), Boys' Day (May 5), Samoan Flag Day (in Aug), Aloha Festivals (Sept–Oct), and Pearl Harbor Day (Dec 7).

> ### Tips Travel Tip
>
> Your best bets for total year-round sun are Maui's south shore (the Kihei–Wailea area) and west shore (from **Lahaina** to **Kapalua**).

MAUI, MOLOKAI & LANAI CALENDAR OF EVENTS

Please note that, as with any schedule of upcoming events, the following information is subject to change; always confirm the details before you plan your trip around an event.

For an exhaustive list of events beyond those listed here, check **www.visitmaui.com**, **www.molokai-hawaii.com**, or **www.visitlanai.net** for events throughout Maui, Molokai, and Lanai. Also consult **http://events.frommers.com**, where you'll find a searchable, up-to-the-minute roster of what's happening in cities all over the world.

January

PGA Mercedes-Benz Championship, Kapalua Resort. Top PGA golfers compete for $1 million. Call ℭ **808/669-2440** or go to www.kapaluamaui.com. January 5 to 11, 2009.

Ka Molokai Makahiki, Kaunakakai Town Baseball Park, Mitchell Pauole Center, Kaunakakai, Molokai. Makahiki, a traditional time of peace in ancient Hawaii, is re-created with performances by Hawaiian music groups and hula *halau* (schools), ancient Hawaiian games, a sporting competition, and Hawaiian crafts and food. It's a wonderful chance to experience the Hawaii of yesteryear. Call ℭ **800/800-6367** or 808/553-3876, or go to www.molokai-hawaii.com. Late January.

Chinese New Year. Lahaina town rolls out the red carpet for this important event with a traditional lion dance at the historic Wo Hing Temple on Front Street, accompanied by fireworks, food booths, and a host of activities. Call ℭ **888/310-1117** or 808/667-9175. Also on Market Street in Wailuku; call ℭ **808/244-3888.** Chinese New Year can fall in January or February; in 2009, January 26 ushers in the year of the ox.

Wendy's Champions Skins Game at Wailea, Wailea Golf Courses, Wailea Resort. Longtime golfing greats participate in this four-man tournament for $770,000 in prize money. Call ℭ **808/875-7450** or go to www.seniorskins wailea.com. Mid-January to early February.

February

Whale Day Celebration, Kalama Park, Kihei. A daylong celebration in the park with a parade of whales, entertainment, a crafts fair, games, and food. Call ℭ **808/249-8811** or go to www.visitmaui.com. Early or mid-February.

Whale Quest Kapalua, Kapalua Resort. This weekend-long event celebrates whales through lectures, interactive displays and events, art and photo exhibitions, and walks. Call ℭ **888/665-9160** or go to www.kapalua.com. Mid-February.

March

Ocean Arts Festival, Lahaina. The entire town of Lahaina celebrates the annual migration of Pacific humpback whales with this festival in Banyan Tree Park. Artists display their best ocean-themed art for sale, while Hawaiian musicians and hula troupes entertain. Enjoy marine-related activities, games, and a Creature Feature touch-pool exhibit for children. Call ℭ **888/310-1117** or 808/667-9194, or go to www.visitlahaina.com. Mid-March.

Run to the Sun, Paia to Haleakala. The world's top ultramarathoners make the journey from sea level to the top of 10,000-foot Haleakala, some 37 miles. Call ☎ **808/280-4893** or go to www.virr.com. Late March.

Molokai Hawaiian Paniolo Heritage Rodeo, Molokai Rodeo Arena, Maunaloa, Molokai. A celebration of Hawaii's *paniolo* (cowboy) heritage. Call ☎ **877/88T-RAIL** (888-7245).

April

East Maui Taro Festival, Hana. Here's your chance to taste taro in many different forms, from poi to chips. The Hawaiian staple food is celebrated through exhibits, music, hula, arts, crafts, and, of course, food. Call ☎ **808/264-3336** or go to www.tarofestival.org. Varying dates in April.

Buddha Day, Lahaina Jodo Mission, Lahaina. Each year on the first Saturday in April, this historic mission holds a flower festival pageant honoring the birth of Buddha. Call ☎ **808/661-4303.** April 4, 2009.

Celebration of the Arts, Ritz-Carlton Kapalua, Kapalua Resort. Contemporary and traditional artists give free hands-on lessons during this 4-day festival, which begins the Thursday before Easter. Call ☎ **808/669-6200** or go to www.celebrationofthearts.org. April 9 to 12, 2009.

Polo Spring Season Begins. For a complete list of all the polo matches in the cool, upcountry area of Maui, call ☎ **808/877-7744** or go to www.visitmaui.com.

David Malo Day, Lahainaluna High School, Lahaina. This daylong event with hula and other Hawaiian cultural celebrations commemorates Hawaii's famous scholar and ends with a luau. Call ☎ **808/662-4000** or go to www.visitmaui.com. Mid- or late April.

Banyan Tree Birthday Party, Lahaina. Come celebrate the birthday of Lahaina's famous Banyan Tree with a weekend of activities. Call ☎ **888/310-1117** or 808/667-9175, or go to www.visitlahaina.com. Generally the end of April.

Earth Day, Kahului and Maalaea. Maui Nui Botanical Gardens in Kahului (☎ **808/249-2798;** www.mnbg.org) and the Harbor Shops in Maalaea (☎ **808/249-8811**) host Earth Day celebrations. Late April.

May

Outrigger Canoe Season, all islands. From May to September, canoe paddlers across the state participate in outrigger canoe races nearly every weekend. Call ☎ **808/383-7790** or go to www.y2kanu.com for this year's schedule of events.

Lei Day Celebration, Fairmont Kea Lani Maui, Wailea. May Day is Lei Day in Hawaii, celebrated with lei-making contests, pageantry, arts and

---

⌒Tips Daylight Saving Time

Since 1966, most of the United States has observed daylight saving time from the first Sunday in April to the last Sunday in October. In 2007, these dates changed, and now daylight saving time lasts from 2am on the second Sunday in March to 2am on the first Sunday in November. **Note that Hawaii does *not* observe daylight saving time.** So when daylight saving time is in effect in most of the U.S., Hawaii is 3 hours behind the West Coast and 6 hours behind the East Coast. When the U.S. reverts to standard time in November, Hawaii is 2 hours behind the West Coast and 5 hours behind the East Coast.

crafts, and concerts throughout the islands. The Fairmont Kea Lani hosts its own royal court procession. Call *©* **808/224-6042** or go to www.visit maui.com. May 1.

Kapalua Jr. Vet/Sr. Tennis Championships, Kapalua Resort. Men and women ages 35 and over compete in singles and doubles championship tournaments. Call *©* **808/669-5677** or go to www.kapaluamaui.com. Early May.

International Festival of Canoes, West Maui. At this celebration of the Pacific islands' seafaring heritage, events include canoe paddling and sailing regattas, a luau feast, cultural demonstrations, canoe-building exhibits, and music. Call *©* **888/310-1117.** Mid- to late May.

Molokai Ka Hula Piko Festival, Papohaku Beach Park, Kaluakoi, Molokai. This daylong celebration of the hula takes place on the island where it was born. It features performances by hula schools, musicians, and singers from across Hawaii, as well as local food and Hawaiian crafts, including quilting, woodworking, feather work, and deer-horn scrimshaw. Call *©* **800/800-6367** or 808/553-3876, or go to www.molokaievents.com. May 16, 2009.

June

Da Kine Classic Windsurfing Event, Kanaha Beach Park, Kahului. This annual windsurfing slalom race takes place at Kanaha Beach Park, west of Kahului Airport in central Maui. Call *©* **808/877-2111.** Early June.

Maui Film Festival, Wailea Resort. Five days and nights of screenings of premieres and special films, along with traditional Hawaiian storytelling, chants, hula, and contemporary music. It begins the Wednesday before Father's Day. Call *©* **808/572-3456** or go to www.mauifilmfestival.com. June 10 to 14, 2009.

King Kamehameha Celebration, statewide. This state holiday (officially June 11, but celebrated on different dates on each island) features a massive floral parade, *hoolaulea* (parties), and much more. Call *©* **888/310-1117** or 808/667-9194, or go to www.visit lahaina.com for Maui events; call *©* **808/567-6361** for Molokai events. Most events in 2009 will be held June 13 to 14.

Hawaiian Slack-Key Guitar Festival, Maui Arts & Cultural Center, Kahului. Great music performed by the best musicians in Hawaii. It's 5 hours long and absolutely free. Call *©* **808/226-2697** or go to www.slackkeyfestival. com. Late June.

Kapalua Clambake Pro-Am Golf Tournament, Kapalua Resort. This tournament, which has taken place every year for more than 2 decades, ends with a giant clambake on the beach. Call *©* **808/669-8802** or go to www.kapalua.com. Late June.

Kapalua Wine & Food Festival, Kapalua Resort. Famous wine and food experts and oenophiles gather at the Ritz-Carlton hotel for formal tastings, panel discussions, and samplings of new releases. Call *©* **800/KAPALUA** (527-2582) or go to www.kapalua resort.com. Late June or early July.

July

Polo Season, Olinda Polo Field, Makawao. Polo matches featuring Hawaii's top players, often joined by famous international players, are held every Sunday at 1pm throughout the summer. Call *©* **808/877-7744** or go to www.mauipolo.com.

Lanai Pineapple Festival, Lanai City, Lanai. This festival on the first Saturday in July celebrates Lanai's history of pineapple plantations and ranching, including a pineapple-eating contest, a pineapple-cooking contest, entertainment, arts and crafts, food, and fireworks. Call ✆ **808/565-7600** or go to www.visitlanai.net. July 4th, 2009.

Fourth of July. Lahaina holds an old-fashioned Independence Day celebration with fireworks lighting the night sky over Lahaina's roadstead. Call ✆ **888/310-1117** or 808/667-9194, or go to www.visitlahaina.com. Kaanapali puts on a grand old celebration with live music, children's activities, and fireworks. Call ✆ **808/661-3271.**

Makawao Parade & Rodeo, Makawao. The annual parade and rodeo event has been taking place in this upcountry cowboy town for generations. Call ✆ **808/572-9565** or go to www.visitmaui.com. July 4.

Bon Dance & Lantern Ceremony, Lahaina. This colorful Buddhist ceremony honors the souls of the dead. Call ✆ **808/661-4304.** Usually early July.

Quiksilver Molokai to Oahu Paddleboard Race, starts on Molokai and finishes on Oahu. Some 70 participants from an international field journey to Molokai to compete in this 32-mile race, considered to be the world championship of long-distance paddleboard racing. The race begins at Kaluakoi Beach on Molokai at 7am and finishes at Maunaloa Bay on Oahu around 12:30pm. Call ✆ **808/638-8208** or go to www.molokai-hawaii.com. Mid- to late July.

August

Maui Onion Festival, Whalers Village, Kaanapali. Everything you ever wanted to know about the sweetest onions in the world. Food, entertainment, tastings, and the Maui Onion cook-off. Call ✆ **808/661-4567** or go to www.whalersvillage.com. Early August.

Hawaii State Windsurfing Championship, Kanaha Beach Park, Kahului. Top windsurfers compete. Call ✆ **808/877-2111.** Early August.

Tahiti Fete, War Memorial Gym, Wailuku. An annual festival with Tahitian dance competition, arts and crafts, and food. Call ✆ **808/244-8088.** Two days in August.

September

Aloha Festivals, various locations. Parades and other events celebrate Hawaiian culture. Call ✆ **800/852-7690** or 808/545-1771, or go to www.alohafestivals.com for a schedule of events.

LifeFest Kapalua, Kapalua Resort. A 3-day health-and-wellness event featuring lectures and panel presentations by leaders in the health-and-wellness field, plus ocean sporting events, fitness activities, a health-and-wellness expo, and sumptuous gala dinners. Area resorts and condominiums offer special package rates. Call ✆ **866/669-2440** or 808/669-2440, or go to www.lifefestmaui.com. Varying dates in September.

A Taste of Lahaina, Lahaina Civic Center, Lahaina. Some 30,000 people show up to sample 40 signature entrees from Maui's premier chefs during this weekend festival, which includes cooking demonstrations, wine tastings, and live entertainment. The event begins Friday night with Maui Chefs Present, a themed dinner/cocktail party featuring about a dozen of Maui's best chefs. Call ✆ **888/310-1117** or go to www.visitmaui.com. Second weekend in September.

Hana Relays, Hana Highway. Hundreds of runners, in relay teams, crowd the Hana Highway from Kahului to Hana (you might want to otherwise avoid the road on this day). Call

Ongoing Events on Maui

Every Friday night from 7 to 10pm, as part of **Friday Night Is Art Night** in Lahaina, the town's galleries open their doors for special shows, demonstrations, and refreshments. There are even strolling musicians wandering the streets.

If you're hungry for Hawaiian music, the **Masters of Hawaiian Slack Key Guitar Series** (© 888/669-3858; www.slackkey.com) features some of the great masters (and some Grammy Award winners) of this guitar style unique to the Hawaiian Islands. Concerts are held every Wednesday night at 7:30pm at the Napili Kai Beach Resort. Tickets are $47; call in advance for reservations.

On the first and third weekends of the month, Hawaiian artists sell and share culture, arts, and crafts under the famous landmark **Banyan Tree** in Lahaina. On the other weekends, the Lahaina Arts Society holds an exhibit and sale of various works of art in the same place.

Every Wednesday at 5:30 and 7:30pm, the **Maui Film Festival** (© 808/ 572-3456 or 579-9244; www.mauifilmfestival.com) presents outstanding contemporary and art films at the Maui Arts & Cultural Center, 1 Cameron Way (just off Kahului Beach Rd.), in Kahului.

You don't have to spend a good chunk of change and order two drinks to experience the Hawaiian art of hula. There are **free hula performances** every week. In **Lahaina**, they take place Saturday and Sunday at 1pm and Tuesday and Thursday at 7pm in the Lahaina Cannery Mall; Wednesday at 2:30pm and Friday at 3:30pm at the Lahaina Center. In **Kaanapali**, they're held every Monday, Wednesday, and Saturday at 6:30pm at the Whalers Village; and every night at 6:30pm at the Kaanapali Beach Hotel. If you would like to try the hula yourself, there are free hula lessons at Whalers Village every Thursday from 3 to 4pm.

It's also fun to check out Maui's **outdoor markets,** where you can find good deals on gifts to bring home, try the grown-on-Maui produce, and meet the locals. Every Saturday from 7am to 1pm, the **Maui Swap Meet** (© 808/877-3100) is held on the campus of the Maui Community College, in Kahului (in an area bounded by Kahului Beach Rd. and Wahine Pio Ave.; access is via Wahine Pio Ave.). This is Maui's largest outdoor market, filled with everything from vegetables to Hawaiian art. For upscale culinary items, stop by the **Aloha Friday Farmers Market,** held every Friday from noon to 6pm at the Maui Community College. Here you'll find gourmet vendors like Surfing Goat Dairy, Waipoli Hydroponic Greens/Pacific Produce, Alii Lavender, and terrific baked goods from the MCC culinary students. At the **Kaahumanu Shopping Center,** on Kaahumanu Avenue in Kahului, the parking lot is filled with bargains every Tuesday, Wednesday, and Friday from 7am to 3pm. At the **Maui Mall,** also on Kaahumanu Avenue in Kahului, you'll get great deals on produce every Tuesday, Wednesday, and Friday from 8am to 5pm. Arrive early to get the best bargains.

© 808/243-9636 or go to www.virr. com. Early September.

Maui Marathon, Kahului to Kaanapali. Runners line up at the Maui Mall before daybreak and head off for Kaanapali. Call © 866/577-8379, or go to www.virr.com or www.mauimarathon. com. Mid- to late September.

Na Wahine O Ke Kai, Molokai. The top women canoe paddlers from across the state will arrive at Hale Lono Harbor on Molokai and paddle across the ocean to Oahu. Call © 808/259-7112 or go to www.molokai-hawaii.com. Mid-September.

Maui County Fair, War Memorial Complex, Wailuku. The oldest county fair in Hawaii features a parade, amusement rides, live entertainment, and exhibits. Call © 800/525-MAUI (6284) (in July, 808/242-2721), or go to www.mauicountyfair.com. Last week in September or first week in October.

October

Aloha Festivals Hoolaulea, Lahaina. This all-day cultural festival, which marks the end of Maui's Aloha Festivals Week, is held at Banyan Tree Park and features Hawaiian food, music, and dance, along with arts and crafts on display and for sale. Call © 888/310-1117 or 808/667-9194, or go to www.visitlahaina.com. September or October.

Molokai Hoe, Molokai to Oahu. This men's 40-mile outrigger contest starts in Molokai and finishes at Fort DeRussy Beach in Waikiki. Call © 808/259-7112 or go to www.molokai-hawaii.com or www.holoholo.com.

Halloween in Lahaina. There's Carnival in Rio, Mardi Gras in New Orleans, and Halloween in Lahaina. Come to this giant costume party (some 20,000 people show up) on the streets of Lahaina; Front Street is closed off for the festivities. Call © 888/310-1117 or 808/667-9194, or go to www.visitlahaina.com. October 31.

November

Hula O Na Keiki, Kaanapali Beach Hotel, Kaanapali. This solo hula competition for children ages 5 to 17 has been held for 2 decades. The weekend festival celebrates Hawaiian dance, arts, and music. Call © 808/661-0011 or go to www.kbhmaui.com. Early November.

Hawaii International Film Festival, various locations. This cinema festival with a cross-cultural spin features filmmakers from Asia, the Pacific Islands, and the United States. Call © 808/550-8457 or go to www.hiff.org. First 2 weeks in November.

EA Sports Maui Invitational Basketball Tournament, Lahaina Civic Center, Lahaina. Top college teams vie in this annual preseason tournament. Call © 847/850-1818 or go to www. mauiinvitational.com. Usually held around Thanksgiving.

December

Hui Noeau Christmas House, Makawao. The festivities in the beautifully decorated Hui mansion include shopping, workshops and art demonstrations, children's activities and visits with Santa, holiday music, fresh-baked goods, and local foods. Call © 808/572-6560 or go to www.huinoeau. com. Late November and early December.

Na Mele O Maui, Kaanapali Beach Resort. Children from Maui and Molokai, in kindergarten through 12th grade, participate in this traditional Hawaiian song competition. Call ©808/661-3271 or go to www.kaanapaliresort. com. Early December.

Festival of Lights, island-wide. Festivities include parades and tree-lighting ceremonies. Marching bands, floats, and Santa roll down Lahaina's Front Street. Call (℃ 808/667-9175 on Maui or 552-2800 on Molokai. Early December.

Festival of Trees, Lahaina Cannery Mall, Lahaina. Look for decorated trees as well as entertainment. Call (℃ 808/661-5304. Early December.

Lighting of the Banyan Tree, Lahaina. At 6:30pm, Lahaina's historic Banyan Tree is lit up with thousands of Christmas lights for the entire holiday season. Santa Claus makes an appearance and choirs sing Christmas carols accompanied by hula. Kids can join a cookie workshop. Call (℃ 808/667-9194 or 667-9194, or go to www.visit lahaina.com. Early December.

Tree Lighting Ceremony, Ritz-Carlton Kapalua, Kapalua Resort. With the flick of a switch, more than 250,000 sparkling lights will illuminate the 25-foot holiday tree and dozens of pine and palm trees around the courtyards of the Ritz-Carlton Kapalua and throughout the resort. Call (℃ 808/669-6200 or go to www.kapalua resort.com. Early December.

Christmas Light Parade, Kaunakakai, Molokai. A light parade with music and holiday arts and crafts. Call (℃ 808/552-2800. Mid-December.

First Light, Maui Arts & Cultural Center, Kahului. The Academy of Motion Pictures holds major screenings of top films. Not to be missed. Call (℃ 808/572-3456 or go to www.mauifilmfestival.com. Late December and early January.

4 Getting There & Getting Around

GETTING TO MAUI

If you think of the island of Maui as the shape of a head and shoulders of a person, you'll probably arrive at its neck, at **Kahului Airport** (OGG). If you're headed for Molokai or Lanai, you'll have to connect through Honolulu.

For complete airline contact information, see the appendix.

At press time, the following airlines fly directly from the U.S. mainland to Kahului: **United Airlines** offers daily nonstop flights from San Francisco and Los Angeles; **Hawaiian Airlines** has direct flights from San Diego, Portland, and Seattle; **Alaska Airlines** offers flights from Anchorage to Seattle to Kahului; **American Airlines** flies direct from Los Angeles and San Jose; **Delta Air Lines** offers direct flights from San Francisco via Los Angeles; and **US Airways** has nonstop service from Las Vegas.

The other carriers—including **Continental Airlines** and **Northwest Airlines**—fly to Honolulu, where you'll have to pick up an interisland flight to Maui. (The airlines listed in the paragraph above also offer many more flights to Honolulu from additional cities on the mainland.) **Hawaiian Airlines** offers jet service from Honolulu.

INTERISLAND FLIGHTS Since September 11, 2001, the major interisland carriers have cut way, way, way back on the number of interisland flights. The airlines warn you to show up at least 90 minutes before your flight, and believe me, with all the security inspections, you will need all 90 minutes to catch your flight. Also, be sure to book your interisland connection from Honolulu to Maui in advance.

In 2008, Hawaii lost one of its three major interisland carriers, Aloha Airlines, but two still remain: **Hawaiian Airlines**

(© **800/367-5320;** www.hawaiianair.
com) and **go!** (© **888/I-FLY-GO-2**
[435-9462]; www.iflygo.com).

Visitors to Molokai and Lanai have
two commuter airlines to choose from.
The carrier go! started commuter service
from Honolulu under the name
go!Express (© **888/I-FLY-GO-2** [435-
9462]; www.iflygo.com), with a fleet of
Cessna Grand Caravan 208B planes.
Pacific Wings began operating a discount
airline called **PW Express** (© **888/
866-5022** or 808/873-0877; www.fly
pwx.com), with daily nonstop flights
between Honolulu and Molokai and
Lanai, plus flights from Kahului, Maui.
And **Island Air** (© **800/323-3345** or
808/484-2222; www.islandair.com) serves
Hawaii's small interisland airports on
Maui, Molokai, and Lanai. However, I
have to warn you that I have not had stellar service on Island Air and recommend
that you book instead on go!Express or
PW Express if you're headed to Molokai
or Lanai.

IMMIGRATION & CUSTOMS

International visitors arriving by air
should cultivate patience and resignation
before setting foot on U.S. soil. U.S. airports have considerably beefed up security clearances in the years since the
terrorist attacks of September 11, and
clearing Customs and Immigration can
take as long as 2 hours.

LANDING AT KAHULUI
AIRPORT

If there's a long wait at baggage claim,
step over to the state-operated **Visitor
Information Center,** where you can ask
about island activities and pick up
brochures and the latest issue of *This
Week Maui,* which features great regional
maps of the islands. After collecting your
bags from the poky, automated carousels,
step out, take a deep breath, proceed to
the curbside rental-car pickup area, and
wait for the appropriate rental-agency

shuttle van to take you ½ mile away to the
rental-car checkout desk. (All major
rental companies have branches at Kahului; see "Getting Around Maui," later in
this chapter.)

If you're not renting a car, the cheapest
way to get to your hotel is via **Speedi
Shuttle** (© **877/242-5777;** www.speedi
shuttle.com), which can take you between
Kahului Airport and all the major resorts
between 6am and 11pm daily. Rates vary,
but figure on $39 for one person to
Wailea (one-way), $54 to Kaanapali, and
$74 to Kapalua. Be sure to call ahead of
time to arrange for pickup.

You'll see taxis outside the airport ter-
minal, but note that they are quite expensive—expect to spend around $60 to $75
for a ride from Kahului to Kaanapali and
$50 to Wailea.

If possible, avoid landing on Maui
between 3 and 6pm, when the working
stiffs on Maui are "pau work" (finished
with work) and a major traffic jam occurs
at the first intersection.

AVOIDING KAHULUI

If you're planning to stay in Kapalua or
Kaanapali, you might consider flying
Island Air (© **800/323-3345;** www.
islandair.com) from Honolulu to the
Kapalua–West Maui Airport. From this
airport, it's only a 10- to 15-minute drive
to most hotels in west Maui, as opposed
to an hour from Kahului.

Pacific Wings (© **888/575-4546** or
808/873-0877; www.pacificwings.com)
flies eight-passenger, twin-engine Cessna
402C aircraft into tiny **Hana Airport,** in
east Maui, and also flies into Kahului.

AGRICULTURAL SCREENING

Note that at all airports in Hawaii, baggage
and passengers bound for the mainland
must be screened by agricultural officials.
Officials will confiscate local produce like
fresh avocados, bananas, and mangoes, in
the name of fruit-fly control. Pineapples,
coconuts, and papayas inspected and

Moments   The Welcoming Lei

Nothing makes you feel more welcome than a lei. The tropical beauty of the delicate garland, the deliciously sweet fragrance of the blossoms, the sensual way the flowers curl softly around your neck—there's no doubt about it: Getting lei'd in Hawaii is a sensuous experience.

Leis are much more than just a decorative necklace of flowers—they're also one of the nicest ways to say "hello," "goodbye," "congratulations," "I salute you," "my sympathies are with you," or "I love you."

During ancient times, leis given to *alii* (royalty) were accompanied by a bow, since it was *kapu* (forbidden) for a commoner to raise his arms higher than the king's head. The presentation of a kiss with a lei didn't come about until World War II; it's generally attributed to an entertainer who kissed an officer on a dare and then quickly presented him with her lei, saying it was an old Hawaiian custom. It wasn't then, but it sure caught on fast.

Lei-making is a tropical art form. All leis are fashioned by hand in a variety of traditional patterns; some are sewn with hundreds of tiny blooms or shells, or bits of ferns and leaves. Some are twisted, some braided, some strung. Every island has its own special flower lei—the lei of the land, so to speak. On Maui, it's the *lokelani*, a small rose; on Molokai, it's the *kukui*, the white blossom of a candlenut tree; and on Lanai, it's the *kaunaoa*, a bright yellow moss. Leis are available at the Kahului Airport, from florists, and even at supermarkets.

Leis are the perfect symbol for the islands: They're given in the moment, and their fragrance and beauty are enjoyed in the moment, but even after they fade, their spirit of aloha lives on. Welcome to Hawaii!

---

certified for export; boxed flowers; leis without seeds; and processed foods (macadamia nuts, coffee, jams, dried fruit, and the like) will pass.

LONG-HAUL FLIGHTS: HOW TO STAY COMFORTABLE

- Your choice of airline and airplane will definitely affect your legroom. Find more details about U.S. airlines at **www.seatguru.com**. For international airlines, the research firm Skytrax has posted a list of average seat pitches at **www.airlinequality.com**.
- Emergency-exit seats and bulkhead seats typically have the most legroom. Emergency-exit seats are usually left unassigned until the day of a flight (to ensure that someone able-bodied

fills the seats); it's worth checking in online at home (if the airline offers that option) or getting to the ticket counter early to snag one of these spots for a long flight. Many passengers find that bulkhead seating offers more legroom, but keep in mind that bulkhead seats have no storage space on the floor in front of you.

- To have two seats for yourself in a three-seat row, try for an aisle seat in a center section toward the back of coach. If you're traveling with a companion, book an aisle and a window seat. Middle seats are usually booked last, so chances are good you'll end up with three seats to yourselves. And in the event that a third passenger is

(Tips Coping with Jet Lag

Jet lag is a pitfall of traveling across time zones. If you're flying north-south and you feel sluggish when you touch down, your symptoms will be the result of dehydration and the general stress of air travel. When you travel east-west or vice versa, however, your body becomes thoroughly confused about what time it is, and everything from your digestive system to your brain is knocked for a loop. Traveling east—say, from San Francisco to Boston—is more difficult on your internal clock than traveling west—say, from Atlanta to Hawaii—because most people's bodies are more inclined to stay up late than to fall asleep early.

Here are some tips for combating jet lag:

- **Reset your watch** to your destination time before you board the plane.
- **Drink lots of water** before, during, and after your flight. Avoid alcohol.
- **Exercise and sleep well** for a few days before your trip.
- If you have trouble sleeping on planes, **fly eastward on morning flights.**
- **Daylight** is the key to resetting your body clock. At the website for **Outside In** (www.bodyclock.com), you can get a customized plan of when to seek and avoid light.

assigned the middle seat, he or she will probably be more than happy to trade for a window or an aisle.

- To sleep, avoid the last row of any section or the row in front of an emergency exit, as these seats are the least likely to recline. Avoid seats near highly trafficked toilet areas. Avoid seats in the back of many jets—these can be narrower than those in the rest of coach. Or reserve a window seat so you can rest your head and avoid being bumped in the aisle.
- Get up, walk around, and stretch every 60 to 90 minutes to keep your blood flowing. This helps avoid **deep-vein thrombosis,** or "economy-class syndrome." See "Avoiding 'Economy Class Syndrome,'" p. 67.
- Drink water before, during, and after your flight to combat the lack of humidity in airplane cabins. Avoid caffeine and alcohol, which will dehydrate you.
- If you're flying with kids, don't forget to carry on toys, books, pacifiers, and snacks and chewing gum to help

them relieve ear pressure buildup during ascent and descent.

GETTING AROUND MAUI

The only way to really see Maui is by rental car. There's no real island-wide public transit.

Maui has only a handful of major roads, and you can expect to encounter a traffic jam or two in the major resort areas. Two of the roads follow the coastline around the two volcanoes that form the island, Haleakala and Puu Kukui (the West Maui Mountains), one road goes up to Haleakala's summit, one road goes to Hana, one goes to Wailea, and one goes to Lahaina. It sounds simple, right? Well, it isn't because the names of the few roads change en route. Study a map before you set out.

BY CAR

Hawaii has some of the lowest car-rental rates in the country—about $47 a day (including all state tax and fees); the national average is about $56. (An exception is the island of Lanai, where they're very expensive.) To rent a car in Hawaii, you must be at least 25 years of age and

Tips Traffic Advisory

The road from central Maui to Kihei and Wailea, **Mokulele Highway (Hwy. 311),** is a dangerous strip that's often the scene of head-on crashes involving intoxicated and speeding drivers. Be careful.

Also be alert on the **Honoapiilani Highway (Hwy. 30)** en route to Lahaina—drivers who spot whales in the channel between Maui and Lanai often slam on the brakes and cause major tie-ups and accidents.

Note that all highways on Maui are packed, bumper-to-bumper, between 7 and 9am and 4 and 6pm, so plan accordingly.

If you get into trouble on Maui's highways, look for the flashing blue strobe lights on 12-foot poles; at the base are emergency solar-powered call boxes (programmed to dial ☎ **911** as soon as you pick up the handset). There are 29 emergency call boxes on the island's busiest highways and remote areas, including along the Hana and Haleakala highways and on the north end of the island in the remote community of Kahakuloa.

Another traffic note: Buckle up your seat belt—Hawaii has stiff fines for noncompliance.

---

have a valid driver's license and credit card. *Note:* If you're visiting from abroad and plan to rent a car in the United States, keep in mind that foreign driver's licenses are usually recognized in the U.S., but you should get an international one if your home license is not in English.

All major car-rental agencies have offices on Maui, usually at both Kahului and West Maui airports. They include **Alamo, Avis, Budget, Dollar, Hertz,** and **National.** For complete rental-agency contact information, see the appendix.

There are also a few frugal car-rental agencies offering older cars at discount prices. **Word of Mouth Rent-a-Car** ✸, in Kahului (☎ **800/533-5929** or 808/877-2436; www.mauirentacar.com), has older cars (1995–2004 Toyotas and Nissans, air-conditioned) that start at $27 a day, including all taxes, with a 3-day minimum, or from $156 a week. Rates include free airport pickup and drop-off. **Maui Cruisers,** in Wailuku (☎ **877/749-7889** or 808/249-2319; www.mauicruisers.net), also offers free airport

pickup and return on its 8- to 10-year-old Nissan Sentras, with rentals starting at $17 a day (3-day minimum) or $119 a week (including tax and insurance).

INSURANCE   Hawaii is a no-fault state, which means that if you don't have collision-damage insurance, you are required to pay for all damages before you leave the state, whether or not the accident was your fault. Your personal car insurance may provide rental-car coverage; check before you leave home. Bring your insurance identification card if you decline the optional insurance, which usually costs from $12 to $20 a day. Obtain the name of your company's local claim representative before you go. Some credit card companies also provide collision-damage insurance for their customers; check with yours before you rent.

DRIVING RULES   Hawaii state law mandates that all car passengers must wear a **seat belt** and all infants must be strapped into a car seat. You'll pay a $50 fine if you don't buckle up. **Pedestrians** always have the right of way, even if they're not in the crosswalk. You can turn

right on red after a full and complete stop, unless otherwise posted.

ROAD MAPS The best and most detailed road maps are published by *This Week* magazine, a free visitor publication available on Maui. Most rental-car maps are pretty good, too.

BY MOTORCYCLE

Don black denim and motorcycle boots, feel the wind on your face, and smell the salt air by riding a Harley, available for rent from **Maui Harley-Davidson,** 150 Dairy Rd., Kahului (© **808/877-7433;** www.mauicarsandbikes.com). Rentals start at $119 for 5 hours or $159 for 24 hours.

BY MOPED

Mopeds are available for rent from **Aloha Toy Store** (www.alohatoystore.com), with locations at 640 Front St., #5, Lahaina (© **888/883-1212** or 808/662-0888), and the Fairway Shops in Kaanapali (© **808/661-9000**). Vespa scooters, which start at $40 for 4 hours and $50 for all day (8am–4pm), are little more than motorized bicycles that get up to around 35 mph (with a good wind at your back), so I suggest using them only locally (to get to the beach or to go shopping). Don't take them out on the highway—they can't keep up with the traffic. Aloha Toy Store also rents motorcycles and dune buggies.

BY TAXI & SHUTTLE

For island-wide 24-hour service, call **Alii Cab Co.** (© 808/661-3688 or 667-2605). You can also try **Kihei Taxi** (© 808/879-3000), **Wailea Taxi** (© 808/874-5000), or **Maui Central Cab** (© 808/244-7278) if you need a ride.

SpeediShuttle (© 877/242-5777; www.speedishuttle.com) can take you between Kahului Airport and all the major resorts from 5am to 11pm daily (for details, see "Landing at Kahului Airport," p. 59).

Maui Public Transit is a public/private partnership that has convenient, economical, and air-conditioned shuttle buses on 11 routes, all operated by Roberts Hawaii (© **808/871-4838;** www.mauicounty.gov/bus). These routes are funded by the County of Maui and provide service in and between various central, west, south, and upcountry Maui communities (including the airport). All routes operate daily. The routes go from as far south as Wailea up to as far north as Kapalua. Fares are $1 to $2.

5 Money & Costs

The most common bills are the $1 (a "buck"), $5, $10, and $20 denominations. There are also $2 bills (seldom encountered), $50 bills, and $100 bills (the last two are usually not welcome as payment for small purchases).

Coins come in seven denominations: 1¢ (1 cent, or a penny); 5¢ (5 cents, or a nickel); 10¢ (10 cents, or a dime); 25¢ (25 cents, or a quarter); 50¢ (50 cents, or a half-dollar); the gold-colored Sacagawea and presidential coins, worth $1; and the rare silver dollar.

It's always advisable to bring money in a variety of forms on a vacation: a mix of cash, credit cards, and traveler's checks. You should also exchange enough petty cash to cover airport incidentals, tipping, and transportation to your hotel before you leave home, or withdraw money upon arrival at an airport ATM.

ATMs

Hawaii pioneered the use of ATMs (automated teller machines) more than 2 decades ago, and now they're everywhere. You'll find them at banks, supermarkets, Longs Drugs, and most resorts and shopping centers. The **Cirrus** (© 800/424-7787; www.mastercard.com) and **PLUS**

Travel in the Age of Bankruptcy

Airlines go bankrupt, so protect yourself by **buying your tickets with a credit card.** The Fair Credit Billing Act guarantees that you can get your money back from the credit card company if a travel supplier goes under (and if you request the refund within 60 days of the bankruptcy). **Travel insurance** can also help, but make sure it covers against "carrier default" for your specific travel provider. And be aware that if a U.S. airline goes bust midtrip, a 2001 federal law requires other carriers to take you to your destination (albeit on a space-available basis) for a fee of no more than $25, provided you rebook within 60 days of the cancellation.

(© **800/843-7587;** www.visa.com) networks span the country. Go to your bank card's website to find ATM locations at your destination. Be sure you know your daily withdrawal limit before you depart.

Note: Many banks impose a fee every time you use a card at another bank's ATM, and that fee is often higher for international transactions (up to $5 or more) than for domestic ones (where they're rarely more than $2). In addition, the bank from which you withdraw cash may charge its own fee. To compare banks' ATM fees within the U.S., use **www.bankrate.com**. Visitors from outside the U.S. should also find out whether their bank assesses a 1% to 3% fee.

CREDIT CARDS & DEBIT CARDS

Credit cards are the most widely used form of payment in the United States: **Visa** (Barclaycard in Britain), **Master-Card** (EuroCard in Europe, Access in Britain, Chargex in Canada), **American Express, Diners Club,** and **Discover.**

They also provide a convenient record of all your expenses and offer relatively good exchange rates. You can withdraw cash advances from your credit cards at banks or ATMs, but high fees make credit card cash advances a pricey way to get cash.

It's highly recommended that you travel with at least one major credit card. You must have a credit card to rent a car, and hotels and airlines usually require a credit card imprint as a deposit against expenses.

ATM cards with major credit card backing, known as **"debit cards,"** are now a commonly acceptable form of payment in most stores and restaurants. Debit cards draw money directly from your checking account. Some stores enable you to receive cash back on your debit card purchases as well. The same is true at most U.S. post offices.

Visitors from outside the U.S. should find out whether their bank assesses a 1% to 3% fee on charges incurred abroad.

6 Health

STAYING HEALTHY
INSECTS & SCORPIONS

Like any tropical climate, Hawaii is home to lots of bugs. Most of them won't harm you. However, watch out for mosquitoes, centipedes, and scorpions, which do sting and may cause anything from mild annoyance to severe swelling and pain.

MOSQUITOES These pesky insects are not native to Hawaii but arrived as larvae stowed away in water barrels on the ship *Wellington* in 1826, when it anchored in Lahaina. There's not a whole lot you can do about them, except to apply commercial repellent, which you can pick up at any drugstore.

What Things Cost on Maui	US$	Euro €	UK£
Cup of coffee	3.00	2.07	1.50
SpeediShuttle from airport to Wailea	39.00	26.90	19.50
SpeediShuttle from airport to Kapalua	74.00	51.03	37.00
Moderate three-course dinner without alcohol	50.00	34.48	25.00
Double room in moderate hotel	125.00– 175.00	86.21– 120.70	62.50– 87.50
Hamburger	6.00	4.14	3.00
Movie ticket (adult)	9.00	6.21	4.50
Movie ticket (child)	5.50	3.79	2.75
Entry to Maui Ocean Center (adult)	24.00	16.55	12.00
Entry to Maui Ocean Center (child)	17.00	11.72	8.50
Entry to Haleakala National Park	5.00	3.45	2.50
Round-trip ferry to Lanai (adult)	50.00	34.48	25.00
Round-trip ferry to Lanai (child)	40.00	27.59	20.00
Basic snorkel-gear rental per week	9.00	6.21	4.50
20-ounce soft drink at drug or convenience store	2.50	1.72	1.25
16-ounce apple juice	3.50	2.41	1.75

CENTIPEDES These segmented bugs with a jillion legs come in two varieties: 6- to 8-inch-long brown ones and 2- to 3-inch-long blue guys. Both can really pack a wallop with their sting. Centipedes are generally found in damp, wet places, such as under wood piles or compost heaps; wearing closed-toe shoes can help prevent stings. If you're stung, apply ice at once to prevent swelling. See a doctor if you experience extreme pain, swelling, nausea, or any other severe reaction.

SCORPIONS Rarely seen, scorpions are found in arid, warm regions; their stings can be serious. Campers in dry areas should always check their boots before putting them on and shake out sleeping bags and bed rolls. Symptoms of a scorpion sting include shortness of breath, hives, swelling, and nausea. In the unlikely event that you're stung, apply diluted household ammonia and cold compresses to the area of the sting and seek medical help immediately.

HIKING SAFETY
In addition to taking the appropriate precautions regarding Hawaii's bug population, hikers should always let someone know where they're heading, when they're going, and when they plan to return; too many hikers get lost in Hawaii because they don't let others know their basic plans.

Before you head out, always check weather conditions. Hike with a pal, never alone. Wear hiking boots, a sun hat, clothes to protect you from the sun and from getting scratches, and high-SPF sunscreen on all exposed areas of skin. Take water. Stay on the trail. Watch your step. It's easy to slip off precipitous trails and into steep canyons. Many experienced hikers and boaters today pack a cellphone in case of emergency; just dial ✆ **911.**

If you're planning a trek to the top of 10,000-foot Haleakala, you'll need to watch for signs of **altitude sickness.** If you experience dizziness, drowsiness, or a

Tips Don't Get Burned: Smart Tanning Tips

Hawaii's Caucasian population has the highest incidence of malignant melanoma (deadly skin cancer) in the world. And nobody is completely safe from the sun's harmful rays: All skin types and races can burn. To ensure that your vacation won't be ruined by a painful sunburn, here are some helpful tips:

- **Wear a strong sunscreen at all times.** Use a sunscreen with an SPF of 15 or higher; people with light complexions should use SPF 30. Apply it liberally (1 tablespoon for each limb), and reapply every 2 hours. The best sunscreens block both UVA and UVB rays. Look for zinc oxide, benzophenone, oxybenzone, sulisobenzone, titanium dioxide, or avobenzone (also known as Parsol 1789) in the list of ingredients.
- **Wear a hat and sunglasses.** Your hat should have a brim all the way around, to cover not only your face but also the sensitive back of your neck. Make sure your sunglasses have UV filters.
- **Protect children from the sun.** Keep infants under 6 months out of the sun completely, and slather older babies and children with strong sunscreen frequently.
- **If it's too late:** The best remedy for a sunburn is to stay out of the sun until all the redness is gone. Aloe vera, cool compresses, cold baths, and anesthetic benzocaine also help with the pain.

sudden headache, consider heading back down the mountain. Pregnant women, heavy smokers, and people with asthma and heart conditions should be especially careful.

VOG

The volcanic haze dubbed *vog* is caused by gases released when molten lava—from the continuous eruption of Kilauea volcano on the Big Island—pours into the ocean. As we went to press, Kilauea had not one but two eruptions going on, spewing out sulfur dioxide. Some people claim that long-term exposure to the hazy, smoglike air has caused bronchial ailments, but it's highly unlikely to cause you any harm in the course of your visit.

There actually is a vog season in Hawaii: the fall and winter months, when the trade winds that blow the fumes out to sea die down. The vog is felt not only on the Big Island, but also as far away as Maui and Oahu.

OCEAN SAFETY

Because most people coming to Hawaii are unfamiliar with the ocean environment, they're often unaware of the natural hazards it holds. With just a few precautions, your ocean experience can be a safe and happy one. An excellent book is *All Stings Considered: First Aid and Medical Treatment of Hawaii's Marine Injuries,* by Craig Thomas and Susan Scott (University of Hawaii Press, 1997).

Note that sharks are not a big problem in Hawaii; in fact, they appear so infrequently that locals look forward to seeing them. Since records have been kept, starting in 1779, there have been only about 100 shark attacks in Hawaii, of which 40% have been fatal. Most attacks occurred after someone fell into the ocean from the shore or from a boat; in these cases, the sharks probably attacked after the person was dead. But general rules for avoiding sharks are: Don't swim at sunrise, at sunset, or where the water is murky due to stream runoff—sharks may mistake you for one of their usual meals. And don't swim where there are bloody fish in the water, as sharks become aggressive around blood.

SEASICKNESS The waters in Hawaii can range from as calm as glass (off the Kona Coast on the Big Island) to downright frightening (in storm conditions); they usually fall somewhere in between. In general, expect rougher conditions in winter than in summer. Some 90% of the population tends toward seasickness. If you've never been out on a boat, or if you've been seasick in the past, you might want to heed the following suggestions:

- The day before you go out on the boat, avoid alcohol, caffeine, citrus and other acidic juices, and greasy, spicy, or hard-to-digest foods.
- Get a good night's sleep the night before.
- Take or use whatever seasickness prevention works best for you—medication, an acupressure wristband, ginger-root tea or capsules, or any combination. But do it *before* **you**

board; once you set sail, it's generally too late.
- While you're on the boat, stay as low and as near the center of the boat as possible. Avoid the fumes (especially if it's a diesel boat); stay out in the fresh air and watch the horizon. Do not read.
- If you start to feel queasy, drink clear fluids like water, and eat something bland, such as a soda cracker.

STINGS The most common stings in Hawaii come from jellyfish, particularly Portuguese man-of-war and box jellyfish. Since the poisons they inject are very different, you need to treat each type of sting differently.

A bluish-purple floating bubble with a long tail, the **Portuguese man-of-war** is responsible for some 6,500 stings a year on Oahu alone. These stings, although painful and a nuisance, are rarely harmful; fewer than 1 in 1,000 requires medical treatment. The best prevention is to watch for these floating bubbles as you snorkel (look for the hanging tentacles below the surface). Get out of the water if anyone near you spots these jellyfish.

Reactions to stings range from mild burning and reddening to severe welts and blisters. *All Stings Considered* recommends the following treatment: First,

Avoiding "Economy Class Syndrome"

Deep vein thrombosis, or "economy-class syndrome" as it's known in the world of flying, is a blood clot that develops in a deep vein. It's a potentially deadly condition that can be caused by sitting in cramped conditions—such as an airplane cabin—for too long. During a flight (especially a long-haul flight), get up, walk around, and stretch your legs every 60 to 90 minutes to keep your blood flowing. Other preventive measures include frequent flexing of the legs while sitting, drinking lots of water, and avoiding alcohol and sleeping pills. If you have a history of deep vein thrombosis, heart disease, or another condition that puts you at high risk, some experts recommend wearing compression stockings or taking anticoagulants when you fly; always ask your physician about the best course for you. Symptoms of deep vein thrombosis include leg pain or swelling, or even shortness of breath.

pick off any visible tentacles with a gloved hand, a stick, or anything handy; then rinse the sting with salt- or fresh water, and apply ice to prevent swelling and to help control pain. Avoid folk remedies like vinegar, baking soda, or urinating on the wound, which may actually cause further damage. Most Portuguese man-of-war stings will disappear by themselves within 15 to 20 minutes if you do nothing at all to treat them. Still, be sure to see a doctor if pain persists or a rash or other symptoms develop.

Transparent, square-shaped **box jellyfish** are nearly impossible to see in the water. Fortunately, they seem to follow a monthly cycle: 8 to 10 days after the full moon, they appear in the waters on the leeward side of each island and hang around for about 3 days. Also, they seem to sting more in the morning hours, when they're on or near the surface.

The stings can cause anything from no visible marks to hivelike welts, blisters, and pain lasting from 10 minutes to 8 hours. *All Stings Considered* recommends the following treatment: First, pour regular household vinegar on the sting; this will stop additional burning. Do not rub the area. Pick off any vinegar-soaked tentacles with a stick. For pain, apply an ice pack. Seek additional medical treatment if you experience shortness of breath, weakness, palpitations, muscle cramps, or any other severe symptoms. Most box-jellyfish stings disappear by themselves without any treatment.

PUNCTURES   Most sea-related punctures come from stepping on or brushing against the needlelike spines of sea urchins (known locally as *wana*). Be careful when you're in the water; don't put your foot down (even if you have booties or fins on) if you can't clearly see the bottom. Waves can push you into *wana* in a surge zone in shallow water. The spines can even puncture a wet suit.

A sea-urchin puncture can result in burning, aching, swelling, and discoloration (black or purple) around the area where the spines entered your skin. The best thing to do is to pull any protruding spines out. The body will absorb the spines within 24 hours to 3 weeks, or the remainder of the spines will work themselves out. Again, contrary to popular wisdom, do not urinate or pour vinegar on the embedded spines—this will not help.

CUTS   All cuts obtained in the marine environment must be taken seriously because the high level of bacteria present in the water can quickly cause the cut to become infected. The best way to prevent cuts is to wear a wet suit, gloves, and reef shoes. Never touch coral; not only can you get cut, but you can also damage a living organism that took decades to grow.

The symptoms of a coral cut can range from a slight scratch to severe welts and blisters. *All Stings Considered* recommends gently pulling the edges of the skin open and removing any embedded coral or grains of sand with tweezers. Next, scrub the cut well with fresh water. If pressing a clean cloth against the wound doesn't stop the bleeding, or the edges of the injury are jagged or gaping, seek medical treatment.

Everything You've Always Wanted to Know about Sharks

The Hawaii State Department of Land and Natural Resources has launched a website, **www.hawaiisharks.com**, that covers the biology, history, and culture of these carnivores. It also provides safety information and data on shark bites in Hawaii.

Enjoying the Ocean & Avoiding Mishaps

The Pacific Whale Foundation has a free brochure called *Enjoying Maui's Unique Ocean Environment* that introduces visitors to Hawaii's ocean, beaches, tide pools, and reefs; it even has maps showing Maui's beaches. It's a great general resource on how to stay safe around the ocean, with hints on how to assess weather before you jump into the water and the best ways to view marine wildlife. To get the brochure, call © **808/244-8390** or visit www.pacificwhale.org.

WHAT TO DO IF YOU GET SICK AWAY FROM HOME

If you suffer from a chronic illness, consult your doctor before your departure. Pack prescription medications in your carry-on luggage, and carry them in their original containers, with pharmacy labels—otherwise, they won't make it through airport security. Visitors from outside the U.S. should carry generic names of prescription drugs. For U.S. travelers, most reliable health-care plans provide coverage if you get sick away from home. Foreign visitors may have to pay all medical costs upfront and be reimbursed later.

See "Medical Insurance," under "Insurance," in the appendix. Doctors, dentists, and emergency numbers are also listed in the appendix.

7 Safety

GENERAL SAFETY

Although tourist areas are generally safe, visitors should always stay alert, even in laid-back Hawaii. It's wise to ask the island tourist office if you're in doubt about which neighborhoods are safe. Avoid deserted areas, especially at night. Don't go into any city park at night unless there's an event that attracts crowds, such as a concert. Generally speaking, you can feel safe in areas where there are many people and open establishments.

Avoid carrying valuables with you on the street, and don't display expensive cameras or electronic equipment. Hold on to your pocketbook, and place your billfold in an inside pocket. In theaters, restaurants, and other public places, keep your possessions in sight.

Remember also that hotels are open to the public and that in a large property, security may not be able to screen everyone entering. Always lock your room door—don't assume that once inside your hotel, you're automatically safe.

DRIVING SAFETY

Recently, burglaries of tourists' rental cars in hotel parking structures and at beach parking lots have become more common. Park in well-lighted and well-traveled areas, if possible. Never leave any packages or valuables visible in the car. If someone attempts to rob you or steal your car, do not try to resist the thief or carjacker—report the incident to the police department immediately. Ask your rental agency about personal safety, and get written directions or a map with the route to your destination clearly marked.

8 Specialized Travel Resources

TRAVELERS WITH DISABILITIES

Most disabilities shouldn't stop anyone from traveling in the U.S. Thanks to provisions in the Americans with Disabilities Act, most public places are required to comply with disability-friendly regulations. There are more options and resources out there than ever before.

Travelers with disabilities are made to feel very welcome in Maui. Hotels are usually equipped with wheelchair-accessible rooms, and tour companies provide many special services. The **Hawaii Center for Independent Living**, 414 Kauwili St., Suite 102, Honolulu, HI 96817 (✆ **808/522-5400;** fax 808/586-8129), can provide information.

The only travel agency in Hawaii specializing in needs for travelers with disabilities is **Access Aloha Travel** (✆ **800/480-1143;** www.accessalohatravel.com), which can book anything, including rental vans, accommodations, tours, cruises, airfare, and anything else you can think of.

If you plan to see Haleakala National Park, check out the **America the Beautiful—National Parks and Federal Recreational Lands Pass—Access Pass** (formerly the **Golden Access Passport**), which gives visually impaired or persons with permanent disabilities (regardless of age) free lifetime entrance to federal recreation sites administered by the National Park Service, including the Fish and Wildlife Service, the Forest Service, the Bureau of Land Management, and the Bureau of Reclamation. This may include national parks, monuments, historic sites, recreation areas, and national wildlife refuges.

The America the Beautiful Access Pass can be obtained only in person at any NPS facility that charges an entrance fee. You need to show proof of medically determined disability. Besides free entry,

the pass offers a 50% discount on some federal-use fees charged for such facilities as camping, swimming, parking, boat launching, and tours. For more information, go to www.nps.gov/fees_passes.htm or call the United States Geological Survey (USGS), which issues the passes, at ✆ **888/275-8747.**

For more on organizations that offer resources to travelers with disabilities, go to Frommers.com.

GAY & LESBIAN TRAVELERS

Hawaii is known for its acceptance of all groups. The number of gay- or lesbian-specific accommodations on the islands is limited, but most properties welcome gays and lesbians like any other travelers. For the latest information on the gay marriage issue, contact the **Hawaii Marriage Project** (✆ 808/532-9000).

Pacific Ocean Holidays, P.O. Box 88245, Honolulu, HI 96830 (✆ **800/735-6600** or 808/944-4700; www.gayhawaiivacations.com), offers vacation packages that feature gay-owned and gay-friendly lodgings. It also has a website (www.gayhawaii.com) with a list of gay-owned and gay-friendly businesses and links throughout the islands.

For more gay and lesbian travel resources, visit Frommers.com.

SENIOR TRAVEL

Discounts for seniors are available at almost all of Maui's major attractions and occasionally at hotels and restaurants. Always ask when making hotel reservations or buying tickets. And always carry identification with proof of your age—it can really pay off.

If you're planning to visit Haleakala National Park, pick up an **America the Beautiful—National Parks and Federal Recreational Lands Pass—Senior Pass** (formerly the **Golden Age Passport**), which gives seniors 62 years or older lifetime entrance to all properties administered by the National Park Service—national parks, monuments, historic sites, recreation areas, and national wildlife refuges—for a one-time processing fee of $10. The pass must be purchased in person at any NPS facility that charges an entrance fee. Besides free entry, the America the Beautiful Senior Pass offers a 50% discount on some federal-use fees charged for such facilities as camping, swimming, parking, boat launching, and tours. For more information, go to www.nps.gov/fees_passes.htm or call the United States Geological Survey (USGS), which issues the passes, at © **888/275-8747.**

Frommers.com offers more information and resources on travel for seniors.

FAMILY TRAVEL

Maui is paradise for children: beaches to run on, water to splash in, and unusual sights to see. To locate accommodations, restaurants, and attractions that are particularly child-friendly, refer to the "Kids" icon throughout this guide, and check out the "Especially for Kids" box in chapter 8. And look for *Frommer's Hawaii with Kids* (Wiley Publishing, Inc.).

The larger hotels and resorts offer supervised programs for children and can refer you to qualified babysitters. By state law, hotels can accept only children ages 5 to 12 in supervised activities programs, but they often accommodate younger kids by simply hiring babysitters to watch over them. You can also contact **People Attentive to Children (PATCH),** which can refer you to babysitters who have taken a training course on child care. On Maui, call © **808/242-9232;** on Molokai and Lanai, call © 800/498-4145; or visit www.patchhawaii.org.

Baby's Away (© **800/942-9030** or 808/875-9030; www.babysaway.com) rents cribs, strollers, highchairs, playpens, infant seats, and the like. The staff will deliver whatever you need to wherever you're staying and pick it up when you're done.

Recommended family-travel websites include **Family Travel Forum** (www.familytravelforum.com), a comprehensive site that offers customized trip planning; **Family Travel Network** (www.familytravelnetwork.com), an online magazine providing travel tips; and **TravelWithYourKids.com** (www.travelwithyourkids.com), a comprehensive site written by parents for parents offering sound advice for long-distance and international travel with children. For a list of more family-friendly travel resources, turn to the experts at Frommers.com.

9 Sustainable Tourism

Sustainable tourism is conscientious travel. It means being careful with the environments you explore and respecting the communities you visit. Two overlapping components of sustainable travel are **ecotourism** and **ethical tourism. The International Ecotourism Society (TIES)** defines ecotourism as responsible travel to natural areas that conserves the environment and improves the well-being of local people. TIES suggests that ecotourists follow these principles:

- Minimize environmental impact.
- Build environmental and cultural awareness and respect.
- Provide positive experiences for both visitors and hosts.
- Provide direct financial benefits for conservation and for local people.
- Raise sensitivity to host countries' political, environmental, and social climates.
- Support international human rights and labor agreements.

Tips It's Easy Being Green

Here are a few simple ways you can help conserve fuel and energy when you travel:

- Each time you take a flight or drive a car, greenhouse gases release into the atmosphere. You can help neutralize this danger to the planet through "carbon offsetting"—paying someone to invest your money in programs that reduce your greenhouse gas emissions by the same amount you've added. Before buying carbon offset credits, just make sure that you're using a reputable company, one with a proven program that invests in renewable energy. Reliable carbon offset companies include **Carbonfund** (www.carbonfund.org), **TerraPass** (www.terrapass.org), and **CoolClimate** (www.carbonneutral.org).

- Whenever possible, choose nonstop flights; they generally require less fuel than indirect flights that stop and take off again. Try to fly during the day—some scientists estimate that nighttime flights are twice as harmful to the environment. And pack light: Each 15 pounds of luggage on a 5,000-mile flight adds up to 50 pounds of carbon dioxide emitted.

- Where you stay during your travels can have a major environmental impact. To determine the green credentials of a property, ask about trash disposal and recycling, water conservation, and energy use; also question if sustainable materials were used in the construction of the property. The website **www.greenhotels.com** recommends green-rated member hotels around the world that fulfill the company's stringent environmental requirements. Also consult **www.environmentallyfriendlyhotels.com** for more green accommodations ratings.

- At hotels, request that your sheets and towels not be changed daily. (Many hotels already have programs like this in place.) Turn off the lights and air-conditioner (or heater) when you leave your room.

- Use public transport where possible—trains, buses, and even taxis are more energy-efficient forms of transport than driving. Even better is to walk or cycle; you'll produce zero emissions and stay fit and healthy on your travels.

- If renting a car is necessary, ask the rental agent for a hybrid, or rent the most fuel-efficient car available. You'll use less gas and save money at the tank.

- Eat at locally owned and operated restaurants that use produce grown in the area. This contributes to the local economy and cuts down on greenhouse gas emissions by supporting restaurants where the food is not flown or trucked in across long distances. Visit **SustainLane** (www.sustainlane.org) to find sustainable eating and drinking choices around the U.S.; also check out **www.eatwellguide.org** for tips on eating sustainably in the U.S. and Canada.

Frommers.com: The Complete Travel Resource

Planning a trip or just returned? Head to **Frommers.com,** voted Best Travel Site by *PC Magazine.* We think you'll find our site indispensable before, during, and after your travels—with expert advice and tips; independent reviews of hotels, restaurants, attractions, and preferred shopping and nightlife venues; vacation giveaways; and an online booking tool. We publish the complete contents of over 135 travel guides in our **Destinations** section, covering over 4,000 places worldwide. Each weekday, we publish original articles that report on **Deals and News** via our free **Frommers.com Newsletters.** What's more, **Arthur Frommer** himself blogs five days a week, with cutting opinions about the state of travel in the modern world. We're betting you'll find our **Events** listings an invaluable resource; it's an up-to-the-minute roster of what's happening in cities everywhere—including concerts, festivals, lectures, and more. We've also added weekly **podcasts, interactive maps,** and hundreds of new images across the site. Finally, don't forget to visit our **Message Boards,** where you can join in conversations with thousands of fellow Frommer's travelers and post your trip report once you return.

You can find some eco-friendly travel tips and statistics, as well as touring companies and associations—listed by destination under "Travel Choice"—at the **TIES** website, www.ecotourism.org. Also check out **Ecotravel.com,** which lets you search for sustainable touring companies in several categories (water based, land based, spiritually oriented, and so on).

While much of the focus of ecotourism is about reducing impacts on the natural environment, ethical tourism concentrates on ways to preserve and enhance local economies and communities, regardless of location. You can embrace ethical tourism by staying at a locally owned hotel or shopping at a store that employs local workers and sells locally produced goods.

Responsible Travel (www.responsible travel.com) is a great source of sustainable travel ideas; the site is run by a spokesperson for ethical tourism in the travel industry. **Sustainable Travel International** (www.sustainabletravelinternational.org) promotes ethical tourism practices and manages an extensive directory of sustainable properties and tour operators around the world.

In the U.K., **Tourism Concern** (www. tourismconcern.org.uk) works to reduce social and environmental problems connected to tourism. The **Association of Independent Tour Operators,** or **AITO** (www.aito.co.uk), is a group of specialist operators leading the field in making holidays sustainable.

Volunteer travel has become increasingly popular among those who want to venture beyond the standard group-tour experience to learn languages, interact with locals, and make a positive difference while on vacation. Volunteer travel usually doesn't require special skills—just a willingness to work hard—and programs vary in length from a few days to a number of weeks. Some programs provide free housing and food, but many require volunteers to pay for travel expenses, which can add up quickly.

Before you commit to a volunteer program, it's important to make sure that any money you're giving is truly going back to the local community, and that the work you'll be doing will be a good fit for you. The **International Volunteer Programs Association** (www.volunteer international.org) has a helpful list of questions to ask to determine the intentions and the nature of a volunteer program.

ANIMAL-RIGHTS ISSUES

Before you get geared up to "swim with the dolphins" or other marine mammals,

realize it is against federal law to harass (which can mean swimming or kayaking with) any marine mammal—and visitors have been prosecuted. For information on animal-friendly issues throughout the world, visit **Tread Lightly** (www.tread lightly.org). For information about the ethics of swimming with dolphins, visit the **Whale and Dolphin Conservation Society** (www.wdcs.org).

10 Packages for the Independent Traveler

Package tours are simply a way to buy the airfare, accommodations, and other elements of your trip (such as car rentals, airport transfers, and sometimes even activities) at the same time and often at discounted prices.

One good source of package deals is the airlines themselves. Most major airlines offer air/land packages, including **American Airlines Vacations** (✆ 800/321-2121; www.aavacations.com), **Continental Airlines Vacations** (✆ 800/301-3800; www.covacations.com), **Delta Vacations** (✆ 800/654-6559; www.delta vacations.com), and **United Vacations** (✆ 888/854-3899; www.unitedvacations. com). Several big online travel agencies—Expedia, Travelocity, Orbitz, Site59, and

Lastminute.com—also do a brisk business in packages.

Some packagers specialize in Hawaiian vacations. **Travelzoo** (www.travelzoo.com) often lists package deals to Hawaii. By far the biggest and most comprehensive packager to Hawaii is **Pleasant Holidays** (✆ **800/2-HAWAII** [242-9244]; www. pleasantholidays.com), which offers an extensive, high-quality collection of 50 condos and hotels in every price range. At press time, Pleasant Holidays featured a package deal that included airfare from Los Angeles to Maui, 5 nights in a one-bedroom condo in Kaanapali (double occupancy), and a 5-day car rental starting at $979 per person.

Tips **Ask Before You Go**

Before you invest in a package deal:

- Always ask about the **cancellation policy.** Can you get your money back? Is there a deposit required?
- Ask about the **accommodations choices** and **prices** for each. Then look up the hotels' reviews in a Frommer's guide and check their rates online for your specific dates of travel. Also find out what types of rooms are offered.
- Look for **hidden expenses.** Ask whether airport departure fees and taxes, for example, are included in the total cost—they rarely are.

Hawaii's top hotel chains offer package deals and special rates as well. Packages may be available for families, seniors, honeymooners, and golfers, and some offer discounts on rental cars or multi-night stays. Check with **Ohana Hotels & Resorts** (© 800/462-6262; www.ohana hotels.com) and its more upscale sibling, **Outrigger Hotels & Resorts** (© 800/ OUTRIGGER [688-7444]; www.outrigger. com); **ResortQuest** (© 800/GO-RELAX [467-3529]; www.resortquest.com); **Marc Resorts Hawaii** (© 800/535-0085; www.

marcresorts.com); and **Castle Resorts & Hotels** (© 800/367-5004; www.castle resorts.com).

Travel packages are also listed in the travel section of your local Sunday newspaper. Or check ads in national travel magazines such as *Arthur Frommer's Budget Travel, Travel + Leisure, National Geographic Traveler,* and *Condé Nast Traveler.*

For more information on package tours and for tips on booking your trip, see Frommers.com.

11 Special-Interest Trips

If all you want is a fabulous beach and a perfectly mixed mai tai, then Maui has what you're looking for. But the island's wealth of natural wonders is equally hard to resist; the year-round tropical climate and spectacular scenery tend to inspire almost everyone to get outside and explore.

If you don't have your own snorkel gear or other watersports equipment, or if you just don't feel like packing it, don't fret: Everything you'll need is available for rent. I've discussed all kinds of places to rent or buy gear in chapter 7.

SETTING OUT ON YOUR OWN VS. USING AN OUTFITTER

There are two ways to go: Plan all the details before you leave and either rent gear or schlep your stuff 2,500 miles across the Pacific, or go with an outfitter or a guide and let someone else worry about the details.

Experienced outdoors enthusiasts may head to coastal campgrounds or even trek

into the rainforest on their own. But in Hawaii, it's often preferable to go with a local guide who is familiar with the conditions at both sea level and summit peaks, knows the land and its flora and fauna in detail, and has all the gear you'll need. It's also good to go with a guide if time is an issue or if you have specialized interests. If you really want to see native birds, for instance, an experienced guide will take you directly to the best areas for sightings. And many forests and valleys in the interior of the islands are either on private property or in wilderness preserves accessible only on guided tours. The downside? If you go with a guide, plan on spending at least $100 a day per person. I've recommended the best local outfitters and tour-guide operators in chapter 7.

But if you have the time, already own the gear, and love doing the research and planning, try exploring on your own. Chapter 7 discusses the best spots to set

Tips Travel Tip

When planning sunset activities, be aware that Maui, like other places close to the equator, has a very short (5–10 min.) twilight period after the sun sets. After that, it's dark. If you hike out to watch the sunset, be sure you can make it back quickly, or else take a flashlight.

out on your own, from the top offshore snorkel and dive spots to great daylong hikes, as well as the federal, state, and county agencies that can help you with hikes on public property. In chapter 2, see "The Lay of the Land" (p. 30) for an overview of birds, plants, and sea life; and "Maui in Popular Culture" (p. 36) for some reference books to help you identify what you're seeing. I recommend that you always use the resources available to inquire about weather, trail, or surf conditions; water availability; and other conditions before you take off on your adventure.

For hikers, a great alternative to hiring a private guide is taking a guided hike offered by the **Nature Conservancy of Hawaii,** Pukalani Square, 81 Makawao Ave., Suite 203A, Makawao, HI 96768 (*C* **808/572-7849** on Maui, 621-2008 on Oahu, or 553-5236 on Molokai), or the **Hawaii Chapter of the Sierra Club,** P.O. Box 2577, Honolulu, HI 96813 (*C* **808/579-9802** on Maui; www.hi.sierra club.org). Both organizations offer guided hikes in preserves and special areas during the year, as well as day- to weeklong work trips to restore habitats and trails and to root out invasive plants. It might not sound like a dream vacation to everyone, but it's a chance to see the "real" Maui— including wilderness areas that are ordinarily off-limits.

All Nature Conservancy hikes and work trips are free (donations are appreciated).

However, you must reserve a spot for yourself, and a deposit is required for guided hikes to ensure that you'll show up; your deposit is refunded once you do. The hikes are generally offered once a month on Maui, Molokai, and Lanai. For all islands, call the Oahu office for reservations. Write for a schedule of guided hikes and other programs.

The Sierra Club offers weekly hikes on Maui. They are led by certified Sierra Club volunteers and are classified as easy, moderate, or strenuous. These half- or all-day affairs cost $1 for Sierra Club members and $3 for nonmembers (bring exact change). For a copy of the club newsletter, which lists all outings and trail-repair work, send $2 to the address above.

USING ACTIVITIES DESKS TO BOOK YOUR ISLAND FUN

If you're unsure of which activity or which outfitter or guide is the right one for you and your family, you might want to consider booking through a discount activities center or activities desk. Not only will they save you money, but good activities centers should also be able to help you find, say, the snorkel cruise that's right for you, or the luau that's most suitable for both you *and* the kids.

Remember, however, that it's in the activities agent's best interest to sign you up with outfitters from which they earn the most commission. Some agents have

Tips Outdoor Etiquette

Act locally, think globally, and carry out what you carry in. Find a trash container for all your litter (including cigarette butts; it's *very* bad form to throw them out of your car window or to use the beach as an ashtray). Observe KAPU (taboo) and NO TRESPASSING signs. Don't climb on ancient Hawaiian *heiau* (temple) walls or carry home rocks, all of which belong to the Hawaiian volcano goddess Pele. Some say it's just a silly superstition, but each year the national and state park services get boxes of lava rocks in the mail that have been sent back to Hawaii by visitors who've experienced unusually bad luck.

(Value) Don't Leave Home Without Your Gold Card

Almost any activity you can think of, from submarine rides to Polynesian luau, can be purchased at a discount by using the **Activities & Attractions Association of Hawaii Gold Card**, 355 Hukilike St., No. 202, Kahului, HI 96732 (© **800/398-9698** or 808/871-7947; fax 808/877-3104; www.hawaii fun.org). The Gold Card, accepted by members on all islands, offers a discount of 10% to 25% off activities and meals for up to four people. It's good for a year from the purchase date and costs $30.

Your Gold Card can lower the regular $149 price of a helicopter ride to only $119, saving you almost $120 for a group of four. And there are hundreds of activities to choose from: dinner cruises, horseback riding, watersports, and more—plus savings on rental cars, restaurants, and golf.

Contact Activities & Attractions to purchase your card. You then contact the outfitter, restaurant, rental-car agency, or other proprietor directly; supply your card number; and receive the discount.

---

no qualms about booking you into any activity if it means an extra buck for them. If an agent tries to push a particular outfitter or activity too hard, be skeptical. Conversely, they'll try to steer you away from outfitters who don't offer big commissions. For example, Trilogy, the company that offers Maui's most popular snorkel cruises to Lanai (and the only one with rights to land at Lanai's Hulopoe Beach), offers only minimum commissions to agents and does not allow agents to offer any discounts at all. As a result, most activities desks will automatically try to steer you away from Trilogy.

Another word of warning: Stay away from activities centers that offer discounts as fronts for timeshare sales presentations. Using a free or discounted snorkel cruise or luau tickets as bait, they'll suck you into a 90-minute presentation—and try

to get you to buy into a Hawaii timeshare in the process. Because their business is timeshares, not activities, they won't be as interested, or as knowledgeable, about which activities might be right for you. These shady deals seem to be particularly rampant on Maui.

On Maui, your best bet is **Tom Barefoot's Tours**, 250 Alamaha St., Kahului (© **800/895-2040** or 808/661-8889; www.tombarefoot.com). Tom offers a 10% discount on all tours, activities, and adventures if you pay using cash, a personal check, or traveler's checks. If you use a credit card, you'll get a 7% discount.

Note that you can reserve activities yourself and save the commission by booking via the Internet. Most outfitters offer 10% to 25% off their prices if you book online.

---

12 Staying Connected

TELEPHONES

Generally, hotel surcharges on both long-distance and local calls are astronomical, so you're better off using your **cellph-one** or a **public pay phone.** Many convenience

groceries and packaging services sell **prepaid calling cards** in denominations up to $50; for international visitors, these can be the least expensive way to call home. Many public pay phones at airports now accept

American Express, MasterCard, and Visa credit cards. In most locales, **local calls** made from pay phones cost 50¢ (no pennies, please).

Most long-distance and international calls can be dialed directly from any phone. All calls on Maui are local calls, whereas calls between the islands are long distance. For **calls from one Hawaiian island to another,** dial 1 followed by the Hawaii area code, 808, and the seven-digit phone number.

For **calls within the United States and to Canada,** dial 1 followed by the area code and the seven-digit number. For **other international calls,** dial 011 followed by the country code, city code, and number you are calling.

Calls to area codes **800, 888, 877,** and **866** are toll-free. However, calls to area codes **700** and **900** (chat lines, bulletin boards, "dating" services, and so on) can be very expensive—usually a charge of 95¢ to $3 or more per minute, and they sometimes have minimum charges that can run as high as $15 or more.

For **reversed-charge** or **collect calls,** and for **person-to-person calls,** dial the number 0 and then the area code and number; an operator will come on the line, and you should specify whether you are calling collect, person-to-person, or both. If your operator-assisted call is international, ask for the overseas operator.

For **local directory assistance** ("information"), dial 411; for long-distance information, dial 1, then the appropriate area code, and 555-1212.

CELLPHONES

Just because your cellphone works at home doesn't mean it'll work everywhere in the U.S. (thanks to our nation's fragmented cellphone system). It's a good bet that your phone will work in major cities, but take a look at your wireless company's coverage map on its website before heading out; T-Mobile, Sprint, and Nextel are particularly weak in rural areas. If you

need to stay in touch at a destination where you know your phone won't work, rent a phone that does from **InTouch USA** (© **800/872-7626;** www.intouch global.com) or a rental-car location, but be aware that you'll pay $1 or more a minute for airtime.

If you're not from the U.S., you'll be appalled at the poor reach of our **GSM (Global System for Mobile Communications) wireless network,** which is used by much of the rest of the world. Your phone will probably work in most major U.S. cities; it definitely won't work in many rural areas. To see where GSM phones work in the U.S., check out www. t-mobile.com/coverage. And you may or may not be able to send SMS (text messaging) home.

VOICE-OVER INTERNET PROTOCOL (VOIP)

If you have Web access while traveling, consider a broadband-based telephone service (in technical terms, **Voice-over Internet Protocol,** or **VoIP**) such as Skype (www.skype.com) or Vonage (www. vonage.com), which allows you to make free international calls from your laptop or in a cybercafe. Neither service requires the people you're calling to also have that service (though there are fees if they do not). Check the websites for details.

INTERNET & E-MAIL
WITH YOUR OWN COMPUTER

More and more hotels, resorts, airports, cafes, and retailers are going wireless, becoming "hot spots" that offer free high-speed Wi-Fi (wireless fidelity) access or charge a small fee for usage. Wi-Fi is even found in campgrounds, RV parks, and entire towns. Most laptops sold today have built-in wireless capability.

Every **Starbucks** in Hawaii has Wi-Fi; for a list of locations, go to www.starbucks. com/retail/find/default.aspx. To find other public Wi-Fi hot spots in your destination, go to **www.jiwire.com**; its

Hotspot Finder holds the world's largest directory of public wireless hot spots.

For dial-up access, most business-class hotels in the U.S. offer dataports for laptop modems, and a few thousand hotels in the U.S. and Europe now offer free high-speed Internet access.

Wherever you go, bring a **connection kit** of the right power and phone adapters, a spare phone cord, and a spare Ethernet network cable—or find out whether your hotel supplies them to guests.

For information on electrical currency conversions, see "Electricity" in the appendix.

WITHOUT YOUR OWN COMPUTER

Most major airports have **Internet kiosks** that provide basic Web access for a per-minute fee that's usually higher than cybercafe prices. Check out copy shops like **FedEx Office** (formerly Kinko's), which offers computer stations with fully loaded software (as well as Wi-Fi). **Hotel business centers** generally provide access, but most charge exorbitant rates.

To find Internet cafes, check **www.cybercaptive.com** or **www.cybercafe.com**. On Maui, **Cyber Buzz Coffee Store** has locations in the Kaahumanu Center in Kahului, Azeka Place II in

Kihei, and Napili, all open daily from 8am to 10pm. **Lighthouse Maui Café,** 70 E. Kaahumanu Ave, Kahului (© **808/871-0875**), is open Monday through Thursday and Saturday from 9am to 6pm, Friday from 9am to 8pm, and Sunday from 10am to 4pm. **Ashley's South Shore Café,** 362 Huku Lii Place, Kihei (© **808/874-8600**), is open daily from 7am to 8pm. **Morning Glories Organic Internet Café,** 137 Hana Hwy., Paia (© **808/579-3336**), is open daily from 7am to 5:30pm.

On every island, branches of the **Hawaii State Public Library System** have free computers with Internet access. To find your closest library or to reserve a computer, check www.librarieshawaii.org/services/pcreservation1.htm. There is no charge for use of the computers, but you must have a Hawaii library card, which is free to Hawaii residents and members of the military. Visitors have a choice of two types of cards: a $25 non-resident card that is good for 5 years (and may be renewed for an additional $25) or a $10 visitor card ($5 for children 18 and under) that is good for 3 months but may not be renewed. To download an application for a library card, go to www.librarieshawaii.org/services/libcard.htm.

13 Tips on Accommodations

Maui offers a tremendous variety of accommodations, from ritzy resorts to simple bed-and-breakfasts. Each type has its pluses and minuses, so before you book, make sure you know what you're getting into. I've also included some tips on how to get the best rates.

TYPES OF ACCOMMODATIONS

HOTELS In Hawaii, the term "hotel" can indicate a wide range of options, from few or no on-site amenities to enough extras to qualify as a resort.

Generally, a hotel offers daily maid service and has a restaurant, on-site laundry facilities, a pool, and a sundries/convenience-type shop (as opposed to the shopping arcades that most resorts have). Top hotels also have activities desks, concierge and valet services, room service, business centers, airport shuttles, bars and/or lounges, and perhaps a few more shops.

The advantages of staying in a hotel are privacy and convenience; the disadvantage is generally noise (either thin walls between rooms or loud music from a lobby lounge late into the night).

RESORTS In Hawaii, a resort offers everything a hotel does—and more. You can expect direct beach access, with beach cabanas and lounge chairs; pools and a Jacuzzi; a spa and fitness center; restaurants, bars, and lounges; a 24-hour front desk; concierge, valet, and bellhop services; room service (often 24-hr.); an activities desk; tennis and golf; ocean activities; a business center; kids' programs; and more.

The advantages of a resort are that you have everything you could possibly want in the way of services and things to do; the disadvantage is that the price generally reflects this. And don't be misled by a name—just because a place is called "ABC Resort" doesn't mean it actually *is* a resort. Make sure you're getting what you pay for.

CONDOS The roominess and convenience of a condo—which is usually a fully equipped, multiple-bedroom apartment—makes this a great choice for families. Condominium properties in Hawaii generally consist of several apartments set in either a single high-rise or a cluster of low-rise units. Condos usually have amenities such as some maid service (ranging from daily to weekly; it may or may not be included in your rate), a pool, and an on-site front desk or a live-in property manager. Condos tend to be clustered in resort areas. There are some very high-end condos, but most are quite affordable, especially if you're traveling in a group.

The advantages of a condo are privacy, space, and conveniences—which usually include a full kitchen, a washer and dryer, a private phone, and more. The downsides are the standard lack of an on-site restaurant and the density of the units (vs. the privacy of a single-unit vacation rental).

BED & BREAKFASTS Hawaii has a wide range of places that call themselves B&Bs: everything from a traditional B&B—several bedrooms in a home, with breakfast served in the morning—to what is essentially a vacation rental on an owner's property that comes with fixings for you to make your own breakfast. Make sure that the B&B you're booking matches your own mental picture. Note that laundry facilities and private phones are not always available. I've reviewed lots of wonderful B&Bs in the chapters that follow. If you have to share a bathroom, I've spelled it out in the listings; otherwise, you can assume that you will have your own.

The advantages of a traditional B&B are its individual style and congenial atmosphere, with a host who's often happy to act as your own private concierge. In addition, they're usually an affordable way to go. The disadvantages are lack of privacy, usually a set time for breakfast, few amenities, and generally no maid service. Also, B&B owners typically require a minimum stay of 2 or 3 nights, and it's often a drive to the beach.

Nickel-and-Dime Charges at High-Priced Hotels

Several upscale resorts in Hawaii engage in a practice that I find distasteful and dishonest: charging a so-called resort fee. This daily fee is added on to your bill for such "complimentary" items as a daily newspaper, local phone calls, and use of the fitness facilities—amenities that the resort has been happily providing free to its guests for years. In most cases, you do not have an option to decline the resort fee—in other words, this is a sneaky way to increase the nightly rate without telling you.

What If Your Dream Hotel Becomes a Nightmare?

To avoid any unpleasant surprises, find out when you make your reservation exactly what the accommodations are offering you: cost, minimum stay, and included amenities. Ask if there's any penalty for leaving early. Discuss what the cancellation policy is if the accommodations fail to meet your expectations—and get this policy in writing.

Upon checking in, if you're not satisfied with your room, notify the front desk or booking agency immediately. Approach the management in a calm, reasonable manner, and suggest a solution (like moving to another unit). Be willing to compromise. Do not leave; if you do, you may not get your deposit back.

If all else fails, when you get home, write to any association the establishment may be a member of (such as the Hawaii Visitors & Convention Bureau or a resort association). Describe your complaint and why the issue was not resolved to your satisfaction. And be sure to let us know if you have a problem with a place recommended in this book!

VACATION RENTALS   This is another great choice for families and for long-term stays. "Vacation rental" usually means that there will be no one on the property where you're staying. The actual accommodations can range from an apartment to an entire fully equipped house. Generally, vacation rentals allow you to settle in and make yourself at home for a while. They have kitchen facilities (at least a kitchenette), on-site laundry facilities, and a phone; some also come with such extras as a TV, VCR or DVD player, and stereo.

The advantages of a vacation rental are complete privacy, your own kitchen (which can save you money on meals), and lots of conveniences. The disadvantages are a lack of an on-site property manager and generally no maid service; often a minimum stay is required (sometimes as much as a week). If you book a vacation rental, be sure that you have a 24-hour contact to call if the toilet won't flush or you can't figure out how to turn on the air-conditioning.

USING A BOOKING AGENCY VS. DOING IT YOURSELF

If you don't have the time to call several places yourself to make sure they offer the amenities you'd like, you might consider a booking agency.

A statewide booking agent for B&Bs is **Bed & Breakfast Hawaii** (© 800/733-1632 or 808/822-7771; fax 808/822-2723; www.bandb-hawaii.com), offering a range of accommodations from vacation homes to bed-and-breakfast inns, starting at $65 a night. For vacation rentals, contact **Hawaii Beachfront Vacation Homes** (© 808/247-3637; fax 808/235-2644). **Hawaii Condo Exchange** (© 800/442-0404; www.myhawaii beachfront.com) acts as a consolidator for condo and vacation-rental properties.

SURFING FOR HOTELS

In addition to the online travel booking sites **Travelocity, Expedia, Orbitz, Priceline,** and **Hotwire,** you can book hotels through **Hotels.com, Quikbook. com,** and **Travelaxe.com.**

Tips B&B Etiquette

In Hawaii, it is traditional and customary to remove your shoes before entering anyone's home. The same is true at most bed-and-breakfast facilities. If this custom is unpleasant to you, a B&B may not be for you.

Hawaii also has a very strict no-smoking law (no smoking in public buildings, restaurants, bars, retail stores, and so on), and more and more hotels, resorts, condos, and vacation rentals generally do *not* allow smoking in the guest rooms (those hotels that still do allow smoking all have nonsmoking rooms available). The majority of bed-and-breakfast units already forbid smoking in the rooms. Be sure to check the policy of your accommodations before you book.

HotelChatter.com is a daily webzine offering smart coverage and critiques of hotels worldwide. **TripAdvisor.com** and **HotelShark.com** offer helpful independent consumer reviews of hotels and resort properties.

It's a good idea to get a confirmation number and make a printout of any online booking transaction.

For more tips on surfing for hotel deals online, visit Frommers.com.

SAVING ON YOUR HOTEL ROOM

The **rack rate** is the maximum rate that a hotel charges for a room. Hardly anybody pays this price, however, except in high season or on holidays.

Rates can sometimes be bargained down, but it depends on the place. The best bargaining can be had at **hotels** and **resorts.** If business is slow and you book directly, some places may give you at least part of the commission they'd normally pay a travel agent. Most hotels and resorts also have local rates for islanders, which they may extend to visitors during slow periods. It never hurts to ask about discounted or local rates; a host of special rates are available for the military, seniors, members of the travel industry, families, corporate travelers, and long-term stays. Also ask about **package deals,** which might include a car rental or free breakfast for the same price as a room by itself.

Hotels and resorts offer packages for everyone: golfers, tennis players, families, honeymooners, and more (see "Packages for the Independent Traveler," earlier in this chapter). I've found that it's worth the extra few cents to make a local call to the hotel; sometimes the local reservations person knows about package deals that the toll-free operators are unaware of. If all else fails, try to get the hotel or resort to upgrade you to a better room for the same price as a budget room, or to waive the parking fee or extra fees for children. Persistence and polite inquiries can pay off.

It's harder to bargain at **bed-and-breakfasts.** You may be able to negotiate down the minimum stay or get a discount if you're staying a week or longer. But generally, a B&B owner has only a few rooms and has already priced the property at a competitive rate; expect to pay what's asked.

You have somewhat more leeway to negotiate at **vacation rentals** and **condos.** In addition to asking for a discount on a multinight stay, ask if they can throw in a rental car to sweeten the deal; believe it or not, they often will.

To lower the cost of your room:

- **Ask about special rates or other discounts.** You may qualify for corporate, student, military, senior, frequent-flier, trade-union, or other discounts.

- **Dial direct.** When booking a room in a chain hotel, you'll often get a better deal by calling the individual hotel's reservation desk rather than the chain's main number.
- **Book online.** Many hotels offer Internet-only discounts or supply rooms to Priceline, Hotwire, or Expedia at rates much lower than the ones you can get through the hotel itself.
- **Remember the law of supply and demand.** Resort hotels are most crowded and, therefore, most expensive on weekends, so discounts are usually available for midweek stays. Business hotels in downtown locations are busiest during the week, so you can expect big discounts over the weekend.
- **Look into group or long-stay discounts.** If you come as part of a large group, you should be able to negotiate a bargain rate. Likewise, if you're planning a long stay (at least 5 days), you might qualify for a discount. As a general rule, expect 1 night free after a 7-night stay.
- **Sidestep excess surcharges and hidden costs.** Many hotels have the unpleasant practice of nickel-and-diming their guests with opaque surcharges. When you book a room, ask what is included in the room rate and what costs extra. Avoid dialing direct from hotel phones, which can have exorbitant rates. And don't be tempted by the room's minibar offerings: Most hotels charge through the nose for water, soda, and snacks. Finally, ask about local taxes and service charges, which can increase the cost of a room by 15% or more.
- **Carefully consider your hotel's meal plan.** If you enjoy eating out and sampling the local cuisine, it makes sense to choose a **Continental Plan (CP),** which includes breakfast only, or a **European Plan (EP),** which doesn't include any meals and allows you maximum flexibility. If you're more interested in saving money, opt for a **Modified American Plan (MAP),** which includes breakfast and one meal, or the **American Plan (AP),** which includes three

---

Tips **What's Happening with B&Bs & Vacation Rentals on Maui?**

Despite all the hoopla in the press, Maui County (which consists of Maui, Molokai, and Lanai) has *not* shut down B&Bs or vacation rentals. However, the Maui County Planning Commission is reviewing the requirements for permits for bed-and-breakfasts and vacation rentals.

As we went to press, neither the Planning Commission (which is a regulatory body that does not make law, only offers suggestions to the County Council) nor the Maui County Council had passed any firm recommendations or laws on how to regulate these two entities in the future.

All of the B&Bs and vacation rentals recommended in this book have been in operation for years, all are reputable, and all have followed the law in paying state and county taxes. However, because there is no predicting what the government will do, please be sure to contact the B&B or vacation rental you are interested in—ideally, way in advance of your trip—to make sure you will get the accommodations of your choice.

meals. If you must choose a MAP, see if you can get a free lunch at your hotel if you decide to do dinner out.

- **Book an efficiency.** A room with a kitchenette allows you to shop for groceries and cook your own meals. This is a big money saver, especially for families on long stays.

- **Consider enrolling in hotel frequent-guest programs,** which are upping the ante lately to win the loyalty of repeat customers. Frequent guests can now accumulate points or credits to earn free hotel nights, airline miles, in-room amenities, merchandise, tickets to concerts and events, and discounts on sporting facilities. Perks are awarded by not only many chain hotels and motels (Hilton HHonors, Marriott Rewards, Wyndham ByRequest, to name a few), but also individual inns and B&Bs. Many chain hotels partner with other hotel chains, car-rental firms, airlines, and credit card companies to give consumers additional incentive to do repeat business.

LANDING THE BEST ROOM

Somebody has to get the best room in the house. It might as well be you. You can start by joining the hotel's frequent-guest program, which may make you eligible for upgrades. A hotel-branded credit card usually gives its owner "silver" or "gold" status in frequent-guest programs for free. Always ask about a corner room. They're often larger and quieter, with more windows and light, and they often cost the same as standard rooms.

When you make your reservation, ask if the hotel is renovating; if it is, request a room away from the construction. If you're a light sleeper, request a quiet room away from vending or ice machines, elevators, restaurants, bars, and discos. Ask for a room that has most recently been renovated or redecorated.

If you aren't happy with your room when you arrive, notify the front desk or booking agency immediately. Approach the management in a calm, reasonable manner and suggest a solution (like moving to another unit). Be willing to compromise. Do not leave; if you do, you may not get your deposit back.

In resort areas, particularly in warm climates, ask the following questions before you book a room:

- What's the view like? Cost-conscious travelers may be willing to pay less for a back room facing the parking lot, especially if they don't plan to spend much time in their room.

- Does the room have air-conditioning or ceiling fans? Do the windows open? If they do, and the nighttime entertainment takes place alfresco, you may want to find out when showtime is over.

- What's included in the price? Your room may be moderately priced, but if you're charged for beach chairs, towels, sports equipment, and other amenities, you could end up spending more than you bargained for.

- How far is the room from the beach and other amenities? If it's far, is there transportation to and from the beach, and is it free?

14 Getting Married on Maui

Maui is a great place for a wedding. Not only does the entire island exude romance and natural beauty, but after the ceremony, you're also already on your honeymoon. And the members of your wedding party will most likely be delighted, since

you've given them the perfect excuse for their own island vacation.

More than 20,000 marriages are performed annually on the islands, mostly on Oahu; nearly half are for couples from somewhere else. The booming wedding business has spawned dozens of companies that can help you organize a long-distance event and stage an unforgettable wedding, Hawaiian style or your style.

The easiest way to plan your wedding is to let someone else handle it at the resort or hotel where you'll be staying. Most Maui resorts and hotels have wedding coordinators who can plan everything from a (relatively) simple low-cost wedding to an extravaganza that people will talk about for years. Resorts can be pricey, though, so be frank with your wedding coordinator if you want to keep costs down. And remember, you don't have to use a coordinator: You can also plan your own island wedding, even from afar, and not spend a fortune doing it.

THE PAPERWORK

The state of Hawaii has some very minimal procedures for obtaining a marriage license. The first thing you should do is contact the **Marriage License Office,** State Department of Health Building, 54 S. High St., Wailuku, HI 96793 (📞 **808/ 984-8210;** www.state.hi.us/doh/records/ vr_marri.html), which is open Monday through Friday from 8am to 4pm. You can download the office's brochure *Getting Married* from the website, which also lists the marriage-licensing agent closest to where you'll be staying on Maui.

Once on Maui, the prospective bride and groom must go together to the marriage-licensing agent to get the license, which costs $60 and is good for 30 days. Both parties must be 15 years of age or older (couples 15–17 years old must have proof of age, written consent of both parents, and written approval of the judge of the family court) and not more closely related than first cousins. That's it.

At this time, gay couples cannot marry in Hawaii. After a protracted legal battle and much discussion in the state legislature, in late 1999 the Hawaii Supreme Court ruled that the state will not issue marriage licenses to same-sex couples.

PLANNING THE WEDDING
DOING IT YOURSELF

The marriage-licensing agents, who range from employees of the governor's satellite office to private individuals, are usually friendly, helpful people who can steer you to a nondenominational minister or marriage performer who's licensed by the state of Hawaii. These marriage performers are great sources of information for budget weddings. They usually know wonderful places to have the ceremony for free or for a nominal fee. For the names and addresses of marriage-licensing agents on Maui, call 📞 **808/984-8210;** on Molokai, 📞 **808/553-3663;** and on Lanai, 📞 **808/565-6411.**

If you don't want to use a wedding planner (see below), but you do want to make arrangements before you arrive on Maui, my best advice is to get a copy of the daily newspaper, the *Maui News,* P.O. Box 550, Wailuku, HI 96793 (📞 **808/244-7691;** www.mauinews. com). People willing and qualified to conduct weddings advertise in the classifieds. They're great sources of information, as they know the best places to have the ceremony and can recommend caterers, florists, and everything else you'll need.

USING A WEDDING PLANNER

Wedding planners—many of whom are marriage-licensing agents as well—can arrange everything for you, from a small, private outdoor affair to a full-blown formal ceremony in a tropical setting. They charge anywhere from $150 to a small fortune—it all depends on what you want.

Planners on Maui include **First Class Weddings** (📞 800/262-8433 or 808/ 877-1411; www.firstclassweddings.com),

A Dream Wedding: Maui Style (© 800/743-2777 or 808/661-1777; fax 808/667-2042; www.maui.net/~dreamwed/dream.html), Romantic Maui Weddings (© 800/808-4144 or 808/874-6444; fax 808/879-5525; www.justmauied.com), Dolphin Dream Weddings (© 800/793-2-WED [793-2933] or 808/661-8535; www.dolphindreamweddings.com), and Simply Married (© 800/291-0110 or 808/572-7898; fax 800/368-6933 or 808/572-1240; www.maui.net/~married). For a more complete list, contact the Maui Visitors Bureau (www.visitmaui.com). Many of the big resorts have their own coordinators on staff as well.

4

Suggested Maui Itineraries

Your vacation time is precious—you have only so many days and you don't want to waste a single one. That's where I come in. Below are several suggestions for what to do and how to spend your time on Maui. I've included ideas if you have 1 week or 2, are traveling with kids, or want a more active vacation. I've also included the best things to see and do on the islands of Molokai and Lanai.

The number-one thing I suggest is this: Don't max out your days. This is Hawaii—allow some time to do nothing but relax. Remember that you most likely will arrive jet-lagged, so it's a good idea to ease into your vacation. In fact, exposure to sunlight can help reset your internal clock, so I include time at the beach on the first day of most of these itineraries.

Also, if this is your first trip to Maui, think of it as a "scouting" trip. Maui is too beautiful, too sensual, too enticing to see just once in a lifetime. You'll be back. You don't need to see and do everything on this trip.

Keep in mind that the following itineraries are designed to appeal to a wide range of travelers. If you're a golf fan or a scuba diver, check out the best golf courses and dive spots in chapter 1 to plan your trip around your passion.

One last thing—you will need a car to get around the island. But plan to get out of the car as much as possible—to smell the sweet perfume of plumeria, to hear the sound of the wind through a bamboo forest, and to plunge into the gentle waters of the Pacific.

1 The Island in Brief

See the "Maui" map on p. 6 to locate the following regions.

CENTRAL MAUI

This flat, often windy corridor between Maui's two volcanoes is where you'll most likely arrive—it's the site of the main airport. It's also home to the majority of the island's population, the heart of the business community, and the local government (courts, cops, and county/state government agencies). You'll find good shopping and dining bargains here but very little in the way of accommodations.

KAHULUI This is "Dream City," home to thousands of former sugar-cane workers whose dream in life was to own their own homes away from the sugar plantations. There's wonderful shopping here (especially at discount stores), and a couple of small hotels near the airport are convenient for 1-night stays if you have a late arrival or early departure, but this is not a place to spend your entire vacation.

WAILUKU Wailuku is like a time capsule, with its faded wooden storefronts, old plantation homes, shops straight out of the 1940s and 1950s, and relaxed way of life. While most people race through on their way to see the natural beauty of **Iao Valley** ✿, this quaint little town is worth a brief visit, if only to see a real place where real people actu-ally appear to be working at something other than a suntan. This is the county seat, so you'll see people in suits on important missions in the tropical heat. Beaches surrounding Wailuku are not great for swimming, but the town has a spectacular view of Haleakala Crater, great budget restaurants, some interesting bungalow architecture, a Frank Lloyd Wright building, a wonderful historic B&B, and the always-endearing Bailey House Museum.

WEST MAUI

This is the fabled Maui you see on postcards. Jagged peaks, green velvet valleys, a wilderness full of native species—the majestic West Maui Mountains are the epitome of earthly paradise. The beaches here are some of Hawaii's best. And it's no secret: This stretch of coastline along Maui's "forehead," from Kapalua to the historic port of Lahaina, is the island's most bustling resort area (with south Maui close behind). Expect a few mainland-style traffic jams.

If you want to book into a resort or condo on this coast, first consider what com-munity you'd like to base yourself in. Starting at the southern end of west Maui and moving northward, the coastal communities look like this:

LAHAINA   This old seaport is a tame version of its former self, a raucous whaling town where sailors swaggered ashore in search of women and grog. Today, the vintage village teems with restaurants, T-shirt shops, and a gallery on nearly every block, and parts of it are downright tacky, but there's a still lot of real history to be found amid the tourist development. Lahaina makes a great base for visitors: A few old hotels (like the restored 1901 Pioneer Inn on the harbor), quaint bed-and-breakfasts, and a hand-ful of oceanfront condos offer a variety of choices. This is the place to stay if you want to be in the center of things—restaurants, shops, and nightlife—but parking can be a problem.

KAANAPALI ⊕   Farther north along the west Maui coast is Hawaii's first master-planned family resort. Pricey mid-rise hotels line nearly 3 miles of lovely gold-sand beach; they're linked by a landscaped parkway and a walking path along the sand. Golf greens wrap around the slope between beachfront and hillside properties. **Whalers Village**—a seaside mall with 48 shops and restaurants, plus the best little whale museum in Hawaii—and other restaurants are easy to reach on foot along the ocean-front walkway or by resort shuttle, which also serves the small West Maui Airport just to the north. Shuttles also go to Lahaina (see above), 3 miles to the south, for shop-ping, dining, entertainment, and boat tours. Kaanapali is popular with convention groups and families—especially those with teenagers, who like all the action.

HONOKOWAI, KAHANA & NAPILI   In the building binge of the 1970s, con-dominiums sprouted along this gorgeous coastline like mushrooms after a rain. Today, these older ocean-side units offer excellent bargains for astute travelers. The great loca-tion—along sandy beaches, within minutes of both the Kapalua and Kaanapali resort areas, and close enough to the goings-on in Lahaina—makes this area a great place to stay for value-conscious travelers. It feels more peaceful and residential than either Kaanapali or Lahaina.

In **Honokowai** and **Mahinahina,** you'll find mostly older units that tend to be cheaper. There's not much shopping here (mostly convenience stores), but you'll have easy access to the shops and restaurants of Kaanapali.

Kahana is a little more upscale than Honokowai and Mahinahina. Most of its condos are big high-rise types, newer than those immediately to the south. You'll find a nice selection of shops and restaurants (including the Maui branch of Roy's) in the area, and Kapalua–West Maui Airport is nearby.

Napili is a much-sought-after area for condo seekers: It's quiet; has great beaches, restaurants, and shops; and is close to Kapalua. Units are generally more expensive here (although I've found a few hidden gems at affordable prices; see the Napili Bay listing on p. 119).

KAPALUA ✿✿ North beyond Kaanapali and the shopping centers of Napili and Kahana, the road starts to climb and the vista opens up to fields of golden-green pineapple and manicured golf fairways. A country lane lined with Pacific pines that leads toward the sea brings you to Kapalua. It's the very exclusive domain of the luxurious Ritz-Carlton Kapalua and expensive condos and villas, set on one of Hawaii's best white-sand beaches, next to two bays that are marine-life preserves (with fabulous surfing in winter).

Even if you don't stay here, you're welcome to come and enjoy Kapalua. The fancy hotel here provides public parking and beach access. The resort has an art school where you can learn local crafts, as well as a golf school, three golf courses, historic features, swanky condos and homes (many available for vacation rental at astronomical prices), and wide-open spaces that include a rainforest preserve—all open to the general public.

Kapalua is a great place to stay put. However, if you plan to "tour" Maui, know that it's a long drive from here to get to many of the island's highlights. You might want to consider a more central place to stay—even Lahaina is a 15-minute drive away.

SOUTH MAUI

This is the hottest, sunniest, driest, most popular coastline on Maui for sun lovers—Arizona by the sea. Rain rarely falls here, and temperatures stick around 85°F (29°C) year-round. On this former scrubland from Maalaea to Makena, where cacti once grew wild and cows grazed, there are now four distinctive areas—Maalaea, Kihei, Wailea, and Makena—and a surprising amount of traffic.

MAALAEA If west Maui is the island's head, Maalaea is just under the chin. This windy oceanfront village centers around a small boat harbor (with a general store, a couple of restaurants, and a huge new mall) and the **Maui Ocean Center** ✿✿, an aquarium/ocean complex. This quaint region offers several condominium units to choose from, but visitors staying here should be aware that it's almost always very windy. All the wind from the Pacific is funneled between the West Maui Mountains and Haleakala, and comes out in Maalaea.

KIHEI Kihei is less a proper town than a nearly continuous series of condos and minimalls lining South Kihei Road. This is Maui's best vacation bargain: Budget travelers swarm like sun-seeking geckos over the eight sandy beaches along this scalloped, condo-packed 7-mile stretch of coast. Kihei is neither charming nor quaint; what it lacks in aesthetics, though, it more than makes up for in sunshine, affordability, and convenience. If you want a latte in the morning, fine beaches in the afternoon, and Hawaii Regional Cuisine in the evening—all at reasonable prices—head to Kihei.

WAILEA ✿✿ Just 3 decades ago, this was wall-to-wall scrub kiawe trees, but now Wailea is a manicured oasis of multimillion-dollar resort hotels along 2 miles of palm-fringed gold coast. It's like Beverly Hills by the sea, except California never had it so good: Wailea has warm, clear water full of tropical fish; year-round golden sunshine and clear blue skies; and hedonistic pleasure palaces on 1,500 acres of black-lava shore indented by five beautiful beaches. It's amazing what a billion dollars can do.

This is the playground of the stretch-limo set. The planned resort development—practically a well-heeled town—has a shopping village, three prized golf courses of its own and three more in close range, and a tennis complex. A growing number of large homes sprawl over the upper hillside, some offering excellent bed-and-breakfast units at reasonable prices. The resorts along this fantasy coast are spectacular, to say the least. Next door to the Four Seasons, the most elegant, is the Grand Wailea Resort Hotel & Spa, a public display of ego by Tokyo mogul Takeshi Sekiguchi, who dropped $600 million in 1991 to create his own mini city. Stop in and take a look—it's so gauche you've gotta see it.

Appealing natural features include the coastal trail, a 3-mile round-trip path along the oceanfront with pleasing views everywhere you look—out to sea and to the neighboring islands, or inland to the broad lawns and gardens of the hotels. The trail's south end borders an extensive garden of native coastal plants, as well as the ruins of ancient lava-rock houses juxtaposed with elegant oceanfront condos. But the chief attractions, of course, are those five outstanding beaches (the best is Wailea Beach).

MAKENA After passing through well-groomed Wailea, suddenly the road enters raw wilderness. After Wailea's overdone density and overmanicured development, the thorny landscape is a welcome relief. Although beautiful, this is an end-of-the-road kind of place: It's a long drive from Makena to anywhere on Maui. If you're looking for an activities-filled vacation or you want to tour a lot of the island, you might want to try somewhere else, or you'll spend most of your time in the car. But if you crave a quiet, relaxing respite, where the biggest trip of the day is from your bed to the gorgeous, pristine beach, Makena is the place.

Beyond Makena, you'll discover Haleakala's last lava flow, which ran to the sea in 1790; the bay named for French explorer La Pérouse; and a chunky lava trail known as the King's Highway, which leads around Maui's empty south shore past ruins and fish camps. Puu Olai stands like Maui's Diamond Head on the shore, where a sunken crater shelters tropical fish, and empty golden-sand beaches stand at the end of dirt roads.

UPCOUNTRY MAUI

After a few days at the beach, you'll probably take notice of the 10,000-foot mountain in the middle of Maui. The slopes of Haleakala ("House of the Sun") are home to cowboys, growers, and other country people who wave at you as you drive by. They're all up here enjoying the crisp air, emerald pastures, eucalyptus, and flower farms of this tropical Olympus—there's even a misty California redwood grove. You can see a thousand tropical sunsets reflected in the windows of houses old and new, strung along a road that runs like a loose hound from Makawao, an old cowboy–turned–New Age village, to Kula, where the road leads up to the crater and **Haleakala National Park** . The rumpled, two-lane blacktop of Hwy. 37 narrows on the other side of Tedeschi Winery, where wine grapes and wild elk flourish on the Ulupalakua Ranch, the biggest on Maui. A stay upcountry is usually affordable, a chance to commune with nature, and a nice contrast to the sizzling beaches and busy resorts below.

MAKAWAO Until recently, this small, two-street upcountry town consisted of little more than a post office, gas station, feed store, bakery, and restaurant/bar serving the cowboys and farmers living in the surrounding community; the hitching posts outside storefronts were really used to tie up horses. As the population of Maui started expanding in the 1970s, a health-food store sprang up, followed by boutiques, a chiropractic clinic, and a host of health-conscious restaurants. The result is an eclectic amalgam of old *paniolo* (cowboy) Hawaii and the baby-boomer trends of transplanted mainlanders. **Hui No'eau Visual Arts Center** ⚘, Hawaii's premier arts collective, is definitely worth a peek. The only accommodations here are reasonably priced bed-and-breakfasts, perfect for those who enjoy great views and don't mind slightly chilly nights.

KULA ⚘ A feeling of pastoral remoteness prevails in this upcountry community of old flower farms, humble cottages, and new suburban ranch houses with million-dollar views that take in the ocean, the isthmus, the West Maui Mountains, and, at night, the lights that run along the gold coast like a string of pearls from Maalaea to Puu Olai. Everything flourishes at a cool 3,000 feet (bring a jacket), just below the cloud line, along a winding road on the way up to Haleakala National Park. Everyone here grows something—Maui onions, carnations, orchids, and proteas (those strange-looking blossoms that look like *Star Trek* props). The local B&Bs cater to guests seeking cool tropic nights, panoramic views, and a rural upland escape. Here you'll find the true peace and quiet that only rural farming country can offer—yet you're still just 30 to 40 minutes away from the beach and an hour's drive from Lahaina.

EAST MAUI

ON THE ROAD TO HANA ⚘⚘⚘ When old sugar towns die, they usually fade away in rust and red dirt. Not **Paia** ⚘⚘. The tangled spaghetti of electrical, phone, and cable wires hanging overhead symbolizes the town's ability to adapt to the times—it may look messy, but it works. Here, trendy restaurants, eclectic boutiques, and high-tech windsurf shops stand next door to a ma-and-pa grocery, a fish market, and storefronts that have been serving customers since plantation days. Hippies took over in the 1970s; although their macrobiotic restaurants and old-style artists' co-ops have made way for Hawaii Regional Cuisine and galleries featuring the works of renowned international artists, Paia still manages to maintain a pleasant granola vibe. The town's main attraction, though, is **Hookipa Beach Park** ⚘, where the wind that roars through the isthmus of Maui brings windsurfers from around the world. A few B&Bs are located just outside Paia in the tiny community of **Kuau.**

Ten minutes down the road from Paia and up the hill from the Hana Highway—the connector road to the entire east side of Maui—is **Haiku.** Once a pineapple-plantation village, complete with a cannery (now a shopping complex), Haiku offers vacation rentals and B&Bs in a quiet, pastoral setting: the perfect base for those who want to get off the beaten path and experience the quieter side of Maui, but don't want to feel too removed (the beach is only 10 min. away).

About 15 to 20 minutes past Haiku is the largely unknown community of **Huelo** ⚘. Every day, thousands of cars whiz by on the road to Hana; most barely glance at the double row of mailboxes overseen by a fading Hawaii Visitors Bureau sign. But if you take the time to stop and head down the gun-metal road, you'll discover a hidden Hawaii—a Hawaii of an earlier time, where Mother Nature is still sensual and wild, where ocean waves pummel soaring lava cliffs, and where an indescribable sense of serenity prevails. Huelo is not for everyone, but those who hunger for a place still largely untouched by "progress" should check in to a B&B or vacation rental here.

HANA ✿✿✿ Set between an emerald rainforest and the blue Pacific is a village probably best defined by what it lacks: golf courses, shopping malls, and McDonald's. Except for a gas station and a bank with an ATM, you'll find little of what passes for progress here. Instead, you'll discover the simple joys of fragrant tropical flowers, the sweet taste of backyard bananas and papayas, and the easy calm and unabashed small-town aloha spirit of old Hawaii. What saved "Heavenly" Hana from the inevitable march of progress? The 52-mile **Hana Highway,** which winds around 600 curves and crosses more than 50 one-lane bridges on its way from Kahului. You can go to Hana for the day—from Kihei and Lahaina, it's a 3-hour drive (and a half-century away)—but 3 days are better. The tiny town has one hotel, a handful of great B&Bs, and some spectacular vacation rentals.

2 A Week on Maui

I've outlined the highlights of Maui for those who have just 7 days and want to see everything. Two suggestions: First, spend 2 nights in Hana, a decision you will not regret, and second, take the Trilogy boat trip to Lanai for the day. I've designed this itinerary assuming you'll stay in west Maui for 5 days. If you are staying elsewhere (like Wailea or Kihei), allow extra driving time.

Day ❶: Arriving & Seeing Kapalua Beach ✿✿✿

After checking in to your hotel, head for **Kapalua Beach** (p. 176). Don't overdo the sun on your first day. After an hour or two at the beach, drive to **Lahaina** (p. 207) and spend a couple of hours walking the historic old town. Go to the **Old Lahaina Luau** (p. 260) at sunset to immerse yourself in Hawaiian culture.

Day ❷: Going Up a 10,000-Foot Volcano & Down Again ✿✿✿

You'll likely wake up early on your first day in Hawaii, so take advantage of it and head up to the 10,000-foot dormant volcano, **Haleakala.** You can **hike in the crater** (p. 190), **speed down the mountain on a bicycle** (p. 200), or just wander about the national park. You don't have to be at the top for sunrise; in fact, it has gotten so congested at sunrise that you may be too busy fighting the crowds to have an awe-inspiring experience. Instead, I'd suggest heading up any time during the day. On your way back down, stop and tour **Upcountry Maui** (p. 165), particularly the communities of **Kula,**

Makawao, and **Paia.** Plan for a sunset dinner in Paia or Kuau.

Day ❸: Driving the Hana Highway ✿✿✿

Pack a lunch and spend the entire day driving the scenic **Hana Highway** (p. 228). Pull over often and get out to take photos, smell the flowers, and jump in the mountain-stream pools. Wave to everyone, move off the road for those speeding by, and breathe in Hawaii. Plan to spend at least 2 nights in Hana (hotel recommendations start on p. 135).

Day ❹: Spending a Day in Heavenly Hana ✿✿✿

You have an entire day in paradise and plenty of things to see. Take an early-morning hike along the black sands of **Waianapanapa State Park** (p. 196); then explore the tiny town of **Hana.** Be sure to see the **Hana Cultural Center & Museum** (p. 236), **Hasegawa General Store** (p. 255), and **Hana Coast Gallery** (p. 254). Get a picnic lunch and drive out to the Kipahulu end of Haleakala National Park at **Oheo Gulch** (p. 240). Hike to the waterfalls and swim in the pools. Splurge

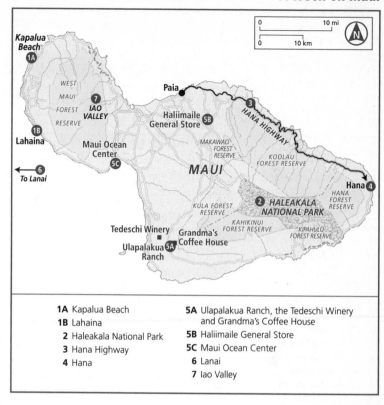

1A Kapalua Beach
1B Lahaina
2 Haleakala National Park
3 Hana Highway
4 Hana
5A Ulapalakua Ranch, the Tedeschi Winery and Grandma's Coffee House
5B Haliimaile General Store
5C Maui Ocean Center
6 Lanai
7 Iao Valley

on dinner at the dining room at the **Hotel Hana-Maui** (p. 137). Spend another night in Hana.

Day ⑤: Enjoying Wine, Food & (Hawaiian) Song

Check to see if the road past Hana is open (it closed after the 2006 earthquake); if it is, continue driving around the island, past Kaupo and up to the **Ulupalakua Ranch** (p. 227) and the **Tedeschi Vineyards and Winery** (p. 227). Stop at **Grandma's Coffee House** (p. 166) for a cup of java and head down the mountain, with a stop for lunch at **Haliimaile General Store** (p. 165). Spend the afternoon at the **Maui Ocean Center,** in Maalaea (p. 220), checking out the sharks and other marine life. Have dinner in Lahaina and see the drama/dance/music show **Ulalena** (p. 260). If the road past Hana is closed, go back along the Hana Highway the way you came, stopping for lunch at Haliimaile, and then follow the rest of the itinerary from there.

Day ⑥: Sailing to Lanai ★★★

Trilogy (p. 180) offers the best sailing/ snorkeling trip in Hawaii, so don't miss it. You'll spend the day (breakfast and lunch included) sailing to Lanai, snorkeling, touring the island, and sailing back to Lahaina. Plus, you still have the afternoon free to shop or take a nap.

Day ⑦: Relaxing & Shopping

Depending on how much time you have on your final day, you can decide to relax on the beach, get pampered in a spa, or shop for souvenirs. Spa-goers have a range of terrific spas to choose from, and shopping aficionados should check out some of my favorite stores (recommendations start on p. 242). If you have a late flight, you might want to check out **Iao Valley** (p. 206).

3 Two Weeks on Maui

Lucky travelers will get 2 weeks to totally relax on the Valley Isle. I'd suggest adding lots of naps, vegging out on the beach, and stopping to smell all the exotic flowers to the 1-week itinerary above. Below are suggestions for your second week on Maui.

Days ❶ to ❼

Follow 1-week itinerary as outlined above.

Day ❽: Flying or Ferrying to Molokai for a Mule Ride 𝒜𝒜𝒜

If you have a spare day or two, head over to the "Friendly Isle" to experience the **Molokai Mule Ride** down into the **Kalaupapa Peninsula** (p. 286). This is an all-day experience that you will remember for the rest of your life. You can either take the ferry over or fly; either way, don't miss this opportunity.

Day ❾: Snorkeling in an Old Volcanic Crater 𝒜𝒜𝒜

Take a day to see the fish inside the **Molokini Crater.** Go in the morning before the wind comes up. If it's whale season and you're lucky, you may spot whales on the way over or back. You'll have to go as part of a tour—my recommendations start on p. 186.

Day ❿: Gliding over the Water in a Kayak 𝒜𝒜𝒜

Kayaking is so easy that you will be paddling away within a few minutes of lessons. One of the best kayak places is **Makena**—it's calm, the water is so clear you can see the fish, and you're protected from the wind. See "Ocean Kayaking" (p. 181) for more suggestions. After a couple hours of kayaking and snorkeling, stop for a picnic lunch at **Makena Landing,** and then explore this area. If you still have energy to spare, hike over to **La Pérouse Monument,** along the rugged shoreline. For coverage of Makena, see p. 221.

Day ⓫: Taking an Offbeat Tour 𝒜

Plan at least one off-the-beaten-path tour while you're on Maui. If you love good food, book the tour of chef James McDonald's **O'o Farm** (p. 152), which includes lunch. Cheese aficionados will love visiting **Surfing Goat Dairy** (p.228) and sampling its cheeses. For a really exotic experience, take the Combo Tour at **Alii Kula Lavender** (p. 227), which includes a tour of the farm and lunch made with lavender products.

Day ⓬: Seeing Maui from a Helicopter 𝒜𝒜𝒜

The feeling of suddenly lifting off straight up in the air and then floating over the island of Maui in a helicopter is a memory that will stay with you forever. Of all the helicopter companies, I recommend booking with **Blue Hawaiian Helicopters** (p. 203) for the most comfortable, informative, and fun tour in the air. After the tour, take some time to explore old **Wailuku** town, wander through the shops (p. 206), stop at the **Bailey House Museum** (p. 206), and then take in **Waikapu** (p. 206), **Kahului** (p. 205), and **Puunene** (p. 205).

Day ⓭: Walking Back in Time in Lahaina 𝒜𝒜

Plan to arrive in this historic town early, before the crowds. Eat a big breakfast, and then put on your walking shoes and take the self-guided **historic walking tour** (p. 212) of the old town. Plan to do some browsing in the quaint stores (recommendations start on p. 246), watch the surfers skim the waves in front of the

1A Kapalua Beach
1B Lahaina

2 Haleakala National Park	**6** Lanai	**12** Wailuku
3 Hana Highway	**7** Iao Valley	**13A** Lahaina
4 Hana	**8** Molokai	**13B** Whalers Village Museum
5A Ulupalakua Ranch, the Tedeschi Winery and Grandma's Coffee House	**9** Molokini Crater	**13C** Kahakuloa
5B Haliimaile General Store	**10** Makena	**13D** Halekii and Pihanakalani Heiau
5C Maui Ocean Center	**11** O'o Farm tour, Surfing Goat Dairy tour, or Alii Kula Lavender tour	

library, and pop over to Kaanapali to the **Whalers Village Museum** (p. 218). Then drive around the head of the island on the **Kahekili Highway** (p. 218), stopping to see the ancient Hawaiian village of **Kahakuloa** and the **Halekii and Pihanakalani Heiau** on the Wailuku side.

Day ⑭: Enjoying Your Last Day
After 13 days of exploring Maui, spend your last day doing what you loved best: beachcombing, snorkeling, hiking, shopping, or whatever your favorite Maui activity is. Pick up a lei before you go to the airport so you will have a little bit of Maui with you as you say aloha.

4 Maui with Kids

Your itinerary is going to depend on the ages of your kids. The number-one rule is *don't plan too much,* especially with young children, who will be fighting jet lag, trying to get adjusted to a new bed (and most likely new food), and possibly dealing with excitement to the point of exhaustion. The 7-day itinerary below is a guide to the various family-friendly activities available on Maui. Pick and choose the ones everyone in your family will enjoy.

Day ❶: Arriving & Enjoying Pool Time 𝒢𝒢

If you have young kids who are not used to the waves, you might consider taking them to the swimming pool at your hotel. They'll be happy playing in the water, and you won't have to introduce them to ocean safety after that long plane ride. Plan an early dinner, with food your kids are used to. If you're in Lahaina, go to **Cheeseburger in Paradise** (p. 150); if you're in Kihei, consider either **Shaka Sandwich & Pizza** (p. 162) or **Stella Blues Cafe** (p. 160). Get to bed early.

Day ❷: Going Up a 10,000-Foot Volcano & Down Again 𝒢𝒢𝒢

Your family will likely be up early, so take advantage of it and head up to the 10,000-foot dormant volcano, **Haleakala.** Depending on the age of your children, you can either **hike in the crater** (p. 190, **speed down the mountain on a bicycle** (p. 200), or just wander about the national park. On your way back down, stop and tour the upcountry communities of **Kula, Makawao,** and **Paia.** Plan to visit the **Surfing Goat Dairy** (p. 228), stop and look at the strange flowers at the **Kula Botanical Garden** (p. 227), or take the 40-minute narrated tram tour at **Maui Tropical Plantation** (p. 206). Grab an early dinner—try **A. K.'s Café** in Wailuku (p. 145), or book a table at the **Mañana Garage** (p. 142) in Kahului.

Day ❸: Seeing Sharks, Stingrays & Starfish without Getting Wet 𝒢𝒢𝒢

After a lazy breakfast, wander over to the **Maui Ocean Center** (p. 220) in Maalaea so your kids can see the fabulous underwater world without having to get wet. Plan to spend the morning immersed in the 5-acre oceanarium. Eat something fishy for lunch. Then head out to **Lahaina,** where you can take the kids underwater in a Jules Verne–type submarine at **Atlantis Adventures** (p. 204), or if

they are too small, hop aboard the **Lahaina/Kaanapali Sugar Cane Train** (p. 204), or rent some snorkel equipment and hit one of the terrific beaches in west Maui (recommendations start on p. 173). Book ahead for the **Old Lahaina Luau** (p. 260) in the evening.

Day ❹: Sailing to Lanai 𝒢𝒢𝒢

Now that the kids have seen the underwater world, take them sailing to Lanai. **Trilogy** (p. 180) offers the best sailing/snorkeling trip in Hawaii, so don't miss it. In the afternoon, wander around Lahaina and see the giant **Banyan Tree** (p. 210), the old **Lahaina Courthouse** (p. 215), and the **old prison** (p. 217).

Day ❺: Driving the Hana Highway 𝒢𝒢𝒢

Pack a lunch and spend the entire day driving the **Hana Highway** (p. 228), the world's most scenic tropical road. Pull over often and get out to take photos, smell the flowers, and jump in the mountain-stream pools. Wave to everyone, move off the road for those speeding by, and breathe in Hawaii. Plan to spend at least 2 nights in Hana (hotel recommendations start on p. 137).

Day ❻: Spending a Day in Heavenly Hana 𝒢𝒢𝒢

You have an entire day in paradise and plenty of things to see. Take an early-morning hike along the black sands of **Waianapanapa State Park** (p. 196); then explore the tiny town of **Hana.** Be sure to see the **Hana Cultural Center & Museum** (p. 236), **Hasegawa General Store** (p. 255), and **Hana Coast Gallery** (p. 254). Get a picnic lunch and drive out to the Kipahulu end of Haleakala National Park at **Oheo Gulch** (p. 240). Hike to the waterfalls and swim in the pools. Splurge on dinner at the dining room at the **Hotel Hana-Maui** (p. 137). Spend another night in Hana.

Maui with Kids

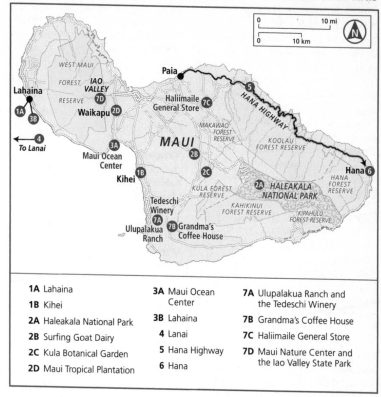

1A Lahaina
1B Kihei
2A Haleakala National Park
2B Surfing Goat Dairy
2C Kula Botanical Garden
2D Maui Tropical Plantation

3A Maui Ocean Center
3B Lahaina
4 Lanai
5 Hana Highway
6 Hana

7A Ulupalakua Ranch and the Tedeschi Winery
7B Grandma's Coffee House
7C Haliimaile General Store
7D Maui Nature Center and the Iao Valley State Park

Day ❼: Seeing the World from a Dragonfly's Point of View ★★

Check to see if the road past Hana is open (it closed after the 2006 earthquake); if it is, continue driving around the island, past Kaupo and up to the **Ulupalakua Ranch** (p. 227) and the **Tedeschi Vineyards and Winery** (p. 227). Stop at **Grandma's Coffee House** (p. 166) for a cup of java and head down the mountain, with a stop for lunch at **Haliimaile General Store** (p. 165). Spend the afternoon at the **Hawaii Nature Center** (p. 207) and the **Iao Valley State Park** (p. 206) next door. If the road past Hana is closed, go back along the Hana Highway the way you came, stopping for lunch at Haliimaile, and then follow the rest of the itinerary from there.

5 Maui for the Adventurous

If you can't stand the thought of just lazing around the beach all day, and your idea of the perfect vacation is to be up, active, and trying new adventures, then Maui is the place for you. This itinerary covers all the basics of what to see on Maui, with added adventures that active people like you will love.

Day ❶: Arriving in Maui & Hitting the Beach ☆☆

Your first stop after you get off the plane should be **Snorkel Bob's** (p. 185) to pick up snorkel gear (the staff will even show you how to use it). Check in to your hotel and then head for the beach. Great snorkeling spots in west Maui include **D. T. Fleming Beach Park, Kapalua Beach, Black Rock on Kaanapali Beach,** and **Wahikuli County Wayside Park.** In south Maui, wonderful snorkeling beaches include the north end of **Oneloa (Big) Beach** in Makena (by the cinder cone), **Ulua Beach** and **Wailea Beach** in Wailea, and **Kamaole III Beach** in Kihei. Beach coverage begins on p. 173. Remember not to overdo the sun on your first day. If you just can't get enough of the underwater world, take a submarine trip with **Atlantis Adventures** (p. 187).

Day ❷: Going Up a 10,000-Foot Volcano & Down Again ☆☆☆

You'll likely wake up early on your first day in Hawaii, so take advantage of it and head up to the 10,000-foot dormant volcano, **Haleakala.** Plan to either **hike in the crater** (p. 190), **speed down the mountain on a bicycle** (p. 200), see the crater on horseback with **Pony Express Tours** (p. 202), or just wander about the national park. You don't have to be at the top for sunrise; in fact, it has gotten so congested at sunrise that you may be too busy fighting the crowds to have an awe-inspiring experience. Instead, I'd suggest heading up any time during the day.

On your way back down, stop and take **Skyline Eco-Adventures' Zipline Haleakala Tour** (p. 191)—not for the faint of heart.

Day ❸: Driving the Hana Highway ☆☆☆

Pack a lunch and spend the entire day driving the scenic **Hana Highway** (p. 228). Pull over often and get out to take photos, smell the flowers, and jump in the mountain-stream pools. Wave to everyone, move off the road for those speeding by, and breathe in Hawaii. Plan to spend at least 2 nights in Hana (hotel recommendations start on p. 137).

Day ❹: Spending a Day in Heavenly Hana ☆☆☆

You have an entire day in paradise and plenty of things to see. Take an early-morning hike along the black sands of **Waianapanapa State Park** (p. 196) and explore the **Piilanihale Heiau** in the **Kahanu Garden** (p. 239). Call **Hana-Maui Sea Sports** and go kayaking (p. 182), or set up a spelunking tour with **Maui Cave Adventures** (p. 9). Get a picnic lunch and drive out to the Kipihulu end of Haleakala National Park at **Oheo Gulch** (p. 240). Hike to the waterfalls and swim in the pools. While you're out there, book a horseback tour with **Maui Stables** (p. 201). Spend another night in Hana.

Day ❺: Trying Something New & Exciting

Check to see if the road past Hana is open (it closed after the 2006 earthquake). If it is, continue driving around the island, past Kaupo and up to the **Ulupalakua Ranch** (p. 227) and the **Tedeschi Winery** (p. 227). Stop at **Grandma's Coffee House** (p. 166) for a cup of java and head down the mountain. Plan to do something you've never tried before, like **learning how to surf** with **Rivers to the Sea** (p. 187), **ocean rafting** with **Capt. Steve's Rafting Excursions** (p. 188), or **windsurfing** (p. 189). If the road past Hana is closed, go back along the Hana Highway the way you came, stopping for lunch at **Haliimaile General Store** (p. 165), and then follow the rest of the itinerary from there.

Day ❻: Sailing to Lanai ☆☆☆

Trilogy (p. 180) offers the best sailing/snorkeling trip in Hawaii, so don't miss it.

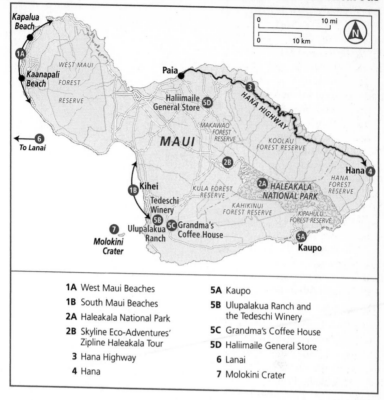

1A West Maui Beaches	**5A** Kaupo
1B South Maui Beaches	**5B** Ulupalakua Ranch and the Tedeschi Winery
2A Haleakala National Park	
2B Skyline Eco-Adventures' Zipline Haleakala Tour	**5C** Grandma's Coffee House
	5D Haliimaile General Store
3 Hana Highway	**6** Lanai
4 Hana	**7** Molokini Crater

You'll spend the day (breakfast and lunch included) sailing to Lanai, snorkeling, touring the island, and sailing back to Lahaina. The really adventurous can also try **scuba diving.**

Day ❼: Enjoying Your Last Chance at Adventure

It's your last chance to do something out of the ordinary. My first pick would be to book a helicopter ride on **Blue Hawaiian Helicopters** (p. 203) to discover what Maui looks like from above. Or if you're a fan of the underwater world, sign up for a **sailing/snorkel tour of Molokini** (p. 180). Even a **guided hike into Maui's rainforest** (p. 190) will remain etched in your memory.

6 A Week on Molokai

The island of Molokai is for people trying to get away from everything or those looking for adventure. There are no direct flights from the mainland to Molokai, so you will have to fly into Honolulu and then take a commuter plane to Molokai.

A Week on Molokai

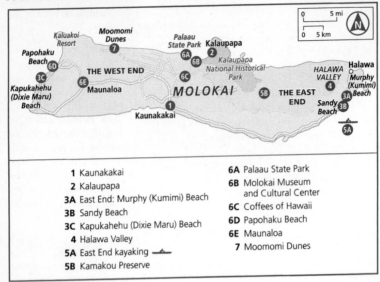

1 Kaunakakai
2 Kalaupapa
3A East End: Murphy (Kumimi) Beach
3B Sandy Beach
3C Kapukahehu (Dixie Maru) Beach
4 Halawa Valley
5A East End kayaking
5B Kamakou Preserve

6A Palaau State Park
6B Molokai Museum and Cultural Center
6C Coffees of Hawaii
6D Papohaku Beach
6E Maunaloa
7 Moomomi Dunes

Day ❶: Arriving & Stopping in Kaunakakai

If you're staying in a condo or vacation rental, head into **Kaunakakai** and stock up on groceries. While you're here, wander around the old two-street town and check out the stores. Be sure to stop at the **Kapuaiwa Coconut Grove/Kiowea Park** (p. 283) and watch the sunset.

Day ❷: Riding a Mule to Kalaupapa 𝒢𝒢𝒢

Your internal clock will still be set to mainland time, so you should have no problem waking up early for the **Molokai Mule Ride** (p. 287). This adventure will take you through 26 switchbacks on a 1,600-foot cliff and give you a chance to tour the **Kalaupapa Peninsula,** where people suffering from leprosy lived for decades.

Day ❸: Heading for the Beach

Molokai has terrific beaches—and on weekdays they are generally empty! Depending on the time of year and the weather, great beaches for snorkeling are

Murphy Beach Park (Kumimi Beach Park) and **Sandy Beach** (both on p. 277) on the East End, and **Kapukahehu (Dixie Maru) Beach** (p. 278) on the West End. Pack a picnic lunch or stop by **Outpost Natural Foods** (p. 275) or the **Sundown Deli** (p. 276), both in Kaunakakai. Stay all day. Relax.

Day ❹: Hiking in a Tropical Valley 𝒢

After a day at the beach, you'll be ready for a hike into the tropical jungle of **Halawa Valley** (p. 290). Bring a picnic lunch for after the hike, and then spend the rest of the day on the beach at Halawa. Stop to see the **fishponds** (p. 289) before you leave the East End.

Day ❺: Exploring the Outdoors 𝒢

Spend a day kayaking, biking, or hiking. **Molokai Outdoors Activities** (p. 278) can set you up with kayaks, mountain bikes, or maps for hiking. My choice would be kayaking along the shallow waters of the East End. Hikers should check out **Pepeopae Trail** (p. 280) or the **Kamakou Preserve** (p. 289).

Day ❻: Touring the West End 🌟🌟
Since you've already seen the East End, spend a day exploring the rest of the island. Start out with a tour of the central part of Molokai by driving out to **Palaau State Park** (p. 285), which overlooks the Kalaupapa Peninsula, and then stop at the **Molokai Museum and Cultural Center** (p. 284) and take a coffee break at **Coffees of Hawaii Plantation Store and Espresso Bar** (p. 292). Next head to the 3-mile-long, white-sand **Papohaku Beach** (p. 277). After an hour or so at the beach, drive up to the cool air in Maunaloa town to see the best store on the

island: the **Big Wind Kite Factory & Plantation Gallery** (p. 293).

Day ❼: Seeing Moomomi Dunes: Archaeology Heaven
Before your flight back, stop by the **Moomomi Dunes** (p. 287), located close to the Hoolehua Airport. This wild, sand-covered coast is a treasure trove for archaeologists. Buried in the mounds are ancient Hawaiian burial sites, fossils, Hawaiian artifacts, and even the bones of prehistoric birds. If you have time, take the 20-minute easy walk west to **Kawaaloa Bay,** the perfect place to say aloha to Molokai.

7 A Week on Lanai

The smallest of all the Hawaiian Islands, Lanai was once a big pineapple plantation and is now home to two exclusive resorts, hundreds of years of history, and just one small town with some of the friendliest people you will ever meet. Like the island of Molokai, there are no direct flights from the mainland to Lanai. You will have to fly into Honolulu and then take a commuter plane to Lanai.

Day ❶: Arriving & Seeing Hulopoe Bay 🌟🌟
After you settle into your hotel, head for the best beach on the island: the marine preserve at **Hulopoe Bay** (p. 304). It's generally safe for swimming, the snorkeling is terrific, and the fish are so friendly you practically have to shoo them away.

Day ❷: Touring the Island in a Four-Wheel-Drive Vehicle
Lanai is a fantastic place to go four-wheeling. Generally you won't need a car if you're staying at one of the two resorts or at the Hotel Lanai (they provide shuttle service), so splurge and rent a four-wheel-drive vehicle for 2 or 3 days. Get a picnic lunch from **Pele's Other Garden** (p. 304) and head out of Lanai City to the **Kanepuu Preserve** (p. 312), a 590-acre dry-land forest. Next stop is **Garden of the Gods** (p. 309) and a picnic lunch at **Polihua Beach** (p. 305), Lanai's largest white-sand beach. The beach generally is not safe for swimming and can be windy,

but it will probably be deserted and you'll have a great view of Molokai in the distance. After lunch, reverse directions and head to **Shipwreck Beach** (p. 306) and then on to **Keomoku Village** (p. 312).

Day ❸: Spending a Day at the Beach
Plan a lazy day at **Hulopoe Beach** (p. 304). Grab a book, watch the kids play in the surf, or take a long walk around the crescent-shaped bay. For lunch, wander over to the **Four Seasons Resort at Manele Bay** and sit poolside at the **Ocean Grill** (p. 302), or else head to the resort's **Challenge at Manele Clubhouse** (p. 302). In the afternoon, plan a nap or try your hand at some Island crafts at the **Lanai Art Center** (p. 314).

Day ❹: Hiking (or Driving) the Munro Trail
If it has not been raining and the ground is dry, do a little exploring. The adventurous can spend the day (plan on at least 7

A Week on Lanai

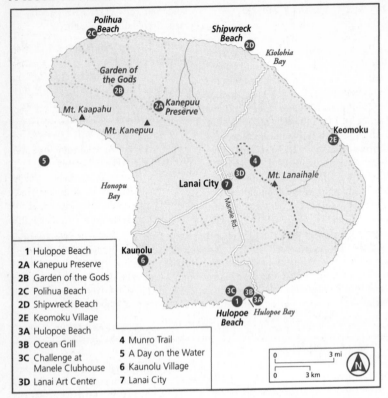

1 Hulopoe Beach
2A Kanepuu Preserve
2B Garden of the Gods
2C Polihua Beach
2D Shipwreck Beach
2E Keomoku Village
3A Hulopoe Beach
3B Ocean Grill
3C Challenge at
 Manele Clubhouse
3D Lanai Art Center

4 Munro Trail
5 A Day on the Water
6 Kaunolu Village
7 Lanai City

hr.) climbing to the top of Lanai on the **Munro Trail** (p. 307). The not-so-adventurous can take a four-wheel-drive vehicle. Soak in a hot tub on your return.

Day ⑤: Enjoying a Day on the Water ⊛⊛

Ring up **Trilogy Lanai Ocean Sports** (p. 306) and book a sailing/snorkeling, whale-watching, or scuba trip.

Day ⑥: Kayaking or Horseback Riding, Followed by a Trip Back in Time

If you can't get enough time on the water, plan a morning kayaking tour with **Trilogy Lanai Ocean Sports** (p. 306). A picnic lunch is included. Horse lovers should arrange a tour of Lanai through the **Stables at Koele** (p. 309). In the afternoon, take a four-wheel-drive vehicle to the historic ruins of the old **Kaunolu Village** (p. 311), on the southwestern side of the island.

Day ⑦: Biking & Shopping

The best way to get around the tiny village of Lanai City is via bicycle. Rent one from the **Four Seasons Resort Lanai, The Lodge at Koele** (p. 300), and ride (downhill) into town. Lanai City has some terrific boutiques that you'll find nowhere else (descriptions of my favorites start on p. 312).

5

Where to Stay

Maui has accommodations to fit every taste and budget, from luxury oceanfront suites and historic bed-and-breakfasts to reasonably priced condos that will sleep a family of four.

The high season, during which rooms are always booked and rates are at the top end, runs from mid-December to March. A second high season, when rates are high but reservations are somewhat easier to get, is summer (late June to early Sept). The off seasons, with fewer tourists and cheaper rates, are April to early June and late September to mid-December.

Remember to add Hawaii's 11.42% accommodations tax to your final bill. Parking is free unless otherwise noted.

Important note: Before you book, be sure to read "The Island in Brief" (p. 87), which will help you choose your ideal location, as well as "Tips on Accommodations" (p. 79). Also check out sections 6, 7, 8, and 9 in chapter 1 for a quick look at my favorite accommodations.

1 Central Maui

KAHULUI

If you're arriving late at night or you have an early-morning flight out, the best choice near Kahului Airport is the **Maui Beach Hotel,** 170 Kaahumanu Ave., Kahului, HI 96732 (© **800/367-5004** or 808/877-0051; fax 808/871-5797; http://castleresorts. com/MBH or www.elleairmaui.com). The nondescript, motel-like rooms (the standard room is so small, you can barely walk around the queen-size bed) start at $120 ($112 if you book online) and include free airport shuttle service (6am–9pm only). It's okay for a night, but it's not a place to spend your entire vacation.

WAILUKU
MODERATE

Old Wailuku Inn at Ulupono ★★ *Finds* This 1924 former plantation manager's home, lovingly restored by innkeepers Janice and Thomas Fairbanks, offers a genuine old Hawaii experience. The theme is Hawaii of the 1920s and 1930s, with decor, design, and landscaping to match. The spacious rooms are gorgeously outfitted with exotic ohia-wood floors, high ceilings, and traditional Hawaiian quilts. The mammoth bathrooms (some with claw-foot tubs, others with Jacuzzis) have plush towels and earth-friendly toiletries on hand. The owners recently added the Vagabond House, a modern three-room complex in the inn's lavishly landscaped backyard. These rooms are decorated in Island designer Sig Zane's floral prints with rare framed prints of indigenous Hawaiian flowers, plus plenty of modern amenities (including an ultra-luxurious multihead shower). You'll feel right at home lounging on the living-room sofa or in an old wicker chair on the enclosed lanai, where a full gourmet breakfast is served in the morning. The inn is located in the historic area of Wailuku, just a few minutes' walk from the Maui County Seat Government Building, the courthouse, and a wonderful stretch of antiques shops.

2199 Kahookele St. (at High St., across from the Wailuku School), Wailuku, HI 96732. © 800/305-4899 or 808/244-5897. Fax 808/242-9600. www.mauiinn.com. 10 units. $150–$190 double. Rates include full breakfast. Extra person $20. 2-night minimum. DC, DISC, MC, V. **Amenities:** Jacuzzi; laundry service; dry cleaning. *In room:* A/C, TV/VCR, dataport, high-speed Internet access, coffeemaker.

INEXPENSIVE

Backpackers should head to **Banana Bungalow Maui,** a funky Happy Valley hostel at 310 N. Market St., Wailuku, HI 96793 (© 800/846-7835 or 808/244-5090; www.mauihostel.com), with $25 dorm rooms and some private rooms ($60 single, $71 double). It provides many free amenities not often found in hostel-type accommodations, such as tours of Maui, high-speed Internet access, airport pickup, beach shuttle, and a Jacuzzi out back. Dorm-style accommodations ($23) and private rooms ($50 single, $60 double) are also available in old Wailuku at the **Northshore Hostel,** 2080 Vineyard St., Wailuku, HI 96793 (© 866/946-7835 or ©/fax 808/986-8095; www.northshorehostel.com). Note, however, that women traveling alone might not feel safe here after dark.

Happy Valley Hale *Value*   The Kong family, owners of Nona Lani Cottages in Kihei (p. 127), have with loving care turned this old plantation home into a tiny oasis in the midst of an economically challenged area. Keep in mind these are budget accommodations—really an alternative to a youth hostel. However, the place is immaculately clean, and the Kongs have made extensive renovations. The four bedrooms—each with twin beds, small fridge, dresser, and closet—share two bathrooms. It's like staying in a family home, with a shared kitchen (no stove, but microwave, griddle, coffeemaker, and so on) and common room with TV. The front yard sports a barbecue and picnic area. The only drawback is that Happy Valley is not exactly a resort area—public housing is just across the street. But for those on extremely tight budgets, it's a good option.

332 Alahee Dr., Wailuku, HI 96793. © 800/733-2688 or 808/357-3737. www.nonalanicottages.com. 4 units. $33 per bed in shared room; $65 double private room; $99 triple private room. MC, V. **Amenities:** Shared kitchen; coin-op washer/dryers. *In room:* Kitchen (in cottages), small fridge, no phone.

2 West Maui

LAHAINA

VERY EXPENSIVE

Hooilo House ⭐   Located just outside Lahaina, about a mile up the West Maui Mountains from Launiupoko Wayside Park, this six-bedroom house is constructed and furnished with materials and furniture from Bali, but the view is all Maui. The atmosphere is relaxing, the rooms are custom decorated with traditional Bali doors and custom beds, there's a private lanai, and the big, big bathrooms have huge tubs and outdoor showers. My favorite rooms are the Kohola and the Nalu (great ocean views). There's also a small swimming pool on the property. My only complaint is that $345 a night seems a bit high for a double room with no hot tub and no fridge. Just a few blocks away is the Guest House (see below), with private hot tubs on private lanais in every room for just $169.

138 Awaiku St., Lahaina, HI 96761. © 808/667-6669. Fax 808/661-7857. www.hooilohouse.com. 6 units. $345 double. Rates include continental breakfast. 3-night minimum. AE, MC, V. **Amenities:** Pool. *In room:* A/C, TV, Wi-Fi, safe.

Where to Stay in Lahaina & Kaanapali

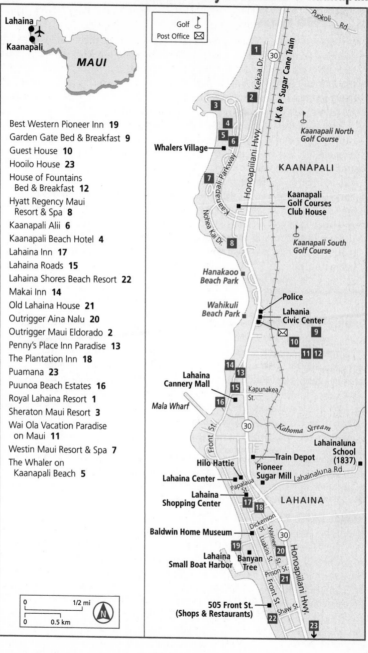

Best Western Pioneer Inn **19**
Garden Gate Bed & Breakfast **9**
Guest House **10**
Hooilo House **23**
House of Fountains
  Bed & Breakfast **12**
Hyatt Regency Maui
  Resort & Spa **8**
Kaanapali Alii **6**
Kaanapali Beach Hotel **4**
Lahaina Inn **17**
Lahaina Roads **15**
Lahaina Shores Beach Resort **22**
Makai Inn **14**
Old Lahaina House **21**
Outrigger Aina Nalu **20**
Outrigger Maui Eldorado **2**
Penny's Place Inn Paradise **13**
The Plantation Inn **18**
Puamana **23**
Puunoa Beach Estates **16**
Royal Lahaina Resort **1**
Sheraton Maui Resort **3**
Wai Ola Vacation Paradise
  on Maui **11**
Westin Maui Resort & Spa **7**
The Whaler on
  Kaanapali Beach **5**

Golf
Post Office

Lahaina
Kaanapali

MAUI

LK & P Sugar Cane Train
Puokoli Rd.
Kekaa Dr.
Honoapiilani Hwy.
Kaanapali North
Golf Course
KAANAPALI
Whalers Village
Kaanapali Parkway
Nohea Kai Dr.
Kaanapali
Golf Courses
Club House
Kaanapali South
Golf Course
Hanakaoo
Beach Park
Wahikuli
Beach Park
Police
Lahania
Civic Center
Lahaina
Cannery Mall
Kapunakea
St.
Mala Wharf
Kahoma Stream
Front St.
Lahainaluna
School
(1837)
Hilo Hattie
Train Depot
Pioneer
Sugar Mill
Lahaina Center
Papalaua
St.
Lahainaluna Rd.
LAHAINA
Lahaina
Shopping Center
Baldwin Home Museum
Dickenson St.
Waineé St.
Luakini St.
Lahaina
Small Boat Harbor
Banyan
Tree
Prison St.
Front St.
Honoapiilani Hwy.
505 Front St.
(Shops & Restaurants)
Shaw St.

0   1/2 mi
0   0.5 km
N

Tips **B&B Etiquette**

In Hawaii, it is traditional and customary to remove your shoes before entering anyone's home. The same is true for most bed-and-breakfast facilities. Most hosts post signs or will politely ask you to remove your shoes before entering the B&B. Not only does this keep the place clean, but you'll also be amazed at how relaxing it is to walk around barefoot. If this custom is unpleasant to you, a B&B may not be for you.

If you've never stayed at a B&B before, here are a few other hints: Generally the hosts live on the property, and their part of the house is off-limits to guests (you do not have the "run of the house"). Most likely there will be a common area that you can use. Don't expect daily maid service. Your host may tidy up, but will not do complete maid service. Also don't expect amenities like little bottles of shampoo and conditioner—this is a B&B, not a resort. Remember you are sharing your accommodations with other guests, so be considerate when you come in late at night.

Some hotels, resorts, condos, and vacation rentals may allow smoking in the guest rooms (most also have nonsmoking rooms available), but the majority of bed-and-breakfasts forbid smoking in the rooms. If this matters to you, be sure to check the policy before you book.

Outrigger Aina Nalu ✿ Set on 9 acres in the middle of Lahaina, this property was totally renovated in 2005. Then the units were sold off to private owners and put into a rental pool. The result is a brand-new first-class property, with all the latest appliances, new furniture, and 21st-century conveniences. The property is on a quiet side street (a rarity in Lahaina) and within walking distance of restaurants, shops, attractions, and the beach (just 3 blocks away). All of the good-size rooms, decorated in tropical-island style, are comfortable and quiet. The complex includes a sun deck and pool, a barbecue, and a picnic area. The aloha-friendly staff will take the time to answer all of your questions.

660 Wainee St. (btw. Dickenson and Prison sts.), Lahaina, HI 96761. ✆ 800/OUTRIGGER (688-7444) or 808/667-9766. Fax 808/661-3733. www.outrigger.com. 197 units. $229–$265 studio with kitchenette; $299–$335 1-bedroom with kitchen (sleeps up to 4); $369–$395 2-bedroom with 1 bathroom and kitchen (sleeps 6); $389–$415 2-bedroom with 2 bathrooms and kitchen (sleeps 6). Extra rollaway bed $18. AE, DC, DISC, MC, V. Parking $5. **Amenities:** Outdoor pool; whirlpool; activities desk; laundry service; dry cleaning. *In room:* A/C, TV, full kitchen (in 1- and 2-bedroom units), kitchenette (in studio), fridge, coffeemaker, hair dryer, iron, safe, washer/dryer (in 1- and 2-bedroom units).

Puunoa Beach Estates ✿✿ *Kids* If you're taking a family to Maui, consider these 10 gorgeous town houses in an exclusive 3-acre enclave on a white-sand beach. The individually owned and decorated two-bedroom units (1,700 sq. ft. and up) all have private beachfront lanais, hardwood floors, marble bathrooms, and modern kitchens. Prices are high, but the amenity list has everything you should want for a first-class vacation rental in a dream location. It's within walking distance of the center of Lahaina, but the residential location makes you feel miles away.

45 Kai Pali Place, Lahaina, HI 96761. Managed by Classic Resorts. ✆ 800/642-6284 or 808/661-3339. Fax 808/667-1145. www.puunoabeachestates.com. 10 units. $800–$1,000 2-bedroom unit (sleeps 4). 3-night minimum. AE, MC, V. **Amenities:** Barbecues; outdoor pool; fitness center; whirlpool; sauna; complimentary snorkeling equipment; concierge; fax service; free Internet access; video library; dry cleaning. *In room:* A/C, TV/VCR, dataport, full kitchen, fridge, coffeemaker, hair dryer, iron, safe, whirlpool tub in master bedroom, washer/dryer, daily maid service.

EXPENSIVE

The Plantation Inn ★★ *Finds* Attention, romance-seeking couples: Look no further. This charming Victorian-style inn, located a couple of blocks from the water, looks like it's been here 100 years or more, but it's actually of 1990s vintage—an artful deception. The rooms are romantic to the max, tastefully done with period furniture, hardwood floors, stained glass, and ceiling fans. There are four-poster canopy beds in some rooms, brass beds and wicker beds in others. All units are soundproof (a plus in Lahaina) and come with a private lanai; the suites have kitchenettes. The rooms wrap around the large pool and deck. Breakfast is served around the pool and in an elegant pavilion lounge. Also on the property is an outstanding French restaurant, Gerard's (p. 148).

174 Lahainaluna Rd. (btw. Wainee and Luakini sts., 1 block from Hwy. 30), Lahaina, HI 96761. © 800/433-6815 or 808/667-9225. Fax 808/667-9293. www.theplantationinn.com. 19 units (some with shower only). $169–$245 double; from $265 suite. Check the website for great package deals. Rates include full breakfast. Extra person $25. AE, DC, DISC, MC, V. **Amenities:** Acclaimed restaurant and bar (Gerard's, p. 148); large outdoor pool; Jacuzzi; concierge; activities desk; coin-op washer/dryers. *In room:* A/C, TV/VCR, kitchenette (in suites), fridge, hair dryer, iron, safe.

Puamana These 28 acres of town houses set right on the water are ideal for those who want to be able to retreat from the crowds and cacophony of downtown Lahaina into the serene quiet of an elegant neighborhood. Private and peaceful are apt descriptions for this complex: Each unit is a privately owned individual home, with no neighbors above or below. Most are exquisitely decorated, and all come with full kitchen, lanai, barbecue, and at least two bathrooms. Puamana was once a private estate in the 1920s, part of the sugar plantations that dominated Lahaina; the plantation manager's house has been converted into a clubhouse with an oceanfront lanai, library, card room, sauna, table-tennis tables, and office. I've found the best rates by booking through Klahani Travel (see below for contact information), but its office is not on-site, which has caused some problems with guests getting assistance. If you'd rather book directly with the Puamana association office, contact Puamana Community Association, 34 Puailima Place, Lahaina, HI 96761 (© **808/661-3423;** fax 808/667-0398; info@Puamana.info).

Front St. (at the extreme southern end of Lahaina, ½ mile from downtown), Lahaina, HI 96761. Reservations c/o Klahani Travel, Lahaina Cannery Mall, 1221 Honoapiilani Hwy., Lahaina, HI 96761. © 800/669-6284 or 808/667-2712. Fax 808/661-5875. www.klahani.com. 40 units. $140–$250 1-bedroom; $160–$350 2-bedroom; $350–$500 3-bedroom. 3-night minimum. AE, DC, DISC, MC, V. **Amenities:** 3 pools (1 for adults only); tennis court; Jacuzzi; game room; activities desk; on-site laundry service. *In room:* TV, kitchen, fridge, coffeemaker, hair dryer, iron, washer/dryer (in some units).

MODERATE

Best Western Pioneer Inn This once-rowdy home away from home for sailors now seems respectable—even charming. The hotel is a two-story plantation-style structure with big verandas that overlook the streets of Lahaina and the harbor, which is just 50 feet away. All rooms have been totally remodeled, with vintage bathrooms and new curtains and carpets. The quietest units face either the garden courtyard—devoted to refined outdoor dining accompanied by live (but quiet) music—or the square-block-size banyan tree next door. I recommend room no. 31, over the banyan court, with a view of the ocean and the harbor. If you want a front-row seat for all the Front Street action, book no. 36 or 49.

658 Wharf St. (in front of Lahaina Pier), Lahaina, HI 96761. ℂ **800/457-5457** or 808/661-3636. Fax 808/667-5708. www.pioneerinnmaui.com. 34 units. $165–$190 double; from $205 suite. Extra person (12 or older) $15. AE, DC, DISC, MC, V. Parking included in room rates. **Amenities:** Restaurant (good for breakfast); bar w/live music; outdoor pool; big shopping arcade; laundry service. *In room:* A/C, TV, fridge, coffeemaker, hair dryer, iron.

Garden Gate Bed & Breakfast
This oasis of a B&B, located on a quiet residential street just outside Lahaina town, is 5 minutes from the beach by car. The six units all have private entrances and a garden or ocean view; the deluxe suites have a deck and a separate pullout sofa for kids. Continental breakfast is served in the garden (Mon–Fri), and hosts Jamie and Bill Mosley are available to answer any questions about things to do or places to eat. Bicycles, boogie boards, beach chairs, and mats are available at no charge. The barbecue area and adjacent laundry facilities are available for guests' use.

67 Kaniau Rd., Lahaina, HI 96761. ℂ **800/939-3217** or 808/661-8800. Fax 808/661-0209. www.gardengatebb.com. 6 units. $129–$179 double. Extra person $15. 3-night minimum. Rates include continental breakfast. AE, DC, DISC, MC, V. *In room:* A/C, TV, VCR (on request), fridge, microwave, coffeemaker, hair dryer, iron.

Guest House ★★ (Finds)
This is one of Lahaina's great bed-and-breakfast deals: a charming house with more amenities than the expensive Kaanapali hotels just down the road. The roomy home features parquet floors and floor-to-ceiling windows; its swimming pool—surrounded by a deck and comfortable lounge chairs—is larger than some at high-priced condos. Every unit has a quiet lanai and a romantic Jacuzzi. Guests share the large, well-equipped kitchen and computers with high-speed Internet access. Scuba divers are welcome here (and provided with places to wash and store their gear). The Guest House also operates Trinity Tours and offers discounts on car rentals and other island activities. Tennis courts are nearby, and the nearest beach is about a block away.

1620 Ainakea Rd. (off Fleming Rd., north of Lahaina town), Lahaina, HI 96761. ℂ **800/621-8942** or 808/661-8085. Fax 808/661-1896. www.mauiguesthouse.com. 4 units. $149 single; $169 double. Rates include full breakfast. MC, V. Take Fleming Rd. off Hwy. 30; turn left on Ainakea; it's 2 blocks down. **Amenities:** Huge outdoor pool; free use of watersports equipment; concierge; activities desk; car-rental desk; self-service washer/dryers. *In room:* A/C, TV/VCR/DVD, wireless Internet access, fridge, Jacuzzi.

House of Fountains Bed & Breakfast (Finds)
This 7,000-square-foot contemporary home, in a quiet residential subdivision at the north end of town, is popular with visitors from around the world. Hostess Daniela Atay keeps the place immaculate; in 2002, she won the prestigious "Most Hawaiian Accommodation" award from the Hawaii Visitors & Convention Bureau. The oversize rooms are fresh and quiet, with white ceramic-tile floors, handmade koa furniture, Hawaiian quilt bedspreads, and a Hawaiian theme; the four downstairs rooms all open onto flower-filled private patios. Guests share a fully equipped kitchen and barbecue area, and are welcome to curl up on the living-room sofa with a book from the library. The nearest beach is about a 5-minute drive away; tennis courts are nearby. Around the pool is a Hawaiian *hale* (house), an *imu* pit for luau, and an area that's perfect for Hawaiian weddings (arrangements available).

1579 Lokia St. (off Fleming Rd., north of Lahaina town), Lahaina, HI 96761. ℂ **800/789-6865** or 808/667-2121. Fax 808/667-2120. www.alohahouse.com. 6 units (all with shower only). $145–$155 double (2 people per room). Rates include full breakfast. AE, MC, V. From Hwy. 30, take the Fleming Rd. exit; turn left on Ainakea; after 2 blocks, turn right on Malanai St.; go 3 blocks, and turn left onto Lokia St. **Amenities:** Outdoor pool; Jacuzzi; washer/dryers. *In room:* A/C, TV/VCR, fridge, hair dryer.

Lahaina Inn ☞ If you like old hotels that have genuine historic touches, you'll love this place. As in many older hotels, some of these antiques-stuffed rooms are small; if that's a problem for you, ask for a larger unit. All come with private bathrooms and lanais. The best room in the house is no. 7, which overlooks the beach, the town, and the island of Lanai. There's an excellent, though unaffiliated, restaurant in the same building (David Paul's Lahaina Grill, p. 146) and a bar downstairs.

127 Lahainaluna Rd. (near Front St.), Lahaina, HI 96761. ℂ 800/669-3444 or 808/661-0577. Fax 808/667-9480. www.lahainainn.com. 12 units (most with shower only). $150–$170 double; from $205 suite. AE, MC, V. Next-door parking $7 per day. **Amenities:** Bar; concierge; activities desk. *In room:* A/C, hair dryer, iron.

Lahaina Roads (*Value* If you dream of an oceanfront condo but your budget is on the slim side, here's your place. This condominium complex offers small, reasonably priced units in an older building located in the quiet part of Lahaina, away from the noisy, crowded downtown area, overlooking the boats in the Mala Wharf roadstead (a protected place to anchor near the shore). The compact units have full kitchens and soundproof walls—a real plus. The bedrooms face the road, while the living rooms and lanais overlook the ocean and the island of Lanai. The building is about 35 years old but well maintained. The only drawbacks are no air-conditioning (it can be boiling hot in Lahaina) and no laundry facilities.

1403 Front St. (1 block north of Lahaina Cannery Mall), Lahaina, HI 96761. Reservations c/o Klahani Travel, Lahaina Cannery Mall, 1221 Honoapiilani Hwy., Lahaina, HI 96761. ℂ 800/669-MAUI [6284] or 808/667-2712. Fax 808/661-5875. www.klahani.com. 17 units. $150 1-bedroom (sleeps up to 4); $225 2-bedroom (sleeps up to 6). 3-night minimum. AE, DC, DISC, MC, V. **Amenities:** Ocean-side outdoor pool. *In room:* TV, kitchen, fridge, coffeemaker, hair dryer, iron.

Lahaina Shores Beach Resort ☞ First there's the location, right on the beach; second there's the location, away from the hustle and bustle of downtown Lahaina; and third there's the location, next door to the 505 Front Street restaurants (with charging privileges) and shops. This recently upgraded condominium project (of studios and one-bedroom units) resembles an old plantation home, with arched colonnades at the entry and an open-air, beachfront lobby. From the moment you step into the airy units (ranging in size from 550–1,430 sq. ft.), you'll feel like you are home. The units all have full kitchens, large lanais, and ocean or mountain views. Ask for an oceanfront unit for that terrific view of the water with the island of Lanai in the distance.

475 Front St., Lahaina, HI 96761. ℂ 800/628-6699 or 808/661-4835. www.lahainashores.com. 145 units. $210–$275 studio double; $290–$340 1-bedroom double; $340–$370 1-bedroom penthouse double. AE, MC, V. Parking $5. **Amenities:** Outdoor pool; tennis courts (across the street); whirlpool; beach activities; barbecue grill; concierge; coin-op washer/dryers; dry cleaning. *In room:* A/C, TV, kitchen, fridge, coffeemaker, iron, hair dryer.

Wai Ola Vacation Paradise on Maui ☞ Just 2 blocks from the beach, in a quiet residential development behind a tall concrete wall, lies this lovely retreat, with shade trees, sitting areas, gardens, a pool, an ocean mural, and a range of accommodations. You can book a small studio, a couple of suites inside the home, a separate honeymoon cottage, a one-bedroom apartment, or the entire 5,000-square-foot house. Hosts Kim and Jim Wicker will gladly provide any information you need to make your vacation fabulous. Every unit has a welcome fruit basket when you arrive, plus coffee beans for the coffeemaker. Kim often surprises her guests with "a little something" from her kitchen, like cheesecake or heavenly brownies. You'll also find a deck, barbecue facilities, and an outdoor wet bar on the property; a great beach and tennis courts are nearby.

1565 Kuuipo St. (P.O. Box 12580), Lahaina, HI 96761. © 800/492-4652 or 808/661-7901. Fax 808/661-1119. www. waiola.com. 5 units. $169–$189 studio; $179 suite; $209 1-bedroom honeymoon cottage for 2. Extra person $15. AE, DISC, MC, V. **Amenities:** Outdoor pool; Jacuzzi; free use of watersports equipment; wireless Internet access; free self-service washer/dryers. *In room:* A/C, TV/DVD/VCR, dataport, kitchenette, fridge, coffeemaker, hair dryer, iron.

INEXPENSIVE

In addition to the following choices, consider value-priced **Old Lahaina House** (© **800/847-0761** or 808/667-4663; fax 808/669-9199; www.oldlahaina.com), which features comfy twin- and king-bedded doubles for just $69 to $139. It's about a 2-minute walk to the water just across Front Street.

Makai Inn *(Value)*   Budget travelers, take note: Here's a small apartment complex located right on the water (okay, no white-sand beach out front, but what do you want at these eye-popping prices?). You can take a 10-minute stroll from this quiet neighborhood to the closest white-sand beach, or walk 20 minutes to the center of Lahaina town. The units are small (400 sq. ft.) but clean and have full kitchens, views of the ocean (from most units), and separate bedrooms. There are no phones or TVs, but there's a public phone by the office. In the middle of the complex is a tropical garden. I recommend the Ginger Hideaway unit, which has windows on two sides overlooking the ocean, for just $156. Families will like the Pineapple "Sweet," the only two-bedroom unit (800 sq. ft.), also priced at $156.

1415 Front St., Lahaina, HI 96761. © **808/662-3200.** Fax 808/661-9027. www.makaiinn.net. 18 units. $105–$180 double. Extra person $15. MC, V. **Amenities:** Coin-op washer/dryers. *In room:* Kitchen, no phone.

Penny's Place Inn Paradise *(Finds)*   No attention to detail has been spared in this Victorian-style bed-and-breakfast, just 50 feet from the water with a fabulous view from the front porch of Molokai and Lanai. Each of the four rooms is uniquely decorated, with themes ranging from contemporary Hawaiian to formal Victorian. Guests are welcome to use the balcony kitchenette (fridge, microwave, toaster, coffeemaker, and ice machine). The only problem is the location—a small island bounded by Honoapiilani Highway on one side and busy Front Street on the other. The house is soundproof, and air-conditioning in each room drowns out the noise inside. Penny recently enclosed the outdoor lanai area, so you can enjoy your breakfast without the highway noise.

1440 Front St., Lahaina, HI 96761. © **877/431-1235** or 808/661-1068. Fax 808/667-7102. www.pennysplace.net. 4 units. $98–$147 double. Rates include continental breakfast Mon–Sat. 3-night minimum. DISC, MC, V. *In room:* A/C, TV, wireless Internet access, iron.

KAANAPALI

Another option to consider, in addition to those below, is the **Royal Lahaina Resort** (© **800/222-5642** or 808/661-3611; fax 808/661-6150; www.hawaiianhotelsand resorts.com). But skip the overpriced hotel rooms: Only stay here if you can get one of the 132 cottages tucked among the well-manicured grounds. Book online, where rates are $195 to $600 (50% off the rack rates).

VERY EXPENSIVE

Hyatt Regency Maui Resort & Spa *(Kids)*   Spa-goers will love this resort. Hawaii's first oceanfront spa, the Spa Moana, opened here in 2000 and boasts 20,000 square feet of facilities, including an exercise floor with an ocean view, 15 treatment rooms, sauna and steam rooms, and a huge menu of massages, body treatments, and therapies. Book your treatment before you leave home—this place is popular.

The management has poured some $19 million in renovations into this fantasy resort, the southernmost of the Kaanapali beachfront properties. It certainly has lots of imaginative touches: a collection of exotic species (pink flamingos, unhappy-looking penguins, and an assortment of loud parrots and macaws in the lobby), nine waterfalls, and an eclectic Asian and Pacific art collection. This huge place covers some 40 acres; even if you don't stay here, you might want to walk through the expansive tree-filled atrium and the parklike grounds, which contain a ½-acre outdoor pool with a 150-foot lava-tube slide, a cocktail bar under the falls, a "honeymooners' cave," and a swinging rope bridge. There's even a kids-only pool with its own beach, tidal pools, and fountains.

The rooms, spread out among three towers, are pleasantly outfitted with an array of amenities and have very comfortable separate sitting areas and private lanais with eye-popping views. The latest, most comfortable bedding (including fluffy feather beds) is now standard in every room. Two Regency Club floors offer a private concierge, complimentary breakfast, sunset cocktails, and snacks.

Families will appreciate Camp Hyatt, a year-round program offering young guests a range of activities, from "Olympic Games" to a scavenger hunt. There's also a game room for kids with video games, pool, Ping-Pong, and air hockey.

200 Nohea Kai Dr., Lahaina, HI 96761. ℂ 800/233-1234 or 808/661-1234. Fax 808/667-4498. www.maui.hyatt. com. 806 units. $485–$755 double; $690–$820 Regency Club double; from $950 suite. Extra person $50 ($75 in Regency Club rooms). Children 18 and under stay free in parent's room using existing bedding. Daily $15 resort fee for access to Moana Athletic Club, local newspaper delivery, local and toll-free calls, and 1-hr. tennis-court time per day. Packages available. AE, DC, DISC, MC, V. Valet parking $10; free self-parking. **Amenities:** 5 restaurants (including Son'z Maui at Swan Court, p. 153); 2 bars; ½-acre outdoor pool; 36-hole golf course; 6 tennis courts; health club w/weight room; state-of-the-art spa; Jacuzzi; watersports equipment rentals; bike rentals; year-round children's program; game room; concierge; activities desk; car-rental desk; business center; shopping arcade; salon; room service; in-room and spa massage; babysitting; coin-op washer/dryers; laundry service; dry cleaning; concierge-level rooms. In room: A/C, TV, dataport, high-speed Internet access ($10 per day), minibar, fridge, coffeemaker, hair dryer, iron, safe, 2-line phone.

Kaanapali Alii 🏖🏖 (Kids)   These luxurious oceanfront condominiums sit on 8 landscaped acres right on Kaanapali Beach. Kaanapali Alii combines the amenities of a luxury hotel (including a 24-hr. front desk) with the conveniences of a condominium. Each of the one-bedroom (1,500 sq. ft.) and two-bedroom (1,900 sq. ft.) units is impeccably decorated and comes with all the comforts of home (fully equipped kitchen, washer/dryer, lanai, two full bathrooms) and then some (room service, daily maid service, complimentary local newspaper). The beachside recreation area includes a swimming pool, a separate children's pool, a whirlpool, gas barbecue grills and picnic areas, exercise rooms, saunas, and tennis courts. You can even take yoga classes on the lawn.

50 Nohea Kai Dr., Lahaina, HI 96761. ℂ 800/642-6284 or 808/661-3330. Fax 808/667-1145. www.kaanapali-alii.com. 264 units. $395–$675 1-bedroom for 4; $590–$975 2-bedroom for 6. AE, DC, DISC, MC, V. **Amenities:** Poolside cafe; 2 outdoor pools; 36-hole golf course; 3 lighted tennis courts; fitness center; Jacuzzi; watersports equipment rentals; children's program; game room; concierge; activities desk; room service; in-room massage; babysitting; same-day dry cleaning. In room: A/C, TV, dataport, kitchen, fridge, coffeemaker, hair dryer, iron, safe, washer/dryer.

Sheraton Maui Resort 🏖🏖 (Kids)   Terrific facilities for families and fitness buffs and a premier beach location make this beautiful resort an all-around great place to stay. The grande dame of Kaanapali Beach is built into the side of a cliff on the curving, white-sand cove next to Black Rock (a lava formation that rises 80 ft. above the beach), where there's excellent snorkeling. The resort comprises six buildings of six stories or fewer set in well-established tropical gardens. The lobby has been elevated to take advantage of panoramic views, and a lagoonlike pool features lava-rock waterways, wooden bridges, and an open-air whirlpool. Cliff divers swan-dive off the torchlit lava-rock headland in a traditional sunset ceremony—a sight to see. And the views of Kaanapali Beach, with Lanai and Molokai in the distance, are some of the best around.

Every unit is outfitted with amenities galore, right down to toothbrushes and toothpaste. Other pluses include the Sweet Sleeper Bed, a private balcony, and a "no-hassle" check-in policy: The valet takes you and your luggage straight to your room. There's also a new emphasis on family appeal, with a class of rooms dedicated to those traveling with kids. These "family suites" have three beds, a sitting room with full-size couch, and two TVs, both equipped with Nintendo. In addition, there's the Keiki Aloha program, with fun activities ranging from Hawaiian games to visits to nearby attractions. Children 12 and younger eat free when dining with one adult.

The Seaside Salon and Day Spa is a tiny boutique spa offering quite an array of services; I recommend the "Beauty in a Blanket" treatment, which gives you a massage, facial, wrap, and scrub.

2605 Kaanapali Pkwy., Lahaina, HI 96761. ② 888/488-3535 or 808/661-0031. Fax 808/661-0458. www.sheraton-maui.com. 510 units. $500–$770 double; from $900 suite. Extra person $70. Children 17 and under stay free in parent's room using existing bedding. Daily $17 resort fee for in-room Internet access, self-parking, local calls and credit card calls up to 60 min., and valet parking on the day of arrival. AE, DC, DISC, MC, V. Valet parking $5; free self-parking. **Amenities:** 2 restaurants; 2 poolside bars; indoor lounge; lagoon-style pool; 36-hole golf course; 3 tennis courts; fitness center; day spa; Jacuzzi; watersports equipment rentals; children's program; lobby and poolside concierge; car-rental desk; business center; room service; babysitting; coin-op washer/dryers; same-day laundry service and dry cleaning; nightly sunset cliff-dive ceremony; beachfront snorkeling at Black Rock; weekly luau. *In room:* A/C, TV, PlayStation, dataport, high-speed Internet access, fridge, coffeemaker, hair dryer, iron, safe.

Westin Maui Resort & Spa ⭐ (Kids)

The 758-room Westin Maui has added a $5-million spa and gym, and in the spirit of having a healthy environment, smoking is no longer allowed in guest rooms. I love the fabulous pillow-top Westin Heavenly Beds, with your choice of five different pillows. If that doesn't give you sweet dreams, nothing will. Once you get up, head to the aquatic playground—an 87,000-square-foot pool area with five free-form heated pools joined by swim-through grottoes, waterfalls, and a 128-foot-long water slide. This is the Disney World of water-park resorts, and your kids will be in water-hog heaven. The fantasy theme extends from the estatelike grounds into the interior's public spaces, which are filled with the shriek of tropical birds and the splash of waterfalls. The oversize architecture and $2-million art collection make a pleasing backdrop for all the action. Most of the rooms in the two 11-story towers overlook the aquatic playground, the ocean, and the island of Lanai in the distance.

2365 Kaanapali Pkwy., Lahaina, HI 96761. ② 888/625-4949 or 808/667-2525. Fax 808/661-5764. www.westin maui.com. 758 units. $515–$795 double; from $1,100 suite. Extra person $70. Daily $20 resort fee for local calls, use of fitness center and spa, a souvenir shopping bag, a 4×6-in. photo, shuttle services to golf and tennis facilities, in-room high-speed Internet access, self-parking, and local newspaper delivery. AE, DC, DISC, MC, V. Valet parking $15; free self-parking. **Amenities:** 5 restaurants; 3 bars; 5 free-form outdoor pools; 36-hole golf course; tennis courts; health club and spa w/aerobics, steam baths, sauna, massages, and body treatments; Jacuzzi; watersports equipment rentals; bike rental; children's program; game room; concierge; activities desk; car-rental desk; business center; shopping arcade; salon; room service; in-room and spa massage; babysitting; same-day laundry service and dry cleaning. *In room:* A/C, TV, dataport, high-speed Internet access, minibar, fridge, coffeemaker, hair dryer, iron, safe.

EXPENSIVE

Outrigger Maui Eldorado ✪ *Kids*   These spacious condominium units—each with full kitchen, washer/dryer, and daily maid service—were built at a time when land in Kaanapali was cheap, contractors took pride in their work, and visitors expected spacious units with views from every window. You'll find it hard to believe that this was one of Kaanapali's first properties in the late 1960s; this first-class choice still looks like new. The Outrigger chain has managed to keep prices reasonable, especially in spring and fall. This is a great choice for families, with its big units, grassy areas that are perfect for running off excess energy, and a beachfront (with beach cabanas and a barbecue area) that's usually safe for swimming. Tennis courts are nearby.

2661 Kekaa Dr., Lahaina, HI 96761. © **800/688-7444** or 808/661-0021. Fax 808/667-7039. www.outrigger.com. 204 units. $279–$329 studio double; $335–$365 1-bedroom (up to 4); $475–$595 2-bedroom (up to 6). Numerous packages available, including 5th night free, rental-car deals, senior rates, and more. Parking $5. AE, DC, DISC, MC, V. **Amenities:** 3 outdoor pools; 36-hole golf course; concierge/activities desk; car-rental desk; some business services; washer/dryers. *In room:* A/C, TV, dataport, kitchen, fridge, coffeemaker, hair dryer, iron, safe, washer/dryer.

The Whaler on Kaanapali Beach ✪   In the heart of Kaanapali, right on the world-famous beach, lies this oasis of elegance, privacy, and luxury. The relaxing atmosphere strikes you as soon as you enter the open-air lobby, where light reflects off the dazzling koi in the meditative lily pond. No expense has been spared on these gorgeous accommodations; every unit has a full kitchen, washer/dryer, marble bathroom, 10-foot beamed ceilings, and blue-tiled lanai—and spectacular views of Kaanapali's gentle waves or the humpback peaks of the West Maui Mountains. Next door is Whalers Village, with numerous restaurants, bars, and shops; Kaanapali Golf Club's 36 holes are across the street.

2481 Kaanapali Pkwy. (next to Whalers Village), Lahaina, HI 96761. © **866/77-HAWAII** (774-2924) or 808/661-4861. Fax 808/661-8315. www.resortquesthawaii.com. 360 units. $255–$330 studio double; $360–$415 1-bedroom (up to 4 people); $305–$760 2-bedroom (up to 6 people). Check website for specials. AE, DC, DISC, MC, V. Parking $10 per day. **Amenities:** Outdoor pool; tennis courts; refurbished fitness room; Hina Mana Salon & Spa (which offers massages, pedicures, and manicures); Jacuzzi; concierge; activities desk; coin-op washer/dryers. *In room:* A/C, TV/VCR/DVD, free dial-up Internet access (fee charged for wireless access), kitchen, fridge, coffeemaker, hair dryer, iron, safe, washer/dryer.

MODERATE

Kaanapali Beach Hotel ✪ *Value*   It's older and less high-tech than its upscale neighbors, but the Kaanapali Beach Hotel has an irresistible local style and a real Hawaiian warmth that's missing from many other Maui properties. Three low-rise wings, bordering a fabulous stretch of beach, are set around a wide, grassy lawn with coco palms and a whale-shaped pool. The spacious, spotless motel-like rooms are done in wicker and rattan, with Hawaiian-style bedspreads and a lanai facing the courtyard and the beach. The beachfront rooms are separated from the water only by Kaanapali's landscaped walking trail.

Old Hawaii values and customs are always close at hand, and the service is some of the friendliest around. Tiki torches, hula, and Hawaiian music create a festive atmosphere every night in the expansive courtyard. As part of the hotel's extensive Hawaiiana program, you can learn to cut pineapple, weave lauhala, and even dance the hula. The children's program is complimentary. There's also an arts-and-crafts fair 4 days a week, a morning welcome reception Monday through Saturday, and a farewell lei ceremony when you depart.

2525 Kaanapali Pkwy., Lahaina, HI 96761. ℂ 800/262-8450 or 808/661-0011. Fax 808/667-5978. www.kbhmaui. com. 430 units. $199–$355 double; from $295 suite. Extra person $30. Car, golf, bed-and-breakfast, and romance packages available, as well as senior discounts. AE, DC, DISC, MC, V. Valet parking $11; self-parking $9. **Amenities:** 2 restaurants (including Tiki Terrace, p. 154); poolside bar (where you can get a mean piña colada); outdoor pool; 36-hole golf course nearby; access to tennis courts; watersports equipment rentals; children's program; concierge/guest services; activities desk; convenience shops; salon; babysitting; coin-op washer/dryers. *In room:* A/C, TV, fridge, coffeemaker, iron, safe.

HONOKOWAI, KAHANA & NAPILI
EXPENSIVE

Also consider **Sands of Kahana** (ℂ **800/326-9874** or 808/669-0423; www.sands-of-kahana.com), an eight-story condo/timeshare complex that's great for families. The one- to three-bedroom units have small kitchens and washer/dryers. The property is loaded with kid-friendly extras, including a large children's pool, a playground, and a stretch of beach that's safe for swimming. Rates range from $150 to $225 for one bedroom, $265 to $450 for two bedrooms, and $375 to $445 for three bedrooms (7-night minimum).

Napili Kai Beach Resort ★★ *Finds*   This comfortable oceanfront complex lies just south of the Kapalua Resort, nestled in a small white-sand cove. The one- and two-story units, with double-hipped Hawaii-style roofs, face a gold-sand beach that's safe for swimming. Many units have a view of the Pacific, with Molokai and Lanai in the distance. Those who prefer air-conditioning should book into the Honolua Building, where you'll get a room set back from the shore around a grassy, parklike lawn and pool. Every unit (except eight hotel rooms) has a fully stocked kitchenette with full-size fridge, cooktop, microwave, toaster oven, washer/dryer, and coffeemaker; some have dishwashers. On-site pluses include daily maid service, even in the condo units; two shuffleboard courts; barbecue areas; complimentary morning coffee and afternoon tea; weekly lei making, hula lessons, and horticultural tours; and a free weekly mai tai party. There are three nearby championship golf courses and excellent tennis courts at the adjacent Kapalua Resort.

5900 Honoapiilani Rd. (at the extreme north end of Napili, next to Kapalua), Lahaina, HI 96761. ℂ 800/367-5030 or 808/669-6271. Fax 808/669-0086. www.napilikai.com. 162 units. $230–$285 hotel room double; $275–$385 studio double (sleeps 3–4); $430–$475 1-bedroom suite (sleeps up to 5); $625–$810 2-bedroom suite (sleeps up to 7). Packages available. AE, DISC, MC, V. **Amenities:** Restaurant (Sea House Restaurant, p. 156); bar; 4 outdoor pools; 2 18-hole putting greens (w/free use of golf putters); tennis courts nearby (and complimentary use of tennis rackets); good-size fitness room; Jacuzzi; complimentary watersports equipment; free children's activities at Easter, June 15–Aug 31, and at Christmas; concierge; activities desk; babysitting; coin-op washer/dryers; laundry service; dry cleaning. *In room:* A/C (in most units), TV, kitchenette (in most units), fridge, coffeemaker, hair dryer, iron, safe.

MODERATE

In addition to the choices below, consider **Polynesian Shores,** 3975 Lower Honoapiilani Rd. (near Kahana and just 2 min. from the Kapalua–West Maui Airport), Lahaina, HI 96761 (ℂ **800/433-6284** or 808/669-6065; fax 808/669-0909; www. polynesianshores.com). Every unit (one to three bedrooms, $150–$285) has floor-to-ceiling sliding-glass doors that open onto a private lanai with an ocean view. There's great snorkeling off the beach out front.

Hale Kai ★ *Kids*   This small two-story condo complex is ideally located, right on the beach and next door to a county park—a great location for those traveling with kids. Shops, restaurants, and ocean activities are all within a 6-mile radius. The units are

Where to Stay & Dine from Honokowai to Kapalua

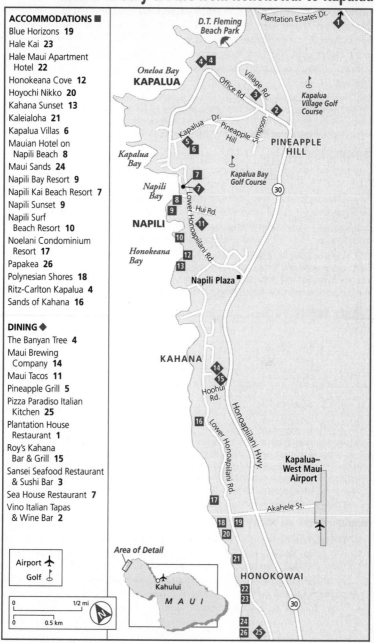

ACCOMMODATIONS ■
Blue Horizons **19**
Hale Kai **23**
Hale Maui Apartment
  Hotel **22**
Honokeana Cove **12**
Hoyochi Nikko **20**
Kahana Sunset **13**
Kaleialoha **21**
Kapalua Villas **6**
Mauian Hotel on
  Napili Beach **8**
Maui Sands **24**
Napili Bay Resort **9**
Napili Kai Beach Resort **7**
Napili Sunset **9**
Napili Surf
  Beach Resort **10**
Noelani Condominium
  Resort **17**
Papakea **26**
Polynesian Shores **18**
Ritz-Carlton Kapalua **4**
Sands of Kahana **16**

DINING ◆
The Banyan Tree **4**
Maui Brewing
  Company **14**
Maui Tacos **11**
Pineapple Grill **5**
Pizza Paradiso Italian
  Kitchen **25**
Plantation House
  Restaurant **1**
Roy's Kahana
  Bar & Grill **15**
Sansei Seafood Restaurant
  & Sushi Bar **3**
Sea House Restaurant **7**
Vino Italian Tapas
  & Wine Bar **2**

Airport ✈
Golf ⛳

0 _____ 1/2 mi
0 _____ 0.5 km

older but in excellent shape; they come with well-equipped kitchens (with dishwasher, disposal, microwave, and blender) and louvered windows that open to the trade winds. Lots of guests clamor for the oceanfront pool units, but I find the park-view units cooler, and they still have ocean views (upstairs units also have cathedral ceilings). This place fills up fast, so book early; repeat guests make up most of the clientele.

3691 Lower Honoapiilani Rd. (in Honokowai), Lahaina, HI 96761. © 800/446-7307 or 808/669-6333. Fax 808/669-7474. www.halekai.com. 25 units. $160 1-bedroom double; $210 2-bedroom (sleeps up to 4); $310 3-bedroom (sleeps up to 6). Extra person $20. 5-night minimum. MC, V. **Amenities:** Outdoor pool; concierge; car-rental desk; coin-op washer/dryers. *In room:* TV/VCR, kitchen, fridge, coffeemaker, hair dryer, iron.

Honokeana Cove *(Value)* These large, secluded units—cozily set around a pool in a lush tropical setting—have fabulous views of Honokeana Cove. The beach here isn't sandy (it's composed of smooth round rocks), but the water just offshore is excellent for snorkeling (turtles have been spotted here) and for whale-watching in winter. The well-appointed units all come with full kitchens and lanais. Amenities include barbecues and deck chairs. The management holds weekly pupu parties so you can meet the other guests. All in all, a well-priced option in an expensive neighborhood.

5255 Lower Honoapiilani Rd. (in Napili), Lahaina, HI 96761. © 800/237-4948 or 808/669-6441. Fax 808/669-8777. www.honokeana-cove.com. 33 units. $189–$205 1-bedroom; $218–$263 2-bedroom (sleeps up to 4); $310 3-bedroom. Extra person $10–$15. 3- to 5-night minimum. MC, V. **Amenities:** Outdoor pool; concierge; coin-op washer/dryers. *In room:* TV/VCR, kitchen, fridge, coffeemaker, iron.

Kahana Sunset *(Kids)* Lying in the crook of a sharp horseshoe curve on Lower Honoapiilani Road is this series of wooden condo units, stair-stepping down the side of a hill to a postcard-perfect white-sand beach. The unique location, nestled between the coastline and the road above, makes this a very private place to stay. In the midst of the buildings sits a grassy lawn with a small pool and Jacuzzi; down by the sandy beach are gazebos and picnic areas. The units feature full kitchens (complete with dishwashers), washer/dryers, large lanais with terrific views, and sleeper sofas. This is a great complex for families: The beach is safe for swimming, the grassy area is away from traffic, and the units are roomy.

4909 Lower Honoapiilani Hwy. (at the northern end of Kahana, almost in Napili), Lahaina, HI 96761. Reservations c/o Premier Properties, P.O. Box 10219, Lahaina, HI 96761. © 800/669-1488 or 808/669-8011. Fax 808/669-9170. www.kahanasunset.com. 79 units. $165–$290 1-bedroom (sleeps up to 4); $225–$465 2-bedroom (sleeps up to 6). AE, MC, V. From Hwy. 30, turn makai (toward the ocean) at the Napili Plaza (Napilihau St.), and then left on Lower Honoapiilani Rd. **Amenities:** 2 outdoor pools (1 for children); concierge. *In room:* TV/DVD/VCR, kitchen, coffeemaker, iron, safe (in some units), washer/dryer.

Mauian Hotel on Napili Beach The Mauian is perched above a beautiful ½-mile-long white-sand beach with great swimming and snorkeling; there's a pool with lounges, umbrellas, and tables on the sun deck; and the verdant grounds burst with tropical color. The rooms feature hardwood floors, Indonesian-style furniture, and big lanais with great views. Thoughtful touches include fresh flowers, plus chilled champagne for guests celebrating a special occasion. There are no phones or TVs in the rooms, but the large *ohana* (family) room does have a TV with a VCR and an extensive library if you need entertainment. There's a barbecue area, great restaurants are just a 5-minute walk away, and Kapalua Resort is up the street. The nightly sunsets off the beach are spectacular.

5441 Lower Honoapiilani Rd. (in Napili), Lahaina, HI 96761. ℭ **800/367-5034** or 808/669-6205. Fax 808/669-0129. www.mauian.com. 44 units. $160–$250 double (sleeps up to 4). Extra person $10. Children 4 and under stay free in parent's room. AE, DISC, MC, V. **Amenities:** Outdoor pool; golf course nearby; tennis courts nearby; shuffleboard court; activities desk; business center w/phones and fax service; free wireless Internet access in family room; coin-op washer/dryers. *In room:* Kitchen, fridge, coffeemaker, no phone.

Napili Sunset *Value*   Housed in three buildings (two on the ocean, one across the street) and located just down the street from Napili Bay (see below), these clean, older, well-maintained units offer good value. At first glance, the plain two-story structures don't look like much, but the location, the moderate prices, and the friendly staff are the real hidden treasures here. In addition to daily maid service, the units all have full kitchens (with dishwashers), ceiling fans (no air-conditioning), sofa beds, small dining rooms, and small bedrooms. The studio units are located in the building off the beach and a few steps up a slight hill; they're a good size, with a full kitchen and either a sofa bed or a Murphy bed, and they overlook the small pool and garden. The one- and two-bedroom units are all on the beach (the downstairs units have lanais that lead right to the sand). The staff makes sure each unit has the basics (paper towels, dishwasher soap, coffee filters, condiments) to get your stay off to a good start. There are restaurants within walking distance. The beach—one of Maui's best—can get a little crowded because the public beach access is through this property (and everyone on Maui seems to want to come here).

46 Hui Rd. (in Napili), Lahaina, HI 96761. ℭ **800/447-9229** or 808/669-8083. Fax 808/669-2730. www.napili sunset.com. 42 units. High season $160 studio double, $310 1-bedroom double, $465 2-bedroom (sleeps up to 4); low season $140 studio, $295 1-bedroom, $450 2-bedroom. Check website for specials. Extra person $15. Children 2 and under stay free in parent's room. 3-night minimum. MC, V. **Amenities:** Small outdoor pool; coin-op washer/ dryers (free detergent supplied). *In room:* TV, kitchen, fridge, coffeemaker.

Napili Surf Beach Resort *Finds*   This well-maintained, superbly landscaped condo complex has a great location on Napili Beach. The well-furnished units (all with full kitchens) were renovated in 2004 with new carpet and new beds, and some units even have all-new kitchens. Free daily maid service, a rarity in condo properties, keeps the place clean. Management encourages socializing: In addition to weekly mai tai parties and coffee socials, the resort hosts annual shuffleboard and golf tournaments, as well as get-togethers on July 4th, Thanksgiving, Christmas, and New Year's. Facilities include three shuffleboard courts and three gas barbecue grills.

50 Napili Place (off Lower Honoapiilani Rd., in Napili), Lahaina, HI 96761. ℭ **800/541-0638** or 808/669-8002. Fax 808/669-8004. www.napilisurf.com. 53 units (some with shower only). $111–$237 studio double (sleeps up to 3); $190–$336 1-bedroom double (sleeps up to 4). Extra person $15. No credit cards. **Amenities:** 2 outdoor pools; shuffleboard courts; coin-op washer/dryers. *In room:* TV/VCR, kitchen, fridge, coffeemaker, iron, safe.

Noelani Condominium Resort *Kids*   This oceanfront condo is a great value, whether you stay in a studio or a three-bedroom unit (ideal for large families). Everything is first class, from the furnishings to the oceanfront location. Though it's on the water, there's no sandy beach here (despite the photos posted on the website)—but right next door is a sandy cove at the county park. There's good snorkeling off the cove, which is frequented by spinner dolphins and turtles in summer and humpback whales in winter. All units feature complete kitchens, entertainment centers, and spectacular views (all except the studio units also have their own washer/dryers and dishwashers). My favorites are in the Anthurium Building, where the condos have oceanfront lanais just 20 feet from the water. Frugal travelers will love the deluxe studios in the Orchid Building, with great ocean views. Guests are invited to a continental breakfast orientation on their first day and mai tai parties at night; there are also oceanfront barbecue grills for guest use.

4095 Lower Honoapiilani Rd. (in Kahana), Lahaina, HI 96761. ℂ **800/367-6030** or 808/669-8374. Fax 808/669-7904. www.noelani-condo-resort.com. 50 units. $125–$175 studio double; $175–$197 1-bedroom (sleeps up to 4); $240–$290 2-bedroom (sleeps up to 6); $330–$335 3-bedroom (sleeps up to 8). Rates include continental breakfast on 1st morning. Extra person $20. Children 17 and under stay free in parent's room. Packages for honeymooners, seniors, and AAA members available. 3-night minimum. AE, MC, V. **Amenities:** 2 freshwater pools (1 heated for night swimming); access to nearby health club; oceanfront Jacuzzi; concierge; activities desk; car-rental desk; coin-op washer/dryers. *In room:* TV/VCR, kitchen, fridge, coffeemaker, hair dryer, iron, safe, washer/dryer (in larger units).

INEXPENSIVE

In addition to the choices below, consider **Hale Maui Apartment Hotel** (ℂ **808/669-6312;** fax 808/669-1302; www.halemauivacationrental.com), a wonderful, tiny place run by Hans and Eva Zimmerman and daughter Marika, whose spirit is 100% aloha. The one-bedroom suites (completely remodeled in 2007), which start at around $95 for a double, come with ceiling fans, private lanais, and complete kitchens. There's no pool, but a private path leads to a great swimming beach.

Another option is **Hoyochi Nikko,** 3901 Lower Honoapiilani Rd. (in Honokowai), Lahaina, HI 96761 (ℂ **800/487-6002,** ext. 1, or 808/669-0089, ext. 1; fax 808/669-3937; www.mauilodging.com), which has 17 older (but well-maintained) one- and two-bedroom units sharing 180 feet of oceanfront ($140–$230 one-bedroom double).

Blue Horizons *(Finds* This is the only bed-and-breakfast on this stretch of west Maui, about a 10-minute drive to Lahaina and about a 5-minute walk to sandy beaches. The four units, in a custom-built home in a subdivision, range from compact to spacious suites with separate bedrooms and a living-room area with sofa bed. Three units have kitchenettes, and all four are air-conditioned, which helps not only with the heat but also with the noise of the subdivision. A lavish breakfast is served in the screened dining area, where the ocean view may distract you from the banana pancakes.

3894 Mahinahina St. (in Kahana, 1 block from Honoapiilani Hwy.), Lahaina, HI 96761. ℂ **800/669-1948** or 808/669-1965. Fax 808/665-1615. www.bluehorizonsmaui.com. 4 units. $109–$149 double. 2-night minimum. Rates include breakfast Mon–Sat. Extra person $15. AE, MC, V. **Amenities:** Small outdoor pool; free use of washer/dryers. *In room:* A/C, TV/VCR (and access to video library), kitchenette (in 3 units), fridge, coffeemaker (in some units).

Kaleialoha This condo complex for the budget-minded has recently been upgraded, with new paint, bedspreads, and drapes in each apartment. Each one-bedroom unit has a sofa bed in the living room, which allows you to comfortably sleep four. All of the Island-style units feature fully equipped kitchens, with everything from dishwashers to washer/dryers (but bring your own beach towels). There's great ocean swimming just off the rock wall (no sandy beach); a protective reef mows waves down and allows even timid swimmers to relax.

3785 Lower Honoapiilani Rd. (in Honokowai), Lahaina, HI 96761. ℂ **800/222-8688** or 808/669-8197. Fax 808/669-2502. www.mauicondosoceanfront.com. 21 units. $185–$215 1-bedroom double. Cleaning fee $75 for stays of under 7 nights. Extra person $10. 3- to 5-night minimum. MC, V. **Amenities:** Outdoor pool; concierge; activities desk; coin-op washer/dryers. *In room:* TV/DVD, kitchen, fridge, coffeemaker, washer/dryer.

Maui Sands The Maui Sands was built back when property wasn't as expensive and developers took the extra time and money to surround their condos with lush landscaping. It's hard to get a unit with a bad view: All face either the ocean (with views of Lanai and Molokai) or tropical gardens blooming with brilliant heliconia, flowering hibiscus,

Nickel-and-Dime Charges at High-Priced Hotels

Several upscale resorts in Hawaii engage in a practice that I find distasteful, dishonest, and downright discouraging: charging a so-called "resort fee." This daily fee (generally $15–$20 a day) is added on to your bill for such "complimentary" items as a daily newspaper, local phone calls, and use of the fitness facilities—amenities that the resort used to happily provide its guests for free. In most cases, you do not have an option to decline the resort fee—in other words, this is a sneaky way to further increase the nightly rate without telling you. I oppose this practice and urge you to voice your complaints to the resort management. Otherwise, what'll be next—a charge for using the tiny bars of soap or miniature shampoo bottles?

and sweet-smelling ginger. Each roomy unit has a lanai and a full kitchen. With two big bedrooms, plus space in the living room for a fifth person (or even a sixth), the larger units are good deals for families. There's a narrow beach out front.

Maui Resort Management, 3600 Lower Honoapiilani Rd. (in Honokowai), Lahaina, HI 96761. © 800/367-5037 or 808/669-1900. Fax 808/878-8790. www.mauiresortmanagement.com. 76 units. $95–$220 1-bedroom (sleeps up to 4). MC, V. **Amenities:** Outdoor pool; coin-op washer/dryers. *In room:* A/C, TV, kitchen, fridge, coffeemaker.

Napili Bay Resort *Finds*   One of Maui's best bargains is this small two-story complex right on Napili's beautiful ½-mile white-sand beach. It's perfect for a romantic getaway: The atmosphere is comfortable and relaxing, the ocean lulls you to sleep at night, and birdsong wakes you in the morning. The beach here is one of the best on the coast, with great swimming and snorkeling—in fact, it's so beautiful that people staying at much more expensive resorts down the road frequently come here. The studio apartments are definitely small, but they pack in everything you need to feel at home, from a full kitchen to a comfortable queen-size bed, plus a roomy lanai that's great for watching the sun set over the Pacific. There's no air-conditioning, but louvered windows and ceiling fans keep the units fairly cool during the day. There are lots of restaurants and a convenience store within walking distance, and you're about 10 to 15 minutes away from Lahaina and some great golf courses.

33 Hui Dr. (off Lower Honoapiilani Hwy., in Napili), Lahaina, HI 96761. Reservations c/o Aloha Condos Hawaii, P.O. Box 396681, Keauhou, HI 96740. © 877/782-5642. www.alohacondos.com. 33 units. $120–$315 double. Cleaning fee $85–$100. 5-night minimum. MC, V. **Amenities:** Coin-op washer/dryers. *In room:* TV, kitchen, fridge, coffeemaker.

Papakea *Value*   Just a mile down the beach from Kaanapali lie these low-rise buildings, surrounded by manicured, landscaped grounds and ocean views galore. Palm trees and tropical plants dot the property, a putting green wraps around two kidney-shaped pools, and a footbridge arches over a lily pond brimming with carp. Each pool has its own private cabana with sauna, Jacuzzi, and barbecue grills; a poolside shop rents snorkel gear for exploring the offshore reefs. All units have dishwashers, big lanais, and washer/dryers. The studios have pull-down beds to save space during the day. Definitely a good value.

Maui Resort Management, 3600 Lower Honoapiilani Rd. (in Honokowai), Lahaina, HI 96761. © 800/367-5037 or 808/669-1900. Fax 808/669-8790. www.mauigetaway.com. 364 units. $115–$155 studio double; $155–$190 1-bedroom (sleeps up to 4); $175–$240 2-bedroom (sleeps up to 6). 7-night minimum. MC, V. **Amenities:** 2 outdoor pools; 3 tennis courts; 2 Jacuzzis; watersports equipment rental; washer/dryer. *In room:* A/C, TV/VCR, kitchen, fridge, coffeemaker, washer/dryer.

KAPALUA

VERY EXPENSIVE

Ritz-Carlton Kapalua *(RRR) (Kids)*   This Ritz is a complete universe, one of those resorts where you can happily sit by the ocean with a book for 2 whole weeks and never leave the grounds. It rises proudly on a knoll, in a singularly spectacular setting between the rainforest and the sea. During construction, the burial sites of hundreds of ancient Hawaiians were discovered in the sand, so the hotel was moved inland to avoid disrupting the graves. The setback gives the hotel a commanding view of Molokai.

In 2008, the Ritz reopened after an extensive $160-million renovation that transformed the place into an even more elegant property, with a focus on a Hawaiian (vs. the former European) theme. All guest rooms now have the latest technology, including flatscreen TVs, DVD players, iPod docking stations, and wireless Internet access (included in the resort fee). Marble bathrooms and private lanais are other nice touches. The penthouse floor has been converted into Residential Suites (with kitchens, living rooms, and separate bedrooms), available for guests. If you can afford it, stay on the **Club Level** *(RRR)*—it offers the best amenities in the state, from French-roast coffee in the morning to a buffet at lunch, from cookies in the afternoon to pupu and drinks at sunset.

Other transformations include upgrades to the signature 10,000-square-foot, three-tiered pool; a new children's pool; an Environmental Education Center; and a new 17,500-square-foot Waihua Spa, with 15 treatment rooms, saunas, whirlpool with lava-stone walls, and fitness center. Your children will enjoy the Ritz Kids program's wide variety of activities, plus the weekly "Ritz Kids Night Out" that allows parents to spend a quiet evening alone.

1 Ritz-Carlton Dr., Kapalua, HI 96761. (C) **800/262-8440** or 808/669-6200. Fax 808/669-1566. www.ritzcarlton.com. 548 units. $599–$649 double; $700–$875 Club Level double; from $759 suite; from $2,000 Club Level suite. Extra person $50 ($150 in Club Level rooms). Daily $20 resort fee for use of fitness center, steam room, and sauna; selected wellness classes; Aloha Friday festivities; cultural-history tours; in-room wireless Internet access; self-parking; resort shuttle service; morning coffee at the Lobby Lounge; preferred tee times; 9-hole putting green; tennis and basketball courts; and games of bocce ball on the lawn. Wedding/honeymoon, golf, and other packages available. AE, DC, DISC, MC, V. Valet parking $18; free self-parking. **Amenities:** 4 restaurants (including the Banyan Tree, p. 157); 4 bars (including 1 serving drinks and light fare next to the beach); outdoor pool; access to the Kapalua Resort's 3 championship golf courses (each w/its own pro shop), golf academy, and deluxe tennis complex; fitness room; spa; 2 outdoor hot tubs; watersports equipment rentals; bike rentals; children's program; game room; concierge; activities desk; car-rental desk; business center; shopping arcade; salon; room service; in-room and spa massage; babysitting; same-day laundry service and dry cleaning; concierge-level rooms (some of Hawaii's best). *In room:* A/C, TV, dataport, wireless Internet access, coffeemaker, hair dryer, iron.

EXPENSIVE

If you're interested in a luxurious condo or town house, consider **Kapalua Villas** (*(C)* **800/545-0018** or 808/669-8088; www.kapaluavillas.com). The palatial units dotting the oceanfront cliffs and fairways of this idyllic coast are a (relative) bargain, especially if you're traveling with a group. The one-bedroom condos go for $279 to $579; two-bedrooms for $389 to $809; and three-bedrooms for $549 to $799, plus a $20 daily resort fee (which covers parking; unlimited local, national, and international calls; and high-speed Internet access). Numerous package deals (which include golf, tennis, honeymoon amenities, and car) can save you even more money.

3 South Maui

I recommend two booking agencies that rent a host of condominiums and unique vacation homes in the Kihei/Wailea/Maalaea area: **Kihei Maui Vacations** (℗ **800/ 541-6284** or 808/879-7581; www.kmvmaui.com) and **Condominium Rentals Hawaii** (℗ **800/367-5242** or 808/879-2778; www.crhmaui.com).

KIHEI
EXPENSIVE

In addition to the choices below, consider the **ResortQuest at the Maui Banyan** (℗ **866/77-HAWAII** [774-2924] or 808/875-0004; www.resortquesthawaii.com), a condo property across the street from Kamaole Beach Park II. The large one- to three-bedroom units are very nicely done and feature full kitchens, air-conditioning, and washer/dryers. Rates start at $175 for hotel rooms ($149 if you book online), $215 for one-bedroom units ($173 online), and $275 for two-bedroom units ($231 online); be sure to ask about packages.

Hale Pau Hana Resort ⚲ ⁽Kids⁾   Located on the sandy shores of Kamaole Beach Park but separated from the white-sand beach by a velvet-green manicured lawn, this is a great condo resort for families. Each of the large units has a private lanai, a terrific ocean view, and a complete kitchen. The management goes above and beyond, personally greeting each guest and acting as your own concierge service. Guests can mingle at the free coffee hour every morning, or at the pupu parties with local Hawaiian entertainment held twice a week at sunset. The location is in the heart of Kihei, close to shopping, restaurants, and activities.

2480 S. Kihei Rd., Kihei, HI 96753. ℗ **800/367-6036** or 808/879-2715. Fax 808/875-0238. www.hphresort.com. 79 units. $249–$349 1-bedroom; $331–$401 2-bedroom. MC, V. **Amenities:** Outdoor pool; concierge; coin-op washer/dryers; barbecue. In room: A/C in bedrooms, TV, full kitchen, fridge, coffeemaker, hair dryer, iron, safe.

Maalaea Surf Resort ⚲   Enjoy a quiet, relaxing vacation on this well-landscaped property, with a beautiful white-sand beach right outside. Located at the quiet end of Kihei Road, this two-story complex sprawls across 5 acres of lush tropical gardens. The luxury town houses all have ocean views, big kitchens (with dishwashers), cable TV, and VCRs. Amenities include maid service (Mon–Sat), shuffleboard, barbecue grills, and discounts on tee times at nearby golf courses; restaurants and shops are within a 5-minute drive.

12 S. Kihei Rd. (at S. Kihei Rd. and Hwy. 350), Kihei, HI 96753. ℗ **800/423-7953** or 808/879-1267. Fax 808/ 874-2884. www.maalaeasurfresort.com. 34 units. $285–$335 1-bedroom (sleeps up to 4); $380–$450 2-bedroom (sleeps up to 6). MC, V. **Amenities:** 2 outdoor pools; 2 tennis courts; concierge; activities desk; car-rental desk; coin-op washer/dryers. In room: A/C, TV/VCR/DVD, kitchen, fridge, coffeemaker, hair dryer, iron, safe.

Maui Coast Hotel ⚲   This place stands out as one of the few hotels in Kihei (which is largely full of affordable condo complexes rather than traditional hotels or resorts). The Extra Value Package gives you a rental car for just a few dollars more than your room rate. The other chief advantage of this hotel is its location, about a block from Kamaole Beach Park I, with plenty of bars, restaurants, and shopping within walking distance, plus a golf course nearby. Guest rooms offer extras such as sitting areas, whirlpool tubs, ceiling fans, and private lanais.

2259 S. Kihei Rd. (1 block from Kamaole Beach Park I), Kihei, HI 96753. © 800/895-6284 or 808/874-6284. Fax 808/875-4731. www.mauicoasthotel.com. 265 units. $265 double; $305 suite; $345 1-bedroom (sleeps up to 4). Children 17 and under stay free in parent's room using existing bedding. Rollaway bed $20. Packages available. AE, DC, DISC, MC, V. **Amenities:** Restaurant; pool bar w/nightly entertainment; outdoor pool (plus children's wading pool); 2 lighted tennis courts; fitness room; concierge; activities desk; room service; washer/dryers; laundry service; dry cleaning. *In room:* A/C, TV, fridge, coffeemaker, hair dryer, iron, safe.

ResortQuest Maui Hill 🐠   If you can't decide between the privacy of a condo and the conveniences of a hotel, try this place. Maui Hill gives you the best of both worlds. Located on a hill above the heat of Kihei town, this large Spanish-style resort (with stucco buildings, red-tile roofs, and arched entries) combines all the amenities and activities of a hotel—pool, hot tub, tennis courts, Hawaiiana classes, maid service, and more—with large luxury condos that have full kitchens and plenty of privacy. Nearly all units have ocean views, dishwashers, washer/dryers, queen-size sofa beds, and big lanais. Beaches, restaurants, and shops are within easy walking distance; a golf course is nearby; and barbecue grills are provided for guests' use. The management here goes out of its way to make sure your stay is perfect. *Note:* Some of the units have converted to timeshares, although no timeshare salesperson bothered me during my stay.

2881 S. Kihei Rd. (across from Kamaole Park III, between Keonekai St. and Kilohana Dr.), Kihei, HI 96753. © 866/77-HAWAII (774-2924) or 808/879-6321. Fax 808/879-8945. www.resortquesthawaii.com. 140 units. $230–$335 1-bedroom ($200–$260 if you book online); $285–$420 2-bedroom (from $236 online); $415–$535 3-bedroom (from $361 online). Extra person $30. AE, DC, DISC, MC, V. **Amenities:** Outdoor pool; putting green; tennis courts; Jacuzzi; concierge; activities desk; car-rental desk; coin-op washer/dryers; laundry service; dry cleaning. *In room:* A/C, TV/VCR, kitchen, fridge, coffeemaker, hair dryer, iron, safe, washer/dryer.

MODERATE

The **Kihei Beach Resorts,** 36 S. Kihei Rd., Kihei, HI 96753 (© 800/367-6034 or 808/879-2744; fax 808/875-0306; www.kiheibeachresort.com), has spacious condos right on the beach. The downside is the constant traffic noise from Kihei Road. Rates are $155 to $180 for a one-bedroom double, $260 to $270 for a two-bedroom (sleeps four); there's a 4-night minimum and a $25 charge per extra person.

Eva Villa 🐠🐠 *(Finds)*   This three-unit bed-and-breakfast is located on ½ acre of lushly landscaped property at the top of the Maui Meadows subdivision. From the rooftop lanai, guests have a spectacular view of the sunset behind Kahoolawe and Lanai, and in the distance the West Maui Mountains. Hosts Rick and Dale Pounds have done everything to make this one of Maui's classiest vacation rentals. From the continental breakfast stocked in the unit's kitchen (fresh fruit, juice, bread, muffins, jam, coffee, and tea) to the decor of the suites, from the heated pool and Jacuzzi to the individual barbecue facilities, this is a great place to stay. The location couldn't be better—just a few minutes' drive to Kihei's sunny beaches, restaurants in Kihei and Wailea, golf courses, and plenty of tennis and shopping. Each unit is a roomy 600 square feet. The separate cottage has a living room, full kitchen, bedroom, and washer/dryer; the poolside studio is a one-room unit with a huge kitchen; and the poolside suite has two bedrooms and a kitchenette. You can't go wrong booking here.

815 Kumulani Dr., Kihei, HI 96753. © 800/824-6409 or 808/874-6407. Fax 808/874-6407. www.mauibnb.com. 3 units. $155–$175 double. Extra person $20. 4-night minimum. No credit cards. **Amenities:** Heated outdoor pool; Jacuzzi. *In room:* TV/DVD, CD player, wireless Internet access, kitchen or kitchenette, fridge, coffeemaker.

Kamaole Nalu Oceanfront Resort   This six-story condominium complex is located between two beach parks, Kamaole I and Kamaole II, and right across the street from a shopping complex. Units have fabulous ocean views, large living rooms,

Where to Stay in South Maui

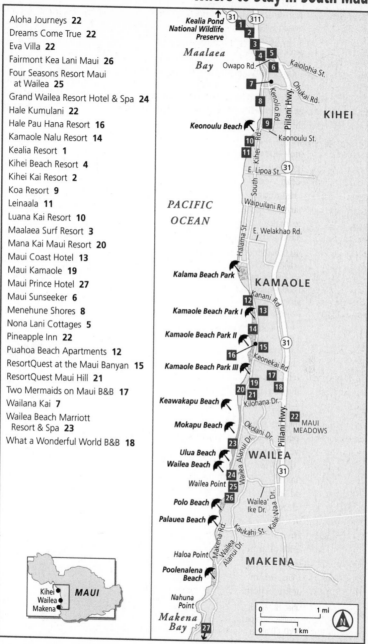

and private lanais; the kitchens are a bit small but come fully equipped. I recommend no. 306 for its wonderful bird's-eye view. The property also has an oceanside pool and great barbecue facilities. Restaurants, bars, a golf course, and tennis courts are nearby. *Warning:* Because the building is right on Kihei Road, it can be noisy.

2450 S. Kihei Rd. (btw. Kanani and Keonekai rds., next to Kamaole Beach Park II), Kihei, HI 96753. © 800/767-1497 or 808/879-1006. Fax 808/879-8693. www.kamaolenalu.com. 36 units. High season $250–$350 double; low season $190–$275 double. Extra person $20. Children 12 and under stay free in parent's room using existing bedding. 5-night minimum. MC, V. **Amenities:** Outdoor pool; activities desk; car-rental desk. *In room:* TV, kitchen, fridge, coffeemaker, hair dryer, iron, safe, washer/dryer.

Kealia Resort (Value) This oceanfront property at the northern end of Kihei is well maintained and nicely furnished—and the prices are excellent. But as tempting as the lower-priced units may sound, don't give in: They face noisy Kihei Road and are near a major junction, so you'll be listening to big trucks downshifting all night. Instead, go for one of the oceanview units, which all have full kitchens and private lanais. The grounds face a 5-mile stretch of white-sand beach. Social gatherings include free coffee-and-doughnut get-togethers every Friday morning and pupu parties on Wednesdays.

191 N. Kihei Rd. (north of Hwy. 31, at the Maalaea end of Kihei), Kihei, HI 96753. © 800/265-0686 or 808/879-0952. Fax 808/875-1540. www.kealiaresort.com. 51 units. $115–$130 studio double; $150–$190 1-bed-room double; $215–$250 2-bedroom (sleeps up to 4). Extra person $10. Children 12 and under stay free in parent's room. 4-night minimum. MC, V. **Amenities:** Outdoor pool. *In room:* TV, kitchen, fridge, coffeemaker, hair dryer, iron, washer/dryer.

Leinaala (★) From Kihei Road, you can't see Leinaala amid the jumble of buildings, but this oceanfront boutique condo offers excellent accommodations at moderate prices. The building is set back from the water, with a county park—an oasis of green grass and tennis courts—in between. A golf course is nearby. The units are compact but filled with everything you need: a full kitchen, sofa bed, and oceanview lanai. (Hideaway beds are available if you need one.)

998 S. Kihei Rd., Kihei, HI 96753. © 800/822-4409 or 808/879-2235. Fax 808/874-6144. www.mauicondo.com. 24 units. $150–$170 1-bedroom double; $195–$220 2-bedroom (sleeps up to 4). 4-night minimum. No credit cards. **Amenities:** Outdoor pool; coin-op washer/dryers. *In room:* A/C, TV, kitchen, fridge, coffeemaker.

Mana Kai Maui Resort (★) (Kids) This eight-story complex, situated on a beautiful white-sand cove, is an unusual combination of hotel and condominium. The hotel rooms, which account for half of the total number of units, are small but nicely fur-nished. Families should consider the condo units, which feature full kitchens and open living rooms with sliding-glass doors that lead to small lanais overlooking the sandy beach and ocean. Some units are beginning to show their age (the building is more than 30 years old), but they're all clean and comfortable. One of the best snor-keling beaches on the coast is just steps away; a golf course and tennis courts are nearby.

2960 S. Kihei Rd. (btw. Kilohana and Keonekai rds., at the Wailea end of Kihei), Kihei, HI 96753. © 800/367-5242 or 808/879-2778. Fax 808/879-7825. www.crhmaui.com. 105 units. $150–$185 hotel room double; $230–$325 1-bedroom (sleeps up to 4); $280–$400 2-bedroom (up to 6). AE, MC, V. **Amenities:** Restaurant (Five Palms, p. 159); bar; outdoor pool; concierge; coin-op washer/dryers. *In room:* A/C (in hotel rooms only), TV, kitchen (in condo units), fridge, coffeemaker, safe.

Maui Kamaole You'll find this condo complex right across the street from the Kihei Public Boat Ramp and beautiful Kamaole Beach Park III, which is great for swimming, snorkeling, and beachcombing. Each roomy, fully furnished unit comes with a private lanai, two bathrooms (even in the one-bedroom units), and an all-electric kitchen. The one-bedroom units—which can comfortably accommodate four—are quite a deal, especially if you're traveling in low season. The grounds are nicely landscaped and offer barbecues. Restaurants and bars are within walking distance; a golf course and tennis courts are also nearby.

2777 S. Kihei Rd. (btw. Keonekai and Kilohana rds., at the Wailea end of Kihei), Kihei, HI 96753. ℂ 800/822-4409 or 808/874-8467. Fax 808/875-9117. www.mauikamaole.com. 62 of the 210 units are in the rental pool. $180–$250 1-bedroom (sleeps up to 4); $240–$320 2-bedroom (sleeps up to 6). AE, MC, V. **Amenities:** 2 outdoor pools; tennis courts; Jacuzzi. *In room:* A/C, TV, kitchen, fridge, coffeemaker, iron, safe (in some units), washer/dryer.

Maui Sunseeker *Finds* This former budget property, located just across the street from a terrific white-sand beach, has a new management team that has spiffed up the studio and one-bedroom units by adding custom furniture, air-conditioning, and other amenities not usually seen at small properties (like high-speed Internet access and concierge services). The redone units have been tastefully decorated. The one-bedrooms, which have a pullout sofa in the living room and new appliances in the kitchen, are a deal during low season. All units have private oceanview lanais and the beach just a few steps away, plus there's a gas barbecue for guests' use. The new owners also bought the apartment complex next door, where they've revamped everything, put slate in the bathrooms and new tile on the floor, bought new furniture, and repainted. The units are small, but the lanais are large and the price is right—and there's even a rooftop lanai where you can sit in the hot tub and enjoy great ocean views.

551 S. Kihei Rd. (P.O. Box 276), Kihei, HI 96753. ℂ 800/532-6284 or 808/879-1261. Fax 808/874-3877. www. mauisunseeker.com. 16 units. $145–$215 hotel room double; $165–$215 studio double; $195–$245 junior suite double; $215–$285 premium junior suite double; $215–$340 1-bedroom double; $365–$585 penthouse apt. Extra person $15. AE, DISC, MC, V. **Amenities:** Hot tub; concierge; coin-op washer/dryers; same-day laundry service. *In room:* A/C, TV/VCR, wireless Internet access, kitchen or kitchenette, coffeemaker, hair dryer, answering machine.

Punahoa Beach Apartments *Value* Book this place! I can't put it any more simply than that. The location—off noisy, traffic-ridden Kihei Road, on a quiet side street with ocean frontage—is fabulous. A grassy lawn rolls about 50 feet down to the beach, where there's great snorkeling just offshore and a popular surfing spot next door; shopping and restaurants are all within walking distance. All of the beautifully decorated units in this small four-story building have fully equipped kitchens and lanais with great ocean views. Rooms go quickly in winter, so reserve early.

2142 Ililili Rd. (off S. Kihei Rd., 300 ft. from Kamaole Beach I), Kihei, HI 96753. ℂ 800/564-4380 or 808/879-2720. Fax 808/875-9147. www.punahoabeach.com. 13 units. $116–$150 studio double; $160–$231 1-bedroom double; $198–$263 2-bedroom double; $188–$258 1-bedroom penthouse. Extra person $15. 5-night minimum. AE, MC, V. **Amenities:** Coin-op washer/dryer. *In room:* TV, kitchen, fridge, coffeemaker, iron.

INEXPENSIVE

In addition to the choices below, also check out **Luana Kai Resort,** 940 S. Kihei Rd., Kihei, HI 96753 (ℂ **800/669-1127** or 808/879-1268; fax 808/879-1455; www. luanakai.com). This older condo complex has 113 units ($109–$209 one-bedroom; $129–$229 two-bedroom; $249–$299 three-bedroom; 4-night minimum).

Kihei Kai Resort, 61 N. Kihei Rd., Kihei, HI 96753 (ℂ **888/778-7717** or 808/891-0780; fax 808/891-9403; www.kiheikai.com), has one-bedroom apartments ($115–$149 double; 4- to 7-night minimum) that are ideal for families.

Aloha Journeys *Finds* Tucked into the residential neighborhood of Maui Meadows (and a 5-min. drive from the nearest good beach), this vacation-home rental, dubbed Hale Alana, is a three-bedroom, three-bathroom Polynesian-style home that comes complete with air-conditioning, three TVs, VCR, stereo, CD player, three cordless phones and an answering machine, full kitchen, open dining room, breakfast bar, and laundry room. It's a terrific deal for a large family or three couples traveling together. The two master bedrooms have California-king-size beds, walk-in closets, and dual sinks and showerheads; the third bedroom has two double beds and a large closet. Skylights, ceiling fans, and an interior lava-rock wall add to the tropical environment. The deck has outdoor tables and chairs, a barbecue grill, and a fabulous hot tub.

490 Mikioi Place (in Maui Meadows), Kihei, HI 96753. (*C*) **800/871-5032** or 808/875-4840. Fax 808/879-3998. www.alohajourneys.com. 1 unit. $350–$420 3-bedroom for 4. Cleaning fee $200. Extra person $35. 7-night minimum. MC, V. **Amenities:** Jacuzzi; laundry facilities. *In room:* A/C, TV/VCR/DVD, kitchen, fridge, coffeemaker, hair dryer.

Dreams Come True on Maui *(Value)*   This bed-and-breakfast (where "you are never just renting a room") was a dream come true for hosts Tom Croly and Denise McKinnon, who, after several years of vacationing to Maui, opened this three-unit property in 2002. It's centrally located in the Maui Meadows subdivision, just a few minutes' drive to golf courses, tennis courts, white-sand beaches, shopping, and restaurants in Kihei and Wailea. The one-bedroom oceanview cottage has its own gourmet kitchen, two TVs, a washer/dryer, a computer with high-speed Internet access, and wraparound decks. Also available are two rooms in the house (one with king-size bed, one with queen-size), each with TV, private entrance, kitchenette, use of washer/dryer, and lots of other amenities not usually found in B&Bs. Guests are invited to use the centrally located oceanview deck; the house living room, which has a computer with high-speed Internet connection; and an outdoor cooking area with barbecue grill, sink, and microwave. Every guest is given personal concierge treatment, from the lowdown on good snorkeling to a tour of the property. In the evenings, Tom shows movies on an 8-foot-wide movie screen and frequently helps guests transfer their digital images to a CD so they can go out and shoot more photos of Maui. The owners recently acquired a one- and two-bedroom condo, across the street from the beach, which they rent for $125 to $169 a night.

3259 Akala Dr., Kihei, HI 96753. (*C*) **877/782-9628** or 808/879-7099. Fax 808/879-7099. www.dreamscometrueon maui.com. 3 units. $89–$109 room double (3- to 4-night minimum); $125–$169 cottage double (6-night minimum; extra person $15). Room rates include breakfast. MC, V. **Amenities:** Concierge service; washer/dryer. *In room:* A/C ($3–$5 per day), TV/VCR, CD player, kitchen or kitchenette, fridge, coffeemaker, hair dryer.

Hale Kumulani *(Finds)*   At the top of the Maui Meadows subdivision, right on the Wailea border and about a 5-minute drive to the beach, lies this ½-acre property, surrounded by a 40,000-acre wilderness area with two quaint units. The first is a darling one-room cottage with full kitchen, wood flooring, high beamed ceilings, living-room area (with king bed and full-size guest sofa/futon), large deck, and outdoor shower. Underneath the main house, but with its own entrance and complete privacy, is the waterfall suite. It has a full kitchen, two bedrooms, two bathrooms, and a living/dining area that opens to a landscaped area with a waterfall plus banana and papaya trees. (It's also wheelchair-accessible.) Both units have access to the organic vegetable garden, numerous fruit trees, and beach equipment. Hosts Ron and Merry couldn't be more gracious in helping you navigate the island. They also have a full-size crib, stroller, and junior beds available for kids.

874 Kumulani Dr. (in Maui Meadows), Kihei, HI 96753. © 808/891-0425. Fax 808/891-0269. www.cottagemaui. com. 2 units. $135 waterfall suite; $155 cottage double. 4-night minimum. MC, V. **Amenities:** 6 championship golf courses within 5 miles; aquatic center w/3 pools nearby (a 7-min. drive). In room: TV/DVD, Wi-Fi, kitchen, fridge, coffeemaker, hair dryer, iron, washer/dryer.

Koa Resort 🌴 (Kids

Located just across the street from the ocean, Koa Resort comprises five two-story wooden buildings on more than 5½ acres of landscaped grounds. There's plenty of room for families, who can enjoy the tennis courts, pool, and putting green. The spacious, privately owned one-, two-, and three-bedroom units are decorated with care and come fully equipped, right down to the dishwasher and disposal in the kitchens. The larger condos have both showers and tubs; the smaller units have showers only. All feature large lanais, ceiling fans, and washer/dryers. For maximum peace and quiet, ask for a unit far from Kihei Road. Bars, restaurants, and a golf course are nearby.

811 S. Kihei Rd. (btw. Kulanihakoi St. and Namauu Place), Kihei, HI 96753. Reservations c/o Bello Realty, P.O. Box 1776, Kihei, HI 96753. © 800/541-3060 or 808/879-3328. Fax 808/875-1483. www.bellomaui.com. 54 units (some with shower only). $99–$115 1-bedroom; $100–$140 2-bedroom; $160–$275 3-bedroom. MC, V. **Amenities:** Outdoor pool; 18-hole putting green; 2 tennis courts; Jacuzzi. In room: TV, kitchen, fridge, coffeemaker, iron, safe, washer/dryer.

Menehune Shores (Value

If you plan to stay on Maui for a week, you might want to look into the car/condo packages here; they're a real deal, especially for families on a budget. The six-story Menehune Shores is more than 4 decades old and is showing its age in some places, but all units are well maintained and have ocean views and lanais. The design is straight out of the 1970s, but the view is timeless. The kitchens are fully equipped, all units have washer/dryers, and the oceanfront location guarantees a steady breeze that keeps the rooms cool (there's no air-conditioning). The building sits in front of the ancient Hawaiian fishponds of Kalepolepo. Some Hawaiians still fish them using traditional throw nets, but generally the pond serves as protection from the ocean waves, making it safe for children (and those unsure of their ability) to swim in the relatively calm waters. There's also a heated pool, shuffleboard courts, and a whale-watching platform on the roof garden. Don't expect the Ritz, but this budget option offers oceanfront units at affordable prices in the heart of Kihei.

760 S. Kihei Rd. (btw. Kaonoulu and Hoonani sts.), P.O. Box 1327, Kihei, HI 96753. © 800/558-9117 or 808/879-3428. Fax 808/879-5218. www.menehunereservations.com. 64 units. $150–$180 1-bedroom double ($1,219 per week with car); $175–$190 2-bedroom for up to 4 ($1,419–$1,529 per week with car); $225–$285 3-bedroom for up to 6 ($1,909 per week with car). 3-night minimum. Extra person $7.50. No credit cards. **Amenities:** Restaurant; bar; outdoor pool. In room: TV/VCR, kitchen, fridge, coffeemaker, washer/dryer.

Nona Lani Cottages 🌴 (Finds

Picture this: a grassy expanse dotted with eight cottages tucked among palm, fruit, and sweet-smelling flower trees, right across the street from a white-sand beach. This is one of the great hidden deals in Kihei. The cottages are tiny but contain everything you'll need: a small but complete kitchen, twin beds that double as couches in the living room, a separate bedroom with a queen-size bed, and a lanai with table and chairs. The cottages were renovated in 2002 with new ceramic flooring. The real attraction, however, is the garden setting next to the beach. There are no phones in the cabins, but there's a public one by the check-in area. There's also a barbecue area. Your hosts, the industrious Kong family, also run Happy Valley Hale (p. 104), hostel accommodations on the other side of the island in Happy Valley, next to Wailuku.

455 S. Kihei Rd. (just south of Hwy. 31), P.O. Box 655, Kihei, HI 96753. © 800/733-2688 or 808/879-2497. www.nonalanicottages.com. 11 units. $105–$150 cottage double. Extra person $15. 7-night minimum in high season. No credit cards. **Amenities:** Coin-op washer/dryers. *In room:* A/C, TV, kitchen, fridge, coffeemaker, no phone.

Pineapple Inn Maui (Finds) Opened in late 2004, this charming inn (four rooms, plus a two-bedroom cottage) is not only an exquisite find, but also a terrific value. Located in the residential Maui Meadows area, with panoramic ocean views, the two-story inn is expertly landscaped, with a lily pond in the front and a giant saltwater pool and Jacuzzi overlooking the ocean. Each of the expertly decorated, soundproof rooms (you won't hear the traffic from nearby Piilani Hwy.) has a private lanai with incredible view, plus a small kitchenette stocked with juice, pastries, and drinks on your arrival. There's also a darling two-bedroom, one-bathroom cottage (wood floors, beautiful artwork) that's landscaped for maximum privacy and has a full kitchen (even a dishwasher), separate bedrooms, phone and answering machine, and private lanai. There's a barbecue area for guests.

3170 Akala Dr., Kihei, HI 96753. © 877/212-MAUI (6284) or 808/298-4403. www.pineappleinnmaui.com. 5 units. $119–$149 double; $195–$215 cottage for 4. 3-night minimum for rooms, 6-night minimum for cottage. No credit cards. **Amenities:** Large saltwater pool; Jacuzzi; complimentary laundry facilities. *In room:* A/C, TV/VCR, wireless Internet access, kitchenette or kitchen, fridge, coffeemaker, hair dryer, no phone.

Two Mermaids on Maui B&B (Finds) The two mermaids, Juddee and Miranda, both avid scuba divers, offer a friendly B&B, professionally decorated with brilliant colors and hand-painted art of the island. It sits in a quiet neighborhood just a 10-minute walk from the beach. My favorite unit is the Ocean Ohana, a large one-bedroom apartment (with the option of a separate connecting bedroom), complete with kitchenette, huge private deck, private entry, and your own giant hot tub. Equally cute is the Poolside Suite, with private entry next to the outdoor pool. This studio (with the option of a separate connecting bedroom) is a living room during the day; at night it converts to a bedroom with a pull-down bed. Continental breakfast, with some of the best homemade bread on the island, is placed on your doorstep every morning (so you can sleep in). Amenities include guitars in every unit, a range of complimentary beach equipment, microwave popcorn, and a barbecue area. If the spirit moves you, Juddee is a licensed minister who can perform weddings.

2840 Umalu Place, Kihei, HI 96753. © 800/598-9550 or 808/874-8687. Fax 808/875-1833. www.twomermaids. com. 2 units. $115 studio double; $140 double 1-bedroom apt; 2-bedroom double $165–$190. Rates include continental breakfast. 3-night minimum. No credit cards. **Amenities:** Outdoor pool; hot tub; golf nearby; tennis courts nearby; massage available; babysitting available. *In room:* TV, VCR/DVD (on request), kitchenette, fridge, coffeemaker, hair dryer, iron, free local calls.

Wailana Kai (Value) Bello Realty has added this renovated two-story apartment building to its collection. Located at the end of a cul-de-sac, and just a 1-minute walk to the beach, the property was totally renovated in 2004. All units have full kitchens and concrete soundproof walls, and the second floor has ocean views. There's also a barbecue area for guests.

34 Wailana Place, Kihei, HI 96753. Reservations c/o Bello Realty, P.O. Box 1776, Kihei, HI 96753. © 800/541-3060 or 808/879-3328. Fax 808/875-1483. www.bellomaui.com. 10 units. $120 1-bedroom; $150 2-bedroom. MC, V. **Amenities:** Outdoor pool; coin-op washer/dryers. *In room:* TV/VCR, kitchen, fridge, coffeemaker, iron.

What a Wonderful World B&B (Value) I couldn't believe what I'd discovered here: an impeccably done B&B with a great location, excellent rates, and thought and care put into every room. Hostess Eva Tantillo has not only a full-service travel agency, but also a master's degree—along with several years of experience—in hotel management. The result? One of Maui's finest bed-and-breakfasts, centrally located in Kihei (½ mile to Kamaole II Beach Park, 5 min. from Wailea golf courses, and convenient to shopping and restaurants). Choose from one of four units: the master suite (with a barbecue grill on the lanai), a studio apartment, or two one-bedroom apartments. Eva serves a gourmet family-style breakfast (eggs Benedict, skillet eggs with mushroom sauce, fruit blintzes, and more) on her lanai, which boasts views of white-sand beaches, the West Maui Mountains, and Haleakala. You're also welcome to use the communal barbecue.

2828 Umalu Place (off Keonakai St., near Hwy. 31), Kihei, HI 96753. (℃) **800/943-5804** or 808/879-9103. Fax 808/874-9352. www.amauibedandbreakfast.com. 4 units. $89–$150 double. Rates include full breakfast. Children 11 and under stay free in parent's room. AE, MC, V. **Amenities:** Hot tub; laundry facilities. *In room:* TV, kitchen (in apartment units), fridge, coffeemaker, hair dryer, iron.

WAILEA

For a complete selection of condo units throughout Wailea and Makena, contact **Destination Resorts Hawaii** (℃) **800/367-5246** or 808/879-1595; fax 808/874-3554; www.drhmaui.com). Its luxury units include studio doubles starting at $230, one-bedroom doubles from $250, two-bedrooms from $280, and three-bedrooms from $420. Those rates include free long-distance calls, high-speed Internet access, and parking; one property, the Polo Beach Club, is completely nonsmoking (indoors and out). Children under 12 stay free; minimum stays vary by property.

VERY EXPENSIVE

The Fairmont Kea Lani Maui ★★★ At first glance, this blinding-white complex of arches and turrets may look a bit out of place in tropical Hawaii (it's a close architectural cousin of Las Hadas, the *Arabian Nights* fantasy resort in Manzanillo, Mexico). But once you enter the flower-filled lobby and see the big blue Pacific outside, there's no doubt you're in Hawaii.

It's not cheap, but for the price of a hotel room in other luxury resorts, you get an entire suite here—plus a few extras. Each unit in the all-suite hotel has a kitchenette, a living room with entertainment center and sofa bed (great if you have the kids in tow), a wet bar, an oversize marble bathroom (with separate shower big enough for a party), a spacious bedroom, and a large lanai that overlooks the pools, lawns, and white-sand beach. The small boutique spa offers the latest in body work in intimate, relaxing surroundings—not to be missed, even if you're staying elsewhere.

The rich and famous stay in the villas—2,000-square-foot two- and three-bedroom fantasy beach bungalows, each with its own plunge pool and gourmet kitchen.

4100 Wailea Alanui Dr., Wailea, HI 96753. (℃) **800/659-4100** or 808/875-4100. Fax 808/875-1200. www.fairmont.com/kealani. 450 units. $525–$1,200 suite (sleeps up to 4); from $1,500 villa. Valet parking $18; free self-parking. AE, DC, DISC, MC, V. **Amenities:** 4 restaurants (including Nick's Fishmarket Maui, p. 163), plus gourmet bakery and deli; 3 bars (w/sunset cocktails and entertainment at the Caffe Ciao Restaurant); 2 large swimming lagoons connected by a 140-ft. water slide and swim-up bar, plus an adults-only pool; nearby Wailea Golf Club's 3 18-hole championship golf courses, as well as the Makena and Elleair golf courses; use of Wailea Tennis Center's 11 courts (3 lit for night play) and pro shop; fine 24-hr. fitness center; excellent full-service spa; 2 whirlpools; watersports equipment rentals; year-round children's program; seasonal (summer and holidays) game room; concierge; activities desk; business center; shopping arcade; full-service salon; 24-hr. room service; in-room and spa massage; babysitting; complimentary self-service laundry; same-day laundry service and dry cleaning. *In room:* A/C, TV/DVD/VCR, CD player, dataport, high-speed Internet access ($14 per day), kitchenette, fridge, microwave, coffeemaker, hair dryer, iron, safe.

Four Seasons Resort Maui at Wailea ✦✦✦ *(Kids)*   If money's no object, this is the place to spend it. It's hard to beat this modern version of a Hawaiian palace by the sea, with a relaxing, casual atmosphere. Although it sits on a glorious beach between two other hotels, you won't feel like you're on resort row: The Four Seasons inhabits its own world, thanks to an open courtyard of pools and gardens. Amenities are first-rate here, including outstanding restaurants and an excellent spa. This may also be the most kid-friendly resort on the island: There's a complete activities program for *keiki* (complimentary, of course), plus other perks like milk and cookies on arrival, kids' menus in all restaurants, infant gear (cribs, strollers, and even toilet-seat locks), and a game room (video games, foosball, and more). You can even prepurchase necessities like diapers and baby food; the hotel will have them waiting for you when you arrive.

The spacious (about 600 sq. ft.) guest rooms feature furnished lanais, nearly all with ocean views, that are great for watching whales in winter and sunsets year-round. The grand bathrooms contain deep marble tubs and showers for two. Service is attentive but not cloying. At the pool, guests lounge in casbahlike tents, pampered with iced Evian and chilled towels. And you'll never see a housekeeping cart in the hall: The cleaning staff works in teams, so they're as unobtrusive as possible and in and out of your room in minutes.

The fabulous spa—which is smaller than the one at the Grand Wailea but has more intimate service—features an incredible menu of treatments ranging from traditional Hawaiian to craniosacral to ayurvedic massage, offered in 13 treatment rooms and three oceanside *hale.*

The ritzy neighborhood surrounding the hotel is home to great restaurants and shopping, the Wailea Tennis Center (known as Wimbledon West), and six golf courses—not to mention that great beach, with gentle waves and islands framing the view on either side.

3900 Wailea Alanui Dr., Wailea, HI 96753. © 800/334-MAUI (6284) or 808/874-8000. Fax 808/874-2222. www.four seasons.com/maui. 380 units. $475–$990 double; $1,065–$1,215 Club Floor double; from $890 suite. Packages available. Extra person $100 ($300 in Club Floor rooms). Children 17 and under stay free in parent's room. Valet parking $12. AE, DC, MC, V. **Amenities:** 3 restaurants (including Spago, p. 163, and Ferraro's at Seaside, p. 164); 3 bars (w/nightly entertainment); 3 fabulous outdoor pools; putting green; use of Wailea Golf Club's 3 18-hole championship golf courses, as well as the nearby Makena and Elleair golf courses; 2 on-site tennis courts (lit for night play); use of Wailea Tennis Center's 11 courts (3 lit for night play); health club featuring outdoor cardiovascular equipment (w/individual TV/VCRs); excellent spa; 2 whirlpools (1 for adults only); beach pavilion w/watersports equipment rentals and 1-hr. free use of snorkel equipment; free use of bicycles; fabulous year-round kids' program; one of Maui's best concierge desks; activities desk; car-rental desk; business center; shopping arcade; salon; room service; in-room, spa, and oceanside massage; babysitting; same-day laundry service and dry cleaning; concierge-level rooms. *In room:* A/C, TV, dataport, high-speed Internet access ($10 per day), minibar, fridge, coffeemaker, hair dryer, iron, safe.

Grand Wailea Resort Hotel & Spa ✦✦✦   Spa aficionados, take note: Hawaii's largest (50,000 sq. ft.) and most elaborate spa is located here, with every kind of body treatment you can imagine. Treatments include use of the numerous baths, hot tubs, mineral pools, saunas, steam rooms, and other relaxation amenities in the his-and-hers spa area.

Built at the pinnacle of Hawaii's brief fling with fantasy megaresorts, the Grand Wailea is extremely popular with families, incentive groups, and conventions; it's the grand prize in Hawaii vacation contests and the dream of many honeymooners. It has a Japanese restaurant decorated with real rocks hewn from the slopes of Mount Fuji; 10,000 tropical plants in the lobby; an intricate pool system with slides, waterfalls, rapids, and a water-powered elevator to take you up to the top; a restaurant in a man-made tide pool; a floating New England–style wedding chapel; and nothing but oceanview, amenity-filled guest rooms. It's all crowned with a $30-million collection of original art, much of it created expressly for the hotel by Hawaii artists and sculptors. Though minimalists may be put off, there's no denying that the Grand Wailea is plush, professional, and pampering, with all the diversions you could imagine. Oh, and did I mention the fantastic beach out front?

Note: All rooms and suites are now nonsmoking. The former smoking rooms have undergone a thorough cleaning and have been deodorized. Smoking is limited to the private lanais outside the rooms.

3850 Wailea Alanui Dr., Wailea, HI 96753. ℂ **800/888-6100** or 808/875-1234. Fax 808/874-2442. www.grand wailea.com. 780 units. $625–$1,180 double; from $1,900 suite; from $1,300 Napua Club Room (in Napua Tower). Daily $25 resort fee for lei greeting on arrival, welcome drink, local calls, use of spa, admission to scuba-diving clinics and water aerobics, art and garden tours, nightly turndown service, in-room high-speed Internet access, self-parking, and shuttle service to Wailea area. Extra person $50 ($100 in Napua Tower). Valet parking $15; free self-parking. AE, DC, DISC, MC, V. **Amenities:** 6 restaurants; 7 bars (including a nightclub w/laser-light shows); 2,000-ft.-long Activity Pool, featuring a swim/ride through mountains and grottoes; use of Wailea Golf Club's 3 18-hole championship golf courses, as well as the nearby Makena and Elleair golf courses; use of Wailea Tennis Center's 11 courts (3 lit for night play) and pro shop; complete fitness center; Hawaii's largest spa; Jacuzzi; watersports equipment rentals; diving and windsurfing lessons; children's program; game room; concierge; activities desk; car-rental desk; business center; shopping arcade; salon; room service; in-room and spa massage; babysitting; same-day laundry service and dry cleaning; concierge-level rooms. *In room:* A/C, TV, dataport, high-speed Internet access, kitchenette, minibar, fridge (fee of $25 per stay), coffeemaker, hair dryer, iron, safe.

EXPENSIVE

Wailea Beach Marriott Resort & Spa 🐾🐾

This classic, open-air, 1970s-style hotel in a tropical garden by the sea gives you a sense of what Maui was like before the big resort boom. It was the first resort built in Wailea (in 1976), and it remains the most Hawaiian of them all. Airy and comfortable, with touches of Hawaiian art throughout and a terrific aquarium that stretches forever behind the front desk, it just feels right. What's truly special about this hotel is how it fits into its environment without overwhelming it. Eight buildings, all low-rise except for an eight-story tower, are spread along 22 gracious acres of lawns and gardens spiked by coco palms, with lots of open space and a half-mile of oceanfront property on a point between Wailea and Ulua beaches. The vast, parklike expanses are a luxury on this now-crowded coast.

The small Mandara Spa offers a long list of treatments, from relaxing massages to aromatherapy wraps to rejuvenating facials in a very Zen atmosphere. My only criticism is the lack (at this time) of a shower facility in the spa.

3700 Wailea Alanui Dr., Wailea, HI 96753. ℂ **800/367-2960** or 808/879-1922. Fax 808/874-8331. www.wailea marriott.com. 545 units. $525–$825 double; from $514 suite. Extra person $40. Packages available. Daily $25 resort fee for self-parking, in-room high-speed Internet access, local calls, daily sunset appetizers, discounts on luau and snorkel-gear rental, and free kids' meals with purchase of adult entree. AE, DC, DISC, MC, V. **Amenities:** 2 restaurants; 2 bars; outdoor pools (including 1 for kids only); use of Wailea Golf Club's 3 18-hole championship golf courses; use of Wailea Tennis Center's 11 courts (3 lit for night play) and pro shop; fitness center; full-service Mandara Spa w/steam rooms and whirlpools; watersports equipment rentals; children's program and recreation center; concierge; activities desk; business center; shopping arcade; salon; room service; in-room and outdoor massages; babysitting; same-day laundry service and dry cleaning. *In room:* A/C, TV, high-speed Internet access, 4-outlet technology console, wet bar, coffeemaker, hair dryer, iron, safe.

MAKENA
EXPENSIVE
Maui Prince Hotel 🐾🐾

If you're looking for a vacation in a beautiful, tranquil spot with a golden-sand beach, here's your place. But if you plan to tour Maui, you might try another hotel. The Maui Prince is at the end of the road, far, far away from anything else on the island, so sightseeing in other areas would require a lot of driving.

When you first see the stark-white hotel, it looks like a high-rise motel stuck in the woods—but only from the outside. Inside, you'll discover an atrium garden with a koi-filled waterfall stream, an ocean view from every guest room, and a simple, clutter-free decor. Rooms are small but come with private lanais with great views.

5400 Makena Alanui, Makena, HI 96753. © 800/321-6284 or 808/874-1111. Fax 808/879-8763. www.mauiprince hotel.com. 310 units. $380–$555 double; from $700 suite. Extra person $60. Packages available. AE, DC, MC, V. **Amenities:** 4 restaurants (including Prince Court, p. 165); 2 bars (w/local Hawaiian music nightly); 2 outdoor pools (1 for adults, 1 for children); 36-hole golf course (designed by Robert Trent Jones, Jr.); 6 Plexipave tennis courts (2 lit for night play); fitness room; Jacuzzi; watersports equipment rentals; children's program; concierge; activities desk; shopping arcade; salon; room service; in-room massage; babysitting; same-day laundry service and dry cleaning. *In room:* A/C, TV, dataport, high-speed Internet access, fridge, hair dryer, iron, safe.

4 Upcountry Maui

MAKAWAO, OLINDA & HALIIMAILE

When you stay in the cooler upcountry climate of Makawao, Olinda, and Haliimaile, on the slopes of Maui's 10,000-foot Haleakala volcano, you'll be (relatively) close to Haleakala National Park. Makawao and Olinda are approximately 90 minutes from the entrance to the park at the 7,000-foot level (you still have 3,000 ft. and another 30–45 min. to get to the top). Staying in Haliimaile adds another 10 to 15 minutes to your drive up to the summit. Accommodations in Kula (reviewed in the next section) are the closest to the summit.

EXPENSIVE

Aloha Cottage 🏵🏵 *(Finds)*   Hidden in the secluded rolling hills of Olinda on a 5-acre parcel of manicured, landscaped tropical foliage are two separate cottages, both designed and decorated by hosts Ron and Ranjana Serle. The Thai Tree House ($245 a night) resembles an upscale Thai home with high vaulted ceilings, teak floors, and a king-size cherrywood bed in the center of the room. The private deck and private soaking tub make this a very romantic lodging. As fabulous as the Thai Tree House is, the Bali Bungalow ($318 a night) is even better. Up a private driveway through a bamboo archway, the Balinese cottage features an octagonal design with multifaceted skylights, a large marble shower built for two, hand-carved teak cabinets in the kitchen area, and Oriental carpets on the hardwood floors. Out on the private deck is a soaking tub for two. Ranjana can arrange weddings, prepare a private dinner, set up personal massages, and even organize a private yoga session for two.

1879 Olinda Rd., Makawao, HI 96765. © 888/328-3330 or 808/573-8555. Fax 808/573-2551. www.alohacottage. com. 2 cottages. $245–$318 double. 3-night minimum. MC, V. *In room:* TV/VCR, CD player, kitchen, fridge, coffeemaker, hair dryer, iron, safe, private soaking tub.

MODERATE

Banyan Tree House 🏵 *(Finds)*   Huge monkeypod trees (complete with swing and hammock) extend their branches over this 2½-acre property like a giant green canopy. The restored 1920s plantation manager's house is decorated with Hawaiian furniture from the 1930s. The house can accommodate a big family or a group of friends; it has three spacious bedrooms and three private marble bathrooms. A fireplace stands at one end of the huge living room, a large lanai runs the entire length of the house, and the hardwood floors shine throughout. The four smaller guest cottages have been totally

Where to Stay in Upcountry & East Maui

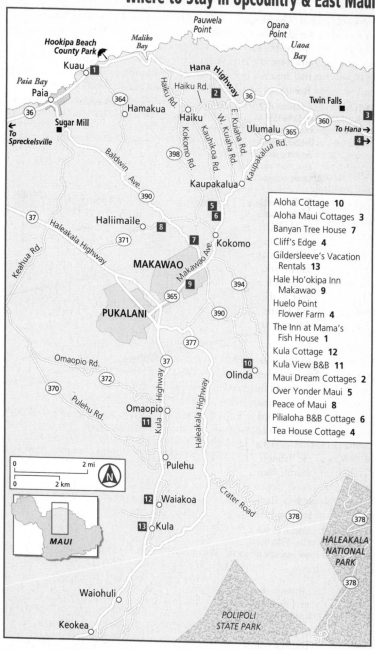

Aloha Cottage **10**

Aloha Maui Cottages **3**

Banyan Tree House **7**

Cliff's Edge **4**

Gildersleeve's Vacation Rentals **13**

Hale Ho'okipa Inn Makawao **9**

Huelo Point Flower Farm **4**

The Inn at Mama's Fish House **1**

Kula Cottage **12**

Kula View B&B **11**

Maui Dream Cottages **2**

Over Yonder Maui **5**

Peace of Maui **8**

Pilialoha B&B Cottage **6**

Tea House Cottage **4**

renovated and also feature hardwood floors and marble bathrooms. Floor plans vary; one has one queen-size bed, the others have two beds (a mix of queen-size, doubles, and twins). The quiet neighborhood and old Hawaii ambience give this place a comfortable, easygoing atmosphere. Restaurants and shops are just minutes away in Makawao, and the beach is a 15-minute drive—but this place is so relaxing that you may want to do nothing but lie in a hammock and watch the clouds float by.

3265 Baldwin Ave. (next to Veterans' Cemetery, less than a mile below Makawao), Makawao, HI 96768. ℂ 808/572-9021. Fax 808/573-5072. www.hawaii-mauirentals.com. 5 units. $165–$170 double room in house; $145–$190 cottage for 2. Extra person $30. Children 12 and under stay in parent's room for $10. 3-night minimum for house. No credit cards. **Amenities:** Outdoor pool; Jacuzzi; babysitting; small charge for washer/dryer. *In room:* TV (in some cottages), kitchen or kitchenette, fridge, coffeemaker.

INEXPENSIVE

If you'd like your own private cottage, consider **Peace of Maui,** 1290 Haliimaile Rd. (just outside Haliimaile town), Haliimaile, HI 96768 (ℂ **888/475-5045** or 808/572-5045; www.peaceofmaui.com), which has a full kitchen, two bedrooms, a day bed, and a large deck. The cottage goes for $120, and children are welcome. The owners also have rooms in the main house (with shared bathroom and kitchen facilities) from $50 single and $55 double.

Hale Ho'okipa Inn Makawao ⊛ (Finds)   Step back in time at this 1924 plantation-style home, rescued by owner Cherie Attix in 1996 and restored to its original charm (and listed on the State and National Historic Registers). Cherie lovingly refurbished the old wooden floors, filled the rooms with furniture from the 1920s, and hung works by local artists on the walls. The result is a charming, serene place to stay, just a 5-minute walk from the shops and restaurants of Makawao, 15 minutes from beaches, and an hour's drive from the top of Haleakala. The guest rooms have separate outside entrances and private bathrooms. The house's front and back porches are wonderful spots for sipping tea and watching the sun set. The Kona Wing is a two-bedroom suite with private bathroom and use of the kitchen.

32 Pakani Place, Makawao, HI 96768. ℂ 877/572-6698 or ℂ/fax 808/572-6698. www.maui-bed-and-breakfast. com. 4 units (2 with shower only). $140–$180 double. Rates include continental breakfast. Extra person $10. MC, V. From Haleakala Hwy., turn left on Makawao Ave., and turn right on the 5th street on the right off Makawao Ave. (Pakani Place); it's the 2nd-to-last house on the right (green house with white picket fence and water tower). *In room:* A/C, TV, wireless Internet access, hair dryer.

KULA

Lodgings in Kula are the closest options to the entrance of Haleakala National Park (about 60 min. away).

INEXPENSIVE

In addition to the options below, consider **Gildersleeve's Vacation Rentals,** formerly known as Elaine's Upcountry Guest Rooms (ℂ **808/878-6623;** fax 808/878-2619; papag@hawaii.rr.com). The warm and welcoming hosts rent three rooms in their spacious pole house ($80 double; 3-night minimum).

Kula Cottage ⊛ (Finds)   I can't imagine having a less-than-fantastic vacation here. Tucked away on a quiet street amid a large grove of blooming papaya and banana trees, Cecilia and Larry Gilbert's romantic honeymoon cottage is very private—it even has its own driveway and carport. The 700-square-foot cottage has a full kitchen (complete with dishwasher) and three huge closets that offer enough storage space for you to move in permanently. The lanai is outfitted with a gas barbecue and an umbrella-covered table and chairs. Cecilia delivers a continental breakfast daily. Groceries and a small takeout lunch counter are within walking distance; it's a 30-minute drive to the beach.

40 Puakea Place (off Lower Kula Rd.), Kula, HI 96790. ℭ 808/878-2043 or 871-6230. Fax 808/871-9187. www.kula cottage.com. 1 unit. $115 double. Rate includes continental breakfast. 2-night minimum. Extra person $15. No credit cards. *In room:* TV, kitchen, fridge, coffeemaker, washer/dryer.

Kula View Bed & Breakfast *Finds*

Hostess and gardener extraordinaire Susan Kauai has this cute private suite (with its own deck and private entrance) upstairs in her home. You are greeted on arrival by George, a big fluffy tabby cat. The roomy studio has a huge deck with a panoramic view of Haleakala. Inside, there's a reading area with a comfy lounge chair and an eating area with table and chairs, toaster oven, coffeemaker, and electric teakettle. Susan serves breakfast in your suite (or will pack a picnic breakfast if you are out early) of tasty breads or muffins, fruit, juice, and tea and coffee. She has plenty of warm jackets, sweaters, and blankets you can borrow if you plan to make the trip to the top of Haleakala. Be sure to take a stroll through her magical garden.

P.O. Box 322, Kula, HI 96790. ℭ 808/878-6736. www.kulaview.com. 1 suite. $115 double. No credit cards. Rates include continental breakfast. 2-night minimum. *In room:* Fridge, coffeemaker.

5 East Maui: On the Road to Hana

KUAU
MODERATE

The Inn at Mama's Fish House *ℛℛ*   The fabulous location (nestled in a coconut grove on secluded Kuau Beach), beautifully decorated interior (with rattan furniture and works by Hawaiian artists), and extras (gas barbecue, 27-in. TVs, and beach toys) make this place a gem for those seeking a centrally located vacation rental. All this, and the fabulous Mama's Fish House restaurant is just next door. The one-bedrooms are nestled in a tropical jungle (red ginger surrounds the garden patio), while the two-bedrooms face the beach. Both have terra-cotta floors, complete kitchens (even dishwashers), sofa beds, and laundry facilities.

799 Poho Place (off the Hana Hwy. in Kuau), Paia, HI 96779. ℭ 800/860-HULA (4852) or 808/579-9764. Fax 808/ 579-8594. www.mamasfishhouse.com. 6 units. $175 garden studio double; $225 1-bedroom (sleeps up to 4); $325–$575 2-bedroom (up to 6). 3-night minimum. AE, DISC, MC, V. **Amenities:** Restaurant. *In room:* A/C, TV/VCR, kitchen, fridge, coffeemaker, hair dryer, iron, washer/dryer.

HAIKU
MODERATE

Pilialoha B&B Cottage *ℛ*   The minute you arrive at this split-level country cottage, set on a large lot with half-century-old eucalyptus trees, you'll see owner Machiko Heyde's artistry at work. Just in front of the quaint cottage (which is great for couples but can sleep up to five) is a garden blooming with some 200 varieties of roses. You'll find more of Machiko's handiwork inside. There's a queen-size bed in the master bedroom, a twin bed in a small adjoining room, and a queen-size sofa bed in the living room. A large lanai extends from the master bedroom. There's a great movie collection for rainy days or cool country nights, plus a garage. If you plan on an early-morning ride to the top of Haleakala, Machiko will make sure you go with a thermos of coffee and her homemade bread.

2512 Kaupakalua Rd. (½ mile from Kokomo intersection), Haiku, HI 96708. (☎ **808/572-1440**. Fax 808/572-4612. 1 unit. $135 double. Extra person $30. 3-night minimum. No cards. **Amenities:** Complimentary use of beach toys (including snorkel equipment); washer/dryer. *In room:* TV, kitchenette, fridge, coffeemaker.

INEXPENSIVE

Maui Dream Cottage *(Value)* Essentially a vacation rental, this country estate is located atop a hill overlooking the ocean. The grounds are dotted with fruit trees (bananas, papayas, and avocados, all free for the picking), and the front lawn is comfortably equipped with a double hammock, chaise longues, and table and chairs. One cottage has two bedrooms, the other just one (plus a sofa bed in the living room). They're both very well maintained and comfortably outfitted with furniture that's attractive but casual. The Haiku location is quiet and restful, offering the opportunity to see how real islanders live. However, you'll have to drive a good 20 to 25 minutes to restaurants in Makawao or Paia. Hookipa Beach is about a 20-minute drive, and Baldwin Beach (good swimming) is 25 minutes away.

265 W. Kuiaha Rd. (1 block from Pauwela Cafe), Haiku, HI 96708. (☎ **808/575-9079**. Fax 808/575-9477. www.mauidreamcottage.com. 2 units (both with shower only). $700 per week double, $100 for each additional night. Extra person $10. 7-night minimum. MC, V. *In room:* TV, kitchen, fridge, coffeemaker, washer/dryer.

Over Yonder Maui If you don't mind sharing a house with the host, this hidden bed-and-breakfast offers a quiet, relaxing vacation on 2 acres in Haiku. Host Neida Cahoj has a perfect eye for decorating and has created an absolutely gorgeous, comfy home. You have your own entrance into the sun room, with floor-to-ceiling windows that overlook the lush tropical jungle of koa, guava, and kukui nut trees. Two bedrooms are available: the antiques-filled Ginger Room and the Plumeria Suite, which features a bathroom with an old Chinese sideboard converted into a sink enclosure. The entire house is decorated with wonderful antiques and one-of-a-kind art and furniture. Guests have use of the living room, sun room, television room, and refrigerator and microwave on the lanai. A breakfast of coffee or tea, cereal, banana bread or toast, and fruit is served every morning. Neida's dog, Dodger, is happy to provide canine company.

2555 Lemi Place, Haiku, HI 96708. (☎ **888/222-2466** or 808/573-5320. www.overyondermaui.com. 2 units. $110–$130 double (10% discount for stays over 4 nights). MC, V. **Amenities:** TV/DVD; use of fridge and microwave; washer/dryer.

TWIN FALLS

INEXPENSIVE

Hidden in a secluded jungle, powered by alternative energy (no utility poles!), the off-the-beaten-path **Tea House Cottage** (☎ **800/215-6130** or 808/572-5610; www.mauiteahouse.com) gives you the chance to get away from it all while still having electricity, phone, and TV—you can even plug in your laptop. Your private cottage has two decks, a screened lanai, a bedroom, a small kitchen, and a unique bathhouse. Rates of $120 single (3-night minimum) and $135 double (2-night minimum) include breakfast. Owner Ann DeWeese is on the property and can provide any helpful tips you need during your vacation.

Aloha Maui Cottages *(Finds)* On 2 acres of jungle, tucked away in the Twin Falls area, sits this budget option. Three separate bungalows offer a back-to-nature experience. The rustic, clean, and well-outfitted cabins are all landscaped to offer privacy and are a good value for the price. They range from the Mango Cottage, with hardwood floors, a full kitchen, and a big bedroom with an ocean view, to the Banana

Room, a small room with kitchenette. All units are stocked with coffee, tea, and locally grown fruit (some come from right outside your front door) in season, and share access to a gas barbecue. Host Ken knows all the hiking and biking trails (he'll loan you his mountain bikes to go exploring) and secret waterfalls.

101 Loomis Rd., Haiku/Huelo (P.O. Box 790210, Paia), HI 96779. (C) 808/572-0298. www.alohamauicottages.com. 3 units (2 with shared bathroom). $70–$135 double. Extra person $5–$7. 3-night minimum. DISC, MC, V. *In room:* Kitchen or kitchenette.

HUELO/WAILUA
EXPENSIVE

Cliff's Edge ★ *Finds*   This B&B and vacation rental couldn't be much closer to the ocean without being underwater. The saltwater swimming pool perches on the edge of a 300-foot cliff in Huelo. The tropically landscaped 2-acre property also has a hot tub and 600-square-foot sun deck. Accommodations include two bedrooms in the main house, a two-bedroom 900-square-foot guesthouse, and a 600-square-foot cottage. The rooms in the B&B range in size from 300 to 600 square feet, all with awesome ocean views, private entries, private lanais, private bathrooms, small kitchenettes (with microwave, coffeemaker, and refrigerator), and ceiling fans. Restaurants and shopping are about 30 minutes away in Paia.

P.O. Box 1095, Haiku, HI 96708. (C) 866/262-6284 or 808/572-4530. www.cliffsedge.com. 4 units. $185–$225 double room in house; $350 cottage. Extra person $25. 3-night minimum. Rates include continental breakfast. No credit cards. **Amenities:** Pool; hot tub; sun deck; Wi-Fi. *In room:* TV (in cottages), stereo/CD player, kitchenette or kitchen, fridge, microwave, coffeemaker.

Huelo Point Flower Farm *Finds*   Here's a little Eden by the sea on a spectacular, remote, 300-foot sea cliff near a waterfall stream. This estate overlooking Waipio Bay has two guest cottages, a guesthouse, and a main house available for rent. The studio-size Gazebo Cottage has three glass walls that make the most of the oceanfront location, a koa-wood captain's bed, a private oceanside patio, a private hot tub, and a half-bathroom with outdoor shower. The new 900-square-foot Carriage House apartment sleeps four and has glass walls facing the mountain and sea, plus a den, decks, and a loft bedroom. The two-bedroom main house contains an exercise room, a fireplace, a sunken Roman bath, cathedral ceilings, and other extras. On the property is a natural pool with a waterfall and an oceanfront hot tub. You're welcome to pick fruit, vegetables, and flowers from the extensive garden. Homemade scones, tree-ripened papayas, and fresh-roasted coffee start your day. The secluded location, off the crooked road to Hana, is just a half-hour from Kahului, or about 20 minutes from Paia's shops and restaurants.

P.O. Box 791808 (off Hana Hwy., btw. mile markers 3 and 4), Paia, HI 96779. (C) 808/572-1850. www.mauiflower farm.com. 4 units. $300 cottage double; $300 Carriage House double; $450 guesthouse double; $600 main house for 4. Extra person $20–$40. 2-night minimum for smaller houses, 5-night minimum for main house. No credit cards. **Amenities:** Outdoor pool; 3 Jacuzzis; washer/dryer. *In room:* TV, kitchenette or kitchen, fridge, coffeemaker, hair dryer.

6 At the End of the Road in East Maui: Hana

Note: To locate the following accommodations, see the "Hana" map on p. 237.

EXPENSIVE

Hotel Hana-Maui ★★★ *Kids*   This hotel sits on 66 rolling seaside acres and offers a wellness center, two pools, and access to one of the best beaches in Hana. This is the atmosphere, the landscape, and the culture of old Hawaii set in 21st-century accommodations. Every unit is excellent, but my favorites are the Sea Ranch Cottages (especially units 215–218 for the best views), where individual duplex bungalows look out over the craggy shoreline to the rolling surf. You step out of the oversize, airy units (with floor-to-ceiling sliding doors) onto a huge lanai with views that will stay with you long after your tan has faded. These comfy units have been totally redecorated with every amenity you can think of, and you won't be nickel-and-dimed for things like coffee and water—everything provided, from the homemade banana bread to the bottled water, is complimentary. Cathedral ceilings, a plush feather bed, a giant soaking tub, Hawaiian artwork, bamboo floors—this is luxury. The white-sand beach (just a 5-min. shuttle away), top-notch wellness center with some of the best massage therapists in Hawaii, and numerous activities (horseback riding, mountain biking, tennis, pitch-and-putt golf) all add up to make this one of the top resorts in the state. There's no TV in the rooms, but the Club Room has a giant-screen TV, plus VCR and Internet access. I highly recommend this little slice of paradise.

5031 Hana Hwy. (P.O. Box 9), Hana, HI 96713. © 800/321-HANA (4262) or 808/248-8211. Fax 808/248-7202. www.hotelhanamaui.com. 66 units. $495–$525 Bay Cottage double; $650–$1,125 Sea Ranch Cottage double; $1,675 2-bedroom suite for 4; from $4,000 2-bedroom Plantation House. Extra person $140. AE, DC, DISC, MC, V. **Amenities:** Restaurant (w/Hawaiian entertainment twice a week); bar (entertainment 4 times a week); 2 outdoor pools; complimentary use of the 3-hole practice golf courses (complimentary use of clubs); tennis courts; fitness center; full-service spa; game room; concierge; activities desk; car-rental desk; business center; small shopping arcade; salon; room service; babysitting; laundry service. *In room:* Dataport, kitchenette, fridge, coffeemaker, hair dryer, iron, safe.

MODERATE
Bamboo Inn This inn shares the same historic site as the Hana Hale Inn (p. 139), and guests have full access to Hana Hale Inn's ancient fishponds and cave. There's access to a nearby rocky beach, which isn't good for swimming but makes a wonderful place to watch the sunset. All accommodations include fully equipped kitchens, bathrooms, bedrooms, living/dining areas, and private lanais. The oceanfront Bamboo Inn contains three units (two studios and a convertible one- or two-bedroom unit).

P.O. Box 374, Hana, HI 96713. © 808/248-7718. www.bambooinn.com. 3 units. $175–$240 double. Extra person $15. 2-night minimum. MC, V. **Amenities:** Jacuzzi. *In room:* TV/DVD, kitchen, fridge, coffeemaker, Jacuzzi.

Ekena ⚐ Just one glance at the 360-degree view, and you can see why hosts Robin and Gaylord gave up their careers on the mainland and moved here. This 8½-acre piece of paradise in rural Hana boasts ocean and rainforest vistas; the floor-to-ceiling glass doors in the spacious Hawaiian-style pole house bring the outside in. The elegant two-story home is exquisitely furnished, from the comfortable U-shaped couch that invites you to relax and take in the view to the top-of-the-line mattress on the king-size bed. The fully equipped kitchen has everything you should need to cook a gourmet meal. Only one floor (and one two-bedroom unit) is rented at any given time to ensure privacy. The grounds are impeccably groomed and dotted with tropical plants and fruit trees. Hiking trails into the rainforest start right on the property, and beaches and waterfalls are just minutes away. Robin places fresh flowers in every room and makes sure you're comfortable; after that, she's available to answer questions, but she also respects your privacy.

P.O. Box 728 (off Hana Hwy., above Hana Airport), Hana, HI 96713. © 808/248-7047. Fax 808/248-7853. www.ekenamaui.com. 2 units. $225 for 2; $295–$400 for 4. Extra person $35. 3-night minimum. Children must be 14 or older. MC, V. **Amenities:** Washer/dryers. *In room:* TV/DVD, CD player, free wireless Internet access, kitchen, fridge, coffeemaker, iron.

Hamoa Bay House & Bungalow 🏆 *Finds*   Down a country lane guarded by two Balinese statues stands a little bit of Indonesia in Hawaii: a carefully crafted bungalow and an Asian-inspired two-bedroom house overlooking Hamoa Bay. This enchanting retreat is just 2 miles beyond Hasegawa General Store on the way to Kipahulu. It sits on 4 verdant acres within walking distance of Hamoa Beach (which James Michener considered one of the most beautiful in the Pacific). The 600-square-foot Balinese-style cottage is distinctly tropical, with elephant-bamboo furniture from Indonesia, batik prints, a king-size bed, a full kitchen, and a screened porch with hot tub and shower. Hidden from the cottage is a 1,300-square-foot home with a soaking tub and private outdoor stone shower. It offers an elephant-bamboo king-size bed in one room, a queen-size bed in another, a screened-in sleeping porch, a full kitchen, and wonderful ocean views.

P.O. Box 773, Hana, HI 96713. © 808/248-7884. Fax 808/248-7853. www.hamoabay.com. 2 units. $225 cottage (sleeps only 2); $285 house for 2; $395 house for 4. 3-night minimum. MC, V. **Amenities:** Hot tub; washer/dryers. *In room:* TV/DVD, CD player, kitchen, fridge, coffeemaker, iron.

Hana Hale Inn *Finds*   Hana Hale Inn sits on a historic site with ancient fishponds and a cave mentioned in ancient chants. Host John takes excellent care of the ponds (you're welcome to watch him feed the fish at 5pm daily) and is fiercely protective of the hidden cave ("It's not a tourist attraction, but a sacred spot"). There's access to a nearby rocky beach, which isn't good for swimming but makes a wonderful place to watch the sunset. All accommodations include fully equipped kitchens, bathrooms, bedrooms, living/dining areas, and private lanais. Next to the fishpond, the Royal Lodge, a 2,600-square-foot architectural masterpiece built entirely of Philippine mahogany, has large skylights the entire length of the house and can be rented as a house or two separate units. The cottages range from the separate two-level Tree House Cottage (with Jacuzzi for two, a Balinese bamboo bed, small kitchen/living area, and deck upstairs) to the Pond View Bungalow (with private outdoor Jacuzzi and shower).

P.O. Box 374, Hana, HI 96713. © 808/248-7641. www.hanahaleinn.com. 5 units. $160–$260 double. Extra person $15. 2-night minimum. MC, V. **Amenities:** Jacuzzi. *In room:* TV/DVD, kitchen, fridge, coffeemaker, Jacuzzi (in all but 1 unit).

Hana Kai Maui Resort   Hana's only vacation condo complex, Hana Kai offers studio and one-bedroom units overlooking Hana Bay. All units have large kitchens and private lanais. Each of the one-bedroom units has a sliding door that separates the bedroom from the living room, plus a sofa bed that sleeps two additional guests. There are no phones or TVs in the units (a pay phone is located on the property), so you can really get away from it all. Ask for a corner unit with wraparound ocean views.

1533 Uakea Rd. (P.O. Box 38), Hana, HI 96713. © 800/346-2772 or 808/248-8426. Fax 808/248-7482. www.hanakaimaui.com. 17 units. $145–$196 studio double; $185–$360 1-bedroom (sleeps up to 4). Children 6 and under stay free in parent's room. MC, V. *In room:* Kitchen, fridge, coffeemaker, no phone.

Hana Oceanfront Cottages 🏆🏆   Just across the street from Hamoa Bay, Hana's premier white-sand beach, lie these two plantation-style units, impeccably decorated in old Hawaii decor. My favorite unit is the romantic cottage, complete with front porch where you can sit and watch the ocean; a separate bedroom (with a bamboo sleigh bed), plus pullout sofa for extra guests; top-notch kitchen appliances; and comfy living room. The 1,000-square-foot vacation suite, located downstairs from hosts Dan and Sandi's home (but totally soundproof—you'll never hear them), has an elegant master bedroom with polished bamboo flooring, a spacious bathroom with custom hand-painted tile, and a fully appointed gourmet kitchen. Outside is a 320-square-foot lanai. The units sit on the road facing Hana's most popular beach, so there is traffic during the day. At night the traffic disappears, the stars come out, and the sound of the ocean lulls you to sleep.

P.O. Box 843, Hana, HI 96713. © 808/248-7558. Fax 808/248-8034. www.hanaoceanfrontcottages.com. 2 units. $250–$275 double. 3-night minimum. MC, V. **Amenities:** Barbecue area. *In room:* TV/VCR/DVD, stereo/CD player, kitchen, fridge, coffeemaker, hair dryer, iron.

Heavenly Hana Inn ★★ *Finds*   This place on the Hana Highway, just a stone's throw from the center of Hana town, is a little bit of heaven, where no attention to detail has been spared. Each suite has a sitting room with futon and couch, polished hardwood floors, and separate bedroom with a raised platform bed (with an excellent, firm mattress). The black-marble bathrooms have huge tubs. Flowers are everywhere, ceiling fans keep the rooms cool, and the delicious gourmet breakfast—worth splurging for—is served in an art-filled setting. The grounds are done in Japanese style with a bamboo fence, tiny bridges over a meandering stream, and Japanese gardens.

P.O. Box 790, Hana, HI 96713. ©/fax 808/248-8442. www.heavenlyhanainn.com. 3 units. $190–$260 suite. Full gourmet breakfast available for $17 per person. 2-night minimum. AE, DISC, MC, V. Children must be 15 or older. *In room:* TV, no phone.

INEXPENSIVE

Mrs. Nakamura has been renting her **Aloha Cottages** (© 808/248-8420) since the 1970s. Located in residential areas near Hana Bay, these five budget rentals are simply but adequately furnished, varying in size from a roomy studio with kitchenette to a three-bedroom, two-bathroom unit. They're all fully equipped, clean, and fairly well kept. Rates run from $70 to $100 double. Not all units have TVs, and none have phones, but Mrs. N. is happy to take messages.

Baby Pigs Crossing Bed & Breakfast ★ *Finds*   If you're looking for a quiet, romantic little cottage, nestled away from it all in old Hawaii but close enough to Hana to drive in for dinner, this is your place. International artist Arabella Gail Ark (formerly known as Gail Bakutis) has created a lovely retreat on her 1-acre parcel of land, which is landscaped in a "fragrance" garden carefully planted with Hawaii's best sweet-smelling plants. The separate guesthouse, with an ocean view from the lanai, is professionally decorated with comfort in mind, from the very cozy rattan furniture to the king-size sofa bed. There's a separate bedroom with a queen-size bed and a small but utilitarian kitchenette. The surprise is the unique bathroom with glass ceiling and walls (with privacy curtains), which opens onto a garden area. Even if you are not staying here, stop by and see the Ark Ceramics Gallery (daily 11am–4pm).

P.O. Box 667, Hana, HI 96713. © 808/248-8890. Fax 808/248-4865. www.mauibandb.com. 1 unit. $250 double for 1 night ($225 per night for 2 nights; $200 per night for 3 nights). AE, MC, V. *In room:* TV/VCR, kitchenette, fridge, coffeemaker, cellphone.

Hana's Tradewind Cottages ★ *Value* *Kids*   Nestled among the ginger and heliconias on a 5-acre flower farm are two separate cottages, each with carport, barbecue, private hot tub, ceiling fans, and sofa bed. The studio cottage sleeps up to four; a bamboo shoji blind separates the sleeping area (with queen-size bed) from the sofa bed in the living room. The Tradewinds Cottage has two bedrooms (with a queen-size bed in one room and two twins in the other), one bathroom (shower only), and a huge front porch. The atmosphere is quiet and relaxing, and hostess Rebecca Buckley, who has been in business for a decade, welcomes families (she has two children, a cat, and a very sweet golden retriever). You can use the laundry facilities at no extra charge.

135 Alalele Place (the airport road), P.O. Box 385, Hana, HI 96713. © **800/327-8097** or 808/248-8980. Fax 808/248-7735. www.hanamaui.net. 2 units. $175 studio double; $175 2-bedroom double. Extra person $15. 2-night minimum. AE, DISC, MC, V. **Amenities:** Washer/dryer. *In room:* TV, kitchen, fridge, coffeemaker, no phone.

Joe's Rentals *(Value* This is as close to a hostel as you can get in Hana. Joe's is a large, rambling house located just spitting distance from Hana Bay. Seven spartan but immaculately clean bedrooms share showers and bathroom; one has private facilities. All guests are welcome to use the large living room with TV and adjoining communal kitchen (free coffee available all day). Other amenities include a rec room, barbecue, and owner Ed Hill himself. He'll tell you the long story about the name if you ask and can also talk about what to do and see in Hana all day if you let him.

4870 Uakea Rd. (P.O. Box 746), Hana, HI 96713. © **808/248-7033**. www.joesrentals.com. 8 units (7 with shared bathroom). $50 double with shared bathroom; $60 double with private bathroom. Extra person $10. MC, V. **Amenities:** TV; kitchen; rec room. *In room:* No phone.

Waianapanapa State Park Cabins *(Value* These 12 rustic cabins are the best lodging deal on Maui. Everyone knows it, too—so make your reservations early (up to 6 months in advance). The cabins are warm and dry, and come complete with kitchen, living room, bedroom, and bathroom with hot shower; furnishings include linens, towels, dishes, and very basic cooking and eating utensils. Don't expect luxury—this is a step above camping, albeit in a beautiful tropical jungle setting. The key attraction at this 120-acre state beach park is the unusual horseshoe-shaped black-sand beach on Pailoa Bay, popular for shore fishing, snorkeling, and swimming. There's an on-site caretaker, along with restrooms, showers, picnic tables, shoreline hiking trails, and historic sites. Bring mosquito protection—this *is* the jungle, after all.

Off Hana Hwy. Reservations c/o State Parks Division, 54 S. High St., Room 101, Wailuku, HI 96793. © **808/984-8109**. 12 units. $45 for 4 (sleeps up to 6). Extra person $5. 5-night maximum. No credit cards. *In room:* Kitchen, fridge, coffeemaker, no phone.

6

Where to Dine

With soaring visitor statistics and a glamorous image, the Valley Isle is fertile ground for Hawaii's famous enterprising chefs (like Roy Yamaguchi of Roy's, Gerard Reversade of Gerard's, James McDonald of I'O and Pacific'O, Peter Merriman of Hula Grill, Mark Ellman of Maui Tacos and Mala Ocean Tavern, D. K. Kodama of Sansei Seafood Restaurant and Vino Italian Tapas, and Beverly Gannon of Haliimaile General Store and Joe's), as well as an international name or two (Wolfgang Puck of Spago). There are also a few newcomers who are cooking up a storm and getting a well-deserved following (Ryan Luckey of Pineapple Grill, Jennifer Nguyen of A Saigon Cafe, Dana Pastula of the Cafe O'Lei restaurants, and Don Ritchey of Moana Bakery & Cafe).

In this dizzying scenario, some things haven't changed: You can still dine well at Lahaina's open-air waterfront watering holes, where the view counts for 50% of the experience. There are still budget eateries, but not many; Maui's old-fashioned, multigenerational mom-and-pop diners are disappearing, eclipsed by the flashy newcomers, or clinging to the edge of existence in the older neighborhoods of central Maui, such as lovable Wailuku. Although you'll have to work harder to find them in the resort areas, you won't have to go far to find creative cuisine, pleasing style, and stellar dining experiences.

In the listings below, reservations are not necessary unless otherwise noted.

1 Central Maui

KAHULUI
MODERATE
Ichiban *(Finds* JAPANESE/SUSHI   What a find: an informal neighborhood restaurant that serves inexpensive, home-cooked Japanese food *and* good sushi at realistic prices. Local residents consider Ichiban a staple for breakfast, lunch, or dinner and a haven of comforts: egg-white omelets; great saimin; combination plates of teriyaki chicken, teriyaki meat, *tonkatsu* (pork cutlet), rice, and pickled cabbage; chicken yakitori; and sushi—everything from unagi and scallop to California roll. The sushi items may not be cheap, but like the specials, such as steamed opakapaka, they're a good value. I love the tempura, miso soup, and spicy-ahi hand roll.

At the Kahului Shopping Center, 47 Kaahumanu Ave., Kahului. (*C*) **808/871-6977.** Main courses $5–$6 breakfast, $8–$12 lunch (combination plates $10), $7–$30 dinner (combination dinner $13, dinner specials from $9). AE, DC, MC, V. Mon–Fri 7am–2pm and 5–9pm; Sat 10:30am–2pm and 5–9pm. Closed 2 weeks around Christmas and New Year's.

Mañana Garage *(Finds* LATIN AMERICAN   Chef Ed Santos is serving up some incomparable fare at this central Maui hot spot. The industrial motif features table bases made from hubcaps, a garage-door divider for private parties, blown-glass chandeliers, and gleaming chrome and cobalt walls with orange accents. The menu is brilliantly conceived and executed. Fried green tomatoes are done just right and served with slivered red onions. Three different kinds of ceviche perfectly balance flavors and textures: lime, cilantro, chile, coconut, and fresh fish. There's even barbecued ribs. Mañana Garage has introduced exciting new flavors to Maui's dining scene—if you are on this side of the island, don't miss this incredible experience.

33 Lono Ave., Kahului. ℃ 808/873-0220. Reservations recommended. Main courses $7–$13 lunch, $16–$31 dinner. AE, DISC, MC, V. Mon, Wed, Sat 11am–1:30am; Tues and Thurs 11am–9pm; Fri 11am–10:30pm; Sun 5–9pm.

Marco's Grill & Deli ITALIAN   Located in the thick of central Maui, where the roads to upcountry, west, and south Maui converge, Marco's is popular among area residents for its homemade Italian fare and friendly informality. Everything—from the meatballs, sausages, and burgers to the sauces, salad dressings, and raviolis—is made in house. The 35 different choices of hot and cold sandwiches and entrees are served all day; some favorites include vodka rigatoni with imported prosciutto and simple pasta with marinara sauce. The antipasto salad and roasted peppers are taste treats, but the meatballs and Italian sausage are famous in central Maui. This is one of those comfortable neighborhood fixtures favored by all generations. It also has a full bar.

At the Dairy Center, 395 Dairy Rd., Kahului. ℃ 808/877-4446. Main courses $11–$27. AE, DISC, MC, V. Daily 7:30am–10pm.

INEXPENSIVE

The **Queen Kaahumanu Center,** the structure that looks like a white *Star Wars* umbrella in the center of Kahului, at 275 Kaahumanu Ave. (5 min. from Kahului Airport on Hwy. 32), has a very popular food court. Eateries include: **Edo Japan,** whose flat Benihana-like grill dispenses marvelous, flavorful teppanyaki; **Panda Express,** which serves tasty Chinese food; and **Alexander's Fish and Chips,** a great place for fast takeout. Outside of the food court, but still in the shopping center, are **Ruby's,** dishing out burgers, fries, and shakes; and **Starbucks.** There's also a branch of **Maui Tacos** (p. 157). When you leave Kaahumanu Center, take a moment to gaze at the West Maui Mountains to your left from the parking lot.

Down to Earth *Value* ORGANIC HEALTH FOOD   If you are looking for a healthy alternative to fast foods, here's your place. Healthful organic ingredients, 90% vegan, appear in scrumptious salads, lasagna, chili, curries, and dozens of tasty dishes, presented at hot and cold serve-yourself stations. Stools line the counters in the simple dining area, where a few tables are available for those who don't want takeout. The food is great: millet cakes, mock tofu chicken, curried tofu, and Greek salad, nearly everything organic and tasty, with herb-tamari marinades and pleasing condiments such as currants or raisins, apples, and cashews. (The fabulous tofu curry has apples, raw cashews, and raisins.) The food is sold by the pound, but you can buy a hearty, wholesome plate for $7. Vitamin supplements, health-food products, fresh produce, and cosmetics fill the rest of the store.

305 Dairy Rd., Kahului. ℃ 808/877-2661. www.downtoearth.org. Self-serve hot buffet and salad bar; food sold by the pound. Average $7–$9 for a plate. AE, MC, V. Mon–Sat 7am–9pm; Sun 8am–8pm.

Restaurant Matsu JAPANESE/LOCAL   Customers have come from Hana (more than 50 miles away) just for Matsu's California rolls, while regulars line up for the cold saimin (julienned cucumber, egg, Chinese-style sweet pork, and red ginger on noodles) and for the bento plates (various assemblages of chicken, teriyaki beef, fish, and rice). The nigiri sushi items are popular, especially among the don't-dally lunch crowd.

Moments   **Roselani: Maui's Best Ice Cream**

For the culinary highlight of your trip to Maui, try **Roselani Ice Cream,** Maui's only made-from-scratch, old-fashioned ice cream. In fact, be sure to try it early in your trip so you can eat your way through this little bit of heaven at restaurants and scooping parlors, or get your own stash at grocery stores. There are more than 40 different flavors, divided into two different brands under the Roselani label: the Premium Parlour Flavors (ranging from the traditional vanilla to the unique black cherry, cappuccino chip, fresh-brewed coffee, and choco-cookie crunch) and the Tropics (with delicious varieties like the best-selling haupia, made from coconut and macadamia nut, or the popular chocolate macadamia nut, Kona mud pie, mango and cream, coconut pineapple, and luau fudge pie). Each rich, creamy flavor contains 12% to 16% butterfat. For a list of hotels, restaurants, ice-cream parlors, and grocery stores that carry Roselani, either call ⓒ 808/244-7951 or check online at www.roselani.com.

The *katsu* pork and chicken, breaded and deep-fried, are other specialties of this casual Formica-style diner. I love the tempura udon and the saimin, steaming mounds of wide and fine noodles swimming in homemade broths and topped with condiments. The daily specials are a changing lineup of home-cooked classics: oxtail soup, roast pork with gravy, teriyaki ahi, miso butterfish, and breaded mahimahi.

161 Alamaha St., Kahului. ⓒ 808/871-0822. Most items under $7. No credit cards. Mon–Thurs 10am–3pm; Fri 10am–8pm; Sat 10am–2pm.

WAILUKU
MODERATE

Class Act ⍟ GLOBAL   Part of a program run by the distinguished Food Service Department of Maui Community College, now housed in a new state-of-the-art, $15-million culinary facility (with floor-to-ceiling windows at one end, exhibition kitchen at the other end), Class Act is a "classroom" restaurant with a huge following. Student chefs show their stuff with a flourish and pull out all the stops to give you a dining experience you will long remember. Linen, china, servers in ties and white shirts, and a four-course lunch make this a unique value. The appetizer, soup, salad, and dessert are set, but you can choose between the regular entrees and a heart-healthy main course prepared in the culinary tradition of the week. The menu roams the globe, with highlights of Italy, Mexico, Maui, Napa Valley, France, New Orleans, and other locales. The filet mignon of French week is popular, as are the New Orleans gumbo and Cajun shrimp, the sesame-crusted mahimahi on taro-leaf pasta, the polenta flan with eggplant, and the bean and green-chile chilaquile.

At Maui Community College, 310 Kaahumanu Ave., Wailuku. ⓒ 808/984-3280. www.mauiculinary.com/academy/class_act.cfm. Reservations recommended. 4-course lunch $27. MC, V. Wed and Fri 11am–12:15pm (last seating). Closed June–Aug for summer vacation. Menu and cuisine type change weekly.

A Saigon Cafe ⍟⍟ *(Finds)* VIETNAMESE   Jennifer Nguyen has stuck to her guns and steadfastly refused to erect a sign, but diners find their way here anyway. That's how good the food is. Fans drive from all over the island for her crisp spiced Dungeness crab, steamed opakapaka with ginger and garlic, and wok-cooked Vietnamese specials tangy with spices, herbs, and lemon grass. There are a dozen different soups, cold and hot noodles (including the popular beef noodle soup called *pho*), and chicken and shrimp cooked in a clay pot. You can create your own Vietnamese "burritos" from a platter of tofu, noodles, and vegetables that you wrap in rice paper and dip in garlic sauce. Among my favorites are the shrimp lemon grass, savory and refreshing, and the tofu curry, swimming in herbs and vegetables straight from the garden. The Nhung Dam—a hearty spread of basil, cucumbers, mint, romaine, bean sprouts, pickled carrots, turnips, and vermicelli, wrapped in rice paper and dipped in a legendary sauce—is cooked at your table.

1792 Main St., Wailuku. ℗ 808/243-9560. Main courses $6.50–$17. DC, MC, V. Mon–Sat 10am–9:30pm; Sun 10am–8:30pm. Heading into Wailuku from Kahului, go over the bridge and take the 1st right onto Central Ave.; then take the 1st right on Nani St. At the next stop sign, look for the building with the neon sign that says OPEN.

INEXPENSIVE

A. K.'s Café ★★ *Value* HEALTHFUL/PLATE LUNCHES   Chef Elaine Rothermel has a winner with this tiny cafe in the industrial district of Wailuku. It may be slightly off the tourist path, but the creative cuisine coming out of the kitchen makes it well worth the effort to find this delicious eatery. Prices are so eye-poppingly cheap, you might find yourself wandering back here during your vacation. Lunches feature everything from grilled chicken with Thai sauce to fish tacos, from hamburger steak to seared ahi sandwich with eggplant tempura. Dinner specials include chicken marsala over noodles, crab cakes with papaya beurre blanc, tofu Napoleon with ginger-basil sauce, and Hunan lamb chops. There are plenty of heart-healthy options to choose from (low in sugar, salt, and fat).

1237 Lower Main St., Wailuku. ℗ 808/244-8774. www.akscafe.com. Plate lunches $6.75–$9.50; dinners $11–$18. MC, V. Tues–Fri 10:30am–2pm; Tues–Sat 5–9pm. Live Hawaiian music Fri–Sat nights.

Main Street Bistro *Value* AMERICAN   Formerly Who's the Boss restaurant and, before that, Iao Café, this popular eatery, located on the main street of Wailuku, is now owned by chef Tom Selman, well known in culinary circles on Maui. He was formerly the chef de cuisine at David Paul's Lahaina Grill and was also corporate chef for the Sansei/Vino restaurants. Main Street Bistro is open only for lunch, but Selman has added a *pau hana* (after-work) menu of tapas like crispy crab and shrimp *gau gee*, mini hamburgers, and barbecued ribs. He calls his cuisine "refined comfort food," with signature items that include onion rings with house-made smoky ketchup, roasted Chinese chicken salad, "mother's roast beef sandwich" (served open-faced on a French roll), Southern-fried chicken, Maryland-style crab cake, and a roasted-veggie sandwich. The chef will happily customize any menu item for those who prefer low-calorie, low-fat, or low-carbohydrate options. Daily specials range from grilled steak to Asian risotto with shrimp, crab, and veggies.

2051 Main St., Wailuku. ℗ 808/244-6816. Entrees $8–$13; daily specials $7–$15. DC, MC, V. Mon–Fri 11am–3pm; tapas menu 3–7pm.

Maui Bake Shop BAKERY/DELI   Sleepy Vineyard Street has seen many a mom-and-pop business come and go, but Maui Bake Shop is here to stay. Maui native Claire Fujii-Krall and her husband, baker José Krall (who was trained in the south of France), are turning out buttery brioches, healthful nine-grain and two-tone rye breads, focaccia, strudels, sumptuous fresh-fruit gâteaux, puff pastries, and dozens of other baked goods and confections. The breads are baked in one of Maui's oldest brick ovens, installed in 1935; a high-tech European diesel oven handles the rest. The front window displays more than 100 bakery and deli items, among them salads, a popular eggplant marinara focaccia, homemade quiches, and an inexpensive calzone filled with chicken, pesto, mushroom, and cheese. Homemade soups (clam chowder, minestrone, cream of asparagus) team up nicely with sandwiches on freshly baked bread. Save room for the ultimate dessert: white-chocolate macadamia-nut cheesecake.

2092 Vineyard St. (at N. Church St.), Wailuku. (C) 808/242-0064. Most items under $7. AE, DISC, MC, V. Tues–Fri 6:30am–2:30pm; Sat 7am–1pm.

Sam Sato's NOODLES/PLATE LUNCHES   Sam Sato's is a Maui institution, not only for its noodles (saimin, dry noodles, chow fun), but also for its flaky baked *manju,* a pastry filled with sweetened lima beans or adzuki beans. Sam opened his family eatery in 1933, and his daughter, Lynne Toma, makes the broth from scratch. The saimin and the dry noodles, with broth that comes in a separate bowl, are big sellers. Eat at the counter, with well-worn wooden stools and homemade salt and pepper shakers. Try the plate lunch with two barbecued meat sticks, two scoops of rice, and macaroni salad. The peach, apple, coconut, and pineapple turnovers fly out the door, as do takeout noodles. *Tip:* If you want them to hold the MSG, be sure to make your request early.

At the Millyard, 1750 Wili Pa Loop, Wailuku. (C) 808/244-7124. Plate lunches $6.50–$7.50. No credit cards. Mon–Sat 7am–2pm.

2 West Maui

LAHAINA
There's a **Maui Tacos** (p. 157) in Lahaina Square ((C) **808/661-8883**). Maui's branch of the **Hard Rock Cafe** is at 900 Front St., in Lahaina ((C) **808/667-7400**).

VERY EXPENSIVE
David Paul's Lahaina Grill ✹✹ NEW AMERICAN   Despite David Paul Johnson's departure, this Lahaina hot spot has maintained its popularity. It's still filled with chic, tanned diners in stylish aloha shirts, and there's still attitude aplenty at the entrance. The signature items remain: tequila shrimp and firecracker rice, Kona coffee–roasted rack of lamb, Maui onion–crusted seared ahi, and kalua-duck quesadilla. As always, a special custom-designed chef's table can be arranged with 72 hours' notice for larger parties. The ambience—black-and-white tile floors, pressed-tin ceilings, eclectic 1890s decor—is striking, and the bar, despite not having an ocean view, is the busiest spot in Lahaina.

127 Lahainaluna Rd. (C) 808/667-5117. Reservations required. Main courses $33–$88. AE, DC, DISC, MC, V. Daily 6–10pm. Bar daily 6–10pm (earlier if it's slow).

The Feast at Lele ✹✹ POLYNESIAN   The owners of the Old Lahaina Luau (see "A Night to Remember: Luau, Maui Style," p. 260) have recruited the culinary prowess of chef James McDonald (I'O and Pacific'O), found the perfect outdoor oceanfront setting, and added the exquisite dancers of the Old Lahaina Luau. The result: a culinary and cultural experience that sizzles. As if the sunset weren't heady enough, dances from Hawaii, New Zealand, Tahiti, and Samoa are presented, up close and personal, in full costumed splendor. Chanting, singing, drumming, dancing, the swish of ti-leaf skirts, the scent of plumeria—it's a full adventure, even for the most

Where to Dine in Lahaina & Kaanapali

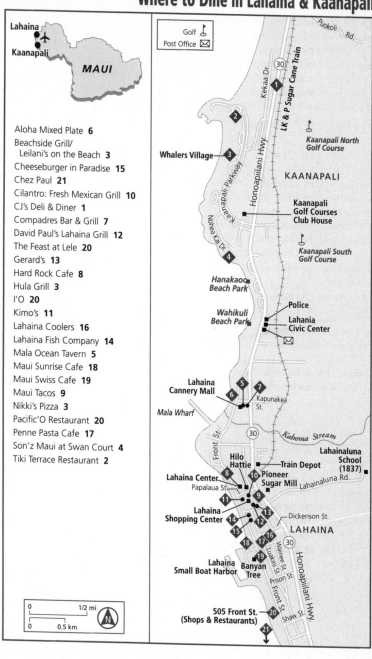

Aloha Mixed Plate **6**
Beachside Grill/
  Leilani's on the Beach **3**
Cheeseburger in Paradise **15**
Chez Paul **21**
Cilantro: Fresh Mexican Grill **10**
CJ's Deli & Diner **1**
Compadres Bar & Grill **7**
David Paul's Lahaina Grill **12**
The Feast at Lele **20**
Gerard's **13**
Hard Rock Cafe **8**
Hula Grill **3**
I'O **20**
Kimo's **11**
Lahaina Coolers **16**
Lahaina Fish Company **14**
Mala Ocean Tavern **5**
Maui Sunrise Cafe **18**
Maui Swiss Cafe **19**
Maui Tacos **9**
Nikki's Pizza **3**
Pacific'O Restaurant **20**
Penne Pasta Cafe **17**
Son'z Maui at Swan Court **4**
Tiki Terrace Restaurant **2**

jaded luau aficionado. Guests sit at white-clothed, candlelit tables set on the sand (unlike the luau, where seating is en masse) and dine on entrees from each island: imu-roasted kalua pig from Hawaii, Maori fishcake from New Zealand, *poisson cru* from Tahiti, and beef with breadfruit from Samoa. Particularly mesmerizing is the evening's opening: A softly lit canoe carries three people ashore to the sound of conch shells.

505 Front St. ℂ **886/244-5353** or 808/667-5353. www.feastatlele.com. Reservations required. Set 5-course menu $110 adults, $80 children 2–12. AE, DISC, MC, V. Apr–Sept daily 6–9pm; Oct–Mar daily 5:30–8:30pm.

EXPENSIVE

Chez Paul 🖈🖈 *(Finds* FRENCH   Chez Paul is located in the middle of nowhere, in Olowalu Village (a blip on the highway—if you blink, you'll miss it). But it's worth the drive to this classic French restaurant, under the helm of chef Patrick Callarec (formerly of the Ritz-Carlton's Anuenue Room). Look forward to such delights as wild-mushroom-and-brie pastry in an aged port-wine sauce, just to get started. Or choose the signature dish of crispy duck with local fruits or fresh Island fish in a champagne-and-cream sauce. Don't miss the pineapple-and-vanilla crème brûlée, served in a pineapple shell. The dress here is Maui casual, which means anything short of tank tops and shorts. Chez Paul has recently added lunch on Sunday starting at 11am.

Olowalu Village, Honoapiilani Hwy., Olowalu. ℂ **808/661-3843**. www.chezpaul.net. Reservations recommended. Main courses $30–$39. DISC, MC, V. Daily 5:30–9pm; Sun 11am–2:30pm.

Gerard's 🖈🖈🖈 *(Finds* FRENCH   The charm of Gerard's—soft lighting, excellent service, Edith Piaf on the sound system—is matched by a menu of uncompromising standards. After more than 2½ decades in Lahaina, Gerard Reversade never runs out of creative offerings, yet stays true to his French roots. Roasted opakapaka with star anise, fennel fondue, and hints of orange and ginger is a stellar entree on a menu of winners. The Kona lobster and avocado salad promises ecstasy, and the spinach salad with scallops is among the finest I've tasted. Gerard's has an excellent appetizer menu, with shiitake and oyster mushrooms in puff pastry, fresh ahi and smoked salmon carpaccio, and a very rich, highly touted escargot ragout with burgundy butter and garlic cream. The restaurant is a frequent winner of the *Wine Spectator* Award of Excellence, as well as the *Wine Enthusiast* 2006 Award of Distinction.

At the Plantation Inn, 174 Lahainaluna Rd. ℂ **808/661-8939**. www.gerardsmaui.com. Reservations recommended. Main courses $33–$54. AE, DC, DISC, MC, V. Daily 6–9pm.

I'O 🖈 PACIFIC RIM   I'O is a fantasy of sleek curves and etched glass, co-owned by chef James McDonald. He offers an impressive selection of appetizers (his strong suit) and some lavish Asian-Polynesian interpretations of seafood, such as his "rainbow catch"—fresh fish of the day topped with lemon-grass pesto, tomatoes, truffle oil, and goat-cheese fondue sauce—or his "scallops ala bondage"—scallops wrapped in sage and jalapeño bacon, served with roasted Japanese eggplant and a ponzu-cream sauce. Unless you're sold on a particular entree, my advice is to go heavy on the superb appetizers, especially the blackened-ahi tower (a tower of ahi, avocado, fruit, and tomatoes), shredded pork in a quesadilla with pepper-jack cheese, or the Siamese shashi rolls (spicy tempura portobello with an orange-mint dipping sauce). McDonald also owns Pacific'O Restaurant (reviewed below) and is the chef for the Feast at Lele (reviewed above).

505 Front St. ℂ **808/661-8422**. www.iomaui.com. Reservations recommended. Main courses $29–$66. AE, DC, DISC, MC, V. Daily 5:30–10pm.

Finds The Ultimate Cookies

Looking for the ultimate taste treat to bring the folks back home? Try mouth-watering **Broke da Mouth Cookies**, 190 Alamaha St., Kahului (℗ **808/873-9255**), open Monday through Friday from 6am to 7pm, Saturday from 7am to 5pm (get here early before the locals buy everything up). These terrific cookies range from chocolate mac-nut, oatmeal raisin, and shortbread to almond, peanut butter, and coconut crunch. While you're here, take a look at the other goodies—the chocolate-haupia pie is to die for, and the *lilikoi* (passion fruit) cake will make your taste buds stand up and applaud.

Pacific'O Restaurant ✪ CONTEMPORARY PACIFIC RIM   You can't get any closer to the ocean than the tables here, which are literally on the beach. With good food complementing this sensational setting, foodies and aesthetes have much to enjoy. The split-level dining starts near the entrance, with a long bar (where you can also order lunch or dinner) and a few tables along the railing. Steps lead down to the outdoor tables, where the award-winning seafood dishes come to you with the back-drop of Lanai across the channel. Favorites include the coconut-and-mac-nut-crusted catch of the day or the pasta moana—fresh fish with bay scallops, rock shrimp, shi-itake mushrooms, roasted peppers, and snap peas in a lobster-Alfredo sauce poured over orecchiette pasta. If you like seafood, sunsets, and touches of India and Indonesia in your fresh-from-the-sea dining choices, you should be happy here.

505 Front St. ℗ 808/667-4341. www.pacificomaui.com. Reservations recommended. Main courses $12–$16 lunch, $30–$40 dinner. AE, DC, MC, V. Daily 11:30am–4pm and 5:30–10pm.

MODERATE
Compadres Bar & Grill MEXICAN   Despite its concrete floor and high industrial ceilings, Compadres exudes good cheer. And that cheer has burgeoned lately with a new open-air seating area and a takeout taqueria window for diners on the run. The food is classic Tex-Mex, good any time of the day, beginning with huevos rancheros, egg burritos, hot cakes, and omelets (the Acapulco is heroic), and progressing to enchiladas and appetizers for the margarita-happy crowd. Stay spare (vegetable enchi-lada in fresh spinach tortilla) or get hefty (Texas T-bone and enchiladas). This is a care-free place with a large capacity for merrymaking. Don't miss Taco Tuesdays, from 4 to 8pm, when margaritas are just $3.

At the Lahaina Cannery Mall, 1221 Honoapiilani Hwy. ℗ 808/661-7189. www.compadresrestaurants.com. Main courses $10–$20. AE, DC, DISC, MC, V. Daily 8am–10pm.

Kimo's STEAK/SEAFOOD   Kimo's has a loyal following that keeps it from falling into the faceless morass of waterfront restaurants serving surf and turf with great sun-set views. It's a formula restaurant (sibling to Leilani's on the Beach and Hula Grill) that works not only because of its oceanfront patio and upstairs dining room, but also because, for the price, there are some satisfying choices. It's always crowded, buzzing with people on a deck offering views of Molokai, Lanai, and Kahoolawe. Burgers and sandwiches are affordable and consistent, and the fresh catch in sweet-basil glaze is a top seller. The waistline-defying hula pie—macadamia-nut ice cream in a chocolate-wafer crust with fudge and whipped cream—originated here.

845 Front St. ☎ **808/661-4811**. www.kimosmaui.com. Reservations recommended for dinner. Main courses $8–$13 lunch, $18–$35 dinner. AE, DC, DISC, MC, V. Daily 11am–3:30pm and 5–10:30pm. Bar 11am–1:30am; light menu 3:30–5pm.

Lahaina Fish Company SEAFOOD   The open-air dining room is literally over the water, with flickering torches after sunset and an affordable menu that covers the seafood-pasta basics. Head to an oceanside table and order a cheeseburger, chicken burger, fish burger, generous basket of peel-and-eat shrimp, or sashimi—lingering is highly recommended. The light lunch/grill menu offers appetizers (sashimi, seared ahi, spring rolls, and pot stickers), salads, and soups. The restaurant has spiffed up its dinner selections to include hand-carved steaks, several pasta choices, and local fare such as stir-fry dishes, teriyaki chicken, and luau-style ribs. The specialty, though, remains the fresh seafood: Four types of fresh fish are offered nightly, in three preparations. Pacific Rim specials include fresh ahi, seared spicy or cooked in a sweet ginger-soy sauce.

831 Front St. ☎ **808/661-3472**. Main courses $8–$15 lunch, $10–$28 dinner. AE, MC, V. Daily 11am–midnight.

Mala Ocean Tavern ★★ *Value* LOCAL/SEAFOOD   Perched right on the ocean, this tiny "tavern" is the brainchild of Mark and Judy Ellman, owners of Maui Tacos and Penne Pasta Café. They use healthy, organically grown food and fresh fish to make intriguing dishes. The atmosphere could not be more enticing, with just a handful of tables out on the oceanfront lanai and several more tables in the warmly decorated interior. The staff is helpful and efficient, and the food is outstanding. If you're in the mood, ask for the exotic martini menu. You can opt for "tavern food" like an ahi burger or a cheeseburger, one of the tempting salads (the beet and Kula goat cheese is divine), or something off the "big plate" menu (like wok-fried moi fish or hoisin-glazed baby back ribs). Don't miss the weekend brunches (I recommend the "killer" French toast). This is a popular place, so try to avoid prime lunch and dinner hours.

1307 Front St. (across from the Lahaina Cannery Mall's Safeway grocery store). ☎ **808/667-9394**. www.malaocean tavern.com. Small plates $5–$17; big plates $15–$26; brunch $6–$12. MC, V. Mon–Fri 11am–10pm; Sat 9am–1pm; Sun 9am–9pm.

INEXPENSIVE

Aloha Mixed Plate ★ *Value* PLATE LUNCHES/BEACHSIDE GRILL   Look for the festive turquoise-and-yellow, plantation-style front with the red corrugated-iron roof and adorable bar, tiny and busy, directly across from the Lahaina Cannery Mall. Grab a picnic table at ocean's edge, in the shade of large kiawe and milo trees, where you can watch the bobbing sailboats and two islands on the near horizon. (On the upper level, there are umbrellas and plumeria trees—just as charming.) Then tuck into inexpensive mahimahi, kalua pig and cabbage, shoyu chicken, teriyaki beef, and other local plate-lunch specials, all at budget-friendly prices, served with macaroni salad and rice. The shoyu chicken is the best I've had, fork-tender and tasty, and the spicy chicken drumettes come from a fabled family recipe. (The bestsellers are the coconut prawns and Aloha Mixed Plate of shoyu chicken, teriyaki beef, and mahimahi.) I don't know of anywhere else where you can order a mai tai with a plate lunch and enjoy table service with an ocean view.

1285 Front St. ☎ **808/661-3322**. www.alohamixedplate.com. Main courses $5–$13. MC, V. Daily 10:30am–10pm.

Cheeseburger in Paradise AMERICAN   Wildly successful, always crowded, highly visible, and very noisy (especially when live music plays in the evenings),

Finds Eat Like a Local

Are you the type of visitor who feels you haven't "experienced" a destination unless you've hit the restaurants where the local residents eat? Or do you enjoy National Public Radio's "Road Food," or any of the Food Network's on-the-road culinary shows? Then sign up for **Tour da Food** ✦✦✦ (© **808/242-8383**; www.tourdafood.com). Pastry chef (and food writer, restaurant publicist, and cookbook author) Bonnie Friedman takes foodies off the tourist path to discover the culinary treasures—from snack shacks to restaurants to markets and manufacturers—that make up Maui's unique cuisine. You will laugh your way across the island with Bonnie's wonderful commentary about Maui's multicultural food options and its colorful history—and you'll also eat some of the island's most yummy food (which you never would have discovered on your own). Check out her website to read about the different tours (from breakfast at an old inn to "lunch like a local" to "plate lunch and picnic with poke"); prices begin at $260 per couple, which includes transportation, a main meal, snacks, an island traditional dessert, a bag of goodies to take home, and Bonnie's personal list of under-the-radar eating places. *Tip:* Book this tour early in your trip, so you have time to follow Bonnie's terrific suggestions of places to eat on Maui.

Cheeseburger is a shrine to the American classic. The home of three-napkin cheeseburgers with attitude, this is burger country, tropical style, with everything from tofu and garden burgers to the biggest, juiciest beef and chicken burgers, served on whole-wheat and sesame buns baked fresh daily. There are good reasons why the two-story green-and-white building next to the sea wall is always packed: good value, good grinds, and a great ocean view. The Cheeseburger in Paradise—a hefty hunk with jack and cheddar cheeses, sautéed onions, lettuce, fresh tomatoes, and Thousand Island dressing—is a paean to the basics. You can build your own burger by adding sautéed mushrooms, bacon, grilled Ortega chiles, and other condiments for an extra charge. Onion rings, chili-cheese fries, and cold beer complete the carefree fantasy.

811 Front St. © **808/661-4855**. www.cheeseburgerland.com. Burgers $9–$13. AE, DISC, MC, V. Daily 8am–10pm.

Cilantro: Fresh Mexican Grill ✦ Finds Kids MEXICAN   This is Maui's best bet for fabulous Mexican food at frugal prices (and winner of the Taste of Lahaina Award each of the last 3 years). And, believe it or not, this fast-food restaurant serves fresh, healthy food. The chef and owner is Paris Nabavi, creator of Maui's Pizza Paradiso Italian Kitchen. He wanted the "challenge of something different," so he took off to Mexico to find out how the Mexicans used to cook in "the old days." He's back on Maui with this unbelievably delicious eatery where everything is made from scratch. Even the corn tortillas are handmade daily. Signature dishes include the citrus-and-herb-marinated chipotle rotisserie chicken, the veggie Mariposa salad, the popular motherclucker flautas, and lip-smacking "al pastor"-style adobo pork. All this at budget-pleasing prices. It's a great place to take the kids; Los Niños menu items are under $4.75.

170 Papalaua Ave. ℂ 808/667-5444. www.cilantrogrill.com. Entrees $5–$13. DISC, MC, V. Mon–Sat 11am–9pm; Sun 11am–8pm.

Lahaina Coolers ℱ AMERICAN/INTERNATIONAL A huge marlin hangs above the bar, epic wave shots and wall sconces made of surfboard fins fill the walls, and open windows line three sides of this ultracasual indoor/outdoor restaurant. This is a great breakfast joint, with feta-cheese Mediterranean omelets; huevos rancheros; and fried rice made with jasmine rice, Kula vegetables, and Portuguese sausage. There are three types of eggs Benedict: the classic, a vegetarian version (with Kula vegetables—excellent), and the Local, with Portuguese sausage and sweetbread. At lunch, burgers rule and the sandwiches, from grilled portobellos to the classic tuna melt, are ideal for casual Lahaina. The pasta, made fresh daily, is prepared Asian style (with chicken and spicy Thai peanut sauce), with pesto, or vegetarian (in a spicy Creole sauce). Pizzas, fresh catch, steak, and enchiladas round out the entrees. Everything can be prepared vegetarian upon request.

180 Dickenson St. ℂ 808/661-7082. Main courses $8.25–$10 breakfast, $8.50–$14 lunch, $10–$25 dinner. AE, DC, DISC, MC, V. Daily 8am–2am (full menu until midnight).

Maui Sunrise Café *(Value)* GOURMET DELI/CAFE If you want to know where to find the best breakfasts or the most filling lunches on a budget, follow the surfers to this teeny-tiny cafe located on Front Street, next door to the library. Eat in the patio garden out back or take your lunch to the beach. You'll find huge breakfasts, delicious gourmet sandwiches, and filling lunch plates all at bargain prices. It's tough to find a parking spot nearby (and you can't park at the library), but you'll probably want a brisk walk after eating here anyway.

693A Front St. ℂ 808/661-8558. Breakfast items under $10; lunch items $6–$10. No credit cards. Daily 6am–3pm.

Maui Swiss Cafe SANDWICHES/PIZZA Newly renovated and double its original size (which was tiny), Swiss Cafe now has five Internet stations and continues to serve excellent sandwiches and continental breakfast. Having gone from a sandwich-and-pizza shop to a European-style sidewalk Internet cafe, it still serves $5 lunch specials and two scoops of ice cream for $2.50 (and sometimes the ice cream is free with the lunch special). Top-quality breads baked fresh daily, Dijon mustard, good Swiss cheese, and keen attention to sandwich fillings and pizza toppings make this a very special sandwich shop. The Swiss owner, Dominique Martin, has imbued this corner of Lahaina with a European flavor, down to the menus printed in English and

---

Chef McDonald Has a Farm, E-I-E-I-O

Here's your chance to see where those delicious greens, sweet basil, and wonderful tropical fruits that make up your dinner at **Pacific'O** and **I'O** restaurants come from. **James McDonald** was the first chef in the state to own and operate a farm for the purpose of supplying his own restaurants. Your visit to **O'o Farm** begins with hot apple cider and pastries. The tour is led by a culinary specialist who helps you handpick items to take with you for a sampler. At the end of the tour, lunch is served. The cost is $50 per person. For more information, call ℂ 808/667-4341 or go to www.oofarm.com.

German and the Swiss breakfast of sliced ham, cheese, hard-boiled egg, and freshly baked croissant. *Tip:* The "signature melt" sandwiches, with imported Emmenthal cheese baked on an Italian Parmesan crust, are something to watch for, and there are excellent vegetarian and turkey sandwiches as well.

640 Front St. ℂ 808/661-6776. www.swisscafe.net. Sandwiches and 8-in. pizzas $6–$8. No credit cards. Daily 9am–8pm.

Penne Pasta Café 🌟 (Finds) ITALIAN/MEDITERRANEAN   Bargain hunters head for this neighborhood cafe, under the helm of chef Mark Ellman (of Maui Tacos and Mala fame). It features delicious Italian and Mediterranean cuisine. You'll get a sit-down meal at takeout prices, and *mama mia!*—those are big plates of pasta, pizzas, salads, and sandwiches. So, what's the catch? No wait help. You order at the counter and the manager delivers your order to your table. Favorites include the *molto bene* linguine pesto, baked penne, and pizza with olives, capers, basil, and roasted pepper. Wine (under $6 a glass) and beer are available, too.

180 Dickenson St. ℂ 808/661-6633. Basic menu items under $10; specials up to $14. AE, DC, DISC, MC, V. Mon–Fri 11am–9:30pm; Sat–Sun 5–9:30pm.

KAANAPALI
EXPENSIVE
Son'z Maui at Swan Court 🌟🌟🌟 CONTEMPORARY EUROPEAN/HAWAII REGIONAL   For 30 years, the Swan Court was *the* dining experience at the Hyatt Regency Maui Resort. When Tri-Star Restaurant Group CEO Aaron Placourakis (who also owns Nick's Fishmarket Maui; p. 163) took over this restaurant, he and executive chef Geno Sarmiento knew they wanted to hit a home run every night with the cuisine. The restaurant already had perhaps the most romantic location in Maui, overlooking a man-made lagoon with white and black swans swimming by and the rolling surf of the Pacific in the distance. Now the combination of the culinary team's creative dishes, fresh local ingredients (Kula corn and strawberries, Ono Farms avocados, Hana hearts of palm, Maui Cattle Company beef, fresh Hawaiian fish, and sweet Maui onions), top-notch service, and relaxing atmosphere makes this one of Maui's best restaurants. My personal picks from the very tempting menu are the Maui Surfing Goat Cheese ravioli appetizer (with Kula corn, edamame, Hamakua mushrooms, prosciutto, and a sherry-vinegar pan sauce) and, for a main course, either the Hawaiian opakapaka piccata (with artichokes, caperberries, Lisbon lemon, sweet-potato hash browns, and tomato purée) or the seared scallops BLT (with bacon and poached cherry tomatoes in a Caesar-salad emulsion, served with truffled potato chips). A beautiful breakfast buffet is also served.

At the Hyatt Regency Maui Resort, 200 Nohea Kai Dr. ℂ 808/667-4506. www.sonzmaui.com. Reservations necessary for dinner. Breakfast buffet $25, entrees $14–$22; dinner entrees $29–$50. AE, DC, DISC, MC, V. Daily 6:30–11am and 5:30–10pm.

MODERATE
Beachside Grill/Leilani's on the Beach STEAK/SEAFOOD   The Beachside Grill is the informal, less expensive room downstairs on the beach, where folks wander in off the sand for a frothy beer and a beachside burger. Leilani's is the dinner-only room, with more expensive but still not outrageously priced steak and seafood offerings. At Leilani's, you can order everything from fresh fish to filet mignon to fried coconut prawns. All of this, of course, comes with an ocean view. There's live music Friday, Saturday, and Sunday from 3 to 5:30pm.

(Finds) The Tiki Terrace

Bravo to the **Kaanapali Beach Hotel** for the low-salt, employee-tested Native Hawaiian diet served in its **Tiki Terrace Restaurant**, 2525 Kaanapali Pkwy. (℗ **808/667-0124**). The Hawaiian Combination features the healthy, traditional diet of fresh fish (you can also order it with chicken breast) and taro greens, flavored with herbs and spices. Fresh mild *limu* (seaweed) adds some natural saltiness, and you can always add your own salt and pepper to taste. The Native Hawaiian menu also includes a salad made from *pohole* fern shoots from Keanae Valley marinated with sweet Maui onions and seaweed and served with ginger-tomato dressing. (With their freshness, pleasing crunch, and mild flavor, fern shoots are one of the most underused greens of Hawaii.) Entree choices are accompanied by steamed sweet potato, taro, and fresh poi made on the premises. The dessert is half a chilled Hana papaya with lemon, grilled bananas, and pineapple slices. The cost for the Hawaiian Combination is $23.

The use of fresh local ingredients is a noteworthy touch in the a la carte menu as well. My favorites are the baked crab and shrimp with artichoke hearts and the coconut shrimp. Try Chef Muromoto's signature Sesame Shoyu dressing on the Kula greens salad—it's a house favorite. The a la carte menu entrees are headed up by the Huki Hukilau, a combination of fresh catch, jumbo prawn, and baby lobster tail. The menu also includes steak, ribs, teriyaki grilled chicken, and rack of lamb.

The dining room is old-fashioned Hawaii, not fancy, with tables on a terrace ringed with plumeria and palm trees. Nightly entertainment is a hula show from 6:30 to 7:30pm and music for dancing under the stars until 9pm.

At Whalers Village, 2435 Kaanapali Pkwy. ℗ **808/661-4495**. www.leilanis.com. Reservations suggested for dinner. Lunch and dinner (Beachside Grill) $10–$17; dinner (Leilani's) $18–$33. AE, DC, DISC, MC, V. Beachside Grill daily 11am–11pm (bar daily until 12:30am). Leilani's daily 5–10pm.

Hula Grill ⚓ HAWAII REGIONAL/SEAFOOD   Who wouldn't want to tuck into a wood-grilled ahi steak or a lemon-ginger roasted chicken at this bistro on the beach at Kaanapali? If you aren't that hungry, you have a choice of sandwiches, entrees, pizzas, appetizers, and salads. There's happy-hour entertainment and Hawaiian music daily. For those wanting a more casual atmosphere, the Barefoot Bar, located on the beach, offers burgers, fish, pizzas, and salads.

At Whalers Village, 2435 Kaanapali Pkwy. ℗ **808/667-6636**. www.hulagrill.com. Reservations recommended for dinner. Lunch and Barefoot Bar menus $8–$18; dinner main courses $17–$35. AE, DC, DISC, MC, V. Daily 11am–11pm.

INEXPENSIVE

Whalers Village, 2435 Kaanapali Pkwy., has a food court where you can get pizza, very good Japanese food (including tempura, soba, and other noodle dishes), Korean plates, and fast-food burgers at serve-yourself counters and courtyard tables. It's

The regular Tiki Terrace breakfast menu presents all the old favorites along with the opportunity to sample Hawaiian food in a familiar context: taro hash browns; three-egg lomi salmon omelet with sweet-potato home fries; a fruit plate of banana baked in ti leaf with lehua honey and macadamia nuts, served with yogurt; and French toast made with taro bread. There are even Hawaiian taro pancakes, and they're wonderful. The Hawaiian **Sunday Champagne Brunch** ($33) features more than 50 items on the buffet, plus stir-fry, carving, and omelet stations, along with Belgian waffles and great desserts, all accompanied by Hawaiian music.

At the resort's buffet-style **Mixed Plate** restaurant, the Hawaiian Friday lunch is widely touted among *Maui News* readers, who voted this the best Hawaiian food: fresh poi, lomi salmon, laulau, kalua pig, and ahi poke for $14. Dinner includes all of the above and prime rib for $17 (with an early-bird rate of $15, 4–6pm).

The hotel also serves guests a complimentary **Ohana Welcome Breakfast** on their first morning at 8am Monday through Saturday, with live music, hula, a buffet breakfast, and advice on how to make the most of a Maui vacation. The hotel's staff greets guests, then takes to the stage for one of their specialties—singing and dancing hulas. Then they are off to work while guests enjoy a tour of hotel events and island activities.

The emphasis on Hawaiian food is only one part of a pervasive spirit of aloha that distinguishes this hotel. Reservations are recommended for dining in the Tiki Terrace (② **808/667-0124**). Dinner is served daily from 6 to 9pm.

an inexpensive alternative and a quick, handy stop for shoppers and Kaanapali beachgoers.

CJ's Deli & Diner ⭑ *(Value* AMERICAN/DELI   If you're staying in Kaanapali, this restaurant is within walking distance from your resort; if you're not staying in Kaanapali, it's worth the drive to sample the "comfort food" (as they call it) at this hip, happening eatery with prices so low you won't believe you're still on Maui. A huge billboard menu hangs from the yellow-and-gold textured wall, and highly polished wooden floors give the roadside eatery a homey feeling. You can eat in or take out (you can even get a "chef-to-go" to come to your accommodations and cook for you), the atmosphere is friendly, and there's a computer with high-speed Internet access to keep the techies humming. Huge, delicious breakfasts are served from 7 to 11am (check out the $4.95 early-bird special of two eggs, bacon or sausage, rice, and coffee). There's a wide selection of egg dishes, plus pancakes and waffles, and don't forget the tempting delights from the bakery. Lunch ranges from deli sandwiches and burgers to pot roast, ribs, and fish dishes. If you are on your way to Hana or up to the top of Haleakala, stop by and get a box lunch. CJ's even has a menu for the kids.

At the Fairway Shops at Kaanapali, 2580 Kekaa Dr. (just off the Honoapiilani Hwy.), Kaanapali. ℂ 808/667-0968. Breakfast items $3–$9.50; lunch items $7–$12; Hana Lunch Box and Air Travel Lunch Box $12 each. AE, MC, V. Daily 7am–8pm.

Nikki's Pizza PIZZA   Formerly Pizza Paradiso, Nikki's has a full menu of pastas, pizzas, and desserts, including smoothies, coffee, and ice cream. This is a welcome addition to the Kaanapali scene, where casual is king and good food doesn't have to be fancy. The pizzas reflect a simple and effective formula that has won acclaim through the years: good crust, true-blue sauces, and toppings loyal to tradition but with just enough edge for those who want it. Create your own pizza with roasted eggplant, mushrooms, anchovies, artichoke hearts, sausage, and a slew of other toppings. Nikki's offers some heroic choices, from the Hawaiian (ham and Maui pineapple) to the Sopranos (roasted chicken, artichoke hearts, sun-dried tomatoes).

At Whalers Village, 2435 Kaanapali Pkwy. ℂ 808/667-0333. Gourmet pizza $3.85–$4.65 by the slice; whole pizzas $12–$27. MC, V. Daily 11am–10pm.

HONOKOWAI, KAHANA & NAPILI

Note: You'll find the following restaurants on the "Where to Stay & Dine from Honokowai to Kapalua" map on p. 115.

EXPENSIVE

Roy's Kahana Bar & Grill 🐟🐟 EURO-ASIAN   Despite the lack of dramatic view and its upstairs location in a shopping mall, Roy's remains crowded and extremely popular for one reason: fabulous food. It bustles with young, hip, impeccably trained servers delivering wasabi/pistachio-crusted ahi steak, hibachi-grilled salmon (with Japanese-style citrus ponzu), and glazed honey-mustard short ribs. You could make a meal of the creative appetizers, such as Roy's original Hawaiian blackened ahi, crab cakes, seared shrimp sticks, crispy shrimp and pork *lumpia*, or Kula baby-spinach salad. Large picture windows open up Roy's Kahana but don't quell the noise, another tireless trait long ago established by Roy's Restaurant in Honolulu, the flagship of Yamaguchi's burgeoning empire.

At the Kahana Gateway Shopping Center, 4405 Honoapiilani Hwy. ℂ 808/669-6999. www.roysrestaurant.com. Reservations strongly recommended. Main courses $27–$42. AE, DC, DISC, MC, V. Daily 5:30–10pm.

Sea House Restaurant ASIAN/PACIFIC RIM   The Sea House is not glamorous, famous, or hip, but it's worth mentioning for its spectacular view of Napili Bay. The Napili Kai Beach Resort, where the Sea House is located, is a charming throwback to the days when hotels blended in with their surroundings, had lush tropical foliage, and were sprawling rather than vertical. Dinner entrees range from "Uncle Frank's" banana Hawaiian snapper (with Hawaiian vanilla bean and coconut-curry essence) to veal piccata. The *keiki* (kids') menu includes hamburgers and chicken nuggets.

At the Napili Kai Beach Resort, 5900 Honoapiilani Hwy. ℂ 808/669-1500. Reservations required for dinner. Main courses $25–$42; appetizer menu $5–$24. AE, DISC, MC, V. Daily 8–10:30am, 11:30am–2pm, and 5:30–9pm.

MODERATE

Maui Brewing Co. SEAFOOD/STEAK   This restaurant consists of a bar, a retail section, and tables. The small retail section sells fresh seafood, while the sit-down menu covers basic tastes: salads, fish and chips, fresh-fish sandwiches, cheeseburgers, and beer—lots of it. At dinner, count on heavier meats and the fresh catch of the day (maybe ahi, mahimahi, or ono), with rotisserie items such as grilled chicken, steaks, and duck. The late-night menu offers shrimp, cheese fries, quesadillas, and lighter fare.

At the Kahana Gateway Shopping Center, 4405 Honoapiilani Hwy. ℂ 808/669-3474. www.mauibrewingco.com. Reservations recommended for dinner. Main courses $8–$14 lunch, $13–$36 dinner. AE, DC, DISC, MC, V. Daily 11am–10pm; late-night menu 10:30pm–1am. Sun brunch 7:30am–3pm during football season (Sept–Jan).

INEXPENSIVE

Maui Tacos MEXICAN   Mark Ellman's Maui Tacos chain has grown faster than you can say "Haleakala." Ellman put gourmet Mexican on paper plates and on the island's culinary map long before Maui became known as Hawaii's center for salsa and chimichangas. Barely more than a takeout counter with a few tables, this and the six other Maui Tacos in Hawaii (five on Maui alone) are popular with hungry surfers, discerning diners, burrito buffs, and Hollywood glitterati like Sharon Stone, whose picture adorns a wall or two. Choices include excellent fresh-fish tacos (garlicky and flavorful), chimichangas, and mouth-breaking compositions such as the Hookipa (a personal favorite): a "surf burrito" of fresh fish, black beans, and salsa. The spinach burrito contains four kinds of beans, rice, and potatoes—it's a knockout, requiring a siesta afterward. Expect good food but not very fast service.

At Napili Plaza, 5095 Napili Hau St. ℂ 808/665-0222. www.mauitacos.com. All items $1.75–$8.50. AE, DISC, MC, V. Mon–Sat 9am–9pm; Sun 9am–8pm. Also in Lahaina Sq., Lahaina (ℂ 808/661-8883); Kamaole Beach Center, Kihei (ℂ 808/879-5005); Piilani Village Shopping Center, Kihei (ℂ 808/875-9340); and Kaahumanu Center, Kahului (ℂ 808/871-7726).

Pizza Paradiso Italian Kitchen PIZZA/ITALIAN   Order at the counter (pastas, gourmet pizza whole or by the slice, paninis, salads, and desserts) and find a seat at one of the few tables. The pasta sauces—marinara, pescatore, Alfredo, Florentine, and pesto, with options and add-ons—are as popular as the pizzas (which took best pizza in the 2005 *Maui News'* reader poll). The Massimo, a pesto sauce with artichoke hearts, sun-dried tomatoes, and capers, comes with a choice of chicken, shrimp, or clams, and is so good it was a Taste of Lahaina winner. Recent additions to the menu include gyros, souvlaki, hummus, and cheesesteak sandwiches. Takeout, dine-in, or delivery (free!), this is a hot spot in the neighborhood.

At the Honokowai Marketplace, 3350 Lower Honoapiilani Rd. ℂ 808/667-2929. www.pizzaparadiso.com. Pastas $10–$11; pizzas $14–$28. DISC, MC, V. Daily 11am–10pm.

KAPALUA

Note: You'll find the following restaurants on the "Where to Stay & Dine from Honokowai to Kapalua" map on p. 115.

VERY EXPENSIVE

The Banyan Tree ASIAN-INSPIRED   The most recent chef de cuisine, in a long line of outstanding chefs chosen from the stables of the Ritz-Carlton resorts around the globe, is Jojo Vasquez. His distinctive menu includes sautéed Kona kampachi with mustard greens, avocado, and poached-shrimp salad; steamed onaga with Chinese black beans and pineapple emulsion; and roasted Muscovy duck breast with snake beans, enoki mushrooms, and pineapple *gastrique*. The four- and five- course tasting menus incorporate Hawaiian gold Kapalua pineapple in every course (pineapple scallops, steamed onaga with spiced essence, crispy duck confit, and pineapple tiramisu). The atmosphere is extremely romantic, overlooking the ocean with the island of Molokai in the distance—get reservations for sunset.

At the Ritz-Carlton Kapalua, 1 Ritz-Carlton Dr. ℂ 808/669-6200. Reservations recommended. Main courses $34–$55; 4-course tasting menu $100; 5-course tasting menu $125. AE, DC, DISC, MC, V. Tues–Sat 5:30–9:30pm.

EXPENSIVE

Pineapple Grill ★★★ PACIFIC ISLAND   If you had only a single night to eat on the island of Maui, this would be the place to go. Up-and-coming young chef Ryan Luckey (a local Lahaina boy) has taken the helm and is winning high praise from both critics and the local residents who flock here nightly. My picks on this creative menu would be ahi steak crusted with pistachios and wasabi peas (served with coconut-scented rice, Hamakua mushrooms, and wasabi-ginger butter), sake-soy grilled mahimahi (in a ginger-carrot emulsion), or the wonderful Maui-style seafood paella (with a hint of Portuguese sausage and Kula herbs). An excellent list of wine pairings by the glass is available. Save room for the Maui gold-pineapple upside-down cake (with Whaler dark-rum sauce and Maui-made Roselani gourmet mac-nut ice cream). There are lots of tasty sandwiches and salads at lunch, and a continental-style breakfast in the morning. Plus, it's all served in a very Maui-like atmosphere, overlooking the rolling hills of the Kapalua golf course out to the Pacific Ocean.

At the Kapalua Golf Club Bay Course, 200 Kapalua Dr. ✆ **808/669-9600.** www.pineapplekapalua.com. Reservations recommended for dinner. Main courses $7–$17 lunch, $10–$45 dinner. AE, MC, V. Daily 8am–10pm.

Plantation House Restaurant ★★ SEAFOOD/HAWAIIAN-MEDITER-RANEAN   With its teak tables, fireplace, and open sides, Plantation House gets stellar marks for atmosphere. The 360-degree view from high among the resort's pine-studded hills takes in Molokai and Lanai, the ocean, the rolling fairways and greens, the northwestern flanks of the West Maui Mountains, and the daily sunset spectacular. Readers of the *Maui News* have deemed this the island's "Best Ambience"—a big honor on an island of wonderful views. It's the best place for breakfast in west Maui, hands down, and one of my top choices for dinner. The eggs Mediterranean makes a superb start to your day, and at lunch, sandwiches (open-faced smoked turkey, roasted vegetable, and goat-cheese wrap) and salads rule. When the sun sets, the menu expands to marvelous starters such as polenta and scampi-style shrimp, crab cakes, and Kula and Mediterranean salads. The menu changes constantly but may include fresh fish prepared several ways—among them, Mediterranean (on roasted Maui onions with couscous), Venice (pressed in panko, with a golden-raisin/pine-nut butter), Maui (pistachio-crusted), Plantation (with sautéed crab and lemon beurre blanc), and Italy (pepper-dusted with olives and caper-berry salsa). Don't forget the numerous vegetarian entrees and wonderful Australian lamb, New Zealand lobster, and a Tuscan-style rib-eye steak you'll long remember.

At the Kapalua Golf Club Plantation Course, 2000 Plantation Club Dr. ✆ **808/669-6299.** www.theplantation house.com. Reservations recommended. Main courses $26–$42. AE, DC, MC, V. Daily 8am–3pm and 5:30–10pm.

MODERATE

Sansei Seafood Restaurant & Sushi Bar ★★ PACIFIC RIM/SUSHI   Perpetual award-winner Sansei offers an extensive menu of Japanese and East-West delicacies. Part fusion, part Hawaii Regional Cuisine, Sansei is tirelessly creative, with a menu that scores higher with adventurous palates than with purists (although there are endless traditional choices as well). If you don't like cilantro, watch out for those complex mango/crab-salad rolls. Other choices include panko-crusted ahi sashimi, sashimi trio, ahi carpaccio, noodle dishes, lobster, Asian shrimp cakes, and sauces that surprise, in creative combinations such as ginger-lime chile butter and cilantro pesto. But there's simpler fare as well, such as shrimp tempura, noodles, and wok-tossed upcountry vegetables. Desserts are not to be missed. If it's autumn, don't pass up the Granny Smith apple tart with vanilla ice cream and homemade caramel sauce. In other seasons, opt for tempura-fried ice cream with chocolate sauce. There's karaoke Thursday and Friday nights from 10pm to 1am. *Money-saving tip:* Eat early; all food is 25% off between 5:30 and 6pm.

600 Office Rd. (*C*) 808/669-6286. www.sanseihawaii.com. Reservations recommended. Main courses $16–$43. AE, DISC, MC, V. Daily 5:30–10pm. Also at Kihei Town Center, Kihei ((*C*) 808/879-0004).

Vino Italian Tapas & Wine Bar *(Finds* ITALIAN   D. K. Kodama (chef and owner of Sansei Seafood Restaurant & Sushi Bar, reviewed above) and Chuck Furuya (Hawaii's only master sommelier) teamed up to create this culinary adventure, which opened in 2003 to big, big accolades. Probably the best Italian food on Maui is served at this exquisite restaurant, overlooking the rolling hills of the Kapalua Golf Club. The menu features more than two dozen tapas (small plates), ranging from the signature asparagus Milanese (just $7) to slow butter-poached Kona lobster ($20). The most popular large-plate dishes include fresh mahimahi with artichokes and grape tomatoes on capellini, crusted pan-fried veal stuffed with prosciutto, and *osso buco* with spinach risotto. Go to Vino's early during your stay on Maui; you most likely will want to return.

At the Kapalua Golf Club Village Course, 2000 Village Rd. (*C*) 808/661-VINO (8466). Reservations recommended. Tapas $6–$20; large plates $19–$38. AE, DISC, MC, V. Daily 11am–2pm and 5–9:30pm.

3 South Maui

KIHEI/MAALAEA

There's a **Maui Tacos** at Kamaole Beach Center, in Kihei ((*C*) 808/879-5005).

EXPENSIVE

Buzz's Wharf AMERICAN   Buzz's is another formula restaurant that offers a superb view, substantial sandwiches, meaty french fries, and surf-and-turf fare—in a word, satisfying but not sensational. Still, this bright, airy dining room makes a fine way station for whale-watching over a cold beer and a mahimahi sandwich. Consider opting for several appetizers (stuffed mushrooms, steamer clams, clam chowder, onion soup) and a salad, and then splurge on dessert. Buzz's prize-winning Tahitian Baked Papaya is a warm, fragrant melding of fresh papaya with vanilla and coconut—the pride of the house.

50 Hauoli St., Maalaea Harbor. (*C*) 808/244-5426. www.buzzswharf.com. Reservations recommended. Main courses $7–$21 lunch, $15–$22 dinner. AE, DC, DISC, MC, V. Daily 11am–9pm.

Five Palms *(* PACIFIC RIM   This is the best lunch spot in Kihei—open air, with tables a few feet from the beach and up-close-and-personal views of Kahoolawe and Molokini. You'll have to walk through a nondescript parking area and the modest entrance of the Mana Kai Maui Resort to reach this unpretentious place. It features a menu of breakfast and lunch items served from 8am to 2:30pm, so if you're jet-lagged and your stomach isn't on Hawaiian time, you can get a crab omelet at 2 in the afternoon or a juicy Kobe beef hamburger at 8 in the morning. At dinner, with the torches lit on the beach and the main dining room open, the ambience shifts to evening romantic, but still casual. Just-caught fish is the star of the dinner menu.

At the Mana Kai Maui Resort, 2960 S. Kihei Rd., Kihei. (*C*) 808/879-2607. www.fivepalmsrestaurant.com. Reservations recommended for dinner. Main courses $8–$19 breakfast and lunch, $28–$45 dinner. AE, DC, MC, V. Daily 8am–2:30pm and 5–9:30pm; pupu menu daily 2:45–6pm.

The Waterfront at Maalaea ★★ SEAFOOD   The family-owned Waterfront has won many prestigious awards for wine excellence, service, and seafood, but its biggest boost is word of mouth. Loyal diners rave about the friendly staff and seafood, fresh off the boat in nearby Maalaea Harbor and prepared with care. The bay and harbor view is one you'll never forget, especially at sunset. There are nine choices of preparations for the several varieties of fresh Hawaiian fish, ranging from *en papillote* (baked in buttered parchment) to Southwestern (smoked chile and cilantro butter) to Island style (sautéed, broiled, poached, or baked and paired with tiger prawns). Other choices: Kula onion soup, an excellent Caesar salad, the signature lobster chowder, and grilled eggplant layered with Maui onions, tomatoes, and spinach, served with red-pepper coulis and feta ravioli. Like the seafood, it's superb.

50 Hauoli St., Maalaea Harbor. ✆ 808/244-9028. www.waterfrontrestaurant.net. Reservations recommended. Main courses $19–$38. AE, DC, DISC, MC, V. Daily 5pm–closing (last seating at 8:30pm).

MODERATE
Cafe O'Lei Kihei ★★ STEAK/SEAFOOD   Chefs Michael and Dana Pastula have had a host of Cafe O'Lei restaurants on Maui (in Makawao, Lahaina, Maalaea, and Napili), and I've loved every one of them. Their latest (in addition to the Maalaea Grill, reviewed below) is in an out-of-the-way location, the not-very-attractive Rainbow Mall. Never mind—you come here for the food, not the view (which is of congested Kihei Rd. and a small bit of ocean between the fence of high-rise condos across the street). Inside, the open and airy room has floor-to-ceiling windows, hardwood floors, a big circular bar in the middle, and, on one side, an exhibition kitchen. The atmosphere is relaxing and inviting. The food is, as usual, not only outstanding, but also a real bargain. You can't beat lunch with fresh fish, rice, and salad for under $12 (arrive early, as the locals will book all the tables in advance). Dinners range from fresh fish to prime rib, mac-nut-crusted chicken breast to roast duck, and even a mushroom-asparagus-pine-nut linguine for the vegetarians. Save room for dessert, such as pineapple upside-down cake or a fudge-brownie sundae (yum, yum).

2439 S. Kihei Rd., Kihei. ✆ 808/891-1368. www.cafeoleirestaurants.com. Reservations recommended. Main courses $7–$13 lunch, $15–$35 dinner. AE, DC, DISC, MC, V. Tues–Sun 10:30am–10pm.

Maalaea Grill ★ ECLECTIC   This relaxing restaurant, with hardwood floors, bamboo dividers, and high ceilings, has one of the best views of the Pacific Ocean in Maalaea. There's a great lanai for sitting outside, but it's rarely used because the near-constant winds in Maalaea are wickedly strong. The lunch menu includes a yummy Asian salad (Oriental veggies and Chinese noodles over organic baby greens with a sesame vinaigrette) for $9, a mac-nut-crusted ono with a ginger-butter sauce for $12, and a range of burgers. At dinner, come before sunset and enjoy a terrific selection of fresh fish (prepared numerous ways), chicken, beef, and pasta. The restaurant is under the helm of Michael and Dana Pastula (who also own Cafe O'Lei, reviewed above). Their philosophy is "good food without hurting your pocketbook."

300 Maalaea Rd., Maalaea Harbor Village. ✆ 808/243-2206. www.cafeoleirestaurants.com/thegrill. Main courses $7–$16 lunch, $13–$33 dinner. AE, DC, DISC, MC. V. Tues–Sun 10:30am–9pm; Mon 10:30am–3pm.

Stella Blues Cafe ★ AMERICAN   Stella Blues gets going at breakfast and continues through to dinner with something for everyone—vegetarians, kids, pasta and sandwich lovers, hefty steak eaters, and sensible diners who go for the inexpensive salad of fresh Maui greens. Grateful Dead posters line the walls, and a covey of gleaming motorcycles is invariably parked outside. It's loud and lively, irreverent and

Where to Dine in South Maui

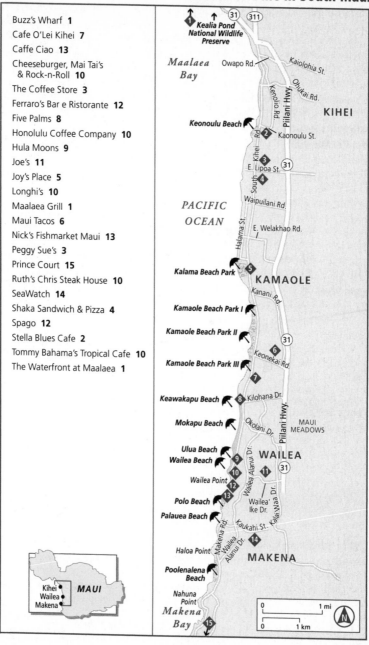

Buzz's Wharf **1**

Cafe O'Lei Kihei **7**

Caffe Ciao **13**

Cheeseburger, Mai Tai's & Rock-n-Roll **10**

The Coffee Store **3**

Ferraro's Bar e Ristorante **12**

Five Palms **8**

Honolulu Coffee Company **10**

Hula Moons **9**

Joe's **11**

Joy's Place **5**

Longhi's **10**

Maalaea Grill **1**

Maui Tacos **6**

Nick's Fishmarket Maui **13**

Peggy Sue's **3**

Prince Court **15**

Ruth's Chris Steak House **10**

SeaWatch **14**

Shaka Sandwich & Pizza **4**

Spago **12**

Stella Blues Cafe **2**

Tommy Bahama's Tropical Cafe **10**

The Waterfront at Maalaea **1**

unpretentious. Sandwiches are the highlight, ranging from Tofu Extraordinaire to grilled chicken to Mom's egg salad on a croissant. Tofu wraps and mountain-size Cobb salads are popular, as are large coffee shakes with mounds of whipped cream. Daily specials include fresh seafood. All of the home-style meals are made from scratch, down to the pesto mayonnaise and herb bread. At dinner, selections are geared toward good-value family dining, from affordable full dinners to pastas and burgers.

At the Azeka Place II Shopping Center, 1279 S. Kihei Rd., Kihei. (C) 808/874-3779. www.stellablues.com. Main courses $18–$31. AE, DC, DISC, MC, V. Daily 7:30am–10pm (happy hour 3:30–5pm).

INEXPENSIVE

The Coffee Store COFFEEHOUSE   This simple, classic coffeehouse for caffeine connoisseurs serves two dozen types of coffee and coffee drinks, from mochas and lattes to cappuccinos, espressos, and toddies. Breakfast items include smoothies, lox and bagels, quiches, granola, and assorted pastries. Salads and sandwiches (tuna, turkey, ham, grilled veggie panini) also move briskly from the takeout counter. The turkey-and-veggie wraps are a local legend. There are only a few small tables, and they fill up fast, often with musicians and artists who've spent the previous evening entertaining at the Wailea and Kihei resorts.

At the Azeka Place II Shopping Center, 1279 S. Kihei Rd., Kihei. (C) 808/875-4244. www.mauicoffee.com. All items under $8.50. AE, MC, V. Mon–Sat 6am–7pm; Sun 6am–5pm.

Joy's Place (Value) HEALTHY DELI/SANDWICHES   If you're in Kihei and looking for a healthy, delicious lunch at a rock-bottom price, it's worth hunting around for Joy's Place. This tiny hole in the wall has humongous sandwiches (turkey and avocado, tuna salad), wheat-free wraps, fresh salads, hot items (falafel burger, veggie burger), soups, and desserts. Most items are organic. There are a few places to sit inside, but the beach is just a couple minutes' walk away.

In the Island Surf Building, 1993 S. Kihei Rd. (entrance on Auhana St.). (C) 808/879-9258. All items under $10. AE, DC, DISC, MC, V. Mon–Sat 10am–3pm.

Peggy Sue's AMERICAN   Just for a moment, forget that diet and take a leap. This 1950s-style diner has oodles of charm and is a swell place to spring for the best chocolate malt on the island. You'll also find sodas, shakes, floats, egg creams, milkshakes, and made-on-Maui Roselani-brand gourmet ice cream. Old-fashioned soda-shop stools, an ELVIS PRESLEY BOULEVARD sign, and jukeboxes on every Formica table serve as a backdrop for the famous burgers (and garden burgers), brushed with teriyaki sauce and served with all the goodies. The fries are great, too.

At the Azeka Place II Shopping Center, 1279 S. Kihei Rd., Kihei. (C) 808/875-8944. Burgers $8.45–$11; plate lunches $7–$16. AE, DISC, MC, V. Sun–Thurs 11am–9pm; Fri–Sat 11am–10pm.

Shaka Sandwich & Pizza PIZZA   How many "best pizzas" are there on Maui? It depends on which shore you're on, the west or the south. This south-shore old-timer recently moved to a new (and much larger) location, but the award-winning pizzas, New York–style heroes, Philly cheesesteaks, calzones, salads, and homemade garlic bread haven't changed. Shaka uses fresh Maui produce, long-simmered sauces, and homemade Italian bread. Choose thin or Sicilian thick crust with gourmet toppings: Maui onions, spinach, anchovies, jalapeños, and a spate of other vegetables. Try the white pizza; with the perfectly balanced flavors of olive oil, garlic, and cheese, you won't even miss the tomato sauce. My favorite, the spinach pizza (with olive oil, spinach, garlic, and mozzarella), is a real treat.

1770 S. Kihei Rd., Kihei. © 808/874-0331. Sandwiches $6–$15; pizzas $17–$29. MC, V. Sun–Thurs 10:30am–9pm; Fri–Sat 10:30am–10pm.

WAILEA

The **Shops at Wailea,** with a sprawling location between the Grand Wailea Resort and Outrigger Wailea Resort, has added a spate of new shops and restaurants to this stretch of south Maui. Five restaurants and dozens of shops, most of them upscale, are among the new tenants of this complex. **Ruth's Chris Steak House** is here, as well as **Tommy Bahama's Tropical Cafe & Emporium; Honolulu Coffee Company; Longhi's;** and **Cheeseburger, Mai Tai's & Rock-n-Roll.** Next door at the Wailea Beach Marriott Resort, **Hula Moons,** the retro-Hawaiian-themed restaurant, has reopened after a $3-million renovation and moved to the upper level of the lobby building, where it serves mid-priced steak and seafood with an ocean view.

VERY EXPENSIVE

Longhi's ⋒ ITALIAN   Unfortunately, the ocean view is now blocked by yet another high-rise, but Longhi's open-air room and its trademark black-and-white checkered floor still make a great backdrop to start the day. Breakfasts here are worth waking up for: perfect baguettes, fresh-baked cinnamon rolls (one is enough for two people), and eggs Benedict or Florentine. Lunch is either an Italian banquet (ahi torino, prawns amaretto, and a wide variety of pastas) or fresh salads and sandwiches. Dinner is where Longhi's shines, with a long list of fresh-made pasta dishes, seafood platters, and beef and chicken dishes (filet mignon with basil, veal scaloppine). Leave room for the daily dessert specials.

At the Shops at Wailea, 3750 Wailea Alanui Dr., Wailea. © 808/891-8883. www.longhi-maui.com. Reservations recommended for dinner. Breakfast items $8.50–$20; lunch items $8.50–$33; dinner main courses $28–$100. AE, DC, DISC, MC, V. Mon–Fri 8am–10pm; Sat–Sun 7:30am–10pm.

Nick's Fishmarket Maui ⋒⋒ SEAFOOD   Here's the place to bring your sweetie to enjoy the moon rise and the sweet smell of the stephanotis growing on the terrace. Fans love this classic seafood restaurant that sticks to the tried and true. The few detractors complain that the food is too old style (circa 1970s), but most agree that there is a high degree of professionalism in both service and preparation, and it's hard to beat the fantasy setting on the south Maui shoreline. The Greek Maui Wowie salad gets my vote as one of the top salads in Hawaii. The rest of the menu features great fresh fish like opakapaka (one of the signature dishes), seared opah, and Hawaiian spiny lobster. There are ample choices for the nonfish-eaters as well, including rack of lamb, roasted chicken, and dry-aged New York steak.

At the Fairmont Kea Lani Maui, 4100 Wailea Alanui Dr. © 808/879-7224. www.tristarrestaurants.com. Reservations recommended. Main courses $30–$80; prix-fixe dinners $55–$85. AE, DC, DISC, MC, V. Daily 5:30–9:45pm. Bar until 11pm.

Spago ⋒⋒ HAWAIIAN/CALIFORNIA/PACIFIC REGIONAL   California meets Hawaii in this contemporary eatery featuring fresh, local Hawaii ingredients prepared under the culinary watch of master chef Wolfgang Puck. The room, formerly Seasons Dining Room, has been stunningly transformed into a sleek modern layout using stone and wood in the open-air setting overlooking the Pacific. The cuisine lives up to Puck's reputation of tweaking traditional Hawaiian dishes with his own brand of cutting-edge innovations. The menu features Hawaiian hapuupuu steamed in ti leaves; pineapple Thai red curry with onaga, mahi, and shrimp; grilled Chinois-style lamb chops; and caramelized pork chops with pineapple and papaya. The wine and beverage list is well thought out and extensive. Make reservations as soon as you land on the island (if not before)—this place is popular.

At the Four Seasons Resort Maui at Wailea, 3900 Wailea Alanui Dr. (C) 808/879-2999. www.fourseasons.com/maui. Reservations required. Main courses $40–$50. AE, DC, DISC, MC, V. Daily 5:30–9:30pm. Bar with pupu daily 5–11pm.

EXPENSIVE

Ferraro's Bar e Ristorante ⋒ ITALIAN

This was a master stroke for the Four Seasons: authentic Italian fare in a casual outdoor tropical setting, with a drop-dead gorgeous view of the ocean and the West Maui Mountains. Ferraro's is not inexpensive, but the food is first rate. Lunch in the open-air restaurant features fabulous salads (my pick is the seared Hawaiian tuna Niçoise salad), sandwiches (from a chicken pita to a grilled sirloin burger), and some Hawaiian classics (try the sesame-crusted salmon). At dinner, the romantic setting, with the sound of the ocean waves, makes for a memorable evening. The fish selection is noteworthy: grilled ahi with a crispy basil risotto roll, candied bell peppers, goat cheese, and a pine-nut dressing, or panfried mahi with basil gnocchi. Make room for dessert—my favorite is the roasted Maui pineapple cobbler with buttermilk-rum ice cream.

At the Four Seasons Resort Maui at Wailea, 3900 Wailea Alanui Dr. (C) 808/874-8000. www.fourseasons.com/maui. Reservations recommended. Main courses $15–$22 lunch, $25–$46 dinner. AE, DC, DISC, MC, V. Daily 11:30am–4pm, 4–6pm (pupu menu), and 6–9pm.

SeaWatch ⋒ ISLAND

Under the same ownership as Kapalua's Plantation House Restaurant (p. 158), SeaWatch is a good choice from morning to evening, and it's one of the more affordable stops in tony Wailea. You'll dine on the terrace or in a high-ceilinged room, from a menu that carries the tee-off-to-19th-hole crowd with ease. From breakfast on, it's a celebration of Island bounty: Crab-cake eggs Benedict or smoked-salmon Benedict is a great way to start your day. Lunch has a range of sandwiches (fresh fish, mango barbecue kalua pork, and traditional burgers), salads, and entrees (blackened fresh catch, stir-fried vegetables with grilled basil chicken). Dinner, with that fabulous ocean view, features five different preparations of the fish of the day, roasted New Zealand lamb, Muscovy duck, and free-range chicken breast.

At the Wailea Golf Club Gold Course, 100 Wailea Golf Club Dr. (C) 808/875-8080. www.seawatchrestaurant.com. Reservations recommended for dinner. Main courses $8.50–$15 breakfast and lunch, $26–$40 dinner. AE, DC, MC, V. Daily 8am–10pm.

MODERATE

Caffe Ciao ⋒ ITALIAN

There are two parts to this charming trattoria: the deli, with a takeout section, and the cafe, with tables under the trees, next to the bar. Rare and wonderful wines, such as Vine Cliff, are sold in the deli, along with ultraluxe rose soaps and other bath products, assorted pastas, pizzas, roasted potatoes, vegetable panini, vegetable lasagna, abundant salads, and an appealing selection of microwavable and takeout goodies. On the terrace under the trees, the tables are cheerfully accented with Italian herbs growing in cachepots. My fave is the linguine pomodoro, with fresh tomatoes, spinach-tomato sauce, and a dollop of mascarpone. Unfortunately, lunch is served only in summer and from mid-December to mid-March, when most of the tourists are around.

At the Fairmont Kea Lani Maui, 4100 Wailea Alanui. (C) 808/875-4100. Reservations recommended. Main courses $13–$20 lunch, $17–$36 dinner; pizzas $17–$19. AE, DC, DISC, MC, V. Lunch (mid-Dec to mid-Mar) daily noon–3pm; dinner (year-round) daily 5:30–10pm. Bar daily 11am–10pm.

Joe's ✹✹ AMERICAN/GRILL   The 270-degree view spans the golf course, tennis courts, ocean, and Haleakala—a worthy setting for Beverly Gannon's style of American home cooking with a regional twist. The hearty staples include excellent mashed potatoes, lobster, fresh fish, and filet mignon, but the meatloaf (a whole loaf, like Mom used to make) seems to upstage them all. The Tuscan white-bean soup is superb, and the tenderloin, with roasted portobellos, mashed potatoes with whole garlic, and a pinot noir demi-glace, is American home cooking at its best. Daily specials could be grilled ahi with white-truffle Yukon gold mashed potatoes or sautéed mahimahi with shrimp bisque and sautéed spinach. If chocolate cake is on the menu, you should definitely spring for it.

At the Wailea Tennis Club, 131 Wailea Ike Place. ✆ **808/875-7767.** www.bevgannonrestaurants.com. Reservations recommended. Main courses $20–$42. AE, DC, DISC, MC, V. Daily 5:30–9pm.

MAKENA
EXPENSIVE
Prince Court ✹✹ CONTEMPORARY ISLAND   Half of the Sunday brunch experience here is the head-turning view of Makena Beach, Molokini islet, and Kahoolawe island. The other half is the fabled Sunday buffet, bountiful and sumptuous, spread over several tables: pasta, omelets, cheeses, pastries, sashimi, crab legs, smoked salmon, fresh Maui produce, and a smashing array of ethnic and Continental foods, plus a few surprises, including assorted dim sum, Thai-style beef curry, specialty pastas, and not-to-be-missed desserts. The dinner menu changes regularly but might include rack of lamb, vegetable risotto, coquilles St. Jacques, or veal scaloppini ala marsala. On a recent visit, I dined on blackened ahi, *pulehu* teriyaki short ribs, and Asian seafood noodles. Don't miss the Friday-night seafood and prime-rib buffet, with one of the largest selections of seafood on ice (fresh sashimi, shrimp, Hawaiian poke, and oysters), a roast-beef carving station, tons of salads (with a Caesar salad bar), and a range of other entrees (fresh fish, grilled chicken, and more).

At the Maui Prince Hotel, 5400 Makena Alanui. ✆ **808/874-1111.** Reservations recommended. Main courses $27–$45; Fri prime-rib and seafood buffet $45 ($25 children 6 and under); Sun brunch $42. AE, MC, V. Sun 9am–1pm (last seating at noon); Fri–Wed 6–9pm (Fri buffet has 5 seatings; call for times).

4 Upcountry Maui

HALIIMAILE (ON THE WAY TO UPCOUNTRY MAUI)
EXPENSIVE
Haliimaile General Store ✹✹✹ HAWAII REGIONAL/AMERICAN   For more than 2 decades, Bev Gannon, one of the original Hawaii Regional Cuisine chefs, has been going strong at her foodie haven in the pineapple fields. You'll dine at tables set on old wood floors under high ceilings (sound ricochets fiercely here), in a peach-colored room emblazoned with works by local artists. The food, a blend of eclectic American with ethnic touches, puts an innovative spin on Hawaii Regional Cuisine. Even the fresh-catch sandwich on the lunch menu is anything but prosaic. Sip the *lilikoi* lemonade and nibble the sashimi napoleon or the house salad (Island greens with mandarin oranges, onions, toasted walnuts, and blue-cheese crumble)—all are notable items on a menu that bridges Hawaii and Gannon's Texas roots.

Haliimaile Rd. ✆ **808/572-2666.** www.haliimailegeneralstore.com. Reservations recommended. Main courses $8–$24 lunch, $24–$42 dinner. AE, DC, MC, V. Mon–Fri 11am–2:30pm; daily 5:30–9:30pm.

MAKAWAO & PUKALANI

MODERATE

Casanova Italian Restaurant ✦ ITALIAN   Look for the tiny veranda with a few stools, always full, in front of a deli at Makawao's busiest intersection—that's the most visible part of the Casanova restaurant and lounge. Makawao's nightlife center contains a stage, dance floor, restaurant, and bar—and food to love and remember. This is pasta heaven; try the spaghetti *fra diavolo* or the spinach gnocchi in a fresh tomato-Gorgonzola sauce. Other options include a huge pizza selection, grilled lamb chops in an Italian mushroom marinade, lots more pasta dishes, and luscious desserts. My personal picks on a stellar menu: garlic spinach topped with Parmesan and pine nuts, and tiramisu, the best on the island.

1188 Makawao Ave. ✆ **808/572-0220.** www.casanovamaui.com. Reservations recommended for dinner. Lunch items $6–$18; dinner main courses $12–$34; pizzas $12–$20; pastas $12–$18. AE, DC, DISC, MC, V. Mon–Sat 11:30am–2pm and 5:30–9:30pm; Sun 5:30–9pm. Dancing Wed–Sat 9:45pm–1am. Lounge daily 5:30pm–12:30am. Deli Mon–Sat 7:30am–6pm; Sun 8:30am–6pm.

KULA (AT THE BASE OF HALEAKALA NATIONAL PARK)

MODERATE

Kula Lodge ✦ HAWAII REGIONAL/AMERICAN   Don't let the dinner prices scare you: The Kula Lodge is equally enjoyable, if not more so, at breakfast and lunch, when the prices are lower and the views through the picture windows have an eye-popping intensity. The million-dollar vista spans the flanks of Haleakala, rolling 3,200 feet down to central Maui, the ocean, and the West Maui Mountains. The Kula Lodge has always been known for its breakfasts: fabulous eggs Benedict, including a vegetarian version with Kula onions, shiitake mushrooms, and scallions; legendary banana/mac-nut pancakes; and a highly recommended tofu scramble with green onions, Kula vegetables, and garlic chives. If possible, go for sunset cocktails and watch the colors change into deep end-of-day hues. When darkness descends, a roaring fire and lodge atmosphere add to the coziness of the room. The dinner menu features "small plates" of Thai summer rolls, seared ahi, and other starters. Sesame-seared ono leads the seafood attractions, but there's also pasta, rack of lamb, filet mignon, and free-range chicken breast.

15200 Haleakala Hwy. (Hwy. 377). ✆ **808/878-2517.** Reservations recommended for dinner. Breakfast items $8–$17; lunch items $10–$18; dinner main courses $14–$35. AE, DC, DISC, MC, V. Daily 6:30am–9pm.

INEXPENSIVE

Cafe 808 AMERICAN/LOCAL   Despite its out-of-the-way location (or perhaps because of it), Cafe 808 has become the universal favorite among upcountry residents of all ages. The breakfast coffee group, the lunchtime crowd, and dinner regulars all know it's the place for tasty home-style cooking with no pretensions: famous burgers (teriyaki, hamburger, cheeseburger, garden burger, mahimahi, taro), roast pork, smoked turkey, and a huge selection of local-style specials. Regulars rave about the chicken *katsu*, saimin, and beef stew. The few tables are sprinkled around a room with linoleum floors, hardwood benches, plastic patio chairs, and old-fashioned booths—rough around the edges in a pleasing way, and very camp.

Lower Kula Rd., past Holy Ghost Church, across from Morihara Store. ✆ **808/878-6874.** Burgers from $4; main courses $5.50–$10. No credit cards. Daily 6am–8pm.

Grandma's Coffee House COFFEEHOUSE/AMERICAN   Alfred Franco's grandmother started what is now a fifth-generation coffee business back in 1918,

Upcountry & East Maui Dining & Attractions

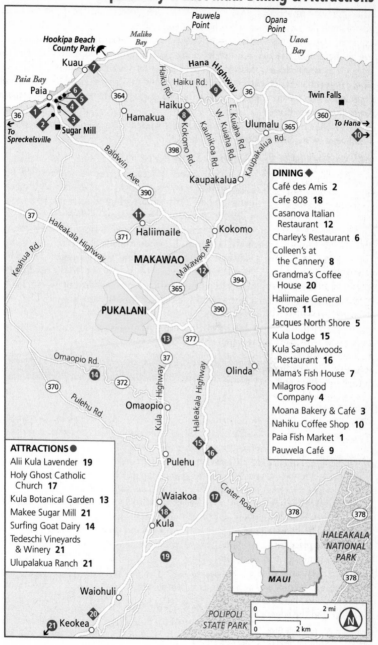

DINING ◆

Café des Amis **2**

Cafe 808 **18**

Casanova Italian
Restaurant **12**

Charley's Restaurant **6**

Colleen's at
the Cannery **8**

Grandma's Coffee
House **20**

Haliimaile General
Store **11**

Jacques North Shore **5**

Kula Lodge **15**

Kula Sandalwoods
Restaurant **16**

Mama's Fish House **7**

Milagros Food
Company **4**

Moana Bakery & Café **3**

Nahiku Coffee Shop **10**

Paia Fish Market **1**

Pauwela Café **9**

ATTRACTIONS ●

Alii Kula Lavender **19**

Holy Ghost Catholic
Church **17**

Kula Botanical Garden **13**

Makee Sugar Mill **21**

Surfing Goat Dairy **14**

Tedeschi Vineyards
& Winery **21**

Ulupalakua Ranch **21**

when she was 16 years old. Today, this tiny wooden coffeehouse, still fueled by home-grown Haleakala coffee beans, is the quintessential roadside oasis. Grandma's offers espresso, hot and cold coffees, home-baked pastries, inexpensive pasta, sandwiches (including sensational avocado garden burgers), homemade soups, fresh juices, and local plate-lunch specials that change daily. Rotating specials include Hawaiian beef stew, ginger chicken, chicken curry, lentil soup, and sandwiches piled high with Kula vegetables. The coffee is legendary, but the real standouts are the lemon squares and the pumpkin bread.

At the end of Hwy. 37, Keokea (about 6 miles before the Tedeschi Vineyards in Ulupalakua). ℂ **808/878-2140**. Most items under $9. AE, DC, MC, V. Daily 7am–5pm.

Kula Sandalwoods Restaurant ⊛ AMERICAN   Chef Eleanor Loui, a graduate of the Culinary Institute of America, makes hollandaise sauce every morning from fresh upcountry egg yolks, sweet butter, and Meyer lemons, which her family grows in the yard above the restaurant. This is Kula cuisine, with produce from the backyard and everything made from scratch, including French toast with home-baked Portuguese sweet bread; hotcakes or Belgian waffles with fresh fruit; open-faced country omelets; hamburgers drenched in a special cheese sauce made with grated sharp cheddar; a killer kalua-pork sandwich; and an outstanding veggie burger. The grilled chicken sandwich is marvelous, served with soup of the day and Kula mixed greens. Dine in the gazebo or on the terrace, with dazzling views in all directions—including, in the spring, a yard dusted with lavender jacaranda flowers and a hillside ablaze with fields of orange akulikuli blossoms.

15427 Haleakala Hwy. (Hwy. 377). ℂ **808/878-3523**. Breakfast $7–$12; lunch $7.25–$12; Sun brunch $7–$12. MC, V. Mon–Sat 6:30am–2:30pm; Sun brunch 6:30am–noon.

5 East Maui: On the Road to Hana

PAIA
MODERATE

Charley's Restaurant ⊛ AMERICAN/MEXICAN   Although Charley's (named after Charley P. Woofer, a Great Dane) serves three meals a day, breakfast is really the time to come here. Located in downtown Paia, Charley's is a cross between a 1960s hippie hangout, a windsurfers' power-breakfast spot, and a honky-tonk bar that gets going after dark. Before you head out to Hana, stop at Charley's for a larger-than-life breakfast (eggs, potatoes, toast, and coffee will set you back only $7). There are plenty of espresso drinks, but the regular coffee is excellent. Lunch is burgers, sandwiches, calzones, and pizza. Dinner is grilled fish and steak—hearty, but nothing to write home about. You'll see all walks of life here, from visitors on their way to Hana at 7am to buff windsurfers chowing down at noon to Willie Nelson on his way to the bar to play a tune.

142 Hana Hwy. ℂ **808/579-9453**. Breakfast items $3.75–$12; lunch items $8–$12; dinner main courses $10–$22. AE, DISC, MC, V. Daily 7am–10pm; food served at the bar until midnight.

Jacques North Shore ⊛⊛ (Value) SEAFOOD/SUSHI   Of the numerous restaurants that have come and gone over the years at this location (right next to Charley's), this eclectic outdoor eatery is my favorite. Jacques is difficult to pin down: Some have called it a hipper, cheaper version of the upscale Mama's Fish House (reviewed below) just down the road; others depict it as an atypical Maui dining experience with excellent food and great prices. The clientele tends to be trendy, hard-body windsurfers;

blonde surfers; and chic north-shore residents. Visitors who wander in generally leave with a smile. The decor is patio dining under a big circus tent. Some might be distracted by the hostess and servers (20-something beauty queens dressed in barely-there clothes), but the main attraction is the food. Do not miss the North Shore pumpkin fish (fish, bananas, and oranges served with a ginger-pumpkin sauce and miso butter), Greek pasta (roasted bell peppers, roasted garlic, and feta cheese over orecchiette), or one of the fabulous vegetarian entrees like the vegetable curry (with tofu, bananas, and oranges). The sushi bar (closed Sun–Mon) whips up a mean spicy-ahi roll and a died-and-gone-to-heaven California roll.

120 Hana Hwy. © 808/579-8844. Reservations not accepted. Main courses $11–$27. AE, DC, DISC, MC, V. Daily 5–10pm. Sushi bar Tues–Sat 5–10pm.

Milagros Food Company ✪ SOUTHWESTERN/SEAFOOD Milagros has gained a following with its great home-style cooking, upbeat atmosphere, and highly touted margaritas. Sit outdoors and watch the parade of Willie Nelson look-alikes ambling by as you tuck into the ahi creation of the evening, a combination of Southwestern and Pacific Rim styles and flavors accompanied by fresh veggies and Kula greens. For breakfast, I recommend the Popeye spinach omelet or the huevos rancheros. Lunch ranges from ahi burgers and Clayton's One-Pound Burger to honey and mac-nut grilled salmon salad. For dinner, options include a grilled ahi burrito, seafood enchiladas, New York strip steak, shrimp pasta, and even Chesapeake Bay crab cakes. I love Paia's tie-dyes, beads, and hippie flavor, and this is the front-row seat for it all. Watch for happy hour, with cheap and fabulous margaritas.

Hana Hwy. and Baldwin Ave. © 808/579-8755. Breakfast items $6–$10; lunch items $7–$12; dinner main courses $14–$25. AE, MC, V. Daily 8am–11pm.

Moana Bakery & Cafe ✪✪ LOCAL/EURO-ASIAN Moana gets high marks for its stylish concrete floors, high ceilings, booths and cafe tables, and fabulous food. Don Ritchey, formerly a chef at Haliimaile General Store, has created the perfect Paia eatery, a casual bakery/cafe that highlights his stellar skills. All the bases are covered: saimin, omelets, wraps, pancakes, and fresh-baked goods in the morning; soups, sandwiches, pasta, and satisfying salads for lunch; and, at dinner, varied selections with Asian and European influences and fresh Island ingredients. The lemon-grass grilled prawns with green-papaya salad are an explosion of flavors and textures; the roasted vegetable napoleon is gourmet fare; and the Thai red curry with coconut milk, served over vegetables, seafood, or tofu, comes atop jasmine rice with crisp rice noodles and fresh sprouts to cool the fire. Ritchey's Thai-style curries are richly spiced and intense. I also vouch for his special gift with fish: The nori-sesame-crusted mahimahi with miso-garlic tapioca pearls is cooked, like the curry, to perfection. There's live jazz most Friday nights.

71 Baldwin Ave. © 808/579-9999. www.members.aol.com/moanacafe. Reservations recommended for dinner. Breakfast items $7–$14; lunch items $6–$13; dinner main courses $7–$32. MC, V. Tues–Sun 8am–9pm; Mon 8am–2:30pm.

INEXPENSIVE

Cafe des Amis ✪✪ *Finds* CREPES/MEDITERRANEAN/INDIAN This tiny eatery is a hidden delight: healthy and tasty breakfasts, lunches, and dinners that are easy on the wallet. Crepes are the star here, and they are popular: spinach with feta cheese, shrimp curry with coconut milk, and dozens more choices, including breakfast crepes and dessert crepes (like banana and chocolate or strawberries and cream).

Equally popular are the Greek salads and smoothies. Dinners feature authentic Indian curries (served with rice, mango chutney, and tomato chutney), such as a vegetable curry with spinach, carrots, cauliflower, and potato with Tamil spices and tomato. You'll also find the best coffee in Paia here.

42 Baldwin Ave. ℭ **808/579-6323.** Breakfast crepes $8–$9; lunch crepes $7.25–$9; dinner entrees $11–$15. MC, V. Daily 8:30am–8:30pm.

Paia Fish Market SEAFOOD   This is a true fish market, with fresh fish to take home and cooked seafood, salads, pastas, fajitas, and quesadillas to take out or enjoy at the few picnic tables inside the restaurant. It's an appealing selection: Cajun-style fresh catch, fresh-fish specials (usually ahi or salmon), fresh-fish tacos and quesadillas, and seafood and chicken pastas. You can also order hamburgers, cheeseburgers, fish and chips (or shrimp and chips), and wonderful lunch and dinner plates that are cheap and tasty. Photos of the number-one sport here, windsurfing, adorn the walls.

110 Hana Hwy. ℭ **808/579-8030.** Lunch and dinner plates $8–$22. DISC, MC, V. Daily 11am–9:30pm.

HAIKU
MODERATE
Colleen's at the Cannery ✸✸✸ *Finds* ECLECTIC   Way, way, way off the beaten path lies this fabulous find in the rural Haiku Cannery Marketplace. Once through the doors, you'll swear you've dropped down in the middle of a hot, chic boutique restaurant in SoHo in Manhattan (only, when you look around at the patrons, they are pure Haiku upcountry residents). It's worth the drive to enjoy Colleen's fabulous culinary creations, like a wild-mushroom ravioli with sautéed portobello mushrooms, tomatoes, herbs, and a roasted-pepper coulis for $14 (not New York City prices); pan-seared ahi for $15; or filet mignon with a side salad for $16. Colleen also serves up smaller meals, such as burgers and fish and chips. Breakfast includes wonderful omelets ($9) and mouthwatering French toast made with Colleen's own homemade bread ($7.75). Lunch stars baguette sandwiches, wraps, salads, and burgers and fries. I only wish Colleen's would take reservations.

At the Haiku Cannery Marketplace, 810 Haiku Rd. ℭ **808/575-9211.** www.colleensinhaiku.com. Reservations not accepted. Breakfast items $5.75–$9; lunch items $6–$15; dinner main courses $10–$33. MC, V. Daily 6am–10pm.

ELSEWHERE ON THE ROAD TO HANA
VERY EXPENSIVE
Mama's Fish House ✸✸✸ SEAFOOD   Okay, it's expensive (maybe the most expensive seafood house on Maui), but if you love fish, this is the place for you. The restaurant's entrance, a cove with windsurfers, tide pools, white sand, and a canoe resting under palm trees, is a South Seas fantasy worthy of Gauguin. The interior features curved lauhala-lined ceilings, walls of split bamboo, lavish arrangements of tropical blooms, and picture windows to let in the view. With servers wearing Polynesian prints and flowers behind their ears, and the sun setting in Kuau Cove, Mama's mood is hard to beat. The fish is fresh (the fishermen are even credited by name on the menu) and prepared either Hawaiian style, with tropical fruit or baked in a crust of macadamia nuts and vanilla beans, or in a number of dishes involving ferns, seaweed, Maui onions, and roasted *kukui* nut. My favorite is mahimahi laulau with luau leaves (taro greens) and Maui onions, baked in ti leaves and served with kalua pig and Hanalei poi. You can get deepwater ahi seared with coconut and lime, or perhaps the

ono "caught by Keith Nakamura along the 40-fathom ledge near Hana" in Hana ginger teriyaki with mac nuts and crisp Maui onion. Other special touches include the use of Molokai sweet potato, organic lettuces, Haiku bananas, and fresh coconut, which evoke the mood and tastes of old Hawaii.

799 Poho Place, just off the Hana Hwy., Kuau. (℄ 808/579-8488. Reservations recommended for lunch, required for dinner. Main courses $29–$54 lunch, $36–$115 dinner. AE, DC, DISC, MC, V. Daily 11am–3pm, 3–4:45pm (light menu), and 4:45–9pm.

INEXPENSIVE

Nahiku Coffee Shop, Smoked Fish Stand, and Ti Gallery *★ (Finds* SMOKED KABOBS   What a delight to stumble across this trio of comforts on the long drive to Hana! The small coffee shop purveys locally made baked goods, several flavors of Maui-grown coffee, organic tropical-fruit smoothies, and the Original and Best Coconut Candy made by Hana character Jungle Johnny. Next door, the Ti Gallery sells locally made Hawaiian arts and crafts, such as pottery and koa-wood vessels.

The barbecue smoker, though, is my favorite part of the operation. It puts out superb smoked and grilled fish, fresh and locally caught, sending seductive aromas out into the moist Nahiku air. These are not jerkylike smoked meats: The process keeps the kabobs moist while retaining the smoke flavor. The breadfruit—sliced, wrapped in banana leaf, and baked—can be bland and starchy (like a baked potato), but it's a stroke of genius to give visitors a taste of this important Polynesian staple. The teriyaki-based marinade, made by the owner, adds a special touch to the fish (such as ono, ahi, and marlin). Among the biggest sellers are the kalua-pig sandwich and the Island-style, two-hand tacos of fish, beef, and chicken, served with about six condiments, including cheese, jalapeños, and salsa. When available, fresh corn on the cob from Kipahulu is grabbed up apace. There are a few roadside picnic tables, or you can take your lunch to go for a beachside picnic in Hana.

Hana Hwy., ½ mile past mile marker 28. No phone. Kabobs $3 each. No credit cards. Fish stand Fri–Wed 10am–5pm. Coffee shop daily 9am–5:30pm. Gallery daily 10am–5pm.

Pauwela Cafe *★ (Finds* INTERNATIONAL   It's easy to get lost while searching out this wonderful cafe, but it's such a find. I never dreamed you could dine so well with such pleasing informality. The tiny cafe, with a few tables indoors and out, has a strong local following for many reasons. Three local boys purchased this well-loved cafe from the original owners in 2004. Chef Brandon Shim (formerly with Tommy Bahama's in Wailea) trained under previous owner Chris Speere at the Maui Community College Culinary Arts School. Chef Brandon certainly has learned well. Nearly everything in this tiny cafe is made from scratch. Breakfasts feature such scrumptious items as *pain perdu* (French bread in orange-vanilla custard) and Belgian waffles. At Sunday brunch, he whips up eggs Benedict on cornbread with lemon hollandaise. Lunch is a great collection of salads and sandwiches, including the scene-stealing kalua-turkey sandwich of moist, smoky shredded turkey with cheese on home-baked French bread, covered with a green-chile and cilantro sauce. For vegetarians, there's a taro burger and veggie burritos. Because this cafe is located in an industrial center of sailboard and surfboard manufacturers, you may find a surf legend dining at the next table. It's a little less than 1½ miles past the Haiku turnoff and ½-mile up on the left.

375 W. Kuiaha Rd. (off Hana Hwy., past Haiku Rd.), Haiku. (℄ 808/575-9242. Breakfast items $4.25–$8.50; lunch items $5.25–$9.50. AE, DISC, MC, V. Mon–Sat 7am–2:30pm; Sun 7am–1pm.

6 At the End of the Road in East Maui: Hana

EXPENSIVE

Hotel Hana-Maui ★★★ LOCAL/ECLECTIC   Although the restaurant's official name is Ka'uiki, everyone in Hana just calls it the Hotel Hana-Maui. Names don't mean much out in this quaint Hawaiian village; in fact, not even Passport Resorts' executive chef, John Cox, who is in charge of developing the daily menu, can put his finger on the delicious type of cuisine served in the open, airy dining room. "I call it cuisine inspired by eastern Maui," he says, pointing to the ingredients-driven menu: the fresh fish caught by local fishermen, the produce brought in by nearby farmers, the fruits that are in season. The result is true Hawaiian food, grown right on the island. Breakfast features an omelet with local Maui onions and a Hana fern salad, almond-crusted French toast, or local papaya with yogurt and homemade granola. Lunch ranges from Maui Cattle Company burgers to just-caught fish sandwiches. Dinner, which changes daily, can include just-picked lettuce for salads (Kula-grown baby romaine with Gruyère crostini and sherry-thyme vinaigrette, or baby greens with Kula citrus, local radishes, and Kalamata olives); a range of soups (such as a chilled Kula cucumber soup); and entrees like seared rare Hana-caught ahi with smoked bacon, forest mushrooms, and wilted greens, or oven-roasted chicken breast with crispy polenta, Nihiku bush beans, and mole sauce. Try the three- or four-course tasting menu or, even better, the Chef's Choice.

Hana Hwy. ✆ **808/248-8211.** www.hotelhanamaui.com. Reservations recommended for Fri–Sat dinner. Main courses $12–$20 breakfast, $10–$21 lunch, $20–$40 dinner. AE, DISC, MC, V. Daily 7:30–10:30am, 11:30am–2:30pm, and 6–9pm. Fri 6–8:30pm Hawaiian show and buffet $50.

MODERATE

Hana Ranch Restaurant *Overrated* AMERICAN   Part of the Hotel Hana-Maui operation, the Hana Ranch Restaurant is the informal alternative to the hotel's dining room. Dinner choices include New York steak, prawns and pasta, and Pacific Rim options like spicy shrimp won tons or the predictable fresh-fish poke. It's not an inspired menu, and the service can be practically nonexistent when the tour buses descend during lunch rush. There are indoor tables as well as two outdoor pavilions that offer distant ocean views. At the adjoining takeout stand, fast-food classics prevail: teriyaki plate lunch, mahimahi sandwich, cheeseburgers, hot dogs, and ice cream.

Hana Hwy. ✆ **808/248-8255.** Reservations required Fri–Sat. Main courses $11–$30. AE, DISC, MC, V. Daily 7–10am and 11am–3pm; Wed and Fri–Sat 6–8:30pm. Takeout counter Sun–Tues and Thurs 6am–7pm; Wed and Fri–Sat 6am–4pm.

7

Fun On & Off the Beach

This is why you've come to Maui—the sun, the sand, and the surf. In this chapter, I'll tell you about the best beaches, from where to soak up the rays to where to plunge beneath the waves. I've covered a range of ocean activities on Maui, as well as my favorite places and outfitters for these marine adventures. Also in this chapter are things to do on dry land, including the best spots for hiking and camping and the greatest golf courses.

1 Beaches

Maui has more than 80 accessible beaches of every conceivable description, from rocky black-sand beaches to powdery golden ones; there's even a rare red-sand beach. What follows is a personal selection of the finest of Maui's beaches, carefully chosen to suit a variety of needs, tastes, and interests.

Hawaii's beaches belong to the people. All beaches, even those in front of exclusive resorts, are public property, and you are welcome to visit. Hawaii state law requires all resorts and hotels to offer public right-of-way access to the beach, along with public parking. So just because a beach fronts a hotel doesn't mean that you can't enjoy the water. Generally, hotels welcome nonguests to their facilities. They frown on nonguests using the beach chairs reserved for guests, but if a nonguest has money and wants to rent gear, buy a drink, or eat a sandwich, well, money is money, and they will gladly accept it from anyone.

For snorkel gear, boogie boards, and other ocean toys, head to one of **Snorkel Bob's** (www.snorkelbob.com) four locations: Dickenson and Wainee streets, Lahaina (© **808/662-0104**); Napili Village, 5425-C Lower Honoapiilani Hwy., Napili (© **808/669-9603**); in North Kihei at Azeka Place II, 1279 S. Kihei Rd. #310 (© **808/875-6188**); and in South Kihei/Wailea at Kamaole Beach Center, 2411 S. Kihei Rd. (© **808/879-7449**). All locations are open daily from 8am to 5pm. If you're island hopping, you can rent from a Snorkel Bob's location on one island and return to a branch on another.

WEST MAUI
D. T. FLEMING BEACH PARK ★★
This quiet, out-of-the-way beach cove, named after the man who started the commercial growing of pineapples on the Valley Isle, is a great place to take the family. The crescent-shaped beach, located north of the Ritz-Carlton hotel, starts at the 16th hole of the Kapalua golf course (Makaluapuna Point) and rolls around to the sea cliffs at the other side. Ironwood trees provide shade on the land side. Offshore, a shallow sandbar extends to the edge of the surf. The waters are generally good for swimming and snorkeling; sometimes, off on the right side near the sea cliffs, the waves build

Beaches & Outdoor Activities

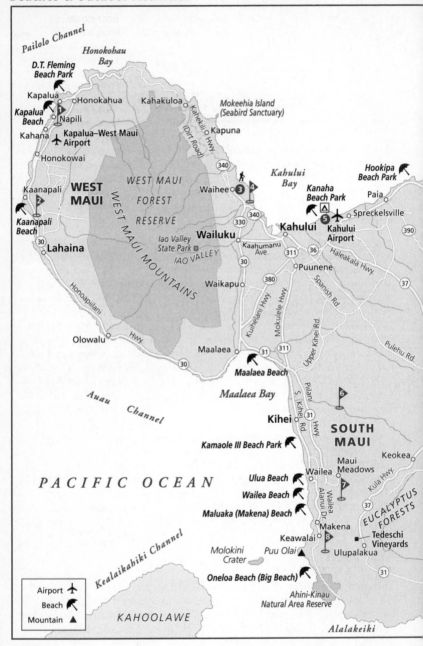

Pailolo Channel

Honokohau Bay

D.T. Fleming Beach Park

Kapalua

Honokahua

Kahakuloa

Mokeehia Island (Seabird Sanctuary)

Kapalua Beach

Napili

Kapuna

Kahana

Kapalua–West Maui Airport

Katekili Hwy. (Dirt Road)

340

Kahului Bay

Hookipa Beach Park

Honokowai

WEST MAUI FOREST RESERVE

Waihee

3

4

Kanaha Beach Park

Paia

Kaanapali

WEST MAUI

WEST MAUI MOUNTAINS

Waihee

340

Kahului

5

Spreckelsville

Kaanapali Beach

330

Kahului Airport

30

Lahaina

Wailuku

Kaahumanu Ave.

36

390

Iao Valley State Park

311

Haleakala Hwy.

IAO VALLEY

Waikapu

380

Puunene

Spanish Rd

37

Honoapiilani Hwy.

Olowalu

Maalaea

30

31

311

Kuihelani Hwy.

Mokulele Hwy.

Upper Kihei Rd.

Pulehu Rd.

Maalaea Beach

Maalaea Bay

Auau Channel

Kihei

31

S. Kihei Rd.

Piilani Hwy.

6

SOUTH MAUI

Kamaole III Beach Park

PACIFIC OCEAN

Ulua Beach

Wailea

Maui Meadows

Keokea

Wailea Beach

Wailea Alanui Dr.

Kula Hwy.

Maluaka (Makena) Beach

37

EUCALYPTUS FORESTS

Makena

Keawalai

8

Tedeschi Vineyards

Molokini Crater

Puu Olai

Ulupalakua

Oneloa Beach (Big Beach)

Kealaikahiki Channel

Ahini-Kinau Natural Area Reserve

31

Airport ✈
Beach 🏖
Mountain ▲

KAHOOLAWE

Alalakeiki

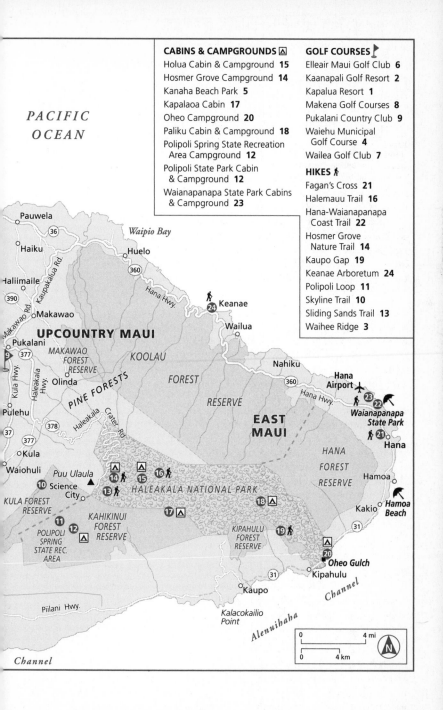

PACIFIC
OCEAN

CABINS & CAMPGROUNDS ⊿
Holua Cabin & Campground **15**
Hosmer Grove Campground **14**
Kanaha Beach Park **5**
Kapalaoa Cabin **17**
Oheo Campground **20**
Paliku Cabin & Campground **18**
Polipoli Spring State Recreation
  Area Campground **12**
Polipoli State Park Cabin
  & Campground **12**
Waianapanapa State Park Cabins
  & Campground **23**

GOLF COURSES ⛳
Elleair Maui Golf Club **6**
Kaanapali Golf Resort **2**
Kapalua Resort **1**
Makena Golf Courses **8**
Pukalani Country Club **9**
Waiehu Municipal
  Golf Course **4**
Wailea Golf Club **7**

HIKES 🚶
Fagan's Cross **21**
Halemauu Trail **16**
Hana-Waianapanapa
  Coast Trail **22**
Hosmer Grove
  Nature Trail **14**
Kaupo Gap **19**
Keanae Arboretum **24**
Polipoli Loop **11**
Skyline Trail **10**
Sliding Sands Trail **13**
Waihee Ridge **3**

Pauwela
Haiku
Haliimaile
Makawao
Pukalani
Olinda
Pulehu
Kula
Waiohuli
Science City
Puu Ulaula

Waipio Bay
Huelo
Keanae
Wailua
Nahiku

Hana
Airport
Waianapanapa
State Park
Hana
Hamoa
Kakio Hamoa
Beach
Kipahulu
Oheo Gulch
Kaupo

Kalacokailio
Point

Hana Hwy.

UPCOUNTRY MAUI

MAKAWAO
FOREST
RESERVE

KOOLAU

FOREST

RESERVE

PINE FORESTS

KULA FOREST
RESERVE

KAHIKINUI
FOREST
RESERVE

POLIPOLI
SPRING
STATE REC.
AREA

HALEAKALA NATIONAL PARK

**EAST
MAUI**

HANA
FOREST
RESERVE

KIPAHULU
FOREST
RESERVE

Piilani Hwy.

Channel

Alenuihaha

Channel

0   4 mi
0   4 km

enough for body boarders and surfers to get a few good rides in. This park has lots of facilities: restrooms, showers, picnic tables, barbecue grills, and a paved parking lot.

KAPALUA BEACH ★★★

The beach cove that fronts the Coconut Grove Villas and the former Kapalua Bay hotel (now in the process of being replaced by condos) is the stuff of dreams: a golden crescent bordered by two palm-studded points. The sandy bottom slopes gently to deep water at the bay mouth; the water's so clear that you can see it turn to green and then deep blue. Protected from strong winds and currents by the lava-rock promontories, Kapalua's calm waters are ideal for swimmers of all ages and abilities, and the bay is big enough to paddle a kayak around in without getting into the more challenging channel that separates Maui from Molokai. Waves come in just right for riding, and fish hang out by the rocks, making it great for snorkeling.

The sandy beach isn't so wide that you'll burn your feet getting in or out of the water, and the inland side is edged by a shady path and cool lawns. Facilities include outdoor showers, restrooms, lifeguards, a rental shack, and plenty of shade. Parking is limited to about 30 spaces in a small lot off Lower Honoapiilani Road, by Napili Kai Beach Resort, so arrive early. Next door is a nice but pricey oceanfront restaurant, Kapalua's Bay Club.

KAANAPALI BEACH ★★

Four-mile-long Kaanapali is one of Maui's best beaches, with grainy gold sand as far as the eye can see. The beach parallels the sea channel through most of its length, and a paved beach walk links hotels and condos, open-air restaurants, and Whalers Village shopping center. Because Kaanapali is so long, and because most hotels have adjacent swimming pools, the beach is crowded only in pockets—there's plenty of room to find seclusion. Summertime swimming is excellent. There's fabulous snorkeling around **Black Rock,** in front of the Sheraton. The water is clear, calm, and populated with clouds of tropical fish. You might even spot a turtle or two.

Facilities include outdoor showers; you can use the restrooms at the hotel pools. Various beach-activity vendors line up in front of the hotels, offering nearly every type of water activity and equipment. Parking is a problem, though. There are two public entrances: At the south end, turn off Honoapiilani Highway into the Kaanapali Resort and pay for parking there, or continue on Honoapiilani Highway, turn off at the last Kaanapali exit at the stoplight near the Maui Kaanapali Villas, and park next to the beach signs indicating public access (this is a little tricky to find and limited to only a few cars, so to save time, you might want to just head to the Sheraton or Whalers Village and plunk down your money).

WAHIKULI COUNTY WAYSIDE PARK

This small stretch of beach, adjacent to Honoapiilani Highway between Lahaina and Kaanapali, is one of Lahaina's most popular beach parks. It's packed on weekends, but during the week it's a great place for swimming, snorkeling, sunbathing, and picnics. Facilities include paved parking, restrooms, showers, and small covered pavilions with picnic tables and barbecue grills.

LAUNIUPOKO STATE WAYSIDE PARK

Families with children will love this small park off Honoapiilani Highway, just south of Lahaina. A large wading pool for kids fronts the shady park, with giant boulders protecting the wading area from the surf outside. Just to the left is a small sandy beach with good swimming when conditions are right. Offshore, the waves are occasionally big enough for surfing. The view from the park is one of the best: You can see the islands of Kahoolawe, Lanai, and Molokai in the distance. Facilities include a paved parking lot, restrooms, showers, picnic tables, and barbecue grills. It's crowded on weekends.

SOUTH MAUI
KAMAOLE III BEACH PARK $\mathcal{R}$
Three beach parks—Kamaole I, II, and III—stand like golden jewels in the front yard of the funky seaside town of Kihei, which is exploding with suburban sprawl. The beaches are the best thing about Kihei; these three are popular with local residents and visitors alike because they're easily accessible. On weekends, they're jam-packed with fishermen, picnickers, swimmers, and snorkelers.

The most popular is Kamaole III, or "Kam-3," as locals say. The biggest of the three beaches, with wide pockets of gold sand, it's the only one with a children's playground and a grassy lawn that meets the sand. Swimming is safe here, but scattered lava rocks are toe-stubbers at the water line, and parents should make sure kids don't venture too far out, as the bottom slopes off quickly. Both the north and south shores are rocky fingers with a surge big enough to attract fish and snorkelers; the winter waves appeal to bodysurfers. Kam-3 is also a wonderful place to watch the sunset. Facilities include restrooms, showers, picnic tables, barbecue grills, and lifeguards. There's plenty of parking on South Kihei Road, across from the Maui Parkshore condos.

ULUA BEACH $\mathcal{R}$
One of the most popular beaches in Wailea, Ulua is a long, wide, crescent-shaped gold-sand beach between two rocky points. When the ocean's calm, Ulua offers Wailea's best snorkeling; when it's rough, the waves are excellent for bodysurfers. The ocean bottom is shallow and gently slopes down to deeper waters, making swimming generally safe. The beach is usually occupied by guests of nearby resorts; in high season (Christmas–Mar and June–Aug), it's carpeted with beach towels and packed with sunbathers like sardines in cocoa butter.

Facilities include showers and restrooms. Beach equipment is available for rent at the nearby Wailea Ocean Activity Center. To find Ulua, look for the blue SHORELINE ACCESS sign on South Kihei Road, near the Renaissance Wailea Beach Resort. There's a tiny parking lot nearby.

WAILEA BEACH $\mathcal{R}\mathcal{R}$
Wailea is the best golden-sand crescent on Maui's sun-baked southwestern coast. One of five beaches within Wailea Resort, Wailea is big, wide, and protected on both sides by black-lava points. It's the front yard of the Four Seasons Resort and the Grand Wailea Resort, Maui's most elegant and outrageous beach hotels, respectively. From the beach, the view out to sea is magnificent, framed by neighboring Kahoolawe and Lanai and the tiny crescent of Molokini, probably the most popular snorkel spot in these parts. The clear waters tumble to shore in waves just the right size for gentle riding, with or without a board. From shore, you can see Pacific humpback whales in season (Dec–Apr) and unreal sunsets nightly. Facilities include restrooms, outdoor showers, and limited free parking at the blue SHORELINE ACCESS sign, on Wailea Alanui Drive, the main drag of this resort.

MALUAKA BEACH (MAKENA BEACH) 🏖🏖

On the southern end of Maui's resort coast, development falls off dramatically, leaving a wild, dry countryside of green kiawe trees. The Maui Prince sits in isolated splendor, sharing Makena Resort's 1,800 acres with only a couple of first-rate golf courses and a necklace of perfect beaches. The strand nearest the hotel is Maluaka Beach, often called Makena, notable for its beauty and its views of Molokini Crater, the offshore islet, and Kahoolawe, the so-called "target" island (it was used as a bombing target from 1945 until the early 1990s). This is a short, wide, palm-fringed crescent of golden, grainy sand set between two black-lava points and bounded by big sand dunes topped by a grassy knoll. The swimming in this mostly calm bay is considered the best on Makena Bay, which is bordered on the south by Puu Olai cinder cone and historic Keawalai Congregational Church. The waters around Makena Landing, at the north end of the bay, are particularly good for snorkeling. Facilities include restrooms, showers, a landscaped park, lifeguards, and roadside parking. Along Makena Alanui, look for the SHORELINE ACCESS sign near the hotel, turn right, and head down to the shore.

ONELOA BEACH (BIG BEACH) 🏖🏖

Oneloa, meaning "long sand" in Hawaiian, is one of the most popular beaches on Maui. Locals call it Big Beach—it's 3,300 feet long and more than 100 feet wide. Mauians come here to swim, fish, sunbathe, surf, and enjoy the view of Kahoolawe and Lanai. Snorkeling is good around the north end, at the foot of Puu Olai, a 360-foot cinder cone. During storms, however, big waves lash the shore and a strong rip current sweeps the sharp drop-off, posing a danger for inexperienced open-ocean swimmers. There are no facilities except for portable toilets, but there's plenty of parking. To get here, drive past the Maui Prince Hotel to the second dirt road, which leads through a kiawe thicket to the beach.

On the other side of Puu Olai is **Little Beach,** a small pocket beach where assorted nudists work on their all-over tans, to the chagrin of uptight authorities. You can get a nasty sunburn and a lewd-conduct ticket, too.

EAST MAUI
BALDWIN PARK

Located off the Hana Highway between Sprecklesville and Paia, this beach park draws lots of Maui residents, especially body-board enthusiasts. It's easy to see why this place is so popular: The surf breaks along the entire length of the white-sand beach, creating perfect conditions for body boarding. On occasion, the waves get big enough for surfing. A couple of swimming areas are safe enough for children: one in the lee of the beach rocks near the large pavilion, and another at the opposite end of the beach, where beach rocks protect a small swimming area. There's a large pavilion with picnic tables and kitchen facilities, barbecue grills, additional picnic tables on the grassy area, restrooms, showers, a semipaved parking area, a baseball diamond, and a soccer field. The park is well used on weekends; weekdays are much quieter.

HOOKIPA BEACH PARK 🏖

Two miles past Paia, on the Hana Highway, is one of the most famous windsurfing sites in the world. Due to its constant winds and endless waves, Hookipa attracts top windsurfers and wave jumpers from around the globe. Surfers and fishermen also enjoy this small gold-sand beach at the foot of a grassy cliff, which provides a natural amphitheater for spectators. Except when competitions are being held, weekdays are the best time to watch the daredevils fly over the waves. When the water is flat,

Tips Safety Tip

Be sure to see the "Health" and "Safety" sections in chapter 3 before setting out on your Maui adventures. You'll find useful information on hiking, camping, and ocean safety, plus how to avoid seasickness and sunburn, and what to do should you get stung by a jellyfish.

snorkelers and divers explore the reef. Facilities include restrooms, showers, pavilions, picnic tables, barbecue grills, and a parking lot.

WAIANAPANAPA STATE PARK 🌟

Four miles before Hana, off the Hana Highway, is this beach park, which takes its name from the legend of the Waianapanapa Cave. Chief Kaakea, a jealous and cruel man, suspected his wife, Popoalaea, of having an affair. Popoalaea left her husband and hid herself in a chamber of the Waianapanapa Cave. A few days later, when Kaakea was passing by the cave, the shadow of a servant gave away Popoalaea's hiding place, and Kaakea killed her. During certain times of the year, the water in the tide pool turns red, commemorating Popoalaea's death. (Scientists claim, less imaginatively, that the water turns red due to the presence of small red shrimp.)

Waianapanapa State Park's 120 acres contain 12 cabins (p. 141), a caretaker's residence, a beach park, picnic tables, barbecue grills, restrooms, showers, a parking lot, a shoreline hiking trail, and a black-sand beach (it's actually small black pebbles). This is a wonderful area for shoreline hikes (mosquitoes are plentiful, so bring insect repellent) and picnicking. Swimming is generally unsafe due to strong waves and rip currents. Waianapanapa is crowded on weekends; weekdays are generally a better bet.

HAMOA BEACH 🌟🌟

This half-moon-shaped, gray-sand beach (a mix of coral and lava) in a truly tropical setting is a favorite among sunbathers seeking rest and refuge. The Hotel Hana-Maui maintains the beach and acts as though it's private, which it isn't—so just march down the lava-rock steps and grab a spot on the sand. James Michener called it "a beach so perfectly formed that I wonder at its comparative obscurity." The 100-foot-wide beach is three football fields long and sits below 30-foot black-lava sea cliffs. Surf on this unprotected beach breaks offshore and rolls in, making it a popular surfing and bodysurfing area. Hamoa is often swept by powerful rip currents, so be careful. The calm left side is best for snorkeling in summer. The hotel has numerous facilities for guests; there are outdoor showers and restrooms for nonguests. Parking is limited. Look for the Hamoa Beach turnoff from Hana Highway.

2 Watersports

Snorkel Bob's (www.snorkelbob.com) rents snorkel gear, boogie boards, and other ocean toys at four locations: Dickenson and Wainee streets, Lahaina (© **808/662-0104**); Napili Village, 5425-C Lower Honoapiilani Hwy., Napili (© **808/669-9603**); in North Kihei at Azeka Place II, 1279 S. Kihei Rd. #310 (© **808/875-6188**); and in South Kihei/Wailea at Kamaole Beach Center, 2411 S. Kihei Rd. (© **808/879-7449**). All locations are open daily from 8am to 5pm. If you're island hopping, you can rent from a Snorkel Bob's location on one island and return to a branch on another.

Boss Frog's Dive and Surf Shops (www.maui-vacation.net) has six locations for rental and other gear: Napili Plaza, next to Subway, in Napili (© **808/669-4949**); Kahana Manor Shops, next to Dollies Pizza, in Kahana (© **808/669-6700**); Kaanapali, 3636 Lower Honoapiilani Rd. (© **808/665-1200**); 150 Lahainaluna Rd., in Lahaina (© **808/661-3333**); Longs Drugs Shopping Center, 1215 Kihei Rd., in North Kihei (© **808/891-0077**); and Dolphin Plaza, 2395 S. Kihei Rd., behind Pizza Hut, in South Kihei (© **808/875-4477**).

BOATING & SAILING

To really appreciate Maui, you need to get off the land and get on the sea. Trade winds off the Lahaina coast and the strong wind that rips through Maui's isthmus make sailing around the island exciting. Many different boats, from a three-masted schooner to spacious trimarans, offer day cruises from Maui.

Later in this section, you can find information on snorkel cruises to Molokini under "Snorkeling," fishing charters under "Sportfishing," and trips that combine snorkeling with whale-watching under "Whale-Watching Cruises."

***Scotch Mist* Sailing Charters** This 50-foot Santa Cruz sailboat offers 2-hour sailing adventures. Prices include snorkel gear, juice, fresh pineapple spears, Maui chips, beer, wine, and soda. Sunset sails are also available.

Lahaina Harbor, slip 2. © 808/661-0386. www.scotchmistsailingcharters.com. Sailing trips $50; sail and snorkel $70; whale-watching trips $40.

DAY CRUISES TO MOLOKAI

You can travel across the seas by ferry from Maui's Lahaina Harbor to Molokai's Kaunakakai Wharf on the ***Molokai Princess*** (© **800/275-6969** or 808/667-6165; www.mauiprincess.com). The 100-foot yacht, certified for 149 passengers, is fitted with the latest generation of gyroscopic stabilizers, making the ride smoother. The ferry makes the 90-minute journey from Lahaina to Kaunakakai daily; the round-trip cost is $85 for adults and $43 for children 3 to 12. Or you can choose to tour the island on one of two different package options: Cruise-Drive, which includes round-trip passage and a rental car for $191 for the driver, $76 per additional adult passenger, and $38 for children; or the Alii Tour, which is a guided tour in an air-conditioned van plus lunch for $191 per adult and $134 per child.

DAY CRUISES TO LANAI

Expeditions Maui–Lanai Passenger Ferry *Value* The cheapest way to Lanai is the ferry, which runs five times a day, 365 days a year. It leaves Lahaina at 6:45am, 9:15am, 12:45pm, 3:15pm, and 5:45pm; the return ferry from Lanai's Manele Bay leaves at 8am, 10:30am, 2pm, 4:30pm, and 6:45pm. The 9-mile channel crossing takes between 45 minutes and an hour, depending on sea conditions. Reservations are strongly recommended. Baggage is limited to two checked bags and one carry-on. Call **Lanai City Service** (© **800/800-4000** or 808/565-7227) to arrange a car rental or bus ride when you arrive.

Ferries depart from Lahaina Harbor; office: 658 Front St., Suite 127, Lahaina. © 800/695-2624 or 808/661-3756. www.go-lanai.com. Round-trip fares from Maui to Lanai $50 adults, $40 children 2–11.

Trilogy *Kids* Trilogy offers my favorite **snorkel-sail trips.** Hop aboard one of the fleet of custom-built catamarans, from 54 to 64 feet long, for a 9-mile sail from Lahaina Harbor to **Lanai's Hulopoe Beach,** a terrific marine preserve, for a fun-filled day of sailing, snorkeling, swimming, and **whale-watching** (in season, of course). This is the only cruise that offers a personalized ground tour of the island and the only one with rights to take you to Hulopoe Beach. The full-day trip costs $203 for adults and $101 for children 3 to 12. Ask about overnighters to Lanai, too.

Trilogy also offers snorkel-sail trips to **Molokini,** one of Hawaii's best snorkel spots. This half-day trip leaves from Maalaea Harbor and costs $118 for adults, $59 for kids 3 to 12, including breakfast and a barbecue lunch. Other options include a late-morning half-day snorkel-sail off Kaanapali Beach for the same price, plus a host of other trips.

These are the most expensive sail-snorkel cruises on Maui, but they're worth every penny. The crews are fun and knowledgeable, and the boats comfortable and well equipped. All trips include breakfast (Mom's homemade cinnamon buns) and a very good barbecue lunch (onboard on the half-day trip, on land on the Lanai trip). Note, however, that you will be required to wear a flotation device no matter how good your swimming skills are; if this bothers you, go with another outfitter.

© **888/MAUI-800** (6284-800) or 808/TRILOGY (874-5649). www.sailtrilogy.com. Prices and departure points vary depending on cruise.

BODY BOARDING (BOOGIE BOARDING) & BODYSURFING

Bodysurfing—riding the waves without a board, becoming one with the rolling water—is a way of life in Hawaii. Some bodysurfers just rely on their hands to ride the waves; others use hand boards (flat, paddlelike gloves). For additional maneuverability, try a boogie board or body board (also known as belly boards or *paipo* boards). These 3-foot-long boards support the upper part of your body and are easy to carry and very maneuverable in the water. Both bodysurfing and body boarding require a pair of open-heeled swim fins to help propel you through the water.

Baldwin Beach, just outside of Paia, has great bodysurfing waves nearly year-round. In winter, Maui's best bodysurfing spot is **Mokuleia Beach,** known locally as Slaughterhouse because of the cattle slaughterhouse that once stood here, not because of the waves—although they are definitely for expert bodysurfers only. To get to Mokuleia, take Honoapiilani Highway just past Kapalua Resort; various hiking trails will take you down to the pocket beach. Storms from the south bring fair bodysurfing conditions and great boogie boarding to the lee side of Maui: **Oneloa Beach (Big Beach)** in Makena, **Ulua Beach** and **Kamaole III Beach Park** in Kihei, and **Kapalua Beach** are all good choices.

OCEAN KAYAKING

Gliding silently over the water, propelled by a paddle, seeing Maui from the sea the way the early Hawaiians did—that's what ocean kayaking is all about. One of Maui's best kayak routes is along the **Kihei Coast,** where there's easy access to calm water. Early mornings are always best, as the wind comes up around 11am, making seas choppy and paddling difficult.

For beginners, my favorite kayak-tour operator is **Makena Kayak & Tours** ⊛ (© **877/879-8426** or 808/879-8426; www.makenakayaks.com). Professional guide Dino Ventura leads a 2½-hour trip from Makena Landing for $55, and loves taking first-timers over the secluded coral reefs and into remote coves. His wonderful tour will be a highlight of your vacation. The 4-hour tour (with lunch) costs $85. Prices include refreshments and snorkel and kayak equipment. Check the website for discounts.

> ### *Tips* An Expert Shares His Secrets: Maui's Best Dives
>
> Ed Robinson, of Ed Robinson's Diving Adventures (see above), knows what makes a great dive. Here are some of his favorites on Maui:
>
> **Hawaiian Reef**   This area off the Kihei-Wailea Coast is so named because it hosts a good cross-section of Hawaiian topography and marine life. Diving to depths of 85 feet, you'll see everything from lava formations and coral reef to sand and rubble, plus a diverse range of both shallow- and deepwater creatures. It's clear why this area was so popular with ancient Hawaiian fishermen: Large helmet shells, a healthy garden of antler coral heads, and big schools of snapper are common.
>
> **Third Tank**   Located off Makena Beach at 80 feet, this World War II tank is one of the most picturesque artificial reefs you're likely to see around Maui. It acts like a fish magnet: Because it's the only large solid object in the area, any fish or invertebrate looking for a safe home comes here. Surrounding the tank is a cloak of schooling snappers and goatfish just waiting for a photographer with a wide-angle lens. Despite its small size, Third Tank is loaded with more marine life per square inch than any site off Maui.
>
> **Molokini Crater**   The backside of the crater is always done as a live boat-drift dive. The vertical wall plummets from more than 150 feet above sea level to around 250 feet below. Looking down to unseen depths gives you a feeling for the vastness of the open ocean. Pelagic fish and sharks are often sighted, and living coral perches on the wall, which is home to lobsters, crabs, and a number of photogenic black-coral trees at 50 feet.
>
> There are actually two great dive sites around Molokini Crater. Named after common chub or rudderfish, **Enenue Side** gently slopes from the surface to about 60 feet and then drops rapidly to deeper waters. The shallower area is an easy dive, with lots of tame butterflyfish. It's also

South Pacific Kayaks, 2439 S. Kihei Rd., Kihei (© **800/776-2326** or 808/875-4848; www.mauikayak.com), is Maui's oldest kayak-tour company. Its experts lead ocean-kayak trips that include lessons, a guided tour, and snorkeling. Tours run from 2½ to 5 hours and range in price from $65 to $139.

In Hana, **Hana-Maui Sea Sports** (© **808/248-7711;** www.hana-maui-seasports.com) runs 2-hour tours of Hana's coastline on wide, stable, no-roll kayaks, with snorkeling, for $89 per person. Kayak surfing lessons are also available for $89.

OCEAN RAFTING

If you're semiadventurous and looking for a more intimate experience with the sea, try ocean rafting. The inflatable rafts hold 6 to 24 passengers. Tours usually include snorkeling and coastal cruising. One of the best (and most reasonable) outfitters is **Hawaii Ocean Rafting** (© **888/677-RAFT** [7238] or 808/667-2191; www.hawaiiocean rafting.com), which operates out of Lahaina Harbor. The best deal is the 5-hour the home of Morgan Bentjaw, one of our friendliest moray eels. Enenue Side is often done as a live boat-drift dive to extend the range of the tour. Diving depths vary. Divers usually do a 50-foot dive, but on occasion advanced divers drop to the 130-foot level to visit the rare boarfish and the shark condos.

Almost every kind of fish found in Hawaii can be seen in the crystalline waters of **Reef's End.** It's an extension of the rim of the crater, which runs for about 600 feet underwater, barely breaking the surface. Reef's End is shallow enough for novice snorkelers and exciting enough for experienced divers. The end and outside of this shoal drop off in dramatic terraces to beyond diving range. In deeper waters, there are shark ledges at varying depths and dozens of eels (some of which are tame), including moray, dragon, snowflake, and garden eels. The shallower inner side is home to Garbanzo, one of the largest and first eels to be tamed. The reef is covered with cauliflower coral; in bright sunlight, it's one of the most dramatic underwater scenes in Hawaii.

La Pérouse Pinnacle In the middle of scenic La Pérouse Bay, site of Haleakala's most recent lava flow, is a pinnacle rising from the 60-foot bottom to about 10 feet below the surface. Getting to the dive site is half the fun: The scenery above water is as exciting as that below the surface. Underwater, you'll enjoy a very diversified dive. Clouds of damselfish and triggerfish will greet you on the surface. Divers can approach even the timid bird wrasse. There are more porcupine puffers here than anywhere else, as well as schools of goatfish and fields of healthy finger coral. La Pérouse is good for snorkeling and long, shallow second dives.

morning tour, which is $74 for adults and $53 for children 5 to 12 (book online and save $11). It includes three snorkeling stops and time spent searching for dolphins, plus continental breakfast and midmorning snacks.

PARASAILING

Soar high above the crowds (at around 400 ft.) for a bird's-eye view of Maui. This ocean adventure sport, which is something of a cross between sky diving and waterskiing, involves sailing through the air, suspended under a large parachute attached by a towline to a speedboat. Keep in mind, though, that parasailing tours don't run during whale season, which is roughly December through May.

I recommend **UFO Parasailing** (© **800/FLY-4-UFO** [359-4836] or 808/661-7-UFO [7836]; www.ufoparasail.net), which picks you up at Kaanapali Beach. UFO offers parasail rides daily from 8am to 2pm. The cost is $65 for the standard flight of 7 minutes of airtime at 400 feet, $75 for a 10-minute ride at 800 feet. You can go up alone or with a friend; no experience is necessary. *Tip:* Take the early-bird special (when the light is fantastic and the price is right) at 8am for just $60 for 400 feet, $70 for 800 feet.

SCUBA DIVING

Some people come to Maui for the sole purpose of plunging into the tropical Pacific and exploring the underwater world. You can see the great variety of tropical marine life (more than 100 endemic species found nowhere else on the planet), explore sea caves, and swim with sea turtles and monk seals in the clear tropical waters off the island. I recommend going early in the morning. Trade winds often rough up the seas in the afternoon, so most dive operators schedule early-morning dives that end at noon, and then take the rest of the day off.

Unsure about scuba diving? Take an introductory dive: Most operators offer no-experience-necessary dives, ranging from $95 to $135. You can learn from this glimpse into the sea world whether diving is for you.

Everyone dives **Molokini**, a marine-life park and one of Hawaii's top dive spots. This crescent-shaped crater has three tiers of diving: a 35-foot plateau inside the crater basin (used by beginning divers and snorkelers), a wall sloping to 70 feet just beyond the inside plateau, and a sheer wall on the outside and backside of the crater that plunges 350 feet. This underwater park is very popular, thanks to calm, clear, protected waters and an abundance of marine life, from manta rays to clouds of yellow butterfly fish.

For personalized diving, **Ed Robinson's Diving Adventures** ⭐ (© 800/635-1273 or 808/879-3584; www.mauiscuba.com) is the only Maui company rated one of *Scuba Diver* magazine's top five best dive operators for 7 years straight. Ed, a widely published underwater photographer, offers specialized charters for small groups. Two-tank dives are $130; his dive boats depart from Kihei Boat Ramp.

If Ed is booked, call **Mike Severns Diving** (© 808/879-6596; www.mikeseverns diving.com) for small (maximum 12 people, divided into two groups of six), personal diving tours on a 38-foot Munson/Hammerhead boat with freshwater shower. Mike and his wife, Pauline Fiene-Severns, are both biologists who make diving in Hawaii educational as well as fun (they have a spectacular underwater photography book called *Molokini Island*). In their 25 years of operation, they have been accident-free. Two-tank dives are $145, including equipment rental, or $130 if you have your own equipment.

Stop by any location of **Maui Dive Shop** ⭐ (www.mauidiveshop.com), Maui's largest diving retailer, with everything from rentals to scuba-diving instruction to dive-boat charters, for a free copy of the 24-page *Maui Dive Guide* (you can also order a copy online). Inside are maps of and details on the 20 best shoreline and offshore dives and snorkel sites, each ranked for beginner, intermediate, or advanced snorkelers/divers. Maui Dive Shop has branches in Kihei at Azeka Place II Shopping Center, 1455 S. Kihei Rd. (© 808/879-3388), Kamaole Shopping Center (© 808/879-1533), and Shops at Wailea (© 808/875-9904); in Lahaina at Lahaina Cannery Mall (© 808/661-5388); and in the Honokowai Marketplace (© 808/661-6166). Other locations include Whalers Village, Kaanapali (© 808/661-5117); Kaanapali Fairway Shops (© 808/551-9663); Maalaea Village (© 808/244-5514); and Kahana Gateway, 4405 Honoapiilani Hwy., Suite 204, Kahana (© 808/669-3800).

SNORKELING

Snorkeling is the main attraction in Maui—and almost anyone can do it. All you need are a mask, a snorkel, fins, and some basic swimming skills. Floating over underwater worlds through colorful clouds of tropical fish is like a dream. In many places all you have to do is wade into the water and look down. If you've never snorkeled before, most resorts and excursion boats offer instruction, but it's plenty easy to figure it out for yourself.

Some snorkel tips: Always go with a buddy. Look up every once in a while to see where you are, how far offshore you are, and whether there's any boat traffic. Don't touch anything; not only can you damage coral, but camouflaged fish and shells with poisonous spines also might surprise you. Always check with a dive shop, lifeguards, and others on the beach about the area in which you plan to snorkel: Are there any dangerous conditions you should know about? What are the current surf, tide, and weather conditions? If you're not a good swimmer, wear a life jacket or other flotation device, which you can rent at most places offering watersports gear.

Snorkel Bob's 🤿 (www.snorkelbob.com) or **Boss Frog's Dive and Surf Shops** (www.maui-vacation.net) will rent you everything you need; see the introduction to this section for locations. Also see "Scuba Diving" (above) for Maui Dive Shop's free booklet on great snorkeling sites.

Maui's best snorkeling spots include **Kapalua Beach;** at **Black Rock at Kaanapali Beach,** in front of the Sheraton; along the Kihei coastline, especially at **Kamaole III Beach Park;** and along the Wailea coastline, particularly at **Ulua Beach.** Mornings are best because local winds don't kick in until around noon. **Olowalu** has great snorkeling around **mile marker 14,** where there is a turtle-cleaning station about 150 to 225 feet out from shore. Turtles line up here to have cleaner wrasses pick off small parasites.

Ahihi-Kinau Natural Preserve is another terrific place. It requires more effort to get here, but it's worth it because it's home to Maui's tropical marine life at its best. You can't miss in Ahihi Bay, a 2,000-acre state natural area reserve in the lee of Cape Kinau, on Maui's rugged south coast, where Haleakala spilled red-hot lava that ran to the sea in 1790. Fishing is strictly *kapu* (forbidden) here, and the fish know it; they're everywhere in this series of rocky coves and black-lava tide pools. The black, barren, lunarlike land stands in stark contrast to the green-blue water. After you snorkel, check out La Pérouse Bay on the south side of Cape Kinau, where the French admiral La Pérouse became the first European to set foot on Maui. A lava-rock pyramid known as Pérouse Monument marks the spot. To get here, drive south of Makena past Puu Olai to Ahihi Bay, where the road turns to gravel (and sometimes seems like it will disappear under the waves). At Cape Kinau, three four-wheel-drive trails lead across the lava flow; take the shortest one, nearest La Pérouse Bay. If you have a standard car, drive as far as you can, park, and walk the remainder of the way.

When the whales aren't around, **Capt. Steve's Rafting Excursions** (© 808/667-5565; www.captainsteves.com) offers 7-hour snorkel trips from Mala Wharf in Lahaina to the waters around **Lanai** (you don't actually land on the island). Discounted online rates of $124 for adults and $89 for children 12 and under include breakfast, lunch, snorkel gear, and wet suits.

If you'd like to head over to Lanai for a day of snorkeling in its pristine waters, see "Day Cruises to Lanai," above.

SNORKEL CRUISES TO MOLOKINI

Like a crescent moon fallen from the sky, the crater of **Molokini** ✸ sits almost midway between Maui and the uninhabited island of Kahoolawe. Tilted so that only the thin rim of its southern side shows above water in a perfect semicircle, Molokini stands like a scoop against the tide, and it serves, on its concave side, as a natural sanctuary for tropical fish and snorkelers, who commute daily in a fleet of dive boats to this marine-life preserve. Note that in high season, Molokini can be crowded with dozens of boats, each carrying scores of snorkelers.

Maui Classic Charters ✸✸   Maui Classic Charters offers morning and afternoon **snorkel-sail cruises to Molokini** on *Four Winds II,* a 55-foot glass-bottom catamaran. Rates for the morning sail are $89 adults and $59 children 3 to 12; in the afternoon, $42 adults and $30 children (book online to save 15%). *Four Winds* trips include continental breakfast; an optional barbecue lunch ($7 extra); complimentary beer, wine, and soda; snorkeling gear and instruction; and sportfishing along the way. Those looking for speed should book a trip on the state-of-the-art catamaran *Maui Magic.* A 5-hour snorkel journey to both Molokini and La Pérouse costs $99 adults and $79 children 5 to 12, including continental breakfast; barbecue lunch; beer, wine, and soda; snorkel gear; and instruction. During whale season (Dec 22–Apr 22), the *Four Winds* has a 3½-hour **whale-watch cruise** that goes for $42 adults and $30 children 3 to 12 (including beverages).

Maalaea Harbor, slip 55 and slip 80. ℭ 800/736-5740 or 808/879-8188. www.mauicharters.com. Prices vary depending on cruise.

Pacific Whale Foundation   This not-for-profit foundation supports its whale research by offering **whale-watch cruises** and **snorkel tours,** some to Molokini and Lanai. There are 15 daily trips to choose from, offered from December through May, out of both Lahaina and Maalaea harbors.

101 N. Kihei Rd., Kihei. ℭ 800/942-5311 or 808/879-8811. www.pacificwhale.org. Trips from $30 adults, $17 children 7–12, free for ages 6 and under; snorkeling cruises from $80 adults, $30 children.

Pride of Maui   For a high-speed, action-packed snorkel-sail experience, consider the *Pride of Maui.* These 5½-hour **snorkel cruises to Molokini** also stop at Turtle Bay and Makena; the cost is $90 for ages 13 and up ($80 if you book online) and $56 for children 3 to 12 ($50 online). Rates include continental breakfast, barbecue lunch, gear, and instruction. Other options include an afternoon Molokini cruise ($42 for ages 13 and up, $27 for children 3–12, with discounts online), an evening sunset cruise ($70 for ages 13 and up, $40 for children 3–12), and, during whale season, a whale-watching cruise ($42 for ages 13 and up, $27 for children 3–12).

Maalaea Harbor. ℭ 877/TO-PRIDE (867-7433) or 808/875-0955. www.prideofmaui.com. Prices vary depending on cruise.

SPORTFISHING

Marlin (as big as 1,200 lb.), tuna, ono, and mahimahi await the baited hook in Maui's coastal and channel waters. No license is required; just book a sportfishing vessel out of Lahaina or Maalaea harbor. Most charter boats that troll for big-game fish carry a maximum of six passengers. You can walk the docks, inspect boats, and talk to captains and crews, or book through an activities desk or one of the outfitters recommended below.

Shop around: Prices vary widely according to the boat, the crowd, and the captain. A shared boat for a half day of fishing starts at $100; a shared full day of fishing starts at around $250. A half-day exclusive (you get the entire boat) starts at $600; a full-day exclusive starts at $900. Also, many boat captains tag and release marlin or keep the fish for themselves (sorry, that's Hawaii style). If you want to eat your mahimahi for dinner or have your marlin mounted, tell the captain before you go.

The best way to book a sportfishing charter is through the experts; the top booking desk in the state is **Sportfish Hawaii** 🛥 (© **877/388-1376** or 808/396-2607; www.sportfishhawaii.com), which books boats on all the islands. These fishing vessels have been inspected and must meet rigorous criteria to guarantee that you'll have a great time. Prices range from $595 to $1,000 for a full-day exclusive charter (you, plus five friends, get the entire boat to yourself); it's $395 to $700 for a half-day exclusive.

SUBMARINE DIVES

Plunging 100 feet below the surface of the sea in a state-of-the-art, high-tech submarine is a great way to experience Maui's magnificent underwater world, especially if you're not a swimmer. **Atlantis Adventures** 🛥, 658 Front St., Lahaina (© **800/548-6262** or 808/667-2224; www.atlantisadventures.com), offers trips out of Lahaina Harbor every hour on the hour from 9am to 2pm; prices are $80 for adults and $41 for children under 12 (children must be at least 3 ft. tall). Book online and save 10%. Allow 2 hours for this underwater adventure. *Warning:* This is not a good choice if you're claustrophobic.

SURFING

The ancient Hawaiian sport of *hee nalu* (wave sliding) is probably the sport most people picture when they think of the islands. If you'd like to give it a shot, just sign up at any one of the recommended surfing schools listed below.

Tide and Kiva Rivers, two local boys (actually twins) who have been surfing since they could walk, operate **Rivers to the Sea** (© **808/280-8795** or 280-6236; www.riverstothesea.com), one of the best surfing schools on Maui. Rates are $75 each for a 2-hour class for a group of three or more, $220 for a couple for a 2-hour class, and $160 for a 2-hour private lesson. All lessons include equipment. The instructor decides where the lesson will take place based on the client's ability and where the surf is on that day. Tide, who has been surfing for 25 years, says he has beginners standing up in their first lesson.

Well-known surfer Nancy Emerson can also teach you how to surf—just call the **Nancy Emerson School of Surfing,** 358 Papa Place, Suite F, Kahului (© **808/244-SURF** [7873] or 662-4445; www.surfclinics.com). Nancy has been surfing since 1961 and has even been a stunt performer for various movies such as *Waterworld*. She's pioneered a new instructional technique called "Learn to Surf in One Lesson" (you can, really). It's $85 per person for a 2-hour group lesson; private 2-hour classes are $175.

WHALE-WATCHING

Every winter, pods of Pacific humpback whales make the 3,000-mile swim from the chilly waters of Alaska to bask in Maui's summery shallows, fluking, spy hopping, spouting, and having an all-around swell time.

The humpback is the star of the annual whale-watching season, which usually begins in December or January and lasts until April or sometimes May. About 1,500 to 3,000 humpback whales appear in Hawaii waters each year. Adults grow to be about 45 feet long and weigh a hefty 40 tons. Humpbacks are officially an endangered species: In 1997, some of the waters around the state were designated the Hawaiian Islands Humpback Whale National Marine Sanctuary, the country's only federal single-species sanctuary.

WHALE-WATCHING FROM SHORE

Between mid-December and April, you can just look out to sea. There's no best time of day for whale-watching, but the whales seem to appear when the sea is glassy and the wind calm. Once you see one, keep watching in the same vicinity; they might stay down for 20 minutes. Bring a book—and binoculars, if you can. Some good whale-watching points on Maui include:

McGregor Point On the way to Lahaina, there's a scenic lookout at mile marker 9 (just before you get to the Lahaina Tunnel); it's a good viewpoint to scan for whales.

Olowalu Reef Along the straight part of Honoapiilani Highway, between McGregor Point and Olowalu, you'll sometimes see whales leap out of the water. Their appearance can bring traffic to a screeching halt: People abandon their cars and run down to the sea to watch, causing a major traffic jam. If you stop, pull off the road so others may pass.

Wailea Beach Marriott Resort On the Wailea coastal walk, stop at this resort to look for whales through the telescope installed as a public service by the Hawaii Island Humpback Whale National Marine Sanctuary.

Puu Olai It's a tough climb up this coastal landmark near the Maui Prince Hotel, but you're likely to be well rewarded: This is the island's best spot for offshore whale-watching. On the 360-foot cinder cone overlooking Makena Beach, you'll be at the right elevation to see Pacific humpbacks as they dodge Molokini and cruise up Alalakeiki Channel between Maui and Kahoolawe. If you don't see one, you'll at least have a whale of a view.

WHALE-WATCHING CRUISES

For a closer look, take a whale-watching cruise. The **Pacific Whale Foundation,** 101 N. Kihei Rd., Kihei (© **800/942-5311** or 808/879-8811; www.pacificwhale.org), is a nonprofit foundation in Kihei that supports its whale research by offering cruises and snorkel tours, some to Molokini and Lanai. It operates a 65-foot power catamaran called the *Ocean Spirit,* a 50-foot sailing catamaran called the *Manute'a,* and other boats. There are 15 daily trips from which to choose, and the rates for a 2-hour whale-watching cruise would make Captain Ahab smile (starting at $30 for adults, $17 for children). Cruises are offered from December through May, out of both Lahaina and Maalaea harbors.

If you want to combine ocean activities, then a snorkel or dive cruise to Molokini, the sunken crater off Maui's south coast, might be just the ticket. You can see whales on the way there, at no extra charge. See "Scuba Diving" and "Boating & Sailing," earlier in this section.

WHALE-WATCHING BY KAYAK & RAFT

Seeing a humpback whale from an ocean kayak or raft is awesome. **Capt. Steve's Rafting Excursions** (© **808/667-5565;** www.captainsteves.com) offers 2-hour

---

Tips **Not So Close! They Hardly Know You**

In your excitement at seeing a whale or a school of dolphins, don't get too close—both are protected under the Marine Mammals Protection Act. Swimmers, kayakers, and windsurfers must stay at least 300 feet away from all whales, dolphins, and other marine mammals. And yes, they have prosecuted visitors for swimming with dolphins! If you have any questions, call the **National Marine Fisheries Service** (© 808/541-2727) or the **Hawaiian Islands Humpback Whale National Marine Sanctuary** (© 800/831-4888).

---

whale-watching excursions out of Lahaina Harbor from $39 for adults, $29 for children 5 to 12. *Tip:* Save $10 by booking the early-bird adventure, which leaves at 7:30am.

WINDSURFING

Maui has Hawaii's best windsurfing beaches. In winter, windsurfers from around the world flock to the town of **Paia** to ride the waves. **Hookipa Beach,** known all over the globe for its brisk winds and excellent waves, is the site of several world-championship contests. **Kanaha Beach,** west of Kahului Airport, also has dependable winds. When the winds turn northerly, **Kihei** is the spot to be; some days, you can spot whales in the distance behind the windsurfers. The northern end of Kihei is best: **Ohukai Park,** the first beach as you enter South Kihei Road from the northern end, has not only good winds, but also parking, a long strip of grass to assemble your gear, and good access to the water. Experienced windsurfers here are found in front of the **Maui Sunset** condo, 1032 S. Kihei Rd., near Waipuilani Street (a block north of McDonald's), which has great windsurfing conditions but a very shallow reef (not good for beginners).

   Hawaiian Island Surf & Sport, 415 Dairy Rd., Kahului (© **800/231-6958** or 808/871-4981; www.hawaiianisland.com), offers lessons (from $79), rentals, and repairs. Other shops that offer rentals and lessons are **Hawaiian Sailboarding Techniques,** 425 Koloa St., Kahului (© **800/968-5423** or 808/871-5423; www.hstwindsurfing.com), with 2½-hour lessons from $79; and **Maui Windsurf Co.,** 22 Hana Hwy., Kahului (© **800/872-0999** or 808/877-4816; www.maui-windsurf.com), which has complete equipment rental (board, sail, rig harness, and roof rack) from $45, plus 1- or 2-hour lessons ranging from $75.

   For daily reports on wind and surf conditions, call the **Wind and Surf Report** at © **808/877-3611.**

3 Hiking & Camping

In the past 3 decades, Maui has grown from a rural island to a fast-paced resort destination, but its natural beauty remains largely inviolate; there are still many places that can be explored only on foot. Those interested in seeing the backcountry—complete with virgin waterfalls, remote wilderness trails, and quiet, meditative settings—should head for Haleakala's upcountry or the tropical Hana Coast.

Camping on Maui can be extreme (inside a volcano) or benign (by the sea in Hana). It can be wet, cold, and rainy, or hot, dry, and windy—often all on the same day. If you're heading for Haleakala, remember that U.S. astronauts trained for the moon inside the volcano: Bring survival gear. Don't forget both your swimsuit and your rain gear if you're bound for Waianapanapa. Bring your own gear, as there are no places to rent camping equipment on Maui.

For more information on Maui camping and hiking trails, and to obtain free maps, contact **Haleakala National Park,** P.O. Box 369, Makawao, HI 96768 (*C* **808/572-4400;** www.nps.gov/hale); or the **State Division of Forestry and Wildlife,** 54 S. High St., Wailuku, HI 96793 (*C* **808/984-8100;** www.hawaii.gov). For information on trails, hikes, camping, and permits for state parks, contact the **Hawaii State Department of Land and Natural Resources,** State Parks Division, P.O. Box 621, Honolulu, HI 96809 (*C* **808/587-0300;** www.state.hi.us/dlnr); note that you can get information from the website but cannot obtain permits there. For Maui County Parks, contact the **Maui County Department of Parks and Recreation,** 1580-C Kaahumanu Ave., Wailuku, HI 96793 (*C* **808/243-7132;** www.co.maui.hi.us/departments/Parks).

TIPS ON SAFE HIKING & CAMPING   Water might be everywhere in Hawaii, but it more than likely isn't safe to drink. Most stream water must be treated because cattle, pigs, and goats have probably contaminated the water upstream. The Department of Health continually warns campers of bacterium leptospirosis, which is found in freshwater streams throughout the state and enters the body through breaks in the skin or through the mucous membranes. It produces flulike symptoms and can be fatal. Make sure that your drinking water is safe by vigorously boiling it, or if boiling is not an option, use tablets with hydroperiodide; portable water filters will not screen out bacterium leptospirosis. Firewood isn't always available, so it's a good idea to carry a small, light backpacking stove, which you can use both to boil water and to cook meals.

Remember, the island is not crime-free: Never leave your valuables (wallet, airline ticket, and so on) unprotected. Carry a day pack if you have a campsite, and never camp alone. Some more dos and don'ts: Do bury personal waste away from streams. Don't eat unknown fruit. Do carry your trash out. And don't forget there is very little twilight in Maui when the sun sets—it gets dark quickly.

See "Health" and "Safety" in chapter 3 for more hiking and camping tips.

GUIDED HIKES   If you'd like a knowledgeable guide to accompany you on a hike, call **Maui Hiking Safaris** *✦* (*C* **888/445-3963** or 808/573-0168; www.maui hikingsafaris.com). Owner Randy Warner takes visitors on half- and full-day hikes into valleys, rainforests, and coastal areas. Randy's been hiking around Maui for more than 25 years and is wise in the ways of Hawaiian history, native flora and fauna, and volcanology. His rates are $59 to $79 for a half-day and $105 to $139 for a full day, which include day packs, rain parkas, snacks, water, and, on full-day hikes, sandwiches.

Maui's oldest hiking-guide company is **Hike Maui** *✦* (*C* **808/879-5270;** www. hikemaui.com), headed by Ken Schmitt, who pioneered guided hikes on the Valley Isle. Hike Maui offers five different hikes a day, ranging from an easy 1-mile, 3-hour hike to a waterfall ($75) to a strenuous full-day hike in Haleakala Crater ($150). All prices include equipment and transportation.

Moments **Zipping Over the Forest Canopy**

For those looking for a different perspective of Haleakala, try **Skyline Eco-Adventures' Zipline Haleakala Tour** (© 808/878-8400; www.skylinehawaii. com), which blends a short hike through a eucalyptus forest with four "zipline" crossings. During the zipline crossing, you'll be outfitted with a seat harness and connected to a cable, then launched from a 70-foot-high platform to "zip" along the cable suspended over the slopes of Haleakala. From this viewpoint, you fly over treetops, valleys, gulches, and waterfalls at 10 to 35 mph. These bird's-eye tours operate daily and take riders from ages 12 and up, weighing between 80 and 300 pounds. The cost is $84.

Venture into the lush West Maui Mountains with an experienced guide on one of the numerous hikes offered by **Maui Eco-Adventures** (© 877/661-7720 or 808/ 661-7720; www.ecomaui.com). I love the Rainforest/Waterfall Hike: After a continental breakfast, you'll hike by streams and waterfalls, through native trees and plants, and on to breathtaking vistas. The tour includes a picnic lunch, swims in secluded pools, and memorable photo ops. The 6-hour excursion costs $120 per person, including meals, a fanny pack with bottled water, and rain gear if necessary. No children under 13 are allowed. An easier jaunt costs just $80.

For information on hikes given by the **Hawaii Sierra Club** on Maui, call © 808/ 573-4147 or go to www.hi.sierraclub.org.

HALEAKALA NATIONAL PARK ★★★

For complete coverage of the national park, see "House of the Sun: Haleakala National Park" (p. 221).

HIKING INTO THE WILDERNESS: SLIDING SANDS & HALEMAUU TRAILS

Hiking into Maui's dormant volcano is the best way to see it. The terrain inside the wilderness area of the volcano, which ranges from burnt-red cinder cones to ebony-black lava flows, is simply spectacular. Inside the crater there are some 27 miles of hiking trails, two camping sites, and three cabins.

Try to arrange to stay at least 1 night in the park; 2 or 3 nights will allow you more time to explore the fascinating interior of the volcano (see below for details on the cabins and campgrounds in the wilderness area of the valley). If you want to venture out on your own, the best route takes in two trails: into the crater along **Sliding Sands Trail** ★, which begins on the rim at 9,800 feet and descends into the belly of the beast, to the valley floor at 6,600 feet; and back out along **Halemauu Trail** ★. Hardy hikers can consider making the 11-mile one-way descent, which takes 9 hours, and the equally long return ascent in a day. The rest of us will need to extend this steep but wonderful hike to 2 days. The descending and ascending trails aren't loops; the trail heads are miles (and several thousand feet in elevation) apart, so you'll need to make advance transportation arrangements to get back to your car, which you'll leave

> **Tips A Word of Warning About the Weather**
>
> The weather at nearly 10,000 feet can change suddenly and without warning. Come prepared for cold, high winds, rain, and even snow in winter. Temperatures can range from 77°F (25°C) down to 26°F (–3°C), and high winds (which make it feel even colder) are frequent. Rainfall varies from 40 inches a year on the west end of the crater to more than 200 inches on the eastern side. Bring boots, waterproof gear, warm clothes, extra layers, and lots of sunscreen—the sun shines very brightly up here.

at the beginning of the hike, about a 30- to 45-minute drive from where the Halemauu Trail ends. You either arrange with someone to pick you up, hitchhike back up to your car, or hook up with other people doing the same thing and drop off one car at each trail head. Before you set out, stop at park headquarters to get camping and hiking updates. See below for details on the cabins and campgrounds in the wilderness area in the valley. There is no registration for day hikers.

The trail head for Sliding Sands is well marked and the trail is easy to follow over lava flows and cinders. As you descend, look around: The view is breathtaking. In the afternoon, waves of clouds flow into the Kaupo and Koolau gaps. Vegetation is sparse to nonexistent at the top, but the closer you get to the crater floor, the more growth you'll see: bracken ferns, pili grass, shrubs, even flowers. On the floor, the trail travels across rough lava flows, passing by rare silversword plants, volcanic vents, and multicolored cinder cones.

The Halemauu Trail goes over red and black lava and past vegetation such as evening primrose as it begins its ascent up the crater wall. Occasionally, riders on horseback use this trail as an entry and exit from the park. The proper etiquette is to step aside and stand quietly next to the trail as the horses pass.

DAY HIKES FROM THE MAIN ENTRANCE

In addition to the difficult hike into the crater, the park has a few shorter and easier options. Anyone can take a .5-mile walk down the **Hosmer Grove Nature Trail** 𝕶, or you can start down **Sliding Sands Trail** for a mile or two to get a hint of what lies ahead (even this short hike can be exhausting at the high altitude). A good day hike is **Halemauu Trail** to Holua Cabin and back, an 8-mile, half-day trip.

A 20-minute orientation presentation is given daily in the Summit Building at 9:30, 10:30, and 11:30am. The park rangers offer two **guided hikes.** The 2-hour, 2-mile **Cinder Desert Hike** takes place Tuesday and Friday at 10am and starts from the Sliding Sands trail head at the end of the Haleakala Visitor Center parking lot. The 3-hour, 3-mile **Waikamoi Cloud Forest Hike** leaves every Monday and Thursday at 9am; it starts at the Hosmer Grove, just inside the park entrance, and traverses through the Nature Conservancy's Waikamoi Preserve. *Always call in advance:* The hikes and briefing sessions may be canceled, so check first. For details, call the park at ✆ **808/572-4400** or visit www.nps.gov/hale.

CAMPING NEAR THE MAIN ENTRANCE

Most people stay at one of two tent campgrounds, unless they get lucky and win the lottery—the lottery, that is, for one of the three wilderness cabins. For more information, contact **Haleakala National Park,** P.O. Box 369, Makawao, HI 96768 (© **808/572-4400;** www.nps.gov/hale).

CABINS   It can get really cold and windy down in the valley (see "A Word of Warning About the Weather," above), so try for a cabin. They're warm, provide protection from the elements, and are reasonably priced. Each has 12 padded bunks (but no bedding; bring your own), a table, chairs, cooking utensils, a two-burner propane stove, and a wood-burning stove with firewood (you might also have a few cockroaches). The cabins are spaced so that each one is an easy walk from the other: Holua cabin is on the Halemauu Trail, Kapalaoa cabin on Sliding Sands Trail, and Paliku cabin on the eastern end by the Kaupo Gap. The rates are $55 a night for groups of one to six, $110 a night for groups of 7 to 12.

The cabins are so popular that the National Park Service has a lottery system for reservations. Requests for cabins must be made 3 months in advance (be sure to request alternate dates). You can request all three cabins at once; you're limited to 2 nights in one cabin and 3 nights total within the wilderness per month.

CAMPGROUNDS   If you don't win the cabin lottery, all is not lost—there are three tent-camping sites that can accommodate you: two in the wilderness area, and one just outside at Hosmer Grove. There is no charge for tent camping.

Hosmer Grove, located at 6,800 feet, is a small, open, grassy area surrounded by a forest. Trees protect campers from the winds, but nights still get quite cold—sometimes there's ice on the ground up here. This is the best place to spend the night in a tent if you want to see the Haleakala sunrise. Come up the day before, enjoy the park, take a day hike, and then turn in early. The enclosed-glass summit building opens at sunrise for those who come to greet the dawn—a welcome windbreak. Facilities at Hosmer Grove include a covered pavilion with picnic tables and grills, chemical toilets, and drinking water. No permits are needed, and there's no charge—but you can stay for only 3 nights in a 30-day period.

The two tent-camping areas inside the volcano are **Holua,** just off Halemauu at 6,920 feet; and **Paliku,** just before the Kaupo Gap at the eastern end of the valley, at 6,380 feet. Facilities at both campgrounds are limited to pit toilets and nonpotable catchment water. Water at Holua is limited, especially in summer. No open fires are allowed inside the volcano, so bring a stove if you plan to cook. Tent camping is restricted to the signed area. No camping is allowed in the horse pasture. The inviting grassy lawn in front of the cabin is off-limits. Camping is free but limited to 2 consecutive nights, and no more than 3 nights a month inside the volcano. Permits are issued at park headquarters daily from 8am to 3pm on a first-come, first-served basis on the day you plan to camp. Occupancy is limited to 25 people in each campground.

HIKING & CAMPING AT KIPAHULU (NEAR HANA)
In the east Maui section of Haleakala National Park, you can set up at **Oheo Campground,** a first-come, first-served, drive-in campground with tent sites for 100 near the ocean. It has a few tables, barbecue grills, and chemical toilets. No permit is required, but there's a 3-night limit. No food or drinking water is available, so bring your own. Bring a tent as well—it rains 75 inches a year here. Contact **Kipahulu Ranger Station,** Haleakala National Park, HI 96713 (© **808/248-7375;** www.nps.gov/hale), for information.

HIKING FROM THE SUMMIT   If you hike from the crater rim down **Kaupo Gap** to the ocean, more than 20 miles away, you'll pass through climate zones ranging from arctic to tropical. On a clear day, you can see every island except Kauai on the trip down.

APPROACHING KIPAHULU FROM HANA   If you drive to Kipahulu, you'll have to approach it from the Hana Highway—it's not accessible from the summit. Always check in at the ranger station before you begin your hike; the staff can inform you of current conditions and share their wonderful stories about the history, culture, flora, and fauna of the area. The entry fee is $10 a car, the same as for the summit atop Haleakala.

There are two hikes you can take here. The first is a short, easy .5-mile loop along the **Kaloa Point Trail** (Kaloa Point is a windy bluff overlooking **Oheo Gulch**), which leads toward the ocean along pools and waterfalls and back to the ranger station. The clearly marked path leaves the parking area and rambles along the flat, grassy peninsula. Along the way you'll see the remnants of an ancient fishing shrine, a house site, and a lauhala-thatched building depicting an earlier time. The pools are above and below the bridge; the best for swimming are usually above the bridge.

The second hike is for the more hardy. Although just a 4-mile round-trip, the trail is steep and you'll want to stop and swim in the pools, so allow 3 hours. You'll be climbing over rocks and up steep trails, so wear hiking boots. Take water, snacks, swim gear, and insect repellent. Always be on the lookout for flash-flood conditions. This walk will pass two magnificent waterfalls, the 181-foot **Makahiku Falls** and the even bigger 400-foot **Waimoku Falls** ⚘. The trail starts at the ranger station, where you'll walk uphill for .5 mile to a fence overlook at the thundering Makahiku Falls. If you're tired, you can turn around here; true adventurers should press on. Behind the lookout, the well-worn trail picks up again and goes directly to a pool on the top of the Makahiku Falls. The pool is safe to swim in as long as the waters aren't rising; if they are, get out and head back to the ranger station. The rest of the trail takes you through a meadow and bamboo forest to Waimoku Falls.

GUIDED HIKES   The rangers at Kipahulu conduct a 1-mile hike to the **Bamboo Forest** ⚘ at 9am daily; .5-mile hikes or orientation talks at noon, 1:30, 2:30, and 3:30pm daily; and a 4-mile round-trip hike to **Waimoku Falls** on Saturday at 9:30am. All programs and hikes begin at the ranger station; they may be canceled, so check in advance by contacting the **Kipahulu Ranger Station,** Haleakala National Park, HI 96713 (✆ **808/248-7375;** www.nps.gov/hale).

SKYLINE TRAIL, POLIPOLI SPRING STATE RECREATION AREA ⚘

This is some hike—strenuous but worth every step. It's 8 miles, all downhill, with a dazzling 100-mile view of the islands dotting the blue Pacific, plus the West Maui Mountains, which seem like a separate island.

The trail is located just outside Haleakala National Park at Polipoli Spring State Recreation Area; however, you access it by going through the national park to the summit. The Skyline Trail starts just beyond the Puu Ulaula summit building on the south side of Science City and follows the southwest rift zone of Haleakala from its lunarlike cinder cones to a cool redwood grove. The trail drops 3,800 feet on a 4-hour hike to the recreation area in the 12,000-acre Kahikinui Forest Reserve. If you'd rather drive, you'll need a four-wheel-drive vehicle.

There's a **campground** at the recreation area, at 6,300 feet. Permits and reservations are required, fees are $5 per campsite per night, and your stay must be limited to 5 nights. One 10-bunk cabin is available for $45 a night for one to four guests ($5 for each additional guest); it has a cold shower and a gas stove, but no electricity or drinking water (bring your own). To reserve, contact the **State Parks Division,** 54 S. High St., Room 101, Wailuku, HI 96793 (© **808/984-8109;** www.hawaiistateparks.org/camping/fees.cfm).

POLIPOLI STATE PARK ☆

You'll find one of the most unusual hiking experiences in the state at Polipoli State Park, part of the 21,000-acre Kula and Kahikinui Forest Reserve on the slope of Haleakala. At Polipoli, it's hard to believe that you're in Hawaii. First of all, it's cold, even in summer, because the loop is up at 5,300 to 6,200 feet. Second, this former forest of native koa, ohia, and mamane trees, which was overlogged in the 1800s, was reforested in the 1930s with introduced species: pine, Monterey cypress, ash, sugi, red alder, redwood, and several varieties of eucalyptus.

The **Polipoli Loop** ☆ is an easy 3.5-mile hike that takes about 3 hours; dress warmly for it. To get here, take the Haleakala Highway (Hwy. 37) to Keokea and turn right onto Hwy. 337; after less than ½ mile, turn on Waipoli Road, which climbs swiftly. After 10 miles, Waipoli Road ends at the Polipoli State Park campground. The well-marked trail head is next to the parking lot, near a stand of Monterey cypress; the tree-lined trail offers the best view of the island.

The Polipoli Loop is really a network of three trails: Haleakala Ridge, Plum Trail, and Redwood Trail. After .5 mile of meandering through groves of eucalyptus, blackwood, swamp mahogany, and hybrid cypress, you'll join the Haleakala Ridge Trail, which, about a mile in, joins with the Plum Trail (named for the plums that ripen in June–July). This trail passes through massive redwoods and by an old Conservation Corps bunkhouse and a run-down cabin before joining up with the Redwood Trail, which climbs through Mexican pine, tropical ash, Port Orford cedar, and, of course, redwood.

Camping is allowed in the park with a $5-per-night permit from the **State Parks Division,** 54 S. High St., Room 101, Wailuku, HI 96793 (© **808/984-8109;** www.hawaiistateparks.org/camping/fees.cfm). There's one cabin, which is available by reservation.

KANAHA BEACH PARK CAMPING

One of the few Maui County camping facilities on the island is at Kanaha Beach Park, located next to the Kahului Airport. The county has two separate areas for camping: 7 tent sites on the beach and an additional 10 tent sites inland. This well-used park is a favorite of windsurfers, who take advantage of the strong winds that roar across this end of the island. Facilities include a paved parking lot, portable toilets, outdoor showers, barbecue grills, and picnic tables. Camping is open 5 days a week (closed Tues–Wed) and limited to no more than 3 consecutive days. Permits, which are $3 per adult and 50¢ per child per night, can be obtained from the **Maui County Parks and Recreation Department,** 700 Halia Nakoa St., Unit 2, Wailuku, HI 96793 (© **808/243-7389;** www.mauimapp.com/information/campingcounty.htm). The 17 sites book up quickly; reserve your dates far in advance (the county will accept reservations a year in advance).

WAIANAPANAPA STATE PARK 🏃🏃

Tucked in a tropical jungle on the outskirts of the little coastal town of Hana is Waianapanapa State Park, a black-sand beach set in an emerald forest.

HANA-WAIANAPANAPA COAST TRAIL 🏃   This is an easy 6-mile hike that takes you back in time. Allow 4 hours to walk along this relatively flat trail, which parallels the sea, along lava cliffs and a forest of lauhala trees. The best time to take the hike is either early morning or late afternoon, when the light on the lava and surf makes for great photos. Midday is the worst time; not only is it hot (lava intensifies the heat), but there's also no shade or potable water available. There's no formal trail head; join the route at any point along the Waianapanapa Campground and go in either direction.

Along the trail, you'll see remains of an ancient *heiau* (temple), stands of lauhala trees, caves, a blowhole, and a remarkable plant, naupaka, that flourishes along the beach. Upon close inspection, you'll see that the naupaka has only half-blossoms; according to Hawaiian legend, a similar plant living in the mountains has the other half of the blossoms. One ancient explanation is that the two plants represent never-to-be-reunited lovers: As the story goes, the couple bickered so much that the gods, fed up with their incessant quarreling, banished one lover to the mountain and the other to the sea.

CAMPING   Waianapanapa has 12 cabins and a tent campground. Go for the cabins (reviewed on p. 141), as it rains torrentially here, sometimes turning the campground into a mud-wrestling arena. Tent camping is $5 per night but limited to 5 nights in a 30-day period. Permits are available from the **State Parks Division,** 54 S. High St., Room 101, Wailuku, HI 96793 (© **808/984-8109;** www.hawaiistate parks.org/camping/fees.cfm). Facilities include restrooms, outdoor showers, drinking water, and picnic tables.

HANA: THE HIKE TO FAGAN'S CROSS

This 3-mile hike to the cross erected in memory of Paul Fagan, the founder of Hana Ranch and Hotel Hana-Maui, offers spectacular views of the Hana Coast, particularly at sunset. The uphill trail starts across Hana Highway from the Hotel Hana-Maui. Enter the pastures at your own risk; they're often occupied by glaring bulls and cows with new calves. Watch your step as you ascend this steep hill on a jeep trail across open pastures to the cross and the breathtaking view.

KEANAE ARBORETUM 🏃

About 47 miles from Kahului, along the Hana Highway and just after the Keanae YMCA Camp (and just before the turnoff to the Keanae Peninsula), is an easy family walk through the Keanae Arboretum, which is maintained by the State Department of Land and Natural Resources, Division of Forestry and Wildlife. The walk, which is just over 2 miles, passes through a forest with both native and introduced plants. Allow 1 to 2 hours, longer if you take time out to swim. Take rain gear and mosquito repellent.

Park at the Keanae Arboretum and pass through the turnstile. Walk along the fairly flat jeep road to the entrance. For .5 mile, you will pass by plants introduced to Hawaii (ornamental timber, pomelo, banana, papaya, hibiscus, and more), all with identifying tags. At the end of this section is a taro patch showing the different varieties that Hawaiians used as their staple crop. After the taro, a 1-mile trail leads through a Hawaiian rainforest. The trail crisscrosses a stream as it meanders through the forest. My favorite swimming hole is just to the left of the first stream crossing, at about 300 feet.

WAIHEE RIDGE 🔆

This strenuous 3- to 4-mile hike, with a 1,500-foot climb, offers spectacular views of the valleys of the West Maui Mountains. Allow 3 to 4 hours for the round-trip hike. Pack a lunch, carry water, and pick a dry day, as this area is very wet. There's a picnic table at the summit with great views.

To get here from Wailuku, turn north on Market Street, which becomes the Kahekilii Highway (Hwy. 340) and passes through Waihee. Go just over 2½ miles from the Waihee Elementary School and look for the turnoff to the Boy Scouts' Camp Maluhia on the left. Turn into the camp and drive nearly a mile to the trail head on the jeep road. About ⅓ mile in, there will be another gate, marking the entrance to the West Maui Forest Reserve. A foot trail, kept in good shape by the State Department of Land and Natural Resources, begins here. The trail climbs to the top of the ridge, offering great views of the various valleys. The trail is marked by a number of switchbacks and can be extremely muddy and wet. In some areas, it's so steep that you have to grab onto the trees and bushes for support. The trail takes you through a swampy area, then up to **Lanilili Peak,** where a picnic table and magnificent views await.

4 Great Golf

In some circles, Maui is synonymous with golf. The island's world-famous golf courses start at the very northern tip of the island and roll right around to Kaanapali, jumping down to Kihei and Wailea in the south. There are also some lesser-known municipal courses that offer challenging play for less than $100.

Golfers new to Maui should know that it's windy here, especially between 10am and 2pm, when winds of 10 to 15 mph are the norm. Play two to three clubs up or down to compensate for the wind factor. I also recommend bringing extra balls—the rough is thicker here and the wind will pick your ball up and drop it in very unappealing places (like water hazards).

If your heart is set on playing on a resort course, book at least a week in advance. For the ardent golfer on a tight budget, consider playing in the afternoon, when discounted twilight rates are in effect. There's no guarantee you'll get 18 holes in, especially in winter when it's dark by 6pm, but you'll have an opportunity to experience these world-famous courses at half the usual fee.

For last-minute and discount tee times, call **Stand-by Golf** (© **888/645-2665;** www.stand-bygolf.com), which offers savings of up to 50% off greens fees, plus guaranteed tee times for same-day or next-day golfing.

Golf Club Rentals (© **808/665-0800;** www.mauiclubrentals.com) has custom-built clubs for men, women, and juniors (both right- and left-handed), which can be delivered island-wide; the rates are $25 a day.

CENTRAL MAUI

Waiehu Municipal Golf Course *(Value* This public, oceanside par-72 golf course is like playing two different courses: The first 9 holes, built in 1930, are set along the dramatic coastline, while the back 9 holes, added in 1966, head toward the mountains. It's a fun course that probably won't challenge your handicap. The only hazard here is the wind, which can rip off the ocean and play havoc with your ball. The only hole that can raise your blood pressure is the 511-yard, par-5 4th hole, which is very narrow and very long. Facilities include a snack bar, driving range, practice greens, club rentals, and clubhouse. Because this is a public course, the greens fees are low—but getting a tee time is tough.

Lower Waiehu Beach Rd., Wailuku. © 808/244-5934. www.co.maui.hi.us/parks/maui/central/WaiehuGolfCourse. htm. Greens fees $50 Mon–Fri, $55 Sat–Sun and holidays. From the Kahului Airport, turn right on the Hana Hwy. (Hwy. 36), which becomes Kaahumanu Ave. (Hwy. 32). Turn right at the stoplight at the junction with Waiehu Beach Rd. (Hwy. 340). Go another 1½ miles and you'll see the entrance on your right.

WEST MAUI

Kaanapali Golf Resort ✦ Both courses at Kaanapali offer a challenge to all golfers, from high-handicappers to near-pros. The par-72, 6,305-yard **North Course** is a true Robert Trent Jones, Sr., design: an abundance of wide bunkers; several long, stretched-out tees; and the largest, most contoured greens on Maui. The tricky 18th hole (par-4, 435 yd.) has a water hazard on the approach to the green. The par-72, 6,250-yard **South Course** is an Arthur Jack Snyder design; although shorter than the North Course, it requires more accuracy on the narrow, hilly fairways. It also has a water hazard on its final hole, so don't tally up your scorecard until you sink the final putt. Facilities at Kaanapali include a driving range, putting course, and clubhouse with dining. You'll have a better chance of getting a tee time on weekdays.

Off Hwy. 30, Kaanapali. © 808/661-3691. www.kaanapali-golf.com. Greens fees: North Course $205 ($170 for Kaanapali guests), twilight rates $110; South Course $175 ($130 for Kaanapali guests), twilight rates $85. At the 1st stoplight in Kaanapali, turn onto Kaanapali Pkwy.; the 1st building on your right is the clubhouse.

Kapalua Resort ✦✦✦ The views from these three championship courses are worth the greens fees alone. The par-72, 6,761-yard **Bay Course** (© 808/669-8820) was designed by Arnold Palmer and Ed Seay. This course is a bit forgiving, with its wide fairways; the greens, however, are difficult to read. The often-photographed 5th overlooks a small ocean cove; even the pros have trouble with this rocky par-3, 205-yard hole. The par-71, 6,632-yard **Village Course** (© 808/669-8830), another Palmer/Seay design, is the most scenic of the three courses. The hole with the best vista is the 6th, which overlooks a lake with the ocean in the distance. But don't get distracted by the view—the tee is between two rows of Cook pines. The **Plantation Course** (© 808/669-8877), site of the PGA Mercedes-Benz Championship, is a Ben Crenshaw/Bill Coore design. This par-73, 6,547-yard course, set on a rolling hillside, is excellent for developing your low shots and precise chipping. Facilities for all three courses include locker rooms, a driving range, and excellent dining. Weekdays are your best bet for tee times.

Off Hwy. 30, Kapalua. © 877/KAPALUA (527-2582). www.kapaluamaui.com. Greens fees: Bay Course $215 ($175 for hotel guests), twilight rates $130; Village Course $185 ($130 for hotel guests), twilight rates $85; Plantation Course $295 ($200 for guests), twilight rates $150.

SOUTH MAUI

Elleair Maui Golf Club Sitting in the foothills of Haleakala, just high enough to afford spectacular ocean vistas from every hole, Elleair (formerly Silversword Golf Club) is a course for golfers who love the views as much as the fairways and greens. It's very forgiving. *Just one caveat:* Go in the morning. Not only is it cooler, but, more important, it's also less windy. In the afternoon, the winds bluster down Haleakala with great gusto. This is a fun course to play, with some challenging holes: The par-5

2nd hole is a virtual minefield of bunkers, and the par-5 8th hole shoots over a swale and then uphill. Facilities include a clubhouse, driving range, putting green, pro shop, and lessons.

1345 Piilani Hwy. (near Lipoa St. turnoff), Kihei. ☎ **808/874-0777**. www.elleairmauigolfclub.com. Greens fees $120; twilight rates $90.

Makena Golf Courses ⭐⭐ Here you'll find 36 holes of "Mr. Hawaii Golf"— Robert Trent Jones, Jr.—at its best. Add to that spectacular views: Molokini islet looms in the background, humpback whales gambol offshore in winter, and the tropical sunsets are spectacular. The par-72, 6,876-yard **South Course** has a couple of holes you'll never forget. The view from the par-4 15th, which shoots from an elevated tee 183 yards downhill to the Pacific, is magnificent. The 16th hole has a two-tiered green that's blind from the tee 383 yards away (that is, if you make it past the gully off the fairway). The par-72, 6,823-yard **North Course** is more difficult and more spectacular. The 13th hole, located partway up the mountain, has a view that makes most golfers stop and stare. The next hole is even more memorable: a 200-foot drop between tee and green. Facilities at Makena include a clubhouse, a driving range, two putting greens, a pro shop, lockers, and lessons. Beware of weekend crowds.

On Makena Alanui Dr., just past the Maui Prince Hotel. ☎ **808/879-3344**. www.makenagolf.com. Greens fees $190 ($120 for Makena Resort guests); twilight rates $115–$150.

Wailea Golf Club ⭐⭐ There are three courses to choose from at Wailea. The **Blue Course,** a par-72, 6,758-yard course designed by Arthur Jack Snyder and dotted with bunkers and water hazards, is for duffers and pros alike. The wide fairways appeal to beginners, while the undulating terrain makes it a course everyone can enjoy. A little more difficult is the par-72, 7,078-yard championship **Gold Course,** with narrow fairways, several tricky dogleg holes, and the classic Robert Trent Jones, Jr., challenges: natural hazards, like lava-rock walls, and native Hawaiian grasses. The **Emerald Course,** also designed by Robert Trent Jones, Jr., is Wailea's newest, with tropical landscaping and a player-friendly design. With 54 holes to play, getting a tee time is slightly easier on weekends than at other resorts, but weekdays are still best (the Emerald Course is usually the toughest to book). Facilities include two pro shops, restaurants, locker rooms, and a complete training facility.

Wailea Alanui Dr. (off Wailea Iki Dr.), Wailea. ☎ **888/328-MAUI** (6284) or 808/875-7450. www.waileagolf.com. Greens fees: Blue Course $165–$185 ($155 for resort guests), twilight rates $130; Gold and Emerald courses $190–$225 ($180 for resort guests), no twilight rates.

UPCOUNTRY MAUI

Pukalani Country Club This cool par-72, 6,962-yard course at 1,100 feet offers a break from the resorts' high greens fees, and it's really fun to play. The 3rd hole offers golfers two different options: a tough (especially into the wind) iron shot from the tee, across a gully (yuck!) to the green; or a shot down the side of the gully across a second green into sand traps below. (Most people choose to shoot down the side of the gully; it's actually easier than shooting across a ravine.) High handicappers will love this course, and more experienced players can make it more challenging by playing from the back tees. Facilities include club and shoe rentals, practice areas, lockers, a pro shop, and a restaurant.

360 Pukalani St., Pukalani. ☎ **808/572-1314**. www.pukalanigolf.com. Greens fees for 18 holes (including cart) $78 before 11am, $73 11am–2pm, $63 after 2pm; 9 holes $44 after 1:30pm only. Take the Hana Hwy. (Hwy. 36) to Haleakala Hwy. (Hwy. 37) to the Pukalani exit; turn right onto Pukalani St. and go 2 blocks.

5 Biking, Horseback Riding & Other Outdoor Activities

BIKING

It's not even close to dawn, but here you are, rubbing your eyes awake, riding in a van up the long, dark road to the top of Maui's dormant volcano. It's colder than you ever thought possible for a tropical island. The air is thin. The place is crowded, packed with people. You stomp your chilly feet while you wait, sipping hot coffee. Then comes the sun, exploding over the yawning Haleakala Crater, which is big enough to swallow Manhattan whole—it's a mystical moment you won't soon forget. Now you know why Hawaiians named the crater the House of the Sun. But there's no time to linger: Decked out in your screaming-yellow parka, you mount your mechanical steed and test its most important feature, the brakes—because you're about to coast 37 miles down a 10,000-foot volcano.

Cruising down Haleakala, from the lunarlike landscape at the top past flower farms, pineapple fields, and eucalyptus groves, is quite an experience—and you don't have to be an expert cyclist to do it. This is a safe trip that requires some stamina in the colder, wetter winter months but is fun for everyone in the warmer months—the key word being *warmer.* In winter and the rainy season, conditions can be harsh, especially on the top, with below-freezing temperatures and 40-mph winds.

Maui's oldest downhill company is **Maui Downhill** ✿ (ⓒ **800/535-BIKE** [2453] or 808/871-2155; www.mauidownhill.com), which offers a sunrise safari bike tour, including continental breakfast and brunch, starting at $125 ($104 if booked online). If it's all booked up, try **Maui Mountain Cruisers** (ⓒ **800/232-6284** or 808/871-6014; www.mauimountaincruisers.com), which has sunrise trips for $144 and midday trips for $110. **Mountain Riders Bike Tours** (ⓒ **800/706-7700** or 808/242-9739; www.mountainriders.com) offers sunrise rides for $155 ($125 if booked online) and midday trips for $120. All rates include hotel pickup, transport to the top, bicycle, safety equipment, and meals. Wear layers of warm clothing—there may be a 30°F (17°C) change in temperature from the top of the mountain to the ocean. Generally, tour groups will not take riders under 12, but younger children can ride along in the van that accompanies the groups, as can pregnant women.

If you want to avoid the crowds and go down the mountain at your own pace, call **Haleakala Bike Company** (ⓒ **888/922-2453;** www.bikemaui.com), which will outfit you with the latest gear and take you up Haleakala.

Note: Not all tours go to the summit. If you want to start your bike ride at the summit, be sure to confirm. The cheapest trip starts at around the 6,500-foot level (about two-thirds up the mountain). After making sure you are secure on the bike, they will let you ride down by yourself at your own pace. Trips range from $60 to $105; bicycle rentals (from $30 a day) are also available if you'd like to tour other parts of Maui on your own.

If you want to venture out on your own, **Maui Sunriders Bike Company,** 71 Baldwin Ave., Paia (ⓒ **866/500-BIKE** [2453]; www.mauibikeride.com), rents bikes from $30 per day or $100 per week.

For information on bikeways and maps, get a copy of the *Maui County Bicycle Map,* which has details on road suitability, climate, trade winds, mileage, elevation changes, bike shops, safety tips, and various bicycling routes. The map is available at bike shops all over the island. A great book for mountain bikers who want to venture out on their own is John Alford's *Mountain Biking the Hawaiian Islands,* published by Ohana Publishing (www.bikehawaii.com).

Moratorium on Bike Tours in Haleakala National Park

As we went to press, the National Park Service issued a moratorium on commercial bicycle tours inside Haleakala National Park due to a September 26, 2007, death of a tourist who lost control of her bicycle and struck a van inside the park.

Some operators of Haleakala's "downhill bike tours" have circumvented this moratorium by staging their bicycle tours outside the park's boundaries. There are also a handful of companies who have "road-based" tour permits, which allows them to transport their clients within the park boundaries by van, but does not allow their clients to bike inside the park. If you want to see the sunrise from the Haleakala Crater, be sure to ask your tour operator if it has a road-based permit; otherwise, you will not be able to get inside the park.

The moratorium does not affect private citizens riding their bikes inside the park boundaries.

HORSEBACK RIDING

Maui offers spectacular adventure rides through rugged ranchlands, into tropical forests, and to remote swimming holes. I recommend riding with **Mendes Ranch & Trail Rides** ★, 3530 Kahekili Hwy., 4 miles past Wailuku (© **808/244-7320;** www.mendesranch.com). The 300-acre Mendes Ranch is a real-life working cowboy ranch that has the essential elements of an earthly paradise—rainbows, waterfalls, palm trees, coral-sand beaches, lagoons, tide pools, a rainforest, and its own volcanic peak (more than a mile high). Allan Mendes, a third-generation wrangler, will take you from the edge of the rainforest out to the sea. On the way, you'll cross tree-studded meadows where Texas longhorns sit in the shade and pass a dusty corral where Allan's father, Ernest, a champion roper, may be breaking in a wild horse. Allan keeps close watch, turning often in his saddle to make sure everyone is happy. He points out flora and fauna and fields questions, but generally just lets you soak up Maui's natural splendor in golden silence. A 2-hour morning or afternoon ride costs $110; add on a barbecue lunch at the corral for an additional $20.

Another one of my favorites is **Piiholo Ranch,** in Makawao (© **866/572-5544** or 808/357-5544; www.piiholo.com). A working cattle ranch owned by the *kamaaina* (long-time resident) Baldwin family, it offers horseback-riding adventures with a variety of different options to suit your ability, from the morning picnic ride (a 3 1/2-hr. ride on the ranch and a picnic lunch for $160 per person) to a 2-hour country ride through a working cattle ranch ($120).

If you're out in Hana, don't pass up **Maui Horseback Tours at Maui Stables** ★★, a mile past Oheo Gulch in Kipahulu (© **808/248-7799;** www.mauistables.com). It offers two rides daily (9:30am and 1pm) through the mountains above Kipahulu Valley—and you get a fantastic historical and cultural tour through the unspoiled landscape, to boot. It is an experience you will not forget. Both rides are $150. If you enjoy your ride, remember to kiss your horse and tip your guide.

For horse lovers looking for the ultimate, check out Frank Levinson's **Maui Horse Whisperer Experience** (© **808/572-6211;** www.mauihorses.com), which includes a seminar on the language of the horse. Prices are $200 for half-day and $300 for full-day workshops. No horse aficionado should pass it up.

HALEAKALA ON HORSEBACK   If you'd like to ride down into Haleakala's crater, contact **Pony Express Tours** ⚔ (© **808/667-2200** or 878-6698; www.pony expresstours.com), which leads a variety of rides down to the crater floor and back up, from $182 per person. Shorter 1- and 2-hour rides are also offered at Haleakala Ranch, located on the beautiful lower slopes of the volcano, for $110. A 1-hour intro-ductory ride is just $65. If you book via the website, you get 10% off. Pony Express provides well-trained horses and experienced guides, and accommodates all riding lev-els. You must be at least 10 years old, weigh no more than 230 pounds, and wear long pants and closed-toe shoes.

SPELUNKING

Don't miss the opportunity to see how the Hawaiian Islands were made by exploring a million-year-old underground lava tube/cave. Chuck Thorne, of **Hana Lava Tube** ⚔ (© **808/248-7308;** www.mauicave.com), offers several tours of this unique geologi-cal feature. After more than 10 years of leading scuba tours through underwater caves around Hawaii, Chuck discovered some caves on land that he wanted to show visitors. When the land surrounding the largest cave on Maui went on the market in 1996, Chuck snapped it up and started his own tour company. Monday through Saturday, between 10:30am and 3:30pm, you can take a self-guided 30- to 45-minute tour for just $12 (free for kids 4 and under).

If you want to combine caving with a tour of Hana, contact **Temptation Tours** (© **808/877-8888;** www.temptationtours.com). Its Cave Quest option costs $199, which covers a 1¼-hour cave tour, an air-conditioned van tour from your hotel to Hana, continental breakfast, beachside picnic lunch, and a stop for a swim.

TENNIS

Maui has excellent public tennis courts; all are free and available from daylight to sun-set (a few are even lit for night play until 10pm). The courts are available on a first-come, first-served basis; when someone's waiting, limit your play to 45 minutes. For a complete list of public courts, call **Maui County Parks and Recreation** (© **808/243-7230**). Because most public courts require a wait and are not conveniently located near the major resort areas, most visitors are likely to pay a fee to play at their own hotels. The exceptions to this are in Kihei (which has courts in Kalama Park on South Kihei Rd., and in Waipualani Park on West Waipualani Rd., behind the Maui Sunset condo), in Lahaina (which has courts in Malu'uou o lele Park, at Front and Shaw sts.), and in Hana (which has courts in Hana Park, on the Hana Hwy.).

Private tennis courts are available at most resorts and hotels on the island. The **Kapalua Tennis Garden and Village Tennis Center,** Kapalua Resort (© **808/669-5677;** www.kapaluamaui.com), is home to the Kapalua Open, which features the largest purse in the state, on Labor Day weekend. Court rentals are $14 per person for resort guests and $18 per person for nonguests. The staff will match you up with a partner if you need one. In Wailea, try the **Wailea Tennis Club,** 131 Wailea Iki Place (© **808/879-1958;** www.waileatennis.com), with 11 Plexipave courts. Court fees are $15 per player.

Seeing the Sights

After a few days of just relaxing on the beach, the itch to explore the rest of Maui sets in: What's on top of Haleakala, looming in the distance? Is the road to Hana really the tropical jungle everyone raves about? What does the inside of a 19th-century whaling boat look like?

There is far more to the Valley Isle than just sun, sand, and surf. Get out and see for yourself the otherworldly interior of a 10,000-foot volcanic crater, watch endangered sea turtles make their way to nesting sites in a wildlife sanctuary, wander back in time to the days when whalers and missionaries fought for the soul of Lahaina, and feel the energy of a thundering waterfall cascade into a serene mountain pool.

1 By Air, Land & Sea: Guided Island Adventures

The adventures below aren't cheap. However, each one offers such a wonderful opportunity to see Maui from a unique perspective that, depending on your interests, you might make one of them the highlight of your trip—it'll be worth every penny.

FLYING HIGH: HELICOPTER RIDES

Only a helicopter can bring you face-to-face with remote sites like Maui's little-known Wall of Tears, near the summit of Puu Kukui in the West Maui Mountains. You'll glide through canyons etched with 1,000-foot waterfalls and over dense rainforests; you'll climb to 10,000 feet, high enough to glimpse the summit of Haleakala, and fly by the dramatic vistas at Molokai.

The first chopper pilots in Hawaii were good ol' boys on their way back from Vietnam—hard-flying, hard-drinking cowboys who cared more about the ride than the scenery. But not anymore. Today's pilots, like the ones at Blue Hawaiian (see below), are an interesting hybrid: part Hawaiian historian, part DJ, part tour guide, and part amusement-ride operator. As you soar through the clouds, you'll learn about the island's flora, fauna, history, and culture.

Among the many helicopter-tour operators on Maui, the best is **Blue Hawaiian Helicopters** 𝕽𝕽, at Kahului Airport (© **800/745-BLUE** [2583] or 808/871-8844; www.bluehawaiian.com), which not only takes you on the ride of your life but also entertains, educates, and leaves you with an experience you'll never forget. Blue Hawaiian is also the only helicopter company in the state to have the latest high-tech, environmentally friendly (and quiet) Eco-Star helicopters, specially designed for air-tour operators. Flight times range from 30 to 100 minutes and cost $150 to $350. A keepsake DVD of your flight is available for $25.

Kids   Especially for Kids

Taking a Submarine Ride   Climb aboard a real sub with **Atlantis Adventures** (© 800/548-6262), which will take you down into the shallow coastal waters off Lahaina to see plenty of fish (maybe even a shark!). Kids will love it, and you'll stay dry the entire time. See "Going Under: Submarine Rides," below, for details.

Riding the Sugar Cane Train   This ride will appeal to small kids as well as train buffs of all ages. A steam engine pulls open passenger cars of the Lahaina/Kaanapali & Pacific Railroad on a 30-minute, 12-mile round-trip through sugar-cane fields between Lahaina and Kaanapali. The conductor sings and calls out the landmarks, and along the way you can see Molokai, Lanai, and the hidden parts of Kaanapali. Tickets are $22 for adults, $15 for kids 3 to 12; book online to save $2 per person. Call © 808/661-0080 or visit www.sugarcanetrain.com for details.

Searching for Stars   The stars over Kaanapali shine big and bright because the tropical sky is almost entirely free of pollutants and the interference of big-city lights. Amateur astronomers can probe the Milky Way, see Saturn's rings and Jupiter's moons, and scan the Sea of Tranquillity in a 60-minute star search on the world's first recreational computer-driven telescope. This cosmic adventure takes place nightly at the **Hyatt Regency Maui Resort,** 200 Nohea Kai Dr. (© 808/661-1234; p. 110), at 8, 9, and 10pm. The cost for hotel guests is $20 for adults and $10 for children 12 and under; nonguests pay $25 for adults and $15 for children.

Seeing Sharks, Stingrays & Starfish   Hawaii's largest aquarium, the **Maui Ocean Center** (© 808/875-1962; p. 220), has a range of sea critters—from tiger sharks to tiny starfish—that are sure to fascinate kids of all ages. At this 5-acre facility in Maalaea, visitors can take a virtual walk from the beach down to the ocean depths via the three dozen tanks, countless exhibits, and 100-foot-long main oceanarium.

Getting a Dragonfly's View   Kids will think this is too much fun to be educational. Don a face mask and get the dizzying perspective of what a dragonfly sees as it flies over a mountain stream, or watch the tiny *oopu* fish climb up a stream at the **Hawaii Nature Center** (© 808/244-6500; p. 207) in beautiful Iao Valley, where you'll find some 30 hands-on, interactive exhibits and displays of Hawaii's natural history.

GOING UNDER: SUBMARINE RIDES

Plunging 100 feet below the surface of the sea in a state-of-the-art, high-tech submarine is a great way to experience Maui's magnificent underwater world, especially if you're not a swimmer. **Atlantis Adventures,** 658 Front St., Lahaina (© 800/548-6262 or 808/667-7816; www.atlantisadventures.com), offers five trips per day out of Lahaina Harbor between 9am and 2pm; prices are $80 for adults and $41 for children under 12 (children must be at least 3 ft. tall). Book online and save 10%. The whole trip takes almost 2 hours; you'll spend about 45 minutes underwater. *Warning:* This is not a good choice if you're claustrophobic.

ECO-TOURS

Venture into the lush West Maui Mountains with an experienced guide on one of the numerous hikes offered by **Maui Eco-Adventures** (*©* 877/661-7720 or 808/661-7720; www.ecomaui.com). After a continental breakfast, you'll hike by streams and waterfalls, through native trees and plants, and on to breathtaking vistas. The tour includes a stop for a picnic lunch, a swim in secluded pools, and memorable photo ops. The 6-hour excursion costs $120 per person, including meals, a fanny pack with bottled water, and rain gear if necessary. No children under 13 are allowed. There's also a shorter, less strenuous jaunt for $80.

2 Central Maui

Central Maui isn't exactly tourist central; this is where real people live. You'll most likely land here and head directly to the beach. However, there are a few sights worth checking out if you feel like a respite from the sun and surf.

KAHULUI

Under the airport flight path, next to Maui's busiest intersection and across from Costco and Kmart in Kahului's new business park, is a most unlikely place: the **Kanaha Wildlife Sanctuary,** Haleakala Highway Extension and Hana Highway (*©* 808/984-8100). Look for the parking area off Haleakala Highway Extension (behind the mall, across the Hana Hwy. from Cutter Automotive), and you'll find a 50-foot trail that meanders along the shore to a shade shelter and lookout. Watch for the sign proclaiming this the permanent home of the endangered black-neck Hawaiian stilt, whose population is now down to about 1,000 to 1,500. Naturalists say this is a good place to see endangered Hawaiian koloa ducks, stilts, coots, and other migrating shorebirds. For a quieter, more natural-looking wildlife preserve, see the **Kealia Pond National Wildlife Preserve,** in Kihei (p. 220).

PUUNENE

This town, located in the middle of the central Maui plains, is nearly gone. Once a thriving sugar-plantation town with hundreds of homes, a school, a shopping area, and a community center, Puunene is little more than a sugar mill, a post office, and a museum today. The Hawaiian Commercial & Sugar Co., owner of the land, has slowly phased out the rental plantation housing to open up more land to plant sugar.

Alexander & Baldwin Sugar Museum This former sugar-mill superintendent's home has been converted into a museum that tells the story of sugar in Hawaii. Exhibits explain how sugar is grown, harvested, and milled. An eye-opening display shows how Samuel Alexander and Henry Baldwin managed to acquire huge chunks of land from the Kingdom of Hawaii, then ruthlessly fought to gain access to water on the other side of the island, making sugar cane an economically viable crop. Allow about half an hour to enjoy the museum.

Puunene Ave. (Hwy. 350) and Hansen Rd. *©* 808/871-8058. www.sugarmuseum.com. Admission $5 adults, $2 children 6–17. Daily 9:30am–4:30pm.

WAIKAPU

Across the sugar-cane fields from Puunene, and about 3 miles south of Wailuku on the Honoapiilani Highway, lies the tiny, one-street village of Waikapu, which has two attractions that are worth a peek, especially if you're trying to kill time before your flight out.

Relive Maui's past by taking a 40-minute narrated tram ride around fields of pineapple, sugar cane, and papaya trees at **Maui Tropical Plantation,** 1670 Honoapiilani Hwy. (© **800/451-6805** or 808/244-7643; www.mauitropicalplantation.com), a real working plantation open daily from 9am to 5pm. A shop sells fresh and dried fruit, and a restaurant serves lunch. Admission is free; the tram tours, which start at 10am and leave about every 45 minutes, are $11 for adults and $4 for kids 3 to 12.

WAILUKU

This historic gateway to Iao Valley (see below) is worth a visit, if only for a brief stop at the Bailey House Museum and some terrific shopping (see chapter 9).

Bailey House Museum ⨀   Missionary and sugar planter Edward Bailey's 1833 home—an architectural hybrid of stones laid by Hawaiian craftsmen and timbers joined in a display of Yankee ingenuity—is a treasure trove of Hawaiiana. Inside, you'll find an eclectic collection, from precontact artifacts like scary temple images, dog-tooth necklaces, and a rare lei made of tree-snail shells to latter-day relics like Duke Kahanamoku's 1919 redwood surfboard and a koa-wood table given to President Ulysses S. Grant, who had to refuse it because he couldn't accept gifts from foreign countries. There's also a gallery devoted to a few of Bailey's landscapes, painted from 1866 to 1896, which capture on canvas a Maui we can only imagine today.

2375-A Main St. © **808/244-3326.** www.mauimuseum.org. Admission $5 adults, $4 seniors, $1 children 7–12. Mon–Sat 10am–4pm.

IAO VALLEY ⨀

A couple of miles north of Wailuku, past the Bailey House Museum, where the little plantation houses stop and the road climbs ever higher, Maui's true nature begins to reveal itself. The transition from suburban sprawl to raw nature is so abrupt that most people who drive up into the valley don't realize they're suddenly in a rainforest. The walls of the canyon begin to close around them, and a 2,250-foot-high needlelike rock pricks gray clouds scudding across the blue sky. The moist, cool air and the shade are a welcome comfort after the hot tropic sun. This is Iao Valley, an eroded volcanic caldera in the West Maui Mountains whose great nature, history, and beauty have been enjoyed by millions of people from around the world for more than a century.

Iao ("Supreme Light") Valley is 10 miles long and encompasses 4,000 acres. The head of the valley is a broad circular amphitheater where four major streams converge into Iao Stream. At the back of the amphitheater is rain-drenched Puu Kukui, the West Maui Mountains' highest point. No other Hawaiian valley lets you go from seacoast to rainforest so easily. This peaceful valley, full of tropical plants, rainbows, waterfalls, swimming holes, and hiking trails, is a place of solitude, reflection, and escape for residents and visitors alike.

To get here from Wailuku, take Main Street; then turn right on Iao Valley Road to the entrance to the state park. The park is open daily from 7am to 7pm. Go early in the morning or late in the afternoon, when the sun's rays slant into the valley and create a mystical atmosphere. You can bring a picnic and spend the day, but be prepared at any time for a tropical cloudburst, which often soaks the valley and swells both waterfalls and streams.

For information, contact the **Division of State Parks,** 54 S. High St., Room 101, Wailuku, HI 96793 (© **808/984-8109;** www.hawaiistateparks.org/parks/maui/index.cfm?park_id=36). The **Hawaii Nature Center** ✿, 875 Iao Valley Rd. (© **808/244-6500;** www.hawaiinaturecenter.org), home of the Iao Valley Nature Center, features interactive exhibits and displays relating the story of Hawaiian natural history; it's an important stop for all who want to explore Iao Valley. Hours are daily from 10am to 4pm. Admission is $6 for adults and $4 for children 4 to 12. **Rainforest Walks** are led Monday through Friday at 11:30am and 1:30pm, Saturday and Sunday at 11am and 2pm. Wear closed-toe shoes (no sandals) suitable for an uneven trail. The cost, which includes a visit to the museum, is $30 for adults and $20 for children 5 and older (younger children not allowed). Book in advance.

You can take the loop trail into the massive green amphitheater of Iao Valley for free. The public walkway crosses the bridge of Iao Stream and continues along the stream itself. The .35-mile paved loop is an easy walk—you can even take your grandmother on this one. A leisurely stroll will allow you to enjoy lovely views of the Iao Needle and the lush vegetation. Others often proceed beyond the state park border and take two trails deeper into the valley, but the trails enter private land, and NO TRESPASSING signs are posted.

The feature known as **Iao Needle** is an erosional remnant consisting of basalt dikes. This phallic rock juts an impressive 2,250 feet above sea level. Youngsters play in **Iao Stream,** a peaceful brook that belies its bloody history. In 1790, King Kamehameha the Great and his men engaged in the battle of Iao Valley to gain control of Maui. When the battle ended, so many bodies blocked Iao Stream that the battle site was named Kepaniwai, or "damming of the waters." An architectural heritage park of Hawaiian, Japanese, Chinese, Filipino, and New England–style houses stands in harmony by Iao Stream at **Kepaniwai Heritage Garden.** This is a good picnic spot, with plenty of tables and benches. You can see ferns, banana trees, and other native and exotic plants in the **Iao Valley Botanic Garden** along the stream.

3 Lahaina & West Maui

OLOWALU

Most people drive right by Olowalu, on the Honoapiilani Highway 5 miles south of Lahaina; there's little to mark the spot but a small general store and Chez Paul (p. 148), an excellent French restaurant. Olowalu ("many hills") was the scene of a bloody massacre in 1790. The Hawaiians stole a skiff from the USS *Eleanora,* took it back to shore here, and burned it for its iron parts. The captain of the ship, Simon Metcalf, was furious and tricked the Hawaiians into sailing out in their canoes to trade with the ship. As the canoes approached, he mowed them down with his cannons, killing 100 people and wounding many others.

Olowalu has great snorkeling around **mile marker 14,** where there is a turtle-cleaning station about 150 to 225 feet out from shore. Turtles line up here to have cleaner wrasses (small bony fish) pick off small parasites.

Lahaina

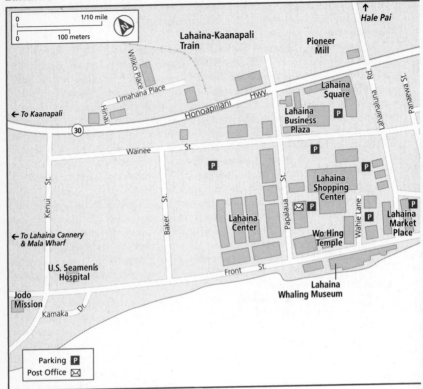

HISTORIC LAHAINA

Located between the West Maui Mountains and the deep azure ocean offshore, Lahaina stands out as one of the few places in Hawaii that has managed to preserve its 19th-century heritage while still accommodating 21st-century guests.

In ancient times, powerful chiefs and kings ruled this hot, dry, oceanside village. At the turn of the 19th century, after King Kamehameha united the Hawaiian Islands, he made Lahaina the royal capital—which it remained until 1845, when Kamehameha III moved the capital to the larger port of Honolulu.

In the 1840s, the whaling industry was at its peak: Hundreds of ships called into Lahaina every year. The streets were filled with sailors 24 hours a day. Even Herman Melville, who later wrote *Moby-Dick,* visited Lahaina.

Just 20 years later, the whaling industry was waning, and sugar had taken over the town. The Pioneer Sugar Mill Co., which still stands but no longer operates today, reigned over Lahaina for the next 100 years.

Today, the drunken and derelict whalers who wandered through Lahaina's streets in search of bars, dance halls, and brothels have been replaced by hordes of tourists crowding into the small mile-long main section of town in search of boutiques, art galleries, and chic gourmet eateries. Lahaina's colorful past continues to have a profound

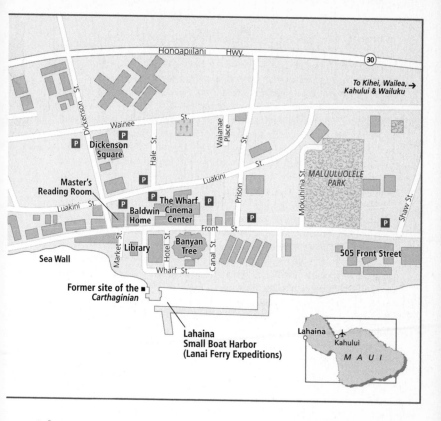

influence. This is no quiet seaside village, but a vibrant, cutting-edge kind of place, filled with a sense of history—but definitely with its mind on the future.

See chapter 7 for details on the various cruises and outfitters operating out of Lahaina.

Baldwin Home Museum ⊛ The oldest house in Lahaina, this coral-and-rock structure was built in 1834 by Rev. Dwight Baldwin, a doctor with the fourth company of American missionaries to sail to Hawaii. Like many missionaries, he came to Hawaii to do good—and did very well for himself. After 17 years of service, Baldwin was granted 2,600 acres in Kapalua for farming and grazing. His ranch manager experimented with what Hawaiians called *hala-kahiki,* or pineapple, on a 4-acre plot; the rest is history. The house looks as if Baldwin has just stepped out for a minute to tend a sick neighbor down the street.

Next door is the **Master's Reading Room,** Maui's oldest building (included with museum admission). This became visiting sea captains' favorite hangout once the missionaries closed down all of Lahaina's grog shops and banned prostitution. By 1844, when hotels and bars started reopening, it lost its appeal. It's now the headquarters of the **Lahaina Restoration Foundation** (© **808/661-3262;** www.lahainarestoration. org), a plucky band of historians who try to keep this town alive and antique at the

Moments   Hoomanao: Step Back in Time to Old Hawaii

As soon as the low wail from the Hawaiian conch shell fills the air, you know that you have entered another time. *Hoomanao* means "to remember," and this 3-hour feast and immersion into ancient Hawaii is something you will definitely remember long after your tan has faded.

Brought to you by the innovative team that stages the Old Lahaina Luau, the Hoomanao takes place in the same oceanfront setting, surrounded by tropical native plants. The feast begins with a breakfast buffet that ranges from stuffed French toast and haupia (coconut) oatmeal to kalua pork and lomi salmon. Hula dancers and chanters entertain, the sun sparkles off the calm ocean water, and a salty breeze is in the air; this is Hawaii at its finest.

Then the fun begins. You get to experience (not just look and listen, but experience hands-on) three aspects of Hawaii: hula, warfare, and ancient Hawaiian life. At the *kulana* (station) for hula, you will learn a few steps of these ancient dances as well as how to play the traditional implements. At the warfare kulana, you will try your hand at tossing a spear or, perhaps, put on a temporary, removable tattoo of a Hawaiian warrior. And at the ancient-life station, you will sample freshly made poi and poke (small pieces of raw fish, salt, seaweed, and *kukui* nut), or practice throwing a fish net.

Hoomanao, on the Old Lahaina Luau grounds, 1251 Front St., Lahaina (© **800/248-5828**; www.oldlahainaluau.com), takes place from 9am to noon on Tuesday and Friday. Tickets are $72 for adults and $71 for children 12 and under. Don't miss it.

same time. Stop in and pick up a self-guided walking-tour map, which will take you to Lahaina's most historic sites.

120 Dickenson St. (at Front St.). © **808/661-3262**. www.lahainarestoration.org. Admission $3 adults, $2 seniors, $5 family. Daily 10am–4pm.

Banyan Tree (Kids   Of all the banyan trees in Hawaii, this is the greatest—so big that you can't get it all in your camera's viewfinder. It was only 8 feet tall when it was planted in 1873 by Maui sheriff William O. Smith to mark the 50th anniversary of Lahaina's first Christian mission. Now it's more than 50 feet tall, has 12 major trunks, and shades two-thirds of an acre in Courthouse Square.

At the Courthouse Building, 649 Wharf St.

Hale Pai   When the missionaries arrived in Hawaii to spread the word of God, they found the Hawaiians had no written language. They quickly rectified the situation by converting the Hawaiian sounds into a written language. They then built the first printing press in order to print educational materials that would assist them on their mission. Hale Pai was the printing house for the Lahainaluna Seminary, the oldest American school west of the Rockies. Today, Lahainaluna is the public high school for the children of west Maui.

Lahainaluna High School Campus, 980 Lahainaluna Rd. (at the top of the mountain). © **808/661-3262**. www. lahainarestoration.org/halepai. Free admission. Mon–Fri by appointment only.

Day Trips to Molokai

It's possible to visit Molokai's famous leper colony (officially known as Kalau-papa National Historical Park) as a day trip from Maui. You won't be able to squeeze in the exhilarating mule ride down the 1,600-foot cliffs (they start at 8am), but you didn't want to sit on your ass all day long anyway, now did you? (Sorry, bad pun.) **Paragon Air** (① 808/244-3356; www.paragon-air.com) offers a $285 package deal that includes round-trip airfare from Maui's Kahului Airport to Molokai's Kalaupapa Airport, a 4-hour tour, lunch, and drinks. All visitors must be at least 16 years old. No tours are given on Sunday, when the national park is closed.

Lahaina Heritage Museum   Located on the second floor of the old Lahaina Courthouse, this museum tells the story of the history and culture of Lahaina. In addition to ever-changing exhibits, there are videos, live demonstrations by cultural artisans, "touch and feel" displays, and interactive exhibits.

648 Wharf St. ① 808/661-1959. www.visitlahaina.com. Free admission. Daily 9am–5pm.

Lahaina Jodo Mission   This site has long been held sacred. The Hawaiians called it Puunoa Point, which means "the hill freed from taboo." Once a small village named *Mala* (garden), this peaceful place was a haven for Japanese immigrants, who came to Hawaii in 1868 as laborers for the sugar-cane plantations. They eventually built a small wooden temple to worship here. In 1968, on the 100th anniversary of Japanese presence in Hawaii, a Great Buddha statue (some 12 ft. high and weighing 3½ tons) was brought here from Japan. The immaculate grounds also contain a replica of the original wooden temple and a 90-foot-tall pagoda.

12 Ala Moana St. (off Front St., near the Mala Wharf). ① 808/661-4304. Free admission. Daily during daylight hours.

Maluuluolele Park   At first glance, this Front Street park appears to be only a hot, dry, dusty softball field. But under home plate is the edge of Mokuula, where a royal compound once stood more than 100 years ago—it's now buried under tons of red dirt and sand. Here, Prince Kauikeaolui, who ascended the throne as King Kamehameha III when he was only 10, lived with the love of his life, his sister, Princess Nahienaena. Missionaries took a dim view of incest, which was acceptable to Hawaiian nobles in order to preserve the royal bloodline. Torn between love for her brother and the new Christian morality, Nahienaena grew despondent and died at the age of 21. King Kamehameha III, who reigned for 29 years—longer than any other Hawaiian monarch—presided over Hawaii as it went from kingdom to constitutional monarchy, and as power over the islands began to shift from island nobles to missionaries, merchants, and sugar planters. Kamehameha died in 1854 at the age of 39. In 1918, his royal compound, containing a mausoleum and artifacts of the kingdom, was demolished and covered with dirt to create a public park. The baseball team from Lahainaluna School now plays games on the site of this royal place, still considered sacred to many Hawaiians.

Front and Shaw sts.

Wo Hing Temple ⓖ   The Chinese were among the various immigrants brought to Hawaii to work in the sugar-cane fields. In 1909, several Chinese workers formed the

Tips **Where to Park for Free—or Next to Free—in Lahaina**

Lahaina is the worst place on Maui for parking. The town was created and filled with shops, restaurants, and historic sites before the throngs of tourists (and their cars) invaded. Street parking is hit or miss. You can either drive around the block for hours looking for a free place to park on the street or park in one of the nearly 20 parking lots. I've divided the lots into three classes: free for customers, discount with validation, and pay.

Free for Customers: The three lots on Papalaua Street are all free for customers. The largest is the Lahaina Shopping Center lot, with 2 free hours. Next in size is the Lahaina Center, across the street (which allows 4 hr. free, but you must get validation from a store in the Lahaina Center). The smallest is the Lahaina Square lot at Wainee Street, which offers 2 free hours for customers.

Discount with Validation: Customers of the Wharf Cinema Center, located on Front Street, can get a discount by parking at either of the theater's two lots—both are between Dickenson and Prison streets, but one is on Wainee Street and the other on Luakini Street.

Pay: Lahaina is filled with pay lots ranging from 50¢ for a half-hour to all-day parking for $8 to $10. Pay lots on Front Street are located between Papalaua and Lahainaluna streets, on the corner of Dickenson Street, and underground at the 505 Front Street shopping center. Pay lots on Luakini Street are located near the Prison Street intersection and near the Lahainaluna Road intersection. Lahainaluna Road has several pay lots between Wainee and Front streets. Dickenson Street has three pay lots between Wainee and Luakini streets.

Wo Hing society, a chapter of the Chee Kun Tong society, which dates from the 17th century. In 1912, they built this social hall for the Chinese community. Completely restored, the Wo Hing Temple contains displays and artifacts on the history of the Chinese in Lahaina. Next door in the old cookhouse is a theater with movies of Hawaii taken by Thomas Edison in 1898 and 1903.

Front St. (btw. Wahie Lane and Papalaua St.). ✆ 808/661-3262. Admission by donation. Daily 10am–4pm.

WALKING TOUR   HISTORIC LAHAINA

Getting There: From the Kahului Airport, take the Kuihelani Highway (Hwy. 38) to the intersection of Honoapiilani Highway (Hwy. 30), where you turn left. Follow Honoapiilani Highway to Lahaina and turn left on Lahainaluna Road. When Lahainaluna Road ends, make a left on Front Street. Dickenson Street is a block down (see the box on parking, above).

Start: Front and Dickenson streets.

Finish: Same location.

Time: About an hour.

Walking Tour: Historic Lahaina

1 Master's Reading Room	**7** Former *Carthaginian* site	**13** Government Market
2 Baldwin Home	**8** Pioneer Inn	**14** Holy Innocents Episcopal Church
3 Richards House	**9** Banyan Tree	**15** Hale Piula
4 Taro Patch	**10** Courthouse	**16** Maluuluolele Park
5 Hauola Stone	**11** Fort	**17** Wainee Church
6 Brick Palace	**12** Canal	**18** Waihee Cemetery

19 Hongwanji Mission	**23** Hale Aloha
20 David Malo's Home	**24** Buddhist Church
21 Old Prison	**25** Luakini Street
22 Episcopal Cemetery	

Back when "there was no God west of the Horn," Lahaina was the capital of Hawaii and the Pacific's wildest port. Today it's a milder version of its old self—mostly a hustle-bustle of whale art, timeshares, and "Just Got Lei'd" T-shirts. I'm not sure the rowdy whalers would be pleased. But if you look hard, you'll still find the historic port town they loved, filled with the kind of history that inspired James Michener to write his best-selling epic novel *Hawaii.*

Members of the Lahaina Restoration Foundation have worked for 3 decades to preserve Lahaina's past. They have labeled a number of historic sites with brown-and-white markers; below, I provide explanations of the significance of each site as you walk through Lahaina's past.

Begin your tour at the:

❶ Master's Reading Room

This coral-and-stone building looks just as it did in 1834, when Rev. William Richards and Rev. E. Spaulding convinced the whaling-ship captains that they needed a place for the ships' masters and captains, many of whom traveled with their families, to stay while they were ashore. The bottom floor was used as a storage area for the mission; the top floor, from which you could see the ships at anchor in the harbor, was for the visiting ships' officers.

Next door is the:

❷ Baldwin Home

Harvard-educated physician Rev. Dwight
Baldwin, with his wife of just a few weeks,
sailed to Hawaii from New England in
1830. Baldwin was first assigned to a
church in Waimea, on the Big Island, and
then to Lahaina's Wainee Church in 1838.
He and his family lived in this house until
1871. The Baldwin Home and the Master's Reading Room are the oldest standing buildings in Lahaina, made from thick
walls of coral and hand-milled timber.
Baldwin also ran his medical office and his
missionary activities out of this house.
(See Baldwin Home Museum, p. 209, for
information on hours and admission.)

On the other side of the Baldwin Home is the
former site of the:

❸ Richards House

The open field is empty today, but it rep-
resents the former home of Lahaina's first
Protestant missionary, Rev. William
Richards. Richards went on to become
the chaplain, teacher, and translator to
Kamehameha III. He was also instrumen-
tal in drafting Hawaii's constitution and
acted as the king's envoy to the United
States and England, seeking recognition
of Hawaii as an independent nation.
After his death in 1847, he was buried in
the Wainee Churchyard.

From here, cross Front Street and walk toward
the ocean, with the Lahaina Public Library on
your right and the green Pioneer Inn on your
left, until you see the:

❹ Taro Patch

The lawn in front of the Lahaina Library
was once a taro patch stretching back to
the Baldwin Home. The taro plant was a
staple of the Hawaiian diet: The root was
used to make poi, and the leaves were
used in cooking. At one time Lahaina
looked like a Venice of the tropics, with
streams, ponds, and waterways flooding
the taro fields. As the population of the
town grew, the water was siphoned off for
drinking use.

Walk away from the Lahaina Harbor toward the
edge of the lawn, where you'll see the:

❺ Hauola Stone

Hawaiians believed that certain stones
placed in sacred places had the power to
heal. *Kahuna* (priests) of medicine used
stones like this to help cure illnesses.

Turn around and walk back toward the Pioneer
Inn; look for the concrete depression in the
ground, which is all that's left of the:

❻ Brick Palace

This structure was begun in 1798 as the
first Western-style building in Hawaii.
King Kamehameha I had this 20×40-
foot, two-story brick structure built for
his wife, Queen Kaahumanu (who is said
to have preferred a grass-thatched house
nearby). Inside, the walls were constructed of wood and the windows were
glazed glass. Kamehameha I lived here
from 1801 to 1802, when he was building his war canoe, *Peleleu,* and preparing
to invade Kauai. A handmade stone sea
wall surrounded the palace to protect it
from the surf. The building stood for 70
years. In addition to being a royal compound, it was also used as a meeting-
house, storeroom, and warehouse.

Behind you, dockside of the loading pier of the
Lahaina Harbor, is the:

❼ Former Site of the *Carthaginian*

This was once the site of a replica of a
19th-century brig that carried commerce
back and forth to Hawaii, and, until
2004, served as a museum and exhibit of
19th-century boating and whaling. The
Carthaginian, which had been plagued
with numerous maintenance problems
for years, has been removed from the slip,
and the Lahaina Restoration Foundation
is in the process of finding a replacement
ship.

Directly opposite the *Carthaginian* site is the:

❽ Pioneer Inn

Lahaina's first hotel was the scene of some
wild parties at the start of the 20th century. George Freeland, of the Royal Canadian Mounted Police, tracked a criminal

to Lahaina and then fell in love with the town. He built the hotel in 1901 but soon discovered that Lahaina wasn't the tourist mecca it is today. To make ends meet, Freeland built a movie theater, which was wildly successful. The Pioneer Inn remained the only hotel in all of west Maui until the 1950s. You can stay at this restored building today (p. 107).

From the Pioneer Inn, cross Hotel Street and walk along Wharf Street, which borders the harbor. On your left is the:

❾ Banyan Tree

This ancient tree has witnessed decades of luau, dances, concerts, private chats, public rallies, and resting sojourners under its mighty boughs. It's hard to believe that this huge tree was only 8 feet tall when it was planted here.

Continue along Wharf Street. Near the edge of the park is the:

❿ Courthouse

In 1858, a violent windstorm destroyed about 20 buildings in Lahaina, including Hale Piula, which served as the courthouse and palace of King Kamehameha III. It was rebuilt immediately, using the stones from the previous building. It served not only as courthouse, but also as custom house, post office, tax collector's office, and government offices. Upstairs on the second floor is the Lahaina Heritage Museum, with exhibits on the history and culture of Lahaina (free admission; open daily 9am–5pm).

Continue down Wharf Street to Canal Street. On the corner are the remains of the:

⓫ Fort

This structure once covered an acre and had 20-foot-high walls. In 1830, some whalers fired a few cannonballs into Lahaina in protest of Rev. William Richards's meddling in their affairs. (Richards had convinced Gov. Hoapili to create a law forbidding the women of Lahaina from swimming out to greet the whaling ships.) The fort was constructed from 1831 to 1832 with coral blocks

taken from the ocean where the Lahaina Harbor sits today. As a further show of strength, cannons were placed along the waterfront, where they remain today. Historical accounts seem to scoff at the "fort," saying it appeared to be more for show than for force. It was later used as a prison, until it was finally torn down in the 1850s; its stones were used for construction of the new prison, Hale Paahao (see no. 21 below).

Cross Canal Street to the:

⓬ Canal

Unlike Honolulu with its natural deepwater harbor, Lahaina was merely a roadstead with no easy access to the shore. Whalers would anchor in deep water offshore, then board smaller boats (which they used to chase down and harpoon whales) to make the passage over the reef to shore. If the surf was up, coming ashore could be dangerous. In the 1840s, the U.S. consular representative recommended digging a canal from one of the freshwater streams that ran through Lahaina and charging a fee to the whalers who wanted to obtain fresh water. In 1913, the canal was filled in to construct Canal Street.

Up Canal Street is the:

⓭ Government Market

A few years after the canal was built, the government built a thatched marketplace with stalls for Hawaiians to sell goods to the sailors. Merchants quickly took advantage of this marketplace and erected drinking establishments, grog shops, and other pastimes of interest nearby. Within a few years, this entire area became known as "Rotten Row."

Make a right onto Front Street and continue down the street, past Kamehameha III Elementary School. Across from the park is:

⓮ Holy Innocents Episcopal Church

When the Episcopal missionaries first came to Lahaina in 1862, they built a church across the street from the current structure. In 1909, the church moved to its present site, which was once a thatched house built for the daughter of King Kamehameha I. The present structure, built in 1927, features unique paintings of a Hawaiian Madonna and birds and plants endemic to Hawaii, executed by DeLos Blackmar in 1940.

Continue down Front Street, and at the next open field, look for the white stones by the ocean, marking the former site of the "iron-roofed house" called:

⓯ Hale Piula

In the 1830s, the two-story stone building with a large surrounding courtyard was built for King Kamehameha III. However, the king preferred sleeping in a small thatched hut nearby, so the structure was never really completed. In the 1840s, Kamehameha moved his capital to Honolulu and wasn't using Hale Piula, so it became the local courthouse. The windstorm of 1858, which destroyed the courthouse on Wharf Street (see no. 10 above), also destroyed the iron-roofed house. The stones from Hale Piula were used to rebuild the courthouse on Wharf Street.

Continue down Front Street; across from the 505 Front Street complex is:

⓰ Maluuluolele Park

This sacred spot to Hawaiians is now the site of a park and ball field. This used to be a village, Mokuhinia, with a sacred pond that was the home of a *moo* (a spirit in the form of a lizard), which the royal family honored as their personal guardian spirit. In the middle of the pond was a small island, Mokuula, home to Maui's top chiefs. After conquering Maui, Kamehameha I claimed this sacred spot as his own; he and his two sons, Kamehameha II and III, lived here when they were in Lahaina. In 1918, in the spirit of progress, the pond was drained and the ground leveled for a park.

Make a left onto Shaw Street and then another left onto Wainee Street. On the left side, just past the cemetery, is:

⓱ Wainee Church

This was the first stone church built in Hawaii (1828–32). At one time the church could seat some 3,000 people, albeit tightly packed together, complete with "calabash spittoons" for the tobacco-chewing Hawaiian chiefs and the ship captains. That structure didn't last long—the 1858 windstorm that destroyed several buildings in Lahaina also blew the roof off the original church, knocked over the belfry, and picked up the church's bell and deposited it 100 feet away. The structure was rebuilt, but that too was destroyed—this time by Hawaiians protesting the 1894 overthrow of the monarchy. Again the church was rebuilt, and again it was destroyed—by fire in 1947. The next incarnation of the church was destroyed by yet another windstorm in 1951. The current church has been standing since 1953. Be sure to walk around to the back of the church: The row of palm trees on the ocean side includes some of the oldest palm trees in Lahaina.

Wander next door to the first Christian cemetery in Hawaii:

⓲ Waihee Cemetery

Established in 1823, this cemetery tells a fascinating story of old Hawaii, with graves of Hawaiian chiefs, commoners, sailors, and missionaries and their families (infant mortality was high then). Enter this ground with respect, because Hawaiians consider it sacred—many members of the royal family were buried here, including Queen Keopuolani, who was wife of King Kamehameha I, mother of kings Kamehameha II and III, and the first Hawaiian baptized as a Protestant. Among the other graves are those of Rev. William Richards (the first missionary in Lahaina) and Princess Nahienaena (sister of kings Kamehameha II and III).

Continue down Waihee Street to the corner of Luakini Street and the:

⓳ Hongwanji Mission

The temple was originally built in 1910 by members of Lahaina's Buddhist sect. The current building was constructed in 1927, housing a temple and language school. The public is welcome to attend the New Year's Eve celebration, Buddha's birthday in April (see "Maui, Molokai & Lanai Calendar of Events," p. 52), and O Bon Memorial Services in August.

Continue down Wainee Street. Just before the intersection with Prison Street, look for the historical marker for:

⓴ David Malo's Home

Although no longer standing, the house that once stood here was the home of Hawaii's first scholar, philosopher, and well-known author. Educated at Lahainaluna School, his book on ancient Hawaiian culture, *Hawaiian Antiquities,* is considered *the* source on Hawaiiana today. His alma mater celebrates David Malo Day every year in April in recognition of his contributions to Hawaii.

Cross Prison Street. On the corner of Prison and Waihee is the:

㉑ Old Prison

The Hawaiians called the prison Hale Paahao ("stuck in irons house"). Sailors who refused to return to their boats at sunset used to be arrested and taken to the old fort (see no. 11 above). In 1851, however, the fort physician told the government that sleeping on the ground at night made the prisoners ill, costing the government quite a bit of money to treat them—so the Kingdom of Hawaii used the prisoners to build a prison from the coral block of the old fort. Most prisoners here had terms of a year or less (those with longer terms were shipped off to Honolulu) and were convicted of crimes like deserting ship, being drunk, or working on Sunday. Today, the grounds of the prison have a much more congenial

atmosphere, and are rented out to community groups for parties.

Continue down Waihee Street, just past Waianae Place, to the small:

㉒ Episcopal Cemetery

This burial ground tells another story in Hawaii's history. During the reign of King Kamehameha IV, his wife, Queen Emma, formed close ties with British royalty. She encouraged Hawaiians to join the Anglican Church after asking the Archbishop of Canterbury to form a church in Hawaii. This cemetery contains the burial sites of many of those early Anglicans.

Next door is:

㉓ Hale Aloha

This "house of love" was built in 1858 by Hawaiians in "commemoration of God's causing Lahaina to escape the smallpox," while it decimated Oahu in 1853, carrying off 5,000 to 6,000 souls. The building served as a church and school until the turn of the 20th century, when it fell into disrepair.

Turn left onto Hale Street and then right onto Luakini Street to the:

㉔ Buddhist Church

This green wooden Shingon Buddhist temple is very typical of myriad Buddhist churches that sprang up all over the island when the Japanese laborers were brought to work in the sugar-cane fields. Some of the churches were little more than elaborate false "temple" fronts on existing buildings.

On the side of Village Galleries, on the corner of Luakini and Dickenson streets, is the historical marker for:

㉕ Luakini Street

"Luakini" translates as a *heiau* (temple) where the ruling chiefs prayed and where human sacrifices were made. This street received its unforgettable name after serving as the route for the funeral procession of Princess Harriet Nahienaena, sister of kings Kamehameha II and III. The princess was a victim of the rapid changes in Hawaiian culture. A convert to Protestantism, she had fallen in love with her brother at an early age. Just 20 years earlier, their relationship would have been nurtured in order to preserve the purity of the royal bloodlines. The missionaries, however, frowned on brother and sister marrying. In August 1836, the couple had a son, who lived only a few short hours. Nahienaena never recovered, and died in December of that same year (the king was said to mourn her death for years, frequently visiting her grave at the Waihee Cemetery; see no. 18 above). The route of her funeral procession through

the breadfruit and koa trees to the cemetery became known as "Luakini," in reference to the gods "sacrificing" the beloved princess.

Turn left on Dickenson and walk down to Front Street, where you'll be back at the starting point.

WINDING DOWN
Ready for some refreshment after your stroll? Head to **Maui Swiss Cafe**, 640 Front St. (✆ 808/661-6776), for tropical smoothies, great espresso, and affordable snacks. Sit in the funky garden area, or get your drink to go and wander over to the sea wall to watch the surfers.

A WHALE OF A PLACE IN KAANAPALI

Heading north from Lahaina, the next resort area you'll come to is Kaanapali, which boasts a gorgeous stretch of beach. If you haven't seen a real whale yet, go to **Whalers Village**, 2435 Kaanapali Pkwy., an oceanfront shopping center that has adopted the whale as its mascot. You can't miss it: A huge, almost life-size metal sculpture of a mother whale and two nursing calves greets you. A few more steps, and you're met by the looming, bleached-white skeleton of a 40-foot sperm whale; it's pretty impressive.

On the second floor of the mall is the **Whalers Village Museum** (✆ 808/661-5992), which celebrates the "Golden Era of Whaling" from 1825 to 1860. Harpoons and scrimshaw are on display; the museum has even re-created the cramped quarters of a whaler's seagoing vessel. It's open during mall hours, daily from 9:30am to 10pm; admission is free.

THE SCENIC ROUTE FROM WEST MAUI TO CENTRAL OR UPCOUNTRY MAUI: THE KAHEKILI HIGHWAY

The usual road from west Maui to Wailuku is the Honoapiilani Highway (Hwy. 30), which runs along the coast and then turns inland at Maalaea. But those in search of a back-to-nature driving experience should go the other way, along the **Kahekili Highway (Hwy. 340)** ✿. (*Highway* is a bit of a euphemism for this paved but somewhat precarious narrow road; check your rental-car agreement before you head out—some companies don't allow their cars on this road. If it is raining or has been raining, skip this road due to mud and rock slides.) The road was named after the great chief Kahekili, who built houses from the skulls of his enemies.

You'll start out on the Honoapiilani Highway (Hwy. 30), which becomes the Kahekili Highway (Hwy. 340) after Honokohau, at the northernmost tip of the island. Around this point are **Honolua Bay** ✿ and **Mokuleia Bay** ✿, which have been designated as Marine Life Conservation Areas (the taking of fish, shells, or anything else is prohibited).

From this point, the quality of the road deteriorates, and you may share the way with roosters, goats, cows, and dogs. The narrow road weaves along for the next 20 miles, following an ancient Hawaiian coastal footpath and showing you the true wild nature of Maui. These are photo opportunities from heaven: steep ravines, rolling pastoral hills, tumbling waterfalls, exploding blowholes, crashing surf, jagged lava coastlines, and a tiny Hawaiian village straight off a postcard.

Just before **mile marker 20,** look for a small turnoff on the mauka ("*mow*-kah," meaning toward the mountain) side of the road, just before the guardrail starts. Park here and walk across the road, and on your left you'll see a spouting **blowhole.** In winter, this is an excellent spot to look for whales.

About 3 miles farther along the road, you'll come to a wide turnoff providing a great photo op: a view of the jagged coastline down to the crashing surf.

Less than half a mile farther along, just before **mile marker 16,** look for the POHAKU KANI sign, marking the huge, 6×6-foot **bell-shaped stone.** To "ring" the bell, look on the side facing Kahakuloa for the deep indentations, and strike the stone with another rock.

Along the route, nestled in a crevice between two steep hills, is the picturesque village of **Kahakuloa** ("the tall hau tree"), with a dozen weather-worn houses, a church with a red-tile roof, and vivid green taro patches. From the northern side of the village, you can look back at the great view of Kahakuloa, the dark boulder beach, and the 636-foot Kahakuloa Head rising in the background.

At various points along the drive are artists' studios nestled into the cliffs and hills. One noteworthy stop is the **Kaukini Gallery,** which features work by more than two dozen local artists, with lots of gifts and crafts to buy in all price ranges. (You may also want to stop here to use one of the few restrooms along the drive.)

When you're approaching Wailuku, stop at the **Halekii and Pihanakalani Heiau,** which visitors rarely see. To get here from Wailuku, turn north from Main Street onto Market Street. Turn right onto Mill Street and follow it until it ends; then make a left on Lower Main Street. Follow Lower Main until it ends at Waiehu Beach Road (Hwy. 340) and turn left. Turn left on Kuhio Street and again at the first left onto Hea Place, and drive through the gates and look for the Hawaii Visitors Bureau marker.

These two *heiau,* built in 1240 from stones carried up from the Iao Stream below, sit on a hill with a commanding view of central Maui and Haleakala. Kahekili, the last chief of Maui, lived here. After the bloody battle at Iao Stream, Kamehameha I reportedly came to the temple here to pay homage to the war god, Ku, with a human sacrifice. Halekii ("house of images") is made of stone walls with a flat grassy top, whereas Pihanakalani ("gathering place of supernatural beings") is a pyramid-shaped mount of stones. If you sit quietly nearby (never walk on any *heiau*—it's considered disrespectful), you'll see that the view alone explains why this spot was chosen.

4 South Maui

MAALAEA

At the bend in the Honoapiilani Highway (Hwy. 30), Maalaea Bay runs along the south side of the isthmus between the West Maui Mountains and Haleakala. This is the windiest area on Maui: Trade winds blowing between the two mountains are funneled across the isthmus, and by the time they reach Maalaea, gusts of 25 to 30 mph are not uncommon.

This creates ideal conditions for **windsurfers** out in Maalaea Bay. Surfers are also seen just outside the small boat harbor in Maalaea, which has one of the fastest breaks in the state.

Maui Ocean Center ★★ *(Kids)*   This 5-acre facility houses the largest aquarium in the state and features one of Hawaii's largest predators: the tiger shark. Exhibits are geared toward the residents of Hawaii's ocean waters. As you walk past the three dozen or so tanks and numerous exhibits, you'll slowly descend from the "beach" to the deepest part of the ocean, without ever getting wet. Start at the surge pool, where you'll see shallow-water marine life like spiny urchins and cauliflower coral; then move on to the reef tanks, turtle pool, touch pool (with starfish and urchins), and eagle-ray pool before reaching the star of the show: the 100-foot-long, 600,000-gallon main tank featuring tiger, gray, and white-tip sharks, as well as tuna, surgeonfish, triggerfish, and numerous others. A walkway goes right through the tank, so you'll be surrounded on three sides by marine creatures. A very cool place, and well worth the time. Some new additions are a hammerhead exhibit and the Shark Dive Maui Program—if you're a certified scuba diver, you can plunge into the aquarium with sharks, stingrays, and tropical fish while friends and family watch safely from the other side of the glass. *Helpful hint:* Buy your tickets online to avoid the long admission lines.

At the Maalaea Harbor Village, 192 Maalaea Rd. (the triangle btw. Honoapiilani Hwy. and Maalaea Rd.). *(©* **808/ 270-7000.** www.mauioceancenter.com. Admission $24 adults, $21 seniors, $17 children 3–12. Daily 9am–5pm (until 6pm July–Aug).

KIHEI

Capt. George Vancouver "discovered" Kihei in 1778, when it was only a collection of fishermen's grass shacks on the hot, dry, dusty coast (hard to believe, eh?). A **totem pole** stands today where he's believed to have landed, across from the Aston Maui Lu Resort, 575 S. Kihei Rd. Vancouver sailed on to what later became British Columbia, where a great international city and harbor now bear his name.

West of the junction of Piilani Highway (Hwy. 31) and Mokulele Highway (Hwy. 350) is **Kealia Pond National Wildlife Preserve** (*©* **808/875-1582**), a 700-acre U.S. Fish and Wildlife wetland preserve where endangered Hawaiian stilts, coots, and ducks hang out and splash. These ponds work two ways: as bird preserves and as sedimentation basins that keep the coral reefs from silting from runoff. You can take a self-guided tour along a boardwalk dotted with interpretive signs and shade shelters, through sand dunes, and around ponds to Maalaea Harbor. The boardwalk starts at the outlet of Kealia Pond on the ocean side of North Kihei Road (near mile marker 2 on Piilani Hwy.). Among the Hawaiian water birds seen here are the black-crowned high heron, Hawaiian coot, Hawaiian duck, and Hawaiian stilt. There are also shorebirds like sanderling, Pacific golden plover, ruddy turnstone, and wandering tattler. From July to December, the hawksbill turtle comes ashore here to lay her eggs. *Tip:* If you're bypassing Kihei, take the Piilani Highway (Hwy. 31), which parallels strip-mall-laden South Kihei Road, and avoid the hassle of stoplights and traffic.

WAILEA

The dividing line between arid Kihei and artificially green Wailea is distinct. Wailea once had the same kiawe-strewn, dusty landscape as Kihei until Alexander & Baldwin Inc. (of sugar-cane fame) began developing a resort here in the 1970s (after piping water from the other side of the island to the desert terrain of Wailea). Today, the manicured 1,450 acres of this affluent resort stand out like an oasis along the normally dry leeward coast.

The best way to explore this golden resort coast is to rise with the sun and head for Wailea's 1.5-mile **coastal nature trail** ★, stretching between the Fairmont Kea Lani and the green grass of the Wailea Beach Marriott. It's a great morning walk on a serpentine path that meanders uphill and down past native plants, old Hawaiian habitats, and a billion dollars' worth of luxury hotels. You can pick up the trail at any of the resorts or from clearly marked SHORELINE ACCESS points along the coast. The best time to go is when you first wake up; by midmorning, the coastal trail is often clogged with joggers and later with beachgoers. As the path crosses several bold black-lava points, it affords vistas of islands and ocean. Benches allow you to pause and contemplate the view across Alalakeiki Channel, where you may see whales in season. Sunset is another good time to hit the trail.

MAKENA

A few miles south of Wailea, the manicured coast changes over to the wilderness of *Makena* (abundance). In the 1800s, cattle were driven down the slope from upland ranches and loaded onto boats that waited to take them to market. Now **Makena Landing** is a beach park with boat-launching facilities, showers, toilets, and picnic tables. It's great for snorkeling and for launching kayaks bound for La Pérouse Bay and Ahihi-Kinau Natural Preserve.

From the landing, go south on Makena Road; on the right is **Keawalai Congregational Church** (© **808/879-5557**), built in 1855 with walls 3 feet thick. Surrounded by ti leaves, which by Hawaiian custom provide protection, and built of lava rock with coral used as mortar, this Protestant church sits on its own cove with a gold-sand beach. It always attracts a Sunday crowd for its 9:30am Hawaiian-language service. Take time to wander through the cemetery; you'll see some tombstones with a ceramic picture of the deceased on them, which is an old custom.

A little farther south on the coast is **La Pérouse Monument**, a pyramid of lava rocks that marks the spot where French explorer Adm. Comte de la Pérouse set foot on Maui in 1786. The first Westerner to "discover" the island, he described the "burning climate" of the leeward coast, observed several fishing villages near Kihei, and sailed on into oblivion, never to be seen again; some believe he may have been eaten by cannibals in what is now Vanuatu. To get here, drive south past Puu Olai to Ahihi Bay, where the road turns to gravel. Go another 2 miles along the coast to La Pérouse Bay; the monument sits amid a clearing in black lava at the end of the dirt road.

The rocky coastline and sometimes rough seas contribute to the lack of appeal for water activities here; **hiking** opportunities, however, are excellent. Bring plenty of water and sun protection, and wear hiking boots that can withstand walking on lava. From La Pérouse Bay, you can pick up the old King's Highway trail, which at one time circled the island. Walk along the sandy beach at La Pérouse and look for the trail indentation in the lava, which leads down to the lighthouse at the tip of Cape Hanamanioa, about a .75-mile round-trip. Or you can continue on the trail as it climbs up the hill for 2 miles, then ventures back toward the ocean, where there are quite a few old Hawaiian home foundations and rocky coral beaches.

5 House of the Sun: Haleakala National Park

At once forbidding and compelling, Haleakala ("House of the Sun") National Park is Maui's main natural attraction. More than 1.3 million people a year ascend the 10,023-foot-high mountain to peer down into the crater of the world's largest dormant volcano. (Haleakala is officially considered active, even though it has not

Impressions

There are few enough places in the world that belong entirely to themselves. The human passion to carry all things everywhere, so that every place is home, seems well on its way to homogenizing our planet, save for the odd unreachable corner. Haleakala crater is one of those corners.
—Barbara Kingsolver, the New York Times

rumbled since 1790.) That hole would hold Manhattan: 3,000 feet deep, 7½ miles long by 2½ miles wide, and encompassing 19 square miles.

The Hawaiians recognized the mountain as a sacred site. Ancient chants tell of Pele, the volcano goddess, and one of her siblings doing battle on the crater floor where *Kawilinau* (Bottomless Pit) now stands. Commoners in ancient Hawaii didn't spend much time here, though. The only people allowed into this sacred area were the *kahuna*, who took their apprentices to live for periods of time in this intensely spiritual place. Today, New Agers also revere Haleakala as one of the earth's powerful energy points, and even the U.S. Air Force has a not-very-well-explained presence here.

But there's more to do here than simply stare into a big black hole: Just going up the mountain is an experience in itself. Where else on the planet can you climb from sea level to 10,000 feet in just 37 miles, or a 2-hour drive? The snaky road passes through big, puffy cumulus clouds to offer magnificent views of the isthmus of Maui, the West Maui Mountains, and the Pacific Ocean.

Many drive up to the summit in predawn darkness to watch the **sunrise over Haleakala;** writer Mark Twain called it "the sublimest spectacle" of his life. Others take a trail ride inside the bleak lunar landscape of the wilderness inside the crater or coast down the 37-mile road from the summit on a bicycle with special brakes (see "Biking," p. 200, and "Horseback Riding," p. 201). Hardy adventurers hike and camp inside the crater's wilderness (see "Hiking & Camping," p. 189). Those bound for the interior should bring their survival gear, for the terrain is raw, rugged, and punishing—not unlike the moon. However, if you choose to experience Haleakala National Park, it will prove memorable—guaranteed.

JUST THE FACTS

Haleakala National Park extends from the summit of Mount Haleakala into the crater, down the volcano's southeast flank to Maui's eastern coast, beyond Hana. There are actually two separate and distinct destinations within the park: **Haleakala Summit** and the **Kipahulu** coast (see "Tropical Haleakala: Oheo Gulch at Kipahulu," p. 240). The summit gets all the publicity, but Kipahulu draws crowds, too—it's lush, green, and tropical, and home to Oheo Gulch (also known as Seven Sacred Pools). No road links the summit and the coast; you have to approach them separately, and you need at least a day to see each place.

WHEN TO GO   At the 10,023-foot summit, weather changes fast. With wind chill, temperatures can be freezing any time of year. Summer can be dry and warm; winter can be wet, windy, and cold. Before you go, get current weather conditions from the park (© **808/572-4400**) or the **National Weather Service** (© **808/871-5054**).

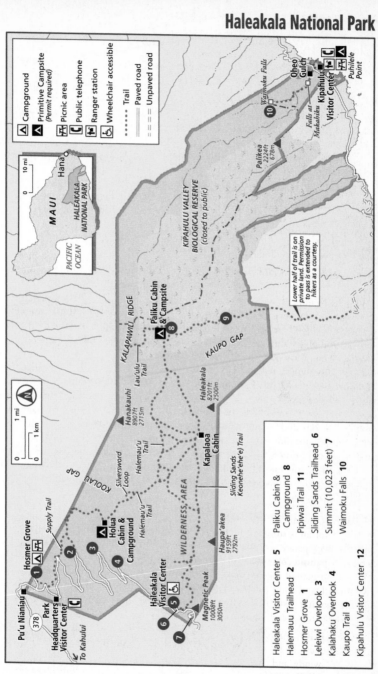

Haleakala National Park

Campground
Primitive Campsite (Permit required)
Picnic area
Public telephone
Ranger station
Wheelchair accessible

• • • • • Trail
━━━━━ Paved road
━ ━ ━ Unpaved road

MAUI

PACIFIC OCEAN

HALEAKALA NATIONAL PARK

Hana

0   10 mi

0   1 mi
0   1 km

N

Waimoku Falls
Oheo Gulch
Kipahulu Visitor Center
Puhilele Point

10

Falls at Makahiku

Palikea
2224ft
678m

KIPAHULU VALLEY BIOLOGICAL RESERVE
(closed to public)

Lower half of trail is on private land. Permission to pass is extended to hikers as a courtesy.

KALAPAWILI RIDGE

Paliku Cabin & Campsite

8

9

KAUPO GAP

Lau'ulu Trail

Hanakauhi
8907ft
2715m

Haleakala
8201ft
2500m

Halemau'u Trail

Silversword Loop

Halemau'u Trail

Kapalaoa Cabin

Sliding Sands
Keoneke'ehe'e) Trail

Hosmer Grove

Supply Trail

2

3

Holua Cabin & Campground

4

KOOLAU GAP

WILDERNESS AREA

Haupa'akea
9159ft
2792m

Pu'u Nianiau

Park Headquarters Visitor Center

378

To Kahului

Haleakala Visitor Center

5

6

7

Magnetic Peak
10008ft
3050m

Haleakala Visitor Center **5**
Halemauu Trailhead **2**
Hosmer Grove **1**
Leleiwi Overlook **3**
Kalahaku Overlook **4**
Kaupo Trail **9**

Paliku Cabin & Campground **8**
Pipiwai Trail **11**
Sliding Sands Trailhead **6**
Summit (10,023 feet) **7**
Waimoku Falls **10**
Kipahulu Visitor Center **12**

223

From sunrise to noon, the light is weak, but the view is usually free of clouds. The best time for photos is in the afternoon, when the sun lights the crater and clouds are few. Go on full-moon nights for spectacular viewing. However, even when the forecast is promising, the weather at Haleakala can change in an instant—be prepared.

ACCESS POINTS **Haleakala Summit** is 37 miles, or a 1½- to 2-hour drive, from Kahului. To get here, take Hwy. 37 to Hwy. 377 to Hwy. 378. For details on the drive, see "The Drive to the Summit," below. Pukalani is the last town for water, food, and gas.

The **Kipahulu** section of Haleakala National Park is on Maui's east end near Hana, 60 miles from Kahului on Hwy. 36 (Hana Hwy.). Due to traffic and rough road conditions, plan on 4 hours for the one-way drive from Kahului. For complete information, see "Driving the Road to Hana," below. Hana is the only nearby town for services, water, gas, food, and overnight lodging; some facilities may not be open after dark.

At both entrances to the park, the admission fee is $5 per person or $10 per car, good for a week of unlimited entry.

INFORMATION, VISITOR CENTERS & RANGER PROGRAMS For information before you go, contact **Haleakala National Park,** P.O. Box 369, Makawao, HI 96768 (*C* **808/572-4400;** www.nps.gov/hale).

One mile from the park entrance, at 7,000 feet, is **Haleakala National Park Headquarters** (*C* **808/572-4400**), open daily from 7:30am to 4pm. Stop here to pick up information on park programs and activities, get camping permits, and, occasionally, see a nene (Hawaiian goose)—one or more are often here to greet visitors. Restrooms, a pay phone, and drinking water are available.

The **Haleakala Visitor Center,** open daily from sunrise to 3pm, is near the summit, 11 miles past the park entrance. It offers a panoramic view of the volcanic landscape, with photos identifying the various features, and exhibits that explain the area's history, ecology, geology, and volcanology. Park staff members are often on hand to answer questions. Restrooms and water are available.

Rangers offer excellent, informative, and free naturalist talks at 9:30, 10:30, and 11:30am daily in the summit building. For information on hiking (including guided hikes) and camping, including cabins and campgrounds in the wilderness itself, see "Hiking & Camping" (p. 189).

THE DRIVE TO THE SUMMIT

If you look on a Maui map, almost in the middle of the part that resembles a torso, there's a black wiggly line that looks like this: WWWWW. That's **Hwy. 378,** also known as **Haleakala Crater Road**—one of the fastest-ascending roads in the world. This grand corniche has at least 33 switchbacks; passes through numerous climate zones; goes under, in, and out of clouds; takes you past rare silversword plants and endangered Hawaiian geese sailing through the clear, thin air; and offers a view that extends for more than 100 miles.

Going to the summit takes 1½ to 2 hours from Kahului. No matter where you start out, you'll follow Hwy. 37 (Haleakala Hwy.) to Pukalani, where you'll pick up Hwy. 377 (which is also Haleakala Hwy.), which you'll take to Hwy. 378. Along the way, expect fog, rain, and wind. You may encounter stray cattle and downhill bicyclists. Fill up your gas tank before you go—the only gas available is 27 miles below the summit

---

(*Fun Fact* **The Legend of the House of the Sun**

According to ancient legend, Haleakala got its name from a very clever trick that the demigod Maui pulled on the sun. Maui's mother, the goddess Hina, complained one day that the sun sped across the sky so quickly that her tapa cloth couldn't dry.

Maui, known as a trickster, devised a plan. The next morning he went to the top of the great mountain and waited for the sun to poke its head above the horizon. Quickly, Maui lassoed the sun, bringing its path across the sky to an abrupt halt.

The sun begged Maui to let go, and Maui said he would on one condition: that the sun slow its trip across the sky to give the island more sunlight. The sun assented. In honor of this agreement, the Hawaiians call the mountain Haleakala, or "House of the Sun."

To this day, the top of Haleakala has about 15 minutes more sunlight than the communities on the coastline below.

---

at Pukalani. There are no facilities beyond the ranger stations, so bring your own food and water.

Remember, you're entering a high-altitude wilderness area. Some people get dizzy due to the lack of oxygen; you might also suffer lightheadedness, shortness of breath, nausea, severe headaches, flatulence, or dehydration. People with asthma, pregnant women, heavy smokers, and those with heart conditions should be especially careful in the rarefied air. Bring water and a jacket or a blanket, especially if you go up for sunrise. Or you might want to go up to the summit for sunset, which is also spectacular.

As you go up the slopes, the temperature drops about 3° every 1,000 feet, so the temperature at the top can be 30° cooler than it was at sea level. Come prepared with sweaters, jackets, and rain gear.

At the **park entrance,** you'll pay an entrance fee of $10 per car (or $5 per person without a vehicle). About a mile from the entrance is **park headquarters,** where an endangered **nene,** or Hawaiian goose, may greet you with its unique call. With its black face, buff cheeks, and partially webbed feet, the gray-brown bird looks like a small Canada goose with zebra stripes; it brays out "nay-nay" (thus its name), doesn't migrate, and prefers lava beds to lakes. The unusual goose clings to a precarious existence on these alpine slopes. Vast populations of more than 25,000 once inhabited Hawaii, but hunters, pigs, feral cats and dogs, and mongooses preyed on the nene; coupled with habitat destruction, these predators nearly caused its extinction. By 1951, there were only 30 left. Now protected as Hawaii's state bird, the wild nene on Haleakala number fewer than 250—and the species remains endangered.

Beyond headquarters are **two scenic overlooks** on the way to the summit; stop at Leleiwi on the way up and Kalahaku on the way back down, if only to get out, stretch, and get accustomed to the heights. Take a deep breath, look around, and pop your ears. If you feel dizzy or drowsy, or get a sudden headache, consider turning around and going back down.

Leleiwi Overlook ⓖ is just beyond mile marker 17. From the parking area, a short trail leads you to a panoramic view of the lunarlike crater. When the clouds are low and the sun is in the right place, usually around sunset, you may experience a phenomenon known as the "Specter of the Brocken"—you can see a reflection of your shadow, ringed by a rainbow, in the clouds below. It's an optical illusion caused by a rare combination of sun, shadow, and fog that occurs in only three places on the planet: Haleakala, Scotland, and Germany.

Two miles farther along is **Kalahaku Overlook** ⓖ, the best place to see a rare **silversword.** You can turn into this overlook only when you are descending from the top. The silversword is the punk of the plant world, its silvery bayonets displaying tiny purple bouquets—like a spacey artichoke with attitude. This botanical wonder proved irresistible to humans, who gathered them in gunnysacks for Chinese potions and British specimen collections, and just for the sheer thrill of having something so rare. Silverswords grow only in Hawaii, take from 4 to 50 years to bloom, and then, usually between May and October, send up a 1- to 6-foot stalk with a purple bouquet of sunflower-like blooms. They're very rare, so don't even think about taking one home.

Continue on, and you'll quickly reach the **Haleakala Visitor Center** ⓖ, which offers spectacular views. You'll feel as if you're at the edge of the earth. But don't turn around here: The actual summit's a little farther on, at **Puu Ulaula Overlook** ⓖ (also known as Red Hill), the volcano's highest point, where you'll find a mysterious cluster of buildings officially known as Haleakala Observatories, but unofficially called **Science City.** If you go up for sunrise, the building at Puu Ulaula Overlook, a triangle of glass that serves as a windbreak, is the best viewing spot. After the daily miracle of sunrise—the sun seems to rise out of the vast crater (hence the name "House of the Sun")—you can see all the way across Alenuihaha Channel to the often-snowcapped summit of Mauna Kea on the Big Island.

MAKING YOUR DESCENT   When driving down the Haleakala Crater Road, be sure to put your car in low gear. That way, you won't destroy your brakes by riding them the whole way down.

6 More in Upcountry Maui

Come upcountry and discover a different side of Maui: On the slopes of Haleakala, cowboys, planters, and other country people make their homes in serene, neighborly communities like **Makawao** and **Kula,** a world away from the bustling beach resorts. Even if you can't spare a day or two in the cool upcountry air, there are some sights that are worth a look on your way to or from the crater. Shoppers and gallery hoppers might want to spend more time here; see chapter 9 for details. For a map of this area, turn to the "Upcountry & East Maui Dining & Attractions" map on p. 167.

On the slopes of Haleakala, Maui's farmers have been producing vegetables since the 1800s. In fact, during the gold rush in California, the Hawaiian farmers in Kula shipped so many potatoes that it was nicknamed Nu Kaleponi, a sort of pidgin Hawaiian pronunciation of "New California." In the late 1800s, Portuguese and Chinese immigrants, who had fulfilled their labor contracts with the sugar-cane companies, moved to this area, drawn by the rural agricultural lifestyle. That lifestyle continues today, among the fancy gentlemen's farms that have sprung up in the past 2 decades. Kula continues to grow its well-known onions, lettuce, tomatoes, carrots, cauliflower, and cabbage. It is also a major source of cut flowers for the state: Most of Hawaii's proteas, as well as nearly all the carnations used in leis, come from Kula.

Moments Stop & Smell the Lavender

While in the upcountry Kula region, stop by **Alii Kula Lavender**, 1100 Waipoli Rd., Kula (© 808/878-3004; www.aliikulalavender.com), which grows several different varieties of lavender, so one species of lavender is always in bloom. There are great tours to take while you're here. On the 30-minute **Lavender Garden Walking Tour** (daily at 9:30, 10:30, 11:30am, 1, and 2:30pm for $12 per person), you're served lavender herb tea with a lavender scone and given a garden and studio tour. My favorite, the **Combo Tour** ($37 per person) combines the walking tour with a lunch basket, which includes a choice of lavender beverage, a delicious lavender-seasoned chicken wrap, lavender gourmet chips, fresh fruit, and a decadent lavender brownie. If you book in advance, try for the **Exclusive Cart Tour with Alii Chang,** offered at 10am and 2pm daily ($25 per person). Five lucky people get to tour the farm through his eyes and hear the stories and history of this legendary farmer who has taken farming to an art form. Seasonal events offered range from a fabulous Valentine's Day Luncheon to a woven-lavender-wand-making workshop in the summer. Be sure to stop by the store and look over the culinary products (lavender seasonings, dressings, scones, honey, jelly, and teas), bath and body goodies (lotions, soaps, bubble baths, bath gels), aromatherapy (oil, candles, eye pillows), and other items (T-shirts, gift baskets, and dried lavender).

To experience a bit of the history of Kula, turn off the Kula Highway (Hwy. 37) onto Lower Kula Road. Well before the turnoff, you'll see a white octagonal building with a silver roof, the **Holy Ghost Catholic Church** (© **808/878-1091**). Hawaii's only eight-sided church, it was built between 1884 and 1897 by Portuguese immigrants. It's worth a stop to see the hand-carved altar and works of art for the Stations of the Cross, with inscriptions in Portuguese.

Kula Botanical Garden ℛ   You can take a self-guided, informative, leisurely stroll through more than 700 native and exotic plants—including three unique collections of orchids, proteas, and bromeliads—at this 5-acre garden. It offers a good overview of Hawaii's exotic flora in one small, cool place.

Hwy. 377, south of Haleakala Crater Rd. (Hwy. 378), ½ mile from Hwy. 37. © 808/878-1715. www.kulabotanical garden.com. Admission $7.50 adults, $2 children 6–12. Daily 9am–4pm.

Tedeschi Vineyards and Winery ℛ   On the southern shoulder of Haleakala is **Ulupalakua Ranch,** a 20,000-acre spread once owned by legendary sea captain James Makee, celebrated in the Hawaiian song and dance "Hula O Makee." Wounded in a Honolulu waterfront brawl in 1843, Makee moved to Maui and bought Ulupalakua. He renamed it Rose Ranch, planted sugar as a cash crop, and grew rich. Still in operation, the ranch is now home to Maui's only winery, established in 1974 by Napa vintner Emil Tedeschi, who began growing California and European grapes here and producing serious still and sparkling wines, plus a silly wine made of pineapple juice. The rustic grounds are the perfect place for a picnic. Pack a basket before you go, and enjoy it with a bottle of Tedeschi wine.

Kids Touring the Surfing Goat Dairy Farm

Just beyond the sugar-cane fields, on the slopes of Haleakala, lies the **Surfing Goat Dairy,** 3661 Omaopio Rd., Kula (© **808/878-2870;** www.surfinggoatdairy. com). Some 140 dairy goats blissfully graze the 42 acres and contribute the milk for 24 different cheeses, which are made every day. If you have kids in tow, they will love the 2-hour **Grand Dairy Tour** ($25)—they get to be a goat herder for a day and even try to milk a goat. They can also play with the kids—goat kids, that is. Meanwhile, mom and dad can learn how to make cheese and sample the different varieties made on the premises. Grand Dairy Tours are scheduled several times each month; call for information. If you don't have a lot of time, drop by for the 20-minute casual dairy tour (Mon–Sat 10am–5pm, Sun 10am–2pm) for just $7 a person. Be sure to sample the goat cheeses (off-the-charts terrific) and buy a bar or two of goat-milk soap.

Across from the winery are the remains of the three smokestacks of the **Makee Sugar Mill,** built in 1878. This is home to Maui artist Reems Mitchell, who carved the mannequins on the front porch of the Ulupalakua Ranch Store: a Filipino with his fighting cock, a cowboy, a farmhand, and a sea captain, all representing the people of Maui's history.

Off Hwy. 37 (Kula Hwy.). © 808/878-6058. www.mauiwine.com. Free tastings daily 9am–5pm. Free tours at 10:30am, 1:30pm, and 3pm.

7 Driving the Road to Hana ★★★

Top down, sunscreen on, radio tuned to a little Hawaiian music on a Maui morning: It's time to head out to Hana along the Hana Highway (Hwy. 36), a wiggle of a road that runs along Maui's northeastern shore. The drive takes at least 3 hours from Lahaina or Kihei—but plan to take all day. Going to Hana is about the journey, not the destination.

There are wilder roads, steeper roads, and more dangerous roads, but in all of Hawaii, no road is more celebrated than this one. It winds 50 miles past taro patches, magnificent seascapes, waterfall pools, botanical gardens, and verdant rainforests, and ends at one of Hawaii's most beautiful tropical places.

The outside world discovered the little village of Hana in 1926, when the narrow coastal road, carved by pickax-wielding convicts, opened. The mud-and-gravel road, often subject to landslides and washouts, was paved in 1962, when tourist traffic began to increase; now more than 1,000 cars traverse the road each day, according to storekeeper Harry Hasegawa. That equals about 500,000 people a year, which is way too many. Go at the wrong time, and you'll be stuck in a bumper-to-bumper rental-car parade—peak traffic hours are midmorning and midafternoon year-round, especially on weekends.

In the rush to "do" Hana in a day, most visitors spin around town in 10 minutes flat and wonder what all the fuss is about. It takes time to take in Hana, play in the waterfalls, sniff the tropical flowers, hike to bamboo forests, and marvel at the spectacular scenery; stay overnight if you can.

However, if you really must do the Hana Highway in a day, go just before sunrise and return after sunset: On a full-moon night, the sea and the waterfalls glow in soft white light, with mysterious shadows appearing in the jungle. And you'll have the road almost to yourself on the way back.

Tips: Forget your mainland road manners. Practice aloha. Give way at one-lane bridges, wave at oncoming motorists, and let the big guys in 4×4s have the right of way—it's just common sense, brah. If the guy behind you blinks his lights, let him pass. And don't honk your horn—in Hawaii, it's considered rude.

THE JOURNEY BEGINS IN PAIA   Before you even start out, fill up your gas tank. Gas in Paia is expensive (even by Maui standards), and it's the last place for gas until you get to Hana, some 42 miles, 54 bridges, and 600 hairpin turns down the road.

The former plantation village of Paia was once a thriving sugar-mill town. The mill is still here, but the population shifted to Kahului in the 1950s when subdivisions opened there, leaving Paia to shrivel up and die. But the town refused to give up and has proven its ability to adapt to the times. Now chic eateries and trendy shops stand next door to the mom-and-pop establishments that have been serving generations of Paia customers.

Plan to be here early, around 7am, when **Charley's** *⁂*, 142 Hana Hwy. (© **808/ 579-9453**), opens. Enjoy a big, hearty breakfast for a reasonable price.

After you leave Paia, just before the bend in the road, you'll pass the Kuau Mart on your left; a small general store, it's the only reminder of the sugar-plantation community of **Kuau.** The road then bends into an S-turn; in the middle of the S is the entrance to **Mama's Fish House,** marked by a restored boat with Mama's logo on the side. Just past the truck on the ocean side is the entrance to Mama's parking lot and adjacent small sandy cove in front of the restaurant. It's not good for swimming— ocean access is over very slippery rocks into strong surf—but the beach is a great place to sit and soak up some sun.

WINDSURFING MECCA   A mile from Mama's, just before mile marker 9, is a place known around the world as one of the greatest windsurfing spots on the planet, **Hookipa Beach Park** *⁂*. *Hookipa* ("hospitality") is where the top-ranked windsurfers come to test themselves against the forces of nature: thunderous surf and forceful wind. World-championship contests are held here (see "Maui, Molokai & Lanai Calendar of Events," p. 52), but on nearly every windy afternoon (the board surfers have the waves in the morning), you can watch dozens of windsurfers twirling and dancing in the wind like colorful butterflies. To watch the windsurfers, do not stop on the highway, but go past the park and turn left at the entrance on the far side of the beach. You can either park on the high grassy bluff or drive down to the sandy beach and park alongside the pavilion. Facilities include restrooms, a shower, picnic tables, and a barbecue area.

INTO THE COUNTRY   Past Hookipa Beach, the road winds down into **Maliko (Budding) Gulch** at mile marker 10. At the bottom of the gulch, look for the road on your right, which will take you out to **Maliko Bay.** Take the first right, which goes under the bridge and past a rodeo arena (scene of competitions by the Maliko Roping Club in summer) and on to the rocky beach. There are no facilities here except a boat-launch ramp. In the 1940s, Maliko had a thriving community at the mouth of the bay, but its residents rebuilt farther inland after a strong tidal wave wiped it out. The bay may not look that special, but if the surf is up, it's a great place to watch the waves.

The Road to Hana

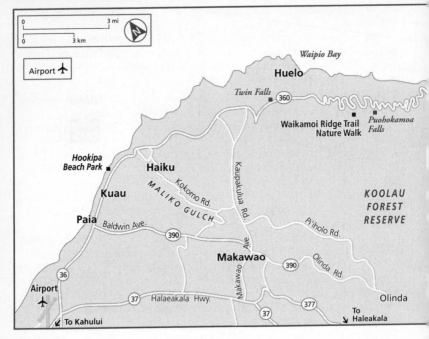

Back on the Hana Highway, as you leave Maliko Gulch, around mile marker 11, you'll pass through the rural area of **Haiku,** where you'll see banana patches, cane grass blowing in the wind, and forests of guava trees, avocados, *kukui* trees, palms, and Christmas berry. Just before mile marker 15 is the **Maui-Grown Market and Deli** (© 808/572-1693), a good stop for drinks or snacks for the ride.

JAWS If it's winter and the waves are up (like 60 ft. or so), here's your chance to watch tow-in surfing off Pauwela Point at an area known as Jaws (because the waves will chew you up), where expert tow-in surfers (who use a personal watercraft to pull a surfer into waves that are bigger than what could be caught by traditional paddling) battle the mammoth waves. To get here, make a small detour off the Hana Highway by turning left at Hahana Road, between mile markers 13 and 14. After the paved road ends, the dirt road is private property (Maui Land & Pine), so you may have to hike in about a mile and a half to get close to the ocean. Practice aloha, do not park in the pineapple fields, and do not pick or even touch the pineapples. Be very careful along the oceanside cliffs.

At mile marker 16, the curves begin, one right after another. Slow down and enjoy the view of bucolic rolling hills, mango trees, and vibrant ferns. After mile marker 16, the road is still called the Hana Highway, but the number changes from Hwy. 36 to Hwy. 360, and the mile markers go back to 0.

A GREAT PLUNGE ALONG THE WAY A dip in a waterfall pool is everybody's tropical-island fantasy. A great place to stop is **Twin Falls** ✦, at mile marker 2. Just before the wide, concrete bridge, pull over on the mountain side and park. There is a NO TRESPASSING sign on the gate. Although you will see several cars parked in the area

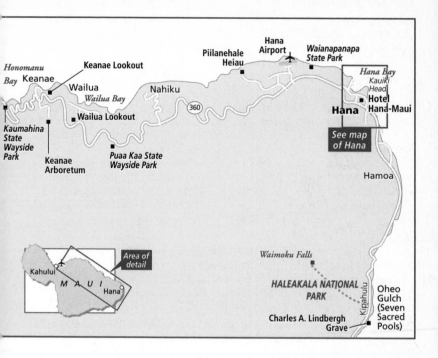

and a steady line of people going up to the falls, be aware that this is private property and trespassing is illegal in Hawaii. If you decide that you want to "risk it," you will walk about 3 to 5 minutes to the waterfall and pool, or continue on another 10 to 15 minutes to the second, larger waterfall and pool (don't go in if it has been raining).

HIDDEN HUELO   Just before mile marker 4 on a blind curve, look for a double row of mailboxes on the left side by the pay phone. Down the road lies a hidden Hawaii of an earlier time, where an indescribable sense of serenity prevails. Hemmed in by Waipo and Hoalua bays is the remote community of **Huelo** 🕊, which means "tail end, last." This fertile area once supported a population of 75,000; today only a few hundred live among the scattered homes here, where a handful of B&Bs and exquisite vacation rentals cater to a trickle of travelers (see p. 137 for my recommendations).

The only reason Huelo is even marked is the historic 1853 **Kaulanapueo Church.** Reminiscent of New England architecture, this coral-and-cement church, topped with a plantation-green steeple and a gray tin roof, is still in use, although services are held just once or twice a month. It still has the same austere interior of 1853: straight-backed benches, a no-nonsense platform for the minister, and no distractions on the walls to tempt you from paying attention to the sermon. Next to the church is a small graveyard, a personal history of this village in concrete and stone.

KOOLAU FOREST RESERVE   After Huelo, the vegetation seems more lush, as though Mother Nature had poured Miracle-Gro on everything. This is the edge of the **Koolau Forest Reserve.** *Koolau* means "windward," and this certainly is one of the greatest examples of a lush windward area: The coastline here gets about 60 to 80 inches of rain a year, as well as runoff from the 200 to 300 inches that falls from farther up the mountain. You'll see trees laden with guavas, as well as mangoes, java plums, and avocados the size of softballs. The spiny, long-leafed plants are *hala* trees, which the Hawaiians used for weaving baskets, mats, and even canoe sails.

From here on out, there's a waterfall (and one-lane bridge) around nearly every turn in the road, so drive slowly and be prepared to stop and yield to oncoming cars.

DANGEROUS CURVES   About ½ mile after mile marker 6, there's a sharp U-curve in the road, going uphill. The road is practically one-lane here, with a brick wall on one side and virtually no maneuvering room. Sound your horn at the start of the U-curve to let approaching cars know you're coming. Take this curve, as well as the few more coming up in the next several miles, very slowly.

Just before mile marker 7 is a forest of waving **bamboo.** The sight is so spectacular that drivers are often tempted to take their eyes off the road. Be very cautious. Wait until just after mile marker 7, at the **Kaaiea Bridge** (literally "breathtaking view") and stream below, to pull over and take a closer look at the hand-hewn stone walls. Then turn around to see the vista of bamboo.

A GREAT FAMILY HIKE   At mile marker 9, there's a small state wayside area with restrooms, picnic tables, and a barbecue area. The sign says KOOLAU FOREST RESERVE, but the real attraction here is the **Waikamoi Ridge Trail** ⋆, an easy .75-mile loop (*Waikamoi* means "waters of the king"). The start of the trail is just behind the QUIET TREES AT WORK sign. The well-marked trail meanders through eucalyptus, ferns, and *hala* trees.

SAFETY WARNING   I used to recommend another waterfall, **Puohokamoa Falls,** at mile marker 11, but not anymore. Unfortunately, what was once a great thing has been overrun by hordes of not-so-polite tourists. You will see cars parking on the already dangerous, barely two-lane Hana Highway ½ mile before the waterfall. Slow down after mile marker 10. As you get close to mile marker 11, the highway becomes a congested one-lane road due to visitors parking on this narrow stretch. Don't add to the congestion by trying to park: There are plenty of other great waterfalls; just drive slowly and safely through this area.

CAN'T-MISS PHOTO OPS   Just past mile marker 12 is the **Kaumahina State Wayside Park** ⋆ (*kaumahina* means "moon rise"). This is not only a good pit stop (restrooms are available) and a wonderful place for a picnic (with tables and a barbecue area), but also a great vista point. The view of the rugged coastline makes an excellent shot—you can see all the way down to the jutting Keanae Peninsula.

Another mile and a couple of bends in the road, and you'll enter the Honomanu Valley, with its beautiful bay. To get to the **Honomanu Bay County Beach Park** ⋆, look for the turnoff on your left, just after mile marker 14, located at a point in the road where you begin your ascent up the other side of the valley. The rutted dirt-and-cinder road takes you down to the rocky black-sand beach. There are no facilities here. Because of the strong rip currents offshore, swimming is best in the stream inland from the ocean. You'll consider the drive down worthwhile as you stand on the beach, well away from the ocean, and turn to look back on the steep cliffs covered with vegetation.

MAUI'S BOTANICAL WORLD   Farther along the winding road, between mile markers 16 and 17, is a cluster of bunkhouses composing the YMCA Camp Keanae. A ¼-mile down is the **Keanae Arboretum** ⋆⋆, where the region's botany is divided into three parts: native forest, introduced forest, and traditional Hawaiian plants, food, and medicine. You can swim in the pools of Piinaau Stream, or press on along a mile-long trail into Keanae Valley, where a lovely tropical rainforest waits at the end (see "Hiking & Camping," in chapter 7).

KEANAE PENINSULA   The old Hawaiian village of **Keanae** *✸✸* ("the mullet") stands out against the Pacific like a place time forgot. Here, on an old lava flow graced by an 1860 stone church and swaying palms, is one of the last coastal enclaves of native Hawaiians. They still grow taro in patches and pound it into poi, the staple of the old Hawaiian diet. And they still pluck opihi (limpet) from tide pools along the jagged coast and cast throw-nets at schools of fish.

The turnoff to the Keanae Peninsula is on the left, just after the arboretum. The road passes by farms as it hugs the peninsula. Where the road bends, there's a small beach where fishermen gather to catch dinner. A ¼ mile farther is the **Keanae Congregational Church** (© **808/248-8040**), built in 1860 of lava rocks and coral mortar, standing in stark contrast to the green fields surrounding it. Beside the church is a small beachfront park, with false *kamani* trees against a backdrop of black lava and a roiling turquoise sea.

For an experience in an untouched Hawaii, follow the road until it ends. Park by the white fence and take the short 5-minute walk along the shoreline over the black lava. Continue along the footpath through the tall California grass to the black rocky beach, separating the freshwater stream, **Pinaau,** which winds back into the Keanae Peninsula, nearly cutting it off from the rest of Maui. This is an excellent place for a picnic and a swim in the cool waters of the stream. There are no facilities here, so be sure you carry everything out with you and use restrooms before you arrive. As you make your way back, notice the white PVC pipes sticking out of the rocks—they're fishing-pole holders for fishermen, usually hoping to catch ulua.

ANOTHER PHOTO OP: KEANAE LOOKOUT   Just past mile marker 17 is a wide spot on the ocean side of the road, where you can see the entire Keanae Peninsula's checkerboard pattern of green taro fields and its ocean boundary etched in black lava. Keanae was the result of a postscript eruption of Haleakala, which flowed through the Koolau Gap and down Keanae Valley and added this geological punctuation to the rugged coastline.

FRUIT & FLOWER STANDS   Around mile marker 18, the road widens; you'll start to see numerous small stands selling fruit or flowers. Many of these stands work on the honor system: You leave your money in the basket and select your purchase. I recommend stopping at **Uncle Harry's,** which you'll find just after the Keanae School around mile marker 18. His family sells a variety of fruits and juices here Monday through Saturday from 9am to 4pm.

WAILUA   Just after Uncle Harry's, look for the Wailua Road off on the left. This will take you through the hamlet of homes and churches of Wailua, which also contains a shrine depicting what the community calls a "miracle." Behind the pink **St. Gabriel's Church** is the smaller, blue-and-white **Coral Miracle Church,** home of the **Our Lady of Fatima Shrine.** According to legend, in 1860 the men of this village were building a church by diving for coral to make the stone. But the coral offshore was in deep water and the men could only come up with a few pieces at a time, making the construction of the church an arduous project. A freak storm hit the area and deposited the coral from the deep on a nearby beach. The Hawaiians gathered what they needed and completed the church. After the church was completed, another freak storm hit the area and swept all the remaining coral on the beach back out to sea.

If you look back at Haleakala from here, on your left you can see the spectacular, near-vertical **Waikani Falls.** On the remainder of the dead-end road is an eclectic collection of old and modern homes. Turning around at the road's end is very difficult, so I suggest you just turn around at the church and head back for the Hana Highway.

Back on the Hana Highway, just before mile marker 19, is the **Wailua Valley State Wayside Park** (*wailua* means "two waters"), on the right side of the road. Climb up the stairs for a view of the Keanae Valley, waterfalls, and Wailua Peninsula. On a really clear day, you can see up the mountain to the Koolau Gap.

For a better view of the Wailua Peninsula, continue down the road about ¼ mile. There's a pull-off area with parking on the ocean side.

PUAA KAA STATE WAYSIDE PARK   You'll hear this park long before you see it, about halfway between mile markers 22 and 23. The sound of waterfalls provides the background music for this small park area with restrooms, a phone, and a picnic area. In fact, *Puaa Kaa* translates as "open laughter." There's a well-marked path to the falls and to a swimming hole. Ginger plants are everywhere: Pick some flowers and put them in your car so that you can travel with that sweet smell.

OLD NAHIKU   Just after mile marker 25 is a narrow 3-mile road leading from the highway, at about 1,000 feet elevation, down to sea level—and to the remains of the old Hawaiian community of **Nahiku.** At one time this was a thriving village of thousands; today, the population has dwindled to fewer than 100—including a few Hawaiian families, but mostly extremely wealthy mainland residents who jet in for a few weeks at a time to their luxurious vacation homes. At the turn of the 20th century, this site saw brief commercial activity as home of the Nahiku Rubber Co., the only commercial rubber plantation in the United States. You can still see rubber trees along the Nahiku Road. However, the amount of rainfall, coupled with the damp conditions, could not support the commercial crop; the plantation closed in 1912, and Nahiku was forgotten until the 1980s, when multimillionaires "discovered" the remote and stunningly beautiful area.

At the end of the road, you can see the remains of the old wharf from the rubber-plantation days. Local residents come down here to shoreline fish; there's a small picnic area off to the side. Dolphins are frequently seen in the bay.

HANA AIRPORT   After mile marker 31, a small sign points to the Hana Airport, down Alalele Road on the left. Commuter airline **Pacific Wings** (© 888/575-4546; www.pacificwings.com) offers three flights daily to and from Hana, with connecting flights from Kahului and traveling on to Honolulu. There is no public transportation in Hana. Car rentals are available through **Dollar Rent A Car** (© 800/800-4000 or 808/248-8237).

WAIANAPANAPA STATE PARK   At mile marker 32, just on the outskirts of Hana, shiny black-sand Waianapanapa Beach appears like a vivid dream, with bright-green jungle foliage on three sides and cobalt-blue water lapping at its feet. The 120-acre park on an ancient *aa* lava flow includes sea cliffs, lava tubes, arches, and the beach, plus 12 cabins, tent camping, picnic pavilions, restrooms, showers, drinking water, and hiking trails. If you're interested in staying here, see p. 141 for a review of the cabins; also see "Beaches" and "Hiking & Camping," in chapter 7.

8 The End of the Road: Heavenly Hana ★★

Green, tropical Hana is a destination all its own, a small coastal village that's probably what you came to Maui in search of. Here you'll find a rainforest dotted with cascading waterfalls and sparkling blue pools, skirted by red- and black-sand beaches.

Beautiful Hana enjoys more than 90 inches of rain a year—more than enough to keep the scenery lush. Banyans, bamboo, breadfruit trees—everything seems larger than life in this small town, especially the flowers, such as wild ginger and plumeria. Several roadside stands offer exotic blooms for $1 a bunch. Just "put money in box." It's the Hana honor system.

A LOOK AT THE PAST

The Hana coast is rich in Hawaiian history and the scene of many turning points in Hawaiian culture. The ancient chants tell of rulers like the 15th-century **Piilani,** who united the island of Maui and built fishponds, irrigation fields, paved roads, and the massive **Piilanihale Heiau,** which still stands today in **Kahanu Garden,** part of the **National Tropical Botanical Garden** (© **808/248-8912;** www.ntbg.org/gardens/kahanu.php). It was Piilani's sons and grandson who finished the *heiau* and built the first road to Hana from west Maui, not only along the coast, but also up the Kaupo Gap and through the Haleakala Crater. For information on visiting the garden, see "Hiking" under "Outdoor Activities," below.

In 1849, the cantankerous sea captain **George Wilfong** brought commerce to this isolated village when he started the first sugar plantation on some 60 acres. Because his harsh personality and set demands for plantation work did not sit well with the Hawaiians, Wilfong brought in the first Chinese immigrants to work his fields.

In 1864, two Danish brothers, **August** and **Oscar Unna,** contributed to the growth of the local sugar industry when they established the Hana Plantation. Four years later they brought in Japanese immigrants to labor in the fields.

By the turn of the 20th century, sugar wasn't the only crop booming in Hana (there were some six plantations in the area): Rubber was being commercially grown in Nahiku, wheat in Kaupo, pineapple in Kipahulu, and tobacco in Ulupalakua.

In the 1920s and 1930s, several self-sufficient towns lined the coast, each with its own general store, school, and churches; some had movie theaters as well. Hana has all of the above plus some 15 stores, a pool hall, and several restaurants.

One can only guess what those towns would have been like today if not for the huge tidal wave that hit the state on April 1, 1946. The damage along the Hana coast was catastrophic: The Keanae Peninsula was swept clear (only the stone church remained), Hamoa was totally wiped out, and entire villages completely disappeared.

After World War II, the labor movement became a powerful force in Hawaii. **C. Brewer,** owner of the largest sugar plantation in Hana, decided to shut down his operation instead of fighting the labor union. The closure of the plantation meant not only the loss of thousands of jobs, but also the loss of plantation-supplied homes and the entire plantation lifestyle. Thankfully, **Paul I. Fagan,** an entrepreneur from San Francisco who had purchased the Hana Sugar Co. from the Unna brothers in the 1930s, became the town's guardian angel.

Fagan wanted to retire here, so he focused his business acumen on the tiny town with big problems. Recognizing that sugar was no longer economically feasible, he looked at the community and saw other opportunities. He bought 14,000 acres of land in Hana, stripped it of sugar cane, planted grass, and shipped in cattle from his ranch on Molokai.

Next he did something that was years ahead of his time: He thought tourism might have a future in Hana, so he established an inn in 1946 that later became the **Hotel Hana-Maui.** Fagan also pulled off a public-relations coup: He brought the entire San Francisco Seals baseball team (which he happened to own) to Hana for spring training, and, more important, he brought out the sportswriters as well. The writers loved Hana and wrote glowing reports about the town; one even gave the town a nickname that stuck: "Heavenly Hana."

In 1962, the state paved the Hana Highway. By the 1970s, tourists had not only "discovered" Maui, but they were also willing to make the long trek out to Hana.

The biggest change to the local lifestyle came in December 1977, when television finally arrived—after a local cable operator spent 6 months laying cable over cinder cones, mountain streams, and cavernous gulches from one side of the island to the other. Some 125 homes tuned in to the tube—and the rural Hawaiian community was never the same. Today, Hana is inhabited by 2,500 people, many part Hawaiian.

SEEING THE SIGHTS

Most visitors zip through Hana, perhaps taking a quick look out their car windows at a few sights before buzzing on down the road. They might think they've seen Hana, but they definitely haven't experienced Hana. Allow at least 2 or 3 days to really let this land of legends show you its beauty and serenity.

Another recommendation: See Hana's attractions, especially the pools, ponds, waterfalls, and hikes, early in the day. You'll have them all to yourself. The day-trippers arrive in Hana around 11am and stay until about 4pm; that's when the area is overrun with hundreds of people in a hurry, who want to see everything in just a few hours.

As you enter Hana, the road splits about ½ mile past mile marker 33, at the police station. Both roads will take you to Hana, but the lower road, Uakea Road, is more scenic. Just before you get to Hana Bay, you'll see the old wood-frame **Hana District Police Station and Courthouse.** Next door is the **Hana Cultural Center & Museum** ⟨★⟩, 4974 Uakea Rd. (© 808/248-8622; www.hookele.com/hccm), usually open daily from 10am to 4pm. This small building has an excellent collection of Hawaiian quilts, artifacts, books, and photos. Also on the grounds are Kauhala O Hana, composed of four *hale* (houses) for living, meeting, cooking, and canoe building or canoe storage.

Cater-cornered from the cultural center is the entrance to **Hana Bay** ⟨★⟩. You can drive right down to the pier and park. There are restrooms, showers, picnic tables, barbecue areas, and even a snack bar here. The 386-foot, red-faced cinder cone beside the bay is **Kauiki Hill,** the scene of numerous fierce battles in ancient Hawaii and the birthplace of Queen Kaahumanu in 1768. A short 5-minute walk will take you to the spot. Look for the trail along the hill on the wharf side, and follow the path through the ironwood trees; the lighthouse on the point will come into view, and you'll see pocket beaches of red cinder below. Grab onto the ironwood trees for support, as the trail has eroded in some areas. This is a perfect place for a secluded picnic, or you can continue on the path out to the lighthouse. To get to the lighthouse, which sits on a small island, watch the water for about 10 minutes to get a sense of how often and from which direction the waves are coming. Between wave sets, either swim or wade in the shallow, sandy bottom channel or hop across the rocks to the island.

Hana

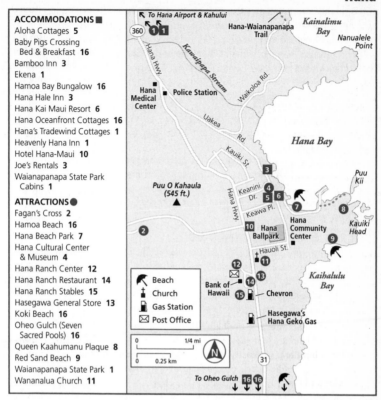

ACCOMMODATIONS ■

Aloha Cottages **5**

Baby Pigs Crossing
  Bed & Breakfast **16**

Bamboo Inn **3**

Ekena **1**

Hamoa Bay Bungalow **16**

Hana Hale Inn **3**

Hana Kai Maui Resort **6**

Hana Oceanfront Cottages **16**

Hana's Tradewind Cottages **1**

Heavenly Hana Inn **1**

Hotel Hana-Maui **10**

Joe's Rentals **3**

Waianapanapa State Park
  Cabins **1**

ATTRACTIONS ●

Fagan's Cross **2**

Hamoa Beach **16**

Hana Beach Park **7**

Hana Cultural Center
  & Museum **4**

Hana Ranch Center **12**

Hana Ranch Restaurant **14**

Hana Ranch Stables **15**

Hasegawa General Store **13**

Koki Beach **16**

Oheo Gulch (Seven
  Sacred Pools) **16**

Queen Kaahumanu Plaque **8**

Red Sand Beach **9**

Waianapanapa State Park **1**

Wananalua Church **11**

To get to the center of town, leave Hana Bay, cross Uakea Road, and drive up Keawa Place; turn left on Hana Highway, and on the corner will be the **Hotel Hana-Maui,** the now-luxurious hotel established by Paul Fagan in 1946. On the green hills above Hotel Hana-Maui stands a 30-foot-high white cross made of lava rock. Citizens erected the cross in memory of Paul Fagan, who founded the Hana Ranch as well as the hotel and helped keep the town alive. The hike up to **Fagan's Cross** provides a gorgeous view of the Hana coast, especially at sunset, when Fagan himself liked to climb this hill (see p. 196 for details).

Back on the Hana Highway, just past Hauoli Road, is the majestic **Wananalua Congregation Church.** It's listed on the National Historic Register not only because of its age (it was built in 1838–42 using coral stones), but also because of its location, atop an old Hawaiian *heiau.*

Just past the church, on the right side of the Hana Highway, is the turnoff to the **Hana Ranch Center,** the commercial center for Hana, with a post office, bank, general store, the Hana Ranch Stables, and a restaurant and snack bar (see "Hana Ranch Restaurant," p. 172). But the real shopping experience is across the Hana Highway at the **Hasegawa General Store** (p. 255), a Maui institution, which carries oodles of merchandise from soda and fine French wines to fishing line and name-brand clothing, plus everything you need for a picnic or a gourmet meal. This is also the place to find out what's going on in Hana: The bulletin board at the entrance has fliers and handwritten notes advertising everything from fundraising activities to classes to community-wide events. Don't miss this unique store.

If you need gas before heading back, fill up at the **Chevron** on the right side of the Hana Highway as you leave town. *Warning:* The price of gas here will take your breath away.

OUTDOOR ACTIVITIES

Hana is one of the best areas on Maui for ocean activities; it also boasts a wealth of nature hikes, remote places to explore on horseback, waterfalls to discover, and even lava tubes to investigate.

For more information on the lava tubes, see **Hana Lava Tube (℗ 808/248-7308)**, on p. 202; for details on horseback riding, see **Maui Horseback Tours at Maui Stables (℗ 808/248-7799)**, on p. 201. If you're a tennis player, you can take advantage of the free public courts located next to the Hotel Hana-Maui, available on a first-come, first-served basis.

BEACHES & OCEAN ACTIVITIES

Hana's beaches come in numerous varieties—white, black, gray, or red sand; perfectly shaped coves, crescents, or long stretches—and they're excellent for just about every kind of ocean activity you can think of. Call **Hana-Maui Sea Sports (℗ 808/248-7711;** www.hana-maui-seasports.com) if you'd like to snorkel or kayak, or venture out on your own at one of my favorite beaches:

HANA BAY   The waters in the Hana Bay are calm most of the time and great for swimming. There's excellent snorkeling and diving by the lighthouse. Strong currents can run through here, so don't venture farther than the lighthouse. See "Seeing the Sights," above, for more details on the facilities and hikes here.

RED SAND BEACH   The Hawaiian name for this beach is Kaihalulu ("roaring sea"). It's truly a sight to see. The beach is on the ocean side of Kauiki Hill, just south of Hana Bay, in a wild, natural setting on a pocket cove, where the volcanic cinder cone lost its seaward wall to erosion and spilled red cinders everywhere to create the red sands. Before you put on your bathing suit, there are three things to know about this beach: You have to trespass to get here (which is against the law); due to recent heavy rains, there have been several serious injuries on the muddy, slippery terrain (enter at your own risk; it can be extremely dangerous); and nudity (also illegal in Hawaii—arrests have been made) is common here.

If you are determined to go, ask for permission at the Hotel Hana-Maui. And ask about conditions on the trail (which drops several stories down to the ocean rocks). To reach the beach, put on solid walking shoes (no flip-flops) and walk south on Uakea Road, past Haoli Street and the Hotel Hana-Maui, to the parking lot for the hotel's Sea Ranch Cottages. Turn left and cross the open field next to the Hana Community Center. Look for the dirt trail and follow it to the huge ironwood tree, where you turn right (do not go ahead to the old Japanese cemetery). Use the ironwood trees to maintain your balance as you follow the ever-eroding cinder footpath a short distance along the shoreline, down the narrow cliff trail (do not attempt this if it's wet). The trail suddenly turns the corner, and into view comes the burnt-red beach, set off by the turquoise waters, black lava, and vivid green ironwood trees.

The lava outcropping protects the bay and makes it safe for swimming. Snorkeling is excellent, and there's a natural whirlpool area on the Hana Bay side of the cove. Stay away from the surge area where the ocean enters the cove.

KOKI BEACH ☆   One of the best surfing and boogie-boarding beaches on the Hana Coast lies just a couple of miles from the Hasegawa General Store in the Oheo Gulch direction. There is a very strong rip current here, so unless it is dead calm and you are a strong swimmer, do not attempt to swim here. However, it's a great place to sit on the white sand and watch the surfers. The only facility is a big parking area. To get here, drive toward Oheo Gulch from Hana, where Hwy. 36 changes to Hwy. 31. About 1½ miles outside of Hana, turn left at Haneoo Road.

HAMOA BEACH ☆☆   For one of Hana's best beaches—great for swimming, boogie boarding, and sunbathing—continue another ½ mile down the Haneoo Road loop to Hamoa Beach. There is easy access from the road down to the sandy beach, and facilities include a small restroom and an outdoor shower. The large pavilion and beach accessories are for Hotel Hana-Maui guests.

WAIOKA POND   Locally, this swimming hole in a series of waterfalls and pools is called Venus Pool. Unfortunately, it has become overrun with impolite tourists who park on the narrow highway, tear down the fence, and aren't very considerate about cleaning up their trash. The land owner, Hana Ranch, has put up NO TRESPASSING signs and is enforcing trespassing laws. (Getting arrested is not a great way to spend your vacation.) I recommend you skip this pond and keep driving to Haleakala National Park down the road. The park has adequate parking as well as restrooms. If you hike just 10 to 15 minutes upstream from the national park's parking lot, you will find much better pools and most likely have them to yourself.

HIKING

Hana is woven with hiking trails along the shoreline, through the rainforest, and up in the mountains. See p. 196 for a discussion of hiking in Waianapanapa and up to Fagan's Cross.

Another excellent hike that takes you back in time is through Kahanu Garden and to **Piilanihale Heiau** ☆☆, one of the largest ancient Hawaiian temples in the state. To get here, look for mile marker 31 on the Hana Highway, make a left on to Ulaino Road, and drive a little over a mile down the paved road (which turns into a dirt road but is still drivable) to the first stream bed (about 1½ miles). If the stream is running with water, do not cross it, as you most likely will get stuck; turn around and go back. If you can forge the stream, cross it and park on the right side of the road by the huge breadfruit trees. The trees are part of the **Kahanu Garden** ☆☆ (© 808/248-8912), owned and operated by the **National Tropical Botanical Garden** (www.ntbg.org). Admission is $10 for adults and free for children 12 and under. The garden is open Monday through Friday from 10am to 2pm. Allow an hour and a half for the self-guided tour. Be sure to wear comfortable walking shoes and long pants, and bring mosquito repellent, a hat for shade, and water.

The 122 acres here encompass plant collections from the Pacific Islands, concentrating on plants of value to the people of Polynesia, Micronesia, and Melanesia. Kahanu Garden contains the largest known collection of breadfruit cultivars from more than 17 Pacific Island groups and Indonesia, the Philippines, and the Seychelles.

The real draw here is the Piilanihale Heiau (see "A Look at the Past," above). Believed to be the largest in the state, it measures 340 feet by 415 feet, and it was built in a unique terrace design not seen anywhere else in Hawaii. The walls are some 50 feet tall and 8 to 10 feet thick. Historians believe that Piilani's two sons and his grandson built the mammoth temple, which was dedicated to war, sometime in the 1500s.

JUST BEYOND HANA
TROPICAL HALEAKALA: OHEO GULCH AT KIPAHULU 𝕽𝕽
If you're thinking about heading out to the so-called Seven Sacred Pools, out past Hana at the Kipahulu end of Haleakala National Park, let's clear this up right now: There are more than 7 pools—about 24, actually—and *all* water in Hawaii is considered sacred. It's all a PR campaign that has spun out of control into contemporary myth. Folks here call the attraction by its rightful name, **Oheo Gulch** 𝕽𝕽𝕽, and visitors sometimes refer to it as Kipahulu, which is actually the name of the area where Oheo Gulch is located. No matter what you call it, it's a beautiful sight. The dazzling series of pools and cataracts cascading into the sea is so popular that it has its own roadside parking lot.

Even though Oheo is part of Haleakala National Park, you cannot drive here from the summit. Even hiking from Haleakala to Oheo is tricky: The access trail out of Haleakala is down Kaupo Gap, which ends at the ocean, a good 6 miles down the coast from Oheo. To drive to Oheo, head for Hana, some 60 miles from Kahului on the Hana Highway (Hwy. 36). Oheo is about 30 to 50 minutes beyond Hana, along Hwy. 31. The Hwy. 31 bridge passes over pools near the ocean; the other pools, plus magnificent 400-foot Waimoku Falls, are reachable via an often-muddy, but rewarding, hourlong uphill hike (see "Hiking & Camping at Kipahulu [near Hana]," p. 193). Expect showers on the Kipahulu coast. The admission fee is $5 per person or $10 per car.

The **Kipahulu Ranger Station** (© **808/248-7375**) is staffed from 9am to 5pm daily. Restrooms are available, but there's no drinking water. Kipahulu rangers offer safety information, exhibits, books, and a variety of walks and hikes year-round. Check with the park rangers before hiking up to or swimming in the pools, and always keep one eye on the water in the streams; the sky can be sunny near the coast, but floodwaters from Kipahulu Valley can cause the pools to rise 4 feet in less than 10 minutes.

There are a number of hikes in the park, and tent camping is allowed. See "Hiking & Camping at Kipahulu (near Hana)," on p. 193, for details.

LINDBERGH'S GRAVE
A mile past Oheo Gulch on the ocean side of the road is **Lindbergh's Grave.** First to fly across the Atlantic Ocean, Charles A. Lindbergh (1902–74) found peace in the Pacific; he settled in Hana, where he died of cancer in 1974. The famous aviator is buried under river stones in a seaside graveyard behind the 1857 **Palapala Hoomau Congregational Church,** where his tombstone is engraved with his favorite words from the 139th Psalm: "If I take the wings of the morning and dwell in the uttermost parts of the sea . . ."

EVEN FARTHER AROUND THE BEND
As we went to press, about 2½ miles past Oheo Gulch, just after Lindbergh's Grave, the road is still closed due to the October 2006 earthquake (there's a huge barrier in the road, and don't even think about going around it). Until the road is repaired, you will have to turn around and drive back the way you came (through Hana and back out on

the Hana Hwy.). Check to see if the road is open by calling the **Maui Public Works Department** (© 808/248-8254) or the **Police Department** (© 808/248-8311).

If the road is open, be careful, as it is unpaved all the way to the fishing village of **Kaupo.** It narrows to one lane at times, wandering in and out of valleys with sharp rock walls and blind bends hugging the ocean cliffs. You may encounter wild pigs and stray cows. About 6 miles and about 60 minutes from Oheo Gulch, you'll see the restored **Huialoha Congregationalist "Circuit" Church,** originally constructed in 1859. Across from the church and down the road a bit is the **Kaupo Store** (© 808/ 248-8054), which marks the center of the ranching community of Kaupo. Store hours are officially Monday through Friday from 7:30am to 4:30pm, but in this arid cattle country, posted hours often prove meaningless. The Kaupo Store is the last of the Soon family stores, which at one time stretched from Kaupo to Keanae.

From the Kaupo Store, the landscape turns into barren, dry desert. In the lee of Haleakala, this area gets little rain. There are no phones or services until you reach **Ulupalakua Ranch** (p. 227), where there are a winery, general store, and gas station, which is likely to be closed.

Between mile markers 29 and 30, look for the ancient lava flow that created an arch as it rolled down Haleakala. Keep an eye peeled for cattle—this is open-range country. Eventually the road will wind uphill, and suddenly the forest and greenery of Ulupalakua come into sight. From here, you're about 45 minutes from Kahului.

Shops & Galleries

Maui is a shopaholic's dream as well as an arts center, with a large number of resident artists who show their works in dozens of galleries and countless gift shops. Maui is also the queen of specialty products, an agricultural cornucopia that includes Kula onions, upcountry protea, Kaanapali coffee, and many other tasty treats that are shipped worldwide.

As with any popular visitor destination, you'll have to wade through bad art and mountains of trinkets, particularly in Lahaina and Kihei, where touristy boutiques line the streets between rare pockets of treasures. If you shop in south or west Maui, expect to pay resort prices, clear down to a bottle of Evian or sunscreen.

With a well-heeled flourish, the **Shops at Wailea,** an upscale shopping-and-restaurant complex, opened in south Maui in 2001. The 16-acre complex features more than 50 shops and five restaurants,

including Louis Vuitton, Tiffany, Gap, Banana Republic, and the ever-popular local retailers Martin & MacArthur and Ki'i Gallery. This is resort shopping much in the vein of **Whalers Village** in Kaanapali, where shopping and restaurant activity is concentrated in a single oceanfront complex.

Don't ignore central Maui, home to some first-rate boutiques. Watch the quaint town of **Wailuku,** which is poised for a resurgence. It has its own antiques alleys, and a major promenade on Main Street is in the works. The **Kaahumanu Center,** in neighboring Kahului, is becoming more fashionable by the month.

Upcountry, the boutiques of **Makawao** are worth seeking out, despite some attitude and high prices. The charm of shopping on Maui has always rested in the small, independent shops and galleries that crop up in surprising places.

1 Central Maui

KAHULUI

Kahului's best shopping is concentrated in two places. Almost all of the shops listed below are at one of the following centers:

The formerly rough-around-the-edges **Maui Mall,** 70 E. Kaahumanu Ave. (© 808/877-7559; www.mauimall.com), is the place of everyday retail, from **Longs Drugs** and **Star Market** to **Tasaka Guri Guri** (the decades-old purveyor of inimitable icy treats that are neither ice cream nor shave ice, but something in between) and Kahului's largest movie theater, a 12-screen megaplex that features current releases as well as art-house films.

Queen Kaahumanu Center, 275 Kaahumanu Ave. (© 808/877-3369; www.queenkaahumanucenter.com), a 10-minute drive from the Kahului Airport on Hwy. 32, offers more than 100 shops, restaurants, and theaters. It covers all the bases, from arts and crafts to a **Foodland** and everything in between: a thriving food court; the island's best beauty supply, **Lisa's Beauty Supply & Salon** (℡ 808/877-6463), and its sister store for cosmetics, **Madison Avenue Day Spa and Boutique** (℡ 808/873-0880); mall standards like **Sunglass Hut, Radio Shack,** and **Local Motion** (surf- and beachwear); standard department stores like **Macy's** and **Sears;** and specialty shops like **Sharper Image.** Its second-floor Plantation District offers home furnishings, accessories, and gifts.

Cost Less Imports   Natural fibers are ubiquitous in this corner of the Maui Mall. Home accessories include lauhala, bamboo blinds, grassy floor and window coverings, shoji-style lamps, burlap yardage, baskets, Balinese cushions, Asian imports, *noreng* (Japanese folk curtains), and made-on-Maui soaps and handicrafts. A good source of tropical and Asian home decor. At the Maui Mall. ℡ 808/877-0300. www.costlessimports-online.com.

Duck Soup *Finds*   Way, way off the beaten path lies this warehouse full of Asian and Indonesian treasures. Owners Judy Bruder and Sandi Stoner definitely have an eye for spotting the unusual and chic. Most of their buying trips to Indonesia are for interior designers, homeowners, and hotels, but they also bring back some incredible jewelry, handbags, and art, all at prices that will put a smile on your face. The location is a bit tricky; call first for directions. Off Mokulele Hwy. (Hwy. 311), about a mile from Puunene, near the Maui Animal Shelter and the Central Maui Baseyard. ℡ 808/871-7875.

Lightning Bolt Maui   Here's an excellent selection of women's board shorts, aloha shirts, swimwear, sandals and shoes, and all the necessary accouterments for fun in the sun. Quality labels such as Horny Toad and City Lights and high-tech, state-of-the-art outdoors gear attract adventurers heading for the chilly hinterlands as well as the sun-drenched shores. 55 E. Kaahumanu Ave. ℡ 808/877-3484. www.lightningboltmaui.com.

Maui Swap Meet   After 17 years on a parcel of land next to the Kahului post office, the popular Maui Swap Meet finally outgrew its home. In November 2008, it moved to the Maui Community College campus, in Kahului, where there is room enough for 300 vendors and plenty of parking. Every Saturday from 7am to 1pm, vendors spread out their wares in booths and under tarps, in a festival-like atmosphere that is pure Maui with a touch of kitsch. The colorful Maui specialties include vegetables from Kula and Keanae, fresh taro, plants, proteas, crafts, household items, homemade ethnic foods, and baked goods, including some fabulous fruit breads. Now students at the community college sell artwork and ceramics; the culinary-arts program has prepared food for sale. Between the cheap Balinese imports and New Age crystals and incense, you may find some vintage John Kelly prints and 1930s collectibles. Admission is 50¢, and if you go early while the vendors are setting up, no one will turn you away. At Maui Community College, in an area bounded by Kahului Beach Rd. and Wahine Pio Ave. (access via Wahine Pio Ave). ℡ 808/877-3100.

Summerhouse   Sleek and chic, tiny Summerhouse is big on style: casual and party dresses, separates by Russ Berens, FLAX, Kiko, and Tencel jeans by Signature—the best. During the holiday season, the selection gets dressy and sassy, but it's a fun browse year-round. I adore the hats, accessories, easy-care clothing, and up-to-the-minute evening dresses. The high-quality T-shirts are always a cut above. The casual selection is well suited to the Island lifestyle. At the Dairy Center, 395 Dairy Rd. ℡ 808/871-1320.

EDIBLES

The **Star Market** and **Longs Drugs** in the Maui Mall, **Foodland** in the Kaahumanu Center, and **Safeway** at 170 E. Kamehameha Ave. will satisfy your ordinary grocery needs. On Saturday, you may want to check out the **Maui Swap Meet** (see above).

Down to Earth Natural Foods, 305 Dairy Rd. (© **808/877-2661**), a health-food staple for many years, has fresh organic produce, a bountiful salad bar, sandwiches and smoothies, vitamins and supplements, fresh-baked goods, snacks, whole grains, and several packed aisles of vegetarian and health foods.

Maui's produce has long been a source of pride for islanders, and **Ohana Farmers Market,** at the Queen Kaahumanu Center (© **808/871-8347**), on Tuesday, Wednesday, and Friday, is the place to find a fresh, inexpensive selection of Maui-grown fruit, vegetables, flowers, and plants. Crafts and gourmet foods add to the event.

WAILUKU

Located at the gateway to Iao Valley, Wailuku is the county seat, the part of Maui where people live and work. Wailuku's attractive vintage architecture, smattering of antiques shops, and mom-and-pop eateries imbue the town with a down-home charm noticeably absent in Maui's resort areas. The community spirit fuels festivals throughout the year and is slowly attracting new businesses, but Wailuku is still a work in progress. It's a mixed bag—of course, there's junk, but a stroll along Main and Market streets usually turns up a treasure or two.

Bailey House Museum Shop　For made-in-Hawaii items, Bailey House is a must-stop. It offers a thoroughly enjoyable browse through authoritative Hawaiiana, in a museum that's one of the finest examples of missionary architecture, dating from 1833. Gracious gardens, rare paintings of early Maui, wonderful programs in Hawaiian arts and culture, and a restored hand-hewn koa canoe await visitors. The shop, a small space of discriminating taste, packs a wallop with its selection of remarkable gift items, from Hawaiian music to exquisite woods, traditional Hawaiian games to pareu and books. Prints by the legendary Hawaii artist Madge Tennent, lauhala hats, hand-sewn pheasant hatbands, jams and jellies, Maui cookbooks, and an occasional Hawaiian quilt are some of the treasures to be found here. At the Bailey House Museum, 2375-A Main St. © 808/244-3326.

Bird of Paradise Unique Antiques　Owner Joe Myhand loves furniture, old Matson liner menus, blue willow china, kimonos for children, and anything nostalgic that happens to be Hawaiian. The furniture ranges from 1940s rattan to wicker and old koa—those items tailor-made for informal Island living and leisurely moments on the lanai. Myhand also collects bottles and mails his license plates all over the world. The collection ebbs and flows with his finds, keeping buyers waiting in the wings for his Depression glass, California pottery from the 1930s and 1940s, old dinnerware, perfume bottles, vintage aloha shirts, and vintage Hawaiian music on cassettes. 56 N. Market St. © 808/242-7699.

Brown-Kobayashi　Graceful living is the theme here. Prices range from a few dollars to the thousands in this 750-square-foot treasure trove. The owners have added a fabulous selection of antique stone garden pieces that mingle quietly with Asian antiques and old and new French, European, and Hawaiian objects. Although the collection is eclectic, there is a strong cohesive aesthetic that sets Brown-Kobayashi apart from other Maui antiques stores. Japanese kimonos and obi, Bakelite and Peking glass

Maui's Own: Ocean Vodka

If you're looking for a souvenir of your fabulous Maui trip to take home, or a unique gift for friends, Maui has its own vodka, called Ocean Vodka. Produced by Hawaii Sea Spirits, this ultrapremium brand is not only USDA certified to contain organic ingredients, but also the water comes from 3,000 feet beneath the ocean off the Kona coast of the Big Island. The deep-sea water is harvested by KOYO USA, producers of MaHaLo Hawaii Deep Sea Water. The desalinated water has become widely popular in Japan, where people swear it has provided beneficial health effects (so far, no scientific studies have backed up this claim). The MaHaLo water is shipped to Maui, where it is blended with organic corn and rye to produce this one-of-a-kind vodka. It's available at restaurants, bars, hotels, and retail shops (for a complete list, see www.oceanvodka.com).

beads, breathtaking Japanese lacquerware, cricket carriers, and cloisonné are among the delights here. Exotic and precious Chinese woods (purple sandalwood and *huanghuali*) glow discreetly from quiet corners, and an occasional monarchy-style lidded milo bowl comes in and flies out. 38 N. Market St. © 808/242-0804.

Gottling Ltd.   Karl Gottling's shop specializes in Asian antique furniture, but you can also find smaller carvings, precious stones, jewelry, netsuke, opium weights, and more. I saw a 17th-century Buddha lending an air of serenity next to a 150-year-old Chinese cabinet. Ming Dynasty ceramics, carved wooden apples ($15), and a Persian rug ($65,000) give you an idea of the range of possibilities here. 34 N. Market St. © 808/244-7779.

Sandell *(Finds*   Since the early 1970s, artist, illustrator, and cartoonist David Sandell has been commenting on Maui through his artwork. Don't miss the opportunity to stop by this shop and "talk story" with the talented artist, who watched Maui go from undiscovered to discovered. His work—from original oils to prints to T-shirts—makes excellent souvenirs to take home. 133 Market St. © 808/249-0234.

EDIBLES

Located in the northern section of Wailuku, **Takamiya Market,** 359 N. Market St. (© 808/244-3404), is much loved by local folks and visitors with adventurous palates, who often drive all the way from Kihei to stock up on picnic fare and mouthwatering ethnic foods for sunset gatherings. Unpretentious home-cooked foods from East and West are prepared daily and served on plastic-foam plates. From the chilled-fish counter come fresh sashimi and poke, and among the renowned assortment of prepared foods are mounds of shoyu chicken, tender fried squid, roast pork, kalua pork, laulau, Chinese noodles, fiddlehead ferns, and Western comfort foods, such as corn bread and potato salad. Fresh produce and paper products are also available, but it's the prepared foods and fresh-fish counter that have made Takamiya a household name in central Maui.

2 West Maui

LAHAINA

Lahaina's merchants and art galleries go all out from 7 to 9pm every Friday, when **Art Night** brings an extra measure of hospitality and community spirit. The Art Night openings are usually marked with live entertainment and refreshments, plus a livelier-than-usual street scene.

If you're in Lahaina on the second or last Thursday of the month, stroll by the front lawn of the **Baldwin Home Museum,** 120 Dickenson St. (at Front St.), for a splendid look at the craft of lei making and an opportunity to meet the gregarious seniors of Lahaina. In a program sponsored by AARP, they gather from 10am to 4pm to demonstrate lei making, to sell their floral creations, and, equally important, to socialize.

What was formerly a big, belching pineapple cannery is now a maze of shops and restaurants at the northern end of Lahaina town, known as the **Lahaina Cannery Mall,** 1221 Honoapiilani Hwy. (📞 808/661-5304; www.lahainacannerymall.com). Find your way through the T-shirt and sportswear shops to coffee at **Starbucks,** or follow your nose to **Compadres Bar & Grill** (p. 149), where the margaritas flow freely and the Mexican food is tasty. At the recently expanded food court, **Compadres Taqueria** sells Mexican food to go, while **L & L Drive-Inn** serves up plate lunches near Greek, pizza, Vietnamese, and Japanese food booths. For film, water, aspirin, groceries, sunscreen, and other things you can't live without, nothing beats **Longs Drugs** and **Safeway** (open 24 hr.), two old standbys. **Footprints Maui** may surprise you with its selection of footwear, everything from running shoes to inexpensive sandals.

The **Lahaina Center,** 900 Front St. (📞 808/667-9216; www.lahainacenter.com), is still a work in progress. It's located north of Lahaina's most congested strip, where Front Street begins. Across the street from the center, the sea wall is a much-sought-after front-row seat to the sunset. There's plenty of free validated parking and easy access to more than 30 shops, a salon, restaurants, a nightclub, and a four-plex movie-theater complex. **Ruth's Chris Steak House** has opened its doors here, and **Hard Rock Cafe** serves lunch and dinner and offers nighttime live music on weekdays. Among the shopping stops: **Hilo Hattie** (a dizzying emporium of aloha wear), **ABC Discount Store,** and a dozen other recreational, dining, and entertainment options.

The conversion of 10,000 square feet of parking space into the re-creation of a traditional Hawaiian village, called **Hale Kahiko,** is a welcome touch of Hawaiiana at the Lahaina Center. With the commercialization of modern Lahaina, it's easy to forget that it was once the capital of the Hawaiian kingdom and a significant historic site. Hale Kahiko features three main houses, called *hale:* a sleeping house, the men's dining house, and the crafts house, where women pounded *hala* (pandanus) strips to weave into mats and baskets. Construction of the houses consumed 10,000 square feet of ohia wood from the island, 20 tons of pili grass, and more than 4 miles of hand-woven coconut sennit for the lashings. Artifacts, weapons, a canoe, and indigenous trees are among the authentic touches in this village; you can take a free guided tour daily between 9am and 6pm.

Banana Wind   Tucked into the Lahaina Cannery, this whimsical store has everything from T-shirts to woven baskets, candles, pareus, shells, and even carved wooden banana trees (just $6,000 and very tricky to transport in your luggage). This is the place to find some great souvenirs to take back home. At the Lahaina Cannery Mall, 1221 Honoapiilani Hwy. 📞 808/661-1600.

David Lee Galleries   This gallery is devoted to the works of David Lee, who uses natural powder colors to paint on silk. The pigments and technique create a luminous, ethereal quality. 712 Front St. ℂ 808/667-7740.

Lahaina Arts Society Galleries   With its membership of more than 185 Maui artists, the nonprofit Lahaina Arts Society is an excellent community resource. Changing monthly exhibits in the Banyan Tree and Old Jail galleries offer a good look at the island's artistic well: two-dimensional art, fiber art, ceramics, sculpture, prints, jewelry, and more. In the shade of the humongous banyan tree in the square across from Pioneer Inn, "Art in the Park" fairs are offered every second and fourth weekend of the month. 648 Wharf St. ℂ 808/661-3228.

Lei Spa Maui   Expanded to include two massage rooms and shower facilities, this day spa offers facials and other therapies. About 95% of the beauty and bath products sold here are made on Maui, and that includes Hawaiian Botanical Pikake shower gel, *kukui* and macadamia-nut oils, Hawaiian potpourris, mud masks with Hawaiian seaweed, and a spate of rejuvenating potions for hair and skin. Aromatherapy body oils and perfumes are popular, as are the handmade soaps and fragrances of torch ginger, plumeria, coconut, tuberose, and sandalwood. Scented candles in coconut shells, inexpensive and fragrant, make great gifts. 505 Front St. ℂ 808/661-1178.

Maggie Coulombe *(Finds*   Imagine a high-fashion store with the unique designs of Maggie Coulombe in the midst of Lahaina. You'll find Maggie's latest couture, jersey, linen, pareu, and shoes, plus accessories, jewelry, purses, and a few surprises. 505 Front St. ℂ 808/662-0696. www.maggiecoulombe.com.

Martin Lawrence Galleries   The front is garish, with pop art, kinetic sculptures, and bright, carnivalesque glass objects. Toward the back of the gallery, however, there's a sizable inventory of two-dimensional art and some plausible choices for collectors of Keith Haring, Andy Warhol, and other pop artists. The originals, limited-edition graphics, and sculptures also include works by Marc Chagall, Pablo Picasso, Joan Miró, Roy Lichtenstein, and other noted artists. At the Lahaina Market Place, 126 Lahainaluna Rd. ℂ 808/661-1788. www.martinlawrence.com.

Old Lahaina Book Emporium   What a bookstore! Chockablock with used books in stacks, on shelves, on counters, and in the aisles, this place is a browser's dream. More than 25,000 quality used books are lovingly housed in this shop, where owner JoAnn Carroll treats both books and customers well. Prices are low, and the selection is diverse, everything from *Li'l Abner* to *Genius and Lust,* old *Mad* magazines, *Aphrodisiac Cookery, Bhagavad Gita, A History of Bicycles,* and *The Cockroach Combat Manual.* The store is 95% used books and 100% delight. Specialties include Hawaiiana, fiction, mystery, sci-fi, and military history, with substantial selections in cookbooks, children's books, and philosophy/religion. You could pay as little as $2 for a quality read, or a whole lot more for that rare first edition. Books on tape, videos, the classics, and old guitar magazines are among the treasures of this two-story emporium. 834 Front St. ℂ 808/661-1399. www.oldlahainabookemporium.com.

Peter Lik Gallery   Australian photographer Peter Lik is known for his spectacular panoramic photos, and his gallery is a lot like his art: spacious, eye-catching, and full of surprises. Stop by just to see his incredible vistas. Even if you can't afford one of his photos, there are posters, cards, books, and other items for sale. 712 Front St. ℂ 808/661-6623. www.peterlik.com.

Village Galleries in Lahaina   The nearly 30-year-old Village Galleries is the oldest continuously running gallery on Maui, and it's esteemed as one of the few galleries with consistently high standards. Art collectors know this as a respectable showcase for regional artists; the selection of mostly original two- and three-dimensional art offers a good look at the quality of work originating on the island. The newer contemporary gallery offers colorful gift items and jewelry. An additional location is at the Ritz-Carlton Kapalua, 1 Ritz-Carlton Dr. (𝄢 **808/669-1800**). 120 and 180 Dickenson St. 𝄢 **808/ 661-4402** or 661-5559.

KAANAPALI

I am somewhat disappointed with upscale **Whalers Village,** 2435 Kaanapali Pkwy. (𝄢 **808/661-4567;** www.whalersvillage.com). Although it offers everything from whale blubber to Prada and Ferragamo, it's short on local shops, and parking at the nearby lot is expensive. The complex is home to the **Whalers Village Museum** (p. 218), with its interactive exhibits, 40-foot sperm-whale skeleton, and sand castles on perpetual display, but shoppers come for the designer thrills and beachfront dining. You can find most of the items featured here in the shops in Lahaina and can avoid the parking hassle and the high prices by skipping Whalers Village.

If you do decide to check it out, don't miss my favorite shoe store, **Sandal Tree** (described below). **Martin & MacArthur** offers a dizzying array of Hawaii crafts: Hawaiian-quilt cushion covers, jewelry, soaps, books, and a stunning selection of woodwork. The always wonderful **Lahaina Printsellers** has a selection of antique prints, maps, paintings, and engravings, including 18th- to 20th-century cartography, all of which offer great browsing and gift potential. You can find award-winning **Kimo Bean** coffee at a kiosk, an expanded **Reyn's** for aloha wear, and **Cinnamon Girl,** a hit in Honolulu for its matching mother-daughter clothing. The return of **Waldenbooks** makes it that much easier to pick up the latest bestseller on the way to the beach. Another mainstay of the village is the busiest **ABC** store in the state, with everything from suntan lotion to takeout sandwiches to cold beer. Once you've stood under the authentic whale skeleton at the museum, you can blow a bundle at **Tiffany, Prada, Chanel, Ferragamo, Louis Vuitton, Coach,** the **Body Shop,** or any of the more than 60 shops and restaurants that have sprouted up in this open-air shopping center. Despite obvious efforts to offer more of a balance between Island-made and designer goods, the chain luxury boutiques still dominate. Whalers Village is open daily from 9:30am to 10pm.

Ki'i Gallery   Some of the works are large and lavish, such as the Toland Sand prisms for just under $5,000 and the John Stokes handblown glass. Those who love glass in all forms, from handblown vessels to jewelry, will love a browse through Ki'i. I found Pat Kazi's work in porcelain and found objects, such as the mermaid in a teacup, inspired by fairy tales and mythology, both fantastic and compelling. The gallery is devoted to glass and original paintings and drawings; roughly half of the artists are from Hawaii. Also at the Grand Wailea Resort (𝄢 **808/874-3059**) and the Shops at Wailea (𝄢 **808/874-1181**). At the Hyatt Regency Maui Resort, 200 Nohea Kai Dr. 𝄢 **808/661-4456.** www.kiigallery.com.

Paul Ropp (𝘧𝘪𝘯𝘥𝘴   The Bali fashion designer's only store outside of Indonesia is found on the ground level at Whalers Village. Ropp sees fashion as a medium, and he calls his creations "sexual clothes." Stop by to check out his sense of fashion (lively and colorful) and eccentric style of dressing, which is perfect for Maui's tropical climate. At Whalers Village, 2435 Kaanapali Pkwy. 𝄢 **808/661-8000.** www.paulropp.com.

A Creative Way to Spend the Day

Make a bowl from clay, or paint a premade one, then fire it, and take it home as a unique souvenir of Maui. The **Art School at Kapalua** (𝒞 808/665-0007; www.kapalua.com/recreation/art_school.php), in a charming 1920s plantation building that was part of an old cannery operation, features local and visiting instructors and is open daily for people of all ages and skill levels. Projects, classes, and workshops at this not-for-profit organization highlight creativity in all forms, including photography, figure drawing, ceramics, landscape painting, painting on silk, and the performing arts (ballet, yoga, creative movement, Pilates). Classes are inexpensive. Call the school to see what's scheduled while you're on Maui.

Sandal Tree   It's unusual for a resort shop to draw local customers on a regular basis, but the Sandal Tree attracts a flock of footwear fanatics who come here from throughout the islands for rubber thongs and Top-Siders, sandals and dressy pumps, athletic shoes and hats, designer footwear, and much more. Sandal Tree also carries a generous selection of Mephisto and Arche comfort sandals, Donald Pliner, Anne Klein, Charles Jourdan, and beachwear and casual footwear for all tastes. Accessories range from fashionable knapsacks to avant-garde geometrical handbags—for town and country, day and evening, kids, women, and men. Prices are realistic, too. Also at the Grand Wailea Resort, 3850 Wailea Alanui Dr., Wailea; and the Hyatt Regency Maui Resort, 200 Nohea Kai Dr., Kaanapali. At Whalers Village, 2435 Kaanapali Pkwy. 𝒞 808/667-5330.

Totally Hawaiian Gift Gallery   This gallery makes a good browse for its selection of Niihau shell jewelry, excellent Hawaiian CDs, Norfolk pine bowls, and Hawaiian quilt kits. Hawaiian quilt patterns sewn in Asia (at least they're honest about it) are labor-intensive, less expensive, and attractive, although not totally Hawaiian. Hawaiian-quilt-patterned gift wraps and tiles, perfumes and soaps, handcrafted dolls, and koa accessories are of good quality, and the artists, such as Kelly Dunn (Norfolk wood bowls), Jerry Kermode (wood), and Pat Coito (wood), are among the tops in their fields. At Whalers Village, 2435 Kaanapali Pkwy. 𝒞 808/667-4070. www.totallyhawaiian.com.

HONOKOWAI, KAHANA & NAPILI

Those driving north of Kaanapali toward Kapalua will notice the **Honokowai Marketplace,** on Lower Honoapiilani Road, only minutes before the Kapalua Airport. It houses restaurants and coffee shops, a dry cleaner, the flagship **Star Market,** a few clothing stores, and the sprawling **Hawaiian Interiors.**

Nearby **Kahana Gateway** is an unimpressive mall built to serve the condominium community that has sprawled along the coastline between Honokowai and Kapalua. If you need women's swimsuits, however, **Rainbow Beach Swimwear** is a find. It carries a selection of suits for all shapes, at lower-than-resort prices, slashed even further during the frequent sales. **Hutton's Fine Jewelry** offers high-end jewelry from designers around the country (lots of platinum and diamonds), reflecting discerning taste for those who can afford it. Tahitian black pearls and jade are among Hutton's specialties.

KAPALUA

Honolua Store   Walk on the old wood floors peppered with holes from golf shoes and find your everyday essentials: bottled water, stationery, mailing tape, jackets, chips, wine, soft drinks, paper products, fresh fruit and produce, and aisles of notions and necessities. With picnic tables on the veranda and a takeout counter offering deli items—more than a dozen types of sandwiches, salads, and budget-friendly breakfasts—there are always long lines of customers. Golfers and surfers love to come here for the morning paper and coffee. 502 Office Rd. (next to the Ritz-Carlton Kapalua). ℭ 808/669-6128.

Village Galleries   Maui's finest artists exhibit their works here and in the other two Village Galleries in Lahaina. Take heart, art lovers: There's no clichéd marine art here. Translucent, delicately turned bowls of Norfolk pine gleam in the light, and George Allan, Betty Hay Freeland, Fred KenKnight, and Pamela Andelin are included in the pantheon of respected artists represented in the tiny gallery. Watercolors, oils, sculptures, handblown glass, Niihau shell leis, jewelry, and other media are represented. The Ritz-Carlton's monthly Artist-in-Residence program features gallery artists in demonstrations and special hands-on workshops that are free, including materials. At the Ritz-Carlton Kapalua, 1 Ritz-Carlton Dr. ℭ 808/669-1800.

3 South Maui

KIHEI
Kihei is one long strip of strip malls. Most of the shopping here is concentrated in the **Azeka Place Shopping Center** on South Kihei Road. Fast foods abound at Azeka, as do tourist-oriented clothing shops like **Crazy Shirts.** Across the street, **Azeka Place II** houses several prominent attractions, including the **Coffee Store** and a cluster of specialty shops with everything from children's clothes to shoes, sunglasses, and swimwear. Also on South Kihei Road is the **Kukui Mall,** with movie theaters, **Waldenbooks,** and **Whaler's General Store.**

Hawaiian Moons Natural Foods   Hawaiian Moons is an exceptional health-food store, as well as a mini supermarket with one of the best selections of Maui products on the island. The tortillas are made on Maui (and good!), and much of the produce here, such as organic vine-ripened tomatoes and organic onions, is grown in the fertile upcountry soil of Kula. There's also locally grown organic coffee, gourmet salsas, Maui shiitake mushrooms, organic lemon grass and okra, Maui Crunch bread, free-range Big Island turkeys and chickens (no antibiotics or artificial nasties), and fresh Maui juices. Cosmetics are top-of-the-line: a staggering selection of sunblock, fragrant floral oils, *kukui*-nut oil from Waialua on Oahu, and Island Essence made-on-Maui mango-coconut and vanilla-papaya lotions, the ultimate in body pampering. The salad bar is one of the most popular food stops on the coast. Also on the west side at 3636 Lower Honoapiilani Rd. (ℭ **808/665-1339**). 2411 S. Kihei Rd. ℭ 808/875-4356.

WAILEA
CY Maui   Women who like flowing clothing in silks, rayons, and natural fibers will love this shop, formerly the popular Manikin in Kahului. If you don't find what you want on the racks of simple bias-cut designs, you can have it made from the bolts of stupendous fabrics lining the store. Except for a few hand-painted silks, everything here is washable. At the Shops at Wailea, 3750 Wailea Alanui Dr. ℭ 808/891-0782. www.cymaui.com.

Fairmont Store   This chic boutique in the Fairmont Kea Lani stands out due to the careful eye of buyer Barbara Cipro, who has an excellent sense of fashion. Here you'll find Michael Stars and Glima T-shirts, Yellow Box and Matisse sandals, Sophia and Chloe jewelry, Helen Kaminski hats, and a range of clothing by Citron, Sigrid

Olsen, and Betsey Johnson. It's definitely worth your time to browse this airy and well-lit shop, with a truly helpful staff. At the Fairmont Kea Lani Maui, 4100 Wailea Alanui Dr. ℂ 808/875-4100, ext. 390.

Grand Wailea Shops   The sprawling Grand Wailea Resort is known for its long arcade of shops and galleries tailored to hefty pocketbooks. However, gift items in all price ranges can be found at Lahaina Printsellers (for old maps and prints), Dolphin Galleries, H. F. Wichman, and Napua Gallery, which houses the private collection of the resort owner. Ki'i Gallery (p. 248) is luminous with studio glass and exquisitely turned woods, and Sandal Tree (p. 249) raises the footwear bar. At the Grand Wailea Resort, 3850 Wailea Alanui Dr. ℂ 808/875-1234.

The Shops at Wailea   This is the big shopping boost that resortgoers have been awaiting for years. The high-end shops sell expensive souvenirs, gifts, clothing, and accessories for a life of perpetual vacations. Chains rule (Gap, Louis Vuitton, Banana Republic, Tiffany, Crazy Shirts, Honolua Surf Co.), but there is still fertile ground for the inveterate shopper in the nearly 60 shops in the complex. **Martin & MacArthur** (furniture and gift gallery; p. 248) has landed in Wailea as part of a retail mix that is similar to Whalers Village. 3750 Wailea Alanui Dr. ℂ 808/891-6770.

4 Upcountry Maui

MAKAWAO

Besides being a shopper's paradise, Makawao is the home of the island's most prominent arts organization, the **Hui No'eau Visual Arts Center** ✆, 2841 Baldwin Ave. (ℂ 808/572-6560; www.huinoeau.com). Designed in 1917 by C. W. Dickey, one of Hawaii's most prominent architects, the two-story, Mediterranean-style stucco home that houses the center is located on a sprawling 9-acre estate called Kaluanui. A legacy of Maui's prominent *kamaaina* (old-timers) Harry and Ethel Baldwin, the estate became an arts center in 1976. Visiting artists offer lectures, classes, and demonstrations, all at reasonable prices, in basketry, jewelry making, ceramics, painting, and other media. Classes on Hawaiian art, culture, and history are also available. Call ahead for schedules and details. The exhibits here are drawn from a wide range of disciplines and multicultural sources, and include both contemporary and traditional art from established and emerging artists. The gift shop, featuring many one-of-a-kind works by local artists and artisans, is worth a stop. Hours are Monday through Saturday from 10am to 4pm.

Collections   This longtime Makawao attraction is showing renewed vigor after more than 2 decades on Baldwin Avenue. It's one of my favorite Makawao stops, full of gift items and spirited clothing reflecting the ease and color of island living. Its selection of sportswear, soaps, jewelry, candles, and tasteful, marvelous miscellany reflects good sense and style. Dresses (including up-to-the-moment Citron in cross-cultural and vintage-looking prints), separates, home and bath accessories, sweaters, and other good things make this a Makawao must. 3677 Baldwin Ave. ℂ 808/572-0781.

Gallery Maui   Follow the sign down the charming shaded pathway to a cozy gallery of top-notch art and crafts. Most of the works here are by Maui artists, and the quality is outstanding. About 30 artists are represented: Wayne Omura and his Norfolk pine bowls, Pamela Hayes's watercolors, Martha Vockrodt and her wonderful paintings, a stunning Steve Hynson dresser of curly koa and ebony. The two- and three-dimensional original works reflect the high standards of gallery owners Deborah and

Robert Zaleski (a painter), who have just added to their roster the talented ceramic artist David Stabley, a two-time American Craft Council juror. 3643-A Baldwin Ave. ℰ 808/572-8092.

Gecko Trading Co. Boutique   The selection in this tiny boutique is eclectic and always changing: One day it's mesh T-shirts in a dragon motif, the next it's Provence soaps and antique lapis jewelry. I've seen everything from handmade crocheted bags from New York to hammered-tin candle holders from Mexico, plus clothing from Spain and France, collectible bottles, toys, and shawls. The prices are reasonable, the service is friendly, and it's more homey than glammy—not as self-conscious as some of the other local boutiques. 3621 Baldwin Ave. ℰ 808/572-0249.

Holiday & Co.   Attractive women's clothing in natural fibers hangs from racks, while jewelry to go with it beckons from the counter. Recent finds include elegant fiber evening bags, luxurious bath gels, easygoing dresses and separates, Dansko clogs, shawls, soaps, aloha shirts, books, picture frames, and jewelry. 3681 Baldwin Ave. ℰ 808/572-1470.

Hot Island Glassblowing Studio & Gallery   You can watch the artist transform molten glass into works of art and utility in this studio at the Makawao Courtyard, where an award-winning family of glass blowers built its own furnaces. It's fascinating to watch the shapes emerge from glass melted at 2,300°F (1,260°C). The colorful works range from small paperweights to large vessels. Four to five artists participate in the demonstrations, which begin when the furnace is heated, about a half-hour before the studio opens at 9am. 3620 Baldwin Ave. ℰ 808/572-4527.

Hurricane   This boutique carries clothing, gifts, accessories, and books that are two steps ahead of the competition. Tommy Bahama aloha shirts and aloha print dresses; Sigrid Olsen's knitted shells, cardigans, and extraordinary silk tank dresses; hats; work by local artists; a notable selection of fragrances for men and women; and hard-to-find, eccentric books and home accessories are part of the Hurricane appeal. 3639 Baldwin Ave. ℰ 808/572-5076.

Maui Hands   Maui hands have made 90% of the items in this shop/gallery. Because it's a consignment shop, you'll find Hawaii-made handicrafts and prices that aren't inflated. The selection includes paintings, prints, jewelry, glass marbles, native-wood bowls, and tchotchkes for every budget. This is an ideal stop for made-on-Maui products and crafts of good quality. The original Maui Hands is in Makawao; another location can be found in Paia at 84 Hana Hwy. (ℰ 808/579-9245). At the Makawao Courtyard, 3620 Baldwin Ave. ℰ 808/572-5194.

The Mercantile   The jewelry, home accessories (especially the Tiffany-style glass-and-shell lamps), dinnerware, Italian linens, plantation-style furniture, and clothing here are a salute to the good life. There's exquisite bedding, rugs, hand-carved armoires, slipcovers, and a large selection of Kiehl's products. The clothing—comfortable cottons and upscale European linens—is for men and women, as are the soaps, which include Maui Herbal Soap products and some unusual finds from France. Maui-made jams, honey, soaps, ceramics, and Jurlique organic facial and body products are among the new winners. 3673 Baldwin Ave. ℰ 808/572-1407.

Sherri Reeve Gallery & Gifts   If you want to take a little bit of the beauty of Maui home with you, stop by this open-air gallery. Artist Sherri Reeve grew up in Hawaii (the local phone book featured her art on the cover one year), and she has captured the vibrant color and feel of the islands. You can find everything from inexpensive cards, hand-painted tiles, and T-shirts to original works and limited editions. 3669 Baldwin Ave. ℂ 808/572-8931. www.sreeve.com.

Tropo Tropo is a magnet for stylish, sensitive, *and* rugged men searching for tasteful aloha wear and comfortable basics. Books, clothing, Tilley hats, and Crabtree & Evelyn products are among the finds here. Men can shop for Tommy Bahama trousers and shorts, tasteful T-shirts, stylish winter wovens by Toes on the Nose, and aloha shirts by Reyn Spooner, Tori Richard, Que, and Kahala. 3643 Baldwin Ave. ℂ 808/573-0356.

Viewpoints Gallery Maui's only fine-arts cooperative showcases the work of 20 established artists in an airy, attractive gallery located in a restored theater with a courtyard, glass-blowing studio, and restaurants. The gallery features two-dimensional art, jewelry, fiber art, stained glass, paper, sculpture, and other media. This is a fine example of what can happen in a collectively supportive artistic environment. 3620 Baldwin Ave. ℂ 808/572-5979.

EDIBLES

Working folks in Makawao pick up spaghetti and lasagna, sandwiches, salads, and changing specials from the **Rodeo General Store,** 3661 Baldwin Ave. (ℂ **808/572-7841**). At the far end of the store is the oenophile's bonanza, a superior wine selection housed in its own temperature-controlled cave.

Down to Earth Natural Foods, 1169 Makawao Ave. (ℂ **808/572-1488**), always has fresh salads and sandwiches, a full section of organic produce (Kula onions, strawberry papayas, mangoes, and lychees in season), herbs, bulk grains, beauty aids, juices, snacks, tofu, seaweed, soy products, and aisles of vegetarian and health foods. Whether it's a smoothie or a salad, Down to Earth has fresh, healthful vegetarian offerings.

In the more than 6 decades that the **T. Komoda Store and Bakery,** 3674 Baldwin Ave. (ℂ **808/572-7261**), has spent in this spot, untold numbers have creaked over the wooden floors to pick up Komoda's famous cream puffs. Old-timers know to come early, before they're sold out. Then the cinnamon rolls, doughnuts, pies, and chocolate cake take over. Pastries are just the beginning: Poi, macadamia-nut candies and cookies, and small bunches of local fruit keep the customers coming.

FRESH FLOWERS IN KULA

Like anthuriums on the Big Island, proteas are a Maui trademark and an abundant crop on Haleakala's rich volcanic slopes. They also travel well, dry beautifully, and can be shipped worldwide with ease. Among Maui's most prominent sources is **Sunrise Protea** (ℂ 808/876-0200; www.sunriseprotea.com), in Kula. It offers a walk-through garden and gift shops, friendly service, and a larger-than-usual selection. Freshly cut flowers arrive from the fields on Tuesday and Friday afternoons. You can order individual blooms, baskets, arrangements, or wreaths for shipping all over the world. (Next door, the Sunrise Country Market offers fresh local fruits, snacks, and sandwiches, with picnic tables for lingering.)

Proteas of Hawaii (ℂ 808/878-2533; www.proteasofhawaii.com), another reliable source, offers regular walking tours of the University of Hawaii Extension Service gardens across the street in Kula.

Outside of Kula, the Saturday-morning **Maui Swap Meet** (p. 243) is among the best and least expensive places for tropical flowers of every stripe.

5 East Maui

ON THE ROAD TO HANA: PAIA

Biasa Rose Boutique   You'll find unusual gift items and clothing with a tropical flair here: capri pants in bark cloth, floating plumeria candles, retro fabrics, dinnerware, handbags and accessories, and stylish vintage-inspired clothes for kids. If the aloha shirts don't get you, the candles and handbags will. You can also custom-order clothing from a selection of washable rayons. 104 Hana Hwy. $\mathcal{C}$ 808/579-8602.

Hemp House   Clothing and accessories made of hemp, a sturdy, eco-friendly fiber, are finally making their way into the mainstream. The Hemp House has as complete a selection as you can expect to see in Hawaii, with "denim" hemp jeans, lightweight linenlike trousers, dresses, shirts, and a full range of sensible, easy-care wear. 16 Baldwin Ave. $\mathcal{C}$ 808/579-8880.

Maui Crafts Guild   The old wooden storefront at the gateway to Paia houses crafts of high quality and in all price ranges, from pit-fired raku to bowls of Norfolk pine and other Maui woods, fashioned by Maui hands. Artist-owned and -operated, the guild claims 25 members who live and work on Maui. Basketry, hand-painted fabrics, jewelry, beadwork, traditional Hawaiian stonework, pressed flowers, fused glass, stained glass, copper sculpture, banana-bark paintings, and pottery of all styles are displayed in the two-story gift gallery. Upstairs, sculptor Arthur Dennis Williams shows his breathtaking work in wood, bronze, and stone. Everything can be shipped. **Aloha Bead Co.** ($\mathcal{C}$ **808/579-9709**), in the back of the gallery, is a treasure trove for bead workers. 43 Hana Hwy. $\mathcal{C}$ 808/579-9697. www.mauicraftsguild.com.

Moonbow Tropics   If you're looking for a tasteful aloha shirt, go to Moonbow. The selection consists of a few carefully culled racks of the top labels in aloha wear, in fabrics ranging from the finest silks and linens to Egyptian cotton and spun rayons. Some of the finds: aloha shirts by Tori Richard, Reyn Spooner, Kamehameha, Paradise Found, Kahala, Tommy Bahama, and other top brands. Silk pants, silk shorts, vintage-print neckwear, and an upgraded women's selection hang on colorful racks. The jewelry pieces, ranging from tanzanite to topaz, rubies to moonstones, are mounted in unique settings made on site. 36 Baldwin Ave. $\mathcal{C}$ 808/579-8592. www.moonbowtropics.com.

HANA

Hana Coast Gallery *(Finds)*   This gallery is a good reason to go to Hana: It's an aesthetic and cultural experience that informs as it enlightens. Tucked away in the posh Hotel Hana-Maui, the gallery is known for its high level of curatorship and commitment to the cultural art of Hawaii. There are no jumping whales or dolphins here, and except for a section of European and Asian masters, the 3,000-square-foot gallery is devoted entirely to Hawaii artists, whose sculptures, paintings, prints, feather work, stonework, and carvings are featured in displays that are so natural, they could well exist in someone's home. In response to the ongoing revival of the American Crafts Movement, director-curator Patrick Robinson (of impeccable artistic integrity) has expanded the selection of koa-wood furniture with a Hawaiian/Japanese influence. Stellar artists Tai Lake from the Big Island and Randall Watkins from Maui are among those represented. Connoisseurs of hand-turned bowls will find the crème de la crème of the genre here: J. Kelly Dunn, Ron Kent, Todd Campbell, Ed Perrira, and Gary Stevens. You won't find a better selection elsewhere under one roof. The award-winning gallery has won accolades from the top travel and arts magazines in the country and has steered clear of trendiness and unfortunate tastes. At the Hotel Hana-Maui. © **808/248-8636**. www. hanacoast.com.

Hasegawa General Store Established in 1910, immortalized in song since 1961, burned to the ground in 1990, and back in business in 1991, this legendary store is indefatigable and more colorful than ever in its fourth generation in business. The aisles are choked with merchandise: coffee specially roasted and blended for the store, Ono Farms organic dried fruit, fishing equipment, every tape and CD that mentions Hana, the best books on Hana to be found, T-shirts, beach and garden essentials, baseball caps, film, baby food, napkins, and other necessities for the Hana life. Hana Hwy. © **808/248-8231**.

10

Maui After Dark

Centered around the $32-million **Maui Arts & Cultural Center (MACC)**, in Kahului (© **808/242-7469;** www.maui arts.org), the performing arts are alive and well on this island. The MACC remains the island's most prestigious entertainment venue, a first-class center for the visual and performing arts. Bonnie Raitt has performed here, as have Hiroshima, Pearl Jam, Ziggy Marley, Tony Bennett, the American Indian Dance Theatre, the Maui Symphony Orchestra, and Jonny Lang, not to mention the finest in local talent. The center boasts a visual-arts gallery, an outdoor amphitheater, offices, rehearsal space, a 300-seat theater for experimental performances, and a 1,200-seat main theater. The center's activities are well publicized locally, so check the *Maui News* or ask your hotel concierge what's going on during your visit.

IN SEARCH OF HAWAIIAN, JAWAIIAN & MORE

Nightlife options on this island are limited. Revelers generally head for **Casanova** in Makawao and **Maui Brews** in Lahaina. Because they are in different parts of this spread-out island, you'll either have to drive a great distance to these clubs or explore what's happening in the major hotels near you. The hotels generally have lobby lounges offering Hawaiian music, soft jazz, or hula shows beginning at sunset.

HAWAIIAN MUSIC The best of Hawaiian music can be heard every Wednesday night at 7:30pm at the Napili Kai Beach Resort's indoor amphitheater, thanks to the Grammy-winning **Masters of Hawaiian Slack Key Guitar Concert Series** (© **888/ 669-3858;** www.slackkey.com). The weekly shows present a side of Hawaii that few visitors ever get to see. Host George Kahumoku, Jr., introduces a new slack-key master every week. Not only is there incredible Hawaiian music and singing, but George and his guest also "talk story" about old Hawaii, music, and Hawaiian culture. Not to be missed. Tickets are $47.

AT THE MOVIES

The 12-screen movie megaplex at the **Maui Mall,** 70 E. Kaahumanu Ave. (© **808/ 249-2222),** in Kahului, features current releases. In June, the not-to-be-missed **Maui Film Festival** ⟨⟨⟨ (© **808/572-3456** or 579-9244; www.mauifilmfestival.com) puts on nights of cinema under the stars in Wailea (see "The Best Place in the World to See a Movie," below). The Maui Film Festival also presents "Academy House" films for the avant-garde, ultrahip movie buff Wednesday nights at the **Maui Arts & Cultural Center,** 1 Cameron Way (just off Kahului Beach Rd.), Kahului, usually followed by live music and poetry readings.

Film buffs can check the local newspapers to see what's playing at the other theaters around the island (or go to www.mauigateway.com/~rw/movie): the **Kaahumanu Theatres,** at the Kaahumanu Center, in Kahului (© **808/873-3133);** the **Kukui Mall**

Moments The Best Place in the World to See a Movie

Imagine lounging on a comfy beach chair on the island of Maui watching the stars come out in the night sky. As soon as it gets dark enough, the biggest outdoor screen you've ever seen comes to life with a film premiere. This has to be the best place in the entire world to watch movies.

If you're headed to Maui in June, plan your travel dates around the **Maui Film Festival** (© **808/572-3456** or 579-9244; www.mauifilmfestival.com), which always starts the Wednesday before Father's Day. This is an event you won't want to miss. The 5-day festival features nightly films in the "Celestial Cinema," an under-the-stars, open-air "outdoor theater" on the Wailea Golf Course. The event features premieres and special advance screenings on a 50-foot-wide screen in Dolby Digital Surround Sound. Festival organizer and film producer Barry Rivers selects "life-affirming" films that often become box-office hits.

In addition to the 5 days and nights of films, film workshops, and filmmaker panels, there's also terrific food: a Taste of Chocolate night, a Taste of Wailea (with Maui's top chefs creating exquisite culinary masterpieces), and a host of other foodie events. For the family, there's a Father's Day concert of contemporary Hawaiian music, a sand-sculpture contest, and picnics. And for those interested in Hawaii culture, the festival presents TheStar Show, where live images of celestial objects are projected onto the screen, as experts in Polynesian astronomy and cultural history take the audience on a tour of the night sky and Polynesian navigational lore.

As Rivers puts it: "Rising stars, shooting stars, movie stars, all under the stars."

Theater, 1819 S. Kihei Rd., in Kihei (© **808/244-8934**); the Wallace Theaters at the **Wharf Cinema Center,** 658 Front St., in Lahaina (© **808/249-2222**); and the **Front Street Theatres** at the Lahaina Center, 900 Front St. (© **808/249-2222**).

AT THE THEATER

It's not Broadway, but Maui does have live community theater at the **Iao Theater,** 68 N. Market St., in Wailuku (© **808/244-8680** or 242-6969 for the box office and program information; www.mauionstage.com). Shows range from locally written productions to well-known plays and musicals.

1 West Maui: Lahaina, Kaanapali & Kapalua

Maui Brews, 900 Front St., Lahaina (© **808/667-7794**), draws the late-night crowd to its corner of the Lahaina Center with swing, salsa, reggae, and jams. There's live music Friday and Monday nights. Hours are daily from 11:30am, with happy hour from 3 to 6pm and nightclub hours from 9pm to 1:30am.

At **Longhi's,** 888 Front St., Lahaina (© **808/667-2288**), live music spills out into the streets from 9:30pm on weekends (with a cover of $5). It's usually salsa or jazz, but call ahead to confirm. Other special gigs can be expected if rock 'n' rollers or jazz musicians

Moments It Begins with Sunset . . .

Nightlife in Maui begins at sunset, when all eyes turn westward to see how the day will end. And what better way to take it all in than over cocktails? With its view of Molokai to the northwest and Lanai to the west, Kaanapali and west Maui boast panoramic vistas unique to this island. In south Maui's resort areas of Wailea and Makena, tiny Kahoolawe and the crescent-shaped Molokini islet are visible on the horizon, and the West Maui Mountains look like an entirely separate island. No matter what your vantage point, you are likely to be treated to an astonishing view.

In Kaanapali, park at Whalers Village and head for **Leilani's on the Beach** (© 808/661-4495) or **Hula Grill** (© 808/667-6636), next to each other on the beach. Both have busy, upbeat bars and tables bordering the sand. These are happy places for great people-watching, gazing over at Lanai, and enjoying mai tais and margaritas. Hula Grill's Barefoot Bar appetizer menu is a cut above. Leilani's has live music Friday through Sunday from 2:30 to 5pm, while at Hula Grill the happy hour starts at 3pm, with live music from 3 to 5pm and hula at 8pm.

Now, Lahaina: It's a sunset-lover's nirvana, lined with restaurants that have elevated mai tais to an art form. If you love loud rock, head for **Cheeseburger in Paradise** (© 808/661-4855). A few doors away, the **Lahaina Fish Company** (© 808/661-3472) and **Kimo's** (© 808/661-4811) are magnets all day long and especially at sunset, when their open decks fill up with revelers.

At the southern end of Lahaina, in the 505 Front Street complex, **Pacific'O** (© 808/667-4341) is a solid hit, with a raised bar, seating on the ocean, and a backdrop of Lanai across the channel. A few steps away, sister restaurant **I'O** shares the same vista, with an appetizer menu and a curved bar that will wow you as much as the drop-dead-gorgeous view.

who are friends of the owner happen to be passing through. There's usually a DJ on Friday nights.

The **Hard Rock Cafe,** 900 Front St., Lahaina (© **808/667-7400**), occasionally offers live music, so it wouldn't hurt to call to see if something's up. Usually it features mainland bands, normally on weekends after 10pm. Cover ranges from $3 to $5.

You won't have to ask what's going on at **Cheeseburger in Paradise,** 811 Front St., Lahaina (© **808/661-4855**), the two-story green-and-white building at the corner of Front and Lahainaluna streets. Just go outside and you'll hear it. Loud, live tropical rock blasts into the streets and out to sea nightly from 4:30 to 11pm (no cover).

Other venues for music in west Maui include the following:

- **B.J.'s Chicago Pizzeria,** 730 Front St., Lahaina (© **808/661-0700**), offers live music from 7:30 to 10pm every night.
- **Cool Cat Café,** 658 Front St., Lahaina (© **808/667-0909**), features live music Tuesday, Thursday, and Saturday from 2 to 4:30pm and 6:30 to 10pm.
- **Hula Grill,** in Whalers Village, Kaanapali (© **808/667-6636**), has live music (usually Hawaiian) from 3 to 5pm and again from 6:30 to 9pm nightly.

In Wailea, the restaurants at the Shops at Wailea, including the highly successful **Tommy Bahama** (© 808/875-9983) and **Longhi's** (© 808/891-8883), are noteworthy additions to the beachfront retail-and-dining scene. **Ferraro's** and **Spago** (© 808/874-8000), both at the neighboring Four Seasons Resort Wailea, have great sunset views to go with their Italian and Pacific Rim menus. Farther south, in Makena, you can't beat the Maui Prince's **Molokini Lounge** (© 808/874-1111), with its casual elegance and unequaled vista of Molokini islet on the ocean side and, on the mauka side, a graceful, serene courtyard with ponds, rock gardens, and lush foliage. Adding to the setting is the appetizer menu, which comes from the esteemed Prince Court kitchen. From 5 to 9:30pm nightly, the *pupu* menu features a Molokini sampler platter for two: honey-glazed baby back ribs, chicken yakitori, and shrimp and crab spring rolls. Live Hawaiian entertainment runs nightly from 6 to 10:30pm, beginning with a mini hula show at 6pm on Monday, Wednesday, and Friday, followed by contemporary Hawaiian music until 10:30pm. Ron Kuala'au plays Sunday, Tuesday, and Thursday; Mele Ohana plays Monday, Wednesday, Friday, and Saturday.

Don't forget the upcountry view: **Kula Lodge** (© 808/878-2517) has a phenomenal one that takes in central Maui, the West Maui Mountains (looking like Shangri-La in the distance), and the coastline. From 3:30 to 5pm, the appetizers-only menu includes everything from Maui onion soup to a host of gourmet salads (the farmers are a stone's throw away), plus pot stickers, summer rolls, seared ahi, and crab cakes. Dinner begins at 5pm, so you can take in the sunset over Cajun ahi, New York steak, and other country-comfort fare.

- **Kimo's,** 845 Front St., Lahaina (© 808/661-4811), has live musicians at various times; call for details.
- **Leilani's on the Beach,** in Whalers Village, Kaanapali (© 808/661-4495), has live music from 4 to 6pm Wednesday through Sunday; the styles range from contemporary Hawaiian to rock.
- **Maui Brewing Co.,** in the Kahana Gateway Shopping Center, Kahana (© 808/669-3474), has live music nightly from 6:30 to 8:30pm (6–9pm in summer).
- **Moose McGillycuddy's,** 844 Front St., Lahaina (© 808/667-7758), offers a DJ some nights from 5:30 to 8:30pm; the schedule varies, so call for details.
- **Pacific'O,** 505 Front St., Lahaina (© 808/667-4341), offers live jazz Friday and Saturday from 9pm to midnight.
- **Paradise Bluz,** 744 Front St., Lahaina (© 808/667-5299), features live music or a DJ every night from 9pm to 2am. Look for special guests like Willie K.
- **Pineapple Grill,** 200 Kapalua Dr., Kapalua (© 808/669-9600), features Hawaiian music on Friday and jazz on Saturday from 7 to 10pm.

- **Pioneer Inn,** 658 Wharf St., Lahaina (✆ **808/661-3636**), offers a variety of live music every night starting at 6pm.
- **Sansei Seafood Restaurant & Sushi Bar,** 600 Office Rd., Kapalua (✆ **808/669-6286**), has karaoke on Thursday and Friday from 10pm to 1am.
- **Sea House Restaurant,** at the Napili Kai Beach Resort, Napili (✆ **808/669-1500**), has live music from 7 to 9pm Wednesday through Monday and a Polynesian dinner show on Tuesday.
- **Spats,** at the Hyatt Regency Maui Resort, Kaanapali (✆ **808/661-1234**), has dancing to a DJ on Saturday from 10pm to 3am.
- **Tropica,** at the Westin Maui Resort, Kaanapali (✆ **808/667-2525**), offers nightly music (call for times).

A NIGHT TO REMEMBER: LUAU, MAUI STYLE

Most of the larger hotels in Maui's major resorts offer luau on a regular basis. You'll pay about $65 to $75 to attend one. Don't expect it to be a homegrown affair prepared in the traditional Hawaiian way. There are, however, commercial luau that capture the romance and spirit of the luau with quality food and entertainment in outdoor settings.

Maui's best choice is indisputably the nightly **Old Lahaina Luau** (✆ **800/248-5828** or 808/667-1998; www.oldlahainaluau.com). On its 1-acre site just ocean side of the Lahaina Cannery, at 1251 Front St., the Old Lahaina Luau maintains its high standards in food and entertainment in a peerless oceanfront setting. Local craftspeople display their wares only a few feet from the water. Seating is provided on lauhala mats for those who wish to dine as the traditional Hawaiians did, but there are tables for everyone else. There's no fire dancing in the program, but you won't miss it (for that, go to the **Feast at Lele,** p. 146). This luau offers a healthy balance of entertainment, showmanship, authentic high-quality food, educational value, and sheer romantic beauty. (No watered-down mai tais, either; these are the real thing.)

The luau begins at sunset and features Tahitian and Hawaiian entertainment, including various forms of hula and an intelligent narrative on the dance's rocky course of survival into modern times. The entertainment is riveting, even for jaded locals. The food, served from an open-air thatched structure, is as much Pacific Rim as authentically Hawaiian: *imu*-roasted kalua pig, baked mahimahi in Maui-onion cream sauce, guava chicken, teriyaki sirloin steak, lomi salmon, poi, dried fish, poke, Hawaiian sweet potato, sautéed vegetables, seafood salad, and the ultimate taste treat, taro leaves with coconut milk. The cost is $96 for adults, $65 for children 12 and under.

ULALENA: HULA, MYTH & MODERN DANCE

The buzz in Lahaina is all about **Ulalena** ⭐, Maui Theatre, 878 Front St., Lahaina (✆ **877/688-4800** or 808/661-9913; www.ulalena.com), a riveting evening of entertainment that weaves Hawaiian mythology with drama, dance, and state-of-the-art multimedia capabilities in a brand-new multimillion-dollar theater. Polynesian dance, original music, acrobatics, and chant, performed by a local and international cast, combine to create an evocative experience that often leaves the audience speechless. It's interactive, with dancers coming down the aisles, drummers and musicians in surprising corners, and mind-boggling stage and lighting effects that draw the audience in. Some special moments: the goddesses dancing on the moon, the white sail of the first Europeans, the wrath of the volcano goddess Pele, the labors of the field-worker immigrants. The story unfolds seamlessly; at the end, you'll be shocked to realize that not a single word of dialogue was spoken. Performances are held Monday through Friday at 6:30pm. Tickets are $60 to $100 for adults, $40 to $70 for children 12 and under.

MAUI-STYLE MAGIC

A very different type of live entertainment is **Warren & Annabelle's,** 900 Front St., Lahaina (© **808/667-6244;** www.warrenandannabelles.com), a magic/comedy cocktail show with illusionist Warren Gibson and "Annabelle," a ghost from the 1800s who plays the grand piano (even taking requests from the audience) as Warren dazzles you with his sleight-of-hand magic. Appetizers, desserts, and cocktails are available (either as a package or a la carte). Check-in is at 5 and 7:30pm. The show-only price is $56; the show plus gourmet appetizers and dessert costs $95. You must be 21 to attend, although occasionally (generally during major school holidays) there is a 4pm family show (minimum age 6) without food or cocktails; call for details.

The **Kaanapali Beach Hotel** has a wonderful show called **Kupanaha** (© **808/661-0011;** www.kbhmaui.com/recreation/kupanaha.html) that is perfect for the entire family. It features the renowned magicians Jody and Kathleen Baran and their entire family, including child-prodigy magicians Katrina and Crystal. The dinner show includes magic, illusions, and the story of the Hawaii fire goddess, Pele, presented through hula and chant performed by the children of the Kano'eau Dance Academy. The shows are Tuesday through Saturday; tickets are $89 to $99 for adults, $57 for ages 13 to 20, and $41 for children 6 to 12. Prices include dinner (entree choices include Island fish, roasted stuffed chicken, steak and shrimp, and a vegetarian dish, with a children's menu available).

2 South Maui: Kihei-Wailea

The Kihei, Wailea, and Maalaea areas in south Maui also feature music in a variety of locations:

- **Bocalino,** 1279 S. Kihei Rd., Kihei (© **808/874-9299**), has live music Monday through Saturday starting at 10pm.
- **Capischi,** at the Diamond Resort, 555 Kaukahi St., Wailea (© **808/879-2224**), has live music Friday and Saturday from 7 to 10pm.
- **Henry's Bar & Grill,** 41 E. Lipoa St., Kihei (© **808/879-2849**), offers live music Thursday through Saturday from 9pm to midnight.
- **Kahale's Beach Club,** 36 Keala Place, Kihei (© **808/875-7711**), offers a potpourri of live music nightly; call for details.
- **Life's a Beach,** 1913 S. Kihei Rd., Kihei (© **808/891-8010**), has nightly live music; call for times.
- **Lobby Lounge,** at the Four Seasons Resort Maui at Wailea (© **808/874-8000**), features nightly live music from 8:30 to 11:30pm.

Hana Nightlife

Nightlife in Hana is pretty sparse. The only exception is the **Hotel Hana-Maui** (© **808/248-8211**), which features Hawaiian music in the Paniolo Lounge Saturday through Monday from 6:30 to 9:30pm, and hosts a dinner hula show every Friday from 7 to 7:45pm in the Main Dining Room.

Watch for the Green Flash

If you're gathered in a crowd on Maui watching a sunset, you may hear someone call out: "Green flash!" If you're lucky, you may get to see it yourself.

The romantic version of the story is the green flash happens when the sun kisses the ocean good night (honeymooners love this version). The scientific version is not quite as dreamy: Light bends as it goes around the curve of the earth. When the sun dips beneath the horizon, it is at the far end of the spectrum. So this refraction of the sunset on the horizon, causes only the color green to be seen in the color spectrum just before the light disappears.

Here's how to view the green flash: First, it has to be a clear day, with no clouds or haze on the horizon. Second, the sun has to set on the ocean (if it sets behind an island, you won't see the flash). Keep checking the sun as it drops (try not to look directly into the sun; just glance at it to assess its position). If the conditions are ideal, just as the sun drops into the blue water, a "flash" or laserlike beam of green will appear to shoot out for an instant.

- **Lulu's,** 1945 S. Kihei Rd., Kihei (© **808/879-9944**), offers entertainment starting at 8pm: karaoke on Wednesday, live music Thursday through Sunday.
- **Maalaea Grill,** in Maalaea Harbor Village, Maalaea (© **808/243-2206**), features live music Thursday to Saturday from 6:30 to 9pm.
- **Mulligan's on the Blue,** 100 Kaukahi St., Wailea (© **808/874-1131**), has live music starting at 9pm Friday and Saturday.
- **Sansei Seafood Restaurant & Sushi Bar,** in Kihei Town Center (© **808/879-0004**), has karaoke Thursday through Saturday from 10pm to 1am.
- **South Shore Tiki Lounge,** 1913 S. Kihei Rd., Kihei (© **808/874-6444**), has live Hawaiian music daily from 4 to 6pm, and dancing from 10pm to 2am.
- **Sports Page Bar,** 2411 S. Kihei Rd., Kihei (© **808/879-0602**), has live music Monday through Saturday starting at 9pm.
- **Yorman's by the Sea,** 760 S. Kihei Rd., Kihei (© **808/874-8385**), generally features jazz Wednesday through Sunday from 6:30pm onward.

3 Upcountry Maui

Upcountry in Makawao, the party never ends at **Casanova,** 1188 Makawao Ave. (© **808/572-0220**), the popular Italian ristorante where the good times roll with the pasta. The newly renovated bar area has large booths, all the better for socializing around the stage and dance floor. If a big-name mainland band is resting up on Maui following a sold-out concert on Oahu, you may find its members setting up for an impromptu night here. DJs take over on Wednesday (ladies' night); on Thursday, Friday, and Saturday, live entertainment draws fun-lovers from even the most remote reaches of the island. Entertainment starts at 9:45pm and continues to 1:30am. Expect good blues, rock 'n' roll, reggae, jazz, Hawaiian, and the top names in local and visiting entertainment. Elvin Bishop, the local duo Hapa, Los Lobos, and many others have taken Casanova's stage. The cover is usually $5. Go Sunday afternoons, from 3 to 6pm, for excellent live jazz.

Another place for live music in the upcountry area is the **Stopwatch Sports Bar,** 1127 Makawao Ave. (© **808/572-1380**), which has live music from 9pm on Friday and Saturday.

4 Paia & Central Maui

In central Maui, **Café Marc Aurel,** 28 N. Market St., Wailuku (© **808/244-0852**), is the place for a range of eclectic music, from folk to Hawaiian to ethnic, and even some open-mic nights; call for information. The **Kahului Ale House,** 355 E. Kamehameha Ave., Kahului (© **808/877-9001**), features karaoke on Sunday, Monday, and Wednesday (10pm–2am); live music on Thursday and Friday (call for times); and a DJ on Saturday from 10pm. At **Sushi Go!,** in the Queen Kaahumanu Center, Kahului (© **808/877-8744**), there's live music Wednesday, Friday, and Saturday. **Mañana Garage,** 33 Lono Ave., Kahului (© **808/873-0220**), has live music Monday and Saturday from 6:30pm and DJs Wednesday and Friday. There's a $10 cover on DJ nights.

In Paia, **Charley's Restaurant,** 142 Hana Hwy. (© **808/579-9453**), features an eclectic selection of music from country and western (Willie Nelson has been seen sitting in) to fusion/reggae to rock 'n' roll; call for details. Also in Paia, the **Moana Bakery & Cafe,** 71 Baldwin Ave. (© **808/579-9999**), has everything from Hawaiian music to cool jazz to sizzling Latin; call for details.

11

Molokai, the Most Hawaiian Isle

Born of volcanic eruptions 1.5 million years ago, Molokai remains a time capsule on the dawn of the 21st century. It has no deluxe resorts, no stoplights, and no buildings taller than a coconut tree. Molokai is the least developed, most "Hawaiian" of all the islands, making it especially attractive to adventure travelers and peace seekers.

Molokai lives up to its reputation as the most Hawaiian place chiefly through its lineage; there are more people here of Hawaiian blood than anywhere else. This slipper-shaped island was birthplace of hula and the ancient science of aquaculture. An aura of ancient mysticism clings to the land here, and the old ways still govern life. The residents survive by taking fish from the sea and hunting wild pigs and axis deer on the range. Some folks still catch fish for dinner by throwing nets and trolling the reef.

Modern Hawaii's high-rise hotels, shopping centers, and other trappings of tourism haven't been able to gain a foothold here. The lone low-rise resort on the island, Kaluakoi—built 30 years ago, now closed and empty—was Molokai's token attempt at contemporary tourism. The only new developments since Kaluakoi were the Molokai Ranch's eco-tourism project of upscale camping in semipermanent "tentalows" (a combination of a bungalow and a tent) and a 22-room lodge on the 65,000-acre ranch—both of which closed in 2008 when the Molokai Ranch shut down all operations.

Not everyone will love Molokai. The slow-paced, simple life of the people and the absence of contemporary landmarks attract those in search of the "real" Hawaii. I once received a letter from a New York City resident who claimed that any "big-city resident" would "blanche" at the lack of "sophistication." But that is exactly the charm of Molokai. This is a place where Mother Nature is wild and uninhibited, with very little intrusion by man. Forget sophistication; this is one of the few spots on the planet where one can stand in awe of the island's diverse natural wonders: Hawaii's highest waterfall and greatest collection of fishponds; the world's tallest sea cliffs; sand dunes, coral reefs, rainforests, and hidden coves; and gloriously empty beaches.

EXPLORING THE "MOST HAWAIIAN" ISLE   Only 38 miles from end to end and just 10 miles wide, Molokai stands like a big green wedge in the blue Pacific. It has an east side, a west side, a backside, and a topside. This long, narrow island is like yin and yang: One side is a flat, austere, arid desert; the other is a lush, green, tropical Eden. Three volcanic eruptions formed Molokai; the last produced the island's "thumb"—a peninsula jutting out of the steep cliffs of the north shore like a punctuation mark on the island's geological story.

On the red-dirt southern plain, where most of the island's 7,000 residents live,

Molokai

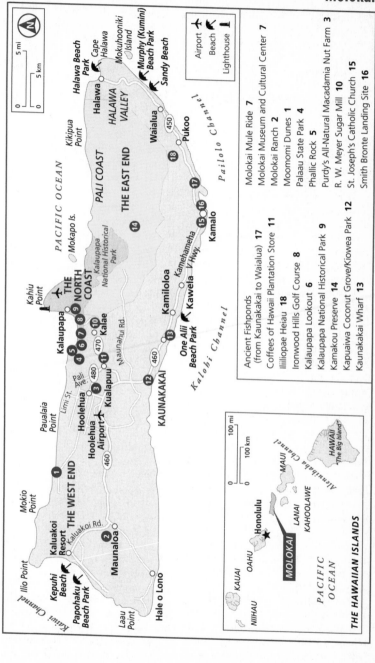

Legend:
- ✈ Airport
- ✈ Beach
- ▮ Lighthouse

Ancient Fishponds (from Kaunakakai to Waialua) **17**
Coffees of Hawaii Plantation Store **11**
Iliiliopae Heiau **18**
Ironwood Hills Golf Course **8**
Kalaupapa Lookout **6**
Kalaupapa National Historical Park **9**
Kamakou Preserve **14**
Kapuaiwa Coconut Grove/Kiowea Park **12**
Kaunakakai Wharf **13**

Molokai Mule Ride **7**
Molokai Museum and Cultural Center **7**
Molokai Ranch **2**
Moomomi Dunes **1**
Palaau State Park **4**
Phallic Rock **5**
Purdy's All-Natural Macadamia Nut Farm **3**
R. W. Meyer Sugar Mill **10**
St. Joseph's Catholic Church **15**
Smith Bronte Landing Site **16**

THE HAWAIIAN ISLANDS

the rustic village of **Kaunakakai** 🐾 looks like the set of an old Hollywood Western, with sun-faded clapboard houses and horses tethered on the side of the road. Mile marker 0, in the center of town, divides the island into east and west.

Eastbound, along the **coastal highway** 🐾🐾🐾 named for King Kamehameha V, are Gauguin-like, palm-shaded cottages set on small coves or near fishponds; spectacular vistas that take in Maui, Lanai, and Kahoolawe; and a fringing coral reef visible through the crystal-clear waves.

Out on the sun-scorched West End, overlooking a gold-sand beach with water usually too rough to swim in, is the island's lone destination resort, **Kaluakoi** (where the hotel is currently closed). The old hilltop plantation town of **Maunaloa** is now a ghost town ever since the Molokai Ranch closed down the expensive lodge and its pricey dining room. Cowboys no longer ride the range on **Molokai Ranch,** a 60,000-acre spread, which was closed in 2008 along with the ranch's accommodations and outdoor-recreation activities.

Elsewhere around the island, in hamlets like **Kualapuu,** old farmhouses with pickup trucks in the yards and sleepy dogs under the shade trees stand amid row crops of papaya, coffee, and corn—just like farm towns in Anywhere, U.S.A.

But that's not all there is. The "backside" of Molokai is a rugged wilderness of spectacular beauty. On the outskirts of **Kaunakakai,** the land rises gradually from sea-level fishponds to cool uplands and the Molokai Forest, long ago stripped of sandalwood for the China trade. All that remains is an indentation in the earth shaped like a ship's hull, a crude matrix that gave them a rough idea of when they'd cut enough sandalwood to fill a ship (it's identified on good maps as *Luanamokuiliahi,* or Sandalwood Boat).

The land inclines sharply to the lofty mountains and the nearly mile-high summit of Mount Kamakou, and then ends abruptly with emerald-green cliffs, which plunge into a lurid aquamarine sea dotted with tiny deserted islets. These breathtaking 3,250-foot **sea cliffs** 🐾🐾, the highest in the world, stretch 14 majestic miles along Molokai's north shore, laced by waterfalls and creased by five valleys once occupied by early Hawaiians who built stone terraces and used waterfalls to irrigate taro patches.

Long after the sea cliffs were formed, a tiny volcano erupted out of the sea at their feet and spread lava into a flat, leaflike peninsula called **Kalaupapa** 🐾🐾🐾—the 1860s leper exile where Father Damien de Veuster of Belgium devoted his life to care for the afflicted. A few people remain in the remote colony by choice, keeping it tidy for visitors.

WHAT A VISIT TO MOLOKAI IS REALLY LIKE   There's plenty of aloha on Molokai, but the so-called "friendly island" remains ambivalent about vacationers. One of the least visited Hawaiian islands, Molokai welcomes about 80,000 visitors annually on its own take-it-or-leave-it terms; it never wanted to attract too big of a crowd, anyway. A sign at the airport offers the first clue: SLOW DOWN, YOU ON MOLOKAI NOW—wisdom to heed on this island, where life proceeds at its own pace.

Rugged, red-dirt Molokai isn't for everyone, but those who like to explore remote places and seek their own adventures should love it. The best of the island can be seen only on foot, bicycle, mule, horseback, kayak, or boat. The sea cliffs are accessible only by sea in summer (when the Pacific is calm) or via a 10-mile trek through the Wailau Valley—an adventure only a handful of hardy hikers attempt each year. The great **Kamakou Preserve** is open just once a month, by special arrangement with the Nature Conservancy. Even **Moomomi,** which holds bony relics of prehistoric flightless birds and other creatures, requires a guide to divulge the secrets of the dunes.

Those in search of nightlife have come to the wrong place; Molokai shuts down after sunset. The only public diversions are softball games under the lights of Mitchell Pauole Field, movies at Maunaloa, and the few restaurants that stay open after dark, often serving local brew and pizza.

The "friendly" island may enchant you as the "real" Hawaii of your dreams. On the other hand, you may leave shaking your head, never to return. Regardless of how you approach Molokai, remember my advice: Take it slow.

1 Orientation

ARRIVING

BY PLANE Molokai has two airports, but you'll most likely fly into **Hoolehua Airport,** which everyone just calls the Molokai Airport. It's on a dusty plain about 6 miles from Kaunakakai town. Twin-engine planes offer daily service.

PW Express (© **888/866-5022** or 808/873-0877; www.pacificwings.com/pw express) has eight daily nonstop flights between Molokai and Honolulu (Oahu), and three daily flights between Molokai and Kahului (Maui). **go!Express** (© **888/I-FLY-GO-2** [435-9462]; www.iflygo.com) provides service from Kona (Big Island), Kahului (Maui), and Honolulu (Oahu) to Molokai. Currently, go!Express offers the best rates and deals among Hawaii's air carriers.

In general, go!Express and PW Express flights are substantially cheaper than those on the twin-engine planes flown by **Island Air** (© **800/323-3345** from the mainland, or 652-6541 interisland; www.islandair.com), with 8 to 10 flights a day from Honolulu. I must warn you that I have gotten less than sterling service from Island Air, which has left me stranded midroute—not once, but twice!

George's Aviation (© **866/834-2120,** 808/834-2120 from Honolulu, or 808/ 893-2120 from Maui; www.georgesaviation.com) has commuter flights on Monday, Friday, and Sunday from Honolulu and Maui to Molokai.

BY BOAT You can travel by ferry from Maui's Lahaina Harbor to Molokai's Kaunakakai Wharf on the *Molokai Princess* (© **800/275-6969** or 808/667-6165; www.mauiprincess.com). The 100-foot, 149-passenger yacht is fitted with the latest generation of gyroscopic stabilizers, making the ride smoother. It makes the 90-minute journey from Lahaina to Kaunakakai daily; the round-trip costs $85 for adults and $43 for children 3 to 12. Or you can choose to tour the island on one of two different package options: Cruise-Drive, which includes round-trip passage and a rental car for $191 for the driver, $76 per additional adult passenger, and $38 per child; or the Alii Tour, a guided tour in an air-conditioned van for $191 per adult and $134 per child, including lunch.

VISITOR INFORMATION

Contact the **Molokai Visitors Association,** P.O. Box 960, Kaunakakai, HI 96748 (© **800/800-6367** from the U.S. mainland and Canada, 800/553-0404 interisland, or 808/553-3876; www.molokai-hawaii.com), or stop by its office in the Moore Center, 2 Kamoi St., Suite 200, Kaunakakai. The staff can give you all the information you need on what to see and do while you're on Molokai.

THE ISLAND IN BRIEF

Kaunakakai 𝒦

Kaunakakai is the closest thing Molokai has to a business district, where dusty vehicles—mostly pickup trucks—park diagonally along Ala Malama Street. Friendly Isle Realty and Friendly Isle Travel offer islanders dream homes and vacations; Rabang's Filipino Food posts bad checks in the window; antlered deer-head trophies guard the grocery aisles at Misaki's Market; and Kanemitsu's, the town's legendary bakery, churns out fresh loaves of onion-cheese bread daily.

Kaunakakai was the royal summer residence of King Kamehameha V. The port town bustled when pineapple and sugar were king, but those days are gone. With its Old West–style storefronts laid out in a 3-block grid on a flat, dusty plain, Kaunakakai is a town from the past. At the end of Wharf Road is Molokai Wharf, a picturesque place to fish, photograph, and just hang out.

Kaunakakai is the dividing point between the lush, green East End and the dry, arid West End. On the west side of town stands a cactus, while on the east side of town there's thick, green vegetation.

The North Coast 𝒦𝒦

Upland from Kaunakakai, the land tilts skyward and turns green, with scented plumeria in yards and glossy coffee trees all in a row, until it blooms into a true forest—and then abruptly ends at a great precipice, falling 3,250 feet to the sea. The green sea cliffs are creased with five V-shaped crevices so deep that light is seldom seen (to paraphrase a Hawaiian poet). The north coast is a remote, forbidding place, with a solitary peninsula—**Kalaupapa** 𝒦𝒦𝒦—that was once the home for exiled lepers (it's now a national historical park). This region is easy on the eyes

but difficult to visit. It lies at a cool elevation, and frequent rain squalls blow in from the ocean. In summer, the ocean is calm, providing great opportunities for kayaking, fishing, and swimming, but during the rest of the year, giant waves come rolling onto the shores.

The West End 𝒦

This end of the island, once home to **Molokai Ranch,** is miles of stark desert terrain, bordered by the most beautiful white-sand beaches in Hawaii. The rugged rolling land slopes down to Molokai's only destination resort, **Kaluakoi,** a cul-de-sac of condos clustered around a 3-decades-old seafront hotel (which closed in 2001 and was still closed when we went to press) near 3-mile-long Papohaku, the island's biggest beach. On the way to Kaluakoi, you'll see **Maunaloa,** a 1920s-era pineapple-plantation town that's now a ghost town since the Molokai Ranch closed all of its operations in 2008, including the upscale lodge, a triplex theater, restaurants, and some shops. The West End is dry, dry, dry. It hardly ever rains, but when it does (usually in the winter), expect a downpour and lots of red mud.

The East End 𝒦𝒦𝒦

The area east of Kaunakakai becomes lush, green, and tropical, with golden pocket beaches and a handful of cottages and condos that are popular with thrifty travelers. With this voluptuous landscape comes rain. However, most storms are brief (15-min.) affairs. Winter is Hawaii's rainy season, so expect more rain from January to March, but even then, the storms are usually brief and the sun comes back out.

Beyond Kaunakakai, the two-lane road curves along the coast past piggeries, palm groves, and a 20-mile string of fishponds as well as an ancient *heiau* (temple), Damien-built churches, and a few contemporary condos by the sea. The road ends in the glorious Halawa Valley ✵, one of Hawaii's most beautiful valleys.

FAST FACTS

Molokai and Lanai are both part of Maui County. For **local emergencies,** call ✆ **911.** For nonemergencies, call the **police** at ✆ **808/553-5355,** the **fire department** at ✆ **808/553-5601,** or **Molokai General Hospital,** in Kaunakakai, at ✆ **808/553-5331.**

Downtown Kaunakakai has a **post office** (✆ **808/553-5845**) and several banks, including the **Bank of Hawaii** (✆ **808/553-3273**), which has a 24-hour ATM.

2 Getting Around

Getting around Molokai isn't easy if you don't have a rental car, and rental cars are often hard to find here. On holiday weekends (see "When to Go," in chapter 3), car-rental agencies simply run out of cars. Book before you go. There's no municipal transit or shuttle service, but a 24-hour taxi service is available (see below).

CAR-RENTAL AGENCIES   Rental cars are available from **Budget** (✆ **808/567-6877**) and **Dollar** (✆ **808/567-6156**); both agencies are located at the Molokai Airport.

TAXI & TOUR SERVICES   **Molokai Off-Road Tours & Taxi** (✆ **808/553-3369;** www.molokai.com/offroad) offers regular taxi service as well as an airport shuttle ($29 for one or two people one-way to Kaunakakai).

3 Where to Stay

Molokai is Hawaii's most affordable island, especially for accommodations. And because the island's restaurants are few, most hotel rooms and condo units come with kitchens, which can save you a bundle on dining costs. The downside is that there aren't too many options—mostly B&Bs, condos, and a few quaint oceanfront vacation rentals. Hardy souls can pitch their own tent at the beach or in the cool upland forest (see "Hiking & Camping," p. 280).

I've listed my top picks below; for additional options, contact **Molokai Vacation Rental,** P.O. Box 1979, Kaunakakai, HI 96748 (✆ **800/367-2984** or 808/553-8334; fax 808/553-3783; www.molokai-vacation-rental.com). *Note:* Taxes of 11.42% will be added to your hotel bill. Parking is free.

KAUNAKAKAI
MODERATE

Hotel Molokai ✵ *Kids*   Since the 2008 closing of the Lodge at Molokai Ranch, this nostalgic Hawaiian motel-like complex is the only hotel on the island. The modest accommodations comprise a series of modified A-frame units, nestled under coco palms along a gray-sand beach that has a great view of Lanai but isn't good for swimming. In 2006, the entire hotel underwent a $1-million renovation, from repaving the parking lot to redoing the kitchen. All rooms have been upgraded and look clean and new, but they aren't fancy—this is still a modest budget hotel. Be sure to ask for a room with a ceiling fan; most units have a lanai. The mattresses are on the soft side, the sheets thin, and the bath towels rough, but you're on Molokai. The front desk is open only from 7am to 8pm; late check-ins or visitors with problems have to go to security.

Kamehameha V Hwy. (P.O. Box 1020), Kaunakakai, HI 96748. 𝄐 **800/367-5004** on the mainland, 800/272-5275 in Hawaii, or 808/553-5347. Fax 800/477-2329. www.hotelmolokai.com. 54 units. $159–$219 double; $229 double with kitchen; from $249 suite. Extra bed/crib $20. AE, DC, DISC, MC, V. **Amenities:** Fairly good and reasonably priced restaurant w/bar; outdoor pool; watersports equipment rentals; bike rentals; activities desk; babysitting; coin-op washer/dryers. *In room:* A/C, TV, dataport, kitchenette (in some units), fridge, coffeemaker, hair dryer, iron, safe.

Molokai Shores *Kids*   Basic units with kitchens and large lanais face a small gold-sand beach in this quiet complex of three-story Polynesian-style buildings, less than a mile from Kaunakakai. Alas, the beach is mostly for show (offshore, it's shallow mud flats underfoot), fishing, or launching kayaks, but the pool and barbecue area come with an ocean view, and the spacious units make this a good choice for families. Well-tended gardens, spreading lawns, and palms frame a restful view of fishponds, offshore reefs, and neighbor islands. The central location is a plus.

There's no daily maid service here, and I have received some letters complaining about the lack of maintenance and cleanliness; the management swears that it's taking steps to correct these deficiencies. On my most recent visit, the grounds and units I saw were clean and well maintained. However, keep in mind that these condos are individually owned, as well as managed by various companies.

Kamehameha V Hwy. (P.O. Box 1037), Kaunakakai, HI 96748. 𝄐 **800/535-0085** or 808/553-5954. Fax 808/553-5954. www.marcresorts.com. 102 units. $190–$210 1-bedroom apt (sleeps up to 4); $250 2-bedroom apt (up to 6). Discounted rates for weekly and extended stays, plus corporate, military, and senior discounts and Internet-only specials. AE, DC, MC, V. **Amenities:** Putting green; salon; coin-op washer/dryers. *In room:* TV, kitchen, fridge, coffeemaker, iron.

INEXPENSIVE

Ka Hale Mala Bed & Breakfast *Value*   In a subdivision just outside town is this large four-room unit, with a private entrance through the garden and a Jacuzzi just outside. Inside, you'll find rattan furnishings, room enough to sleep four, and a full kitchen. The helpful owners meet all guests at the airport like long-lost relatives, provide a couple of bikes as well as snorkel and picnic gear, and happily share their home-grown organic produce; I recommend paying the extra $5 each for breakfast here.

7 Kamakana Place (P.O. Box 1582), off Kamehameha V Hwy. (before mile marker 5), Kaunakakai, HI 96748. 𝄐/fax **808/553-9009**. www.molokai-bnb.com. 1 unit. $80 double without breakfast; $90 double with breakfast. Extra person $15 without breakfast, $20 with breakfast. No credit cards. **Amenities:** Jacuzzi. *In room:* TV, kitchen, fridge, coffeemaker.

THE WEST END
MODERATE

Paniolo Hale *Kids* *Finds*   Tucked into a verdant garden on the dry West End, this condo complex has the advantage of being next door to a white-sand beach. The two-story, old Hawaii ranch-house design is airy and homey, with oak floors and folding-glass doors that open to huge screened verandas. All units are spacious and well equipped. The whole place overlooks the Kaluakoi Golf Course (which closed in 2008), a green barrier that separates these condos from the rest of the rapidly fading Kaluakoi Resort. Out front, Kepuhi Beach is a scenic place for walkers and beach-combers, but the seas are too hazardous for most swimmers. A pool, paddle tennis, and barbecue facilities are on the property, which adjoins open grassland countryside.

As with most condominiums in a rental pool, the quality and upkeep of the individually owned units can vary widely. When booking, spend some time talking with the friendly people at Molokai Vacation Rental so that you get a top-quality condo that has been renovated recently.

Lio Place (next door to Kaluakoi Resort), Kaluakoi, HI 96770. Reservations c/o Molokai Vacation Rental, P.O. Box 1979, Kaunakakai, HI 96748. 𝄐 **800/367-2984** or 808/553-8334. Fax 808/553-3783. www.molokai-vacation-rental.com

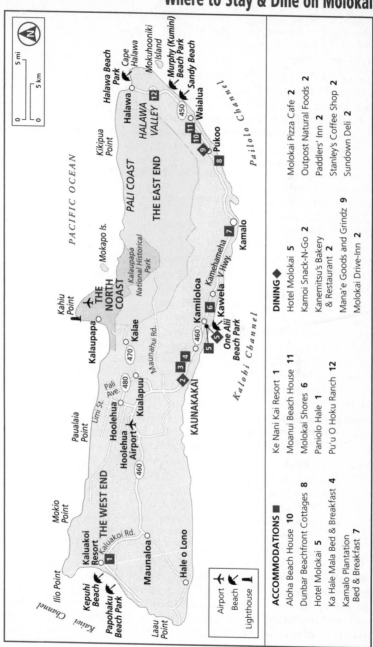

PACIFIC OCEAN

Kaiwi Channel

Ilio Point

Mokio Point

THE WEST END

Kaluakoi Resort **1**

Kepuhi Beach

Papohaku Beach Park

Maunaloa

Hale o Lono

Laau Point

Kaluakoi Rd.

Paualaia Point

Hoolehua

Hoolehua Airport

Kualapuu

Kalaupapa

Kahiu Point

THE NORTH COAST

Kalae

Kalaupapa National Historical Park

Mokapo Is.

Kikipua Point

PALI COAST

Maunahui Rd.

Pali Ave.

Limi St.

KAUNAKAKAI

Kamiloloa

Kamehameha V Hwy.

Kalohi Channel

One Alii Beach Park

Kawela

Kamalo

THE EAST END

HALAWA VALLEY

Halawa

Halawa Beach Park

Cape Halawa

Mokuhooniki Island

Murphy (Kuminil) Beach Park

Sandy Beach

Waialua

Pukoo

Pailolo Channel

Airport
Beach
Lighthouse

ACCOMMODATIONS

Aloha Beach House **10**
Dunbar Beachfront Cottages **8**
Hotel Molokai **5**
Ka Hale Mala Bed & Breakfast **4**
Kamalo Plantation
Bed & Breakfast **7**

Ke Nani Kai Resort **1**
Moanui Beach House **11**
Molokai Shores **6**
Paniolo Hale **1**
Pu'u O Hoku Ranch **12**

DINING

Hotel Molokai **5**
Kamoi Snack-N-Go **2**
Kanemitsu's Bakery & Restaurant **2**
Mana'e Goods and Grindz **9**
Molokai Drive-Inn **2**

Molokai Pizza Cafe **2**
Outpost Natural Foods **2**
Paddlers' Inn **2**
Stanley's Coffee Shop **2**
Sundown Deli **2**

or www.paniolohale.org. 77 units. $120–$150 studio double; $130–$350 1-bedroom apt (sleeps up to 4); $275 2-bedroom apt (up to 6). 3-night minimum; 1-week minimum Dec 20–Jan 5. AE, MC, V. **Amenities:** Outdoor pool. *In room:* TV, kitchen, fridge, coffeemaker, washer/dryer.

INEXPENSIVE

Ke Nani Kai Resort ⚜ *Kids*   These large apartments are set up for full-time living with real kitchens, attractive furnishings, and breezy lanais. There's a huge pool, a volleyball court, and tennis courts. These condos are farther from the sea than other local accommodations, but are still just a brief walk to the beach. The two-story buildings are surrounded by parking and garden areas. The only downside: Maid service is only every third day.

At the Kaluakoi Resort development, Kaluakoi Rd., off Hwy. 460 (P.O. Box 289), Maunaloa, HI 96770. Reservations c/o Molokai Vacation Rental, P.O. Box 1979, Kaunakakai, HI 96748. ℂ 800/367-2984 or 808/553-8334. Fax 808/553-3783. www.molokai-vacation-rental.com. 100 units. $135 1-bedroom apt (sleeps up to 4); $140–$195 2-bedroom apt (up to 6). 3-night minimum. AE, DC, DISC, MC, V. **Amenities:** Outdoor pool; 2 tennis courts; Jacuzzi. *In room:* TV/VCR, kitchen, fridge, coffeemaker, washer/dryer.

THE EAST END
MODERATE

Aloha Beach House ⚜⚜ *Finds* *Kids*   This Hawaiian-style beach house sits right on the white-sand beach of Waialua in the lush East End. Perfect for families, the impeccably decorated two-bedroom, 1,600-square-foot property has a huge, airy living/dining/kitchen area that opens onto an old-fashioned porch for meals or just sitting in the comfy chairs and watching the clouds roll by. The place is fully equipped, from the complete kitchen (including a dishwasher) to a VCR (plus a library of videos) to all the beach toys you can think of. It's located close to Mana'e Goods and Grindz (p. 276).

Located just after mile marker 19. Reservations c/o the Rietows, P.O. Box 79, Kilauea, HI 96754. ℂ 888/828-1008 or 808/828-1100. Fax 808/828-2199. www.molokaivacation.com. 1 unit. $290 double. Cleaning fee $175 for 2 people. Extra person $20 plus additional cleaning fee. 3-night minimum. No credit cards. *In room:* TV/VCR, kitchen, fridge, coffeemaker, washer/dryer.

Dunbar Beachfront Cottages ⚜⚜ *Kids*   This is one of the most peaceful, comfortable, and elegant properties on Molokai's East End, and the setting is simply stunning. Each of these two green-and-white plantation-style cottages sits on its own secluded beach (good for swimming)—you'll feel like you're on your own private island. Both cottages have ceiling fans, comfortable tropical furniture, large furnished decks (perfect for whale-watching in winter), and views of Maui, Lanai, and Kahoolawe across the channel.

Kamehameha V Hwy., past mile marker 18. Reservations c/o Matt and Genesis Dunbar, HC01 Box 738, Kaunakakai, HI 96748. ℂ 800/673-0520 or 808/558-8153. www.molokai-beachfront-cottages.com. 2 units. $170 cottage (sleeps up to 4). Cleaning fee $75. 3-night minimum. No credit cards. *In room:* TV/VCR, kitchen, fridge, coffeemaker, washer/dryer.

Moanui Beach House ⚜ *Kids*   If you're looking for a quiet, remote beach house, this is it. The genial Fosters (no relation to the author), who have lived on the islands for many years, run the popular Kamalo Plantation B&B (see below). They recently renovated the kitchen in this two-bedroom beach house, right across the street from a secluded white-sand cove beach. The A-frame has a shaded lanai facing the ocean, a screened-in lanai on the side of the house, and an ocean view that's worth the price alone—it's a great place for families to spread out and relax. The Fosters leave a "starter supply" of breakfast foods for guests (fruit basket, home-baked bread, tropical fruit juices, tea, and coffee).

Kamehameha V Hwy., at mile marker 20. Reservations c/o Glenn and Akiko Foster, HC01, Box 300, Kaunakakai, HI 96748. ©/fax **808/558-8236**. 1 unit. $150 double. Extra person $50. 3-night minimum. No credit cards. *In room:* TV, kitchen, fridge, coffeemaker, hair dryer, iron, washer/dryer.

Pu'u O Hoku Ranch ⊛ (*Kids*)   *Pu'u o Hoku* ("Star Hill") Ranch, which spreads across 14,000 acres of pasture and forests, is the last place to stay before Halawa Valley—it's at least an hour's drive from Kaunakakai along the shoreline. Two acres of tropically landscaped property circle the ranch's rustic Sunrise Cottage, which boasts breathtaking views of rolling hills and the Pacific. The wooden cottage features comfortable country furniture, a full kitchen, two bedrooms (one with a double bed, one with two twins), two bathrooms, and a separate dining room on the enclosed lanai. Stargaze at night, watch the sunrise in the morning, and hike, swim, or play croquet in the afternoon. Horseback riding is available at the ranch (see "Horseback Riding," p. 281). Kids will have plenty of room to run around and explore.

For larger parties, there's also a four-bedroom, three-bathroom house (sleeps up to eight) and an 11-room lodge on the property.

Kamehameha V Hwy., at mile marker 25. Reservations c/o P.O. Box 1889, Kaunakakai, HI 96748. © **808/558-8109.** Fax 808/558-8100. www.puuohoku.com. 2 units. $140 double. Cleaning fee $75. Extra person $20. 2-night minimum. No credit cards. **Amenities:** Outdoor pool. *In room:* TV/VCR (on request), kitchen, fridge, coffeemaker.

INEXPENSIVE

Kamalo Plantation Bed & Breakfast ⊛ (*Value*)   Glenn and Akiko Foster's 5-acre spread includes an ancient *heiau* ruin in the front yard, plus leafy tropical gardens and a working fruit orchard. Their Eden-like property is easy to find: It's right across the East End road from Father Damien's historic St. Joseph's Church. The plantation-style cottage is tucked under flowering trees and surrounded by swaying palms. It has its own lanai, a big living room with a queen-size sofa bed, and a separate bedroom with a king-size bed, so it can sleep four comfortably. The kitchen is fully equipped (it even has spices), and there's a barbecue outside. A breakfast of fruit and freshly baked bread is served every morning. There's no TV reception, but the cottage does have a VCR, a radio, and a CD and cassette player.

Kamehameha V Hwy., just past mile marker 10 (HC01, Box 300), Kaunakakai, HI 96748. ©/fax **808/558-8236.** 1 unit. $100 cottage double. Rate includes continental breakfast. Extra person $10. 2-night minimum. No credit cards. *In room:* Kitchen, fridge, coffeemaker, hair dryer.

4 Where to Dine

The good news is that on Molokai, you won't find long lines at overbooked, self-important restaurants. The bad news is that Molokai's culinary offerings are spare.

A lot of people like it that way and acknowledge that the island's character is unchangeably rugged and natural. But a few years ago, when the renovated Hotel Molokai unveiled a tropical fantasy of an oceanfront dining room, the islanders thought this was the height of culinary pleasure. And it quickly became the island's busiest restaurant.

Even with such developments, however, Molokai has retained its glacial pace of change. Its culinary offerings are dominated by mom-and-pop eateries, most of them fast-food or takeout places, and many of them with a home-cooked touch. Personally, I like the unpretentiousness of Molokai; it's an oasis in a state where plastic aloha abounds. But sybarites, foodies, and pampered oenophiles had best lower their expectations upon arrival.

You'll even find a certain defiant stance against the trappings of modernity. Although some of the best produce in Hawaii is grown on this island, you're not likely to find much of it served in its restaurants, other than in the takeout items at Outpost Natural Foods, or at the Molokai Pizza Cafe (one of the most pleasing eateries on the island) and the Hotel Molokai. The rest of the time, content yourself with ethnic or diner fare—or by cooking for yourself. The many visitors who stay in condos find that it doesn't take long to sniff out the best sources of produce, groceries, and fresh fish to fire up at home when the island's other dining options are exhausted. The "Edibles" sections under "Shopping" (later in this chapter) will point you in the right direction.

Molokai's restaurants are inexpensive or moderately priced, and several of them do not accept credit cards. Regardless of where you eat, you certainly won't have to dress up. In most cases, I've listed just the town rather than the street address because, as you'll see, street addresses are as meaningless on this island as fancy cars and sequins. Reservations are not accepted unless otherwise noted.

Note: You'll find the restaurants reviewed in this chapter on the "Where to Stay & Dine on Molokai" map (p. 271).

KAUNAKAKAI
INEXPENSIVE
Hotel Molokai ℱ AMERICAN/ISLAND   Set on the ocean, with a view of Lanai, torches flickering under palm trees, and tiny fairy lights lining the room and the neighboring pool area, the Hotel Molokai's dining room evokes the romance of a South Seas fantasy. It's a casual room and, since its 1999 reopening, provides the only nightlife in Kaunakakai (see "Molokai After Dark," p. 293) and the most pleasing ambience on the island. Lunch choices consist of the basics; most promising are salads (Big Island organic greens) and sandwiches, from roast beef to grilled mahimahi. As the sun sets and the torches are lit for dinner, the menu turns to heavier meats, ribs, fish, and pasta. Try the fresh catch, *kalbi* ribs, barbecued pork ribs, New York steak, or lip-smacking coconut shrimp. Temper your expectations of culinary excellence, and you're sure to enjoy a pleasing dinner in an atmosphere that's unequaled on the island.

On Kamehameha V Hwy. ℂ 808/553-5347. Reservations recommended for dinner. Main courses $8–$15 lunch, $15–$25 dinner. AE, DC, MC, V. Daily 7am–2pm and 6–9pm. Bar until 10:30pm.

Kamoi Snack-N-Go ICE CREAM/SNACKS   The Kamoi specialty: sweets and icy treats. Ice cream made by Dave's on Oahu comes in flavors such as green tea, litchi sherbet, *ube* (made from Okinawan sweet potato), haupia, mango, and many others. Lines form for the cones, shakes, sundaes, and popular Icee floats served at this tiny snack shop. If the ice cream doesn't tempt you, browse the aisles full of candies. It's takeout only (no tables).

At the Kamoi Professional Center. ℂ 808/553-3742. Ice cream $2.25–$4.15; sundaes $3.60–$6.40. MC, V. Mon–Fri 10am–9pm; Sat 9am–9pm; Sun noon–9pm.

Kanemitsu's Bakery & Restaurant ℱ BAKERY/DELI   Morning, noon, and night, this local legend fills the Kaunakakai air with the sweet smells of baking. Taro lavosh is the hot seller, joining Molokai bread—developed in 1935 in a cast-iron, kiawe-fired oven—as a Kanemitsu signature. Flavors range from apricot-pineapple to coconut or strawberry, but the white, wheat, cheese, sweet, and onion-cheese breads are classics. The bread mixes offer a way to take Molokai home. In the adjoining coffee shop/deli, the hamburgers and egg-salad sandwiches are popular and cheap.

Kanemitsu's has a life after dark, too. Whenever anyone on Molokai mentions "hot bread," he's talking about the hot-bread run at Kanemitsu's, the surreal late-night ritual for die-hard bread lovers. Those in the know line up at the bakery's back door beginning at 10pm, when the bread is whisked hot out of the oven and into waiting hands. You can order your fresh bread with butter, jelly, cinnamon, or cream cheese, and the bakers will cut the hot loaves down the middle and slather on the works so it melts in the bread. The cream-cheese-and-jelly bread makes a fine substitute for dessert.

79 Ala Malama St. ⓒ 808/553-5855. Most items under $5.50. AE, MC, V. Restaurant Wed–Mon 5:30am–noon. Bakery Wed–Mon 5:30am–6:30pm. Hot-bread run Tues–Sun at 10pm.

Molokai Drive-Inn AMERICAN/TAKEOUT   It is a greasy spoon, but it's one of the rare drive-up places with fresh akule (mackerel) and ahi (when available), plus fried saimin at budget-friendly prices. The honey-dipped fried chicken is a favorite among residents, who also come here for the floats, shakes, and other artery-clogging choices. But don't expect much in terms of ambience: This is a fast-food takeout counter, and it doesn't pretend to be otherwise.

Kaunakakai. ⓒ 808/553-5655. Most items under $9. No credit cards. Mon–Thurs 6am–9pm; Fri–Sun 6:30am–10:30pm.

Molokai Pizza Cafe ⓡ PIZZA   This gathering place serves excellent pizzas and sandwiches that have made it a Kaunakakai staple as well as one of my favorite eateries on the island. The bestsellers are the Molokai (pepperoni and cheese), the Big Island (pepperoni, ham, mushroom, Italian sausage, bacon, and vegetables), and the Molokini (plain cheese slices). My personal fave is the vegetarian Maui pizza, but others tout the fresh-baked submarine and pocket sandwiches and the gyro pocket with spinach pie. Pastas and new "gourmet" hamburgers on homemade buns round out the menu. Sunday is prime-rib day; Wednesday is Mexican. Coin-operated cars and a toy airplane follow the children's theme, but adults should feel equally at home with the very popular barbecued baby back ribs and the fresh-fish dinners.

At the Kahua Center, on the old Wharf Rd. ⓒ 808/553-3288. Large pizzas $18–$23. No credit cards. Sun 11am–10pm; Mon–Thurs 10am–10pm; Fri–Sat 10am–11pm.

Outpost Natural Foods ⓡ VEGETARIAN   The healthiest and freshest food on the island is served at the counter of this health-food store, around the corner from the main drag on the ocean side of Kaunakakai town. The tiny store abounds in Molokai papayas, bananas, herbs, potatoes, watermelon, and other local produce. The salads, burritos, tempeh sandwiches, tofu-spinach lasagna, and mock chicken, turkey, and meatloaf served at the lunch counter are testament to the fact that vegetarian food need not be boring. A must for health-conscious diners and shoppers.

70 Makaena Place. ⓒ 808/553-3377. Entrees $12–$15. AE, DISC, MC, V. Sun 10am–5pm; Mon–Thurs 9am–6pm; Fri 9am–4pm.

Paddlers' Inn AMERICAN/LOCAL   If you want to meet local residents, come to this friendly diner. Breakfast features specials like homemade biscuits with sausage gravy. At lunch, it's filled with hungry folks grinding on ⅓-pound all-beef burgers or plate lunches. Vegetarians will find a few items here, but not a lot. Call ahead for dinner specials. Later on, the small cafe becomes a hot spot for Molokai entertainment (p. 293).

10 Mohala St. ⓒ 808/553-5256. Breakfast items $5–$12; lunch items $6–$22; dinner main courses $10–$30. AE, DC, DISC, MC, V. Mon–Fri 6:30am–9pm; Sat 9am–9:30pm; Sun 9am–9pm.

Stanley's Coffee Shop & Gallery COFFEE SHOP   Breakfast, coffee, and sandwiches are on tap at this tiny cafe, located across from the Triangle Park and next to St. Sophia Church. If you need Internet access, it can supply that, too (at 10¢ per minute). Upstairs is the small gallery, which also does framing. Breakfast items range from Belgian waffles to eggs; lunch has a host of sandwiches and the strongest espresso in Kaunakakai.

125 Puali St. ☎ 808/553-9966. Breakfast items under $6; lunch items under $9. MC, V on bills of $20 or more. Mon–Fri 6:30am–4pm; Sat 6:30am–2pm.

Sundown Deli ✹ DELI   From "gourmet saimin" to spinach pie, Sundown's offerings are home-cooked and healthful, with daily specials that include quiche, vegetarian lasagna, and club sandwiches. Grab a sandwich (smoked turkey, chicken salad) or salad (Caesar, Oriental, stuffed tomato) or the daily soup (clam chowder, Portuguese bean, cream of broccoli). Vitamins, T-shirts, and snacks are also sold in this tiny cafe, but most of the business is takeout.

145 Puali St. (across the street from Veteran's Memorial Park). ☎ 808/553-3713. Sandwiches, soups, and salads $4–$7.50. No credit cards. Mon–Fri 7:30am–3:30pm.

THE EAST END
INEXPENSIVE
Mana'e Goods and Grindz ✹ AMERICAN   Formerly the Neighborhood Store, this place has a new name, but it's still the same quick-stop market/lunch counter. It's nothing fancy, and that's what I love about it. Near mile marker 16 in the Pukoo area en route to the East End, this tiny store appears like a mirage, complete with a large parking area and picnic tables. The place serves omelets, Portuguese sausage, and other breakfast specials (brunch is very popular); it then segues into sandwiches, salads, and varied lunch offerings, served on paper plates with plastic utensils. Favorites include the mahimahi plate lunch, the chicken *katsu,* and the Mexican plate. There are daily specials, ethnic dishes, and some vegetarian options, as well as a killer veggie burger, saimin, and legendary desserts. Made-on-Maui Roselani ice cream is a featured attraction. A Molokai treasure, this is the only grocery store on the East End (see the shopping review on p. 293).

Pukoo. ☎ 808/558-8498. Most items under $10. MC, V. Daily store hours 8am–5pm; food service Mon–Fri 9am–5pm and Sat–Sun 8am–5pm.

5 Beaches

With imposing sea cliffs on one side and lazy fishponds on the other, Molokai has little room for beaches along its 106-mile coast. Still, a big gold-sand beach flourishes on the West End, and you'll find tiny pocket beaches on the East End. The emptiness of Molokai's beaches is both a blessing and a curse: The seclusion means no lifeguards on any of the beaches. To locate them, see the "Molokai" map (p. 265).

KAUNAKAKAI
ONE ALII BEACH PARK
This thin strip of sand, once reserved for the *alii* (chiefs), is the oldest public beach park on Molokai. You'll find One Alii Beach Park (*One* is pronounced "*o*-nay," not "*won*") by a coconut grove on the outskirts of Kaunakakai. Safe for swimmers of all ages and abilities, it's often crowded with families on weekends, but it can be all yours on weekdays. Facilities include outdoor showers, restrooms, and free parking.

THE WEST END
KEPUHI BEACH

Sunbathers like this picturesque golden strand's semiprivate grassy dunes—they're seldom, if ever, crowded. Beachcombers often find what they're looking for here, but swimmers have to dodge lava rocks and risk riptides. There are no facilities or lifeguards, but cold drinks and restrooms are handy at the resort.

PAPOHAKU BEACH 🍂🍂

Nearly 3 miles long and 300 feet wide, gold-sand Papohaku Beach is one of the biggest in Hawaii (17-mile-long Polihale Beach on Kauai is the biggest). It's great for walking, beachcombing, picnics, and sunset-watching year-round. The big surf and riptides make swimming risky except in summer, when the waters are calmer. Go early in the day, when the tropic sun is less fierce and the winds are calm. The beach is so vast that you may never see another soul. Facilities include outdoor showers, restrooms, picnic grounds, and free parking.

THE EAST END
HALAWA BEACH PARK 🍂

At the foot of scenic Halawa Valley is this beautiful black-sand beach with a palm-fringed lagoon, a wave-lashed island offshore, and a distant view of the West Maui Mountains across the Pailolo Channel. The swimming is safe in the shallows close to shore, but where the waterfall stream meets the sea, the ocean is often murky and unnerving. A winter swell creases the mouth of Halawa Valley on the north side of the bay and attracts a crowd of local surfers. Facilities are minimal; bring your own water. To get here, take King Kamehameha V Highway (Hwy. 450) east to the end.

MURPHY BEACH PARK (KUMIMI BEACH PARK)

In 1970, the Molokai Jaycees wanted to create a sandy beach park with a good swimming area for the children of the East End. They chose a section known as Kumimi Beach, which was owned by the Pu'u o Hoku Ranch. The beach was a dump—literally. The ranch owner, George Murphy, gave his permission to use the site as a park, and the Jaycees cleaned it up and built three small pavilions, plus picnic tables and barbecue grills. Officially, the park is called the George Murphy Beach Park (shortened to Murphy Beach Park), but some old-timers still call it Kumimi Beach, and, just to make things really confusing, some people call it Jaycees Park.

No matter what you call it, this small park is shaded by ironwood trees that line a white-sand beach. It's generally a very safe swimming area, and on calm days snorkeling and diving are great outside the reef. Fishermen also come here to look for papio and other Island fish.

SANDY BEACH 🍂

Molokai's most popular swimming beach—ideal for families with small kids—is a roadside pocket of gold sand protected by a reef, with a great view of Maui and Lanai. You'll find it off the King Kamehameha V Highway (Hwy. 450) at mile marker 20. There are no facilities—just you, the sun, the sand, and the surf.

6 Watersports

Molokai Fish & Dive, Kaunakakai (© 808/553-5926; www.molokaifishanddive. com), rents snorkeling gear, fishing gear, and even ice chests. This is also a hot spot for fishing news and tips on what's running where.

Molokai's Best Snorkel Spots

Most Molokai beaches are too dangerous for snorkeling in winter, when big waves and strong currents are generated by storms that sweep down from Alaska. From mid-September to April, stick to Murphy Beach Park (also known as Kumimi Beach Park) on the East End. In summer, roughly May to mid-September, the Pacific Ocean turns into a flat lake, and the whole west coast of Molokai opens up for snorkeling. Mike Holmes, of Molokai Ranch & Fun Hogs Hawaii, says the best spots are as follows:

Kawaikiunui, Ilio Point & Pohaku Moiliili (West End) These are all special places seldom seen by even those who live on Molokai. You can reach Kawaikiunui and Pohaku Moiliili on foot after a long, hot, dusty ride in a four-wheel-drive vehicle, but it's much easier and quicker to go by sea. See above for places to rent a kayak and get advice. It's about 2 miles as the crow flies from Pohaku Moiliili to Ilio Point.

Kapukahehu (Dixie Maru) Beach (West End) This gold-sand family beach is well protected, and the reef is close and shallow. The name Dixie Maru comes from a 1920s Japanese fishing boat stranded off the rocky shore. One of the Molokai Ranch cowboys hung the wrecked boat's nameplate on a gate by Kapukahehu Beach, and the name stuck. To get here, take Kaluakoi Road to the end of the pavement, and then follow the footpath 300 feet to the beach.

Murphy (Kumimi) Beach Park ✿ (East End) This beach is located between mile markers 20 and 21, off Kamehameha V Highway. The reef here is easily reachable, and the waters are calm year-round.

BODY BOARDING (BOOGIE BOARDING) & BODYSURFING

Molokai has only three beaches that offer ridable waves for body boarding and bodysurfing: Papohaku, Kepuhi, and Halawa. Even these beaches are only for experienced bodysurfers, due to the strength of the rip currents and undertows. You can rent boogie boards with fins for just $5 a day or $20 a week at **Molokai Outdoors Activities** (✆ 877/553-4477 or 808/553-4477; www.molokai-outdoors.com).

OCEAN KAYAKING

During the summer, when the waters on the north shore are calm, Molokai offers some of the most spectacular kayaking in Hawaii. However, most of Molokai is for the experienced kayaker only. You must be adept in paddling through open ocean swells and rough waves. **Molokai Outdoors Activities** (✆ 877/553-4477 or 808/553-4477; www.molokai-outdoors.com) has a "downwinder" tour: See 6 miles of Molokai's reef as you paddle downwind ($89 per person, plus $10 for lunch). It also rents kayaks starting at $26 a day.

SCUBA DIVING

Want to see turtles or manta rays up close? How about sharks? Molokai resident Bill Kapuni has been diving the waters around the island his entire life; he'll be happy to show you whatever you're brave enough to encounter. You can book him through **Molokai Fish & Dive** (© 808/553-5926; www.molokaifishanddive.com), which offers scuba-diving trips from $135 (two-tank dive) to $275 (three-tank dive).

SNORKELING

When the waters are calm, Molokai offers excellent snorkeling; you'll see a wide range of butterflyfish, tangs, and angelfish. Good snorkeling can be found—when conditions are right—at many of Molokai's beaches (see "Molokai's Best Snorkel Spots," below). **Molokai Outdoors Activities** (© 877/553-4477 or 808/553-4477; www.molokai-outdoors.com) has the best rental prices ($6 a day or $24 a week for fins, mask, and snorkel). It also offers snorkel tours for $69 per person.

For snorkeling tours on a boat, Walter Naki of **Molokai Action Adventures** (© 808/558-8184) offers leisurely snorkeling, diving, and swimming trips in his 21-foot Boston whaler for $50 per person for a 4- to 6-hour custom tour.

SPORTFISHING

Molokai's waters can provide prime sporting opportunities, whether you're looking for big-game sportfishing or bottom fishing. I recommend going with Captain Clay of **Hallelujah Hou Fishing** (© 808/336-1870; www.hallelujahhoufishing.com), who leads light-tackle guided fishing trips on his 24-foot power catamaran. The price is $395 to $495 for up to four adults for a half-day. He provides all tackle and bottled water; you bring the sunscreen. If you catch something, he'll even filet it for dinner. *Note:* There's no "head" (toilet) on the boat.

When customers are scarce, Capt. Joe Reich goes commercial fishing, so he always knows where the fish are biting. He runs **Alyce C Sportfishing,** out of Kaunakakai Harbor (© 808/558-8377; ace@aloha.net). A full day for up to six people is $500, three-quarters of a day is $450, and a half-day is $400. You can usually persuade him to do a whale-watching cruise during the winter months.

For fly-fishing or light-tackle reef-fish trolling, contact Walter Naki at **Molokai Action Adventures** (© 808/558-8184). A full-day trip in his 21-foot Boston whaler, for up to four people, goes for $400.

Molokai Fish & Dive, Kaunakakai (© 808/553-5926; www.molokaifishanddive. com), has fishing tours for $400 for a half-day, $600 for a full day.

For deep-sea fishing, contact **Fun Hogs Hawaii,** which books through Molokai Outdoors Activities (see below). Excursions for six passengers on a fully equipped, 27-foot sportfishing vessel cost $400 for 4 hours, $417 for 6 hours, and $521 for 8 hours.

If you just want to try your luck casting along the shoreline, **Molokai Outdoors Activities** (© 877/553-4477 or 808/553-4477; www.molokai-outdoors.com) offers the least expensive fishing poles for rent ($5 a day or $24 a week) and can tell you where they're biting.

SURFING

Depending on the time of year and the wave conditions, Molokai can offer some great surfing for the beginner as well as the expert. **Molokai Outdoors Activities** (© 877/553-4477 or 808/553-4477; www.molokai-outdoors.com) not only knows where the waves are, but also rents soft surfboards for $13 a day. Good surfing spots include Kaunakakai Wharf in town, Hale O Lono Beach and Papohaku Beach on the West End, and Halawa Beach on the East End.

7 Hiking & Camping

HIKING

THE PEPEOPAE TRAIL 🌺🌺

Molokai's most awesome hike is the Pepeopae Trail, which takes you back a few million years. On the cloud-draped trail (actually a boardwalk across the bog), you'll see mosses, sedges, native violets, knee-high ancient ohia, and lichens that evolved in total isolation over eons. Eerie intermittent mists blowing in and out will give you an idea of this island at its creation.

The narrow boardwalk, built by volunteers, protects the bog and keeps you out of the primal ooze. Don't venture off it; you could damage this fragile environment or get lost. The 3-mile round-trip takes about 90 minutes to hike—but first you have to drive about 20 miles from Kaunakakai, deep into the Kamakou Preserve, on a four-wheel-drive road. Plan a full day for this outing. Better yet, go on a guided nature hike with the **Nature Conservancy of Hawaii,** which guards this unusual ecosystem. For information, write to the Nature Conservancy at 1116 Smith St., Suite 201, Honolulu, HI 96817. No permit is required for this easy hike. Call ahead (© **808/537-4508** or 553-5236; www.nature.org/wherewework/northamerica/states/hawaii/travel/art16727.html) to check on the condition of the ungraded, red-dirt road that leads to the trail head and to let people know that you'll be up here. *Warning:* Don't try this with a regular rental car.

To get here, take Hwy. 460 west from Kaunakakai for 3½ miles and turn right before the Maunawainui Bridge onto the unmarked Molokai Forest Reserve Road (sorry, there aren't any road signs). The pavement ends at the cemetery; continue on the dirt road. After about 2 to 2½ miles, you'll see a sign telling you that you are now in the Molokai Forest Reserve. At the Waikolu Lookout and picnic area, which is just over 9 miles on the Molokai Forest Reserve Road, sign in at the box near the entrance. Continue on the road for another 5 miles to a fork in the road with the sign PUU KOLEKOLE pointing to the right side of the fork. Do not turn right; instead, continue straight at the fork, which leads to the clearly marked trail head. The drive will take about 45 minutes.

THE TRAIL TO KALAUPAPA 🌺🌺

This hike to the site of Molokai's famous leper colony is like going down a switchback staircase with what seems like a million steps. You don't always see the breathtaking view because you're too busy watching your step. It's easier going down (surprise!)—in about an hour, you'll go 2½ miles, from 2,000 feet to sea level. The trip up sometimes takes twice as long. The trail head starts on the mauka (inland) side of Hwy. 470, just past the Mule Barn. Check in here at 7:30am, get a permit, and go before the mule train departs. You must be 16 or older (it's an old state law that kept kids out of the leper colony) and should be in good shape. Wear good hiking boots or sneakers.

THE WEST END

Molokai Outdoors Activities (© **877/553-4477** or 808/553-4477; www.molokai-outdoors.com) offers an all-day (6–8 hr.) Halawa Cultural Hike full of historical information on East Molokai. The hike is rated intermediate to advanced, with a distance of 2.2 miles. It has two river crossings and some rocky areas along the trails, with possible fallen trees after a storm. The cost is $78 per person and includes a picnic lunch. **Molokai Fish & Dive** (© **808/553-5926;** www.molokaifishanddive.com) offers a hike into Halawa Valley for $75 (see "Halawa Valley: A Hike Back in History," p. 290).

CAMPING

Bring your own camping equipment, as none is available for rent on the island.

AT THE BEACH

One of the best year-round places to camp on Molokai is **Papohaku Beach Park**, on the island's West End. This drive-up seaside site makes a great getaway. Facilities include restrooms, drinking water, outdoor showers, barbecue grills, and picnic tables. Groceries and gas are available in Maunaloa, 6 miles away. Kaluakoi Resort is a mile away. Get camping permits by contacting **Maui County Parks Department**, P.O. Box 526, Kaunakakai, HI 96748 (② **808/553-3204;** www.co.maui.hi.us/parks/permits/parkspermits.htm). Camping is limited to 3 days, but if nobody else has applied, the time limit is waived. The cost is $3 a person per night.

IN AN IRONWOOD FOREST

At the end of Hwy. 470 is the 234-acre piney woods known as **Palaau State Park**, home to the Kalaupapa Lookout (the best vantage point for seeing the historic leper colony if you're not hiking or riding a mule in). It's airy and cool in the park's ironwood forest, where many love to camp at the designated state campground. Camping fees for Hawaii State Parks are $5 per campsite per night, and you'll need a permit from the **State Division of Parks** (② **808/567-6618;** www.hawaiistateparks.org/camping/maui.cfm). For more on the park, see p. 285.

8 Golf & Other Outdoor Activities

GOLF

Golfing on Molokai is challenging and fun, tee times are open, and the rates are lower than your score will be. **Ironwood Hills Golf Course,** off Kalae Highway (② **808/567-6000**), is located just before the Molokai Mule Ride Mule Barn, on the road to the Lookout. Built in 1929 by Del Monte Plantation for its executives, it's one of the oldest courses in the state. This unusual course, which sits in the cool air at 1,200 feet, delights with its rich foliage, open fairways, and spectacular views of the rest of the island. *Tip:* After teeing off on the 6th hole, just take whatever clubs you need to finish playing the hole and a driver for the 7th hole, and park your bag under a tree. The climb to the 7th hole is steep—you'll be glad that you're carrying only a few clubs. Greens fees are $31 for 18 holes.

BIKING

Molokai is a great place to see by bicycle. The roads are not very busy, and there are great places to pull off the road and take a quick dip. **Molokai Bicycle,** 80 Mohala St., Kaunakakai (② **808/553-3931;** www.bikehawaii.com/molokaibicycle), offers bike rentals for $15 a day, or $70 a week, including helmet and lock. Owner Phillip Kikukawa is schoolteacher, so call him in late afternoon when he's in the shop.

HORSEBACK RIDING

One of the most scenic places to go riding on Molokai is **Pu'u O Hoku Ranch** (② **808/558-8109;** www.puuohoku.com), about 25 miles outside Kaunakakai on the East End. Guided trail rides pass through green pasture and then head up into the high mountain forest. Don't forget your camera: There are plenty of scenic views of waterfalls, the Pacific Ocean, and the islands of Maui and Lanai in the distance. Rates are $55 for a 1-hour ride, $75 for a 2-hour ride, and $120 for a beach adventure.

Frommer's Favorite Molokai Experiences

Riding a Mule into a Leper Colony: Don't pass up the opportunity to see this hauntingly beautiful peninsula. Buzzy Sproat's mules (p. 286) go up and down the 3-mile Kalaupapa Trail to Molokai's famous leper colony. The views are breathtaking: You'll see the world's highest sea cliffs (over 300 stories tall) and waterfalls plunging thousands of feet into the ocean. If you're afraid of heights, catch the views from the Kalaupapa Lookout.

Venturing into the Garden of Eden: Drive the 30 miles along Molokai's East End. Take your time. Stop to smell the flowers and pick guavas by the side of the road. Pull over for a swim. Wave at every car you pass and every person you see. At the end of the road, stand on the beach at Halawa Valley and see Hawaii as it must have looked in A.D. 650, when the first people arrived on the islands.

Celebrating the Ancient Hula: Hula is the heartbeat of Hawaiian culture, and Molokai is its birthplace. Although most visitors to Hawaii never get to experience the real thing, it's possible to see it here—once a year, on the third Saturday in May, when Molokai celebrates the birth of the hula at its **Ka Hula Piko Festival.** The daylong affair includes dance, music, food, and crafts. For details, contact the Molokai Visitors Association (© **800/800-6367** or 808/553-3876; www.molokai-hawaii.com).

Strolling the Sands at Papohaku: Go early, when the tropical sun isn't so fierce, and stroll this 3-mile stretch of unspoiled golden sand on Molokai's West End. It's one of the longest beaches in Hawaii. The big surf and riptides make swimming somewhat risky, but Papohaku is perfect for walking, beachcombing, and, in the evening, sunset watching.

Traveling Back in Time on the Pepeopae Trail: This awesome hike takes you through the Molokai Forest Reserve (p. 280) and back a few million years in time. Along the misty trail (actually a boardwalk across the bog), expect close encounters of the botanical kind: mosses, sedges, violets, lichens, and knee-high ancient ohia.

Soaking in the Warm Waters off Sandy Beach: On the East End, about 20 miles outside Kaunakakai—just before the road starts to climb to Halawa Valley—lies a small pocket of white sand known as Sandy Beach. Submerging yourself here in the warm, calm waters (an outer reef protects the cove) is a sensuous experience par excellence.

TENNIS

The only two courts on Molokai are located at the **Mitchell Pauole Center,** in Kaunakakai (© **808/553-5141**). Both are lit for night play and are available free on a first-come, first-served basis, with a 45-minute time limit if someone is waiting. You can also rent tennis rackets ($5 a day, $24 a week) and balls ($3 a day, $12 a week) from **Molokai Outdoors Activities** (© **877/553-4477** or 808/553-4477; www.molokai-outdoors.com).

Snorkeling among Clouds of Butterflyfish: The calm waters off Murphy (Kumimi) Beach, on the East End, are perfect for snorkelers. Just don your gear and head to the reef, where you'll find lots of exotic tropical fish, including long-nosed butterflyfish, saddle wrasses, and convict tangs.

Kayaking along the North Shore: This is the Hawaii of your dreams: waterfalls thundering down sheer cliffs, remote sand beaches, miles of tropical vegetation, and the wind whispering in your ear. The best times to go are late March and early April, or in summer, especially August to September, when the normally galloping ocean lies down flat.

Watching the Sunset from a Coconut Grove: Kapuaiwa Coconut Grove/Kiowea Park (see below), off Maunaloa Highway (Hwy. 460), is a perfect place to watch the sunset. The sky behind the coconut trees fills with a kaleidoscope of colors as the sun sinks into the Pacific. Be careful where you sit, though: Falling coconuts could have you seeing stars well before dusk.

Sampling the Local Brew: Saunter up to the Espresso Bar at the Coffees of Hawaii Plantation Store (p. 292), in Kualapuu, for a fresh cup of java made from beans that were grown, processed, and packed on this 450-acre plantation. While you sip, survey the vast collection of native crafts.

Tasting Aloha at a Macadamia-Nut Farm: It could be the owner, Tuddie Purdy, and his friendly disposition that make the macadamia nuts here taste so good. Or it could be his years of practice in growing, harvesting, and shelling them on his 1½-acre farm. Either way, Purdy produces a perfect crop. See how he does it on a short, free tour of Purdy's All-Natural Macadamia Nut Farm (p. 284), in Hoolehua, just a nut's throw from the airport.

Talking Story with the Locals: The number-one favorite pastime of most islanders is "talking story," or exchanging experiences and knowledge. You can probably find residents more than willing to share their wisdom with you while fishing from the wharf at Kaunakakai, hanging out at Molokai Fish & Dive (p. 291), or having coffee at any of the island's restaurants.

Posting a Nut: Why send a picturesque postcard to your friends and family back home when you can send a coconut? The Hoolehua Post Office (p. 284) will supply the coconuts if you'll supply the postage fee of $7.50 to $11.

9 Seeing the Sights

Note: You'll find the following attractions on the "Molokai" map (p. 265).

IN & AROUND KAUNAKAKAI

Kapuaiwa Coconut Grove/Kiowea Park 🧒 *Kids* This royal grove—1,000 coconut trees on 10 acres planted in 1863 by the island's high chief Kapuaiwa (later King Kamehameha V)—is a major roadside attraction. The shoreline park is a favorite subject of sunset photographers and visitors, who delight in a hand-lettered sign that warns: DANGER: FALLING COCONUTS. In its backyard, across the highway, stands Church Row: seven churches, each a different denomination—clear evidence of the missionary impact on Hawaii.

Along Maunaloa Hwy. (Hwy. 460), 2 miles west of Kaunakakai.

Post-A-Nut ⭐   The postmaster on Molokai will help you say "Aloha" with a Molokai coconut. Just write a message on the coconut with a felt-tip pen, and she'll send it via U.S. mail. Coconuts are free, but postage averages $7.50 to $11 for a mainland-bound coconut.

Hoolehua Post Office, Puu Peelua Ave. (Hwy. 480), near Maunaloa Hwy. (Hwy. 460). © 808/567-6144. Mon–Fri 7:30–11:30am and 12:30–4:30pm.

Purdy's All-Natural Macadamia Nut Farm (Na Hua O'Ka Aina) ⭐ *Finds*   The Purdys have made buying macadamia nuts an entertainment event, offering tours of the homestead and giving lively demonstrations of nutshell cracking in the shade of their towering trees. The tour of the 70-year-old nut farm explains the growth, bearing, harvesting, and shelling processes.

Lihi Pali Ave. (behind Molokai High School), Hoolehua. © 808/567-6601. www.molokai-aloha.com/macnuts. Free admission. Mon–Fri 9:30am–3:30pm; Sat 10am–2pm. Closed on holidays.

THE NORTH COAST

Even if you don't get a chance to see Hawaii's most dramatic coast in its entirety—not many people do—you shouldn't miss the opportunity to glimpse it from the **Kalaupapa Lookout**, at Palaau State Park. On the way, there are a few diversions (arranged here in geographical order).

EN ROUTE TO THE NORTH COAST

Coffees of Hawaii   The defunct Del Monte pineapple town of Kualapuu is rising again—only this time, coffee is the catch, not pineapple. Located in the cool foothills, Coffees of Hawaii has planted coffee beans on 600 acres of former pineapple land. The plantation irrigates the plants with a high-tech, continuous water-and-fertilizer drip system. You can see it all on the self-guided walking tour or the guided Morning Espresso Tour, which shows visitors the sorting facility and processing procedures. The less physically motivated should try the Mule Drawn Wagon Tour, great for families. The 2-hour tour is led by a guide and two mules (Moana and Leila or Lilo and Loke) through the coffee fields and around the reservoir. Afternoon adventures include a 2½-hour hike through the coffee fields to the top of Kualapuu Hill for a terrific view of Molokai. The Plantation Store sells arts and crafts from Molokai. Stop by the Espresso Bar for a Mocha Mama, an intoxicating blend of coffee, ice cream, and chocolate that will keep you going all day—maybe even all night.

1630 Farrington Ave. (near the junction of Hwy. 470), Kualapuu. © 877/322-FARM (3276) or 808/567-9490, ext. 26. www.coffeesofhawaii.com. Mon–Fri 8am–5pm; Sat 8am–4pm; Sun 8am–2pm. Self-guided tour free. Morning Espresso Tour Mon–Fri 10am; $20 adults, $10 kids 5–10. Mule Drawn Wagon Tour Mon–Fri 8am and 1pm, Sat–Sun 8am; $35 adults, $10 kids 5–10. Afternoon Hiking Adventures daily 3–5:30pm; free.

Molokai Museum and Cultural Center   En route to the California Gold Rush in 1849, Rudolph W. Meyer (a German professor) came to Molokai, married the high chiefess Kalama, and began to operate a small sugar plantation near his home. Now on the National Register of Historic Places, this restored 1878 sugar mill, with its century-old steam engine, mule-driven cane crusher, copper clarifiers, and redwood evaporating

(Kids) Especially for Kids

Flying a Kite (p. 293): Not only can you get a guaranteed-to-fly kite at the **Big Wind Kite Factory** (© 808/552-2634) in Maunaloa, but kite designer Jonathan Socher also offers free kite-flying classes to kids, who'll learn how to make their kites soar, swoop, and, most important, stay in the air for more than 5 minutes.

Spending the Day at Murphy (Kumimi) Beach Park (p. 277): Just beyond Waialua on the East End is this small wayside park that's perfect for kids. You'll find safe swimming conditions, plenty of shade from the ironwood trees, and small pavilions with picnic tables and barbecue grills.

pan (all in working order), is the last of its kind in Hawaii. The mill also houses a museum that traces the history of sugar growing on Molokai and has special events, such as wine tastings, taro festivals, an annual music festival, and occasional classes in ukulele making, loom weaving, and sewing. Call for a schedule.

Meyer Sugar Mill, Hwy. 470 (just after the turnoff for the Ironwood Hills Golf Course and 2 miles below Kalaupapa Overlook), Kalae. © 808/567-6436. Admission $2.50 adults, $1 students. Mon–Sat 10am–2pm.

Palaau State Park ☆   This 234-acre piney-woods park, 8 miles out of Kaunakakai, doesn't look like much until you get out of the car and take a hike, which literally puts you between a rock and a hard place. Go right, and you end up on the edge of Molokai's magnificent sea cliffs, with its panoramic view of the well-known Kalaupapa leper colony; go left, and you come face to face with a stone phallus.

If you have no plans to scale the cliffs by mule or on foot (see "Hiking & Camping," p. 280), the **Kalaupapa Lookout** ☆☆☆ is the only place from which to see the former place of exile. The trail is marked, and historic photos and interpretive signs will explain what you're seeing.

It's airy and cool in the ironwood forest, where camping is free at the designated state campground. You'll need a permit from the **State Division of Parks** (© 808/567-6618). Not many people seem to camp here, perhaps because of the legend associated with the **Phallic Rock** ☆. Six feet high and pointed at an angle that means business, Molokai's famous Phallic Rock is a legendary fertility tool: According to Hawaiian legend, a woman who wishes to become pregnant need only spend the night near the rock and . . . *voilà!*

Phallic Rock is at the end of a well-worn uphill path that passes an ironwood grove and several other rocks that vaguely resemble sexual body parts. No mistaking the big guy, though. It supposedly belonged to Nanahoa, a demigod who quarreled with his wife, Kawahuna, over a pretty girl. In the tussle, Kawahuna was thrown over the cliff, and both husband and wife were turned to stone. Of all the phallic rocks in Hawaii and the Pacific, this is the one to see. It's featured on a postcard with a tiny, awestruck Japanese woman standing next to it.

At the end of Hwy. 470.

THE LEGACY OF FATHER DAMIEN: KALAUPAPA NATIONAL HISTORICAL PARK ★★★

Kalaupapa, an old tongue of lava that sticks out to form a peninsula, became infamous because of man's inhumanity to victims of a formerly incurable contagious disease.

King Kamehameha V sent the first lepers—nine men and three women—into exile on this isolated shore, at the base of ramparts that rise like temples against the Pacific, on January 6, 1866. By 1874, more than 11,000 lepers had been dispatched to die in one of the world's most beautiful—and lonely—places. They called it Kalaupapa, "The Place of the Living Dead."

Leprosy is actually one of the world's least contagious diseases, transmitted only by direct, repetitive contact over a long period of time. It's caused by a bacterium, *Mycobacterium leprae*, that attacks the nerves, skin, and eyes, and is found mainly, but not exclusively, in tropical regions. American scientists found a cure for the disease in the 1940s.

Before science intervened, there was Father Damien. Born to wealth in Belgium, Joseph de Veuster traded a life of excess for exile among lepers, devoting himself to caring for the afflicted at Kalaupapa. Horrified by the conditions in the leper colony, Father Damien worked at Kalaupapa for 11 years, building houses, schools, and churches, and giving hope to his patients. He died on April 15, 1889, in Kalaupapa, of leprosy. He was 49.

A hero nominated for Catholic sainthood, Father Damien is buried not in his tomb next to Molokai's St. Philomena Church, but in his native Belgium. Well, most of him, anyway. His hand was recently returned to Molokai and was reinterred at Kalaupapa as a relic of his martyrdom.

This small peninsula is the final resting place of possibly more than 11,000 souls. The sand dunes are littered with grave markers, sorted by the religious affiliation—Catholic, Protestant, Buddhist—of those who died here. But so many are buried in unmarked graves that no accurate census of the dead exists.

Kalaupapa is now a national historical park (© **808/567-6802;** www.nps.gov/kala) and one of Hawaii's richest archaeological preserves, with sites that date from A.D. 1000. About 60 former patients chose to remain in this tidy village, where statues of angels stand in the yards of the whitewashed houses. The original name for their former affliction, leprosy, was officially banned in Hawaii by the state legislature in 1981. The name used now is "Hansen's disease," for Dr. Gerhard Hansen of Norway, who discovered the bacterium in 1873.

Kalaupapa welcomes visitors who arrive on foot, by mule, or by small plane. Father Damien's St. Philomena Church, built in 1872, is open to visitors, who can see it from a yellow school bus driven by resident tour guide Richard Marks, an ex-seaman and sheriff who survived the disease. You won't be able to roam freely, and you'll be allowed to enter only the museum, the crafts shop, and the church.

MULE RIDES TO KALAUPAPA ★★★   The first turn's a gasp, and it's all downhill from there. You can close your eyes and hold on for dear life, or slip the reins over the pommel and sit back, letting the mule do the walking down the precipitous path to Kalaupapa National Historical Park.

Even if you have only a day to spend on Molokai, spend it on a mule. This is a once-in-a-lifetime ride. The cliffs are taller than a 300-story skyscraper, but Buzzy Sproat's mules go safely up and down the narrow 3-mile trail daily, rain or shine. Starting at the top of the nearly perpendicular ridge (1,600 ft. high), the surefooted mules step down the muddy trail, pausing often on the 26 switchbacks to calculate their next move—and always, it seems to me, veering a little too close to the edge. Each switchback is numbered; by the time you get to number four, you'll catch your breath, put the mule on cruise control, and begin to enjoy Hawaii's most awesome trail ride.

The mule tours are offered once a day Monday through Saturday; the park is closed on Sunday. Tours start at 8am and last until about 3:30pm. It costs $165 per person for the all-day adventure, which includes the round-trip mule ride, a guided tour of the settlement, a visit to Father Damien's church and tomb, lunch at Kalawao, and souvenirs. Book in advance, as these tours often fill up. To go, you must be at least 16 years old and physically fit, and weigh less than 250 pounds. Contact **Molokai Mule Ride** ✦✦✦, 100 Kalae Hwy., Suite 104, on Hwy. 470, 5 miles north of Hwy. 460 (© **800/567-7550,** or 808/567-6088 8am–10pm; www.muleride.com). Advance reservations (at least 2 weeks ahead) are required.

SEEING KALAUPAPA BY PLANE   The fastest and easiest way to get to Kalaupapa is by hopping on a plane and zipping to Kalaupapa Airport. From here, you can pick up the same Kalaupapa tour that the mule riders and hikers take. **Molokai Mule Ride** (see above) will pick you up at the Kalaupapa Airport and take you to some of the area's most scenic spots, including Kalawao, where Father Damien's church still stands, and the town of Kalaupapa. The package includes round-trip airfare from Honolulu, hotel pickup, guided mule tour, entry permits, tour of the historical park, and a picnic lunch; it costs $319 per person, with a two-person minimum.

If you are coming from Maui, your choices are either to take the ferry (where you will hike in and back out in 1 day, or join the mule ride and then stay overnight, due to the ferry's schedule) or to go by plane (call them and they can help set up a charter plane).

If you are on Molokai and want to fly directly into Kalaupapa, Molokai Mule Ride will book you from the Molokai Airport to Kalaupapa and include entry permits, a park tour with Damien Tours, and a light picnic lunch for $130 per person, with a two-person minimum.

SEEING KALAUPAPA BY FERRY/HIKING   From Maui, take the *Molokai Princess* (© **800/275-6969** or 808/667-6165; www.mauiprincess.com) to Molokai, where you'll be met and transported by van to the top of the 1,700-foot sea cliffs. Here you hike down the 3-mile trail to the Kalaupapa National Historical Park; at the park, you are met by Damien Tours and given a van tour of the peninsula, during which you'll visit Father Damien's St. Philomena Church, see his early gravesite, and hear the stories of struggle and courage of the residents of Kalaupapa. The only catch is you have to hike back up the 1,700-foot cliffs, where you are picked up by van and returned to the ferry dock for the trip back to Maui. This fabulous experience really should be undertaken only by the physically fit (it will take about an hour to hike down and another 90 min. to hike back up). Cost for ferry, transportation, tour, and lunch is $277 (participants must be at least 16 years old).

THE WEST END
MAUNALOA
In the first and only attempt at urban renewal on Molokai, the 1920s-era pineapple-plantation town of Maunaloa has become a ghost town ever since the Molokai Ranch closed all of its operations in 2008 (including the movie theater, restaurant, lodge, and some shops).

ON THE NORTHWEST SHORE: MOOMOMI DUNES
Undisturbed for centuries, the Moomomi Dunes, on Molokai's northwest shore, are a unique treasure chest of great scientific value. The area may look like just a pile of sand

as you fly over on the final approach to Hoolehua Airport, but Moomomi Dunes is much more than that. Archaeologists have found adz quarries, ancient Hawaiian burial sites, and shelter caves; botanists have identified five endangered plant species; and marine biologists are finding evidence that endangered green sea turtles are coming out from the waters once again to lay eggs here. The greatest discovery, however, belongs to Smithsonian Institute ornithologists, who have found bones of prehistoric birds—some of them flightless—that existed nowhere else on earth.

Accessible by jeep trails that thread downhill to the shore, this wild coast is buffeted by strong afternoon breezes. It's hot, dry, and windy, so take water, sunscreen, and a windbreaker. At Kawaaloa Bay, a 20-minute walk to the west, there's a broad golden beach that you can have all to yourself. (*Warning:* Due to the rough seas, stay out of the water.) Within the dunes, there's a 920-acre preserve accessible via monthly guided nature tours led by the **Nature Conservancy of Hawaii;** call © **808/553-5236** or 524-0779 for an exact schedule and details.

To get here, take Hwy. 460 (Maunaloa Hwy.) from Kaunakakai; turn right onto Hwy. 470, and follow it to Kualapuu. At Kualapuu, turn left on Hwy. 480 and go through Hoolehua Village; it's 3 miles to the bay.

THE EAST END

The East End is a cool and inviting green place that's worth a drive to the end of King Kamehameha V Highway (Hwy. 450). Unfortunately, the trail that leads into the area's greatest natural attraction, Halawa Valley, is now off-limits.

A HORSEBACK RIDE TO ILIILIOPAE HEIAU

On horseback (where the elevated view is magnificent), you bump along a dirt trail through an incredible mango grove, bound for an ancient temple of human sacrifice. This temple of doom—right out of *Indiana Jones*—is Iliiliopae, a huge rectangle of stone made of 90 million rocks, overlooking the once-important village of Mapulehu and four ancient fishponds. The horses trek under the perfumed mangoes and then head uphill through a kiawe forest filled with Java plums to the *heiau* (temple), which stands across a dry stream bed under cloud-spiked Kaunolu, the 4,970-foot island summit.

Hawaii's most powerful *heiau* attracted *kahuna* (priests) from all over the islands. They came to learn the rules of human sacrifice at this university of sacred rites. Contrary to Hollywood's version, historians say that the victims here were always men, not young virgins, and that they were strangled, not thrown into a volcano, while priests sat on lauhala mats watching silently. Spooky, eh?

This is the biggest, oldest, and most famous *heiau* on Molokai. The massive 22-foot-high stone altar is dedicated to Lono, the Hawaiian god of fertility. The *heiau* resonates with *mana* (power) strong enough to lean on. Legend says Iliiliopae was built in a single night by a thousand men who passed rocks hand over hand through the Wailau Valley from the other side of the island; in exchange for the *ili'ili* (rock), each received an *'opae* (shrimp). Others say it was built by *menehune,* mythic elves who accomplished Herculean feats.

After the visit to the temple, your horse takes you back to the mango grove. Contact **Molokai Wagon Rides,** King Kamehameha V Highway (Hwy. 450), at mile marker 15, Kaunakakai (© **808/558-8380**). The tour and horseback ride costs $37 per person. The hour-long ride goes up to the *heiau,* then beyond it to the top of the mountain for those breathtaking views, and finally back down to the beach.

KAMAKOU PRESERVE

It's hard to believe, but close to the nearly mile-high summit here, it rains more than 80 inches a year—enough to qualify as a rainforest. The Molokai Forest, as it was historically known, is the source of 60% of Molokai's water. Nearly 3,000 acres, from the summit to the lowland forests of eucalyptus and pine, are now held by the Nature Conservancy, which has identified 219 Hawaiian plants that grow here exclusively. The preserve is also the last stand of the endangered *olomao* (Molokai thrush) and *kawawahie* (Molokai creeper).

To get to the preserve, take the Molokai Forest Reserve Road from Kaunakakai. It's a 45-minute four-wheel-drive trip on a dirt trail to Waikolu Lookout Campground; from here, you can venture into the wilderness preserve on foot across a boardwalk on a 1½-hour hike (see "The Pepeopae Trail," p. 280). For more information, contact the **Nature Conservancy** (© **808/553-5236;** www.nature.org).

EN ROUTE TO HALAWA VALLEY

No visit to Molokai is complete without at least a passing glance at the island's **ancient fishponds,** a singular achievement in Pacific aquaculture. With their hunger for fresh fish and lack of ice and refrigeration, Hawaiians perfected aquaculture in A.D. 1400, before Christopher Columbus "discovered" America. They built gated, U-shaped stone and coral walls on the shore to catch fish on the incoming tide; they would then raise them in captivity. The result: a constant, ready supply of fresh fish.

The ponds, which stretch for 20 miles along Molokai's south shore and are visible from Kamehameha V Highway (Hwy. 450), offer insight into the island's ancient population. It took something like a thousand people to tend a single fishpond, and more than 60 ponds once existed on this coast. Some are silted in by red-dirt runoff from south-coast gulches; others are in use by folks who raise fish and seaweed.

The largest, 54-acre **Keawa Nui Pond,** is surrounded by a 3-foot-high, 2,000-foot-long stone wall. **Alii Fish Pond,** reserved for kings, is visible through the coconut groves at One Alii Beach Park (p. 276). From the road, you can see **Kalokoeli Pond,** 6 miles east of Kaunakakai on the highway.

Our Lady of Sorrows Catholic Church, one of five built by Father Damien on Molokai and the first outside Kalaupapa, sits across the highway from a fishpond. Park in the church lot (except on Sun) for a closer look.

St. Joseph's Catholic Church   The afternoon sun strikes St. Joseph's Church with such a bold ray of light that it looks as if God is about to perform a miracle. This little 1876 wood-frame church is one of four Father Damien built "topside" on Molokai. Restored in 1971, the church stands beside a seaside cemetery, where feral cats play under the gaze of a Damien statue amid gravestones decorated with flower leis. King Kamehameha V Hwy. (Hwy. 450), just after mile marker 10.

Smith Bronte Landing Site   In 1927, Charles Lindbergh soloed across the Atlantic Ocean in a plane called *The Spirit of St. Louis* and became an American hero. That same year, Ernie Smith and Emory B. Bronte took off from Oakland, California, on July 14, in a single-engine Travelair aircraft named *The City of Oakland,* headed across the Pacific Ocean for Honolulu, 2,397 miles away. The next day, after running out of fuel, they crash-landed upside-down in a kiawe thicket on Molokai, but emerged unhurt to become the first civilians to fly to Hawaii from the U.S. mainland. The 25-hour, 2-minute flight landed Smith and Bronte a place in aviation history—and a roadside marker on Molokai. King Kamehameha V Hwy. (Hwy. 450), at mile marker 11, on the makai (ocean) side.

Moments Halawa Valley: A Hike Back in History

"There are things on Molokai, sacred things, that you may not be able to see or may not hear, but they are there," says Pilipo Solotario, who was born and raised in Halawa Valley and survived the 1946 tsunami that barreled into the ancient valley. "As Hawaiians, we respect these things." Solotario feels it is important that visitors learn about the history and culture of Molokai; that is part of the secret of appreciating the island.

"I see my role, and I'm nearly 70 years old, as educating people, outsiders, on our culture, our history," he said at the beginning of this cultural hike into his family property in Halawa Valley. "To really appreciate Molokai, you need to understand and know things so that you are *pono*, you are right with the land and don't disrespect the culture. Then you see the real Molokai."

Solotario and his family, who own the land in the valley, are the only people allowed to hike into Halawa. They lead daily tours, which begin at the county park pavilion, with a history of the valley, a discussion of Hawaiian culture, and a display of the fruits, trees, and other flora you will see. Along the hike, Solotario stops to point out historical and cultural aspects, including chanting in Hawaiian before entering a sacred *heiau*. At the waterfalls, visitors can swim in the brisk water. Cost for the 4-hour tour is $75. Book through **Molokai Fish & Dive** (© **808/553-5926**; www.molokaifishanddive.com). Bring insect repellent, water, a snack, and a swimsuit. Don't forget your camera.

Note that if you venture away from the county park into the valley on your own, you will be trespassing and can be prosecuted.

HALAWA VALLEY ⊛

Of the five great valleys of Molokai, only Halawa—with its two waterfalls, golden beach, sleepy lagoon, great surf, and offshore island—is easily accessible. Unfortunately, the trail through fertile Halawa Valley, which was inhabited for centuries, and on to the 250-foot Moaula Falls has been closed for some time. There is one operator who conducts hikes to the falls (see below).

You can spend a day at Halawa Beach Park (p. 277), but do not venture into the valley on your own. In a kind of 21st-century *kapu*, the private landowners in the valley, worried about slip-and-fall lawsuits, have posted NO TRESPASSING signs on their properties.

To get to Halawa Valley, drive north from Kaunakakai on Hwy. 450 for 30 miles along the coast to the end of the road, which descends into the valley past Jersalema Hou Church. If you'd just like a glimpse of the valley on your way to the beach, there's a scenic overlook along the road: After Pu'u o Hoku Ranch at mile marker 25, the narrow two-lane road widens at a hairpin curve, and you'll find the overlook on your right; it's 2 miles more to the valley floor.

10 Shopping

KAUNAKAKAI

Molokai Surf, Molokai Island Creations, and **Lourdes** are clothing and gift shops close to one another in downtown Kaunakakai, where most of the retail shops sell

T-shirts, muumuu, surf wear, and informal apparel. For food shopping, there are several good options—and because many visitors stay in condos, knowing the grocery stores is especially important. Other than that, serious shoppers will be disappointed, unless they love kites or native-wood vessels. The following are Kaunakakai's notable stores.

Bamboo Pantry It's hard to believe this creative kitchenware, cutlery, and specialty-foods store is located in the heart of Kaunakakai. It has everything from dishes, woven baskets, and glassware to high-end cookware and gourmet food. 107 Ala Malama St., Kaunakakai. ⓒ 808/553-3300.

Imamura Store Wilfred Imamura, whose mother founded this store, recalls the old railroad track that stretched from the pier to a spot across the street. "We brought our household things from the pier on a hand-pumped vehicle," he recalls. His store, appropriately, is a leap into the past, a marvelous amalgam of precious old-fashioned things. Rubber boots, Hawaiian-print tablecloths, ukulele cases, plastic slippers, and even coconut bikini tops line the shelves. But it's not all nostalgia: The Molokai T-shirts, jeans, and *palaka* shorts are of good quality and inexpensive, and the pareu fabrics are a find. In Kaunakakai. ⓒ 808/553-5615.

Molokai Drugs David Mikami, whose father-in-law founded this pharmacy in 1935, has made this more than a drugstore. It's a friendly stop full of life's basic necessities, with generous amenities such as a phone and a restroom for passersby. Here you'll find the best selection of guidebooks, books about Molokai, and maps, as well as paperbacks, cassette players, flip-flops, and every imaginable essential. The Mikamis are a household name on the island, not only because of their pharmacy, but also because the family has shown exceptional kindness to the often economically strapped Molokaians. At the Kamoi Professional Center. ⓒ 808/553-5790.

Molokai Fine Arts Gallery ⓐⓐ (Finds) If you shop in only one store in Kaunakakai, make it this one. The expanded gallery (it recently moved to a much bigger and better space) features the very best of Molokai artists and craftspeople. Peruse the myriad forms of art, such as exquisite handmade jewelry (from contemporary gold earrings, necklaces, and rings to Molokai shell leis), scenic paintings, batik on wood, photos, etched glass, carved bowls, and even feather leis. 2 Kamoi St., Suite 300, Kaunakakai. ⓒ 808/553-8520. www.molokaifinearts.com.

Molokai Fish & Dive Here you'll find the island's largest selection of T-shirts and souvenirs, crammed in among fishing, snorkeling, and outdoor gear that you can rent or buy. Find your way around the fish nets, boogie boards, bamboo rakes, beach towels, juices and soft drinks, disposable cameras, and staggering miscellany of this store. One entire wall is lined with T-shirts, and the selection of Molokai books and souvenirs is extensive. The staff is happy to point out the best snorkeling spots of the day. In Kaunakakai. ⓒ 808/553-5926. www.molokaifishanddive.com.

Molokai Surf This wooden building houses Molokai Surf and its selection of skateboards, surf shorts, sweatshirts, sunglasses, T-shirts, footwear, boogie boards, backpacks, and a broad range of clothing and accessories for life in the surf and sun. 130 Kamehameha V Hwy., Kaunakakai. ⓒ 808/553-5093.

Take's Variety Store If you need luggage tags, buzz saws, toys, candy, cloth dolls, canned goods, canteens, camping equipment, hardware, batteries, candles, fishing supplies—whew!—and other products for work and play, this variety store—which has

The Perfect Molokai Souvenir

It's small, it's easy to pack, and it's made only on Molokai: It's Molokai salt. The Hawaii Kai Corporation (www.hawaiikaico.com) has two product lines featuring Molokai salt: the gourmet **Soul of the Sea** ($18 for 12 oz.) and the **Palm Island Premium** ($6 for 6 oz.). Soul of the Sea salt is hand-harvested from some of the cleanest ocean water in the state, hand-processed and hand-packed on Molokai. It comes in three varietals: Papohaku White, Kilauea Black, and Haleakala Red. While making Soul of the Sea salt, Hawaii Kai Corporation got a byproduct it calls Ocean Essence, which it blends with Molokai salt to restore trace minerals lost in the heating process. The result is Palm Island Premium, which comes in White Silver, Red Gold, Black Lava, and Bamboo Jade. The newest line is **Hawaii Kai Gourmet,** which comes in white, red, black, and green blends.

been around more than 50 years—is the answer. You may suffer from claustrophobia in the crowded, dusty aisles, but Take's carries everything. In Kaunakakai. ℭ **808/553-5442.**

EDIBLES

For fresh-baked goods, see **Kanemitsu's Bakery & Restaurant** (p. 274).

Friendly Market Center   You can't miss this salmon-colored wooden storefront on the main drag of "downtown" Kaunakakai, where people of all generations can be found just talking story. Friendly's carries everything from local poi to Glenlivet. Blue-corn tortilla chips, soy milk, and Kumu Farms macadamia-nut pesto, the island's stellar gourmet food, are among the items that surpass standard grocery-store fare. In Kaunakakai. ℭ **808/553-5595.**

Misaki's Grocery and Dry Goods   Established in 1922, this third-generation local legend is one of Kaunakakai's two grocery stores. Some of its notable items: fresh luau leaves (taro greens), fresh okra, Boca Burgers, large Korean chestnuts in season, gorgeous bananas, and an ATM. The fish section includes akule and ahi, fresh and dried. Liquor, stationery, candies, and paper products round out the selection in this full-service grocery. In Kaunakakai. ℭ **808/553-5505.**

Molokai Wines & Spirits   This is your best bet on the island for a decent bottle of wine. The shop offers 200 labels, including Caymus, Silver Oak, Joseph Phelps, Heitz, and Bonny Doon. The snack options include imported cheeses, salami, and Carr's biscuits. In Kaunakakai. ℭ **808/553-5009.**

EN ROUTE TO THE NORTH COAST

Coffees of Hawaii Plantation Store and Espresso Bar   This is a fairly slick—for Molokai—combination coffee bar, store, and gallery for more than 30 artists and craftspeople from Hawaii. Sold here are the Malulani Estate and Muleskinner coffees that are grown on the 500-acre plantation surrounding the shop (see p. 284 for plantation tours). The gift items are worth a look: pikake and plumeria soaps from Kauai, pure beeswax candles from Maui, koa bookmarks and hair sticks, pottery, and baskets. Hwy. 480 (near Hwy. 470), Kualapuu. ℭ **800/709-BEAN** (2326) or 808/567-9023.

Molokai Museum Gift Shop   This restored 1878 sugar mill sits 1,500 feet above the town of Kualapuu. It's a considerable drive from town, but a good cause for those who'd like to support the museum and the handful of local artisans who sell their crafts, fabrics, cookbooks, quilt sets, and other gift items in the tiny shop. There's also a modest selection of cards, T-shirts, coloring books, and, at Christmas, handmade ornaments made of lauhala and koa. Meyer Sugar Mill, Hwy. 470 (just after the turnoff for the Ironwood Hills Golf Course and 2 miles below Kalaupapa Overlook), Kalae. ℂ 808/567-6436.

EDIBLES

Kualapuu Market   This market, in its third generation, is a stone's throw from the Coffees of Hawaii store. It's a scaled-down, one-stop shop with wine, food, and necessities—and a surprisingly presentable, albeit small, assortment of produce, from Molokai sweet potatoes to Ka'u navel oranges in season. The shelves are filled with canned goods, propane, rope, hoses, paper products, and baking goods, reflecting the rural lifestyle of the area. In Kualapuu. ℂ 808/567-6243.

THE WEST END

Big Wind Kite Factory & Plantation Gallery 𝄞𝄞   Jonathan and Daphne Socher, kite designers and inveterate Bali-philes, have combined their interests in a kite factory/import shop that dominates the commercial landscape of Maunaloa, the reconstituted plantation town. Maunaloa's naturally windy conditions make it ideal for kite-flying classes (offered free when conditions are right). The adjoining gallery features local handicrafts such as milo-wood bowls, locally made T-shirts, sandblasted glassware, lauhala baskets, and Hawaiian-music CDs. There are also many Balinese handicrafts, from jewelry to clothing and fabrics. In Maunaloa. ℂ 808/552-2364.

A Touch of Molokai 𝄞   Even though the Kalaukoi Hotel is closed, this fabulous shop remains open. It is well worth the drive. The surf shorts and aloha shirts sold here are better than the norm, with attractive, up-to-date choices by Jams, Quiksilver, and other brands. Tencel dresses, South Pacific shell necklaces (up to $400), and a magnificent hand-turned milo bowl also caught my attention. Most impressive are the *wiliwili, kamani,* and soapberry leis and a handsome array of lauhala bags, all made on Molokai. At Kaluakoi Hotel & Golf Club. ℂ 808/552-0133.

THE EAST END
EDIBLES

Mana'e Goods and Grindz   Formerly the Neighborhood Store 'N Counter, the only grocery on the East End sells batteries, film, aspirin, cookies, beer, Molokai produce, candies, paper products, and other sundries. There's good food pouring out of the kitchen at the breakfast and lunch counter, too. See p. 276 for a restaurant review. In Pukoo. ℂ 808/558-8498.

11 Molokai After Dark

Hotel Molokai, in Kaunakakai (ℂ **808/553-5347;** www.hotelmolokai.com), offers live entertainment poolside and in the dining room every night. At Aloha Fridays, every Friday from 4 to 6pm, the musicians of Molokai who have been performing here for decades show you why locals love their music and hula. With its South Seas ambience and poolside setting, this has become the island's premier venue for local and visiting entertainers.

The **Paddlers' Inn,** also in Kaunakakai (ℂ **808/553-5256**), has recently become a nightspot for live Hawaiian music, comedy acts, and other entertainment such as karaoke; see the website for the current schedule.

12

Lanai, a Different Kind of Paradise

Lanai is not an easy place to reach. There are no direct flights from the mainland. It's almost as if this quiet, gentle oasis—known, paradoxically, for both its small-town feel and its celebrity appeal—demands that its visitors go to great lengths to get here in order to ensure that they will appreciate it.

Lanai (pronounced lah-*nigh*-ee), the nation's biggest defunct pineapple patch, now claims to be one of the world's top tropical destinations. It's a bold claim because so little is here; Lanai has even fewer dining and accommodations choices than Molokai. There are no stoplights and barely 30 miles of paved road. This almost virgin island is unspoiled by what passes for progress, except for a tiny 1920s-era plantation village—and, of course, the village's fancy new arrivals: two first-class luxury hotels where room rates average $400-plus a night.

As soon as you arrive on Lanai, you'll feel the small-town coziness. People wave to every car, residents stop to "talk story" with their friends, fishing and working in the garden are considered priorities in life, and leaving the keys in your car's ignition is standard practice.

For generations, Lanai was little more than a small village, owned and operated by the pineapple company, surrounded by acres of pineapple fields. The few visitors to the island were either relatives of the residents or occasional weekend hunters. Life in the 1960s was pretty much the

same as in the 1930s. But all that changed in 1990, when the Lodge at Koele, a 102-room hotel resembling an opulent English Tudor mansion, opened its doors, followed a year later by the 250-room Manele Bay, a Mediterranean-style luxury resort overlooking Hulopoe Bay. Overnight the isolated island was transformed: Corporate jets streamed into tiny Lanai Airport, former plantation workers were retrained in the art of serving gourmet meals, and the population of 2,500 swelled with transient visitors and outsiders coming to work in the island's new hospitality industry. Microsoft billionaire Bill Gates chose the island for his lavish wedding, booking all of its hotel rooms to fend off the press—and uncomplicated Lanai went on the map as a vacation spot for the rich and powerful.

But this island is also a place where people come looking for dramatic beauty, quiet, solitude, and an experience with nature. The sojourners who find their way to Lanai seek out the dramatic views, the tropical fusion of stars at night, and the chance to be alone with the elements.

They also come for the wealth of activities: snorkeling and swimming in the marine preserve known as Hulopoe Bay, hiking on 100 miles of remote trails, talking story with the friendly locals, and beachcombing and whale-watching along stretches of otherwise deserted sand. For the adventurous, there's horseback riding in the forest, scuba diving in caves, playing

Lanai

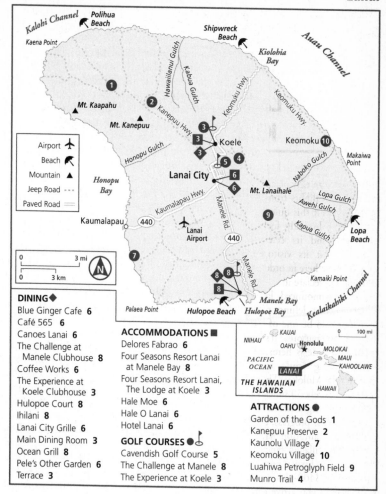

DINING ◆
Blue Ginger Cafe **6**
Café 565 **6**
Canoes Lanai **6**
The Challenge at
  Manele Clubhouse **8**
Coffee Works **6**
The Experience at
  Koele Clubhouse **3**
Hulopoe Court **8**
Ihilani **8**
Lanai City Grille **6**
Main Dining Room **3**
Ocean Grill **8**
Pele's Other Garden **6**
Terrace **3**

ACCOMMODATIONS ■
Delores Fabrao **6**
Four Seasons Resort Lanai
  at Manele Bay **8**
Four Seasons Resort Lanai,
  The Lodge at Koele **3**
Hale Moe **6**
Hale O Lanai **6**
Hotel Lanai **6**

GOLF COURSES ●⛳
Cavendish Golf Course **5**
The Challenge at Manele **8**
The Experience at Koele **3**

ATTRACTIONS ●
Garden of the Gods **1**
Kanepuu Preserve **2**
Kaunolu Village **7**
Keomoku Village **10**
Luahiwa Petroglyph Field **9**
Munro Trail **4**

golf on courses with stunning ocean views, or renting a four-wheel-drive vehicle for the day and discovering wild plains where spotted deer run free.

In a single decade, a plain red-dirt pineapple patch has become one of Hawaii's top fantasy destinations. But the real Lanai is a multifaceted place that's so much more than a luxury resort—and it's the traveler who comes to discover the island's natural wonders, local lifestyle, and other inherent joys who's bound to have the most genuine island experience.

THE PINEAPPLE ISLAND'S UNUSUAL PAST
This old shield volcano in the rain shadow of Maui has a history of resisting change in a big way. Early Polynesians, fierce Hawaiian kings, European explorers, 20th-century farmers—the island has seen them all and sent most of them packing, empty-handed

and broken. The ancient Hawaiians believed that the island was haunted by spirits so wily and vicious that no human could survive here. People didn't settle here until around A.D. 1400.

But those spirits never really went away, it seems. In 1778, the king of the Big Island, Kalaniopuu, invaded Lanai in what was called "the war of loose bowels." His men slaughtered every warrior, cut down trees, and set fire to all that was left except a bitter fern whose roots gave them all dysentery.

In 1802, Wu Tsin made the first attempt to harvest a crop on the island, but he ultimately abandoned his cane fields and went away. Charles Gay acquired 600 acres at public auction to experiment with pineapple as a crop, but a 3-year drought left him bankrupt. Others tried in vain to grow cotton, sisal, and sugar beets; they started a dairy and a piggery and raised sheep for wool. But all enterprises failed, mostly for lack of water.

Harry Baldwin, a missionary's grandson, was the first to succeed on Lanai. He bought Lanai for $588,000 in 1917, developed a 20-mile water pipeline between Koele and Manele, and sold the island 5 years later to Jim Dole for $1.1 million.

Dole planted and irrigated 18,000 acres of pineapple, built Lanai City, blasted out a harbor, and turned the island into a fancy fruit plantation. For a half-century, he enjoyed great success. Even Dole was ultimately vanquished, however: Cheaper pineapple production in Asia brought an end to Lanai's heyday.

The island still resembles old photographs taken in the glory days of Dole. Any minute now, you half expect to look up and see old Jim Dole himself rattling up the road in a Model-T truck with a load of fresh-picked pineapples. Only now, there's a new lord of the manor, and his name is David Murdock.

Of all who have looked at Lanai with a gleam in their eye, nobody has succeeded quite like Murdock, a self-made billionaire who acquired the island in a merger more than a decade ago. About 97% of it is now his private holding.

Murdock spent $400 million to build two grand hotels on the island: the Lodge at Koele, which resembles an English country retreat, and the Four Seasons Resort Lanai at Manele Bay, a green tile-roofed Mediterranean palazzo by the sea. Murdock recycled the former field hands into waitstaff, even summoning a London butler to school the natives in the fine art of service, and carved a pair of daunting golf courses, one in the island's interior and the other along the wave-lashed coast. He then set out to attract tourists by touting Lanai as "the private island."

Murdock is now trying to make all this pay for itself by selling vacation homes and condos, all in the million-dollar range, next door to the two resorts.

The redevelopment of this tiny rock should have been a pushover for the big-time tycoon, but island-style politics have continually thwarted his schemes. GO SLOW, a sun-faded sign at Dole's old maintenance shed once said. Murdock might have heeded the warning because his grandiose plans are taking twice as long to accomplish as he had expected. Lanai is under the political thumb of many who believe that the island's precious water supply shouldn't all be diverted to championship golf courses and Jacuzzis, and there remains opposition from Lanaians for Sensible Growth, who advocate affordable housing, alternative water systems, and civic improvements that benefit residents.

Lanai residents might have lived in a rural setting, but they certainly haven't been isolated. Having watched the other islands in Hawaii attempt the balancing act of economic growth and the maintenance of an island lifestyle, the residents of Lanai are cautiously welcoming visitors, but at a pace that is still easy for this former plantation community to digest.

1 Orientation

ARRIVING

BY PLANE   No matter where you're coming from, you'll have to make a connection in Honolulu (on Oahu) or Kahului (on Maui), where you can catch a plane for the 25-minute flight to Lanai's airport. You'll touch down in Puuwai Basin, once the world's largest pineapple plantation; it's about 10 minutes by car to Lanai City and 25 minutes to Manele Bay.

Commuter airline Pacific Wings operates a discount airline, **PW Express** (© 888/866-5022 or 808/873-0877; www.pacificwings.com/pwexpress), with daily nonstop flights between Lanai and Honolulu. Another inexpensive air carrier, **go!** (© 888/I-FLY-GO-2 [435-9462]; www.iflygo.com), in conjunction with Mokulele Airlines, provides service from Kahului (Maui) and Honolulu (Oahu) to Lanai under the name **go!Express,** on its new fleet of Cessna Grand Caravan 208B planes. Currently, go!Express offers the best rates and deals among Hawaii's air carriers.

Also offering service to Lanai is **Island Air** (© 800/323-3345 from the mainland, 800/652-6541 interisland, or 808/565-6744; www.islandair.com), with daily flights from Honolulu. I must warn you, however, that I have gotten less than sterling service from Island Air, which has left me stranded midroute—not once, but twice!

BY BOAT   A round-trip on **Expeditions Maui–Lanai Passenger Ferry** (© 808/661-3756; www.go-lanai.com) takes you between Maui and Lanai for $25 adults and $20 children, each way. The ferry runs five times a day, 365 days a year, between Lahaina (on Maui) and Lanai's Manele Bay harbor. The 9-mile channel crossing takes 45 minutes to an hour, depending on sea conditions. Reservations are strongly recommended; call or book online. Baggage is limited to two checked bags and one carry-on.

VISITOR INFORMATION

Lanai Visitors Bureau, P.O. Box 631436, Lanai City, HI 96763; or 431 Seventh St., Suite A, Lanai City (© **800/947-4774** or 808/565-7600; fax 808/565-9316; www.visitlanai.net), and the **Hawaii Visitors & Convention Bureau** (© **800/GO-HAWAII** [464-2924] or 808/923-1811; www.gohawaii.com) provide brochures, maps, and island guides.

THE ISLAND IN BRIEF

Inhabited Lanai is divided into three parts—Lanai City, Koele, and Manele—and two distinct climate zones: hot and dry, and cool and misty.

Lanai City (pop. 3,200) sits at the heart of the island at 1,645 feet above sea level. It's the only place on the island where you'll find services. Built in 1924, this plantation village is a tidy grid of quaint tin-roofed cottages in bright pastels, with tropical gardens of banana, *lilikoi,* and papaya. Many of the residents are Filipino immigrants who once worked the pineapple fields. Their clapboard homes, now worth $500,000 or more (for a 1,000-sq.-ft. home, built in 1935, on a tiny 5,000-sq.-ft. lot), are excellent examples of historic preservation; the whole town looks like it's been kept under a bell jar.

Around Dole Park, a charming village square lined with towering Norfolk and Cook Island pines, plantation buildings house general stores selling basic necessities, a post office (where people stop to chat), two banks, three restaurants, an art gallery, an arts center, a whimsical shop, and a coffee shop that outshines any Starbucks. A victim of "progress" was the local one-room police station with a jail that consisted of three blue-and-white wooden outhouse-size cells with padlocks. It's now a block from the square with "modern facilities," including regulation-size jail cells.

In the nearby cool upland district of **Koele** is the Lodge at Koele (now managed by the Four Seasons Resort), standing alone on a knoll overlooking pastures and the sea at the edge of a pine forest, like a grand European manor.

The other bastion of indulgence, the Four Seasons Resort Lanai at Manele Bay, is on the sunny southwestern tip of the island at **Manele.** You'll get more of what you expect from Hawaii here—beaches, swaying palms, mai tais, and the like.

FAST FACTS

Lanai is part of Maui County. In case of **emergencies,** call the police, fire department, or ambulance services at ℭ **911,** or the **Poison Control Center** at ℭ **800/362-3585.** For nonemergencies, call the **police** at ℭ **808/565-6428.**

For emergency dental care, call **Dr. James Sagawa** (ℭ **808/565-6418**). If you need a doctor, contact the **Lanai Family Health Center** (ℭ **808/565-6423**) or the **Lanai Community Hospital** (ℭ **808/565-6411**).

For a weather report, call the **National Weather Service** at ℭ **808/565-6033.**

2 Getting Around

With so few paved roads here, you'll need a four-wheel-drive vehicle if you plan to explore the island's remote shores, its interior, or the summit of Mount Lanaihale. Even if you have only a day on Lanai, rent one and see the island. Both standard cars and four-wheel-drive vehicles are available at the **Dollar Rent-A-Car** desk at **Lanai City Service/Lanai Plantation Store,** 1036 Lanai Ave. (ℭ **800/588-7808** for Dollar reservations, or 808/565-7227 for Lanai City Service). Expect to pay about $139 a day for a four-wheel-drive jeep.

Warning: Gas is expensive on Lanai, and those four-wheel-drive vehicles get terrible mileage. Because everything in Lanai City is within walking distance, it makes sense to rent a jeep only for the days you want to explore the island.

Though it's fun to rent a car and explore the island, it is possible to stay here and get to the beach without one. The two big resort hotels run shuttle vans to the Four Seasons Resort Lanai at Manele Bay; from there, you can walk to Hulopoe Beach. When you want to return, you just catch the hourly shuttle (it may run on the half-hour from Four Seasons Resort Lanai at Manele Bay) back to Lanai City.

If you're staying elsewhere, you can walk to everything in Lanai City and take a taxi to the beach. **Lanai Plantation Store** (ℭ **808/565-7227**) will provide transportation from Lanai City to Hulopoe Beach for $10 per person one-way (you can arrange in advance when you want to be picked up, or walk over to the Four Seasons Resort Lanai at Manele Bay and phone them to come and get you—or you can most likely get a ride back up to Lanai City with a local). Whether or not you rent a car, sooner or later you'll find yourself at Lanai City Service/Lanai Plantation Store. This all-in-one grocery store, gas station, rental-car agency, and souvenir shop serves as the island's Grand Central Terminal—you can pick up information, directions, maps, and all the local gossip here.

3 Where to Stay

The majority of the accommodations are located "in the village," as residents call Lanai City. Above the village is the luxurious Four Seasons Resort Lanai, the Lodge at Koele, while down the hill at Hulopoe Bay are two options: the equally luxurious Four Seasons Resort Lanai at Manele Bay or tent camping under the stars at the park. In Lanai City, Hotel Lanai is the only hotel, or you can choose from several B&Bs and vacation rentals.

In addition to the choices listed below, consider the B&B accommodations offered by **Delores Fabrao** (✆ **808/565-6134;** dmfabrao@hotmail.com), who has two guest rooms in her home: a double with a shared bathroom and a family room that sleeps up to six with a private bathroom. This is the best deal on Lanai, with prices unchanged for the last 10 years ($55 double, $100 for four); she says she considers it a service to the community. She doesn't provide breakfast, but you'll have the run of the entire house, including the kitchen. If she has any of her homemade jams or jellies for sale, buy as many jars as you can! At **Hale Moe** (✆ **808/565-9520** or 565-6656; www.staylanai.com), host and Lanai native Momi Suzuki makes three bedrooms in her Lanai City home available to guests; all have private bathrooms ($80–$90 double). Guests are welcome to use the entertainment center, the large deck, and her bicycle. She also has a vacation rental house for $300. **Hale O Lanai,** in Lanai City (✆ **808/247-3637;** www.hibeach.com), has a fully equipped two-bedroom vacation rental that sleeps up to six; rates range from $115 to $135.

Don't forget to add 11.42% in taxes to all accommodations bills. Parking is free.

EXPENSIVE

Four Seasons Resort Lanai at Manele Bay ✦✦✦   The well-known luxury hotel chain Four Seasons took over management of this 236-unit oceanside resort after a $50-million makeover. Every Four Seasons resort is spectacular, but this one really stands out. Located on a sun-washed southern bluff overlooking Hulopoe Beach, one of Hawaii's best stretches of golden sand, this U-shaped hotel steps down the hillside to the pool and the beach, and then fans out in oceanfront wings separated by gardens with lush flora, man-made waterfalls, lotus ponds, and streams. On the other side, it's bordered by golf greens. The place is a real oasis against the dry Arizona-like heat of Lanai's south coast.

Designed as a traditional luxury beachfront hotel, it features open, airy rooms, each with a breathtaking view of the big blue Pacific. Murals depicting scenes from Hawaiian history, sea charts, potted palms, soft camel-hued club chairs, and hand-woven kilim rugs fill the lobby. Redone in the clean, crisp style of an elegant Hawaiian resort, the oversize guest rooms have 40-inch flatscreen LCD TVs, huge marble bathrooms, and semiprivate lanais. This resort is much less formal than the Lodge at Koele up the hill and attracts more families. Speaking of families, in addition to the "Kids for All Seasons" child-care programs, the hotel features a teen center with video games, computers, a small pool table, and a 54-inch TV.

The new spa facility offers a variety of massages, facials, wraps, and scrubs (don't miss the signature Ali'i banana-coconut scrub). In addition, the Four Seasons has added a 1,500-square-foot fitness center (with one of the best ocean views in the resort) that has the latest cardiovascular and strength-training equipment, free weights, and a wood-floored studio for classes (spinning, yoga, Pilates, and meditation).

1 Manele Bay Rd., P.O. Box 631380, Lanai City, HI 96763. ✆ **800/321-4666** or 808/565-2000. Fax 808/565-2483. www.fourseasons.com/lanai. 236 units. $445–$1,370 double; from $1,600 suite. Extra person $75. Children 17 and

under stay free in parent's room. Numerous packages available. AE, DC, MC, V. Airport shuttle $33 round-trip. **Amenities:** 4 restaurants (Ihilani, p. 301; Hulopoe Court, p. 302; Ocean Grill, p. 302; and Challenge at Manele Clubhouse, p. 302); bar w/breathtaking views; large outdoor pool; golf at the Jack Nicklaus–designed Challenge at Manele; tennis courts; fitness center w/classes; full spa; Jacuzzi; complimentary snorkeling equipment; children's program; game room; concierge; activities desk; business center; retail store; salon; room service; massage; babysitting; laundry service; dry cleaning. *In room:* A/C, TV/DVD, dataport, wireless Internet access ($10 per day), minibar, coffeemaker, hair dryer, iron, safe.

Four Seasons Resort Lanai, The Lodge at Koele ★★★ After some $50 million in renovations, the luxury resort chain Four Seasons took over the management of the former Lodge at Koele. This inn, which resembles a grand English country estate, was built in 1991 and needed the makeover—the new look is spectacular. All 102 guest rooms were totally redone, a game room was added, the grounds have been spruced up, and a pagoda imported from China has been constructed on the sprawling English gardens' grounds (not my taste, but I'm sure it will be the backdrop for hundreds of wedding photos).

Inside, heavy timbers, beamed ceilings, and the two huge stone fireplaces of the Great Hall complete the look. Overstuffed furniture sits invitingly around the fireplaces, richly patterned rugs adorn the floor, and museum-quality art hangs on the walls. The guest rooms continue the English theme with four-poster beds, sitting areas (complete with window seats), formal writing desks, and bathrooms with oversize tubs. All rooms now have new carpeting and furniture, glass bath partitions, signature Four Seasons beds, 42-inch LCD flatscreen televisions, and high-speed Internet access.

The Four Seasons also retrained the staff to their level of excellent service. Don't expect the "sophisticated" service you'd get in most Four Seasons around the world—most of the staff have lived on Lanai for generations. Instead, you'll find a charming display of aloha spirit and a strong desire to make sure your vacation is perfect.

Before you reach for the phone, understand that this hotel is not located at the beach (see the Manele Bay resort, above), but rather in the cool mist of the mountains, on 21 acres at 1,700 feet above sea level, 8 miles inland from any beach. In the winter, temperatures can drop into the 50s (don't worry, the rooms have heat as well as air-conditioning). Most guests here are looking for relaxation: sitting on the rattan lawn chairs on the porch, reading, watching the turkeys mosey across the manicured lawns, strolling through the Japanese hillside garden, or watching the sun sink into the Pacific.

There are plenty of activities here and at the sister resort down the hill, Manele, so you'll get the best of both hotels. Other pluses include complimentary shuttle to the golf courses, beach, and Four Seasons Resort Lanai at Manele Bay; complimentary coffee and tea in the lobby; formal afternoon tea; and twice-daily maid service. Guests can also take advantage of the croquet lawns, horseback riding, hiking trails, and garden walks.

1 Keomoku Hwy., P.O. Box 631380, Lanai City, HI 96763. © **800/321-4666** or 808/565-4000. Fax 808/565-4561. www.fourseasons.com/lanai. 102 units. $345–$770 double; from $850 suite. Extra person $75. Children 17 and under stay free in parent's room. Numerous packages available. AE, DC, MC, V. Airport shuttle $33 round-trip. **Amenities:** 3 restaurants (including the Main Dining Room, p. 301, and Terrace, p. 302); bar w/live music; outdoor pool; golf at Greg Norman–designed Experience at Koele (p. 303); tennis courts; fitness room; Jacuzzi; complimentary snorkeling equipment at Four Seasons Resort Lanai at Manele Bay; bike rentals; children's program; game room; concierge; activities desk; retail store; room service; massage; babysitting; laundry service; dry cleaning. *In room:* A/C, TV/DVD, dataport, wireless Internet access ($10 per day), minibar, fridge, coffeemaker, hair dryer, iron, safe.

MODERATE

Hotel Lanai ★ *Kids* This hotel lacks the facilities of the two resorts described above, but it's perfect for families and other vacationers who can't afford to spend $400 (and up) a night. In fact, if you're looking for the old-fashioned aloha that Lanai City is famous for, this is the place to stay. Built in the 1920s for VIP plantation guests, this clapboard plantation-era relic has retained its quaint character and lives on as a country inn.

In 2005, the entire hotel underwent renovations—repainting, remodeling, and a general sprucing up. The guest rooms, although extremely small, are clean and newly outfitted with Hawaiian quilts, wood furniture, and ceiling fans (but no air-conditioning or TVs). The most popular are the lanai units, which feature a shared lanai with the room next door. All rooms have private shower-only bathrooms. The one-bedroom cottage, with a TV and bathtub, is perfect for a small family.

The hotel serves as a down-home crossroads where total strangers meet local folks on the lanai to drink beer and talk story or play the ukulele and sing into the dark, tropical night. Often a curious visitor in search of an authentic experience will join the party and discover Lanai's very Hawaiian heart. Guests have the use of the complimentary shuttle to the Four Seasons Lodge at Koele, the Four Seasons Lanai at Manele Bay, the golf courses (at which they get the same lower rates given to guests at the two resorts), and the beach.

828 Lanai Ave. (P.O. Box 630520), Lanai City, HI 96763. ② **800/795-7211** or 808/565-7211. Fax 808/565-6450. www.hotellanai.com. 11 units. $139–$159 double; $209 cottage double. Rates include continental breakfast. Extra person $10. 2-night minimum. AE, MC, V. Airport shuttle $33 round-trip. **Amenities:** Excellent restaurant (Lanai City Grille, p. 303); intimate bar; access to 2 resort golf courses on the island; nearby tennis courts; complimentary snorkeling equipment.

4 Where to Dine

Lanai is a curious mix of innocence and sophistication, with strong cross-cultural elements that liven up its culinary offerings. You can dine like a sultan on this island, but be prepared for high prices. The tony hotel restaurants require deep pockets, and there are only a handful of other options.

Note: You'll find the restaurants reviewed in this chapter on the map on p. 295.

VERY EXPENSIVE

Ihilani ✶✶✶ ITALIAN   A number of top Hawaii chefs (such as Philippe Padovani and Edwin Goto) have added bits of their own style to the inspiring menu, which melds Mediterranean with Island cuisine. The result is one of Lanai's top gourmet restaurants. The latest incarnation of this classy, formal restaurant, overlooking the resort and the ocean beyond, is traditional Italian cuisine. Try the perfect homemade spinach gnocchi or the lobster risotto. My other favorites include the osso buco, rare ahi alla caponata, and onaga alla puttanesca with artichoke purée and a spicy tomato and caper sauce. Be sure to leave room for the scrumptious desserts.

At the Four Seasons Resort Lanai at Manele Bay. ② **808/565-2296.** www.fourseasons.com/manelebay/dining. Reservations strongly recommended. Resort attire recommended. Main courses $31–$50; set menu $106 without wine, $160 with wine. AE, MC, V. Tues–Sat 6–9:30pm.

Main Dining Room ✶✶✶ NEW AMERICAN   The former Formal Dining Room has been revamped under the Four Seasons management and has a new menu. However, they did retain the relaxing setting, with a roaring fire, bountiful sprays of orchids, sienna-colored walls, and a team of waitstaff serving in hushed voices. The menu highlights American favorites. The appetizers are so tempting, you could make a meal from the variety of choices: seared diver scallops with cauliflower purée, foie gras torchon with a toasted brioche with roasted pineapple and vanilla compote, and lava-rock-seared Lanai venison. The entrees vary according to the season; when I dined here, the menu included Maui lavender-honey roasted duck breast, mustard-and-herb-roasted rack of lamb, and a buttered poached lobster from the Big Island. The service is impeccable, the atmosphere relaxing. But don't forget your platinum credit card—you'll need it.

At the Four Seasons Resort Lanai, the Lodge at Koele. (C) **808/565-4580**. www.fourseasons.com/koele/dining. Reservations required. Resort attire recommended; collared shirts and closed-toe footwear requested for men. Main courses $50–$65. AE, DC, MC, V. Daily 6–9:30pm.

EXPENSIVE

Hulopoe Court ✸✸ HAWAII REGIONAL   This is the Manele Bay's informal dining room. It serves one of the best breakfast buffets I've seen in Hawaii, with everything from an omelet station to breakfast meats, daily pancakes, potatoes, rice, and local tropical fruit. The dinner menu showcases local ingredients—examples include the steamed Hawaiian seafood laulau (with mahimahi, sea bass, shrimp, Molokai sweet potatoes, and local vegetables), grilled opakapaka with Lanai greens and a mango sauce, and Hawaiian-style short ribs and pork chops.

At the Four Seasons Resort Lanai at Manele Bay. (C) **808/565-2290**. www.fourseasons.com/manelebay/dining. Reservations recommended for dinner. Resort attire recommended. Breakfast main courses $19–$23, buffet $31; dinner main courses $31–$41. AE, MC, V. Daily 7–11am and 6–9:30pm.

Ocean Grill ✸ SEAFOOD   The former Pool Grille has been remodeled and expanded, and is now open for lunch and dinner. Located just off the pool, the casual, open-air, Hawaii-style bistro serves interesting lunches like wraps and sandwiches (such as a veggie wrap with portobello mushrooms, red bell peppers, provolone cheese, avocado, and roasted garlic hummus), a great selection of salads (including a yummy calamari salad), and a range of entrees such as kalua-pork and cheese quesadilla or mahimahi fish and chips. At dinner, watch the sun set and the stars come out as you dine on fresh local fish, steak, free-range chicken, or small-plate entrees such as Hawaiian kampachi, crab cakes, lobster, and red-curry chowder.

At the Four Seasons Resort Lanai at Manele Bay. (C) **808/565-2093**. www.fourseasons.com/manelebay/dining. Main courses $15–$20 lunch, $35–$50 dinner. AE, MC, V. Daily 11am–5pm; Thurs–Mon 5:30–9pm.

Terrace ✸✸ AMERICAN   Located next to the Main Dining Room in the Lodge at Koele, between the 35-foot-high Great Hall and a wall of glass looking out over prim English gardens, this wonderful spot is the Lodge's "casual" dining room. The Terrace is far from your typical hotel restaurant—the menu may be fancy for comfort food, but it does, indeed, comfort. Hearty breakfasts of waffles and cereals, fresh pineapple from the nearby Palawai Basin, frittata, and blue-crab Benedict make a grand start to the day. Dinner choices include slow-roasted lamb shank, grilled beef filet, roasted pork chops, fresh fish of the day, and a couple of vegetarian selections (garganelli pasta with sautéed mushrooms and white truffle butter; a teriyaki-glazed vegetable and tofu brochette with zucchini couscous).

At the Four Seasons Resort Lanai, the Lodge at Koele. (C) **808/565-4580**. www.fourseasons.com/koele/dining. Reservations recommended. Resort attire recommended. Full breakfast $16–$27; main courses $14–$25 lunch, $28–$40 dinner. AE, DC, MC, V. Daily 7–11am breakfast, 11am–2pm lunch, and 6–9:30pm dinner.

MODERATE

The Challenge at Manele Clubhouse ✸ PACIFIC RIM   The view from the alfresco tables here may be the best on the island, encompassing Kahoolawe,

Haleakala (on Maui), and, on an especially clear day, the peaks of Mauna Kea and Mauna Loa on the Big Island. You can lunch on salads and sandwiches (Asian tuna salad with grilled ahi, turkey club sandwich, clubhouse burgers with caramelized onions and cheese) or on more substantial entrees, ranging from fish and chips to kalbi beef. The clubhouse is casual, the view of the ocean is awe inspiring, and it's a great gathering place.

At the Challenge at Manele Golf Course. © 808/565-2230. www.fourseasons.com/manelebay/dining. Reservations recommended. Main courses $14–$20. AE, DC, MC, V. Daily 10:30am–4:30pm.

The Experience at Koele Clubhouse AMERICAN This tiny eatery overlooks the verdant, rolling hills of the Experience at Koele Golf Course. Most of your fellow diners will have just finished a round of golf; you can join them at one of a handful of tables inside or on the lanai overlooking the pastoral view. Soups, salads, and over-size sandwiches rule here, everything from a delicious portobello mushroom on toasted focaccia to open-faced chicken salad (with a yummy mango-avocado salsa), smoked turkey club, or charbroiled cheddar burger.

At the Experience at Koele Golf Course. © 808/565-4605. www.fourseasons.com/koele/dining. Main courses $10–$19. AE, DC, MC, V. Daily 10:30am–4:30pm.

Lanai City Grille ★★ CAJUN/COUNTRY Celebrated Maui chef Bev Gannon (Haliimaile General Store, Joe's Restaurant) redesigned the menu in this cute eatery, where the decor consists of pine-paneled walls, chintz curtains, and a fireplace. The menu sticks to whatever is in season and fresh that day, from the fish and seafood to meats and rotisserie chicken.

At the Hotel Lanai, 828 Lanai Ave., Lanai City. © 808/565-7211. www.hotellanai.com. Main courses $14–$38. AE, MC, V. Daily 5:30–9pm.

INEXPENSIVE

Blue Ginger Cafe COFFEE SHOP Famous for its mahimahi sandwiches and inexpensive omelets, Blue Ginger is a very local, very casual, and very reasonably priced alternative to Lanai's fancy hotel restaurants. The four tables on the front porch face the cool Norfolk pines of Dole Park and are always filled with locals who talk story from morning to night. The offerings are solid, no-nonsense, everyday fare: fried saimin (no MSG), very popular burgers on homemade buns, and mahimahi with capers and mushrooms. Blue Ginger also serves a tasty French toast made with home-made bread and a surprisingly good stir-fried vegetable dish.

409 Seventh St. (at Ilima St.), Lanai City. © 808/565-6363. Breakfast and lunch items under $13; dinner main courses under $16. No credit cards. Daily 6am–8pm.

Café 565 PIZZA/SUBS Diners at this colorful pizzeria (named after Lanai's phone prefix, 565) spill out of the old house and into the umbrella tables in the front yard. The pizzas here are the real thing, baked in pizza ovens. The subs, made with fresh-baked rolls, range from hot (like Philly cheesesteak) to cold (Genoa salami, capicollo, mortadella, and provolone). Daily plate-lunch specials and great salads complete the menu.

408 Eighth St. (at Ilima St.), Lanai City. © 808/565-6622. Sub sandwiches $5–$10; pizzas $14–$20; most dinner main courses under $9. No credit cards. Mon–Fri 10am–3pm and 5–8pm; Sat 10am–3pm.

Canoes Lanai LOCAL This ma-and-pa eatery may have changed its name (it used to be Tanigawa's), but it remains the landmark that it's been since the 1920s. In those days, the tiny storefront sold canned goods and cigarettes; the 10 tables, hamburgers, and Filipino food came later. This hole in the wall is a local institution, with a reputation for serving local-style breakfasts. The fare—fried rice, omelets, short stack, and simple ham and eggs—is more greasy spoon than gourmet, but it's definitely budget friendly.

419 Seventh St., Lanai City. © 808/565-6537. Reservations not accepted. Breakfast items under $8.50; sandwiches $2.50–$8.50; burgers $2–$5. No credit cards. Thurs–Tues 6:30am–1pm.

Coffee Works ⚱★ COFFEEHOUSE   Oahu's popular Ward Warehouse coffeehouse has opened a new branch on Lanai, with a menu of espresso drinks, ice cream (including local brands), and a small selection of pastries. It's Lanai City's new gathering place, a tiny cafe with tables and benches on a pleasing wooden deck just a stone's throw from Dole Park. Formerly a plantation house, the structure fits in with the surrounding homes in the heart of town. There are some nice gift items available, including T-shirts, tea infusers, teapots, cookies, and gourmet coffees.

604 Ilima St., Lanai City (across from the post office). © 808/565-6962. Most items under $5. AE, DC, DISC, MC, V. Mon–Sat 6am–4pm; Sun 6am–noon.

Pele's Other Garden ⚱★★ DELI/BISTRO   This popular eatery has added a patio with umbrella tables and expanded the kitchen in the back, so there's a lot more seating than there used to be—and a fuller menu to match. Owners Mark and Barbara have turned this small sandwich shop into a full-scale deli and bistro. Daily soup and menu specials, excellent pizza, fresh organic produce, and special items such as top-quality black-bean burritos and stuffed grape leaves make Pele's Other Garden a Lanai City must. Sandwiches are made as wraps or with whole-wheat, rye, sourdough, or French bread, all baked on the island and delivered fresh daily. In the evening, you can dine on china at cloth-covered tables, and the menu expands to include pastas (bowtie pasta with butterflied garlic shrimp; fettuccine with smoked salmon), pizza, and salads. Beer and wines by the glass (from $4.25) were recently added.

Dole Park, 811 Houston St., Lanai City. © 808/565-9628. Lunch items under $8; pizzas from $7; dinner main courses $17–$20. AE, DISC, MC, V. Mon–Fri 10am–2pm and 5–8pm.

5 Beaches

If you like big, wide, empty, gold-sand beaches and crystal-clear, cobalt-blue water full of bright tropical fish—and who doesn't?—go to Lanai. With 18 miles of sandy shoreline, Lanai has some of Hawaii's least crowded and most interesting beaches.

HULOPOE BEACH ⚱★★

In 1997, Dr. Stephen Leatherman of the University of Maryland (a professional beach surveyor who's also known as "Dr. Beach") ranked Hulopoe the best beach in the United States. It's easy to see why. This palm-fringed, gold-sand beach is bordered by black-lava fingers, protecting swimmers from ocean currents. In summer, Hulopoe is perfect for swimming, snorkeling, or just lolling about; the water temperature is usually in the mid-70s (mid-20s Celsius). Swimming is usually safe, except when swells kick up in winter. The bay at the foot of the Four Seasons Resort Lanai at Manele Bay is a protected marine preserve, with schools of colorful fish and spinner dolphins. Humpback whales cruise by here in winter. Hulopoe is also Lanai's premier beach park, with a grassy lawn, picnic tables, barbecue grills, restrooms, showers, and ample parking. You can camp here, too.

(Moments) Frommer's Favorite Lanai Experiences

Snorkeling Hulopoe Beach: Crystal-clear waters teem with brilliant tropical fish off one of Hawaii's best beaches. There are tide pools to explore, waves to play in, and other surprises—like a pod of spinner dolphins that often makes a splashy entrance.

Exploring the Garden of the Gods: Eroded by wind, rain, and time, these geologic badlands (p. 309) are worth visiting at sunrise or sunset, when the low light plays tricks on the land—and your mind.

Hiking the Munro Trail: The 11-mile Munro Trail (p. 307) is a lofty, rigorous hike along the rim of an old volcano. You'll get great views of the nearby islands. Take a four-wheel-drive vehicle if you want to spend more time on top of the island.

Four-Wheeling It: Four-wheeling is a way of life on Lanai because there are only 30 miles of pavement on the whole island. Plenty of rugged trails lead to deserted beaches, abandoned villages, and valleys filled with wild game.

Camping Under the Stars: The campsites (p. 308) at Hulopoe Beach Park are about as close to the heavens as you can get. The crashing surf will lull you to sleep at night, and chirping birds will wake you in the morning. If you're into roughing it, this is a great way to experience Lanai.

Watching the Whales at Polihua Beach: Located on the north shore, this beach—which gets its name from the turtles that nest here—is a great place to watch for whales during the winter months.

HULOPOE'S TIDE POOLS   Some of the best lava-rock tide pools in Hawaii are found along the south shore of Hulopoe Bay. These miniature SeaWorlds are full of strange creatures such as asteroids (sea stars) and holothurians (sea cucumbers), not to mention spaghetti worms, Barber Pole shrimp, and Hawaii's favorite local delicacy, the opihi, a tasty morsel also known as the limpet. Youngsters enjoy swimming in the enlarged tide pool at the eastern edge of the bay. When you explore tide pools, do so at low tide. Never turn your back on the waves. Wear tennis shoes or reef walkers, as wet rocks are slippery. Collecting specimens in this marine preserve is forbidden, so don't take any souvenirs home.

POLIHUA BEACH ⊛

So many sea turtles once hauled themselves out of the water to lay their eggs in the sunbaked sand on Lanai's northwestern shore that Hawaiians named the beach here *Polihua*, or "egg nest." Although the endangered green sea turtles are making a comeback, they're seldom seen here now. You're more likely to spot an offshore whale (in season) or the perennial litter that washes up onto this deserted beach at the end of Polihua Road, a 4-mile jeep trail. This strand is ideal for beachcombing (those little green-glass Japanese fishing-net floats often show up here), fishing, or just being alone. There are no facilities except fishermen's huts and driftwood shelters. Bring water and sunscreen. Beware of the strong currents, which make the water unsafe for swimming.

SHIPWRECK BEACH ⚓

This 8-mile-long windswept strand on Lanai's northeastern shore—named for the rusty ship *Liberty* stuck on the coral reef—is a sailor's nightmare and a beachcomber's dream. The strong currents yield all sorts of flotsam, from Japanese handblown-glass fish floats and rare pelagic paper nautilus shells to lots of junk. This is also a great place to spot whales from December to April, when the Pacific humpbacks cruise in from Alaska. The road to the beach is paved most of the way, but you really need a four-wheel-drive to get down here.

6 Watersports

Lanai has Hawaii's best water clarity because it lacks major development, it has low rainfall and runoff, and its coast is washed clean daily by the sea current (known as "The Way to Tahiti"). But the strong sea currents pose a threat to swimmers, and there are few good surf breaks. Most of the aquatic adventures—swimming, snorkeling, scuba diving—are centered on the somewhat protected south shore, around Hulopoe Bay.

The only outfitter for watersports is **Trilogy Lanai Ocean Sports** ★★★ (© 888/ MAUI-800 [6284]; www.visitlanai.com).

SAILING & SNORKELING

Trilogy Lanai Ocean Sports (see above), which has built a well-deserved reputation as the leader in sailing/snorkeling cruises in Hawaii, offers both a morning and an afternoon **snorkel sailing trip** on board its luxury custom sailing catamarans or its 32-foot jet-drive rigid aluminum-inflatable vessel. The trips along Lanai's protected coastline sail past hundreds of spinner dolphins and into some of the best snorkeling sites in the world for $203 (half-price for children 3–15) and include lunch, sodas, snorkel gear, and instruction.

If you just want to snorkel on your own, Hulopoe is Lanai's best snorkeling spot. Fish are abundant in the marine-life conservation area. Try the lava-rock points at either end of the beach and around the lava pools.

SCUBA DIVING

Two of Hawaii's best-known dive spots are found in Lanai's clear waters, just off the south shore: **Cathedrals I** and **II,** so named because the sun lights up an underwater grotto like a magnificent church. **Trilogy Lanai Ocean Sports** (see above for contact information) offers several kinds of sailing, diving, and snorkeling trips on catamarans and from its new 32-foot high-tech jet-drive ocean raft. It has its own version of "sunrise services" at the Cathedrals—not only is this the best time of day to dive this incredible area, but there also are virtually no other dive boats in the water at this time. Cost is $169 to $199 for a two-tank dive, $79 for nondivers. Beach dives are available for $95 (one-tank dive) for certified divers and $95 for an introductory dive for noncertified divers.

SPORTFISHING

Spinning Dolphin Charters of Lanai (© 808/565-7676; www.sportfishinglanai.com) offers sportfishing on a 42-foot Hatteras boat. It will take up to six passengers for $700 for 4 hours ($110 for each additional hour), or you can share a boat for $150 each for 4 hours.

SURFING

If you've ever wanted to learn how to surf, let instructor Nick Palumbo, a surfing champion, take you on a four-wheel-drive surfing safari to a secluded surf spot. He'll have you up and riding the waves in no time. His **Lanai Surf School & Surf Safari** (© 808/565-7258; www.lanaisurfsafari.com) offers a package that includes a 2½-hour lesson with surfboard, four-wheel-drive transportation, refreshments, and "a really good time" for $185 per person.

WHALE-WATCHING

During whale season, from December to April, **Trilogy Lanai Ocean Sports** (see above for contact information) takes passengers out on its 26-passenger, rigid-hulled inflatable boat, a 32-foot jet-drive Zodiac named *Manele Kai,* for a 2-hour ocean adventure that explores some of the remote and unspoiled sites in Hawaii. Lanai is also home to one of Hawaii's largest schools of spinner dolphins and a haven for North Pacific humpback whales. The captains and crew are Certified Island Naturalists who make each trip educational as well as entertaining, and they can usually find these wonderful and playful mammals. The cost is $75 (half-price for children 3–15), which includes soft drinks.

7 Hiking & Camping

HIKING

A LEISURELY MORNING HIKE

The 3-hour self-guided **Koele Nature Hike** starts by the reflecting pool in the back-yard of the Lodge at Koele and takes you on a 5-mile loop through Norfolk Island pines, into Hulopoe Valley, past wild ginger, and up to Koloiki Ridge, with its panoramic view of Maunalei Valley and of Molokai and Maui in the distance. You're welcome to take the hike even if you're not a guest at the Lodge. The path isn't clearly marked, so ask the concierge for a free map. Do this hike in the morning; by after-noon, the clouds usually roll in, marring visibility at the top and increasing your chance of being caught in a downpour.

THE CHALLENGING MUNRO TRAIL

This tough 11-mile (round-trip) uphill climb through the groves of Norfolk pines is a lung-buster, but if you reach the top, you'll be rewarded with a breathtaking view of Molokai, Maui, Kahoolawe, the peaks of the Big Island, and—on a really clear day—Oahu in the distance. Figure on 7 hours. The trail begins at Lanai Cemetery along Keomoku Road (Hwy. 44) and follows Lanai's ancient caldera rim, ending up at the island's highest point, Lanaihale. Go in the morning for the best visibility. After 4 miles, you'll get a view of Lanai City. The weary retrace their steps from here, while the more determined go the last 1.25 miles to the top. Die-hards head down Lanai's steep south-crater rim to join the highway to Manele Bay. For more details on the Munro Trail—including information on four-wheel-driving it to the top—see "Five Islands at a Single Glance: The Munro Trail" (p. 310).

A SELF-GUIDED NATURE TRAIL

This self-guided nature trail in the Kanepuu Preserve (described below) is about a 10- to 15-minute walk through eight stations, with interpretive signs explaining the nat-ural or cultural significance of what you're seeing. The trail head is clearly marked on the Polihua Road on the way to the Garden of the Gods. Kanepuu is one of the last remaining examples of the type of forest that once covered the dry lowlands through-out the state. There are some 49 plant species here that are found only in Hawaii. The **Nature Conservancy** (✆ 808/565-7430) conducts guided hikes every month; call for details.

GUIDED HIKES

The **Lodge at Koele** (✆ 808/565-4552; www.fourseasons.com/lanai) offers a 2½-hour Koloiki Ridge Nature hike through 5 miles of the upland forests of Koele at 11am daily. Fee is $15. It's considered moderate, with some uphill and downhill hiking.

The **Four Seasons Resort Lanai at Manele Bay** (✆ 808/565-2000; www.four seasons.com/lanai) has a free 1½-hour fitness hike along an old fishermen's trail at 9am Tuesday and Friday, led by Joe West, wildlife and outdoor photographer extraordi-naire. Bring your camera and ask Joe for photography tips. This hike will expose you to Lanai's unique geography. Along the way, you'll see the island's natural beauty and breathtaking coastline.

CAMPING AT HULOPOE BEACH PARK

There is only one legal place to camp on Lanai: **Hulopoe Beach Park,** which is owned by Castle and Cooke Resorts. To camp in this exquisite beach park, with its crescent-shaped white-sand beach bordered by kiawe trees, contact **Wendell Sarme–Park Manager,** Castle and Cooke Resorts, P.O. Box 630310, Lanai City, HI 96763 (✆ 808/565-2970). There's a $5 registration fee, plus a charge of $5 per person, per night. Hulopoe has six campsites; each can accommodate up to six people. Facilities include restrooms, running water, showers, barbecue areas, and picnic tables.

8 Golf & Other Outdoor Activities

GOLF

Cavendish Golf Course *(Finds* This quirky par-36, 9-hole public course lacks not only a clubhouse and club pros, but also tee times, scorecards, and club rentals. To play, just show up, put a donation into the little wooden box next to the first tee, and hit away. The 3,071-yard, E. B. Cavendish–designed course was built by the Dole plantation in 1947 for its employees. The greens are a bit bumpy, but the views of Lanai are great and the temperatures usually quite mild.

Next to the Lodge at Koele in Lanai City. No phone. Greens fees $5–$10 suggested donation.

The Challenge at Manele *★★* This target-style, desert-links course, designed by Jack Nicklaus, is one of the most challenging courses in the state. Check out the local rules: "No retrieving golf balls from the 150-foot cliffs on the ocean holes 12, 13, or 17," and "All whales, axis deer, and other wild animals are considered immovable obstruc-tions." That's just a hint of the unique experience you'll have on this course, which is routed among lava outcroppings, archaeological sites, kiawe groves, and *ilima* trees. The five sets of staggered tees pose a challenge to everyone from the casual golfer to the pro. Facilities include a clubhouse, pro shop, rentals, practice area, lockers, and showers.

Next to the Four Seasons Resort Lanai at Manele Bay. ✆ 800/321-4666 or 808/565-2222. Greens fees $225 ($220 for guests).

The Experience at Koele *★★* This traditional par-72 course, designed by Greg Norman with fairway architecture by Ted Robinson, has very different front and back 9 holes. Mother Nature reigns throughout: You'll see Cook Island and Norfolk pines, indigenous plants, and lots of water—seven lakes, flowing streams, cascading water-falls, and one green (the 17th) completely surrounded by a lake. All goes well until you hit the signature hole, number 8, where you tee off from a 250-foot elevated tee to a fairway bordered by a lake on the right and trees and dense shrubs on the left. After that, the back 9 holes drop dramatically through ravines filled with pine, koa, and eucalyptus trees. The grand finale, the par-5 18th, features a green rimmed by waterfalls that flow into a lake on the left side. To level the playing field, there are four different sets of tees. Facilities include a clubhouse, pro shop, rentals, practice area, lockers, and showers.

Next to the Lodge at Koele in Lanai City. (© 800/321-4666 or 808/565-4653. Greens fees $225 ($210 for guests).

BIKING

The **Lodge at Koele** (© 808/565-4552) rents mountain bikes for $8 an hour.

HORSEBACK RIDING

Horses can take you to many places in Lanai's unique landscape that are otherwise unreachable. The **Four Seasons Lanai Resort's Stables at Koele** (© 808/565-4424) offers various daily rides (9am and 1:30pm), including slow, gentle group excursions starting at $95 for a 1½-hour **Paniolo Trail Ride,** which takes you into the hills sur-rounding Koele. You'll meander through guava groves and ironwood trees; catch glimpses of axis deer, quail, wild turkeys, and Santa Gertrudis cattle; and end with panoramic views of Maui and Lanai. Private 2-hour rides can be arranged for $160 per person; 1½-hour sunset rides go for $190 per person. Kids will love the 15-minute pony rides; parents will love the price of $10 per person. Long pants and closed-toe shoes (like running shoes) are required, and safety helmets are provided. Bring a jacket—the weather is chilly and rain is frequent. Children must be at least 9 years old and 4 feet tall, and riders cannot weigh more than 225 pounds.

TENNIS

Public courts, lit for night play, are available in Lanai City at no charge; call © 808/565-6979 for reservations. If you're staying at the Lodge at Koele or at Manele Bay, you can take advantage of the Lodge's three new Premiere Cushion outdoor hard courts, with complimentary use of Wilson racquets, balls, and bottled water. You're also invited to experience the tennis center at the Four Seasons Resort Lanai at Manele Bay, which offers a full pro shop, use of a ball machine, and weekly tennis mixers and tournaments. Courts are $20 per person for hotel guests (not open to nonguests). For information, call © 808/565-2072.

9 Seeing the Sights

You'll need a four-wheel-drive vehicle to reach all the sights listed below. Renting a jeep is an expensive proposition on Lanai—from $139 to $179 a day—so I suggest renting one just for the day (or days) you plan on sightseeing; otherwise, it's easy enough to get to the beach and around Lanai City without your own wheels. For details on vehicle rentals, see "Getting Around" (p. 298).

Note: You'll find the following attractions on the map on p. 295.

GARDEN OF THE GODS ✪

A dirt four-wheel-drive road leads out of Lanai City, through the now uncultivated pineapple fields, past the Kanepuu Preserve (a dry-land forest preserve teeming with

Kids **Especially for Kids**

Exploring Hulopoe's Tide Pools (p. 305): An entire world of marine life lives in the tide pools on the eastern side of Hulopoe Bay. Everything in the water, including the tiny fish, is small—kid size. After examining the wonders of the tide pool, check out the larger swimming holes in the lava rock, perfect for children.

Hunting for Petroglyphs (p. 311): The Luahiwa Petroglyph Field, located just outside Lanai City, is spread out over a 3-acre site. Make it a game: Whoever finds the most petroglyphs gets ice cream from the Pine Isle Market.

Listening to Storytellers: Check with the Lanai Library, on Fraser Avenue near Fifth Street, in Lanai City (© 808/565-6996), to see if any storytelling or other children's activities are scheduled. The events are usually free and open to everyone.

rare plant and animal life) to the so-called Garden of the Gods, out on Lanai's north shore. This rugged, barren, beautiful place is full of rocks strewn by volcanic forces and shaped by the elements into a variety of shapes and colors—brilliant reds, oranges, ochers, and yellows.

Ancient Hawaiians considered this desolate, windswept place an entirely supernatural phenomenon. Scientists, however, have other, less colorful explanations. Some call the area an "ongoing posterosional event"; others say it's just "plain and simple badlands." Take a four-wheel-drive ride out here and decide for yourself.

Go early in the morning or just before sunset, when the light casts eerie shadows on the mysterious lava formations. Drive west from the Lodge at Koele on Polihua Road; in about 2 miles, you'll see a hand-painted sign that'll point left down a one-lane, red-dirt road through a kiawe forest to the site.

FIVE ISLANDS AT A SINGLE GLANCE: THE MUNRO TRAIL ⊛

In the first golden rays of dawn, when lone owls swoop over abandoned pineapple fields, hop into a 4×4 and head out on the two-lane blacktop toward Mount Lanaihale, the 3,370-foot summit of Lanai. Your destination is the Munro Trail, the narrow, winding ridge trail that runs across Lanai's razorback spine to the summit. From here, you may get a rare Hawaii treat: On a clear day, you can see all of the main islands in the Hawaiian chain except Kauai.

When it rains, the Munro Trail becomes slick and boggy with major washouts. Rainy-day excursions often end with a rental jeep on the hook of the island's lone tow truck—and a $250 tow charge. You could even slide off into a major gulch and never be found, so don't try it. But in late August and September, when trade winds stop and the air over the islands stalls in what's called a *kona* condition, Mount Lanaihale's suddenly visible peak becomes an irresistible attraction.

When you're on Lanai, look to the summit. If it's clear in the morning, rent a four-wheel-drive vehicle and take the Munro Trail to the top. Look for a red-dirt road off Manele Road (Hwy. 440), about 5 miles south of Lanai City; turn left and head up the ridge line. No sign marks the peak, so you'll have to keep an eye out. Look for a wide spot in the road and a clearing that falls sharply to the sea.

Perfect for a Rainy Day: Lanai Art Center

A perfect activity for a rainy day in Lanai City is the **Lanai Art Center,** 339 Seventh St., located in the heart of the small town. Top artists from across Hawaii frequently visit this homegrown art program and teach a variety of classes, ranging from raku (Japanese pottery), silk printing, silk screening, pareu making (creating your own design on this islanders' wrap), *gyotaku* (printing a real fish on your own T-shirt), and watercolor drawing to a variety of other island crafts. The cost for the 2- to 3-hour classes is usually in the $15-to-$70 range (materials are extra). For information, call C **808/565-7503** or visit www.lanaiart.org.

From here you can see Kahoolawe, Maui, the Big Island of Hawaii, and Molokini's tiny crescent. Even the summits show. You can also see the silver domes of Space City on Haleakala in Maui; Puu Moaulanui, the tongue-twisting summit of Kahoolawe; and, looming above the clouds, Mauna Kea on the Big Island. At another clearing farther along the thickly forested ridge, all of Molokai, including the 4,961-foot summit of Kamakou and the faint outline of Oahu (more than 30 miles across the sea), are visible. You actually can't see all five islands in a single glance anymore because a thriving pine forest blocks the view. For details on hiking the trail, see "Hiking & Camping" (p. 307).

LUAHIWA PETROGLYPH FIELD

Lanai is second only to the Big Island in its wealth of prehistoric rock art, but you'll have to search a little to find it. Some of the best examples are on the outskirts of Lanai City, on a hillside site known as Luahiwa Petroglyph Field. The characters you'll see incised on 13 boulders in this grassy 3-acre knoll include a running man, a deer, a turtle, a bird, a goat, and even a rare curly-tailed Polynesian dog (a latter-day wag has put a leash on him—some joke).

To get here, take the road to Hulopoe Beach. About 2 miles out of Lanai City, look to the left, up on the slopes of the crater, for a cluster of reddish-tan boulders (believed to form a rain *heiau,* or shrine, where people called up the gods Ku and Hina to nourish their crops). A cluster of spiky century plants marks the spot. Look for the Norfolk pines on the left side of the highway, turn left on the dirt road that veers across the abandoned pineapple fields, and after about 1 mile, take a sharp left by the water tanks. Drive for another ½ mile and then veer to the right at the V in the road. Stay on this upper road for about ¼ mile; you'll come to a large cluster of boulders on the right side. It's just a short walk up the cliffs (wear walking or hiking shoes) to the petroglyphs. Exit the same way you came. Go between 3pm and sunset for ideal viewing and photo ops.

KAUNOLU VILLAGE

Out on Lanai's nearly vertical, Gibraltar-like sea cliffs is an old royal compound and fishing village. Now a national historic landmark and one of Hawaii's most treasured ruins, it's believed to have been inhabited by King Kamehameha the Great and hundreds of his closest followers about 200 years ago. It's a hot, dry, dusty, slow-going, 3-mile 4×4 drive from Lanai City to Kaunolu, but the mini-expedition is worth it. Take plenty of water, don a hat for protection against the sun, and wear sturdy shoes.

Ruins of 86 house platforms and 35 stone shelters have been identified on both sides of Kaunolu Gulch. The residential complex also includes the Halulu Heiau temple, named after a mythical man-eating bird. The king's royal retreat is thought to have stood on the eastern edge of Kaunolu Gulch, overlooking the rocky shore facing Kahekili's Leap, a 62-foot-high bluff named for the mighty Maui chief who leaped off cliffs as a show of bravado. Nearby are burial caves, a fishing shrine, a lookout tower, and many warrior-like stick figures carved on boulders. Just offshore stands the telltale fin of little Shark Island, a popular dive spot that teems with bright tropical fish and, frequently, sharks.

Excavations are underway to discover more about how ancient Hawaiians lived, worked, and worshipped on Lanai's leeward coast. Who knows? The royal fishing village may yet yield the bones of King Kamehameha. His burial site, according to legend, is known only to the moon and the stars.

KANEPUU PRESERVE

This ancient forest on the island's western plateau is so fragile, you can visit only once a month, and even then only on a guided hike. Kanepuu, which has 48 species of plants unique to Hawaii, survives under the Nature Conservancy's protective wing. Botanists say the 590-acre forest is the last dry lowland forest in Hawaii; the others have all vanished, trashed by axis deer, agriculture, or "progress." Among the botanical marvels of this dry forest are the remains of *olopua* (native olive), *lama* (native ebony), *mau hau hele* (a native hibiscus), and the rare *'aiea* trees, which were used for canoe parts.

Due to the forest's fragile nature, guided hikes are led only 12 times a year, on a monthly, reservations-only basis. Contact the **Nature Conservancy Oahu Land Preserve** manager at 1116 Smith St., Suite 201, Honolulu, HI 96817 (© **808/537-4508**), to reserve.

OFF THE TOURIST TRAIL: KEOMOKU VILLAGE

If you're sunburned lobster red, have read all the books you packed, and are starting to get island fever, take a little drive to Keomoku Village, on Lanai's east coast. You'll really be off the tourist path here. All that's in Keomoku, a ghost town since the mid-1950s, is a 1903 clapboard church in disrepair, an overgrown graveyard, an excellent view across the 9-mile Auau Channel to Maui's crowded Kaanapali Beach, and some very empty beaches that are perfect for a picnic or a snorkel. This former ranching and fishing village of 2,000 was the first non-Hawaiian settlement on Lanai, but it dried up after droughts killed off the Maunalei Sugar Company. The village, such as it is, is a great little escape from Lanai City. Follow Keomoku Road for 8 miles to the coast, turn right on the sandy road, and keep going for 5¾ miles.

10 Shopping

Central Bakery ★ (Finds)   This is the mother lode of the island's baked delights, the bakery that is, well, central to Lanai's dining pleasure. If you've noshed on the fantastic sandwiches at the Terrace at the Lodge at Koele or any of the stellar desserts at the Lodge's Main Dining Room or at the Four Seasons Resort Lanai at Manele Bay, you've enjoyed goodies from Central Bakery. The bakery supplies all breads, all breakfast pastries, specialty ice creams and sorbets, all banquet desserts, and restaurant desserts on the island. Although it's not your standard retail outlet, you can call in advance, place your order, and pick it up. The staff prefers as much notice as possible (preferably 48 hr.), but, in a pinch, will take a 24-hour order. Breads (most priced at $4.50) range from walnut onion to roasted potato bacon to olive onion. The bakery also has cookies (chocolate chip, oatmeal, coconut—all for 50¢), brownies, muffins, croissants (including chocolate croissants), Danishes, and scones, plus an assortment of breakfast pastries (pineapple turnover, hazelnut roll, mascarpone apricot Danish, pistachio chocolate roll, and others). 1311 Fraser Ave., Lanai City. ✆ 808/565-3920.

Dis 'N Dat ⭐⭐ (Finds)   Dis (Barry) and Dat (Susie) visited Lanai from Florida to look at buying a retirement home. They found their home and moved to Lanai to retire. Retirement didn't last. A few years later, outgoing Barry and his wife started searching for unusual, finely crafted teak and exotic wood sculptures and carvings. Along the way, they took a shine to mobiles and wind chimes—the more outrageous, the better. Then they started collecting handmade jewelry, stained glass, and unique garden ornaments and home decor. All this led to this eclectic store, which you have to see to believe. Meeting Barry is worth the trip alone. You'll find T-shirts, pottery, ceramics, batik scarves, hula lamps and whimsical dragonfly lamps, woven baskets, and even waterfalls. This is also the biggest collection of Hawaii slipper necklaces, earrings, anklets, and bracelets. You can't miss the vivid green shop with hanging chimes and mobiles leading the way to the front door. 418 Eighth Ave. (at Kilele St.), Lanai City. ✆ 866/DIS-N-DAT (347-6328) or 808/565-9170.

Gifts with Aloha ⭐   Phoenix and Kimberly Dupree's store of treasures has blossomed since they moved to a larger location on the other side of Dole Park. They are now shipping minigardens and lamps to the mainland, and selling fabulously stylish hats, locally made clothing, T-shirts, swimwear, quilts, Jams World dresses, children's clothes, toys, Hawaii-themed CDs, DVDs, music, books, pareu, candles, aloha shirts, picture frames, handbags, ceramics, and art by local artists (including some of the most beautiful jewelry in the islands). The sumptuous honey from the Big Island is available here, as are jams and jellies by Lanai's Fabrao House. The made-on-Maui soaps and bath products—in gardenia, pikake, and plumeria fragrances—make great gifts. Dole Park, 363 Seventh St. (at Ilima St.), Lanai City. ✆ 808/565-6589. www.giftswithaloha.com.

Heart of Lanai Gallery   Denise Hennig, the resident artist at Hotel Lanai, displays her own photographs and watercolors of landscapes, people, and the lifestyle of Lanai's plantation past, as well as the work of other local Lanai artists, at her afternoon teas, Tuesday through Saturday from 2:30 to 4:30pm. You can drop by and enjoy a cup of tea with her as she shows you the art on display that week. Her home/gallery is located behind the hospital in a bright yellow house. 758 Queens St., Lanai City. ✆ 808/565-7815. www.lanaionline.com/Merchants/heart_of_lanai.htm.

High Lights   Located just a block off Seventh Street, across from Coffee Works, is this island-style beauty salon and supply store. Owner Katharina Oriol has been working in salons since 1975 and offers a full-service menu of haircuts, styling, highlights, manicures, pedicures, waxing, and so on. She also carries a wide selection of products for hair and skin, plus cosmetics. Walk-ins are welcome. 617 Ilima Ave., Lanai City. ✆ 808/565-7207.

International Food & Clothing   This store sells the basics: groceries, housewares, T-shirts, hunting and fishing supplies, over-the-counter drugs, wine and liquor, paper goods, and hardware, and even has a takeout lunch counter. I was pleasantly surprised by the extraordinary candy and bubble-gum section, the beautiful local bananas in the small produce section, the surprisingly extensive selection of yuppie soft drinks (Sobe,

Snapple, and others), and the best knife-sharpener I've seen. 833 Ilima Ave., Lanai City. © 808/565-6433.

Lanai Art Center ⚡ *(Finds)*   This wonderful center was organized in 1989 to provide a place where both residents and visitors can come to create art. The center offers classes and studio time in ceramics, painting and drawing, calligraphy, woodworking, photography, silk and textile painting, watercolor, and glass. There's an impressive schedule of visiting instructors, from writers to folk artists (quilting, lei making, and instrument making) to oil painters. Check out the reasonably priced classes (generally in the $25 range) or browse the gallery for excellent deals on works by Lanai residents. 339 Seventh St., Lanai City. © 808/565-7503. www.lanaiart.org.

Lanai Marketplace   Everyone on Lanai, it seems, is a backyard farmer. From 7 to 11am or noon on Saturday, they all head to this shady square to sell their dewy-fresh produce, home-baked breads, plate lunches, and handicrafts. This is Lanai's version of the green market: petite in scale (like the island) but charming, and growing.

Dolores Fabrao's jams and jellies, under the label **Fabrao House** (© **808/565-6134** for special orders), are a big seller at the market and at resort gift shops. Flavors include pineapple-coconut, pineapple-mango, papaya, guaivi (strawberry guava), *poha* (gooseberry), passion fruit, Surinam cherry, and the very tart karamay jelly. All fruits are grown on the island. Dole Park, Lanai City.

The Local Gentry ⚡⚡ *(Finds)*   Jenna (Gentry) Majkus's wonderful boutique, open since 1999, is the first of its kind on the island, featuring clothing and accessories that are not the standard resort-shop fare. (Visiting and local women alike make a beeline for this store.) You'll find fabulous silk aloha shirts by Tiki, mahogany lamps, mermaids and hula girls, inexpensive sarongs, and fabulous socks. There are also great T-shirts, jewelry, bath products, picture frames, jeans, and offbeat sandals. The most recent additions are wonderful children's clothes. 363 Seventh St. (behind Gifts with Aloha, facing Ilima St.), Lanai City. © 808/565-9130.

Mike Carroll Gallery   If he is on the island, you'll find Mike Carroll at work here on his original oil paintings. After a successful 22-year career as a professional artist in Chicago, Carroll moved to Lanai and has been painting the beauty and the lifestyle of the island ever since. You'll find an extensive selection of his original work, some limited editions, prints and notecards, plus a dozen or so of Maui's and Lanai's top artists and even some locally made, one-of-a-kind jewelry. 443 Seventh St., Lanai City. © 808/565-7122. www.mikecarrollgallery.com.

Pine Isle Market   A local landmark for two generations, Pine Isle specializes in locally caught fresh fish, but you can also find fresh herbs and spices, canned goods, electronic games, ice cream, toys, zoris, diapers, paint, cigars, and other basic essentials of work and play. The fishing section is outstanding, with every lure imaginable. 356 Eighth St., Lanai City. © 808/565-6488.

Richard's Shopping Center   The Tamashiros' family business has been on the square since 1946; not much has changed over the years. This "shopping center" is, in fact, a general store with a grocery section, paper products, ethnic foods, meats (mostly frozen), liquor, toys, film, cosmetics, fishing gear, sunscreens, clothing, kitchen utensils, T-shirts, and other miscellany. Half a wall is lined with an extraordinary selection of fish hooks and anglers' needs. Aloha shirts, aloha-print zoris, fold-up lauhala mats, and gourmet breads from the Central Bakery (see above) are among the countless good things at Richard's. 434 Eighth St., Lanai City. © 808/565-6047.

11 Lanai After Dark

The only regular nightlife venues are the Lanai Playhouse, at the corner of Seventh and Lanai avenues in Lanai City, and the two resorts, the Four Seasons Resort Lodge at Koele and Four Seasons Resort Lanai at Manele Bay.

The **Lanai Playhouse** (© 808/565-7500) is a historic 1920s building that has won awards for its renovations. When it opened in 1993, the 150-seat venue stunned residents by offering first-run movies with Dolby sound—quite contemporary for anachronistic Lanai. The Lanai Playhouse usually, but not always, shows two movies each evening from Friday to Tuesday (to Wed in summer), at 6:30 and 8:30pm, with occasional Sunday and Monday matinees; if a 3-hour movie is on, it's shown at 7:30pm. Tickets are $8 for adults ($5 for matinees) and $5 for kids and seniors. The playhouse is also the venue for occasional special events.

The **Lodge at Koele** has stepped up its live entertainment. In front of the manorial fireplaces in the Great Hall, local artists serenade listeners, who sip port and fine liqueurs while sinking into plush chairs, with contemporary Hawaiian, classical, and other genres of music. The special programs are on weekends, but some form of nightly entertainment takes place throughout the week, from 7 to 10pm.

The **Lanai Art Center** features "Stars Under the Stars," free outdoor screenings of classic films (plus a cartoon) in Dole Park. They start at sunset on the first Thursday of the month. Bring your own blankets, beach chairs, and a picnic dinner. For more information, go to www.visitlanai.net.

Occasionally, special events will bring in a few more nightlife options. During the annual **Pineapple Festival,** generally the first weekend in July, some of Hawaii's best musicians arrive to show their support for Lanai (see "Maui, Molokai & Lanai Calendar of Events," p. 52). **Aloha Festivals** (www.alohafestivals.com) takes place in the end of September or the first week in October, and the **Christmas Festival** is held on the first Saturday in December. For details on these festivals, contact the **Lanai Visitors Bureau,** P.O. Box 631436, Lanai City, HI 96763; or 431 Seventh St., Suite A, Lanai City (© 800/947-4774 or 808/565-7600; fax 808/565-9316; www.visitlanai.net).

Appendix:
Fast Facts, Toll-Free
Numbers & Websites

1 Fast Facts: Maui

AMERICAN EXPRESS For 24-hour traveler's-check refunds and purchase information, call ℭ **800/221-7282.** Offices are located in south Maui at the Grand Wailea Resort Hotel & Spa (ℭ **808/875-4526**), and in west Maui at the Westin Maui Resort & Spa at Kaanapali Beach (ℭ **808/661-7155**).

AREA CODES All of the Hawaiian Islands are in the **808** area code. Note that if you're calling one island from another, you'll have to dial "1-808" before the local number (and you'll be billed long-distance rates).

ATM NETWORKS/CASHPOINTS See "Money & Costs," p. 63.

AUTOMOBILE ORGANIZATIONS There is no AAA office located on Maui.

BUSINESS HOURS Most offices are open Monday through Friday from 8am to 5pm. Bank hours are Monday through Thursday from 8:30am to 3pm and Friday from 8:30am to 6pm; some banks are open on Saturday as well. Shopping centers are open Monday through Friday from 10am to 9pm, Saturday from 10am to 5:30pm, and Sunday from noon to 5 or 6pm.

CAR RENTALS See "Getting Around Maui," p. 61, and "Toll-Free Numbers & Websites," p. 322.

DENTISTS Emergency dental care is available at **Kihei Dental Center,** 1847 S. Kihei Rd., Kihei (ℭ **808/874-8401**), and at **Aloha Lahaina Dentists,** 134 Luakini St. (in the Maui Medical Group Building), Lahaina (ℭ **808/661-4005**).

DOCTORS The **West Maui Healthcare Center,** Whalers Village, 2435 Kaanapali Pkwy., Suite H-7 (near Leilani's on the Beach), Kaanapali (ℭ **808/667-9721**), is open 365 days a year; no appointment is necessary. In Kihei, call **Urgent Care Maui,** 1325 S. Kihei Rd., Suite 103 (at Lipoa St., across from Star Market), Kihei (ℭ **808/879-7781**).

DRINKING LAWS The legal age for purchase and consumption of alcoholic beverages is 21; proof of age is required and often requested at bars, nightclubs, and restaurants, so it's always a good idea to bring ID when you go out.

Bars are allowed to stay open daily until 2am; places with cabaret licenses are able to keep the booze flowing until 4am. Grocery and convenience stores are allowed to sell beer, wine, and liquor 7 days a week.

Do not carry open containers of alcohol in your car or any public area that isn't zoned for alcohol consumption. The police can fine you on the spot. And nothing will ruin your trip faster than getting a citation for DUI ("driving under the influence"), so don't even think about driving while intoxicated.

DRIVING RULES See "Getting There & Getting Around," p. 58.

ELECTRICITY Like Canada, the United States uses 110 to 120 volts AC (60 cycles), compared to 220 to 240 volts AC (50 cycles) in most of Europe, Australia, and New Zealand. Downward converters that change 220–240 volts to 110–120 volts are difficult to find in the United States, so bring one with you.

EMBASSIES & CONSULATES   All embassies are located in the nation's capital, Washington, D.C. Some consulates are located in major U.S. cities, and most nations have a mission to the United Nations in New York City. If your country isn't listed below, call for directory information in Washington, D.C. (© 202/555-1212), or check www.embassy.org/embassies.

The embassy of **Australia** is at 1601 Massachusetts Ave. NW, Washington, DC 20036 (© 202/797-3000; www.usa.embassy.gov.au). There are consulates in New York, Honolulu, Houston, Los Angeles, and San Francisco.

The embassy of **Canada** is at 501 Pennsylvania Ave. NW, Washington, DC 20001 (© 202/682-1740; www.canadianembassy.org). Other Canadian consulates are in Buffalo (New York), Detroit, Los Angeles, New York, and Seattle.

The embassy of **Ireland** is at 2234 Massachusetts Ave. NW, Washington, DC 20008 (© 202/462-3939; www.irelandemb.org). Irish consulates are in Boston, Chicago, New York, San Francisco, and other cities. See the website for a complete listing.

The embassy of **New Zealand** is at 37 Observatory Circle NW, Washington, DC 20008 (© 202/328-4800; www.nzembassy.com). New Zealand consulates are in Los Angeles, Salt Lake City, San Francisco, and Seattle.

The embassy of the **United Kingdom** is at 3100 Massachusetts Ave. NW, Washington, DC 20008 (© 202/588-7800; www.britainusa.com). Other British consulates are in Atlanta, Boston, Chicago, Cleveland, Houston, Los Angeles, New York, San Francisco, and Seattle.

EMERGENCIES   Dial © 911 for police, fire, or ambulance. Police district stations are located in Lahaina (© 808/661-4441) and in Hana (© 808/248-8311). For the Poison Control Center, call © 800/362-3585.

GASOLINE (PETROL)   At press time, the cost of gasoline (also known as gas, but never petrol), is abnormally high in the U.S. At this writing, average prices for regular gas in Maui are about $4.43 per gallon. Note that taxes are already included in the printed price. One U.S. gallon equals 3.8 liters or .85 imperial gallons. Fill-up locations are known as gas or service stations.

HOLIDAYS   Banks, government offices, post offices, and many stores, restaurants, and museums are closed on the following legal national holidays: January 1 (New Year's Day), the third Monday in January (Martin Luther King, Jr., Day), the third Monday in February (Presidents' Day), the last Monday in May (Memorial Day), July 4 (Independence Day), the first Monday in September (Labor Day), the second Monday in October (Columbus Day), November 11 (Veterans' Day/Armistice Day), the fourth Thursday in November (Thanksgiving Day), and December 25 (Christmas). The Tuesday after the first Monday in November is Election Day, a federal government holiday in presidential-election years (held every 4 years, and next in 2008 and 2012).

State and county offices are also closed on local holidays. For more information, go to "Holidays" and "Maui, Molokai & Lanai Calendar of Events" in the "When to Go" section on p. 50.

HOSPITALS   In central Maui, **Maui Memorial Hospital** is at 221 Mahalani, Wailuku (© 808/244-9056). East Maui's **Hana Medical Center** is on the Hana Highway (© 808/248-8924). In upcountry Maui, **Kula Hospital** is at 204 Kula Hwy., Kula (© 808/878-1221).

INSURANCE   Medical   Insurance
Although it's not required of travelers, health insurance is highly recommended. Most health insurance policies cover you if you get sick away from home—but check your coverage before you leave.

International visitors to the U.S. should note that, unlike many European countries, the United States does not usually offer free or low-cost medical care to its citizens or visitors. Doctors and hospitals are expensive and, in most cases, will require advance payment or proof of coverage before they render their services. Good policies will cover the costs of an accident, repatriation, or death. Packages such as **Europ Assistance's "Worldwide Healthcare Plan"** are sold by European automobile clubs and travel agencies at attractive rates. **Europ Assistance USA** (© 800/777-8710; www.europassistance-usa.com) is the agent in the United States. Though lack of health insurance may prevent you from being admitted to a hospital in nonemergencies, don't worry about being left on a street corner to die: The American way is to fix you now and bill the daylights out of you later.

If you're ever hospitalized more than 150 miles from home, **MedjetAssist** (© 800/527-7478; www.medjetassistance.com) will pick you up and fly you to the hospital of your choice in a medically equipped and staffed aircraft 24 hours a day, 7 days a week. Annual memberships are $225 individual, $350 family; you can also purchase short-term memberships.

Citizens of **Canada** should check with their provincial health plan offices or call **Health Canada** (© 866/225-0709; www.hc-sc.gc.ca) to find out the extent of their coverage and what documentation and receipts they must take home in case they are treated in the United States.

Travelers from the **U.K.** should carry their European Health Insurance Card (EHIC), which replaced the E111 form as proof of entitlement to free/reduced-cost medical treatment abroad (© **0845 606 2030;** www.ehic.org.uk). Note, however, that the EHIC covers only "necessary medical treatment," and for repatriation costs, lost money, baggage, or cancellation, travel insurance from a reputable company should always be sought (www.travelinsuranceweb.com).

Travel Insurance   The cost of travel insurance varies widely, depending on the destination, the cost and length of your trip, your age and health, and the type of trip you're taking, but expect to pay between 5% and 8% of the vacation itself. You can get estimates from various providers through **InsureMyTrip.com.** Enter your trip cost and dates, your age, and other information, for prices from more than a dozen companies.

U.K. citizens and their families who make more than one trip abroad per year may find that an annual travel insurance policy works out cheaper. Check **www.moneysupermarket.com**, which compares prices across a wide range of providers for single-trip and multitrip policies.

Most big travel agents offer their own insurance and will probably try to sell you their package when you book a holiday. Think before you sign. **Britain's Consumers' Association** recommends that you insist on seeing the policy and reading the fine print before buying travel insurance. The **Association of British Insurers** (© 020/7600-3333; www.abi.org.uk) gives advice by phone and publishes *Holiday Insurance,* a free guide to policy provisions and prices. You might also shop around for better deals: Try **Columbus Direct** (© 0870/033-9988; www.columbusdirect.net).

Trip-Cancellation Insurance   Trip-cancellation insurance will help retrieve your money if you have to back out of a trip or depart early, or if your travel supplier goes bankrupt. Trip cancellation traditionally covers such events as sickness, natural disasters, and State Department advisories. The latest news in trip-cancellation insurance is the availability of **expanded hurricane coverage** and the **"any-reason" cancellation coverage**—which costs more but covers cancellations made for any reason. You won't get back 100% of your prepaid trip cost, but you'll be refunded a substantial portion. **TravelSafe** (© **888/885-7233;** www.travelsafe.com) offers both types of coverage. Expedia also offers any-reason cancellation coverage for its air/hotel packages. For details, contact one of the following recommended insurers: **Access America** (© 866/807-3982; www.access america.com), **AIG Travel Guard** (© 800/ 826-4919; www.travelguard.com), **Travel Insured International** (© 800/243-3174; www.travelinsured.com), or **Travelex Insurance Services** (© 888/457-4602; www.travelex-insurance.com).

INTERNET ACCESS   See "Staying Connected," p. 77.

LEGAL AID   If you are "pulled over" for a minor infraction (such as speeding), never attempt to pay the fine directly to a police officer; this could be construed as attempted bribery, a much more serious crime. Pay fines by mail, or directly into the hands of the clerk of the court. If accused of a more serious offense, say and do nothing before consulting a lawyer. Here the burden is on the state to prove a person's guilt beyond a reasonable doubt, and everyone has the right to remain silent, whether he or she is suspected of a crime or actually arrested. Once arrested, a person can make one telephone call to a party of his or her choice. International visitors should call their embassy or consulate.

LOST & FOUND   Be sure to tell all of your credit card companies the minute you discover your wallet has been lost or stolen, and file a report at the nearest police precinct. Your credit card company or insurer may require a police report number or record of the loss. Most credit card companies have an emergency toll-free number to call if your card is lost or stolen; they may be able to wire you a cash advance immediately or deliver an emergency credit card in a day or two. Visa's U.S. emergency number is © **800/ 847-2911** or 410/581-9994. American Express cardholders and traveler's-check holders should call © **800/221-7282.** MasterCard holders should call © **800/ 307-7309** or 636/722-7111. For other credit cards, call the toll-free number directory at © **800/555-1212.**

If you need emergency cash over the weekend when all banks and American Express offices are closed, you can have money wired to you via **Western Union** (© **800/325-6000;** www.westernunion. com).

MAIL   At press time, domestic postage rates were 27¢ for a postcard and 42¢ for a letter. For international mail, a first-class letter of up to 1 ounce costs 94¢ (72¢ to Canada and Mexico); a first-class postcard costs the same as a letter. For more information, go to **www.usps.com** and click on "Calculate Postage."

In Lahaina, there are post offices at the Lahaina Civic Center, 1760 Honoapiilani Hwy., and at the Lahaina Shopping Center, 132 Papalaua St. In Kahului, there's a branch at 138 S. Puunene Ave., and in Kihei, there's one at 1254 S. Kihei Rd.

If you aren't sure what your address will be in the United States, mail can be sent to you, in your name, c/o General Delivery at the main post office of the city or region where you expect to be. (Call © **800/275-8777** for information on the nearest post office.) The addressee must pick up mail in person and must produce proof of identity (driver's license, passport, and such). Most post offices will hold your mail for up to 1 month, and are open Monday to Friday from 8am to 6pm, and Saturday from 9am to 3pm.

Always include zip codes when mailing items in the U.S. If you don't know your zip code, visit www.usps.com/zip4.

MAPS See "Getting Around Maui," p. 61.

MEASUREMENTS See the chart on the inside front cover of this book for details on converting metric measurements to nonmetric equivalents.

MEDICAL CONDITIONS If you have a medical condition that requires **syringe-administered medications,** carry a valid signed prescription from your physician; syringes in carry-on baggage will be inspected. Insulin in any form should have the proper pharmaceutical documentation. If you have a disease that requires treatment with **narcotics,** you should also carry documented proof with you—smuggling narcotics aboard a plane carries severe penalties in the U.S.

For **HIV-positive visitors,** requirements for entering the United States are somewhat vague and change frequently. For up-to-the-minute information, contact **AIDSinfo** (© 800/448-0440, or 301/519-6616 outside the U.S.; www.aidsinfo.nih.gov) or the **Gay Men's Health Crisis** (© 212/367-1000; www.gmhc.org).

NEWSPAPERS & MAGAZINES The island's daily newspaper is the *Maui News,* P.O. Box 550, Wailuku, HI 96793 (© 808/244-3981; www.mauinews.com).

Publications for visitors include *This Week Maui* (www.thisweek.com), *Maui Visitor Magazine* (www.visitormagazines.com), and *101 Things to Do.*

PASSPORTS The websites listed provide downloadable passport applications as well as the current fees for processing applications. For an up-to-date, country-by-country listing of passport requirements around the world, go to the "International Travel" tab of the U.S. State Department at **http://travel.state.gov**. International visitors to the U.S. can obtain a visa application at the same website. *Note:* Children are required to present a passport when entering the United States at airports. More information on obtaining a passport for a minor can be found at http://travel.state.gov. Allow plenty of time before your trip to apply for a passport; processing normally takes 4 to 6 weeks (3 weeks for expedited service) but can take longer during busy periods (especially spring). And keep in mind that if you need a passport in a hurry, you'll pay a higher processing fee.

For Residents of Australia You can pick up an application from your local post office or any branch of Passports Australia, but you must schedule an interview at the passport office to present your application materials. Call the **Australian Passport Information Service** at © 131-232, or visit the government website at www.passports.gov.au.

For Residents of Canada Passport applications are available at travel agencies throughout Canada or from the central **Passport Office,** Department of Foreign Affairs and International Trade, Ottawa, ON K1A 0G3 (© 800/567-6868; www.ppt.gc.ca). *Note:* Canadian children who travel must have their own passport. However, if you hold a valid Canadian passport issued before December 11, 2001, that bears the name of your child, the passport remains valid for you and your child until it expires.

For Residents of Ireland You can apply for a 10-year passport at the **Passport Office,** Setanta Centre, Molesworth Street, Dublin 2 (© 01/671-1633; www.irlgov.ie/iveagh). Those under age 18 and over 65 must apply for a 3-year passport. You can also apply at 1A South Mall, Cork (© 21/494-4700), or at most main post offices.

For Residents of New Zealand You can pick up a passport application at any

New Zealand Passports Office or download it from the website. Contact the **Passports Office** at © **0800/225-050** (in New Zealand) or 04/474-8100, or log on to www.passports.govt.nz.

For Residents of the United Kingdom To pick up an application for a standard 10-year passport (5-year passport for children under 16), visit your nearest passport office, major post office, or travel agency, or contact the **United Kingdom Passport Service** at © **0870/521-0410** or go to www.ukpa.gov.uk.

POLICE In an emergency, dial © **911** for police. For nonemergencies, call the district station in Lahaina (© **808/661-4441**) or Hana (© **808/248-8311**).

SMOKING It's against the law to smoke in public buildings, including airports, shopping malls, grocery stores, retail shops, buses, movie theaters, banks, convention facilities, and all government buildings and facilities. There is no smoking in restaurants, bars, and nightclubs. Most bed-and-breakfasts prohibit smoking indoors, and more and more hotels and resorts are becoming nonsmoking even in public areas. Also, there is no smoking within 20 feet of a doorway, window, or ventilation intake (so no hanging around outside a bar to smoke—you must go 20 ft. away).

TAXES The United States has no value-added tax (VAT) or other indirect tax at the national level. Every state, county, and city may levy its own local tax on all purchases, including hotel and restaurant checks and airline tickets. Hawaii state general excise tax is 4%. The hotel-occupancy tax is 7.25%, and hoteliers are allowed by the state to tack on an additional .1666% excise tax. Thus, expect taxes of about 11.42% to be added to your hotel bill.

TELEPHONES See "Staying Connected," p. 77.

TELEGRAPH, TELEX & FAX **Telegraph** and **telex** services are provided primarily by **Western Union** (© **800/325-6000;** www.westernunion.com). You can telegraph (wire) money, or have it telegraphed to you, very quickly over the Western Union system, but this service can cost as much as 15% to 20% of the amount sent.

Most hotels have **fax machines** available for guests' use (be sure to ask about the charge to use them). Many hotel rooms are wired for guests' fax machines. A less expensive way to send and receive faxes may be at stores such as the **UPS Store** (formerly Mail Boxes Etc.).

TIME The continental United States is divided into **four time zones:** Eastern Standard Time (EST), Central Standard Time (CST), Mountain Standard Time (MST), and Pacific Standard Time (PST). Alaska and Hawaii have their own zones. For example, when it's 9am in Los Angeles (PST), it's 7am in Honolulu (HST), 10am in Denver (MST), 11am in Chicago (CST), noon in New York City (EST), 5pm in London (GMT), and 2am the next day in Sydney.

Daylight saving time is in effect from 2am on the second Sunday in March to 2am on the first Sunday in November, except in Arizona, Hawaii, the U.S. Virgin Islands, and Puerto Rico. Daylight saving time moves the clock 1 hour ahead of standard time. Note that when the rest of the U.S. observes daylight saving time, Hawaii is 3 hours behind the West Coast and 6 hours behind the East Coast.

TIPPING Tips are a very important part of certain workers' income, and gratuities are the standard way of showing appreciation for services provided. (Tipping is certainly not compulsory if the service is poor!) In hotels, tip **bellhops** at least $1 per bag ($2–$3 if you have a lot of luggage) and tip the **chamber staff** $1 to $2 per day (more if you've left a disaster area for him or her to clean up). Tip the **door-man** or **concierge** only if he or she has provided you with some specific service (for example, calling a cab for you or obtaining difficult-to-get theater tickets). Tip the **valet-parking attendant** $1 every time you get your car.

In restaurants, bars, and nightclubs, tip **service staff** 15% to 20% of the check, tip **bartenders** 10% to 15%, tip **check-room attendants** $1 per garment, and tip **valet-parking attendants** $1 per vehicle.

As for other service personnel, tip **cab drivers** 15% of the fare, tip **skycaps** at airports at least $1 per bag ($2–$3 if you have a lot of luggage), and tip **hair-dressers** and **barbers** 15% to 20%.

TOILETS   You won't find public toilets or "restrooms" on the streets in most U.S. cities but they can be found in hotel lobbies, bars, restaurants, museums, department stores, bus stations, and service stations. Large hotels and fast-food restaurants are often the best bet for clean facilities. If possible, avoid the toilets at parks and beaches, which tend to be dirty; some may be unsafe. Restaurants and bars in resorts or heavily visited areas may reserve their restrooms for patrons.

VISAS   For information on U.S. visas, go to **http://travel.state.gov** and click on "Visas." Or go to one of the following websites:

Australian citizens can obtain up-to-date visa information from the **U.S. Embassy Canberra,** Moonah Place, Yarralumla, ACT 2600 (© 02/6214-5600), or by checking the U.S. Diplomatic Mission's website at http://us embassy-australia.state.gov/consular.

British subjects can obtain up-to-date visa information by calling the **U.S. Embassy Visa Information Line** (© 0891/200-290) or by visiting the "Visas to the U.S." section of the American Embassy London's website at www.us embassy.org.uk.

Irish citizens can obtain up-to-date visa information through the **Embassy of the USA Dublin,** 42 Elgin Rd., Dublin 4, Ireland (© 353/1-668-8777), or by checking the "Visas to the U.S." section of the website at http://dublin.usembassy.gov.

Citizens of **New Zealand** can obtain up-to-date visa information by contacting the **U.S. Embassy New Zealand,** 29 Fitzherbert Terrace, Thorndon, Wellington (© 644/472-2068), or get the information directly from the website at http://wellington.usembassy.gov.

2 Toll-Free Numbers & Websites

MAJOR U.S. AIRLINES
(*flies internationally as well)

Alaska Airlines
© 800/252-7522
www.alaskaair.com

American Airlines*
© 800/433-7300 (in U.S. and Canada)
© 020/7365-0777 (in U.K.)
www.aa.com

Continental Airlines*
© 800/523-3273 (in U.S. and Canada)
© 084/5607-6760 (in U.K.)
www.continental.com

Delta Air Lines*
© 800/221-1212 (in U.S. and Canada)
© 084/5600-0950 (in U.K.)
www.delta.com

go!
© 888/435-9462
www.iflygo.com
(interisland Hawaii only)

Hawaiian Airlines*
© 800/367-5320 (in U.S. and Canada)
www.hawaiianair.com

Northwest Airlines
© 800/225-2525 (in U.S.)
© 870/0507-4074 (in U.K.)
www.nwa.com

United Airlines*
© 800/864-8331 (in U.S. and Canada)

MAJOR INTERNATIONAL AIRLINES

Air Canada
© 888/247-2262 (in U.S. and Canada)
www.aircanada.com

Air France
© 800/237-2747 (in U.S.)
© 800/375-8723 (in U.S. and Canada)
© 087/0142-4343 (in U.K.)
www.airfrance.com

Air New Zealand
© 800/262-1234 (in U.S.)
© 800/663-5494 (in Canada)
© 0800/028-4149 (in U.K.)
© 0800/737-000 (in New Zealand)
www.airnewzealand.com

Air Pacific
© 800/227-4446 (in U.S. and Canada)
www.airpacific.com

Air Tahiti Nui
© 877/824-4846 (in U.S. and Canada)
www.airtahitinui-usa.com

Alitalia
© 800/223-5730 (in U.S.)
© 800/361-8336 (in Canada)
© 087/0608-6003 (in U.K.)
www.alitalia.com

All Nippon Airways (ANA)
© 800/235-9262 (in U.S. and Canada)
© 03/5489-1212 (in Japan)
www.fly-ana.com

American Airlines
© 800/433-7300 (in U.S. and Canada)
© 020/7365-0777 (in U.K.)
www.aa.com

British Airways
© 800/247-9297 (in U.S. and Canada)
© 087/0850-9850 (in U.K.)
www.british-airways.com

© 084/5844-4777 (in U.K.)
www.united.com

US Airways*
© 800/428-4322 (in U.S. and Canada)
© 084/5600-3300 (in U.K.)
www.usairways.com

China Airlines
© 800/227-5118 (in U.S.)
© 022/715-1212 (in Taiwan)
www.china-airlines.com

Continental Airlines
© 800/523-3273 (in U.S. and Canada)
© 084/5607-6760 (in U.K.)
www.continental.com

Delta Air Lines
© 800/221-1212 (in U.S. and Canada)
© 084/5600-0950 (in U.K.)
www.delta.com

Hawaiian Airlines
© 800/367-5320 (in U.S. and Canada)
www.hawaiianair.com

Japan Airlines
© 800/525-3663 (in U.S. and Canada)
© 012/025-5931 (international)
www.jal.co.jp

Korean Air
© 800/438-5000 (in U.S. and Canada)
© 0800/413-000 (in U.K.)
© 02/656-2000 (in Korea)
www.koreanair.com

Philippine Airlines
© 800/435-9725 (in U.S. and Canada)
© 632/855-8888 (in Philippines)
www.philippineairlines.com

Qantas Airways
© 800/227-4500 (in U.S.)
© 084/5774-7767 (in U.K. and Canada)
© 13 13 13 (in Australia)
www.qantas.com

United Airlines*
© 800/864-8331 (in U.S. and Canada)
© 084/5844-4777 (in U.K.)
www.united.com

US Airways*
© 800/428-4322 (in U.S. and Canada)
© 084/5600-3300 (in U.K.)
www.usairways.com

CAR-RENTAL AGENCIES

Alamo
© 800/GO-ALAMO (462-5266)
www.alamo.com

Avis
© 800/331-1212 (in U.S. and Canada)
© 084/4581-8181 (in U.K.)
www.avis.com

Budget
© 800/527-0700 (in U.S.)
© 800/268-8900 (in Canada)
© 087/0156-5656 (in U.K.)
www.budget.com

Dollar
© 800/800-4000 (in U.S.)
© 800/848-8268 (in Canada)
© 080/8234-7524 (in U.K.)
www.dollar.com

Enterprise
© 800/261-7331 (in U.S.)
© 514/355-4028 (in Canada)

Virgin Atlantic Airways
© 800/821-5438 (in U.S. and Canada)
© 087/0574-7747 (in U.K.)
www.virgin-atlantic.com

© 012/9360-9090 (in U.K.)
www.enterprise.com

Hertz
© 800/654-3131 (in U.S. and Canada)
© 800/654-3001 (for international reservations)
www.hertz.com

National
© 800/CAR-RENT (227-7368)
www.nationalcar.com

Rent-A-Wreck
© 800/535-1391
www.rentawreck.com

Thrifty
© 800/367-2277 (in U.S. and Canada)
© 918/669-2168 (international)
www.thrifty.com

MAJOR HOTEL & MOTEL CHAINS

Best Western International
© 800/780-7234 (in U.S. and Canada)
© 0800/393-130 (in U.K.)
www.bestwestern.com

Four Seasons
© 800/819-5053 (in U.S. and Canada)
© 0800/6488-6488 (in U.K.)
www.fourseasons.com

Hilton Hotels
© 800/HILTONS (445-8667) (in U.S. and Canada)
© 087/0590-9090 (in U.K.)
www.hilton.com

Hyatt
© 888/591-1234 (in U.S. and Canada)
© 084/5888-1234 (in U.K.)
www.hyatt.com

Marriott
© 877/236-2427 (in U.S. and Canada)
© 0800/221-222 (in U.K.)
www.marriott.com

Renaissance
© 888/236-2427
www.renaissance.com

Sheraton Hotels & Resorts
© 800/325-3535 (in U.S.)
© 800/543-4300 (in Canada)
© 0800/3253-5353 (in U.K.)
www.starwoodhotels.com/sheraton

Westin Hotels & Resorts
© 800/937-8461 (in U.S. and Canada)
© 0800/3259-5959 (in U.K.)
www.starwoodhotels.com/westin

Index

See also Accommodations and Restaurant indexes, below.

ACCOMMODATIONS

RESTAURANTS

The new way to
get AROUND town.

Make the most of your stay. Go Day by Day!

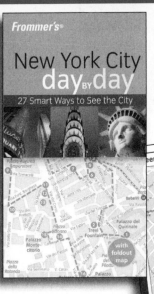

The all-new Day by Day series shows you the best places to visit and the best way to see them.

- Full-color throughout, with hundreds of photos and maps
- Packed with 1–to–3–day itineraries, neighborhood walks, and thematic tours
- Museums, literary haunts, offbeat places, and more
- Star-rated hotel and restaurant listings
- Sturdy foldout map in reclosable plastic wallet
- Foldout front covers with at-a-glance maps and info

The best trips start here.

Frommer's®
A Branded Imprint of ⊛WILEY
Now you know.

A Guide for Every Type of Traveler

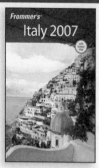

Frommer's Complete Guides
For those who value complete coverage, candid advice, and lots of choices in all price ranges.

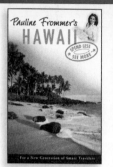

Pauline Frommer's Guides
For those who want to experience a culture, meet locals, and save money along the way.

MTV Guides
For hip, youthful travelers who want a fresh perspective on today's hottest cities and destinations.

Day by Day Guides
For leisure or business travelers who want to organize their time to get the most out of a trip.

Frommer's With Kids Guides
For families traveling with children ages 2 to 14 seeking kid-friendly hotels, restaurants, and activities.

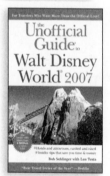

Unofficial Guides
For honeymooners, families, business travelers, and others who value no-nonsense, *Consumer Reports*–style advice.

For Dummies Travel Guides
For curious, independent travelers looking for a fun and easy way to plan a trip.

Visit Frommers.com

Now you know.

FROMMER'S® COMPLETE TRAVEL GUIDES

Alaska
Amalfi Coast
American Southwest
Amsterdam
Argentina
Arizona
Atlanta
Australia
Austria
Bahamas
Barcelona
Beijing
Belgium, Holland & Luxembourg
Belize
Bermuda
Boston
Brazil
British Columbia & the Canadian
    Rockies
Brussels & Bruges
Budapest & the Best of Hungary
Buenos Aires
Calgary
California
Canada
Cancún, Cozumel & the Yucatán
Cape Cod, Nantucket & Martha's
    Vineyard
Caribbean
Caribbean Ports of Call
Carolinas & Georgia
Chicago
Chile & Easter Island
China
Colorado
Costa Rica
Croatia
Cuba
Denmark
Denver, Boulder & Colorado Springs
Eastern Europe
Ecuador & the Galapagos Islands
Edinburgh & Glasgow
England
Europe
Europe by Rail

Florence, Tuscany & Umbria
Florida
France
Germany
Greece
Greek Islands
Guatemala
Hawaii
Hong Kong
Honolulu, Waikiki & Oahu
India
Ireland
Israel
Italy
Jamaica
Japan
Kauai
Las Vegas
London
Los Angeles
Los Cabos & Baja
Madrid
Maine Coast
Maryland & Delaware
Maui
Mexico
Montana & Wyoming
Montréal & Québec City
Morocco
Moscow & St. Petersburg
Munich & the Bavarian Alps
Nashville & Memphis
New England
Newfoundland & Labrador
New Mexico
New Orleans
New York City
New York State
New Zealand
Northern Italy
Norway
Nova Scotia, New Brunswick &
    Prince Edward Island
Oregon
Paris
Peru

Philadelphia & the Amish Country
Portugal
Prague & the Best of the Czech
    Republic
Provence & the Riviera
Puerto Rico
Rome
San Antonio & Austin
San Diego
San Francisco
Santa Fe, Taos & Albuquerque
Scandinavia
Scotland
Seattle
Seville, Granada & the Best of
    Andalusia
Shanghai
Sicily
Singapore & Malaysia
South Africa
South America
South Florida
South Korea
South Pacific
Southeast Asia
Spain
Sweden
Switzerland
Tahiti & French Polynesia
Texas
Thailand
Tokyo
Toronto
Turkey
USA
Utah
Vancouver & Victoria
Vermont, New Hampshire & Maine
Vienna & the Danube Valley
Vietnam
Virgin Islands
Virginia
Walt Disney World® & Orlando
Washington, D.C.
Washington State

FROMMER'S® DAY BY DAY GUIDES

Amsterdam
Barcelona
Beijing
Boston
Cancun & the Yucatan
Chicago
Florence & Tuscany

Hong Kong
Honolulu & Oahu
London
Maui
Montréal
Napa & Sonoma
New York City

Paris
Provence & the Riviera
Rome
San Francisco
Venice
Washington D.C.

PAULINE FROMMER'S GUIDES: SEE MORE. SPEND LESS.

Alaska
Hawaii
Italy

Las Vegas
London
New York City

Paris
Walt Disney World®
Washington D.C.

FROMMER'S® PORTABLE GUIDES

Acapulco, Ixtapa & Zihuatanejo
Amsterdam
Aruba, Bonaire & Curacao
Australia's Great Barrier Reef
Bahamas
Big Island of Hawaii
Boston
California Wine Country
Cancún
Cayman Islands
Charleston
Chicago
Dominican Republic

Florence
Las Vegas
Las Vegas for Non-Gamblers
London
Maui
Nantucket & Martha's Vineyard
New Orleans
New York City
Paris
Portland
Puerto Rico
Puerto Vallarta, Manzanillo &
  Guadalajara

Rio de Janeiro
San Diego
San Francisco
Savannah
St. Martin, Sint Maarten, Anguila &
  St. Bart's
Turks & Caicos
Vancouver
Venice
Virgin Islands
Washington, D.C.
Whistler

FROMMER'S® CRUISE GUIDES

Alaska Cruises & Ports of Call

Cruises & Ports of Call

European Cruises & Ports of Call

FROMMER'S® NATIONAL PARK GUIDES

Algonquin Provincial Park
Banff & Jasper
Grand Canyon

National Parks of the American West
Rocky Mountain
Yellowstone & Grand Teton

Yosemite and Sequoia & Kings
  Canyon
Zion & Bryce Canyon

FROMMER'S® WITH KIDS GUIDES

Chicago
Hawaii
Las Vegas
London

National Parks
New York City
San Francisco

Toronto
Walt Disney World® & Orlando
Washington, D.C.

FROMMER'S® PHRASEFINDER DICTIONARY GUIDES

Chinese
French

German
Italian

Japanese
Spanish

SUZY GERSHMAN'S BORN TO SHOP GUIDES

France
Hong Kong, Shanghai & Beijing
Italy

London
New York
Paris

San Francisco
Where to Buy the Best of Everything.

FROMMER'S® BEST-LOVED DRIVING TOURS

Britain
California
France
Germany

Ireland
Italy
New England
Northern Italy

Scotland
Spain
Tuscany & Umbria

THE UNOFFICIAL GUIDES®

Adventure Travel in Alaska
Beyond Disney
California with Kids
Central Italy
Chicago
Cruises
Disneyland®
England
Hawaii

Ireland
Las Vegas
London
Maui
Mexico's Best Beach Resorts
Mini Mickey
New Orleans
New York City
Paris

San Francisco
South Florida including Miami &
  the Keys
Walt Disney World®
Walt Disney World® for
  Grown-ups
Walt Disney World® with Kids
Washington, D.C.

SPECIAL-INTEREST TITLES

Athens Past & Present
Best Places to Raise Your Family
Cities Ranked & Rated
500 Places to Take Your Kids Before They Grow Up
Frommer's Best Day Trips from London
Frommer's Best RV & Tent Campgrounds in the U.S.A.

Frommer's Exploring America by RV
Frommer's NYC Free & Dirt Cheap
Frommer's Road Atlas Europe
Frommer's Road Atlas Ireland
Retirement Places Rated